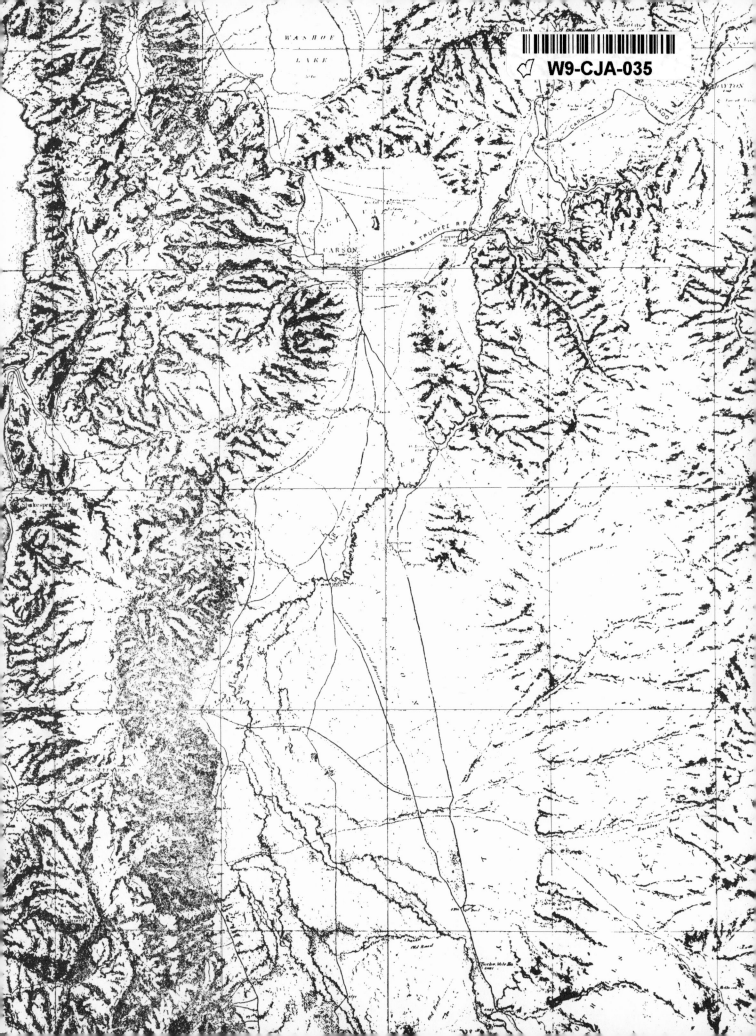

THE SAGA OF LAKE TAHOE

The Saga of
LAKE
TAHOE

By EDWARD B. SCOTT

A complete documentation of Lake Tahoe's development over the last one hundred years.

Published by

SIERRA-TAHOE PUBLISHING CO.

Crystal Bay, Lake Tahoe, Nevada

Printed by

HAYWOOD PUBLISHING COMPANY
OF INDIANA

Lafayette, Indiana

DEDICATED TO THE PIONEERS OF LAKE TAHOE

AND THEIR DESCENDANTS,

WHOSE NAMES ARE LEGEND UPON HER

WATERS, SHORES AND MOUNTAINS

ACKNOWLEDGMENTS

Invaluable assistance from the sons, daughters, grandsons and granddaughters of the early pioneer families at Lake Tahoe is gratefully acknowledged: the late Harry Oswald Comstock; his daughters, Velma Comstock Eden and Gladys Comstock Bennett, Maillard Bennett and Harry P. O'Callaghan of Brockway Hot Springs; George and the late David Chambers of Chambers' Lodge; Benjamin F. Callender, the Donald Huffs and J. P. Obexers of Homewood; Ernest Henry Pomin of Tahoe Pines and John Ernest Pomin of Idlewild; Jeanette Pomin Watson, the Robert H. Watsons, A. M. Henrys, Mr. and Mrs. A. M. Anderson, John Starrett, Harry Johanson, Carl Andrew Bechdolt, Sr., Judge and Mrs. C. W. Vernon, Mrs. Eleanor Swanson, Mrs. Alice Gebhardt and Jeanette Mitchell, George and Bliss Hinkle, all originally from Tahoe City.

Mrs. Charles R. Young, the George Andersons, Melvin F. Springmeyers and Jack Meyn of Bijou; Mrs. Frank Celio, Hazel Celio Taylor and Norman Celio of Tahoe and Lake valleys; Mrs. Rose Chubbuck Dodson, Joseph Rochon, Charles Oliver, the Ellis J. Folsoms, William Lindsey, Mrs. Edward McFaul and the late George D. Oliver of Carson City, Nevada; David Wallace Park of Edgewood; William Rabe of old Hobart, Lake Tahoe; Jack Van Sickle and Harry James of Lakeside; Frances Price Craven of Fallen Leaf Lake; Dixwell Pierce of Sacramento; Mrs. Ralph C. Graves, Mrs. Lewis L. Cox and Lloyd Tevis of Carmel; Grant Merrill of Woodfords, California; Mrs. Emma Jewel Clifford, Mrs. Jane Barnes Clark and Mrs. Grace Jellerson McCleary of Reno.

Mrs. Laura McFaul Allerman and the Edwin V. Fettics of Genoa, Nevada; Mr. and Mrs. James M. Leonard of Virginia City; "Red" McGovern of Lakeview Station, Nevada; Miss Jessie Armstrong of Oakland, California; William M. Bliss, the late Walter Danforth Bliss and William Fenton Ham of Glenbrook, Nevada; George Kehlet, Captain Fred Kehlet and Arnold Luneman of Meeks Bay; Mrs. Fannie Rowland Barton, Miss Catherine Patterson, Dr. Frank Tahoe McClaskey, Judge Peter J. Shields and Matt Green of Sacramento; Mrs. Ouida Kyburz Barton of Tahoe Valley, and Jack Bell of Sparks, Nevada.

The Sydney Ehrmans and Mrs. Claude Lazard of Sugar Pine Point, Lake Tahoe; the William Wallace Meins and Dr. Cabot Brown of Sunnyside Bay, Lake Tahoe; Mrs. Katherine Brigham Ebright of Cascade Lake; Mrs. Hattie Belle Colwell Almstaden, Joseph McKee and Mrs. Donald Goodrich of Placerville; Mrs. Alice Elaine Lyon and Mrs. Mehetable Jane Sickels of Phillips Station; Joe King of King's Beach; Mrs. Minnie Lyons Creighton of San Mateo; Lloyd Saxon of San Jose; Mrs. Harry Murphy Lawson of Sacramento; Mrs. W. F. Lampe of Gardnerville, Nevada; Mr. and Mrs. Edward Grover Chandler of Berkeley; Miss Marion Otis Mitchell of Alameda; Dr. Clark Burnham of Piedmont, California; Locke T. Harper of San Francisco, and Mr. and Mrs. Frank Globin of Al Tahoe.

The courtesy and cooperation extended by these men and women of California and Nevada have made this historical on Lake Tahoe possible.

The author's grateful appreciation goes to the able staff of the Bancroft Library, University of California, Berkeley; Mr. Allan R. Ottley and his co-workers in the California Section of the California State Library, Sacramento; the Nevada State Historical Society, Reno, Nevada; the University of Nevada School of Mines, Reno, and the Nevada State Museum, Carson City. All furnished photographic reproduction assistance and important documentary material.

Valuable reference data were also found in the Berkeley Public Library, the Oakland Public Library, the Harrison Library, Carmel, the Monterey Public Library, Monterey, California, and the Huntington Library, Pasadena, California.

The county recorder's offices of Placer and El Dorado counties in California, and Washoe, Ormsby and Douglas counties in Nevada cooperated with names, dates, deeds, and mortgage records from their Assessment Rolls and Great Registers.

A particular indebtedness is felt toward C. O. Valentine of Costa Mesa, California, and the late George D. Oliver of Carson City for furnishing classic early photographs of Lake Tahoe, in which they captured clear-cut panoramas, steamer silhouettes, winter and summer views and early resort locations. Mrs. Gladys Comstock Bennett, Mrs. Velma Comstock Eden, Miss Catherine Patterson, Mrs. Charles P. Young, Mrs. A. M. Henry, Kathleen Starratt, Eleanor Swanson, Mrs. Fannie Rowland Barton, and Mrs. Mima Widup of The Filmer Brothers Press were among those who also graciously contributed photographs of the times and other valuable assistance.

CONTENTS

ACKNOWLEDGMENTS vii

INTRODUCTION xi

Chapter One   SQUAW VALLEY 1

Chapter Two   TRUCKEE RIVER CANYON 11

Chapter Three   DEER PARK SPRINGS 19

Chapter Four   TAHOE CITY 23

Chapter Five   TAHOE TAVERN 51

Chapter Six   TAHOE PARK 57

Chapter Seven   TAHOE PINES 63

Chapter Eight   HOMEWOOD 69

Chapter Nine   RUBICON SPRINGS 75

Chapter Ten   CHAMBERS' LODGE 81

Chapter Eleven   MOANA VILLA 91

Chapter Twelve   TAHOMA 95

Chapter Thirteen   MAY-AH-MEE LODGE 97

Chapter Fourteen   SUGAR PINE POINT 101

Chapter Fifteen   MEEKS BAY 109

Chapter Sixteen   RUBICON PARK AND BAY 115

Chapter Seventeen   RUBICON POINT 119

Chapter Eighteen   EMERALD BAY 121

Chapter Nineteen   CASCADE LAKE 137

Chapter Twenty   FALLEN LEAF LAKE 143

Chapter Twenty-one   GLEN ALPINE SPRINGS 147

Chapter Twenty-two   TALLAC 151

Chapter Twenty-three   CASCADE HOUSE 167

Chapter Twenty-four   CAMP RICHARDSON 171

Chapter Twenty-five   ECHO LAKE 175

Chapter Twenty-six	LAKE VALLEY	179
Chapter Twenty-seven	MEYERS	189
Chapter Twenty-eight	SIERRA HOUSE	197
Chapter Twenty-nine	AL TAHOE	203
Chapter Thirty	BIJOU	211
Chapter Thirty-one	LAKESIDE	221
Chapter Thirty-two	EDGEWOOD	231
Chapter Thirty-three	HOBART	239
Chapter Thirty-four	MARLA BAY	243
Chapter Thirty-five	ZEPHYR COVE	245
Chapter Thirty-six	CAVE ROCK	251
Chapter Thirty-seven	LOGAN HOUSE	257
Chapter Thirty-eight	SHAKESPEARE ROCK	261
Chapter Thirty-nine	GLENBROOK	263
Chapter Forty	SPOONER STATION AND SUMMIT CAMP	291
Chapter Forty-one	MARLETTE LAKE	299
Chapter Forty-two	INCLINE	305
Chapter Forty-three	CRYSTAL BAY	313
Chapter Forty-four	BROCKWAY HOTEL AND HOT SPRINGS	319
Chapter Forty-five	KING'S BEACH	331
Chapter Forty-six	TAHOE VISTA	335
Chapter Forty-seven	AGATE BAY	339
Chapter Forty-eight	CARNELIAN BAY	343
Chapter Forty-nine	DOLLAR'S POINT	351
Chapter Fifty	LAKE FOREST	355
Chapter Fifty-one	THE GREAT BONANZA ROAD TO WASHOE	359
Section I	WAY STATIONS ON THE BONANZA ROAD TO WASHOE	377
Section II	EARLY MARINE HISTORY OF LAKE TAHOE	385
	MARINE ACTIVITY . . .	
	THE GAY '90's INTO THE ATOMIC 1950's	436
Section III	FISHING FACTS AND FANCY	443
Section IV	FACTS OF LAKE TAHOE	453
	BIBLIOGRAPHY	469
	CHAPTER NOTES	471
	INDEX	499

INTRODUCTION

Any attempt to chronicle the history of Lake Tahoe from the time of its discovery by Captain John Charles Fremont and Charles Preuss on St. Valentine's Day, February 14, 1844, down to the present day is comparable to fitting together a complex jig-saw puzzle composed of fact, fiction, documentation and hearsay.

Early magazine articles, county court house records, musty diaries, hotel registers, regional histories, letters and photographs furnish much of the substance for the Tahoe story.

A basic part of the subject matter lies buried in the tinderous newsprint of the times, newspapers of settlements and cities that ring Lake Tahoe—Truckee, Reno, Virginia City, Carson City, Gold Hill, Genoa, Placerville—with additional material hidden in the fine print of early Sacramento Valley, East Bay and San Francisco dailies.

Virginia City's famous *Territorial Enterprise*, sounding board of Mark Twain, Dan DeQuille and Joe Goodman, offers illuminating sunstreaks of information.

Another on the spot pulsebeat is found in Tahoe's first paper, the *Tahoe Tattler*, that skyrocketed across the lake in the summer of 1881, only to sputter out in its second year of publication. Over a half century was to pass before this postage stamp daily would again be revived, but the original tissue sheets are filled with whimsical nostalgia, sparkling vignettes and blunt editorial scoldings that capture the tone of the Bonanza days at Tahoe.

Add to this the dedicated, unsparing helpfulness of the pioneer Tahoe residents and gradually the hodge-podge of pieces that make up this picture of the world's greatest Alpine lake fall into place.

The general misconception that Lake Tahoe was a no-man's land in early California-Nevada history, because it lay between the two main arteries of mass migration moving westward in the late 1840's and early 1850's, has been the convenient excuse offered for ignoring Tahoe's vital, colorful contribution to the growth of the Far West and America. Pack trails and wagon roads—five routes in all —skirted Tahoe and were used by the emigrants. The Great Bonanza Road to Washoe, carrying a floodtide of animals, men and materials to the Nevada mines, ran along the lake's southern shore. This turnpike constituted the "main stem" of the West from 1859 to 1868.

Obviously the natural beauty of Mark Twain's and Dan DeQuille's "Lake of the Sky" overshadows man's development of the Tahoe region. However, a backdrop of Washoe and Paiute Indian tribes fighting for control of the "Big Water's" fishing and hunting grounds—the nearly forgotten arterials, Pony Express riders, teamsters, and drivers of ox-cart and Concord coach alike, all furnish the nucleus for a story that is pertinent to Tahoe itself.

Of major importance were the extensive lumbering operations and vast water projects spawned by, and furnishing lifeblood to, the Comstock Lode—the small armadas of sailing, steam, and at the turn

"In the early morning one watches the silent battle of dawn and darkness on the waters of Tahoe with a placid interest but when the shadows skulk away and one by one the hidden beauties of the shore unfold themselves in the full splendor of noon; when the smooth surface is belted like a rainbow with broad bars of blue and green and white, half the distance from circumference to center, when in the lazy summer afternoon, he lies in a boat far out to where the dead blue of the deep water begins and smokes the pipe of peace and idly winks at the distant crags and patches of snow from under his cap brim; when the boat drifts shoreward to the white water, and he lolls over the gunwale and gazes by the hour down through the crystal depths and notes the color of the pebbles and reviews the finny armies gliding in procession a hundred feet below; when at night he sees moon and stars, mountain ridges feathered with pines, jutting white capes, bold promontories, grand sweeps of rugged scenery topped with bald glimmering peaks, all magnificently pictured in the polished mirror of the lake, in richest, softest detail the tranquil interest that was born with the morning deepens and deepens, by sure degrees, till it culminates at last in resistless fascination."

MARK TWAIN

INTRODUCTION

Aɴʏ ᴀᴛᴛᴇᴍᴘᴛ to chronicle the history of Lake Tahoe from the time of its discovery by Captain John Charles Fremont and Charles Preuss on St. Valentine's Day, February 14, 1844, down to the present day is comparable to fitting together a complex jig-saw puzzle composed of fact, fiction, documentation and hearsay.

Early magazine articles, county court house records, musty diaries, hotel registers, regional histories, letters and photographs furnish much of the substance for the Tahoe story.

A basic part of the subject matter lies buried in the tinderous newsprint of the times, newspapers of settlements and cities that ring Lake Tahoe—Truckee, Reno, Virginia City, Carson City, Gold Hill, Genoa, Placerville—with additional material hidden in the fine print of early Sacramento Valley, East Bay and San Francisco dailies.

Virginia City's famous *Territorial Enterprise*, sounding board of Mark Twain, Dan DeQuille and Joe Goodman, offers illuminating sunstreaks of information.

Another on the spot pulsebeat is found in Tahoe's first paper, the *Tahoe Tattler*, that skyrocketed across the lake in the summer of 1881, only to sputter out in its second year of publication. Over a half century was to pass before this postage stamp daily would again be revived, but the original tissue sheets are filled with whimsical nostalgia, sparkling vignettes and blunt editorial scoldings that capture the tone of the Bonanza days at Tahoe.

Add to this the dedicated, unsparing helpfulness of the pioneer Tahoe residents and gradually the hodge-podge of pieces that make up this picture of the world's greatest Alpine lake fall into place.

The general misconception that Lake Tahoe was a no-man's land in early California-Nevada history, because it lay between the two main arteries of mass migration moving westward in the late 1840's and early 1850's, has been the convenient excuse offered for ignoring Tahoe's vital, colorful contribution to the growth of the Far West and America. Pack trails and wagon roads—five routes in all—skirted Tahoe and were used by the emigrants. The Great Bonanza Road to Washoe, carrying a floodtide of animals, men and materials to the Nevada mines, ran along the lake's southern shore. This turnpike constituted the "main stem" of the West from 1859 to 1868.

Obviously the natural beauty of Mark Twain's and Dan DeQuille's "Lake of the Sky" overshadows man's development of the Tahoe region. However, a backdrop of Washoe and Paiute Indian tribes fighting for control of the "Big Water's" fishing and hunting grounds—the nearly forgotten arterials, Pony Express riders, teamsters, and drivers of ox-cart and Concord coach alike, all furnish the nucleus for a story that is pertinent to Tahoe itself.

Of major importance were the extensive lumbering operations and vast water projects spawned by, and furnishing lifeblood to, the Comstock Lode—the small armadas of sailing, steam, and at the turn of the century, gasoline-powered vessels, moving out upon the waters of the lake—the trappers' cabins growing to trading posts, expanding into wayside inns and Wells Fargo Express stations and finally luxurious "Saratogas of the Pacific"—gold and silver boom towns that exploded into activity and then disappeared in a handful of sundowns—bright ribbons of railroad iron winding through the forestland and serving the gigantic lumbering combines for decades—a nationally famous trout fishing industry that, each year, took hundreds of tons of native silvers and cutthroat from the lake's waters—and some of the finest High Sierra farm and ranch land, producing record yields of timothy hay, outsize vegetables, beef and dairy cattle.

All played an essential part in the growth and expansion of the old Central Overland Trail where it branched out and crossed the twin Sierra Nevada barrier over Eagle Valley, Daggett, Luther and Johnson passes, all served to assure the Comstock Lode's development, and each lent a significance to Lake Tahoe that has been largely overlooked.

Factual roots of the Tahoe area are buried deep and the fanciful and legendary are easily confused with the veritable, thus gaining erroneous stature and acceptance. The myth, the imaginary, the tall-tale is, however, a definite part of the Tahoe narrative and is therefore treated as an obvious partner to the authentic.

This great inland sea that is Lake Tahoe has a rewarding story to offer the historian—a story that is not alone concerned with sweeping panoramas, vast mountain reaches, roiling snow water and blue horizons.

The true saga of Tahoe is found in the pioneer laker's struggle to carve out an all-year existence from this wilderness high altitude land of contrary extremes—blinding blizzards and telescopic clarity —frozen winter wastes and penetrating summer sunshine—gale-whipped peaks and quiet coves.

The shoreline and waters of this immense indigo basin have seen little more than a century of the white man's activity, but mountain men, emigrants, lumberjacks, Washoe nabobs, innkeepers, timber barons, windjamming "salts," steamer captains and scores of others from every walk of life have left their imprint on the Tahoe region.

Such homespun and brocade furnishes the patchwork for this many-colored crazy quilt that constitutes The Saga of Lake Tahoe.

THE SAGA OF LAKE TAHOE

"In the early morning one watches the silent battle of dawn and darkness on the waters of Tahoe with a placid interest but when the shadows skulk away and one by one the hidden beauties of the shore unfold themselves in the full splendor of noon; when the smooth surface is belted like a rainbow with broad bars of blue and green and white, half the distance from circumference to center, when in the lazy summer afternoon, he lies in a boat far out to where the dead blue of the deep water begins and smokes the pipe of peace and idly winks at the distant crags and patches of snow from under his cap brim; when the boat drifts shoreward to the white water, and he lolls over the gunwale and gazes by the hour down through the crystal depths and notes the color of the pebbles and reviews the finny armies gliding in procession a hundred feet below; when at night he sees moon and stars, mountain ridges feathered with pines, jutting white capes, bold promontories, grand sweeps of rugged scenery topped with bald glimmering peaks, all magnificently pictured in the polished mirror of the lake, in richest, softest detail the tranquil interest that was born with the morning deepens and deepens, by sure degrees, till it culminates at last in resistless fascination."

MARK TWAIN

Chapter One

SQUAW VALLEY

In STINGING RAIN that was gradually turning to sleet and a blanketing fall of snow, Ethan Allen Grosch a young prospector from one of the Western Utah camps (Virginia City), and his companion, Richard W. Bucke, struggled downriver from the outlet of Lake Tahoe (Bigler).[1] It was the afternoon of November 22, 1858. Strapped to the back of their single pack mule were the keys to the Comstock Lode's secret—specimens, charts, claims, and assays.

Their supplies were rapidly diminishing and the trail to Truckee Lake was obliterated.[2] Donner Pass, they knew, would be buried in deep drifts. Doggedly the two miners turned west and fought their way along the ice-bound creek into Squaw Valley. Ahead lay a formidable barrier of mountain peaks, with walls of snow towering on all sides.

Scarcely a month earlier Grosch had buried his brother, Hosea, under Sun Mountain.[3] After scraping together enough money for provisions, equipment and a jenny, he and Bucke had left Washoe on November 4 to cross the northwestern rim of the Sierra Nevada through the first swirling flakes of a growing snowstorm.

Following an Indian trail they reached a summit divide and dropped from 9,000 feet to the shores of Tahoe. Skirting its northern shoreline to the lake's outlet, they now were trying desperately to break through to the Middle Fork of the American River and Mud Springs.[4] Squaw Valley was the gateway to the western Sierra's bleak divide, but the soft fall of white death was closing in on them. It commenced to rain again, then grew colder. The wind increased and a blizzard funneled out of the canyon ahead. After making several futile attempts to scale the ridge, they built a crude shelter of pine branches and willows at the base of the snow barricade.

Provisions were now exhausted. Survival became their primary thought. They shot the burro and roasted her flesh. They fabricated crude snowshoes. Grosch threw his heavy ore samples into the drifts, keeping only his claims and assay reports.

Taking advantage of a break in the storm the following morning, the two men started across the fresh powder snow toward the pinnacles above them. After zigzagging upwards for hours they finally staggered over the pass. Ahead lay Mud Springs, but their hazardous trip was barely half completed.[5]

Another storm broke. Their blankets, great coats and gunpowder became soaked and useless. They threw them away, cursing. Grosch located a fallen pine. Wrapping his precious claims and assays in canvas he deposited them in a hollow of the tree. After carving a crude cross to mark the spot, they pushed on.

Once they discovered tracks in the snow ahead. But hope turned to despair. The footprints were their own. They had been traveling in a circle. Dazed and despairing they stumbled on, miraculously reaching the Middle Fork of the American River on December 5. Cold, hunger and exposure

1

brought them to their knees after they had wandered aimlessly through the rugged canyon for two days. Crawling on all fours the two men finally collapsed in the lee of some rocks.

Bucke was aroused from his stupor by gunshots. He struggled to his feet, only to slump into the arms of a party of Mexican miners who were deer hunting. They laid the two men on sleds and pulled them into Last Chance, a nearby gold mining camp.

Grosch died while fighting off the attempts of helping hands to amputate his frozen, gangrenous legs. No doctor was available, no anesthetic; just a hunting knife and saw. His last words were a delirious babbling about "Sun Mountain . . . Gold Canyon . . . blue stuff . . . the Company . . ."

Bucke's life was saved when the miners hacked off one leg, then his other foot. After months spent recuperating, he returned to his home in Canada. Later he became one of the Dominion's leading medical men. Richard Bucke had turned his back on the hundreds of millions in gold and silver that lay waiting in the Comstock Lode—the treasure thousands of stampeding miners were to discover later that same year.[6]

Grosch and his brother had been the Comstock's first quartz prospectors—the true discoverers of what would become the world-shaking Big Bonanza. Squaw Valley, so formidably guarded by the great Sierra Nevada, had connived with winter to keep the secret a few months longer. Sleeping with Allen Grosch was his discovery of pure silver hidden in the blue clay once cursed and discarded by the gold miners of Six Mile Canyon.

The tragedy of Grosch and Bucke pointed up the near impossibility of successfully crossing over the Squaw Valley route in mid-winter, although they were not the first to negotiate the Sierra at this point. As early as 1849 this shortcut to the Valley of the Sacramento had been known as "Scott's Route." It struck west from Eagle Valley Ranch (Carson City) over the Carson Range to the shores of Lake Tahoe, skirting its northern side to the outlet, then passing over the western Sierra by way of Squaw Valley to Fork House.[7]

To divert the growing overland emigrant travel through Placer County the trail had to be improved. On June 8, 1852, $13,000 was appropriated, and during the summer and fall of that year the money was spent clearing and grading. An additional $7,000 debt was run up before completion of what became known as the Placer County Emigrant Route. During the next three years this road was used as an alternate east-west crossing of the Sierra, however, the easier Donner, Johnson and Carson passes dried up traffic on the Placer County road and it fell into disrepair.[8]

"SNOWSHOE" CROSSING THE SNOWY RANGE

John "Snowshoe" Thompson on Norwegian snowshoes (skis) carrying the mails in 1856.

With the passage of the California Wagon Road Act in 1855, Placer County again bid for the central overland travel. In August of 1856 Thomas A. Young, official surveyor for the county, led a party of six men out of Fork House[9] and they headed northeast to determine both the condition of the road and approximate cost of putting the "Old Ridge Route" into usable shape again. Eight miles of travel and they had passed Secret Springs House, Canadian Hill, Damascus and Weaverville and arrived at Robinson's Flat.

The party moved on, climbing steadily "by easy grade" along a passable road following the ridge to the Sierra summit west of Tahoe. Young reported a "fine view of the lake was obtained from here," estimating its distance as seven air miles away. From the summit, under Squaw Peak, the men dropped three miles down the divide into the northwest end of Squaw Valley. Here Young recommended that the road be rerouted to the lower end of the valley, making the descent more gradual.

The surveyor's enthusiasm over the sight spread out below inspired him to note: "Squaw Valley is the most beautiful valley the eye of man has ever beheld. It is covered with luxuriant grasses, and the soil is of the most productive nature. It is completely surrounded by mountains, there being about five hundred acres of tillable land available. From the upper end of Squaw a nearly level road runs two miles to the crossing of the Truckee River. Here the ford is good, being two feet deep and thirty feet wide, with the current rapid and a solid stream bed. From the crossing of the Truckee the road extends along the east bank of the stream five miles to the headwaters of Lake Bigler.

"Very little labor will be required to make a good turnpike, allowing sixty feet of grade to the mile. The head of the Truckee River (Bigler Lake outlet) is four feet deep and ninety feet wide, running in a northerly direction. Bigler is a magnificent sheet of water, forty-five miles in length by fifteen miles

SQUAW VALLEY'S FIRST

The barn and stable of Fish, Ferguson, Smith and Coggins Company, built in 1862 and located on the west side of the valley. This view was taken in May, 1883, after Lowell and Locke acquired the ranch.

California State Library

SNOWSHOE RACING IN THE SIERRA NEVADA

This early sketch, from the Mining and Scientific Press of 1886, shows the racers' "schuss technique," bolstered with courage instilled by the whiskey keg, and contestants "doping" their skis.

in breadth (sic), with soft granite rock deposits of sand and round washed gravel on the shoreline and lake bottom."

Young also commented on the vivid colors and clarity of the lake, marveling at its suggestion of tremendous depth.[10]

The surveyor's report continues: "The road now runs nearly parallel with the western shore to the north end of Lake Bigler for twenty miles and here sidehill cutting will be necessary. Several pieces of good meadowland are passed enroute.[11] From the north end of the lake, the road commences ascending the east summit of the Sierra Nevada." The ascent was described as "easy, the surface smooth, with good grass." After reaching the eastern summit the party passed down the five-mile drop, through Little Valley, to Washoe.

Young further pointed out that the (Little Valley) road, for the most part, "has been worked here with much sidehill cutting already done." Of a slide of loose granite rock he said "five men in one week's time will place this part of the road in its original condition."

Obviously optimistic about opening the route, Young noted that the total distance from Fork House, by way of Squaw Valley over the twin Sierra barrier to Washoe, was only sixty-two miles, making it the shortest trans-Sierra crossing.[12]

The surveyor and his men found only Mormon settlers in the vicinity of Washoe Sink, where Brigham Young's Judge of Probate, Orson Hyde, was building a flour mill near the present site of Franktown. Young reported Hyde as "being in favor of the road improvement," and he indicated that a mere $8,000 would put the Ridge Route or Squaw Valley road "in the best of condition." He stressed the fact it crossed only one stream exceeding five feet in width (the Truckee River at its junction with Squaw Valley) and opined that a "sixty-foot wooden span above high water mark" would be all that was required there.

Young's findings electrified the supervisors and residents of Placer County. Immediate plans were made to appropriate funds necessary to put the route in "turnpike shape." Emigrant travel flowing again through Placer County was envisioned. Beautiful Squaw Valley would be transformed into what was unusually described as "a ladies' paradise."

Suddenly on July 8, 1857, the road improvement program was dropped, its supporters explaining that "insufficient money had been raised." It was an unexpected and bitter defeat for Young.[13]

However, with the discovery of the Great Comstock two years later the Ridge Route again came up for consideration and on February 11, 1860, the Placer County and Washoe Turnpike Company was organized with $50,000 in capital stock issued. Now everybody was certain the new thoroughfare would become an actuality and operate as a toll road.[14] But once again it was shelved and a direct, high level wagon and stage route to the mines by way of Squaw failed to materialize. Construction of the Central Pacific Railroad, across the Sierra at Donner Pass to the north, ended all possibility of the Placer County-Washoe road improvement.

Today the course of the early emigrant's ox-drawn Conestoga "sail tops" can still be traced from the tracks cut by massive iron-banded wheel rims into the granite road bed. Before usage partially improved the trail, wagons often had to be dismantled and dragged with block and tackle up the near vertical cliffs. Draft animals would be double-teamed to haul the vehicles on the easier stretches toward the summit and giant pines on the route still show the marks of the snubbing ropes and chains.

Before the advent of white settlers, Squaw Valley was a summer tribal ground for the native Washoe Indians. Many theories have been advanced as to the origin of the name. Among them is the legend of the faithful squaw waiting patiently in the valley for her warrior brave to return, not knowing he had been killed in battle with the Paiutes. Another is the fanciful story of one "Indian Charlie" who murdered his common law wife in the valley during a game of "squaw poker." Unanimously acquitted by a jury of his fellow Washoe tribesmen, after it was decided the white man's red-eye had blinded him to what he was doing, he is said to have become known as "Squaw Valley Charlie" and left his nickname on the valley.

A logical source of the name is based on fact. When the first emigrants moved through the valley in 1849-50 they were surprised to find only squaws and children at the summer encampment. The bucks were away on a trek to Long Valley, sixteen miles to the southeast over the granite ridge from Lower Hell Hole and the Rubicon River. There they hunted the "picket pin" gopher and caught grasshoppers to augment the tribe's food supply. Since the emigrants found a majority of squaws in the base camp they named it Squaw Valley.[15]

In 1862, Fish, Ferguson, Smith and Coggins settled on Federal lands in Squaw, calling their meadowland sections Squaw Valley Ranch.[16] During the summer and fall seasons more than 125 tons of wild hay were cut. After baling it in a crude hand press the partners transported the bales by high-bed stake wagon over the new $500 Truckee River bridge and a passable road five miles to the lake's outlet.

No record of a boom development at Squaw Valley is recorded until June of the year 1863. At that time two prospectors, John Keiser and Shannon Knox, made their way from Yankee Jim's over the Squaw Valley summit pass into the mountain meadow.[17] Originally Georgetowners, they were vaguely headed in the general direction of Washoe. Near a flat across the Truckee and northwest of the mouth of Squaw Creek, the miners located outcroppings of rich-looking reddish ore. A mile upstream additional "color" was discovered.

The news spread through the Mother Lode like wildfire. Tales of fabulous wealth touched off a

SPEEDSTERS ON THE SLOPE

A quintet of single-poled, star-hatted members of a pioneer Sierra Nevada skiing group are crouched and ready for action in the 1880's.

William Berry

stampede that threatened to depopulate the settlements of Placer County. Miners, merchants, saloon keepers, mechanics, gamblers and "gentlemen at large" (more commonly called "bummers") hurried in companies, squads and single file to Squaw Valley. The magic call echoed through the mountains. This was the new El Dorado with "ledges of the richest silver, rivaling and even surpassing those of the Comstock Lode itself."

First Knoxville, named for Shannon Knox, sprang into life adjoining the site of the first "strike." Then Claraville mushroomed overnight upriver, near the location of the second discovery. By August of 1863 a wilderness had been transformed into bustling, thriving settlements. From two prospectors the district's population had grown in six weeks to six hundred frenzied miners.[18]

Actually the settlements were only collections of hastily thrown together, rough shacks. "Hotels" had dirt floors. Chairs, tables and beds were constructed on the spot. Not even a horse and wagon had been driven down the narrow trail that connected the two centers of activity and passed for a main street.

Everybody was speculating in mining footage. Town lots that had sold for $10 apiece a few weeks before skyrocketed to $200.

But it was the opinion of one shrewd observer that "he surely would not invest in any mine he had seen there, and he had visited eight or nine of the best." "I'd give $25 for a good photograph of both main streets," he declared, "particularly if it included Knoxville's Union Clothing Store, a shanty in the shade of a tree with brush for a roof." He stared in amazement at the Union Hotel: "You could see clean through the walls and its roof was equally divided between canvas and bushes," he reported. Looking further, he discovered bearded men and scampering chipmunks by the hundreds in the "diggings," but not a single woman or child.[19]

Assay reports on the ore were pending and it appeared that most everything but a proven bonanza was available.[20] A legend persists that Shannon Knox originally "salted" his claim. Salted or not, Knox was inoculated with the fever and dug frantically like all the rest.

Johnson King, a Tennessee outlaw, terrorized Knoxville and it is said James Tracey, diminutive storekeeper and solid citizen, trumped this King with a revolver bullet between the eyes. King was "laid away with a spade" and Tracey lost a customer—a loss witnesses testified he preferred to forfeiting his own life.[21]

Suddenly the fatal word flashed between Knoxville and Claraville. Ore samples had failed to prove up. The bubble exploded. Once again a stampede began, this time in reverse. The high-pitched excitement died out as quickly as it had started. Another would-be El Dorado vanished, its streets, shacks and mines deserted before the year was out.

However, this abortive bonanza served an unexpected purpose. It set the stage for the establishment of Tahoe City five miles upstream and spread a handful of disgruntled miners along the western shores of Lake Tahoe.[22] Nor was the valley itself neglected. Wild hay was plentiful. Choice timber stands ran from the meadow's edge up the mountains on all sides. In addition, the snow-fed waters of Squaw Creek offered water power and trout in abundance. Excellent hunting was also reported. Two grizzlies had been seen in the valley and three nimrods with Henry rifles immediately set out "seeking an interview."[23]

By April of 1864 the Prescott brothers had improved the "Squaw Valley Trail" from Forest Hill over the western summit into the valley. It was now termed "a usable thoroughfare." Lots in Knoxville and Claraville were purchased at bargain prices by the Prescotts, who hoped to build a permanent settlement with farming and lumbering.

In the spring of 1872 Lowell and Locke, who had settled at the lake's outlet, acquired the Squaw Valley Ranch and properties held by the Prescott brothers. A mowing machine, three wagons and

Ernie Mack

"GRASS AND WATER . . . PLENTY"

Springtime in Squaw, "the most beautiful valley the eye of man has ever beheld." Here the Washoe Indians set up their summer encampments in the fertile meadowland bordering Squaw Creek, and the emigrants rested their stock before crossing the barrier range to the Valley of the Sacramento.

dairy cows were added. Timothy hay and other ranch products were raised on their 320 acres and shipped into Truckee.[24] By 1879 Casper Shock's water-powered shingle mill was operating in the valley, and 275,000 cedar shakes were turned out before winter set in.[25]

Three years later Squaw Valley was being described as the "Gem of the Mountains" situated in "rarefied, pure air at 6,126 feet above sea level, with the little farming community raising hay, vegetables, berries, and kegging butter and cheese in white fir firkins made by local coopers." The valley was now acknowledged to be "the best butter producing and dairy farming location in the Sierra, with a ready market found for products—at the hotels around the lake and the sawmills of the region. . . ."[26]

During the next half century, however, Squaw dropped from its position as a major High Sierra farming settlement to little more than a secluded summer range for running cattle.

In 1949, nearly eighty years after the mining rush to the area, Squaw Valley Development Company took title to much of the acreage in the valley and leased the surrounding mountain land. Squaw now stood on the threshold of substantial growth. This was no silver strike boom, lumbering operation, or farming project. The natural amphitheater was about to become one of America's finest ski resorts.

SETTING FOR THE 1960 WINTER OLYMPICS

Aerial view of Squaw Valley, looking southwest. Eight thousand nine hundred sixty-foot Squaw Peak, known as Sugar Loaf in the 1870's, stands in the center background flanked by Silver Peak, Needle Peak and Granite Chief. Squaw Valley Lodge, which burned and was rebuilt in 1956, lies at the terminus of the road (center foreground).

William Briner

A spacious, modern lodge was constructed. Outlying guest chalets were built to take care of the burgeoning winter business. Up the side of the mountain toward Squaw Peak, its steel towers anchored to the precipitous slope, rose a double chair lift, largest in the world at the time. Today Squaw Valley rivals Idaho's Sun Valley, Colorado's Aspen and the Continent's finest resorts in Switzerland and the Austrian Tyrol.[27]

Final laurels have now been added.

Squaw Valley's manager, Alexander Cushing, with the cooperative backing of California's Governor Goodwin J. Knight and other personages, flew to Europe in the spring of 1955 and appeared before the International Olympic Committee where he presented such a convincing picture of the facilities and snow conditions existing in the region that the valley was selected for the 1960 Winter Olympic Games. By the spring of 1956 the necessary multi-million dollar appropriation had been voted by the California Legislature and added to an original commitment.

Paradoxically, the bonanza that failed to materialize nearly a century ago is now assured and Squaw Valley has embarked on another tremendous expansion program—one that would cause the grizzled miners of the early 1860's to gape in wonderment and shake their heads in stunned disbelief.

FORERUNNER OF THE MIRACLES TO COME

Original Squaw Valley Lodge as it appeared in the early spring of 1954; looking down Squaw Valley northeast toward the Truckee River.

William Briner

Chapter Two

TRUCKEE RIVER CANYON

"O<small>N A CLEAN THROW</small>, the sawlogs jump away like cannon balls, picking up speed with lightning rapidity down the 1700-foot dry chute that drops to the terminal pond in the Truckee River a half mile distant."

C. F. McGlashan, editor of the *Truckee Republican*, was leaning against the vertically grooved bark of a massive cedar tree high above the gorge. It was the summer of 1876, and McGlashan was jotting down notes on this man-made sensation of the Sierra Nevada, the log chute. He continued to write:

"Tons of sugar pine move faster and faster, forty—fifty—sixty—then seventy miles an hour, now leaving a rocket's trail as sparks and clouds of smoke fan out behind the hurtling missiles, caused by the frictional heat generated as they thunder down the greased runway. Often the ground on which the log chutes lie is irregular, and the whistling projectiles make gigantic leaps into the air, sometimes even jumping clear of the track, to pin-wheel over and over down the mountainside. Ahead is the deep water pool at the bottom of the canyon, and the screaming logs careen off into space, a sunstreak of motion, cracking into the water barrier with an ear-splitting report heard over a mile distant. An arching sheet of spray is driven into the air to a height of nearly 100 feet, spreading a feathered rainbow against the canyon walls and hanging, a transparent curtain of sparkling diamonds, before falling back into the pond.

"The logs have traversed the chute, with a perpendicular drop of 700 feet, in fourteen seconds, averaging over a hundred feet per second and traveling more than twice that speed when they strike the water. At times these deadly, screeching timbers carom off another log in the receiving pond. Then they snap end over end a half dozen times as easily as a thrown lead pencil.

"Brickell and Krueger recall seeing 4-foot by 20-foot logs leap into the air in a soaring arc and carry cleanly across the river, rebounding on the further bank to bury themselves a full half of their length, 150 feet up the mountain."[1]

Several years later a correspondent from the *Reno Evening Gazette* reported with obvious amazement, "Record speeds of saw logs down the chutes have been carefully checked, and Brickell clocked one massive log when it flashed one-half mile *in five seconds!*"[2]

At certain locations on the Truckee River, the paths of the log chutes crossed the wagon and stage road. Here speeding logs were sometimes trestled overhead but more often they leaped the intervening space before rocketing on down the steep slope. The "free-carry" practice was abandoned after a span of horses had been crushed to death by a log that hurtled out of control—the driver of the team experiencing a hairbreadth escape.

With such expeditious transportation available from high line logging camps to the river, it was

ITS GATES WERE BACKBREAKERS

Colonel Von Schmidt's Tahoe outlet dam built in the spring of 1870. The gates were raised and lowered by hand. Photograph was taken in 1898 from the old wooden bridge, looking east toward Tahoe.

a foregone conclusion that the more daring lumberjacks would eventually "have a go" at riding the logs down the chutes. Contemporary sketches glorified the intrepid, if addle-brained, cleat-booted stalwarts who took off on the steep downgrade run, their hair streaming out in the breeze. Successfully negotiating the leap away from the log at that split second before it drove into the pond, the thrill-seekers would emerge soaking wet and half drowned but triumphant.[3]

Indeed, the dry chute, perfected in the early 1860's, offered blood-stirring excitement peculiar to back country logging camps. Oxen were originally used to drag-chain the logs down an improvised road to the Truckee River. Crude skidways superseded this method. Three, four, or often five, logs were laid on the ground to form a base for the logway, with two additional logs spiked on top. This was a costly, time-consuming installation.

The development of the dual log chute logically followed, and brought timbering in the high country to a fine degree of perfection. Truckee River Canyon shared in the pioneering of the dual log chute, with Brickell and Krueger's Truckee River Lumber Company installing their first "gravitation chutes" in 1864.[4] The cost was nominal, approximating $1.00 a foot. Very little labor was involved as trees felled at the site were laid end to end across flat terrain, and down steep declivities. Some of the drops ranged as high as 65 degrees. A shallow trench was usually dug first, then the logs were rolled in and anchored to the ground where necessary. Particular care was taken to butt the log ends smoothly and securely together with the lower end of the chute, if on an incline, resting against a stump or granite slab. Once

---

George D. Oliver

CALK BOOTED "JACKS" AND SAW LOGS

Breaking a log jam with peaveys on the Truckee River near Rampart, August 3, 1896.

the logs were paralleled their inner surfaces were faced off to form a trough. Greasing of the ways by a "tallow boy" was the final step.

A typical large scale logging operation was noted in the *Truckee Republican* during July of 1873:

"Up river from the Truckee River Lumber Company's double mill, bluffs run back above the gorge a full half mile into the heavy stands of timber. Here high line logging camps are established, each camp consisting of the gang boss, a forty-odd man crew of fallers, trimmers, teamsters, swampers, a blacksmith, cook, tallow boy, and draft animals. French-Canadian lumberjacks are dropping the mammoth six- and seven-foot-through sugar pine, averaging one down every three minutes, and the great forest kings are crashing in every direction. Before the dust even settles around a fallen monarch, a swarm of trimmers are cleaning off the limbs. The air resounds to the monotonous rasp of two-man hand saws, the sharp ring of double-edged axes, and the long-drawn-out 'wheehoes' of the bullwhackers and skinners. Through the din may be heard the steady grinding rasp of the heavy log sections as they are dragged onto the feeder ramps preparatory to starting their run down the mountainside. When three to four logs have been positioned in the upper logway, a team of six, hitched in tandem by a 'chain gearing,' moves in with a 'breaker' riding the wheel animal. A large iron hook is faced into the butt of the last log in the chute, secured by trace-chains to the horses or mules.

"With a sharp crack of the buckskin lash's 'popper' the team is off at a trot toward the edge of the steep bluff, pulling eight tons of logs easily down the greased chute. The tallow boy is running up and down the sides of the trough, slopping brushfuls of animal fat onto the running surfaces.[5] At the top of the precipitous fall to the river, the hook is thrown and the logs plunge over the rim of the canyon wall and down the chute. This is accomplished without stopping the team or breaking their gait.

"Accidents are expected. Sometimes the animals are crushed when their drag chains entangle in the moving logs. Again a train of fast-moving logs may overtake those ahead, with disastrous effect. When the hook is embedded too deeply into the butt of the 'mover' log death is riding with the breaker and his animals. If the hook cannot be snapped free, the horses' feet are jerked out from under them and they fall heavily in a thrashing mass."

The *Reno Evening Gazette*, in an article titled "Delivering Logs," gives a somewhat different picture of logging above the Truckee Canyon during the summer of 1881:

"Teams of six and eight animals are being used to snake the fallen timber to the upper end of the log chutes. Trees are scattered and the work is expensive. Horse 'gangs' of three and four animals are also at work dragging logs on the level spots where they will not slide under their own momentum.

"These are referred to as 'horse railways.' A total of thirty chutes, the longest three miles in length, are in use on the river and loggers are constantly on the watch for fire from the whistling logs smoking down the terminal chute."

The invention of the ingenious V-flume in 1867 and earlier adaptation of the box-type watercourses served to complement the use of the dry log chutes. As water flumes were primarily used to move cordwood and lumber to the staging yards, the fast, reliable log chute, along with the logging wagon, was the first step in starting saw logs on their way to the mills.

Apart from lumbering, the Truckee River Canyon has had its share of Washoe Indian legends. One of the better known tales concerns the fable of Lover's Leap. High above Big Chief Camp on the river road and half way between Tahoe City and Truckee stands the profile of Big Chief "No-Name." Clearly visible is his aquiline nose, stern mouth, and majestic forehead. Nearly every county and state in the country boasts a Lover's Leap. This is Tahoe's.[6] Legend reaches back to an early Washoe Indian known as Charlie Smith, who passed the story on for posterity. Charley had been given the tribal name "Lame Horse" but quickly changed it to Smith. His explanation: "Everybody knows a lame horse can't get anybody anywhere, anytime, so what kind of a name is that?" he asked.

Centuries before the advent of the white man, "Lame Horse's" ancestors camped on the shores of Tahoe at what is now Carnelian Bay. They hunted the back country in the vicinity of Mount Watson and Pluto, Bear Trap, and the Big Gorge (Truckee Canyon). Wearing skins of the mountain cougar, black bear, and whitetailed deer, they feasted on grasshopper soup and a tasty, spicy sauce made from myriads of red ants. The tribe's chieftain, so proficient in his leadership that words could not describe his abilities, was given the title "No-Name." "No-Name's" only daughter, fragile and beautiful Cedar Heart, lived under the watchful, jealous eye of her father. She was forbidden to marry, yet the Chief wished her to carry on his mighty tribal customs and follow him as leader of the Washoes when the Great Spirit called him to the Happy Hunting Grounds. But the inevitable young Indian brave stepped in and won Cedar Heart's love. No-Name's rage was terrible to see, and he called for the warrior's death. The young lovers took to the forest with Big Chief No-Name and his tribe in hot pursuit. Moving swiftly over a game trail toward the Truckee River they were heading for Squaw Valley Pass in an attempt to escape to the Valley of Grass beyond. The Great Spirit, moved by the plight of the terrified couple, caused a tremendous storm to sweep the forest. Thunder rolled. Stinging rain drove through the massive tree tops. Still No-Name and his warriors followed. Suddenly Cedar Heart and her lover found themselves on the edge of the Truckee Gorge. Hundreds of feet below, sharp granite rocks thrust up from the bottom of the sheer cliff. The howling warriors closed in rapidly with No-Name in the lead

George D. Oliver

TOURING ON THE TRUCKEE TURNPIKE

The George D. Oliver family from Hobart Mills, headed for Tahoe City on July 8, 1909, in their wooden spoked, acetylene lamped Mitchell "sports runabout." Photograph taken alongside the narrow gauge railroad east of present Deer Park Lodge.

HARVESTING BLUE ICE ON THE RIVER

"Red" Anderson, Robert Watson, Charlie Watson, Bob Harkness, Carl Bechdolt, Sr., Bert Watson and Johnnie Karnack cutting and chuting ice blocks to the road in 1927, at the first pool downstream from Tahoe's outlet.

flourishing his flint-headed ax. All chance of escape was cut off. Only one choice remained. The pursued threw their arms around each other and leaped off into space, dropping to their death in the chasm. Chief No-name rushed to the edge of the cliff. Kneeling, he peered into the void beneath him, his face contorting in horror and shame. The great Chief's warriors, seeing the convulsive despair of their leader, melted into the blackness of the forest. Wind howled and moaned around No-Name, and rain beat down upon his once proud head. It appeared as though the Great Spirit were holding him on the rocky summit instead of sweeping him off into the gorge. He clung to the promontory, his eyes straining for some sign of his daughter and her Indian brave. At last the Chief attempted to rise, but the Great Spirit had frozen him to the red-brown rock. A thousand arrows of remorse struck through his heart, and he twisted and turned in his grief. No-Name lifted his face toward the heavens imploring help, but no help came. Slowly he sank back into the rock until only his profile remained. His destiny would be to look forever into eternity.[7]

Historically, the Truckee River Canyon (or Gorge) combines legend and lumbering, staging, and "natural wonders." A debate still smoulders over the actual source of the name Truckee, and the word carries nearly as many interpretations as are found in the Tahoe controversy.

V-PLOW AND DOUBLE-HEADER

On April 17, 1922, it took two locomotives and a push plow 21 days to break through the 20-foot snowdrifts from Tahoe City to Truckee.

Originally the Truckee River was given the name Salmon Trout by Captain John Charles Fremont, during his Pacific Coast exploratory probe in January of 1844, when he discovered "two to four foot" land-locked salmon in the river. One authority pursues the thought that "Truckee, son of Chief Winnemucca, was the first to lead Fremont across the mountains (Sierra Nevada) and that his name was given to the river, by the pathfinder, in gratitude." The same source indicates that Truckee Lake (Donner) was first called "Snow Lake" or "Lake Wood" by Fremont.[8] Both statements are erroneous, as Fremont did not strike west up the Truckee Gorge but moved south instead to what later became the Carson River and Pass.[9]

A more acceptable version of the name Truckee is found in mountain man Stephen Hall Meek's testimony. He indicated that "Truckee" was a French-Canadian trapper traveling with the Bonneville-Walker group in the 1830's.[10]

In November of 1844, Matthew Harbin, a member of the Stevens-Townsend-Murphy emigrant party, the first to cross the Central Sierra with wagons, named their Paiute Indian guide Truckee after this same French-Canadian trapper whom Harbin was reported to have known. Although Dr. John Townsend is said to have attempted to name the river the "Stevens" in honor of his associate, "Truckey" stuck from the beginning.[11]

Gudde, in his "Place Names of California," mentions that the Spanish name for trout is *trucha*, and hints that it could have passed to the Paiute Indians previous to the time of the white trappers and explorers and thence to the river. In spite of the Donner party tragedy at "Truckey" Lake in the winter of 1846, the lake contined to be known as "Truckey," "Trucky" and "Truckey's Lake" through the 1850's and early 60's. In 1876 it was officially changed to Donner on the Wheeler Survey map. But the name Truckee was retained on the river "to become one of the most notable place names in the West."[12]

Strangely enough, the town of Truckee did not receive its present name until the year 1869. Joseph Gray built the first log house there in 1863 as a stage station to serve the Dutch Flat Wagon Road traffic spewing over Donner Pass. J. McConnell followed Gray in 1864, settling on ground half a mile west of Gray's cabin, and sold out to one Coburn, who gave his name to the settlement. When the Central Pacific Railroad pushed its rails past Coburn's Station four years later the railroad magnates bestowed the established local place name, Truckee, on the location.[13]

The lumbering and railroad town has survived fires, bloodletting, racial purges and carousing to lift its head in the last few decades toward creditable self-improvement. An unimpressed newsman offered the following sneer in the fall of 1870: "Truckee is a straggling town of some 1200 inhabitants —several sawmills employ a portion of the population, with the rest standing around and watching the others work."[14]

Today the opposite is true and Truckee is expanding west toward Donner Lake with a new Tahoe-Truckee high school, hospital, and shopping center already completed. Active service organizations and clubs bolster civic pride and the little town with the famous name is on its way.

TWENTY-FIVE YEARS YOUNG

Engine Number One (formerly the "TAHOE" at Glenbrook) takes a breather near Deer Park Springs station in the summer of 1901 before continuing her downgrade run to Truckee. Engineer Frank Titus, Sr., and fireman seated between the drive wheels.

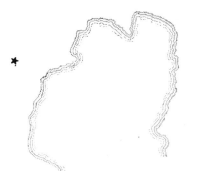

Chapter Three

DEER PARK SPRINGS

J<small>IM</small> M<small>C</small>N<small>UTT</small> wasn't much of a hand with the ladies but he was known as one hell of a good mountain man. McNutt could take a pair of springy hickory staves, rub their running surfaces smooth, smear them with bear fat, pick a steep tree-covered slope of powder snow and leave both the guff-and-blow braggart and experienced cross country skier behind in a whirling white barrage.

As all-year caretaker for the John Brown Scott family, owner-developers of Deer Park Inn during the late 1880's, McNutt had the opportunity to embellish his reputation as a crack shot, skillful trapper and the "hardest man to follow in the Sierra."[1]

From his winter headquarters at the Inn he made trapping forays into the back country where he pelted fisher, marten, silver and red fox. On one of these expeditions McNutt learned from bitter experience never to roll up in his moth-eaten blanket and lie down on the snow. At the time he made this mistake, the heat generated by the vast number of whiskey nightcaps he'd downed melted his snowy mattress, lowering him gently to the icy ground while he snored. In the morning he awoke to find himself surrounded by the walls of a frozen mausoleum. After this "sobering" experience Jim McNutt slept on a slab of fir bark so he could, as he put it, "remain on top of the situation." It also placed him in a position of readiness in case a "devil beast" (wolverine) entered his camp to make off with his meager supply of grub, or worse, threatened his jug of raw spirits.

Whether it was summer or winter, insomnia never bothered McNutt. On deer hunting trips during the fall season he would curl up in his single tattered blanket, take a last long pull from his gallon demijohn, pull his slouch hat down over his ears, tuck his nose and chin into his beard and sleep like a log.[2]

A somewhat different slant on Deer Park Inn and Springs was given by Edwin Markham in his *California the Wonderful* when he bowed to the resort in nostalgic prose, describing it as a "canyon'd and cascaded slope where the joy hunters gather."[3]

Actually the original Inn and Springs, located south over the ridge from Squaw Valley, afforded a mountain meadow retreat that attracted porch sitters and outdoorsmen alike for nearly half a century. Relaxation and the healthy approach to living were emphasized. Only two miles from the Truckee River, the resort was situated in a grove of yellow pine and tamarack bordering Bear Creek. Deer Park served as a gateway to Five Lakes, Upper and Lower Hell Hole, and the Rubicon wilderness country.

Before the establishment of the hotel, John P. Scott, owner of a large cattle ranch in Sacramento County, found that his summer grazing range in Alpine's Hope Valley failed to provide sufficient pasturage for his expanding herd. It was the summer of 1880, and he and his wife, Alice Riggins Scott, rode north on horseback along the western Sierra Nevada rim above Tahoe, looking for new high country meadowland to which they could drive their stock. After picking their way down the old Placer County Emigrant Road into Squaw Valley they here discovered bottomland and waist-high wild grass. Their search had ended.

The Scotts then acquired several quarter sections of grazing land from Casper Shock, Lowell and Locke and other landholders in the valley.[4] The new location proved ideal for a dairy ranch and "their business prospered after the manner of the times."[5]

In the autumn of 1882 Scott encountered rigorous weather as he was driving his cattle from summer range to the Sacramento Valley. As a result of exposure he died that October, leaving his widow and their three sons, Ed, Herbert, and J. Chester, to carry on the business.[6]

During the mid-1880's Mrs. Scott married John Brown Scott. Her second husband was no relation to John P. Scott, nor was he a cattle man. He did recognize, however, that the Bear Valley area directly to the south of Squaw Valley contained many natural features that made it a logical choice for a summer resort. There was a beautiful amphitheater carpeted with wild flowers. Above rose lofty granite peaks, and a snow-fed stream meandered through the meadow. All that it needed was someone to exploit its possibilities.

Scott and his wife purchased the land, and in the summer of 1888 they completed a large three-story, twenty-room hotel. Eight outlying cabins were added within the next three years, including a log and shake roofed "social hall." Southeast across the creek from the Inn the Scotts had previously come upon iron, sulphur and soda mineral springs. This discovery was hailed with delight, as natural mineral waters were then considered a "must" for any self-respecting summer health establishment.

Various names were given to the cabins, such as "Forty Nine" after the forty-nine steps leading to its heavy pine door, and "Tamarack" for the surrounding grove of trees. A stable and barn were built on granite rock foundations, then a log corral was added. Here the Scotts' horses and milk cows were kept.[7]

FLAGS AND THE FOURTH

Social Hall at Deer Park Springs decked out for a shivaree on the Fourth of July, 1889, looking southwest up the side of the mountain.

California State Library

"ACCOMMODATIONS FOR MAN OR BEAST"

Two and one-half story Deer Park Springs Inn (Hotel), famous high country health hostelry, as it appeared in August, 1919. View taken facing southeast in the direction of Tahoe.

Mrs. E. G. Chandler

During the 1890's John Brown Scott or his oldest stepson, Ed, staged to Truckee to meet guests arriving on the railroad from San Francisco and the valley towns. On April 18, 1900, a post office was authorized for the up-and-coming resort, and in the summer of the same year, a station placed at the junction of Deer Park road and the Lake Tahoe Railway and Transportation Company's new narrow-gauge line.[8] Being closer to civilization than were rival Rubicon Springs and Glen Alpine, yet offering the same seclusion, Deer Park now attracted school marms, hunters, fishermen and other health seekers. Here, more than a mile above sea level, all sought the salutary effects of rarefied air and mineral water. Pioneer California families, among them the George B. Wilcuts, Tallants, Crockers and Williams, reserved cabins year after year for one and two month periods.[9]

A touch of High Sierra levity was exhibited on a large sign that hung above the entrance to the hotel. It read: "Accommodations for man or beast." Visitors chuckled with appreciation, but old-timers uneasily derided the quip, fancying it carried unfavorable personal insinuations.

Although other resorts in the Lake Tahoe region at the turn of the century advertised "homelike, family style accommodations," Deer Park was the one that came closest to fulfilling the boast.[10] From their dairy in Squaw Valley the Scott boys supplied milk daily to the Springs in five-gallon cans. Prime steaks are recalled as mouth-watering delicacies and no liquor was served. Even crusty old mountain man Jim McNutt, normally unconcerned by guests whether "man *or* beast," nevertheless felt constrained to do his drinking behind the barn. Mrs. Scott considered a full ten hours' sleep essential to the well-being of her patrons and personally made the rounds with a flickering kerosene lamp each night at 10 o'clock sharp to make sure all were bedded down. At mealtimes the strident clanging of the triangle brought guests stampeding to the dining hall adjoining the creek, where steaming hot meals were served ranch style. Providing hot water presented a problem. Guests sometimes had to wait until 3:00 in the afternoon for the massive iron water barrel to heat up from the bonfire started beneath it early the same morning.[11]

Deer Park Springs had but one recorded fatality, and this occurred during the winter of 1909. The caretaker, a Scandinavian who finally replaced the durable McNutt, made his customary trip into Tahoe City on snowshoes to pick up the mail. Here he availed himself of this excellent opportunity to get solidly drunk. That night he staggered down river carrying a jug under one arm and a mail sack under the other. Several days passed and when he failed to appear at the post office a search party, led by Robert Montgomery Watson, set out to find him. On the snow-covered bank of Bear Creek they came upon what the wolves had left of his frozen body. The following spring Watson buried the remains alongside the road leading into Deer Park Springs, placing a white cross to mark the spot.[12]

Upon John Brown Scott's death, shortly after the turn of the century, Miss Katherine Chandler, a writer and teacher of botany from San Francisco, California, took over the Inn. A semi-invalid, she was unable to run the resort with the same bustling thoroughness and hearty manner shown by the indefatigable Scott family. However, Miss Chandler added new facilities as well as improving existing ones at Deer Park Springs. A dam had been thrown across Bear Creek by the Scotts, and small boats placed upon the artificial lake thus formed. A tennis court and croquet grounds were now added. Music and the serving of iced lemonade became a regular part of the afternoon program. Well kept rock-bordered paths led to the mineral springs which were enclosed by a log pergola. Young "Bud" Chandler, nephew of Miss Chandler, gained a measure of fame when he was "quarantined" in the ice house during a spell of measles. Some years later he would achieve national recognition as a tennis player.[13]

Miss Chandler had taken over the resort in 1905 and several other owners subsequently acquired Deer Park Springs. Included were the C. J. Smiths, the Vincent Whitneys, and Ellery Arms, all of San Francisco. At the close of the 1920's the San Francisco Board of Trade foreclosed on the land and improvements.[14]

During the last two decades Deer Park has gradually reverted to the primitive and today the years have erased the buildings. A few fallen timbers mark the old stable and a sagging cabin straddles the creek.

At "Big Bend," just south of Bear Creek's inlet into the Truckee River, a new Deer Park Lodge was built. Run as an all-year resort, under the management of Mr. and Mrs. Gerald Dee Waters, it offered a High Sierra retreat for the summer outdoorsman and winter ski enthusiast. In 1964 the Lodge was purchased by San Francisco-Tahoe financier Gardner W. Mein who renamed it River Ranch and later resold the establishment.

Chapter Four

TAHOE CITY

O N A FROSTY October morning in 1876 one of James Cardwell's six-horse stages was loading in front of the Grand Central Hotel, preparatory to making its scheduled run down canyon to Truckee. The unmatched spans of horseflesh, their nostrils steaming the crisp air, were anything but a blooded show team, yet they appeared well fed and powerful.

A. J. Bayley, proprietor of the Central, stood at the high step placed in front of the coach's open door personally handing his departing guests aboard.[1] Ticket agent Lloyd Hawthorne scurried about in a frenzied state of excitement, endeavoring to seat as many passengers as possible in the rapidly diminishing available space.[2] Desperation finally prompted him to line five of the party together over the rear seat. Then he requested that they all sit down when he gave the word. A loud chorus of groans resulted from this action, for, when they were seated, a shoehorn couldn't have been passed between them without difficulty.

Porters swarmed to the top of the conveyance strapping down valises, haversacks, suit cases, Gladstone bags and assorted bandboxes. Even a huge Saratoga trunk was upended on the rear boot of the vehicle. Finally sixteen wayfarers had been squeezed aboard with two of the male passengers sitting atop the mountain of baggage. The massive coach now sagged heavily on its thoroughbraces.

Jack Hanscomb, locally famous "Knight of the Lash," climbed to the box and Cardwell swung up alongside onto the leather-covered, excelsior-filled cushion reserved for the company agent. At this moment the syncopated beat of hooves was heard to the north. The sound grew in volume and a rolling cloud swirled down the turnpike toward the Central—W. B. Campbell's Hot Springs Flyer with Burke handling the ribbons was coming![3]

The coach and four careened into town at a gallop. Passenger heads appeared at the windows and a succession of catcalls were tossed at the big Bonanza Lines coach as Campbell's high-wheeler flashed by.

Hanscomb grimly reset his light hat, buttoned his linen duster and snapped the whipstock from its socket with a gloved hand. "Gee-app," he bawled out over the heads of his geldings, his voice resounding across the icy Commons. They squatted into the traces and then the triple span was away at a smart trot down the slope toward the river.

"We'll eat dust all the way to Truckee, Jim," Hanscomb muttered. "Mebbe we can pass Burke at 'Big Hill'," Cardwell answered.[4] He pulled a heavy gold chronometer from his fob pocket, glanced at it and frowned. They were nearly ten minutes late on the down-river run that would connect with the westbound Central Pacific, and Cardwell knew the train was already past Lake Station (Reno).

Hanscomb sensed the urgency. He swung the four-foot hickory stock back and the long buckskin lash curled over the top of the stage, circled, and its popper cracked as it snaked out above the heads of his leaders. They strained forward, pulling the swing and wheel horses into a gallop. The coach swayed

THE MAIN STEM—1874

*Looking southwest down the
80-foot wide thoroughfare at Tahoe
City toward the Truckee River.
Buildings, from left to right:
Tahoe House and bar,
Frank Trueworthy's, Cardwell's
bowling alley and billiard rooms,
Grand Central Meat Market,
Grand Central Saloon, Grand
Central Hotel and J. A.
Todman's.*

California State Library

and rocked, rolling in and rattling out of the deep ruts in the road and shaking up the passengers with bone-crushing effect.

Ahead they could see the Hot Springs Express throwing gravel, and bobbing and weaving as Burke fought to maintain his lead. Four, then five miles, swept by under the whirling wheels and Hanscomb managed to close the distance by several hundred yards. Now they were approaching Big Hill, rising abruptly to the north of the river.

"He's going to take it up and over, Jack," Cardwell shouted excitedly. "Lay it on and we'll try Huntington's new cut around the side."

Without slackening speed, Hanscomb skillfully reined his pounding team into the turnoff, holding his off-leader close to the right bank. Above them he could see Burke's coach slowing to a laboring walk as the animals buckled into the load on the steep pitch.

"We've got him," Cardwell exulted, but Hanscomb was too busy "taking an extra reef in the tines" to listen. Where the detour joined the turnpike again, it called for a heavy foot on the brake and Hanscomb set himself, waiting for the right moment. He knew that they would have to slide through the turn fast to be out in front.

The ponderous vehicle hurtled into the dog-leg just as Burke crested the divide and started down grade. Hanscomb slammed on the drag and a shower of sparks pin-wheeled around the iron rims of the coach's rear wheels. There was a sharp report like a rifle crack—the brake staff had broken under his high-heeled boot. Out of control now, the stage surged forward onto the crossarm, its full weight thrown upon the horses who panicked in terror. The overloaded vehicle careened across the road in a skidding lunge, canted, hung for an instant on two wheels, then overturned, dragging the animals sideways off the turnpike as though they were a handful of jackstraws.

Cardwell and the two passengers riding the baggage jumped clear but Hanscomb held to the box rail as the coach plunged down a 30-foot slope. Stupefied but unhurt, the men who had leaped to safety saw the stage disappear over the bank in a cloud of spiraling dust, spinning wheels and thrashing horses. Half way down the steep embankment a gnarled tamarack jutted above a small meadow. As the coach plummeted into space its full weight was caught by the tree trunk, which broke its fall. Doors splintered and flew open, sidings cracked like matchwood and the top sailed off into space, followed by baggage, and passengers catapulted in all directions.

The Hot Springs Flyer had ground to a halt and Cardwell, trailed by Burke, stumbled down the bank to assist the injured travelers and cut the animals loose. After assuring himself that his passengers were more alive than dead, Cardwell leaped astride one of his bays and galloped back to the Central to telegraph Truckee for assistance.

Providence must have been riding on the coach that day as, incredibly enough, all sixteen passengers survived, although Hanscomb and several of the party sustained near fatal injuries.

The *Truckee Republican* bannered the story under the screaming headline: "A FEARSOME ACCIDENT ON THE TRUCKEE-TAHOE TURNPIKE." The bend at "Big Hill" was immediately renamed "Cardwell's Curve," and the tree that had caught the stage became a tourist attraction overnight.

Durable Hanscomb continued to drive for Cardwell, although he was unfairly dubbed "a reckless fellow." Some weeks later he was heard to admit across the Grand Central bar: "That damn nightmare

ADJOINING POMIN'S WAS A BRASS RAIL—

William Pomin(e)'s Tahoe House and Bar, built in 1868 on what became the location of Tahoe Inn. Pomin family standing on porch. Augustus H. Saxton in white shirt back of Cardwell's freight wagon. Photograph taken July, 1873, looking northwest up Main (Lake) Street.

was the closest handshake with the hereafter I ever expect to experience until Gabriel prods me with his golden spur." Such were the unforeseen hazards of the road leading from Tahoe City to Truckee.[5]

Known in the early post office records as "Tahoe," and with the word "City" periodically questioned by Truckee residents fifteen miles downstream, Tahoe City lies on the lake's western shore directly north of the Truckee River's headwaters.

In 1860, John A. Huntington constructed the Tahoe-Truckee Toll Road, a winding improved trail at best—rocky, rutted and single-buggy width. John McCormick was appointed agent for the road and Placer County delivered a staggering slap at the struggling turnpike by assessing it at a valuation of $800.[6] During the heavy winter of 1861 a lone trapper froze to death near the river's outlet, the tragedy serving to point up the fact that Tahoe was wild, undeveloped country.[7]

By the summer of 1862, Fish, Ferguson, Coggins and Smith Company were harvesting shoulder-high hay on the flatlands bordering the present site of the town, combining their cuttings with those from Squaw Valley to take out 240 tons during the season.[8] The company's 60-foot, two-masted schooner, *Iron Duke*, transported bales to the south end of the lake and the cove at the river's outlet served as home port for the vessel as well as a mooring for Fish and Ferguson's 28-foot whaleboat. The *Iron Duke* was Tahoe's first strictly commercial hull of record and it helped to supply the thousands of animals moving over the Sierra on the newly completed Johnson Pass-Kingsbury Grade cut-off to Virginia City's Comstock Lode.

The company's schooner enterprise was a lucrative business, as hay brought $250 a ton during the summer of 1862 at Lapham's Landing and Lake House Fisheries wharf on the southeast side of Tahoe.

Undocumented reports indicate that William Pomin(e) from Forest Hill surveyed and established the site of Tahoe City in the fall of 1863.[9] It is also erroneously believed that he built the city's first hotel, Tahoe House, the following year, and later became the father of the first white child born at the lake and appropriately christened Tahoe Pomin.[10]

In June of 1864, James C. Chesroon, native of Pennsylvania and '49er from Georgetown, California, completed a 100-foot wharf fronting on what would become, four years later, the Tahoe Commons.[11] Other pioneer landholders in Tahoe City during 1863-64 were M. L. King, Augustus H. Saxton, Lou and John Huntington, Charles Johnson, J. A. Hatch, G. T. Richer, Frank Trueworthy, William Wallace, Thomas G. Wilton and Ward Rush. Their occupations—hotel and store owners, lumbermen, toll road keepers, fishermen and ranchers.[12]

The Truckee River Lumber Company had been formed by Brickell and Kreuger, and $200 worth of shingles were stacked at the city.[13] Town lots sold at the going rate of $50 each with trenches dug around the properties to designate boundary lines. William Ferguson and James Tracey from Squaw Valley pre-empted 800 acres of land two miles north of Tahoe City, calling it the Tahoe Ranch. Their property adjoined Homer D. Burton's Island Farm on the lakeshore and D. Holten's and Sellers' ten acres running to the outskirts of the settlement. Edward Vischer's *Pictorial Views of California* gives a comprehensive sketch of Tahoe City in 1867: "It is unmistakably the sailors' nook of the lake. A dozen small craft lie at anchor near the wharf, strictly an amphibious population not alone confined to the Portuguese and Italian fishermen who in summer make a living from the waters. Everybody (settler, trader and backwoodsman) is trained to use the paddle. At the river's outlet cove, several fine pleasure yachts are moored, owned by residents of Bay City (San Francisco) and Virginia (City) who have summer villas at the lake.[14] A neat little ferry boat (the *Governor Blaisdel*), running between Tahoe City and Glenbrook, passes several large steam-powered mills (sic) at the mouth of creeks on the western shore, and a couple of hours' run, touching at some of the larger mill landings, brings you to Glenbrook House and stage station."

SO OPULENT NO SIGN WAS NEEDED

A. J. Bayley's Grand Central Hotel, formerly M. L. King's Tahoe City Hotel, was the finest establishment between San Francisco and Virginia City when this picture was taken in August of 1874. On the south side of the 3½-story edifice stands the Grand Central Saloon.

California State Library

Colonel A. W. Von Schmidt had assumed the presidency of the Lake Tahoe and San Francisco Water Company, incorporated in 1865 and capitalized at $20,000,000.[15] For $3.00 per acre, he acquired a half section of land surrounding the Truckee River outlet, along with the right to appropriate 500 cubic second feet of Tahoe and Truckee river water to be "perfected and perpetuated by a dam one hundred and fifty yards downstream from the lake's outlet."[16]

Another powerful combine, the Donner Lumber and Boom Company, headed by Mark Hopkins and Leland Stanford, was granted authority by the California Legislature on April 4, 1870, to construct a dam on the same location.

Although temporarily balked by Von Schmidt, the "Big Four" secured a 20-year franchise on the exclusive use of the river channel for flotation of logs and cordwood to Truckee. The stream channel was cleared and tolls of 50 cents a thousand for saw logs and 25 cents a cord for wood were levied.[17]

Von Schmidt had completed his crib dam of timber and stone fill by the fall of 1870 and the following year he proposed a grandiose scheme for running a combination railroad tunnel and aqueduct through the Sierra. It was to start at the head of Cold Stream west of Truckee and near the loop of the Central Pacific's Horseshoe Bend. Two six-foot conduits would be fed by a diversion dam on the river, capable of carrying 200,000,000 gallons of water daily. San Francisco and Oakland were to be served by way of the Sacramento Valley, and branch aqueducts would supply the mines of Yankee Jim's, Forest Hill and Michigan Bluff.

It would also shorten the railroad's line by seven miles, lower its elevation by 1,000 feet and eliminate 20 miles of snowsheds. According to Von Schmidt, the project would be completed in five years.[18] The City of San Francisco dismissed Von Schmidt's plan as impractical and the directors of the Central Pacific, who also controlled the Donner Lumber and Boom Company, obviously had no interest in it either. They had already blasted their tunnels and run their rails over Donner Summit.

Von Schmidt persisted in his efforts. On March 15, 1875, he announced the completion of a diversion dam five miles down the Truckee River at a point near Bear Creek. From here he now planned to run a canal, paralleling the river on its western side, to Hardscramble Creek (Deep Creek). All the waters of Bear, Squaw and Deer Creeks, plus those of Hardscramble itself and a large part of the Truckee Rivers' flow, were to be collected. At the mouth of Hardscramble the water was to enter a five-mile tunnel running under the Sierra crest and emerge at Soda Springs, near the headwaters of the North Fork of the American River. Fluming and piping would then carry it to San Francisco.[19]

The citizens of northwestern Nevada, being dependent upon the river's water, swore that "Von Schmidt should most certainly be the one damned instead of damming the Truckee" because he proposed to take away most of the waters that were a "God given grant to the Silver State." Tahoe City's townspeople ignored the clamor, even though Von Schmidt's new dam backed the water up so high that the Tahoe-Truckee Toll Road had to be realigned farther up the side of the canyon.[20]

The timber and rock fill obstruction in the river, however, was of help to the lumbermen. They could now "set 200,000 feet of logs behind the dam, open the gates when a head of water had been collected and be sure that the timber would carry on down stream to the mills without continuously jamming." Von Schmidt had been unable to obtain financial backing for his latest water project and the control of the Truckee River outlet dam and surrounding property eventually passed to the Donner Lumber and Boom Company.

Before the fiery Russian left the Tahoe scene he sponsored two other unsuccessful promotions. His first was an attempt to place the James Lick Observatory on Chinquapin Point.[21] Secondly, Von Schmidt contracted to run the Nevada-California boundary survey from the Oregon line across the east side of Lake Tahoe to the Arizona border. Although a capable, brilliant engineer, many of his imaginative schemes miscarried.

Meanwhile Tahoe City was expanding. The Truckee River and Tahoe Lake Turnpike Company had been formed, supplanting John Huntington's Tahoe-Truckee Toll Road organization. Along with the new, high sounding name there was also a representative list of Tahoe and Truckee residents who owned and ran it.[22]

Lou and John Huntington had taken over Tracey and Ferguson's Tahoe Ranch and added the Whippoorwill Farm, another extensive acreage on the outskirts of town. In addition, they bought six lots in the city itself. Pioneer Ward Rush was operating a shingle mill one mile downriver from the settlement[23] and M. L. King, with his son Fred, were owner-managers of the largest hostelry on the western shore of the lake, Tahoe City Hotel. They were adding 60 feet to the establishment, with ten carpenters working around the clock to assure its completion by June 1 of 1869.[24] "King's Castle," as it was also known, boasted "fifty commodious suites and luxurious apartments, two dining rooms, a dance salon, and bowling alley."

Adjoining the hotel to the south was Robert Kincaid's saloon, operating in friendly competition with William Pomin's Tahoe House Bar.[25] Fishing boats were available from Prentiss Pringle and Jeremiah Hurley at the outlet and the *Governor Stanford*, a wood-burning sidewheeler, now crossed the lake three times a week carrying passengers and freight.

Sawmill operators in the vicinity were loud in their demands for an extension of the Central Pacific's rails up the Truckee River canyon. It was pointed out that an easy 40 foot to the mile grade existed and that revenue derived from saw logs, charcoal, shingles, freight and passenger traffic practically guaranteed the profitability of the enterprise.[26]

Toll gates had been placed across Tahoe City's 80-foot-wide thoroughfare, Lake Street (Main) and two of its side streets were barred by obstructions and buildings before the startled townspeople awoke to the infringement on their rights and had the barriers removed. Citizens were predicting that the summer of 1870 would find Tahoe City only eight hours away from Sacramento owing to accelerated train schedules. The more daring young ladies in the growing settlement flaunted their disregard for distance by side-saddling the 30-mile round trip to Truckee in one afternoon.

Theatrical talent was noted as being rounded up on Saturday nights and giving fine entertainment at the Tahoe House with the amateur plays, "In and Out of Place" and "Shoo-Fly," being done with variations. On Sunday, "Dr. Dwinell talked to the wicked of Tahoe" (City).[27]

A correspondent from the San Francisco *Daily California Alta* arrived in town during the fall of 1870. He described his stage trip up the canyon "as being made over an excellent road with Burke handling the thoroughbrace." Correctly he noted that "beautiful Tahoe was Bigler by an act of Legislature," and rhapsodized about this "vast inland sea of unknown depth (sic)." His disappointment with the settlement was apparent when stagedriver Burke pointed out "a fine large hotel (King's) and outbuildings—only this and nothing more—that is the City."

The reporter, however, discovered another lodging place (Pomin's) and mentioned, "I sat on the piazza of Tahoe House." He continued:

"Your correspondent has a weakness for a trotting horse, so the livery stable keeper was requested to furnish blooded and fiery steeds for two gents and a lady to make the ride to Cornelian Bay.[28] 'You can just bet your life I'll give you ones that can git up and git,' said he. Resting content with the promise, we retired to prepare for our ride.

"Upon our reappearance the chargers were waiting. Their appearance almost caused us to turn our eyes heavenward to see if the vultures were already gathering. The one allotted to me was a curious specimen. Tall and lank, architecturally built with a hand railing on back to hang on to, plus all other modern conveniences—wall eyes which wore a villainous expression—and, to cap the climax, almost completely covered by a pair of huge *macheres* which entirely precluded the possibility of a foothold in the stirrups. Complaints were useless, however, so, hoping for the best, we sprang lightly into our saddles and dashed off—as far as the stables, beyond which my noble charger refused to advance. On undertaking to lay down the law to him, and show the advisability of an onward movement, he executed an immense number of pirouettes, and finally succeeded in striking me—full in the face—with his head, after which movement he went madly forward until, coming to a steep hill, he planted his forefeet firmly in the soil and came to a dead halt, doubtless expecting that the laws of motion would assert their power, and somebody would do some 'ground' and lofty tumbling. The maneuver being a total failure the steed gave up all hope and plodded along for the remainder of the—two hour—ride to Cornelian."[29]

In the summer of 1871, the California and Nevada newspapers heralded with unprecedented fanfare Tahoe City's answer to the elegant Glen Brook House across the lake. The swank Grand Central Hotel was about to open its doors to the traveling public's elite. Actually the establishment was none other than M. L. King's former Tahoe City Hotel, refurbished and enlarged, but now owned and run by A. J. Bayley, of Pilot Hill, California. Bayley proudly advertised that he could accommodate "one hundred and sixty discriminating guests at a rate of $20.00 each per week, three meals a day included."[30]

The Central exploded upon the Tahoe scene with heretofore unknown magnificence. It sported a new $800 kitchen range, shining black walnut furniture in every room, a cherrywood piano and expensive Brussels carpets. Balconies ringed the L-shaped three and one-half story building. Here guests could take their ease and view the panorama of lake and mountains to the east. White fir trees had even been cut in the backwoods and "planted" to the south of the porticoed entranceway, adding what was considered to be a deft touch of sweet scented High Sierra atmosphere.

Tahoe Tattler.

Published Every Evening, Sunday Excepted,
in the
GRAND CENTRAL HOTEL.

Subscription, Fifty Cents per one Month.

WEDNESDAY :   :   : July 20

The Santa Cruz Sentinel, one of, if not the best, country paper in the State, comes to us as an exchange. It is a thirty-six column paper, large enough to make fifteen numbers of the *Tattler*, and one would suppose that such a big-bug would take little notice of so small a sheet, but McPherson is a man of large perceptive faculties, and soon sees that disseminating news of our wonderful lake will assist in bringing travel to the State, and when here they certainly will not miss seeing the prettiest town on the sea coast, Santa Cruz.

Any person catching over 50 trout in one-half day will be entitled to the *Tattler* for one month.

Fishing for silver trout has now been going on in Lake Tahoe for more than twenty years, but the old fishermen and residents of this vicinity say there never yet has been a season when more have been taken than in this, hence we may safely argue that they grow faster than they can be taken out, and the supply is practically inexhaustible, so long as no other means than the hook is resorted to for taking them.

The *Tattler* exchange list is increasing daily. Space will not permit of our publishing the many flattering news we are receiving at the hands of well established papers, but suffice is to say that we are becoming widely circulated and extensively copied throughout the Pacific States and ere long we expect to hear from some of the leading papers in the Great East.

Tahoe Tattler.

WEDNESDAY :   :   : July 20

JOTTINGS.

—Miss Wentworth, of the Soda Springs, is visiting her friends the Misses Bayley.

—The weather pleasant this morning and the lake just right for fishing.

—The steward of the Grand Central lately shot a deer within a mile of Tahoe, and Thomas Ross, the porter, brought it in.

—R. E. wood, the photographer, is spending a couple of days at the southern end of the lake, taking views of the scenery.

—That string of fifty-two fish, caught by R. G. Smith, of Candelaria, and F. M. Smith, of Oakland, on the 16th, is supposed by old residents to be the largest catch ever made on the lake in the same length of time.

—Mrs. LaMott and her son Howard caught ten silver trout this morning on the Truckee steps.

—Twelve passengers on the steamer.

—P. McShane, Esq., proprietor of the Occidental Hotel, San Francisco, is a guest of the Grand Central.

—All of Mayo & Harley's and Morgan & Co.'s row boats were engaged last evening, owing, no doubt, to their advertisement in the *Tattler.*

—Four or five beautiful strings of trout meet our gaze whenever we step out from our office in search of items.

—The Grand Central Hotel boasts of the best baker.

—Don't you forget that Bill Pomin keeps good cigars at the Tahoe Saloon.

—Extra copies of the *Tattler* 10 cents.

Grand Central Arrivals.—James Wormser and wf, Mrs Charles Miller, Misses Mary, Maude and Blanche Miller, San Francisco; Daisy Rose, Los Angeles.

A game of ten pins was played yesterday on the Grand Central alley between Mrs. Taylor and Mr. and Mrs. Loomis on one side, and Miss Fay, Miss Taylor and Captain Freeman on the other. The party of the second part came out winner, Miss Fay being champion.

J. I. Felter, of Sacramento, captured Mayo and his boat yesterday afternoon, and Mrs. Tozer went along to show them how to fish. The instructress pulled out 11 to Mr. Felter's 8, and Mayo caught 1 to make it an even 20 for the boat.

A load of stray shot entered the office this morning and nearly squelched us. The devil vanished, and has not been heard of since.

Bancroft Library

NEWSY—NOISY—AND NOSEY

Robert E. Wood's Tahoe Tattler, *the small postage stamp daily published at Tahoe City in 1881 and early 1882. Wood's hard-hitting reporting and editorial scoldings faithfully recorded the pulse of high living at Tahoe during the Bonanza days.*

From the date of its opening all-night celebration, over the next two decades the Grand Central would be recognized as the leading and most luxurious hostelry between Sacramento and Virginia City. It lived up to its reputation even though the portable sewage tank, in the rear of the hotel, had to be hauled away by a span of horses and dumped whenever necessity demanded.

The time had come for Tahoe City to again take stock of its accomplishments.

Fifty houses constituted the settlement. Two hotels were operating to capacity summer crowds. Three saloons, including "Big Mose" Staples' Big Bonanza Bar, were doing a brisk business, with all-night poker games in full swing. Joseph B. Campbell and James Olmstead Forbes had purchased Wilton's general merchandise store and built a new wharf and over-water combination saloon, post office and billiard parlors in front of the Grand Central. As it became the *custom* for residents of the city and transients alike to take a drink when they passed through the doors, its owners called this backwoods bistro the Custom House.[31]

James Cardwell and his partner Gordon owned 12 buildings in town along with a bar, butcher shop, stables, bowling alley, croquet grounds, laundry, billiard rooms and swimming baths on the Commons. Cardwell's stage line, with George McIntyre and Jack Hanscomb alternately sitting the "high box," connected with Truckee Hotel and Donner Summit House on a regular daily schedule. As Cardwell put it: "Everything is available for the *rational* use and enjoyment of our visitors."

Those "lightning strikers," A. R. Shiveley from Truckee and A. A. Bayley of Woodland, had run the first telegraph line to the lake, stringing the wire on trees between Tahoe City and the railroad town, with its eastern terminus in the Grand Central. On June 20, 1873, the initial message came through "heralded with great rejoicing and followed by a torch parade."[32] The general jollification of the citizens at Tahoe City continued until sun-up, with many of the less temperate finding themselves with their heads in the watering trough along toward afternoon.

James Cardwell and his partner were exerting every effort to establish a reputation as the "split second stage and express line." Their ironclad motto—"Get the passengers to their destination or kill a horse trying." When a bangtail actually dropped dead in the traces after a record breaking stage run down canyon to connect with the Central Pacific, everybody agreed that conclusive evidence of policy had been furnished.

On another occasion one of Cardwell's "mud wagons" pulled up at the Grand Central just as the luxurious *Governor Stanford* backed away from the wharf. A single passenger jumped from the stage and dashed for the pier in an unsuccessful attempt to board the vessel. Cardwell immediately readied a Whitehall boat with four husky oarsmen at the sweeps and rowed the amazed traveler fourteen miles across the water to Glenbrook. With time to spare, the tourist connected with "Doc" Benton's Carson bound coach and four, and profuse in his thanks tried to pay for his passage and the unprecedented extra service. This offer was waved aside by one of the oarsmen with the remark: "That, sir, is just another courtesy of Mr. Cardwell's."

Ben Holladay's new steamer, the *Emerald I*, now joined the *Blaisdel* and *Stanford* in making daily cruises around and across the lake. Two Italians, Flores and Salado, leased "Billy" Morgan's and Joe Pomin's pier and fishing boats, supplying a Quadrille Band that played every afternoon for their foot-stomping patrons. After the concert the customers trolled for silvers, speckled and salmon trout.

Even an ice skating rink opened in the spring of 1873 down at the river's outlet. The *Truckee Republican* insisted that a surgeon was now indispensable, pointing out: "It is amusing to watch the subdued expression that steals across a lady skater's face as she changes from the perpendicular to a recumbent position on the ice, but the onlooker quickly changes his attitude to one of dismay when the fall is coupled with a violence that loosens teeth and drives her spinal column up through her cap."

In the summer of 1873, S. C. Davis and W. C. Noteware of Glenbrook and Carson leased Camp-

THE LITTLE TISSUE SHEET THAT CARRIED A BIG STICK

Anybody who was anybody, on the western and southern shores of Lake Tahoe in 1881, advertised in the TATTLER and everything from an aromatic Havana cigar to a luxurious bridal suite could be located after scanning its pages.

bell and Forbes' mercantile store at the head of the Custom House pier, freighting in 1,500 tons of grain and 40 tons of liquors from Truckee during the season. Many prominent people were doing more than just cast an eye toward Tahoe City. Darius Ogden Mills, Charles Crocker, William Ralston, William Alvord, L. L. Robinson and S. F. Butterworth, financial tycoons from San Francisco and Virginia City, contemplated the purchase of town lots with the intention of building summer mansions. Celebrities also added their praises to the acknowledged magnificence of the lake. The famous "Jersey Lily" Langtry, original "sweater girl," ravishing beauty and leading actress of her day, took a long, appreciative look at the tri-colored expanse of Tahoe from the city's high ground. "I'll buy a parcel or two of land next year, as Tahoe is the beauty spot of the world," was her unsolicited trilly statement. This, coming from an entertainer of kings and knaves alike, was considered *something*, and the lakers beamed.

Generals Ulysses S. Grant and Philip H. Sheridan, riding high on the crest of the victorious Union cause, added their praises. A lesser, but none the less voluble personage, Mrs. Charles McGlaughlin from San Francisco, advised the press that she had been a European traveler for years, but that Tahoe was the equal, yes, actually the superior, of anything to be found abroad. This profound statement was respectfully recorded as being submitted by an "unquestionable authority." The *Truckee Republican*, reporting the interview, concluded with a smidge of pompous, down the nose dignity: "Mrs. McGlaughlin is worth four million dollars."

The "color of the nut brown maid" had become ultra-fashionable for young ladies at the Grand Central, who bared their wrists and faces to the high altitude sunshine with reckless abandon. A quaint but thoroughly admirable touch was added when Miss Lulu Campbell established her "School for Little Folk" at the city, with "swings, whirligigs and such like."

But all was not uninterrupted sweetness and light at Tahoe City. A few minutes walk from Lake Street took adventurers into the wilderness country of forest and canyon. Here a handful of lumberjacks and cordwood splitters, working in the timber stands, had chosen this outpost of civilization for various private reasons.

One such man was hotblooded, cold-eyed James Stewart. Powerful, unpredictable and gun crazy, Stewart had drifted around the lake from Glenbrook, where it was said Bliss' gang boss paid him 50 cents more each day provided he would stay out of the settlement during his off-hours. Stewart had bought property in Tahoe City and gone to work as a "faller" at Lonely Gulch above Rubicon Bay. When sober, he could fell two trees to the average lumberjack's one, but when drunk he enjoyed nothing more than shooting up the city with his six-guns. After he had killed several men in questionable gun fights, his arrival in town was the signal for residents to make for their homes.

One early spring morning in 1874 Stewart rode slowly into the settlement with the townspeople deserting Main Street as he approached. He went directly to Campbell's Custom House on the wharf and started drinking. It appeared to bartender Fred A. Scott that Stewart intended to empty every bottle in the establishment, and along toward noon Stewart's steady imbibing began to have its effect. He became abusive, then sullen. Fixing a glowering eye on Scott, he roared: "I'll be ready for you when I get back." Then the gunman stumbled through the doorway and up the pier.

The terrified barkeep loaded a double-barreled shotgun with buckshot, ran down the planks, and hid in the shadows between Davis and Noteware's store and warehouse. Stewart soon weaved back down the walkway. Scott waited until he was nearly opposite him, then fired both barrels, dropping Stewart on the boards and killing him instantly. The blast brought most of the male population of the City down the pier on the run and Stewart's body was laid out on the Custom House floor. Surprisingly enough, he was found to have been unarmed.

Bayley from the Grand Central immediately called an inquest, with Jeremiah Hurley acting as defense counsel. Scott explained the circumstances leading up to the killing and the jury, composed of Saxton, Morgan, Campbell and Forbes, deliberated. After a hurried conference, Morgan whispered in Bayley's ear, whereupon Bayley rose and cleared his throat: "Gentlemen," he began, "it is unanimously opined that the deceased met his death from something close to what may be considered an act of the Almighty. Bless us all for this timely deliverance from a mean, unscrupulous blackguard. I hereby declare the case closed and the drinks on me." Coroner, counsel and jury made a headlong rush for the bar and Stewart's body was later buried in an unmarked grave north of the Commons.[33]

On January 3 of the same year J. B. Campbell reported that 15 residents remained in the city. During the long winter months they hunted the white hare and trapped fox and marten in lulls between howling blizzards. Campbell snowshoed into Truckee, making the 16-mile trip over the frozen turnpike in six hours and he discovered only one habitation on the way, Tahoe Fish Ranch and Toll House, north of the present location of Big Chief Camp. Its lone, bearded occupant had engulfed him in small talk, for he hadn't seen another face in two and one-half months. Those who said business at Tahoe City had slowed to a walk were making a generous understatement.

In the spring of 1877, A. J. Bayley took over the stage line from Cardwell. Elijah "Pop" Church and a relief driver replaced George McIntyre and John Hanscomb on the ribbons, reining the colorful Bonanza Lines coach and six over the toll road daily. At Truckee Station, Church picked up tourists, gold seekers, lumbermen, "drummers," excursionists, mail and Wells Fargo express, then rolled back up canyon on his two and one-half hour return trip. The swing through the gorge was consid-

THIS WAS NO BLOODED SHOW TEAM "BUT THE HORSES HAD WHAT IT TOOK TO HAUL THROUGH"

With master whip, Elijah "Pop" Church, at the multiple reins, eleven passengers crowded into the fringe-topped thoroughbrace, and a mountain of baggage piled onto the rear boot, Bayley's Tahoe-Truckee Flyer is poised, in the summer of 1880, for its down-river run to the Central Pacific Railroad.

Author's collection

ered one of the most scenic trips in the Far West with both "natural and man-made wonders combining to amaze the traveler." "Pop," a hard-swearing Knight of the Lash, had a name for all the points of interest—Devil's Armchair, Devil's Post Pile, Devil's Anvil, ad infinitum. He entertained his passengers with the story of Big Chief No-Name and Lover's Leap, and pointed out the Indian burial ground, where "750 native sons were laid to rest some three hundred years before, giving a true account and history of same."[34]

The abandoned towns, Knoxville and Claraville, and the cannonading log chutes that made the Celestials cry out "What for? What for?" also received their share of Church's enthusiastic attention. On the towering cliffs above the river he showed the tourists "profiles of Belva Lockwood, Roscoe Conkling and the Duke of Wellington along with the 'Old Woman' and the 'Old Man'." The "splash dams" along the river were hailed by Church as "great undertakings of the age." One admiring female passenger, riding the company agent's seat alongside the driver, gushed: "All stages on this run should have nothing but front seats so that everyone can hear 'Pop's' stories."[35]

One autumn morning, as Church was hightailing it back up the canyon, a masked highwayman suddenly leaped into the road and leveled a shotgun over the heads of the leaders. "Pop" laid into the brake iron and skidded to a stop in front of his own self-styled "Devil's Bluff," some four miles southeast of Truckee. The road agent, a flour sack covering his head, motioned Church off the box and ordered the passengers out. Pockets were turned inside out and purses opened, but it was a paltry showing. Muttering under his breath the gunman backed slowly away and disappeared into the pine forest.

"Pop" was livid. Being a versatile linguist, he promptly rose to the occasion and split the air for the next five minutes with a masterful sequence of choice swear words. He ended his tirade by renaming the rocky abutment "Robber's Roost." It was learned later that one Lyman, a lake fisherman from Truckee and somewhat down on his luck, had brandished the scattergun in "Pop's" face, obtaining for his first and last attempt at stage robbery a miserable $15.00 in gold and silver coin.[36]

Church always had some trick up the sleeve of his linen duster to sustain the interest of his passengers. One season he spent the better part of a month feeding a family of woodchucks at a point on his run so they would come at his whistle to be admired by his passengers while he breathed his team. "It's a miracle how them little wild things take to strangers," he would tell the gaping tourists. "Why, hell, even wildcats and mountain lions in the forest would do the same if I could coax 'em off the ridges."

July 9, 1881, saw the advent of Tahoe's first newspaper, the *Tahoe Tattler*.[37] It was a miniature sheet published daily except Sunday at Bayley's Grand Central by Robert E. Wood, who at first was copy writer, printer's devil, news runner and editor all rolled into one. In addition he was the only commercial photographer at the lake. The little tissue sheet made up in text interest for what it lacked in size. Selling for ten cents a copy, it chronicled the high life of the 1881 season.

Among other things, the *Tattler* predicted swimming would become a popular amusement at Tahoe, because the temperature of the water was six degrees warmer than the ocean at that time of year.

Pursuing this thought further, the editor promised to keep his readers advised on the exploits of a Miss Anna Head, "the most noted lady swimmer on the Pacific Coast," who, if good weather continued, would *possibly* try her skill in the lake, and thus refute the fact that bodies were supposed to sink like a rock in Tahoe's crystal clear waters. Miss Head must have seriously doubted her ability to stay afloat, for nothing more was written about her proposed venture. This, however, coincided with the paper's announcement, which may have had a deterring effect: "Colds are very prevalent right now and handkerchiefs are in great demand."

The *Tattler* was genuinely concerned about finding some way to attract San Francisco society to the lake. Wood acknowledged that a yoke of oxen could not drag them away once they were there but to get the bluebloods to Tahoe, short of binding and gagging them—*that* was the problem.

Style at the city brought hearty side-splitting buffs from the transient loggers and teamsters; two Saratoga trunks and the "five a day change" being not uncommon for the more genteel ladies staying at the Grand Central. The feminine targets of this unkind criticism were amply rewarded, however, by the many "flattering puffs bestowed upon them by young gallants at the hotel during the evening promenade."

The Custom House wharf was being extended on rock cribbing another 250 feet out into the lake from the over-water establishment, and it was proudly noted that soon facilities for mooring all the boats and steamers on Tahoe right in front of the city would be available.

Dr. Paul T. Kirby of Carson City and Emerald Bay launched what he claimed to be "the fastest sailboat in the Sierra Nevada." Skidded into the water from the Commons, it was christened the *Fleeter* and Kirby immediately tossed a challenge at Elias J. "Lucky" Baldwin of Tallac, suggesting that he participate in a flat out race. On an August afternoon in 1881 Baldwin accepted Kirby's request to engage in a blue water contest and the *Tattler* foresightedly placed a reporter on each boat to be sure the paper would represent a winner. Not a breath of wind stirred at the starting line in front of Tahoe City and, as the use of oars was ruled out, the sailing match resulted in a dead heat.

Another spectacle now engaged the interest of the townspeople and the *Tattler* focused upon it. George Loomis, acknowledged to be the bravest as well as the luckiest man in the city, was stagger-

OUTLET POINT IN 1901

Log cribbing and a boathouse contained the white domicile of Jeremiah Hurley and the clapboard of "Billy" Morgan. Here Dat-So-La-Lee later settled to create her world-famous ceremonial baskets. In the upper left background stands old Tahoe Inn (House) and to the right of Morgan's dwelling is Tahoe City's over-water Custom House, general store, warehouse, post office and Toy-Yat Club. Private homes lie above on the bluff.

Author's collection

LAKE TAHOE.

MOGUL ON THE MAINLINE

Engine Number 5 "deadheading" south from the machine shops across Tahoe City's trestle pier toward the Commons and Custom House wharf in July of 1911.

ing under the chaperonage of nine attractive young ladies who were sojourning at the Central. To keep them occupied and healthy, a trip was planned for the gay group each morning. Loomis even went so far as to take them by coach and six to the nearest snowline, where they playfully buried their dainty feet in its white coldness, "sans striped hose."

The Grand Central was always thrown open to the public in the red carpet manner on the first day of May, closing with a thud on October 1. In conjunction with Pomin's Tahoe House, the management sponsored fishing matches, taffy pulls, amateur theatricals, billiard "strikes," the Tallac Glee Club, and even a ladies' decorative class without charge to participants, the only stipulation being "agreeable company."

In the spring of 1882, J. F. Moody, proprietor of the railroad town's Truckee Hotel, purchased the Tahoe and Truckee stage line and immediately set about improving its rolling stock. He placed a massive, dark maroon 18-passenger, open sided coach on the run. Built by Kimball Manufacturing Company, it was considered the last word in leather slung luxury. Moody took over the mail and express contract from Bayley, and his driver, Al Nichols, often strapped to the box after a prolonged bout with the bottle, continued to wheel the stage daily during the season to and from Truckee, connecting with the packet steamer *Governor Stanford* at the city's wharf.

Promptly at 10 o'clock every morning the sidewheeler would back slowly away from her mooring, with a shrill blast of the steam whistle announcing the boat's departure for McKinney's, Tallac, Rowland's, Glenbrook and the Hot Springs. Four dollars per person was charged for the complete cruise around the lake, but excursionists could cross to Glenbrook for half price whenever the vessel made the direct run.[38]

J. B. Campbell was now sole owner of the Custom House at the Grand Central's eastern stairway approach. Here he sold steamer tickets, sorted and stacked mail in his dockside post office, supervised the operation of his two billiard parlors—one for the ladies and the other for the "gents" (the "gent's" table was used to sleep off a good drunk as often as it was used to lay a cue on)—and served up Boca, Tahoe and Milwaukee lager along with the choicest of liquors in his saloon.[39] Campbell advertised "Open 24 hours a day, with eatables and drinkables at the coziest spot on the lake," and as it was a one-man operation where men with a thirst could "buck the tiger" or "see the elephant" any time of day or night, none could determine when their untiring host found time to sleep.

F. W. McQueen's fruit store, located in the Big Bonanza Saloon building, reminded the townspeople that fresh fruit could be delivered to any point on the lake by steamer 24 hours after it had been picked from the trees. Everybody marveled at the speed of this modern age and wondered vaguely what future wonders lay ahead.[40]

The fiery little editorials in R. E. Wood's *Tahoe Tattler* were gone from the scene along with the paper, which had discontinued publication on January 21, 1882, after Wood wryly confessed: "It (the paper) possessed a healthy stomach that could not be satisfied by faith without dumplings." Many residents in the city recalled his heated admonitions. Once he had brewed up a storm by laying down the law to his readers with Ordinance Number One.

"No more lying about our lake," he had thundered. "Eight and ten-pound trout caught daily, bears chasing and devouring men leaving only the sole of a boot, or parts of spectacles by which to recognize one party, and nothing else for friends to cry over." "Don't impose any more rash stories upon an outside world. The truth is good enough for average humanity." Wood had crossed swords with the editor of the *Gold Hill News*, the lakers remembered, after the Washoe sheet mentioned: "A small newspaper, about the size of a large beer stamp, is being published at Tahoe City, California." The *Tattler's* editor replied testily: "This is the person who growled about our small beer mugs, and now our barkeepers always serve him with a ten-pound lard can."

Deftly changing pace, he had then lauded the many improvements taking place at the Grand Central Hotel: "A magnificent bridal chamber will be arranged and furnished in first class style, pre-

A WHITE CROSS STANDS ABOVE THE CITY

William Boyle's funeral on February 4, 1912, when the "boys" (see insert) fulfilled his wish to be buried on the mountain west of the City. Among the group of Boyle's pallbearers: Arthur and Edgar Wehrman, Ernest H. Pomin, Bert Watson, Andrew Jackson Sumpter, Captain Edmund Hunkin, Leonard Wehrman, Robert Montgomery Watson and Art Smith. Charles Keyser is standing with two unidentified men to the right of Boyle's coffin. View looking northeast across Tahoe.

Carl Bechdolt, Sr.

suming the people of the country are going to perpetuate the one-ing institution," and then a bow to the lakers generally: "People of Tahoe allow nothing or anybody to supersede them in enterprise and go-a-head-a-tive-ness."

Most of the residents of the city agreed that it was too bad Bob Wood had to discontinue publication of the *Tattler*. Some wondered if its demise had not been caused by the crusading editor's hard-hitting reporting. All remembered the time a discordant note had been struck with one reader, as Wood had alarmingly printed: "A load of buckshot entered the office this morning and nearly squelched us. The devil vanished and has not been heard of since."

No matter what the cause, the paper was laid to rest and it would be missed.

Two trout farms were operating, Lake Fishery at the outlet, known as the "Pisicultural Establishment of Morgan, Pringle and Early" (sic), and Tahoe Fish Ranch and Toll House ten miles downstream from the settlement. But what was the sense in raising trout, people asked. Everybody knew the supply was limitless in the lake. The townspeople were both bewildered and impressed by high-sounding geological phrases saddled upon the surrounding terrain by visiting scientists: "Masses of scoriacious rock, strewn along the banks of the river and a small conical mound, a creation of solfa-tares," were pointed out. All the lakers really wanted to know was did these formations conceal any gold or silver?

William Pomin, proprietor of the Tahoe House, was erroneously reported to be building a brewery when he was actually only enlarging his hotel and saloon.[41] "Why in hell don't outsiders get things straight?" asked the city fathers. John Huntington, by now the oldest pioneer in the city, continued to maintain the Tahoe City-Truckee turnpike during the summer and carry the mails twice a week over the deep snow to the railroad town during the winter.

Lumbering furnished the lifeblood of the community. Log chutes and flumes grooved the surrounding mountains and ravines. Nat Stein's logging camp to the south of town averaged better than 21,000 feet of saw logs per day with 645,000 feet cut in the month of July, 1882. Tahoe City also took credit for the largest log boom ever assembled up to that time, when 380,000 feet of logs were cabled together at Hurricane Bay, just south of Ward Creek, and rafted to Glenbrook by the *Meteor*.

Summer evenings at Tahoe House were enlivened by raffling off fishing boats. Thirty-five chances at $2.00 apiece constituted the usual drawing and on one occasion three skiffs in a row, the *Eva*, *Freddie*, and *Susie*, went to commercial fishermen "Billy" Morgan and Joe Pomin with loud cries of "rigged raffle" and "get those thieves" splitting the night air.

On April 14, 1883, two French-Canadian lumberjacks drowned while crossing the lake from the city when a sudden squall swamped their boat. Their bodies were never recovered, mysteriously adding to a growing list of those claimed by the great deep of Tahoe.[42] A. J. Bayley was still "Mine Host" at the Grand Central and described as that "genial old German who spends his winters in the Sierra and therefore has sore eyes."[43]

In June of the year a terrific storm struck the lake, recalled later as the "Tahoe Typhoon." Thunderheads rolled out of the east and the pounding waves appeared to "climb the mountains with solid walls of water breaking high on the shoreline." Piers were smashed to kindling and the old excursion barge *Pavillion* was driven aground at the outlet.[44] Twenty-four hours later the beach at the city was a shambles of broken log booms and smashed fishing boats tossed high and dry.

The *Truckee Republican* felt obliged to apologize for its exaggerated coverage of the catastrophe, as it had mentioned that the city was completely washed away. The paper's informant was a member of the California Legislature, the *Republican's* editor lamely explained and therefore it was self-evident *why* the story proved to be somewhat far-fetched.

During the spring thaw of the following year another quirk of nature was blamed for an unusual

occurrence. It snowed angle worms, one of the lakers testified. Not just a dozen or so, but hundreds. A skeptical reporter from Reno suggested that the townspeople at Tahoe City should immediately start an oil factory, as everyone knew that angle worms were a positive cure for rheumatism.[45]

Such were the facts and fancies served up to the public in the 1880's at the settlement.

In the year 1887, Robert Montgomery Watson, who had come to the lake in the bonanza year of 1875, purchased the Tahoe House from William Pomin.[46] Watson went on to become a Yukon gold-seeker in 1897 and returned to Tahoe City as trail blazer, mountaineer, conservationist and High Sierra guide. His name became famous throughout the Tahoe region and today it remains on Mount Watson and Watson Lake.

Tahoe House continued to stand for another half century under changing management. However, a fire swept through the fabulous Grand Central Hotel in the fall of 1895, leveling the structure to its granite foundations and symbolizing an end to the Bonanza period in which it had been built.[47]

By the late fall of 1898 the rolling stock and equipment from Glenbrook's Lake Tahoe Railroad and the Lake Valley Line (Bijou) had been moved across the lake on 104-foot cordwood barges and unloaded at Tahoe City. This included used narrow gauge track, 45 platform cars (flats) and the little locomotive *Tahoe* from the lumbering settlement. Twenty-five flat cars, 555 tons of secondhand rails and the locomotives *Santa Cruz* and *Engine Number Three* had been barged over from Bijou.[48] Maintenance buildings, machine shops and employees' houses would follow in 1900.

A railroad right-of-way was surveyed down the Truckee Canyon by William Seth Bliss in the summer of 1898 and laying of narrow gauge track began in the spring of 1899, with the road opened for regular service early in 1900.[49]

Consolidation of the former Carson and Tahoe Lumber and Fluming Company's Glenbrook and Bijou railroads called for the elimination of some equipment and the addition of other rolling stock. The Bliss family's newly-formed Lake Tahoe Railway and Transportation Company needed closed cars and, as the narrow gauge Alameda-Santa Cruz Railway was changing to broad gauge, four box cars and passenger coaches were purchased from the coast line. Two passenger coaches (known as cars 60 and 61) and two baggage cars, one a combination baggage car and smoker (Number 24) were later bought from the Texas Railroad. Also added was an open-air observation car known as the "Rattler."[50]

The pride of the new line was the garish parlor car acquired from the Carson and Colorado Line. Its drab brindle brown exterior gave no hint of the wonders within. Each plush seat was numbered in gold leaf, shutters framed curtained windows and an ice box allowed cool refreshments to be served. All equipment on the road was "link and coupling" and hand-braking was still in use.

Within the next decade a secondhand Mogul locomotive, with higher drive wheels than the others, was added. Known as *Engine Number Five*, it was followed by the *Number Thirteen*, a still larger combination coal and wood burner purchased from the Tonopah Line.

Engineers included John E. Dunlap, handling throttle on the *Thirteen*, Frank Titus at the controls of the old *Number One* (formerly the *Tahoe*) and Charlie Keyser in the cab of *Number Five*. Conductor Jack Bell, Frank Pomin, and brakeman Scott were among the regular crew members.[51]

On the day of the railroad's official opening run down canyon to Truckee, Don Goodrich of Al

---

G. D. Oliver

HERE THE NARROW GAUGE TRAINS WHISTLED TO A STOP

The Bliss Company's General Merchandise over-water store and post office (formerly Davis and Noteware's) at the head of the Custom House wharf bordering the Tahoe City Commons. The handcar (center foreground) carried mail and freight from the trains to the steamers. Photograph taken looking north toward "Swallows Bank" and the machine shops, in the summer of 1908.

Tahoe was accorded the honor of driving the last spike on the 16-mile line, because of his untiring efforts in pushing the rails to completion. He always contended that one of his legs had grown several inches longer than the other from walking the edge of the ties during construction work on the road.[52]

In order to maintain a gradient of 90 feet to the mile, the railroad crossed and recrossed the river eight times. One mile of track above Old Road Station bridged the Truckee five times and in places crib piers were required along the right-of-way to secure the road bed. The longest trestle work ran between the old Custom House wharf and the company's shops to the north.

Locomotives on the line doubled as "steam winches," hauling the company vessels onto the marine ways. Backing down the track, they pulled the cable, secured at right angles to the cradle of the hull coming out of the water, through an iron block.

Upon completion of the railroad, new timber areas were opened up along the western slopes of Tahoe. A spur was laid south to Ward Creek and into the canyon for two miles. Another track was run along the north side of Squaw Valley and a third built to a log landing at what is now a winter skiing mecca—Granlibaken.

Near the eastern end of the main line it bridged the river one-eighth of a mile below the outlet dam and then climbed a short, steep rise west of Tahoe Tavern in back of the present telephone office. At times the little locomotive with its trainload of passengers failed to make the stiff pull on the first attempt. It would then back down for another full throttle try, with the cheers of the excited passengers lending moral support to the engineer's efforts. Upon reaching the top of the rise, the train went into a switchback that brought it out directly in front of the western entrance to the hotel.

Here guests and luggage were unloaded, then the locomotive and cars backed down to the switch, taking the main track again to the freight and express office adjoining the Tavern casino. From here the train moved out above the water on an eighth of a mile long trestle pier to its terminus where the company's steamers were moored, adjoining the over-water warehouse.

Mail and freight destined for ports of call around the lake, were transferred to the steamers *Tahoe* or *Nevada*. Conductor and brakeman then changed their headgear for pursers' caps and boarded the vessel that would make the scheduled trip that day.[53]

Before the last bridge crossing of the Truckee River another spur track ran across the Tahoe City Y and Commons, passing company carbarns, the Tahoe Mercantile (the "Merc"), the Toy-Yat Club, post office, warehouses, and the Bliss store.[54]

The Tahoe Mercantile was a large two-story rustic building with wide porches that paralleled the railroad. Part of the structure was built out on rock cribbing over the water. Along with the other company buildings and private houses, it violated the township's rights on the Commons. This infringement was tolerated because of the business brought in by the railroad.[55] The "Merc" was destroyed by fire, rumored to have been the work of an arsonist, on October 21, 1937, three years after old Tahoe House (Tahoe Inn) on the bluffs above had gone up in a blaze that ended 70 years of hospitality.

The early 1900's had witnessed some macabre happenings at the city. In the year 1908 Robert Montgomery Watson, his son Bob, and others were unearthing caskets from the old cemetery north of the present John L. Merrill home (original C. T. Bliss residence) and moving them to their present site back of the Tahoe City golf course. As the bodies were exhumed, many were found to be "metalized and fossilized" which was attributed to the seepage of snow water into the graves. Mrs. J. B. Campbell's body, laid to rest some 30 years before, now weighed over 400 pounds. Surprisingly enough her fine black silk dress, in which she had been buried, showed no signs of deterioration. R. M. Watson had placed the Dunlap baby's body in the graveyard several decades previously and it now gave off a metallic ring when tapped on the forehead. Jeremiah "Johnny" Hurley still had his shock of black hair and, according to one eyewitness, "he looked surprisingly fit."[56]

Such strange revelations from the past were fortunately the exception to the rule at the city.

The disinterring of Hurley's body recalled to one oldtimer's mind the days when "Old John" was operating his commercial naphthene launch at the river's outlet. Its cranky engine actually broke down more often than it ran, placing Hurley in a financially embarrassing predicament. He began to think more in dollars lost than in distances covered and when approached one summer morning by a tourist and asked how far it was to Cave Rock he immediately answered: "$20.00 is the distance, sir."[57]

In the early 1900's a traveler from Georgia made his way to Tahoe and settled in the city. His name was William Boyle and he became known as an easy-going, likeable "Southern cracker," with a dry sense of humor. The townspeople had taken to him on sight and, as he was a skilled carpenter, Boyle turned his hand to building fishing boats and selling them to his neighbors at give-away prices.

Bill was a follower of Izaak Walton and the fish had to be biting poorly in the lake before he would settle down to boatbuilding. He reached out with his friendship to everybody, including the Washoe Indians camped down by the Truckee River outlet, but he was in no sense of the word a "squaw man."

Boyle's drollery appealed to the youngsters of the settlement and when he passed the word around that he had "baked up an acre of pie and a cord of doughnuts" the children were the first to make a dash for his lakeshore cabin. Bill was not a steady drinking man but on occasion he "bucked the tiger" at the Custom House wharf. The last time this happened he was dumped unceremoniously into a skiff by three of his companions who rowed him home. Partially sobering up upon his arrival, Boyle demanded that they cut his hair. This they proceeded to do, shaving him bare from ear to ear. The following morning Bill happened to glance in the mirror and when he realized that the shiny-pated apparition staring back at him was himself he swore off drinking for good.

Boyle kept his pledge but that did not stop him from seeing that his friends were well taken care of across the bar.

One afternoon in the summer of 1906, he was stretched out comfortably on Campbell's billiard table. J. B. Campbell had died and his younger brother Frank was in charge. Frank shook Boyle and asked him if he would tend bar while he took his spring wagon and span down to George Murphy's at McKinney's to pick up some bear meat. Bill roused himself and took over.

When Campbell returned several hours later he was barely able to shoulder his way through a boisterous crowd of male customers who packed his Custom House. Frank was all smiles, thinking he had struck a business bonanza. He immediately joined in the festivities. Suddenly Campbell realized that he failed to detect a familiar sound. Drinks were flowing across the bar—but there was no heart-warming ring of the cash register.

Panic-stricken, he questioned Boyle, who quietly advised him that he had felt it was high time *somebody* gave a party for the "boys" and—well—he had more or less indicated that the celebration was on Frank. "Look at the happy glow on their faces," enthused Bill. "Have you ever seen a more deserving bunch enjoying your hospitality?" Campbell dropped his shot glass and sprayed a fine stream of liquor across the bar, but finally he was talked into going along with the "mine host" role, although it cost him several cases of sour mash whiskey.[58]

Boyle always told his friends that he wanted to be buried on the mountain overlooking the city and Tahoe so that he could, as he put it, "keep an eye on those other 'crackers' down below." When he died on a snowy February morning in 1912 the "boys" decided to fulfill his often expressed wish.

On the morning of February 4, a group of his old friends gathered at Tahoe House, and, after fortifying themselves internally for the rugged trip up the ice-encrusted mountain, they made the climb to summit, dragging Bill's coffin behind on a sled.

Today a white cross, 500 feet above the city, marks the grave of William Boyle.

The winter of 1908 had found horses in tandem drawing sleighs between Tahoe City and Truckee

to break the road, and traffic continued to move by snowshoe, dog sled, or sledge. Opening of the rail-road in the spring presented almost insurmountable problems following heavy winters. In April of 1922 it took two locomotives 21 days to break through the snow and ice pack to the city. A V-pilot plow on a low-bed car with flanger attached enabled the engines to make progress down the track, foot by foot and a Johnson bar was used to lift the plow after the engines had made a run at the 12- to 15-foot drifts covering the railbed. Then the little wood-burners would back off down the rails and smash into the snow embankment again.

The old Von Schmidt and Donner Lumber and Boom Company dam was becoming costly to main-tain and by 1909 its gates, that had to be winched open by hand, had become obsolete. Construction of the present concrete structure was begun at that time and when completed it allowed lake water to crest at 6229.35, more than six feet higher than the natural rim.

By the summer of 1925 the Bliss interests, a name that had been synonymous with the develop-ment of Tahoe since 1873, were bowing out of the picture on the western side of the lake. A group of San Francisco capitalists, Bruce Dohrmann, Milton Esberg, John Drum and Herbert Fleishhacker, Sr., in combination with the Linnard Hotel interests, assumed management of Tahoe Tavern Properties. On June 30 of the same year, Southern Pacific and the Blisses reached an understanding. For an annual payment of one silver dollar the Bliss family turned over the narrow gauge railroad to the South-ern Pacific on a 99-year lease. In return the Southern Pacific agreed to convert the line to standard gauge and offer over-night service between San Francisco and Tahoe City.[59]

Broad gauge track was laid down the canyon in 1926 following the roadbed surveyed in 1898. By the following summer the Blisses considered that all provisions of the lease had been fulfilled and in an informal ceremony William S. Bliss handed the deed to the Southern Pacific's attorney and received in return a shiny new silver dollar.[60]

An extensive publicity campaign was now launched by the Linnard interests and the Southern Pacific. Tahoe was promoted as an all-year playground, the name of the railroad's main line was changed from Overland to Lake Tahoe and Snow Ball Specials ran during the winter out of San Fran-cisco. Even with the heavier equipment used on broad gauge track, one of the ski trains bogged down in six-foot drifts between Truckee and Tahoe City during February of 1928. Sleighs and tractors were sent out to rescue the marooned passengers and crew.

Most of the narrow gauge equipment had been loaded aboard flat cars and shipped out and in the fall of 1936 the little Mogul locomotive, *Number One*, that had lain at the machine shops in the city since 1925, was moved to the Grass Valley Line.[61]

Competition from passenger and freight travel on the new highways slowly throttled the railroad's business and a profitable operation finally became impossible. Service on the Tahoe-Truckee railroad was discontinued in 1942 and the rails were torn up and used for scrap iron in World War II. From that time forward mail, express and Tahoe-bound travelers have been carried over the paved highways.

During the early 1920's an old log cabin that had stood to the north of Tahoe Inn for decades was leased from Carl A. Bechdolt, Sr., by Ed Reusenberg of Reno and his partner, Frank Hardin.

The "boys" set up a wide open High Sierra speakeasy in the log and mortar structure with Joe King of Truckee supplying the hand-rocked bootleg whiskey, aged at his "goat ranch" down the

C. O. Valentine

SUN AND SHADOW ALONG THE SHORELINE

Ski tracks in the fresh powder snow leading north on Tahoe City's railroad pier toward the L. T. R. & T. Company's maintenance shops; early spring of 1910.

Author's collection

SNOWDRIFTS PILED TO
30 AND 40 FEET—

*Tahoe City's Mercantile
in the spring of 1925,
viewed from the Commons
looking west.*

Truckee River. In prohibition days purveyors of alcoholic stimulants had to move fast to keep one step ahead of the Federal "Prohis" and it was extremely helpful if one's landlord stood well with the county sheriff.

As this was the only back-country bistro operating in the region at the time, it did a flourishing business with the liquid white heat served across the bar at $1.00 a shot considered to be the best "red eye" in the Sierra. At least there was no recorded case of a patron passing out of the picture from sniffing the cork of a bottle at the establishment. Customers were allowed to cross the threshold of this "blind pig" without undue scrutiny, and the customary heavy barred door and peephole were nonexistent.

In the early 1930's a second Log Cabin was built west of the Inn to take care of the customers overflowing Log Cabin Number One. Johnny Rayburn and Freddie Reiselt were partners in this smoke-filled pleasure palace that offered the glamor of a tarnished Indian head penny, and Tom Sutton

CONFLAGRATION
ON THE COMMONS

*On the night of October 21, 1937,
Tahoe City's Mercantile (the"Merc")
vanished in a sheet of flame that
signalized the closing years
of the railroad's operation.*

C. W. Vernon

ELUSIVE WAS THE WORD FOR FREMONT'S CANNON

Fremont's (nee Pray's) brass 12-pounder at Glenbrook, Fourth of July, 1888, 10 years before it was installed on the bluff above the Tahoe City Commons. Included in the group standing behind the fieldpiece are Johnny Griffin, his son Ralph and blacksmith, George Allen.

Author's collection

managed the place. Here it is recalled that the serving of gagging potables was reinforced with a little fast and fancy gaming. If a weaving patron ever had the phenomenal luck to make more than one pass with the dice or, bug-eyed, saw his number come up on the wheel, it is said that the worried owners immediately adjourned to the back room to find out "what in hell had gone wrong." Log Cabins Number One and Two operated for more than a decade and the Federal revenue agents never did discover any appreciable quantity of liquor in either of them.[62]

The baffling secret lay in the ingenuity of the "boys." Behind Log Cabin Number Two's bar, squares of black and white linoleum covered the floor. Under one of the 8-inch black squares and beneath a cutout in the floor stood a five-gallon copper can. Here lay the secondary source of the whiskey. In one of Tahoe Inn's cabins stood the primary source, aging in 50-gallon charred oak barrels filled with shavings and "cooking" with the dubious assistance of an electric heater.

Log Cabin Number One burned like a kerosene saturated wick when Tahoe Inn went up in smoke during April of 1934. The second Log Cabin was moved, piece by piece, to North Stateline during the early part of World War II. It now stands to the east of Northshore Club.

When Log Cabin Number Two had been dismantled and the foundations examined it was reported that the "batteries, wires and general underfloor arrangements" that strangely enough appeared to run in the general direction of the "games of chance," resembled a front line, barbed wire outpost in the Battle of the Bulge.[63]

Placement of the famous Fremont (nee Pray) cannon on the bluff above the Tahoe City Commons pointed up a story that would constitute a book in itself.

After thousands of miles of cross country travel, this historic field piece, originally issued by the United States Armory in Saint Louis, was abandoned by Captain John C. Fremont on January 29, 1844, when Fremont's exploration party struggled west on the last leg of its journey that would take him, Christopher "Kit" Carson and their men over the Carson Pass to Sutter's Fort in the Valley of the Sacramento. The gun had served the explorers well, providing a visible show of armed strength. Only when Fremont was confronted with the problem of dragging the gun through deep Sierra snows did he decide to abandon it.

He then discarded the brass 12-pounder between Fales Hot Springs, California, and a point on the east bank of the Walker River, ten miles southeast of the present town of Coleville, California.

Historians disagree on the rediscovery of the cannon, with fact and fiction combining to shadow its travels from that time forward. In July of 1861 the gun was said to have been found in the vicinity of the West Walker by a man named Sheldon. Early Walker River settlers insisted, however, that it was located near some abandoned emigrant wagons at the head of Lost Canyon.

The United States Geological Service placed enough credence in the latter report to name the creek running through the canyon "Lost Cannon Creek" and the peak at its head, "Lost Cannon Peak." Richard Watkins, another pioneer who settled in the region in 1861, said the cannon was found on the trail leading from Pickle Meadows to Sonora Pass. Both canyons lie west of the Walker River and all reports agree that Fremont left his field piece at some point east of the river. Sheldon's cannon appears to be the one he tried to sell at Gold Hill, but if it was actually Fremont's it must have been moved from its original resting place.[64] This howitzer ended up in Virginia City and stood for years in "Cannon Corner" in the National Guard Hall. It was fired several times and its last recorded detonation was in 1873 when water came through to Virginia City from the Carson Range of the Sierra.[65]

It is generally believed that this gun, or what might be called the "Sheldon Cannon," was the one moved to Glenbrook by Captain Augustus W. Pray.

The "Pray Cannon" attracted as many conflicting stories as the "Sheldon Cannon." One is that the gun was unmounted when Pray took it to Glenbrook, another, that it was mounted but that Pray removed the wheels and used them on a hay wagon.[66] A third version is that J. S. Whitten and his partner sold it to Pray for $2.50, complete with running gear. Another story offers the thought that the gun passed through the hands of several people before Pray obtained it.

At least it is known that the "Pray Cannon" was fired at the lumbering settlement to celebrate Fourth of July and other special occasions—among these Captain Todman's marriage, the opening of the Lake Tahoe Railroad and launching of the steamer *Tahoe*. A Fourth of July photograph taken in the 1880's shows the howitzer at Glenbrook mounted on a low carriage.

Upon Pray's death in the late 1890's his widow tried to sell the relic and it is reported that a junk dealer had backed his wagon into Mrs. Pray's yard at Glenbrook and was preparing to cart off the field piece when it was retrieved by residents Dick Hesse, John Griffin and Jack Quill, who hid it under a chicken house.[67]

When the Blisses moved their equipment out of Glenbrook in 1898-99, the unmounted barrel of the cannon was placed on a bargeload of scrap that Nat Stein was hauling to Tahoe City. The gun was salvaged and bedded on a 12-inch by 18-inch 5-foot wooden carriage and installed on the bluff above the Commons as a "salute gun." Contrary to general belief, the cannon was never fired at Tahoe City, as Gus Rother, former postmaster at Glenbrook and later storekeeper at Tahoe City, drove the narrow end of a file into the touchhole of the gun, fearing it might explode if discharged.[68]

An interesting sidelight is thrown upon the Pray Cannon by Robert H. Watson of Tahoe City. Watson indicates that Pray moved the original carriage to his logging camp on Observatory Point (Old Lousy) in the early 1890's where it was used as a cordwood wagon. The wheels' hand-forged iron rims were in the possession of Watson in 1956.

Pray's Cannon became the source of numerous forays by well-meaning historical societies bent on claiming it. Local patrotism ran high in each instance and the gun always seemed to vanish into thin air upon the approach of determined claimant groups from Auburn, Reno or Carson City. It is said that the cannon was quietly and successively moved to an office vault, a flour barrel, the Tahoe Tavern pantry, and at one time buried in the Tavern grounds. This, according to a reliable source, is sheer window dressing.[69]

The elusive 12-pounder was actually hidden behind the stairway of the help's quarters at Tahoe Tavern after being removed for the last time from the Tahoe City Commons. Here it was discovered by Ernest Henry Pomin while he was helping Tavern manager Jack Mathews move out an assorted stock of groceries. Pomin smuggled the cannon to A. M. "Joe" Henry's garage in the city and, later, Ernest Pomin, acting as the new custodian of the relic, presented it to Will M. Bliss of Glenbrook. Bliss, in turn, donated it to the Nevada State Museum at Carson City.

There it rests today after being the subject of a heated California-Nevada controversy for nearly three-quarters of a century. Whether it be the Fremont Cannon or not, the legend is more impressive than reality itself as the brass field piece represents a successful human attempt by Tahoe oldtimers to wrest some tangible reminder of the past from creeping oblivion that overtakes all mortal monuments in the region.[70]

Once again Tahoe City is experiencing a business upswing. Tahoe Inn is expanding its facilities, additional motels have been built and other enterprises are springing up. The Tahoe City golf course and Tahoe Boat Company marina are among the finest to be found around the lake. A new development is mushrooming at the Truckee River's outlet, and the Tahoe City Commons is now a public picnic ground.

In the shallows of the lake, bordering the city, rock cribbing and pilings that supported the over-water buildings and piers through the decades stand as fast disappearing reminders of the old settlement.

Here "propellers" and side-wheelers whistled in and docked for nearly three-quarters of a century and the narrow gauge trains puffed into town below the bluff to discharge passengers, freight and mail.

Today this is only a colorful memory that echoes in the hearts of the city's early pioneers.

NARROW GAUGE AT THE CITY

Engine Number Three, baggage car and passenger coach unloading at the Tahoe City Commons, August 12, 1907, View taken from Custom House Wharf looking southwest with old Tahoe Inn in the background.

George D. Oliver

Carl Bechdolt, Sr.

HEADED FOR OLYMPIC HILL

"Red" Anderson (driving), his plumed six-horse team and sleigh leaving Tahoe Tavern's west entrance for the toboggan run and ski jump-ing hill with guests dressed to the teeth; winter of 1931.

Chapter Five

TAHOE TAVERN

A FAMILIAR FIGURE in rumpled suit was standing self-consciously before a select group of state governors and other notables who were gathered around a scrubby yellow pine on the Tahoe Tavern grounds. The day was warm—July of 1933—and a dedication was in progress. The celebrity brushed a shock of hair back from his forehead and twisted the wide brim of his Stetson between thumb and forefinger. He shuffled booted feet and glanced around sheepishly.

Harry Comstock, president of the Lake Tahoe Sierra Association, stepped forward and tied a small bronze plaque around the scrawny tree. Turning, he ceremoniously shook hands with the man in the disheveled suit.

"I give you, 'Governor at Large' Rogers, your own Sierra 'giant'," Comstock said with a smile.

Will Rogers managed a shy grin and hung his head characteristically. Then he glanced at the pine. "A good cow pony could pull this sapling out roots and all," he observed wryly. "There's no money in lumber right now, anyway, and mebbe this fledgling will be worth something bye and bye when it grows up." Rogers bowed, acknowledging the applause of his distinguished audience.[1]

To the west of the gathering rose a large four-story, many-gabled hotel, Tahoe Tavern. A small, self-contained community—internationally famous Tahoe Tavern had taken up where the equally world-renowned Tallac House left off.

Designed by Walter Danforth Bliss and constructed for the Duane L. Bliss family in 1901, the hostelry is located one-half mile south of Tahoe City on a knoll above the lake, surrounded by a grove of pine and cedar. The Tavern Annex, south of the main hotel, was added in 1906 and the Casino, north and below the main building, was put up in the fall of 1907. By 1925 additional accommodations were required and a new $200,000 south wing was built the following year.[2]

Before construction began on the Tavern itself a one-eighth of a mile long trestle pier had been run out into Lake Tahoe for the Bliss Company's steamers and narrow-gauge railroad. When completed, the Tavern, with its brown shingled exterior, wide porches and stretches of lawn and flower beds, became the show place of Tahoe. A laundry, steam plant, water system that included piping water from above Tahoe City, and consultation offices for a resident physician were provided.

The Casino offered a bowling alley, novelty and barber shop, with a ballroom and stage on the second floor. In the 1920's and 30's the Casino was managed by the late Tim Butler. During Butler's time the ballroom was turned into a motion picture theater and a cocktail bar and coffee shop added.

A swimming pool adjoins the Casino. There is a sundeck and a pleasure pier with its cribbed and rocked-in boat wells. Tennis courts, shops, commercial boating and a car livery complete the facilities. For years the Tavern was considered a luxury hotel catering to the carriage trade who desired a combination of comfort and good cuisine when vacationing in the Sierra Nevada. Now it is a popular priced resort.

The Horatio Alger story of Matt Green of Sacramento is part of Tahoe Tavern's history. Coming to the lake in 1901, Green worked as a carpenter in the building of the new hotel. Thirty-five years later he became a stockholder, moved up to become president of the Lake Tahoe Development Company, and finally acquired control.[3]

Green saw a long line of managers come and go, including Jack Mathews, Walter Rounsevel and Glenn Greene. In 1945 Matt sold out to East Bay businessmen A. J. and John Flagg, Lawrence Curtola and Louis Navone. In the following year the Tavern was again sold, this time to a group headed by Albert and Fred Ichelson of San Francisco.

During the fifty-five years the Tavern has operated the great and near great have passed through her doors. Today she is like an aging dowager that still carries her head high in spite of youthful competition springing up around her. Here many of the lake's resort owners learned their trade, among them Carl A. Bechdolt, Sr., of Tahoe Inn and the late Al Richardson of Camp Richardson.

Unknown musicians and bands found the Tavern ballroom a springboard to national success. Fourth floor riots in the employees' rooms, sparked by gallon jugs of warm pink gin, were not uncommon in the prohibition days of the "Roaring 20's," and on many evenings during the summer season it was touch and go whether members of the band would all make the bandstand together.

A high point in the summer season was the Venetian Water Carnival. The Tavern pier was converted into a Venetian bridge for the occasion and the theme completed by strolling musicians, colorful lanterns and a flotilla of gayly decorated commercial and private boats from around the lake.

To the west of the Tavern a ski jump and toboggan run were laid out during the 1930's for use as a Winter Olympic Games qualifying hill. Proper garb for the novice skier and spectator alike were

GABLED MAGNIFICENCE IN THE HIGH SIERRA

Tahoe Tavern's east entrance in the summer of 1914 before the lower section of the main hotel had been glassed in. View taken looking north with the dining room wing on the right.

C. O. Valentine

knickers or riding pants tucked into hiking boots, and turtle-neck sweaters topped off with stocking caps.

Scotty Allen, the famous Alaskan dog sled driver, pitched his "igloo" and housed his malamutes on the frozen Tavern grounds. Cross country races were a feature of the day. When the hotel remained open for winter sports, the garage was turned into an ice rink (Tavern owners groaned loudly over the enormous heating bills) and sleighs drawn by six horses (approaching dray dimensions) shuttled excited guests to and from "Olympic Hill."

For several summers a two-by-four bar flourished in the cloakroom adjoining the dining room entrance. It was replaced in the 1930's and 40's by slot machines that were whisked to a safe hiding place whenever the county sheriff telephoned to say he was about to make a raid.

"Muchie" and Johnny Bezoni were the favorite fishing guides to see at the head of the railroad pier and trout of "getaway" size could always be produced for the unlucky fisherman at a moment's notice. Private gasoline launches, with crews in starched whites, met their affluent owners when they arrived on the narrow-gauge train at the end of the Tavern pier. The launches then churned away to Idlewild, Sugar Pine, Rubicon and other points on the lake.

Picnic parties visited Page Meadows and wondered vaguely how it had received its name. The Page family from Clarksville, El Dorado County, had built the original wagon road into the meadows to run cattle during the summer and it has been said that John, brother of Lou and Sam Page, was hanged for slitting a horse's throat, but only after it was discovered he had topped this off by murdering the rider.[4]

At Outlet Point, adjoining the Tavern grounds to the north, an unmercifully commercialized old

WHERE RAIL AND WATER MET

Engine Number 3, baggage car and "Rattler" at the end of Tahoe Tavern's railroad trestle pier in August, 1905, with freight, baggage and mail being transferred to the steamer TAHOE.

Marie Henry

ICICLES AND A BLANKET OF WHITE

Tahoe Tavern's north wing, looking southeast, beneath 35-foot drifts on March 16, 1922.

Author's collection

Washoe Indian woman with the given name of Louisa Keyser, sat cross-legged at the door of William Morgan's former home on the water's edge. Better known as Dat-So-La-Lee, she wove and shaped intricate ceremonial baskets, moaning pitifully at times during the summer season: "Dat-So-La-Lee getting old."

Said to have been born in Eagle Valley (Carson) in the early 1830's, this illiterate woman possessed a spark of genius that created basket art recognized as the finest of its kind ever to be fabricated by a North American Indian. Since her mother had worked for Dr. S. L. Lee in Carson City, the source of her nickname is obvious.[5] Trained for nearly half a century in the craftsmanship of basketry, Dat-So-La-Lee combined patience with artistic talent to produce what have now become museum pieces. Abraham Cohen, also of Carson, recognized this creative ability and, whether for exploitation or because of his genuine feeling for her art, brought her to the lake at the turn of the century. Dat-So-La-Lee practiced her art of fine basket weaving at both the Truckee River outlet and Tahoe Tavern. During the spring of the year she wandered the shore and back trails of Tahoe, gathering and curing roots and branches of willow, incense cedar, red fir and tamarack. From these she made the strands and dyes required for her painstaking work. She cured many materials used in her baskets for as long as twelve years before starting to weave her finest creations.

In the late 1890's her best works brought upwards of $50 a basket. Considered high at the time, this was only a fraction of their value in later years. So carefully did she plan her work that not one of her versatile designs was a duplication. Her most amazing faculty was a perfect knowledge

Author's collection

A STYGIAN CLOUD BLACKENS THE SIERRA SKY

The railroad pier's warehouse goes up in smoke during the early 1930's with the steamers TAHOE and NEVADA standing by.

of perspective and symmetry. To this was added an innate mastery of precise craftsmanship and blending of colors.

Thirty-five of Dat-So-La-Lee's masterpieces and at least 75 of her minor pieces are known to exist. Her best work has eighty warps to the inch and another of her more famous baskets, which took two years to complete, contains 84,500 tightly woven stitches.

Unfortunately Dat-So-La-Lee was the last of her line, leaving no imitator or successor when she died in Carson City in 1925 after living 96 winters. Two-thirds of her life had been devoted to creating and perfecting her art. Until the time of her death Dat-So-La-Lee's gnarled hands, seemingly more suitable for plowing than intricate weaving, were busy turning out these perfections. The "L. K." (Louisa Keyser) baskets, as they are known today, may be seen at the Nevada State Historical Society

OUT OVER THE LAKE OF THE SKY

The only known aerial view, taken in the early 1930's, showing the L. T. R. & T. Company's one-eighth of a mile long transportation pier, standard gauge track (changed over from narrow gauge in 1926) and train, steamer TAHOE *in her slip, Tavern Casino (behind white smoke of engine), Tahoe Tavern, express offices, and Johnny Bezoni's fishing shack at the head of the trestle.*

Fred Main

Museum in Reno, and the Nevada State Museum in Carson City. One of her finer ceremonial works is in the Carnegie Museum, Pittsburgh, Pennsylvania.[6]

The general public probably would have been unable to view many of these masterpieces if Abe Cohen's salesmanship had not misfired. One summer afternoon in the early 1920's, a prosperous group of seasonal Tahoe residents, consisting of Walter Hobart, Jr., John Drum, Sr., and others, stopped at the "Basketry" to admire Dat-So-La-Lee's art. Cohen, always on the alert for business, jotted down the names of his wealthy visitors and the following day dispatched a letter to Hobart offering all of Dat-So-La-Lee's work to him for $25,000.

Upon reading the bluntly commercial missive, Hobart immediately called in his secretary. Never at a loss for the ready, if off-beat answer, Hobart dictated the following: "Dear Basket, Today I am only buying 'A's' . . ." at this point he reached for a dictionary and ordered his stenographer to copy the first three pages, starting with "Aaron." Then he continued, "Possibly in the near future I will be purchasing in the 'B's' at which time I will most certainly contact you, (signed) Walter Scott Hobart, Jr."[7]

Thus abruptly were concluded the "basket" negotiations between Cohen and Hobart. Cohen, however, might have had the final chuckle, as several of Dat-So-La-Lee's finest ceremonial baskets are valued as high as $10,000 each today.

BASKET BARGAINS
—UP TO $10,000 APIECE

*Dat-So-La-Lee (Louisa Keyser)
shown in the early 1900's
standing beside two of her
hand woven ceremonial
masterpieces.
This Washoe Indian's intricate
handiwork is now considered
the finest creative basketry
ever to be fabricated in the
Western Hemisphere.*

Chapter Six

TAHOE PARK

"**D**AMN IT THEN, I'll agree to 40 cents a tie, laid down at Coburn's Station, and 50 cents each if the contract is completed on schedule. The Central won't go any higher, so take it or leave it."

The heavy set, square-jawed man, standing in the slushy snow back of Saxton's Mill that early spring morning in 1866, hunched his shoulders and drove his clenched right fist into the palm of his left hand. The collar of a thick, nearly ankle-length great coat crept up his neck in tight folds, tipping the man's bowler over bushy eyebrows. With a show of annoyance he reset his hat. He had flung his ultimatum at a powerful red-shirted logger, Augustus H. Saxton, owner of the mill.[1] Saxton scrutinized the lumber buyer with amusement and grudging respect. Then Saxton reached out calloused fingers and picked up a soggy pine needle branch. He bent it double and snapped it in a whirring arc toward the lake before turning again to the fidgeting buyer from the Central Pacific Railroad, who now pulled at his mutton-chop whiskers.

"Agreed, Mister Huntington," said Saxton. He was a man of few words.

Collis P. Huntington, guiding genius of the new Central Pacific Railroad's colossal gamble, hurriedly shook Saxton's hand, then stomped north down the trail through the melting drifts, his outsize coat "caboosing" behind. Huntington congratulated himself. Once again he figured he'd closed a deal with "scrupulous dishonesty."[2]

Not until the "Big Four's" financial wizard had disappeared among the pines did Saxton allow himself the satisfaction of open gloating. Then Saxton's face broke into a toothy smile. He considered the contract price for milling the Central's railroad ties to be fantastic and he envisioned immediate wealth. Let the deep rock miners in Virginia City struggle for their gold and silver. His bonanza towered to the skies of Tahoe — a vast forest of sugar and yellow pine. "What is all that ox-dung about Huntington, the shrewd trader?" Saxton asked himself. The ties weren't worth one quarter of the agreed price. He remembered what the boys had said down at that collection of shacks grandly known as Tahoe City. Saxton set his jaw. Barely three years before they had pegged him for just another "crazy miner from Volcanoville." But things were different now, he mused happily. His eyes lit up—he was thinking: "I wonder what they'll say now?"

In the fall of 1863 Saxton had taken title to a large section of timberland, two and one half miles south of the "City." His land ran west from the bay's shoreline and included all of Ward Creek Canyon.[3]

Before the heavy snows set in that winter, he constructed a water-powered sawmill. In order to drive the machinery that turned his double circular saws, Saxton built a gigantic 54-foot high overshot wheel. One and three quarters of a mile up the canyon he threw a diversion dam part way across Ward Creek. After digging the long millrace he released the water into the ditch. Saxton was in business.[4]

ENOUGH DUST FOR 10,000 GESUNDHEITS

Five span of yoked oxen moving downgrade along Ward Creek to Saxton's Mill, engulfing the bullwhacker, behind the off-wheel animal, in a cloud of talcum-fine dust. Summer of 1871.

Author's collection

By June 15, 1864, he had yarded a miserable 10,000 feet of lumber, worth only $200 on the going market. A single yoke of oxen constituted Saxton's sole means of moving saw logs to his mill, which was valued at $3,000. With meticulous attention to detail, the Placer County assessor listed seven hens, worth $7.00, and one non-taxable male dog. This was the lumberman's only personal property. The customary gold watch, upon which every tax collector of the day pounced, was missing from Saxton's frayed vest pocket.

One year later Saxton's improvements had nearly doubled his mill's value, and now eight head of oxen and a crew of "fallers" were working the back country. Eighteen hundred dollars worth of lumber was stacked on his racks.[5]

In the spring of 1866, the Central Pacific Railroad was still racing east in an attempt to out-rail the Union Pacific and the fierce competition between the two lines brought into reality Saxton's fabulous windfall: the milling of railroad ties.

"Splash dams" were built in the Truckee River to back up water sufficient to float the timbers to Coburn's Station (Truckee).[6] Extra crews of lumberjacks worked from sunup to darkness. Then Saxton ran into difficulties. He had not counted on the green lumber sinking to the bottom of the stream, but it did. "Pushers" and "breakers" were rushed to the river to keep the ties moving. Double rafts were hurriedly constructed to raise the bunched, sunken lumber, but they only compounded Saxton's troubles. Cumbersome and unwieldy, these miniature "Go-Devils" were often swept down stream, blocking the river and creating more complications. Saxton's costs shot up. Then the thought suddenly struck him. Huntington *must* have foreseen these problems when he offered that "fantastic" price and nailed it down with his fast delivery requirement. " 'Cagey Collis' was pretty shrewd after all," Saxton admitted disgustedly.

Then he got mad. "Stack 'em on wagons," bellowed Saxton. This only added to his headaches. It took four and one-half hours for his creaking, slow-moving lumber carriers to make the winding trip down the gorge to Truckee, a mere 16 miles.

Finally Saxton completed his contract, but instead of realizing the handsome profit he had expected, he found himself nearly bankrupt. "I could have carried every last one of them damn ties to the railroad on my own back easier and quicker and made a few double gold eagles," he is said to have muttered.[7]

In June of 1867 the value of Saxton's mill somehow had increased to $8,000 and he was now turning out 8,000 board feet of lumber a day.[8] Six months later, however, the Central Pacific's demands fell off sharply. In spite of this loss of business, Saxton ran 75,000 ties through his circular saws the following season. These floated. Saxton had learned, through bitter experience, and stacked and dried his cut the preceding winter. Ruben R. Saxton, A. H. Saxton's son, was now old enough to help out at the mill, and Saxton Sr. left his boy in charge while he made the trip to Virginia City. Here he obtained a contract to supply lagging for the Con-Virginia mine.[9]

The Saxtons worked their way higher into the heavy timber stands surrounding Ward Peak. They leased additional land from the Central Pacific, which had acquired railroad grants to the west in the vicinity of Twin Peaks, Bear Pen, and Grouse Canyon and built logging chutes that dropped into Ward Creek Canyon, skidding and dragging the saw logs down canyon to the mill.

In the summer of 1871 a lumberman named Edwards was taken in by the Saxtons as a partner. He suggested they convert the mill to steam power. But "Rube" and his father refused. Even with their outmoded water-driven machinery they were still able to produce 50,000 feet of lumber during the months of July and August, 1873.[10]

Captain J. A. Todman from Glenbrook leased Saxton's Mill in April of 1877 and Edwards dropped out as a partner. Todman, the "Fleet-builder of Lake Tahoe," turned out planking and square-finished ribs for the 104-foot cordwood barges he was constructing for the Carson and Tahoe Lumber and Fluming Company. It was a disastrous year for Todman and the Saxtons. During the summer a giant forest fire swept the mountain slopes from the Truckee Gorge to Idlewild. Burning unchecked for nearly two full weeks, it destroyed most of the choice timber reserves in the vicinity of the mill. This catastrophe ended extensive logging operations at Saxton's.[11]

By the spring of 1881 the old mill had become a tourist attraction, pointed out to steamer passengers as "that extinct mill which had supplied the first ties for the railroad east of Donner Summit." It was also erroneously described as "the site of that extensive logging camp of the Central Pacific Railroad during the period of its construction."[12]

Although Saxton's Mill was closed down, early records indicate that the site was used for a wood camp until 1887.

Augustus H. Saxton died in the winter of 1886.[13] The following summer James C. Titus of Glenbrook purchased the mill from Rube Saxton for $250. For another $250 Rube offered Titus 640 adjacent acres, including a half mile of bayshore frontage. Titus scoffed at this proposal. Everybody knew that this cut-over and burned-out land was worthless. He laughingly suggested that Rube look for and sell it to a drunken Washoe nabob. Then Titus tore down the mill and barged the hand-hewn, wooden pegged timbers across the lake. Here they were flumed to Carson Valley for use in the building of farm houses.[14]

Activity at Saxton's Mill over the years had not been confined to lumbering alone. In September of 1866, a number of "Lakers" witnessed the appearance of a 5- to 6-foot cone-shaped column of water, rising like an artesian well out of Tahoe, just offshore from the millsite. When the column subsided, a whirlpool 10 feet in width developed and continued for two days. There was a depression eighty feet deep in the lake bottom at this point, although soundings showed the surrounding depth to be only forty feet. The residents of Tahoe immediately considered this to be indisputable proof that subterranean outlets existed on the floor of the lake. They also theorized that the geyser of water "had issued from the crater of an extinct volcano."[15]

Mrs. Hayes, claimed as a resident by both the Golden and Silver States, is credited with naming the bay when she built Sunnyside Cottage, boathouse and pier at the influx of Ward Creek.[16] The cove became a favorite fishing spot for "Lakers" and summer vacationists as thousands of trout migrated up the creek each year. In the summer of 1881 the *Tahoe Tattler* reported that a "Miss Carrie Stevenson and M. T. Benham took 15 silversides in one and one-half hours of trolling with very little effort." An anonymous fishing guide in another boat was described as suffering from a "severe case of jim-jaws." This was attributed to the fact that he had been tipping the bottle the previous night and, "immeasurably worse," was a former resident of Reno.

Thomas McMurtrey, living south of the old millsite on Sunnyside Bay, had the fastest rowboat on the lake.[17] Named the *Brightbird*, it was moored at Saxton's crumbling wharf where the bay residents

Author's collection

"BLACK BART" STRAPPED INTO THE SHOEING STALL

One of A. J. Saxton's "stag" lead oxen getting a new set of split shoes at Lake Camp on snow-covered ground in early May, 1875.

admired its graceful lines and marveled at its six-mile-an-hour speed with only one oarsman at the sweeps. Old-timers at the lake, however, remember McMurtrey more for his lack of nautical prowess than for his boat. McMurtrey established his questionable marine reputation when he pushed off from Saxton's wharf one calm Sunday morning in the late 1880's. He was standing upright in the gleaming *Brightbird* and waving enthusiastically to the envious watchers ashore. Their admiring exclamations over the new boat and its fortunate owner quickly turned into warning shouts and frantic arm signals as they saw McMurtrey's craft rapidly bearing down on a piling hidden from his view. With a resounding crash, the bow of the speedster caught the piling nose on, catapulting its startled occupant over the side of the boat into the icy waters. This was the last trip the embryonic mariner ever made in the *Brightbird*, but his unexpected plunge into Tahoe had served a purpose. McMurtrey had learned to swim—the hard way.[18]

Ward Canyon also contributed to the lighter side of life when a dance platform, built at Tahoe City, proved distracting to the townspeople. It was moved on the Bliss railroad's Ward Creek spur to a spring up the canyon. But its popularity only survived two or three excursion trips. Sarsaparilla had been served instead of hard liquor and the recreation center in the wilderness died a natural death . . . from thirst.[19]

In 1910, 50 by 100 foot lots were selling along the lakeshore for $50 each. The Bliss family now owned most of the land from Tahoe Tavern to Ward Creek. They had sold some of the choicer parcels to the Bissells (property later purchased by the William Wallace Meins), Spencer Blacks, James F. Moffitts, and other prominent San Francisco and East Bay families, who built "mansion houses" above the lake. The Blisses also offered some plots to their employees for $10.00 down and $1.00 a month. Few took advantage of the offer. "What good is a lakefront lot now that the big timber is gone?" they asked.[20]

The Ward Creek spur of the L. T. R. and T. Company was the scene of a tragedy several summers later. Two Italian woodcutters, Frank Pizini and one "Barnie," were walking the ties toward Sunnyside in a blissful alcoholic fog when the 4 o'clock logging train whistled around a curve. Pizini was killed instantly but Barnie escaped with his life, although his right leg was amputated. Several months later Robert H. Watson from Tahoe City happened to meet Barnie in Truckee, where the Italian was hobbling down the street with the aid of a crutch.

"Too bad you had to lose your leg," Watson sympathized.

With a show of flashing white teeth Barnie drew a finger across his throat. "Yes," he agreed, "but the other fellow he losa *his* leg *up to here!*"[21]

In the 1920's, Chris Nielson, locally famous Danish fishing guide, operated a small marine ways and winter storage business just south of what is now Sunnyside Lodge. A hard trader, and master of the art of making corrosive home-brew, old Chris was obsessed with a gnawing ambition — he had to take the largest cutthroat trout swimming in the waters of Lake Tahoe.[22] When he finally gaffed a 26½-pound scarlet-gilled beauty, Nielson thought he had made it, but after repeated "thumb-on-the-scale" weighings the monstrous trout was still found to be three pounds under the lake record. Chris therefore had to be satisfied with landing the biggest cutthroat ever caught on the *west* side of Tahoe. Chris had another weakness. He ignored the meal-time clanging of the triangle and spent most of his spare time trolling on Sunnyside Bay. But his wife Hulda, whom he had met and married while she was a chambermaid at Tallac, had a remedy. She would project a clarion call, punctuated with choice and juicy expletives, out across the waters of Tahoe. This never failed to bring Chris racing in at breakneck speed. Young old-timers at Tahoe City who remember Hulda insist that they could hear her shrill summons just as plainly as though she were standing alongside their pier instead of being some two and one-half miles away.[23]

INTO THE HIGH COUNTRY AFTER SUGAR PINE

Augustus H. Saxton standing at the brake arm and ratchet of his solid-wheeled logging truck, hauled by 16 animals yoked and trace-chained to the carrier. Above Ward Creek in the summer of 1876.

Today the large acreage that now constitutes Tahoe Park (owned at various times by the Saxtons, Bliss family, William Kents, Lamberts and others) stretches back into Ward Creek Canyon from Sunnyside Bay. Here a small community of stores, motels and private residences has sprung up. The former Charles Kendrick home is now Sunnyside Lodge, originally operated by Ralph Sears and his family. Among the private estates that lie to the south are those owned by the Thieriot, Murphy, Gamble, Poett, Dohrmann, Ducato, Saroni, Marsten, Towne and McClatchy families. Northeast of the Lodge now stand the summer homes of the Millers, Browns, Meins, Fays, Scotts, Bechdolts and Kings, with many of these places changing hands over the years.

At the site of Saxton's old wharf, saw logs, scantling and slashing are visible to a depth of 100 feet in the crystal clear water, where they were discarded as worthless mill waste nearly a century ago. Here enough water-logged lumber now lies on the lake bottom to build a small settlement of homes.

NARROW GAUGE SPUR AND SUNNYSIDE BAY

Looking south in May of 1915. Railroad track (foreground) leading into Ward Creek Canyon, with Ward Creek Point, Mt. Ellis, Burton(s) Pass and the Rubicon Range in the distance.

Chapter Seven

TAHOE PINES

Dapper Mr. R. Porter Ashe of the Bay City recoiled in horror at the sight advancing toward him down the trail. "Back, ladies," he shouted at the group of young socialites he was squiring up Blackwood Creek Canyon. "Get back of me at once."

They turned and, with their ground-sweeping dresses tripping them at every step, ran screaming down the path in the direction of Idlewild.

Ashe had come face to face with a "monstrous black bear" and her cub ambling through the forest shade. The color drained from his face as the big animal cuffed her offspring aside, broke into a shuffling charge and rapidly bore down on him. He barely had time to pull out his "Bull Dog British revolver" before the snarling brute attacked, fastening her great teeth on his left arm. Luckily, he was somewhat protected by a heavy hunting jacket. With his free arm, he leveled the gun at the "growling devil and shot the bear five times in the chest, killing her instantly."

After this magnificent display of heroism, Ashe proceeded to faint dead away. Reviving soon afterward, he was assisted to a nearby log by several of the admiring and breathless ladies who had paused in their flight to witness the encounter. It was reported he "lit up his Meerschaum pipe, and accepted the plaudits of the little group."[1]

Meeting the challenge of nature in the raw in the 1880's was, fortunately, the exception to the rule at Idlewild. Generally days and nights were spent by the gay San Francisco and Virginia City social set canoeing, promenading, trolling for silversides on the tranquil waters of McKinney Bay, botanizing and studying the brilliant stars overhead. The boldest of the blazered, peg-bottom trousered "blades" of the era took the shy-eyed, wasp-waisted ladies of their choice in a spring wagon along the narrow dirt road leading to Sugar Pine Point. The vehicle usually held two, but as a chaperone was looked upon as an unfortunate necessity, she took her place on an improvised "dickey seat" forward of the tailgate.[2]

High society had blossomed on the shores of Lake Tahoe and Mrs. Edwin B. Crocker was the acknowledged leader of the summer whirl in her "sumptuous home" at Idlewild.

Barker's Peak had even taken on a high-sounding pronunciation, being shown on a map of the times as "Bawker's."[3] Wags at the earthy settlement of Tahoe City doubled up with laughter and vowed that Bill Barker, the lately-deceased old rancher, "would sure be tossed around in his white pine box if he could hear that one."[4]

Many of Tahoe's pioneer residents insisted that it seemed as though a full century had passed since Hampton Craig Blackwood settled in the region. Actually it was only 15 years. In the late fall of 1863 Blackwood, a native of North Carolina who had traveled the alkali death trail by way of the Humboldt Sink cut-off as one of the envied '49ers, left the phantom silver strike in Squaw Valley

HERE HIGH SOCIETY BLOSSOMED

Judge and Mrs. Edwin B. Crocker's summer retreat at Idlewild in the fall of 1883, where their daughter Aimeé led the gay, seasonal social whirl. Looking northwest toward Eagle Rock from Tahoe.

and moved south along Tahoe's shoreline to the creek which now bears his name. Mud Springs (El Dorado) was this miner's California home but the canyon and high country grazing land, to the west of the creek's influx into the lake, offered fine pasturage for sheep or cattle. He decided to put it to summer range.[5]

During May of the following year Blackwood interested El Dorado rancher William Andrew Barker in "the finest grazing land in the High Sierra" and together they ran Barker's stock in the canyon and fertile meadowland to the west. After fattening on wild timothy grass and bunch clover, the animals were driven in the fall down through the canyons to the foothills above Sacramento Valley.

Today Blackwood's name is on the creek and canyon, while Barker's remains on the peak, meadow and pass.[6]

William Samuel Cothrin was another pioneer stockman of the 1860's, coming from White Oaks Township near Clarksville, El Dorado County, where he ran "Cothrin's Store." He pastured sheep in the back country on range land to the south of Barker and Blackwood's holding, leaving his name on "Cothrin Cove."

In the year 1868 Thomas McConnell of Sacramento located on the lakeshore at Blackwood Creek's outlet. He acquired 388 acres of lake frontage and forested back country, running from a point north of Eagle Rock along Upson Bay (McKinney) one-quarter of a mile past the present settlement of Homewood.[7]

McConnell is said to have obtained his holdings from a homesteader (possibly Blackwood) who shot and killed one of the Washoe tribesmen for setting a fish trap on the creek. Fearing the tribe's vengeance, the squatter considered it a good bargain to obtain the few dollars offered by McConnell for his half section.[8]

By the spring of 1873 George Connors was running a sheep camp in the upper reaches of Blackwood, and during the same year McConnell doubled his acreage which gave him two miles of lake front alone.

The Ferdinand von Leicht and J. D. Hoffmann *Topographical Map of Lake Tahoe* (1874) shows "McConnel" (sic) located on the north side of Blackwood Creek, with a trail leading along Upson Bay to the south. Wheeler's United States Geographical Map of 1876-77, however, ignores McConnell's entirely, even placing the pack trail back one-eighth of a mile from the location of his house on the lakeshore.[9]

By the year 1880 McConnell had sold off tracts of land adjoining Blackwood Creek's outlet into Tahoe. Henry Marvin Yerington of Glenbrook, Edwin B. Crocker and Fred K. Birdsall of Sacramento, N. D. Rideout and the Lubeck family from San Francisco were the purchasers. Property surrounding Tom McConnell's "Lake House" became the exclusive residential section of Tahoe during the summer and was known as Idlewild.[10]

Birdsall's cottage, when completed in the spring of 1881, was described as "palatial" and "one of the finest on the lake" by the admiring *Tahoe Tattler* editor, R. E. Wood. Constructed at a cost of $3,000, it immediately elevated its owner to the "esquire" listing at the Tahoe City post office.

During the summer of the same year the *Truckee Republican* noted that "one hundred and twenty excursionists embarked from the *Governor Stanford* at McConnell's for luncheon, after the boat had whistled grandly into the wharf."[11] The primary reason for the stopover was to obtain a closeup view of Eagle Rock, rising an abrupt 250 feet above Idlewild, and to climb to its summit.[12]

Although McConnell's was not considered a resort, it did have picnic grounds, a dance floor under the pines, summer cottages and a steamer wharf. A chronicler described the location as a "delightful spot on the shore under the shadow of 'Eagle Bluff' and two miles beyond Sunnyside, with Mrs. E. B. Crocker's summer resort located thereon," adding with the customary inaccuracy of the times, "the highest mountain in the background is Tinker's Knob."[13]

Thomas McConnell was not without competition in the picnic grounds and dance hall business. In the late 1870's he sold a strip of lakeshore property to H. S. Brooks of Sacramento, who located approximately one mile south of Idlewild. Brooks advertised regular dances on Saturday night, boast-

EXIT THE CROCKERS — ENTER THE KOHLS

The Crocker home, facing the lake, in the winter of 1905, before it was moved to the west of Frederick Kohl's new "mansion house," shown under construction at the extreme left of the picture. John Ernest Pomin standing with his back to the camera.

John Ernest Pomin

Joseph McKee

SMOKING LOGS STRUCK AT MORE THAN A MILE A MINUTE AND SPRAY FEATHERED 100 FEET INTO THE AIR

The terminal point of logger "Winnie" Smith's log chute where it entered Tahoe's Hurricane Bay, one-half mile north of Idlewild. Here saw logs were V-boomed and rafted to Glenbrook's mills in 1891. Ward Creek Point, center left.

ing the "largest dance platform on the west side of Tahoe." Set among towering cedars and adjoining the wagon road from Tahoe City to McKinney's, it was known as Cedar Grove.[14]

For nearly a quarter of a century Idlewild symbolized the pinnacle of social activity at Lake Tahoe. Aimeé Crocker Ashe Gillig Gouraud Miskinoff (Princess Alexander Galitzine), daughter of Judge and Mrs. Edwin B. Crocker, set the pace for the gay, carefree whirl. It appears that Mrs. Miskinoff was more than qualified for this position. She was generally considered to be a worldly, tempestuous adventuress. Her deft handling of the male of the species, evidenced by her collection of husbands, was later pointed up in her eyebrow-raising book, *I'd Do It Again*, a scorching account of her successes that immediately gained acceptance as "a super spry book." This was shortly followed by *Paula Loves Pearls*, a racy tome inspired by Aimeé's cruise to the South Pacific, where, it is reported, "the great sacrifice was made to a South Sea Island chief in exchange for a magnificent black pearl."[15] These lurid goings-on, which are said to have provided the material for her private printings decades later, did, indeed, add zest to life at Idlewild in the Gay '90's.

In the summer of 1905 Frederick C. Kohl of San Francisco purchased the Crocker home at Tahoe, moving the old place back from the lake toward Eagle Rock after constructing a large two-story, U-shaped house to the west.[16] Cliff Weatherwax, who later met death mysteriously at the Ritz Carlton Hotel in New York, is said to have extended every effort to carry on the traditions of high living at Idlewild. The young dandy became violently enamored of the attractive Mrs. Kohl, the home thereafter becoming known in back parlor conversation as "Cliff's Kohling Station."

In 1926, Herbert Fleishhacker, Sr., San Francisco capitalist, bought the Kohl estate together with extensive sections up Blackwood Canyon. An enclosed swimming pool in the lake and shoreline cottages were added, along with two speedboats to complement the 60-foot cruiser *Idlewild* originally built for Kohl. The new additions in the marine line were for his sons, Herbert, Jr. and Allen. As this was during the expansive 1920's, it was not uncommon to find formal banquets being held in the picnic grounds adjoining Blackwood Creek. Waiters, resplendent in white tie and tails, moved incongruously among the pines, serving roasted suckling pig, wild duck and other delicacies from a glowing barbecue pit.[17]

During the early 1930's the Everts Mills family acquired the Fleishhacker interests at Idlewild. Much of the original holding was subdivided and the old home, with its north wing removed, belongs today to the A. R. Bradleys.

Idlewild officially became Tahoe Pines on March 21, 1912, with the establishment of a post office. Mail pouches were made up daily in Truckee and Tahoe City, then dispatched by packet boat with Tahoe Pines the first stop on the mail boat's counter-clockwise run around the lake.

During the deer season a decade later Tom Walker's mountain speakeasy in Blackwood Canyon, known as the "Bucket of Blood," supplied the thirsty hunter and served also as a lookout post for the State game warden. The sight of one Schumacher, warden for the district, taking his ease in front of a roaring fire at the bar and checking out the day's kill brought in by bone-tired nimrods, gradually built up a resentment in the local gentry.

One fall afternoon in the early 1920's a group of hunters, enlivened by several long drinks at Walker's bar and still smarting from the detailed scrutiny given their truck by Schumacher, watched him through field glasses as he climbed to a vantage point on the south side of the canyon. There he could obtain a clear view of "illegal shooting." Picking up their rifles, the group took turns ringing Schumacher with "carry" shots that brought him down the mountain with express train speed, ranting and cursing. He crashed through the saloon door, stormed up to the innocent looking hunters and swore he would have the lot of them in the county jail before nightfall. Unfortunately for the warden's plans, no one seemed to have the vaguest idea who had done the shooting.[18]

On the northern ridge of Blackwood Canyon near Stanford Rock, directly above the present Town and Country Lodge, a choice stand of red fir grew untouched until 1890. In that year logger "Winnie" Smith from Tahoe City ran a two and one-quarter mile log chute from the 8500-foot summit down into what was then Hurricane Bay. The steep drop sent the saw logs smoking down the chute at such speed that square-headed spikes had to be driven into the runway to slow them down and ribbons of peeled bark streamed out in back of the timbers like serpentine as they pounded down the log way. The course of the old chute can still be traced up the side of the mountain when it is viewed from out on the water.[19]

Numerous private homes are today scattered along the protected shoreline of Homewood Bay. One of the more fabulous private estates on Lake Tahoe is located on the lakeshore between old Idlewild and Homewood. This is Henry J. Kaiser's "Fleur du Lac."[20] The estate's six native stone chalets were built on a willow and yellow pine-covered marshy lowland south of Blackwood Creek. In the year 1939 a crew of nearly 300 workmen descended upon this swamp. Steam shovels, dragline equipment, piledrivers, masons, carpenters, engineers, plasterers, decorators and day laborers worked around the clock. The marsh was cleared. Dump trucks and power shovels moved thousands of cubic yards of fill to raise and increase the lake frontage. Roads, pathways and stone bridges were laid out, and even a diversion of Blackwood Creek was dredged. Completed in the record time of 29 days, the equivalent of a medium-sized settlement of shake-roofed, low-lying buildings rose where scrub brush and a sand spit formerly stood.

In addition, a rocked-in inland waterway, native red brownstone breakwater with lighthouse, drive-in boat storage, double swimming pool, amphibious plane landing and water ski take-off were built. Central heating was piped underground to all units. Rolling lawns and flower beds throughout the property completed this beautiful mountain estate. Originally constructed as a meeting place for The Six Companies executives, "Fleur du Lac" became the private summer home of Mr. and Mrs. Henry J. Kaiser and family.

Kathleen Haine

BUILT IN THE RECORD TIME OF 29 DAYS

Henry J. Kaiser's "FLEUR DU LAC"; palatial Tahoe retreat completed in 1939 where Blackwood Canyon fans out to the lake.

Chapter Eight

HOMEWOOD

IT MUST HAVE BEEN a storm-swept day with thunderheads rolling over the mountains when Martin Lowe arrived at Lake Tahoe. This well-educated behemoth of a man was to set in motion an explosive series of personal exploits that practically demanded a rumbling reception from the elements. Lowe's 260-pound bulk arrived on the Tahoe scene shortly after the turn of the century. He immediately settled in the marshland adjoining Blackwood Creek, his residence consisting of a weatherbeaten shack with a burlap-shrouded entrance and no windows.

Lowe soon talked himself into a partnership with market-fisherman Bill "El Campo" Johnson of Homewood. Reports indicate that this ponderous individual considered the life of shuttling across the water in his skiff from Blackwood Creek to the resorts on McKinney Bay entirely suited to his particular talents. Events were shaping up that would place the dubious mantle of "character" around his hulking shoulders. In retrospect, one must conclude that Lowe was a man of infinite capacity, with the ability to enjoy life fully. It is even more of a certainty that his inner expansiveness pointed consistently in one clearly-defined direction—namely, that of regularly downing two quarts of whiskey a day, cadging drinks to meet his quota whenever necessary, and unhesitatingly accepting all that were offered.

The sale of his early morning catch of trout to George Murphy of McKinney's or Ralph Colwell, proprietor of Moana Villa, was the signal for a personal celebration. It soon became this prodigious man's custom to meet the steamer *Tahoe*, with its hundred or so passengers, when the vessel docked at Homewood or McKinney's pier. Normally this would have passed for commendable fellowship and astute public relations, but in most instances Lowe's condition was the same—roaring drunk.

This state of body and mind allowed him the utmost freedom of expression. He immediately became a brother to all men when the boat arrived, shouting at the passengers to throw something of "color" into the water so that he could retrieve it. Although momentarily thunderstruck, the vacationers never failed to enter into the spirit of the occasion, assuming the quick tolerance that marks the true excursionist. Coins were invariably tossed in the direction of the trembling mountain of flesh waiting at the end of the wharf. A five dollar gold piece was naturally the most acceptable offering, but Martin was not proud. Assured as a water ouzel of his prowess, he would dive for anything that sank and swim for objects which floated. There were times when three horizons showed in front of his befuddled eyes, but the chill waters of the lake always seemed to bring him around, provided he missed the end of the pier on his initial dive.

One afternoon he took off in a leaping swan dive but, unfortunately, dropped like a plummet onto the guard rail of the steamer, smashing his bulbous nose before bouncing off into the water. Feeling the impact, those passengers remaining on the lee side of the steel hull rushed to the railing where Martin had disappeared. They talked excitedly and peered intently down into the clear water. Lowe was nowhere to be seen!

Fear gripped the spectators. Five minutes dragged by—then ten. Still no Lowe. Young Ben Callender of Homewood raced to the beach and commandeered a boat. He rowed swiftly to the spot where the Bacchus of Tahoe had disappeared. A crowd had collected on the wharf and Lowe, the inebriate, was rapidly assuming the hallowed role of good old Martin, lifelong companion and stalwart friend of all who knew him.

Suddenly it occurred to Callender to row to the other side of the vessel. He rounded the stern of the *Tahoe* and there, floating like a playful porpoise, was Lowe, a grin splitting his face from ear to ear. Before Callender could cry out, the balloon-like apparition upended and disappeared under the hull. Ben next heard cries of relief from the passengers and shouts from the crowd on the pier. Martin was showered with coins and allowed himself to be hauled, coughing and blowing, onto the landing.

Only Callender caught Lowe's sidelong glance that clearly seemed to say, "You know I've been on the bottom all this time, don't you, son?" A few moments later Martin was accepting, with unbecoming modesty and downcast eyes, the back slaps and jiggers of whiskey pressed upon a man who had come back from the depths of a lake which, every one knew, never gave up its dead. It was a miracle, they said, and Martin was the first to agree.[1]

From that day forward Lowe was acknowledged to be the greatest deep-water diver on Tahoe. Ladies' purses, steamer trunks, iron stoves—anything in the way of sunken freight or personal belongings—became his specialty. The frantic call for Martin was sounded so often that his main source of livelihood changed overnight from trolling for trout to salvaging lost objects.

SUNDOWNS AND SWEEPING SKIRTS

Reception Day at Hotel Homewood, August 4, 1914, with the large gathering shown on the establishment's north porch, a forerunner of the Horseless Carriage Caravan that now makes Homewood a stopover point each season.

C. O. Valentine

Several months after his "miraculous return from the bottom of Tahoe," a stylishly dressed woman passenger arrived at Homewood and, as she stepped off the steamer, accidently dropped her gold mesh handbag overboard. It could be seen clearly in about 25 feet of water and the call went out for Lowe. He galloped to the edge of the pier and squinted carefully at the purse, sizing it up from all angles. Glancing thoughtfully at the group which had gathered, his rheumy eyes wandered to the afternoon sun dropping behind the western rim of the Sierra. "Too late," he muttered finally; "tomorrow will do."

The owner of the purse was extremely disturbed. She explained that her rings, money and other jewelry were inside. Lowe stood firm. "Too cold," he insisted, eyeing the nearby bar. Lowe's decision was grudgingly accepted.

Wagering ran heavy that evening on the number of dives it would take the amphibious clown to recover the purse, and the smart money was betting Martin would bring it up on the first attempt. Early the following morning the anxious owner of the purse and an eager crowd were on hand for the maestro's aquatic performance. In his grandest reeling style Lowe took off from "high point," a ten-foot piling extending above the pier. He soared into space and struck the water with a detonating splash, throwing up a small tidal wave that thoroughly drenched his onlookers.

When he surfaced, a few moments later, the purse was clutched in one hamlike fist. A resounding cheer went up and money changed hands as Martin restored the handbag to its owner. Upon opening it she slipped to the wharf in a dead faint. Lowe was the first to assist in carrying her back to the hotel, where she was placed on a couch. Then they all crowded around the open purse.

"It's empty!" gasped Lowe, his eyes rolling in amazement. Everybody appeared baffled but none more so than the revived victim. She was speechless. The crowd unanimously agreed that she must

CHINESE LANTERNS, LATTICED INTERIOR AND A POLISHED FLOOR

Homewood's Dance Casino that stood across the road from the hotel and catered to the Lakers for three decades until it was leveled by heavy snows in the winter of 1938.

have misplaced her money and jewelry, and the men complained that it was "just like a woman." The loudest laments came from Lowe, who blubbered about the loss of his reward money.

On the very day the woman concluded her stay at the resort, a strange metamorphosis came over Martin. The bartender was astonished to hear him bellow that he would stand drinks for the house— an unprecedented, world-shaking phenomenon. It was further noted that Lowe lacked energy for anything more trying than lifting a whiskey bottle to fill his shot glass. What was even more remarkable, he was able to pay for the bottle.

For weeks on end Martin haughtily disregarded any and all salvage calls and considered the mere suggestion of going fishing an insult. Lowe spent all his time draped across the bar, bottle in one hand, jigger in the other. Finally he discarded the jigger entirely. The mellower he became the more thoughtful he appeared. Between fistfulls of free pretzels he would shake his head slowly from side to side and repeat at regular intervals, "That poor woman! And Murphy says her husband is only worth several million dollars. That poor, poor woman!"[2]

Martin Lowe's versatility extended into fields other than swimming, diving and acting a part that temporarily filled his pocket. A fire in McKinney's commissary, which destroyed all the labels on the canned goods, gave him the opportunity to exercise both his ingenuity and his gambling instinct. Raising $10 by the beg, borrow and steal method, Martin paid George Murphy cash for the lot, carting it off like a pack rat to his shack at Blackwood. Each morning after concluding his fishing he settled back in his cabin and surveyed the tiers of shining cans stacked to the ceiling. Then with the help of a long, hooked stick he would topple down two or three cans selected at random and open them with an anticipatory gleam in his eye. Sometimes his diet would consist of canned asparagus and pigs feet for breakfast, black currants for lunch and condensed milk with sauerkraut juice for dinner. It was an intriguing game for Martin until the supply ran out. After nudging the last can off the shelf he advised all and sundry that he was now conditioned to eat anything, anywhere, at any time.[3]

On another occasion, Lowe was helping George Murphy hang sides of beef in a screened meat house near Homewood. Being in his usual unsteady condition, he slipped on the sawdust-covered floor, clutched wildly for a handhold and skewered his right hand on one of the curved meat hooks lining the wall. Grabbing up a grimy gunny sack, Lowe carefully wrapped his profusely bleeding hand and took off at a fast trot for Homewood, where Dr. Etta Smith Duffy Farmer, from Folsom, gave him all the medical attention he would allow. She sternly warned him to take to his bed for a week and attempt nothing in the way of heavy work until the wound had healed.

Martin, completely unconcerned, was up with the sun the following morning. Fortified with a long pull from a demijohn hidden in its accustomed place under his bed, he climbed into his skiff, set the liquor crock on the forward seat and rowed 13 miles to Glenbrook to dig for angle worms that were bringing one cent each as trout bait. The whiskey he neglected to consume on the trip he sloshed over his injured hand, and upon his return he proudly displayed it as "cured" . . . loudly proclaiming to everyone, that medicine, unless self-administered, was strictly for the squirrels.

Another time the Olympic Club of San Francisco sent its champion oarsman to the lake and Lowe was chosen to defend the honor of Tahoe in a rowing contest. On a five-mile course, circling McKinney Bay and ending at Homewood, Martin soundly trounced the stripe-shirted challenger by 300 yards. It took four strong men to carry their hero into the bar, where he claimed the prize—a full gallon of spirits.[4]

J. P. Obexer of Homewood called upon Lowe in the winter of 1912 after Martin had moved his market fishing activities to Meeks Bay. Lowe crunched across the snow and ice in his bare feet down to the wharf, where he welcomed Obexer. There he stood for over half an hour without noticeable discomfort, haggling over the price of trout. Finally Lowe settled for 25 cents a fish. It also was common practice for Martin to roll up on the wet, icy ground in front of his cabin and sleep off an alcoholic spree, with the pouring rain soaking him to the skin. No man physically punished himself more.[5]

At times Lowe wandered as far afield as Tahoe City, and one afternoon early in the spring of 1914, he was passing the lake outlet when he noticed a party of duck hunters with scatter guns who had crumpled three birds out of a flock of mallards onto the frozen river. As the thin ice would not hold a man's weight, they were hopelessly debating their chances of recovering the game. Lowe shuffled down to the party and the offer of a quart of whiskey spurred him into immediate action. Without bothering to remove his clothes, he plunged into the river, leaping forward onto the crust of ice ahead of him like a hunted polar bear. Windmilling his feet and crushing the ice with his clasped hands, he retrieved the birds with less trouble than a trained water spaniel would have encountered in open water.

In spite of Lowe's braggadocio, intemperance and shiftlessness, there were occasions, admittedly rare, when he was a sober, reasonable individual with a sense of fair play. Three times during his years at Lake Tahoe he is known to have rescued drowning people. Martin once brought a man up from 30 feet of water and then broke down and cried like a baby when the body was pronounced lifeless.[6]

Martin Lowe did have courage—usually the kind born of the bottle. Once a brother tipster threw a bucket of water on him while he was pulling up a pant leg to show the assembled gathering his twisted left leg that had been run over by a logger's wagon wheel years before. (When doctors decided to amputate, Lowe had left the hospital by way of the window.) Martin lunged at his tormentor, who grabbed up a heavy bar stool and splintered it across Lowe's head and back. It was enough to fell an ox, but Lowe laid into his antagonist without appearing to notice the crushing blow. When he finally dropped the man with a knee to the stomach, onlookers swore that, chair and all, Martin looked better than his attacker.[7]

In later years he slipped into a hermit's existence, shuttling between Meeks Bay and Tahoe City and living like a Digger Indian in squalid tepees. Fishing and handouts became his only means of livelihood. His garb was reduced to loin cloth and moccasins, and he let his hair and beard grow in a tangled mass. Martin Lowe died at Auburn, California, in 1921, while returning to the lake which had tolerantly permitted him a way of life of his own choosing.[8]

Previous to the 1880's Homewood, as such, did not exist. Early settlers by-passed this spot, locating on creek outlets flowing from heavily forested canyons.[9] This allowed the pioneer logger, mill owner, hunter, fisherman and trapper accessibility to timberland, water power, and trout migrating up the streams. Slightly over a mile to the southeast lay old McKinney's (Chambers' Lodge) at the fan-out of Burton (McKinney) Creek, and two miles to the north, Idlewild. The lake settlement of Homewood was located between these two points.

On July 31, 1909, a post office was established at Homewood to serve the first residents.[10] These included Ed Farmer and his wife Dr. Etta Farmer, Senator Voorhees, Adolph Mueller, "Peg Leg" Saunders, who owned the water company, the Prentiss family, the Holabirds (Holabird's Nest), and the Blacks. The following summer, Annie and Arthur C. Jost started construction of Hotel Homewood, living in a tent on the shoreline until the new resort and a small pier were completed. Several seasons later the Josts added a large casino and dance floor across the road from the hotel. Built by Matt Green of Tahoe City, its lattice work interior and Chinese lanterns rivaled and nearly duplicated those to be found at Tahoe Tavern's entertainment center.[11]

After the death of Arthur Jost in the early 1920's, Annie Jost continued to operate the hotel, advertising it as "Homewood—all the name implies."[12] In 1938 Mr. and Mrs. Donald Huff of Woodland, California, purchased the property, renovating and adding to the establishment to make it a comfortable family resort. Today Homewood Resort offers a snack bar on the water's edge at the head of the pier, a cocktail lounge adjoining the knotty pine lobby of the hotel, and remodeled guest cottages.

A chronicler of the late 1920's mentions Homewooders of the day: the Osbornes, "Uncle Jimmie" Horace Gardner (who had bull-whacked teams of oxen for his father 50 years before in Lake Valley), the Bushes, Hamels, Breezes, Harriet Lewis (the school teacher), Fred Grimshaw (a descendant of the Donner party), the Doods, Mrs. Arthur Jost (who had no time for publicity), Ben and Howard Callender (the commercial boating operators) and J. P. "Jake" Obexer ("Mr. Red Crown") with his store, boathouse and boats.

Also placed is "El Campo," a campground run by "Old Bill" Johnson, market hunter, commercial fisherman and the "prohi's" deadly enemy.[13] It was common knowledge that Johnson hid a bottle of "Sierra chain lightning" under a different log each day, barely keeping one log ahead of the Federal officers. "Old Bill," an angular, deceptively powerful man, formerly an expert blacksmith in Sacramento, was recognized as one of the few men who could whip man-mountain Martin Lowe, provided he could stay away from Lowe's bear-hug. He was also reported to yodel with the best of them and to be "quick tempered, but generous at all times."[14]

Another resident of Homewood during 1929 was George McConnell, whose father, Thomas McConnell, "once owned all of Homewood."[15]

Walter Hobart, Jr.'s "ugly red boathouse" dominated the lakeshore. Here Hobart had eight to ten sumptuously furnished second floor rooms, served by an elevator and adjoining a replica of a ship's galley. It was whispered that Hobart brought over girls from "the line" at Truckee and installed them as more than just window dressing in the establishment.

Mr. Carol Skinner was a new neighbor on the outskirts of town, and lakeshore property sold for $50 a front foot in the summer of 1929, when the leveling depression that fall was still something that could never happen.

In 1931, a fire wiped out a section of "Jake" Obexer's new marine pier, but hard trading "Mr. Red Crown" came up with a novel method of protecting his interests. The fire started when Obexer climbed into the forward cockpit of his Gar Wood runabout, pressed the starter button and was nearly blown through the boathouse roof. As the Standard Oil Company had participated equally with Jake in the pier's construction, he approached Kingsbury, the company's president, and carefully explained, with characteristic gestures, that the *company's* portion of the structure had been the part that burned to the water line. Kingsbury waived an argument and had the damaged section rebuilt at Standard's expense.[16]

Damage by fire was not the only threat to property. During the winter heavy snows, common to this section of Tahoe, took their regular toll. Hunter's Lodge on the outskirts of Homewood (500 feet north of The Hut, which burned in the winter of 1955) collapsed in March of 1931 under ten feet of snow and ice. It had cost $7,500 to build and was never opened for business. The Homewood Casino was also leveled in the winter of 1936 and Ben Callender used its timbers to build The Hut.[17]

A representative group of Tahoe pioneers and young old-timers now form the nucleus of today's Homewood that is situated in one of the more secluded and sheltered sections of the lake.

Chapter Nine

RUBICON SPRINGS

"CALL FOR A DRINK, it's better than whiskey!" was the popular slogan that publicized Rubicon Springs mineral water in the early 1880's. The magic words brought in so much business that R. E. Wood, editor of the *Tahoe Tattler*, dolefully complained: "That old fizz king (George Hunsucker) is doing so well no advertisement is needed in *my* paper."

These famous springs on Rubicon River were probably located by the early day trappers, explorers, and survey parties traveling the Georgetown-Lake Bigler Indian trail during the 1850's.[1] The credit for their official discovery goes, however, to John and George Hunsucker.[2] The Hunsuckers were miners from Kelsey, El Dorado County, California, who settled in this desolate Rubicon region during the summer of 1867. Here the brothers felled pine and built a hewn log cabin in the meadow south of the springs, bordering on Rubicon River.

The Hunsuckers could not have chosen a wilder setting as it was situated at the foot of Rubicon's frowning granite gorge and studded with mammoth trees. It appears to have presented a challenge to these mountain men, because the remoteness of the springs necessitated transporting supplies and equipment over the mountains by pack mule train.

By the year 1877 the two mountaineers had added outlying shacks, and a pine sapling corral for their stock. The *Virginia Territorial Enterprise* reported that "hunting (at the Springs) was excellent, game plentiful, and the scenery grand."[3] The hunting must have been unparalleled, for mule-tail deer were slaughtered by the hundreds. Market hunters ranged from the Springs to Lower Hell Hole, taking the hides and leaving the carcasses for vulture and coyote.[4] There was no mention of the diamond-back rattlesnakes that infested the region.

Three years later the Hunsuckers began bottling Rubicon Springs water, packing it out by mule train to Georgetown and McKinney's, and during the summer of 1881 they were hard pressed to fill the skyrocketing demand.

Health seekers from Nevada now discovered the Springs, and it required only the effort and enterprise of a hardworking person to expand the facilities into a prosperous resort. Early in the summer of 1886 an energetic woman filling these requirements bought out the Hunsuckers and added Clark Potter's Springs one mile east up the canyon. She was Mrs. Sierra Nevada Phillips Clark, daughter of Joseph W. D. Phillips, who owned Phillips Station on the Johnson Pass road.

"Vade," as she was familiarly known, rolled up her sleeves and went to work. At the time only an improved trail led from McKinney's over Burton's Pass to Rubicon, continuing on by way of Wentworth Springs to Georgetown. Vade enlisted the aid of El Dorado County and a circuitous, one-way road was pushed through to completion the following year. Even then, wagons attempting the trip in early spring had to be let down into the gorge over heavy snowdrifts by means of snubline, block and

RUBICON SPRINGS . . . WILD, REMOTE, REMEDIAL

John and George Hunsucker's original log cabin "hotel" (center) and outbuildings in the fall of 1888, two years after the brothers had sold the Springs to Mrs. Sierra Nevada Phillips Clark (later Bryson). Seated on the freight wagon in the left foreground, J. W. D. Phillips, Dan Phillips, John Meloche; in front, Mehetable Jane Phillips, Alice Blair, Mr. and Mrs. Joy, Sierra Nevada Phillips Clark, May Kenny, Warren Dipple and Mrs. Knapp. Looking west toward Rubicon River.

tackle. Teams coming up the gorge were forced to swim the river and the vehicles "dead X'd" across the fast-moving water.[5]

In three summers Vade Clark changed the face of Rubicon Springs. Lumber for the two and a half story hotel that now stood in the meadow bordering on the river had been unloaded from wood barges and hauled over the pass from McKinney's wharf. For its day and location, the inn was a creditable feat of construction. Curtained glass windows set off the first and second floors. Sixteen small rooms were available in the main building. Bedsteads were built on the spot. A downstairs parlor lent an air of elegance to the hotel. To the bone-tired guests arriving from Tahoe and Georgetown, the horsehair furniture and foot-pedal organ were objects of eye-opening splendor. Over the northeast entrance, the words "Virginia City" were painted to make the Comstock Lode visitors feel more at home.

Vade Clark was indefatigable. She quickly established a reputation as the finest cook in the Sierra. White linen tablecloths, polished silverware and generous quantities of substantial food enticed her patrons three times a day, and it was commonplace for Vade to whip up a meal for one hundred of her ravenous guests.[6]

DANIEL ABBOTT CARRIED THE THREATENING CRAYON

This crude but effective sign was nailed on the entrance door of Rubicon Springs Hotel at the close of the 1903 season to discourage prowlers.

Mehetable Jane Sickels

ALL CAME TO DRINK OF THE CURATIVE MINERAL WATERS

Looking north, in the summer of 1890, at "The Rubicon Springs" (beneath the shelter) and a large group of health seekers. Warren Dipple, in white apron on the far right, Mrs. Sierra Nevada Clark (black dress) seated to his right next to Colonel Boyle (hat and white goatee), Mrs. Boyle (white skirt and straw hat), Mehetable Jane Clark standing below man in the top center of the picture.

THE FOUR-HORSE POSTERIOR-PUNISHING RUBICON FLYER

Stage departing from Rubicon Springs Hotel for Moana Villa in July, 1909, with a group of Ralph Colwell's guests on hand to speed seekers after the salubrious on their way. Rubicon River side of the establishment looking northwest.

When vacationists, and others seeking cures from the mineral water, arrived on week ends the hotel usually filled to capacity, and additional sleeping space had to be found somehow. Often four protesting males were squeezed into one small room. Meadow grass was stuffed into pillow slips to make improvised mattresses for use on the downstairs floor and dining room table. Cabins and tents ringing the meadow were spoken for, and guests spilled out into the open, where they curled up in bed-rolls or slept on blanketed pine boughs.

A Sacramento Valley news-paper advised: "At the present time there is a rush from all parts of the Sagebrush State (Nevada) to Rubicon Springs. They must now take the water about as fast as it makes its appearance. It is a mineral

RUBICON'S SNORTING "GREEN DRAGON"

Ralph Colwell, in the tonneau of his green Pierce Arrow stage, the Springs caretaker and high-booted passengers at Rubicon during the fall of 1919.

Hattie Belle Colwell Almstaden

spring only, about the smallest in the Sierra, with its whole flow coming through a hole in the rock about the size of a lead pencil. Waters come hissing up with gases, and it is all the stronger for being a small quantity. It is pleasant to the taste, and impregnated with minerals. Those who drink the water soon want four square meals a day. California has not discovered the virtues of the Spring as yet, but it is nonsense to cross the ocean to spas while Rubicon continues to flow."[7]

Such superlative publicity was of great commercial benefit and Rubicon soon grew from a weekend watering spot into a summer retreat that was filled day after day all through the season. Vade Clark now placed a six-passenger, leather-slung coach and four on the road to McKinney's and daily her bearded driver "dustered" guests over the divide to and from the Springs. Those who could not find space aboard the coach made the trip by carriage or horseback, taking some two and one-half hours to cover the nine miles.

All supplies were brought in by wagon or stage but laundry was taken care of at the resort. Linens were run through the hardwood rollers of a tremendous mangle presided over by "Marty," one of Vade's helpers. Vade could usually count on the arrival of fifteen or twenty extra guests without advance reservations, and the hotel continued to burst at the seams. Twenty milk cows were pastured in the surrounding meadowland, but often there was not enough cream and butter to go around. After the evening meal, Vade would have the downstairs parlor cleared of furniture and seat herself at the piano to play for dancing. In spite of minor inconveniences most people enjoyed the informality of Rubicon Springs Hotel and the resort prospered.

In the summer of 1890 an authority on health resorts observed: "The Springs are situated in a beautiful garden valley on Rubicon River some eleven miles (sic) from Tahoe. These waters are good for consumptives, asthmatics, persons suffering from chronic bronchitis, catarrh, etc." Not wishing to overlook any other possible benefits, the reporter went on to describe the action of Rubicon's mineral water as "dimetric, detergent, asperient and anti-acid." To these highly edifying remarks he added an afterthought: "The Springs are 6,200 feet above sea level."[8]

California's aged and infirm began converging on this back country wilderness, competing with the Nevada oldsters for accommodations. One enthusiastic imbiber of the waters announced proudly "that his appetite was now so good he could eat a horse and cart and chase the driver." This was considered by many to be a definite improvement on the usual version of the motheaten story. The witticism, widely circulated around Tahoe, lost little of its publicity value even after it was discovered that one of Vade Clark's hired hands and not a regular patron had been responsible for the quip.

The hope of immediate cures from the magical mineral water at Rubicon continued to draw health seekers to the resort for three more decades. Sometimes referred to as "gullible, goofed, and gouty," these pursuers of the salubrious descended into this isolated canyon as though convinced they had at last discovered the illusive Fountain of Youth. The fortitude shown by the elderly and ailing who made the rugged trip to the Springs is still the object of admiration and amazement. This jarring, spine-twisting stage jaunt, that slewed around tortuous curves and rattled over rocky terrain euphemistically described as a road was, in itself, enough to kill or cure.

Old timers from San Francisco recall ferrying across the bay to the Oakland Mole, boarding the Overland sleeper, and making the long, smoky train shuttle over the Sierra Nevada to Truckee. Here they first staged, then after 1900, boarded the wood-burning narrow gauge "rattler" for Tahoe Tavern pier. Again they transferred, this time to the steamer *Tahoe* or *Nevada* and churned down the lake to McKinney's or Moana Villa. After dragging themselves down the wharf, many of the more experienced males fortified themselves with several quick pulls from a bottle (usually containing "Old Monogram, smooth as corn silk"), and then struggled aboard the four-horse "Rubicon Flyer." Ten and sometimes twelve passengers—gauntleted, veiled, and lap-robed—were crammed into the highwheeler. As the contraption rocked on its thoroughbraces, the group steeled themselves for what has been realistically described as the "damndest ride ever invented" over a road conceded by many to have been "the worst in Creation."[9] A gee-up from the driver, and leaders and wheelers strained into their traces, grinding up Burton's Canyon through clouds of choking dust, the vehicle sliding and clattering off two-foot high solid granite rock centers in the rutted thoroughfare. By an apparently malicious contrivance of the roadkeeper, every hairpin turn was strewn with boulders over which the stage swayed, bounced and leaped. Passengers inside and out were tossed about indiscriminately in a "disgraceful, devil-may-care manner."[10]

Compounding this torture was the fiendish handiwork of the stagemaker's "trimmer." Cushions on the seats of the vehicle were two-inch thick leather-covered pads of excelsior sneakily decorated with flint-hard buttons. Sitting on these excruciations was comparable to sliding about on a gravel pile. How the posteriors of those old folks took the physical beating is a matter for conjecture to this day. But they did, and their owners came back for more punishment year after year.[11]

Vade Clark operated Rubicon Springs Hotel for nearly fifteen seasons, establishing it solidly on the map of California. In May of 1901, a post office was sanctioned for the Springs and in the same year Vade sold the property to Daniel Abbott.[12] Abbott is remembered as a cantankerous introvert who replaced the friendly welcome with a policy of "enter at yur' own peril." Vade Clark had remarried and was now Mrs. Bryson. She leased the hotel from Abbott in 1904 and left Rubicon Springs permanently four years later.

In October, 1908, a flash flood swept down the gorge and the river rose eight feet overnight. The following morning the meadow at the Springs was a torrent of mud and debris with water running through the barn two feet deep. The hotel and outbuildings were nearly washed from their foundations.[13] "Mike," one of the resort's best riding horses, drowned and floated away on the crest. A dripping cow-hand watched the animal as it disappeared downriver and mumbled a resigned amen. He guessed that old Mike would probably end up in Hell Hole some seven miles down the gorge.[13]

In May, 1908, Ralph Colwell of Moana Villa purchased Rubicon Springs Hotel and became owner-manager of both resorts. Colwell and his sons continued to carry passengers, mail and freight daily over the divide from Tahoe into the Springs. The old stage was replaced several years later by a four-cylinder Dodge four-door, equipped with special low gears to enable the disc-wheeler to pull up the steep grade out of Rubicon. A battered sign at the summit of Cape Horn carried a timely warning: "Enter all cars at your own risk. Fee for towing out $25.00," and few but the Colwells attempted the trip by automobile.

Later the Dodge was superseded by a racy, dark green Pierce Arrow touring car proudly driven by George Colwell, who wore out a set of non-skids with monotonous regularity every two weeks.

The outmoded horse-drawn Rubicon Flyer, that frightening "bun-bun-buster" which had tested the mettle of thousands of passengers in its heyday, stood in the barn at Moana Villa until the Colwells sold out their lakeshore resort to David Chambers. In the early 1950's the thoroughbrace was purchased by the Whitney brothers at the beach in San Francisco, where it may be seen today.[14]

An attempt was made to operate Rubicon Springs Hotel through the 1920's, but the back country health resort had lost its magical appeal and Ralph Colwell sold the land and improvements to the Sierra Power Company in 1930. The hotel stood until 1953 with foundations crumbling and doors sagging on their hinges. Heavy snows that blanketed the Sierra that winter leveled the 65-year-old structure and in the spring of 1954 nothing remained but splintered timbers and a pile of rubble.[15]

Although Rubicon's "Fountain of Youth" continues to flow, the inevitable creep of age which the health-seekers hoped to retard has finally overtaken the famous resort itself.

Chapter Ten

CHAMBERS LODGE

"Dresses in white, in black, in red, in lawn, striped and unstriped, with drapery, without drapery, big hats, small hats, hats that sat perched on top of a fair head, hats in all styles and shades; and those cute faces underneath. It was nearly too much for any man, be he single or married." So enthused a fledgling reporter in the summer of 1887 as he stood on the wharf at McKinney's and watched the steamer *Tod Goodwin* backing and filling as it maneuvered for a landing. Later, when the deep-throated whistle announced the vessel's departure and a plume of white steam drifted across the afterdeck, the neophyte newsman noted admiringly, "Even the boat appeared to leave the pier reluctantly because of the beautiful display of feminine pulchritude that had gathered to flutter handkerchiefs and wave goodbye."[1]

The daily arrival and departure of the steamer constituted an occasion, and John Washington McKinney, owner-proprietor of the resort, could always be counted upon to be on hand.[2] New guests had to be welcomed, and old friends sent on their way. Canvas sacks of mail required attention.[3] Deer and bear meat lay stacked on the wharf awaiting shipment to the market in Truckee and lake trout were to be forwarded in oblong, white pine boxes. "Old John" was the man who saw that everything went off smoothly. He was a giant, standing six-feet-six in his beaded Indian moccasins and fringed buckskins.

Silent, powerful and self-sufficient, McKinney had tramped the western shores of Tahoe more than a quarter of a century earlier, to choose the most suitable location for a hunting and fishing cabin. Two years before the booming Squaw Valley "Silver Rush" of 1863, he and another Georgetown pioneer, John Wren, established a hay ranch on the summit of Burton's Pass, adjoining the El Dorado-Placer County line. In the spring of 1862, McKinney moved down the canyon to Burton Creek's inlet into Tahoe, settling on its western side.[4]

It has been said that John McKinney hadn't even seen a match until he was 13 years of age, and that he could not read or write. On these points his contemporaries were agreed, but what was so strange about that, they asked. After all, didn't they also sign their names with an X and use flint and steel? But find a mountain man, they insisted, who could match McKinney in the backwoods, and you'd have somebody. Carrying a handful of jerky in his buckskin jacket for food, he could slip into the tall timber with his hunting dogs and Sharps buffalo rifle and track down a grizzly, cinnamon bear or eight-point buck in half the time it would take an ordinary man just to get started. Those who knew him well would stake their reputations on McKinney's uncanny ability in the forest.

"Old John" had chosen his location well. The south side of Upson Bay (McKinney's)[5] offered sheltered beach frontage protected by Sugar Pine Point to the east. Ample running water churned in the creek and an abundance of game roamed through the heavy timber stands that extended from the

HIGH-STACKER DOCKSIDE AT THE CLUB HOUSE

Passengers, including two "belle dames," boarding the sidewheel steamer GOVERNOR STANFORD *at McKinney's wharf in the fall of 1876, with McKinney's* TRANSIT *hauled out and boarded over for the winter in back of a pile of cordwood (right foreground).*

shoreline back into high country. In the summer of 1863 McKinney established Hunter's Retreat; a log cabin, tents, sapling pier, and three or four small fishing boats.[6] In June of the following year he turned his hand to felling giant cedar and splitting the heartwood. At the end of the season a "quantity of rough shake shingles were stacked on the lakeshore and assessed."[7]

By 1869 his tract of land comprised 160 acres, 13 of which ran to the lake,[8] and Hunter's Retreat catered to Nevada's mining nabobs, who were drawn by what was claimed to be the finest hunting and fishing found in the Sierra Nevada. Twenty tourist cabins and numerous tents were now available, but the rugged outdoor accommodations, free to all comers, appealed to the majority of the guests, and they slept on the ground wrapped up in bedrolls. John Muir was a regular guest at McKinney's and the famous California naturalist and outdoorsman aptly described the stately sugar pines surrounding the resort as "priests of the forest extending their arms in benediction over the congregation."

The small finger pier at the resort had been rebuilt and lengthened, and fishing boats and sailboats were now available to guests without charge. By 1873 John McKinney's taxable personal property, excluding his land and improvements, consisted of three sailboats and several fishing boats valued at $100, and one silver watch worth $40.[9] One of the first boathouses at the lake was built on the wharf two years later, and it doubled as a bar and clubhouse.[10]

McKinney stayed in every winter, and the snows of 1879 were the severest in two decades. Thirty to forty foot drifts lay in the canyon below Burton's Pass. With the coming of spring the lake rose

Jeanette Pomin Watson

"OLD JOHN" WOULD RUN UP SAIL WITH ANYONE

Earliest known photograph of McKinney's Hunters Retreat, taken from the METEOR *in 1877 showing John McKinney's crack sailing hull, the* TRANSIT *(right center), Captain Howland's* CHALLENGE *under single canvas, Club House to left and shoreline cottages.*

an average of one-half inch a day for 42 days to set a new record.[11] George Hunsucker, owner of Rubicon Springs, wintered with McKinney. Their hunting and trapping forays brought in silver and cross-breed foxes, stone marten, mink, and American sable, all taken within a few miles of the resort.[12]

The summer of 1880 sparked talk of another bonanza when a silver outcropping was discovered seven miles up Burton Creek canyon in the vicinity of Sourdough Hill. The ore failed to prove out under assay, so "Old John" added five more cottages to Hunter's Retreat, an enterprise that offered a more assured return for his efforts.[13]

A correspondent of the era, writing on the wonders of Tahoe, could find only one cloud on the horizon—the hordes of mosquitoes that made the early spring days miserable. McKinney brushed this slanderous persiflage aside with the comment that the critters would all disappear when the snows

NIMRODS SET FOR THE SPIKED HEADS

John Washington McKinney (far left), four back country marksmen and guests at Hunter's Retreat previous to the shikari's departure in pursuit of Tahoe's mule-tail deer. August, 1887, after the season's first light fall of snow.

Charles Oliver

POISED FOR THE TROUTING GROUNDS

The Murphy brothers and Morgan carried on McKinney's tradition of free fishing boats for guests at the resort, and here anglers, both male and female, are preparing to troll for the flashing silversides. Summer of 1899, looking south from the Club House. The resort's hotel, formerly Glenbrook House, was moved across the lake in 1897.

melted, adroitly drawing the scribe's attention to the sailboats and fishing boats lying at the wharf. "Ten yards offshore you can't find one of those stinging miseries," he advised. "Come along with me and I'll take you for a trip on my *Transit*."[14]

John was known as a man who would lay everything down to put up sail with anybody, and when the constant challenger, Elias J. "Lucky" Baldwin of Tallac, threw both his hat and sailboat into the ring, McKinney accepted the taunting offer to race. Little wind was stirring across the water on the day of the great event, but experienced sailor McKinney soundly trounced the multi-millionaire by cramming on all the canvas his small sloop would carry and heaving mightily on the oars, an unexpected maneuver that assured his crossing the finish line in the lead.[15] Baldwin, somewhat rankled by his defeat at the hands of a man who rowed as well as sailed, directed a sharp barb at "Old John's" custom of providing free boats for all his guests. "Lucky" snorted that Tallac House charged only for the *comforts* that were obviously lacking at McKinney's. "Our low prices," insisted Baldwin, "cover rugs, cushions, parasols, tackle, bait, and competent guides. Reasonable as hell," he added. McKinney only smiled. He was doing just fine.[16]

Quail Lake, an artificial body of water one mile up the canyon and source of the resort's water supply, had been stocked with brook trout by McKinney and George Hunsucker in 1879. Three years later anglers were taking two and a half pound scarlet-bellied beauties from under the lily pads on wet fly and light tackle. Mule-tail deer were also plentiful in the back country. Nine bucks were packed out of Gray Horse Valley and Lower Hell Hole in the vicinity of Rubicon River by William Bliss, Tom Clark and four other hunters from Glenbrook on a single outing. McKinney hung the six and eight-pointers on a pole rack alongside the milk house as visible proof that his resort was the logical starting place for any hunting trip in the Sierra.

McKinney had his own vegetable garden and dairy on Burton's Creek near the spot where it flowed into the lake. The clubhouse and pier were now a regular stop for the sidewheel steamer *Governor Stanford* and an intermittent layover point for the steam tug *Meteor*. McKinney's was also the eastern terminus of the Georgetown-Rubicon Springs-Tahoe pack trail and during the season bartender Patrick Bingham constantly scurried around behind the polished maple, "setting 'em up" for the be-whiskered and mustachioed trade crowding the brass rail.

Although poisonous reptiles were (and are) nonexistent at Lake Tahoe, the canyons and floor of Rubicon River Gorge were infested with snakes. One four and a half foot diamond-back with 18 rattles was killed and brought to McKinney's Club House, where it was placed on display. A prominent sign clearly explained that it had come from Rubicon Springs, thereby proving the area to be a good place to stay away from. No holds were barred in the free-for-all bid for the tourist trade. Virginia, Gold Hill and Carson City vacationists rediscovered Hunter's Retreat in the summer of 1881, and anything pertaining to snakes and other hazards of the wilderness back country only served as a challenge to the citizens from the sand and sagebrush state.

Glowing accounts of the resort were now reaching the reading public. One writer of the times wrote enthusiastically: "Handsome Hunter's Home is nine miles from Tahoe City. It is a village of 18 pretty brown cottages, situated in a pine grove immediately on the shore of the lake. Genial host McKinney has accommodations for 60 guests, and the old Georgetown Trail runs ten miles south to Rubicon Mineral Springs."[17]

Another more generous chronicler located "twenty-five comfortable cottages bordering a clean, pebbly beach away from the reach of high water, a main building that includes a dining hall, and 200 feet of wharf leading out into the lake to admit steamers, upon which is built a 22 x 32-foot saloon two stories high." The correspondent went on to explain that "the 'Old Pioneer' treats his guests well, with sailboats and rowboats available for yachting and fishing parties, and a semi-daily steamer stop for mail and passengers is made." He ended his observations with the statement that "Old John's crack *Transit* is the fastest sailer on the lake."[18]

A reporter from the *Sacramento Union* during the same year endeavored to account for the resort's amazing popularity and, after due deliberation, came up with his findings: "The degree of social equality displayed at McKinney's is indeed refreshing, no noses being turned up on the promenade, and particularly no little, refined, sarcastic cuts being met with; in other words, a wholesome, well-met type of place."

When fishing, hunting, riding and steamboating paled, McKinney always took the time to amuse his guests with "factual" stories such as the one related to him by one Clem Anderson. "Clem," McKinney assured his listeners, "is a sober, trustworthy sort of individual, and sure enough if he hasn't seen a mammoth trout in the lake."

"I was told," continued McKinney cautiously, "that it would go, without stretchin', eight or nine feet in length with a girth the size of a pony barrel of bock, and weigh in around a hundred pounds when caught." The tremendous fish was not lying on the wharf just then as proof, McKinney admitted, but Clem was a man of integrity and he would produce that fish yet. Stories such as this proved to be an excellent source of advertising for the resort, and if one of McKinney's tall tales were questioned he would draw himself up to his full six-feet-six and quietly ask the doubting Thomas to "just show him where it warn't possible."

In the fall of 1887 bachelor John McKinney sprang the surprise of the season at a "grand ball" given by Ephraim "Yank" Clement. The festivities took place in Yank's new Cascade House near Tallac on the south end of the lake.[19] It was reported by the *Carson City Appeal* to have been a "smash" affair attended by some 50 guests from Washoe and Tahoe. The Reverend Dr. Davis of Carson City raised his hand for silence in the midst of the circling dancers, beckoned McKinney and his partner, Mrs. Minnie Bates, to the front of the room and joined them in marriage on the spot. A Truckee correspondent covering the celebration wrote: "The old-fashioned house warming was considerably enlivened by this event, unlooked for by many, but adding much interest to the occasion, particularly in the estimation of the ladies."[20] The newspiece implied that a choice bit of gossip had been

BIDDING FOR THE TOURIST TRADE WAS FIERCE AND
COMPETITION PROMPTED GIVE-AWAY BENEFITS

CHANGED IN NAME ONLY

With the exception of the Dance Pavilion (left foreground), leveled by snows in 1953, the New Chambers' Lodge of 1956 was substantially the same as this view of McKinney's in 1909.

Author's collection

launched that would keep the good ladies' tongues wagging for weeks to come, as Mrs. Bates was said to be a dashing grass widow.

Carson City's *Appeal* gave John McKinney and his new wife a fitting editorial sendoff: "Bonfires were lighted on the mountains, rockets shot to the skies, and anvils rung when he (McKinney) took his blushing bride back across the waters of Tahoe on the *Tod Goodwin*, the course of the steamer being marked by empty champagne bottles that danced in the wake for miles." No flags were reported flown at half mast, although it was definitely recorded that "Old John's" housekeeper at the resort had to be forcibly restrained from running the Red, White and Blue partially up the flagpole.

The year 1889 found McKinney's listed as one of the principal resorts on the lake, with a dockside post office and barber shop adjoining the over-water saloon. A man could read his mail, have a haircut or shave and down several shot glasses of whiskey while reclining in the chair. A San Francisco company was even experimenting with a water wheel that would furnish power from water flowing out of Quail Lake. Here was a new wonder—electric lighting! Several hundred feet to the east of the Club House, one of the lakeshore cottages had been extended out over the lake. This became the popular new dance pavilion. McKinney's now boasted 30 cottages. The pier had again been lengthened, and plans were afoot to build a large main hotel and dining room.

McKinney was now a living legend of Tahoe, respected by "Lakers" and summer residents alike. Unfortunately, he had one fault: he was a poor businessman. John was so kind-hearted that he often carried past due accounts for years at a time and then scratched the debts off a ledger which only he could decipher. McKinney answered friendly criticism of this practice by saying, "If somebody don't want to pay me what's owed, you only make an enemy by trying to collect." Then he would add, "I only want friends."

In the fall of 1892 a character cut from different cloth than McKinney stepped in. For a miserable $600 whiskey bill, William Westhoff, a spirits drummer from Sacramento, took over the property, and John, too proud to go to his friends for help, lost the resort. After this disheartening setback he moved to a bathhouse bordering the Commons at Tahoe City. Broken in spirit, John Washington McKinney died shortly after the turn of the century at the Auburn County Hospital, California.[21]

George and James Murphy, pioneer El Dorado cattlemen, in partnership with their brother-in-law, Luke Daniel Morgan, from Georgetown, leased McKinney's from William and Louise Westhoff in 1893. They advertised rates of $10 and $12 per week and announced that accommodations were now

THE STEAMER'S ARRIVAL WAS INDEED AN OCCASION

During the summer season Tahoe's "Queen of the Lake" ran on a regular schedule. This photograph, taken on the morning of July 28, 1903, looking northwest from McKinney's Club House, shows the flurry of activity resulting from the loading and unloading of passengers, baggage, and freight.

available for 125 vacationists.[22] Free fishing boats were still available, with tackle tossed in for good measure, and the resort's brochures pointed up the now familiar slogan: "No rattlesnakes, poison oak, or harmful insects are to be found at Lake Tahoe." Morgan and the Murphys also uncovered two new attractions to lure the undecided summer tourist: "a fine new photographic room and iron and magnesia springs," the latter "rediscovered" after years of being ignored.[23]

During the fall of 1897 Westhoff and the Murphy brothers were offered historic Glenbrook House by the Bliss and Yerington interests, provided the purchasers stood the cost of moving it across the lake on one of the lumbering combine's 104-foot cordwood barges. This transaction was agreed upon, and the two and one-half story wayside inn, that had stood since the early 1860's bordering the Great Bonanza road, was partially dismantled, towed across Tahoe and set on new foundations at McKinney's.[24]

A decade later the Murphys still had McKinney's under lease (with James Murphy listed as postmaster), but they turned it back to the Westhoffs in 1919. A year later David Henry Chambers, formerly manager of Brockway Hot Springs, purchased the hotel, cottages and surrounding land. Chambers renamed the resort "Chambers' Lodge" and continued the 60-year policy of maintaining an "old-fashioned mountain inn, but not a dressy place."[25]

"Dave," as he was known to his intimates, modernized the cottages and made other improvements, but the atmosphere of the hotel and Club House remained substantially unchanged from the days when the sidewheelers and "propellers" whistled in for a landing.

Like McKinney and the Murphy brothers, Dave Chambers left his imprint on Tahoe. A familiar figure with cane, cigar and bulldog, he was, in keeping with established tradition, always the first to greet new arrivals at the Lodge. His reputation for kindliness was proved by his generosity to his friends. As acting fire chief in the region, Dave relished nothing more than the opportunity to jump into his bright red fire engine and race to every conflagration in the vicinity. In his eagerness to serve the community it is known that the little matter of closed garage doors seldom stood in the way of his performance of duty once the fire alarm had sounded.[26] Dave Chambers passed away in the winter of 1952, and his brother, George C. Chambers, operated the Lodge until its sale to Thomas G. Stone in the spring of 1956. Stone formed a corporation, bringing in Ernest Kettenhofen from San Francisco and Samuel W. Gardner of Marin County, California. It is now known as the New Chambers' Lodge.

Today the oldest hotel still standing on Lake Tahoe is flanked by cottages and outbuildings, several of which date back to the 1860's. The original structures have distinguishing sharply-angled roofs and thin cedar shakes and are canted at various degrees. Set on pilings above the water is the same old Club House. Here the venerable bartender prides himself on the fact that he is the only one who actually dispenses alcoholic spirits commercially *on* the lake. He also delights in recalling stories of the days when good sour mash whiskey was 10 cents for a full two-ounce shot glass across the bar, and a "pony" of the best obtainable, an extravagant 15 cents.[27]

C. O. Valentine

SUNSET AND SHIMMERING WATER

This photograph, taken to the west of Moana Villa in the late summer of 1911,
with a box camera on a tripod, was made seconds before the sun
dropped behind the western Sierra.

Chapter Eleven

MOANA VILLA

ALTHOUGH the sharp crack of the buckskin lash, arching over the heads of the leaders and wheelers, is heard no more, and the high-wheeled stage that rolled out of Moana Villa is only a recollection, the old Burton Pass road and bordering back country have changed little during the last three-quarters of a century. The rutted, rock-strewn thoroughfare still follows the same dusty, winding course up the canyon which was then known as the "Sluice Box." After rising in sinuous grade from McKinney Creek, it passes McKinney and Lily Lake before lifting again to Miller Lake at the western Sierra summit. Here the road skirts Miller Meadow (Mud Lake), breaks out high above forbidding Rubicon Gorge and circles "Cape Horn" before falling in a near vertical drop to Rubicon Springs and River.[1]

For over forty years Moana Villa derived a substantial share of its business from the traffic moving over this narrow arterial.

During the fall of 1862 the first recorded use of the land by white settlers shows that Burton and Company cut 75 tons of wild hay from the narrow strip of meadowland flanking Burton's Creek (McKinney's).[2] After baling, it was shipped on Homer T. Burton's *Edith Batty* to the south end of Lake Tahoe.[3]

Five years later, Augustus Colwell, a native of New York State who listed himself as a "miller-merchant" from Mud Springs, El Dorado County, pre-empted more than 900 acres of timberland fronting on Upson Bay (McKinney's). Colwell's lakeshore holdings ran from McKinney's property line at Burton's Creek one and one-quarter miles east to Sugar Pine Point.[4] Near the site of what later became Moana Villa, he built a steam-powered sawmill. Colwell, with surprising foresight, left much of the shoreline timber, cutting instead along the southwest slopes of Burton Canyon, then east over the mountain toward Meeks Bay.[5]

During the winter of 1867, the south shore of Upson Bay established its place in Tahoe history when eight feet of snow fell in one 12-hour period to set a Tahoe-Sierra record that has never been equalled.[6]

Colwell operated his mill for another decade. In the summer of 1874 he was disgruntled to learn that two blundering topographers had erroneously changed the name of his lumber and shingle producer from Colwell's to "Casnells Mill." His ruffled feelings were assuaged, however, when he discovered that the map-makers hadn't even mentioned neighbor John McKinney's Hunter's Retreat, had wiped the last "l" from Thomas McConnell's location on Blackwood Creek and garbled Meeks Bay to "Micks Bay."[7]

In 1875, the C. and T. L. and F. Company reached across Tahoe for additional timber stands to supply their mills. It was now more profitable for Augustus Colwell to sell his pine and cedar logs directly to Bliss and Yerington's combine or extend timber leases. Two seasons later he closed down his sawmill and gradually sold off his acreage, holding only the land adjoining McKinney's.

Here, in the spring of 1894, Augustus Colwell's oldest son, Ralph Lewis Colwell, built Moana Villa. The hotel was set in a clearing facing the lake, surrounded by the dense grove of yellow pine that his father had left uncut. The establishment consisted of a two and one-half story lodge, single room cottages and tents, a clubhouse over the water and 500 feet of pier for a steamer landing. To the west, on the lakeshore, stood a bathing house and white-washed picket fence with a high arch entrance. The fence marked the division line between Colwell's and McKinney's properties as well as the El Dorado-Placer county line.[8]

Before Ralph Colwell opened Moana Villa, John W. McKinney at Hunter's Retreat hosted the wayfarers who crossed from Tahoe to Rubicon Springs. In the summer of 1894, a friendly rivalry sprang up between the two establishments and it continued until Colwell purchased the Springs from Daniel Abbott in 1909. Colwell's acquisition of Rubicon Springs was a shrewd business move, as it enabled him to combine Moana with a health resort and in the management of the two resorts he was assisted by his three sons, Albert, George and Elmer.

Martin Lowe, the hell-raising egomaniac from Blackwood Creek and Homewood, was no stranger to Moana Villa.

One placid afternoon in the summer of 1910, he was lounging on Moana's wharf with the Colwell boys, discoursing at great length on his ability as a High Sierra mountain climber. Elmer Colwell nudged his brothers and they burst into raucous guffaws. Lowe was insulted. He swung to his feet and started back down the pier. Then he stopped and turned.

HOME OF THE HATTIE BELLE

Earliest existing picture known of Moana Villa, taken in the summer of 1895 looking southwest down the 500-foot pier to the hotel and cottages. White picket fence to the right of the shoreline bathhouse marks the El Dorado-Placer County division line.

Hattie Belle Colwell Almstaden

"I'll prove it and take witnesses, you dam' pack of howlin' cayuses," he roared.

"Make it tomorrow then if you think you can stand on your feet that long," Albert shouted derisively.

Lowe didn't even bother to answer. He was fighting mad. He'd show those wallopers.

The taunts of the Colwells had finally driven Martin to a desperate measure. He would now have to abandon his well-worn seat at the bar and embark on a grueling pilgrimage. Suddenly he discovered his stomach! Years of overeating, combined with an incredible consumption of alcohol, had built up voluminous rolls of flesh around his huge frame. A week of hiking would do the trick, he mused. His anger cooled. Then he chuckled. Upon his return he would be the *new* Lowe—the svelte, hardened mountain man. Martin struck off west toward his shack. If he was to leave in the morning he had work to do.

That evening Lowe carefully checked a well-worn map and decided that Buck Lake would serve as his base camp. He needed those witnesses so he asked young Ben Callender of Homewood to bring a friend and join him.

Sunup found Martin loaded down with nearly 100 pounds of equipment—pup tent, duffle bag, pots and pans and provisions, liquid as well as solid. The boys joined him, and on ponderous piano-like legs he reeled off down the road toward Moana Villa and the Burton Pass road, looking more like a drummer for an outdoor equipment house than the rugged pathfinder he considered himself to be. After an hour of steady going Martin and his teen-age companions left the pass road and started up the steep trail toward Buck Lake. Here the boys were called upon to assist the puffing pioneer. Their combined efforts provided that needed extra push and the trio finally topped the divide. Dripping with perspiration, they staggered around the south side of the small lake and pitched camp beneath a

LETTERS IN YELLOW-GREEN MOSS WELCOMED THE MARINE TRAVELER
Social hall and cottages viewed from Moana Villa's pier in the spring of 1912.

C. O. Valentine

granite outcropping. Lowe dropped exhausted under a sugar pine, after first making certain that a full bottle was within arm's reach.

Ben Callender, genuinely concerned that the Sierra safari would dissolve into a leaderless fiasco if Lowe drank *anything*, stealthily managed to overturn the bottle, spilling all but a few drops. When the hulking outdoorsman awoke, reached for the whiskey and discovered his loss, his bellows resounded across the water and echoed from the rocky amphitheater under Mount Ellis. He stomped up and down on the pine needles like an enraged bull, cursing the fates that had intervened and overturned his liquor.

After a frantic search, Lowe was flabbergasted to find that he had somehow neglected to bring another bottle along. Catsup, vinegar, chili sauce, yes, but no whiskey. This was a catastrophic oversight that triggered another tantrum. He kicked savagely at the bottles filled with condiments and with one clutching sweep of his arms demolished the tent set up by the boys while he slept.

Without so much as a backward glance he deserted his companions and took off down the trail. At the rim of the canyon he left the path and barrelled down the mountain, carrying away everything movable that blocked his path. Now he was yelling at the top of his lungs in the wild hope that George Colwell, driver of the Rubicon Flyer, would hear him, stop, and return him post-haste to the sanctuary of McKinney's saloon. The astonished youngsters followed, but were left far behind to trace Lowe's progress down the steep ravine by the sound of his thrashings through the underbrush.

If Lowe succeeded in flagging down the stage it is ·unrecorded, but that evening he was at his accustomed place at the Club House bar. Filling the air with his piteous tale, he shuddered violently every time he thought of *that* horrible predicament. Mountain man? To hell with the Colwell boys. He could prove that any time.[9]

During the summer of 1910, Frank Pomin, who was soon to build Pomin's Lodge, leased Moana Villa and for the next three years the Colwells concentrated on the Rubicon Springs operation. Pomin was followed by several other lessees before Carl Andrew Bechdolt, Sr., acquired Moana in 1925.

A highlight of Bechdolt's opening was the appearance of Anson Week's band, then starting its climb to fame with a summer booking at Tahoe Tavern. Another fledgling orchestra, Dick Jurgens' seven-piece College of the Pacific combination, later played throughout the season at the Villa.[10]

These were the prohibition days—the high-flying 20's. Bechdolt leased a cabin south of the hotel to young businessman-rancher Joe King, who opened a shadowy speakeasy, calling it "Squirrel Inn." Opposite the "Inn" was the house occupied by Aimee Semple McPherson when she held revival meetings in Moana Villa's dance hall. In Aimee's absence, the cabin housed King's stock of locally-produced barleycorn. This product deserves special mention, as it is generally conceded that nothing manufactured before or since could leave such a stomach-punishing, head-splitting aftermath.[11]

During 1927 the Rim of the Lake highway was widened and paved. On the lakeshore at Moana Villa a large dining room and hotel annex were under construction and a stage left for Rubicon daily, sagging with passengers and mail.[12]

Due to Moana Villa's proximity to Chambers' (McKinney's) it was often mistaken for a part of the Lodge but in the early 1930's David Chambers, owner of Chambers' Lodge, put an end to this misconception by purchasing Moana and adding it to his resort.

Today many of the original buildings are still standing at old Moana, and when Chambers' Lodge is filled to capacity with guests the rooms are used to accommodate the overflow.[13] The wharf and overwater clubhouse have disappeared, however, and the day is only a memory when passengers could step off the steamers *Tahoe*, *Nevada*, or *Hattie Belle* and saunter down the pier beneath an archway that proudly spelled out the name Moana Villa in yellow-green letters of pine moss.

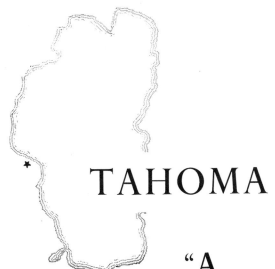

Chapter Twelve

TAHOMA

"A MASSIVE WAGON loaded with five great logs and drawn by seven yoke of oxen stood here on the shores of the lake as we passed on the steamer . . ." Paolo Sioli was leaning across the railing on the upper deck of the *Governor Stanford* jotting down notes for his forthcoming El Dorado historical. It was the summer of 1882 and Sioli observed a logging wagon on the shoreline of Augustus Colwell's timber holding, where Nat Stein, Rube Saxton and Michel Spooner had established a lumber camp.[1]

Some 35 years later, Ralph Colwell, who acquired the property from his father, sold a parcel of lakeshore land between Moana Villa and Pomin's Lodge to his brother-in-law, Joseph Bishop, an affluent San Francisco chimney sweep. Bishop is said to have named the site "Tahoma," interpreted, according to its owner, as a "place away from home that would mean home to his guests." Tahoma is also considered to mean "high mountain" in the Washoe Indian dialect, but the word's definition, as applied to this location on the south side of McKinney Bay, is difficult to reconcile. If such is the true native interpretation of "Tahoma," only the resort's setting on a bluff above the water could have prompted the name, as the closest peaks are Ellis, four miles distant, and Lost Corner Mountain, six air miles away.

After building Tahoma in 1916, Joe Bishop operated the hotel and cottages until the year 1920 and then leased the resort to Mr. and Mrs. John J. Planett and family for two seasons. The Planetts first came to Tahoe on the Fourth of July, 1919. As accommodations were unavailable over this crowded holiday week-end, their disappointing introduction to the lake was a choice between sleeping in the lobby of McKinney's Hotel or under the stars. They chose the lobby and moved to Tahoma the next day.[2]

Between 1922 and 1926, the management of Tahoma see-sawed between Bishop and the Planetts. Then it was sold to Frank Swind of Los Angeles. Swind placed well-liked and capable Marcel Maes in charge as manager.

Tahoma now boasted a large dance hall and dining room, a rocked-in swimming pool built out into the lake, and a renovated two and one-half story hotel, along with the usual cottages and tents.[3]

Over the next decade a sizable list of owners and managers juggled Tahoma around, and in the early 1940's the Schumachers bought the resort.

The spring of 1925 had ushered in the development of Tahoe Cedars Tract by H. L. Henry. It was extensive, second growth forest land, south across the state highway from Tahoma Resort and bounded on the east by the property of Richard Kirman and I. W. Hellman. When completed the subdivision included nearly 1,000 lots. Several of these were sold to Hollywood notables of the time and other public personages, as Henry intended to start a motion picture colony here. Included among the original

TAHOMA FOR THE TOURIST

*This imaginative artist's sketch purported
to show Tahoma Hotel and cottages
as they existed in 1921
and was entitled "Tahoma Resort
on the Lincoln Highway."*

purchasers of property were Lon Chaney, Lina Basquette, Ernest Belcher, the ballet master, and writer Francis Rawling Illes. Streets were laid out, power lines run, and a water system installed.[4]

During the time Henry was developing his subdivision, two of Aimee Semple McPherson's followers in the Four Square Gospel (Angelus Temple) approached him regarding purchase of the property for a summer bible school and colony. It was the spring of 1927, times were good and Henry agreed to sell provided he could obtain his price. Sixty lots were to be used as camping grounds for members of Mrs. McPherson's Angelus Temple who could not afford to buy land, and the balance of the tract was to be sold to disciples of the church who were spread throughout the world.

That July, hundreds of the faithful and curious flocked to the opening of Aimee's summer Gospel Camp. A thirty-nine-piece band took part in the pageantry. Everything moved along in true revival hysteria until a reported disagreement developed between Aimee and her mother, Mrs. Kennedy, over the famous "kidnapping" of the star of this incredible cult. All plans for a Four Square Gospel settlement were then dissolved and H. L. Henry reopened his subdivision to the public.[5]

Aimee's attempts to spread the "good word" at Tahoma failed, but at least the fiery evangelist had introduced her followers to Tahoe's great outdoors. With a refreshing frankness, one young old-timer recalls that "Mrs. McPherson possessed a magnetic personality all right, but she sure had a pair of piano legs that dam' near offset it."[6]

As Tahoma was located in a section of Tahoe that was subject to the heaviest winter snows, opening of the state highway in the spring of the year presented an extremely difficult problem. The late 1920's were still days of back-breaking hand shoveling as snow plows were not available. A truck would start out from the house farthest south, bucking its way through the shallow drifts and picking up volunteers as it went along. The men cleared the road ahead with more and more helpers joining the group and they were spurred on by exuberant residents who pressed liquid refreshments on the workers as they moved slowly toward Tahoe City.[7]

In the year 1929 a Tahoe correspondent singled out Tahoma and with unbecoming candor described the resort as a "small cluster of houses, famous only because their owners are continually trying to sell the place, but never completing the deal."[8] This barb does not apply today for the resort offers a new knotty pine store, post office, summer cabins and a beach and boat landing.[9] Owned in the 1950's by the S. D. Sartor's it is today in the center of a burgeoning community.

SEVEN MILES OF
HAND-SHOVELING LAY AHEAD

*Winter residents joined forces on May 8, 1927,
to clear the road of snow and ice between Tahoma and
Tahoe City. Among the group are: Jake Obexer,
Bill Warwick, Charlie Swanson, Charlie Winslow,
George Colwell, Fred Voight, Lee Allen, Albert
Colwell, Frank Pomin, Art White, George Cameron
of the S. F. CHRONICLE, Jack Hale,
Joe Henry and Bill Hughes.*

Chapter Thirteen

MAY-AH-MEE LODGE

THE YELLOW pine sapling bent and swayed as though whipped by a hurricane. In its upper branches sheepherder Lugi Barnetto hung on, frozen in terror, his eyelids pinched tight. The shirt had been torn from his back. Five deep crimson slashes streaked from shoulder to wide leather belt. Dust and sweat caked his forehead, ran down his face. He alternately prayed and screamed in hysterical gasps. On the trampled ground beneath Barnetto, 800 pounds of snarling, gray-flecked fury clawed at the spindly tree and long strips of bark curled from its trunk with each scythe-like sweep of the grizzly's forepaws.[1] Spittle slavered out of the bear's gaping jaws, and a series of deep coughing roars resounded through the forest. Lifting to its haunches, the maddened brute reached higher—clutching, shaking, slapping. Vise-like teeth fastened on the Basque's right foot, tearing his heavy boot away. His grip was broken, and with an agonized yell he started falling, grasping wildly for another hold as he dropped. With arms and legs flailing, Barnetto was seized and dragged to the ground by the enraged animal.

The following morning a search party broke into the clearing where the death struggle had taken place. It presented a gruesome sight. Near the center of the meadow stood a lone, scarred tree. The bark had been stripped cleanly to a height of nearly nine feet. Underneath, bunch grass was torn up and flattened. Uprooted scrub brush also attested to the violence. Blackening pools of blood stained the surrounding area. Shreds of clothing, scattered bones and a tuft of black hair were all that remained of Lugi Barnetto.[2]

The men laid their Henry rifles aside. Dropping to their knees they carefully examined the tracks of the monstrous beast. Two toes were missing from the right front paw and the other imprints measured 11 inches across and 14 inches in length. One of the older mountain men whistled softly. "Old Brin!" he muttered. Another in the party spoke up, "That dam' grizzly's been ten summers in our Tay-ho-Sierry country, and we're next if we don't get him."[3] The others nodded. They collected Barnetto's pitiful remains, scraped out a hollow grave and erected a crude rock cairn to mark its location.

As the killer's trail pointed southeast toward Meeks and Lonely Gulch, several of the better shots immediately set off to track down the animal. After trailing the grizzly many miles through rough, mountainous country, they caught up with him in heavy manzanita and sugar pine high above Rubicon Point. As he disappeared, in a shuffling roll, around a rocky abutment, the hunters "got a shot at nearly one ton of bear, but missed."[4]

Close to the spot where Barnetto lost his life an occurrence of a different nature took place 45 years later. Standing upon a raised platform facing a chanting audience of summer visitors was a piercing-eyed young woman dressed in flowing white robes. Aimee Semple McPherson was launching a revival meeting at Lake Tahoe. She had chosen the pine-scented forest as her cathedral, and her arms

C. O. Valentine

FRANK'S HORSE "OLD BILL" DID MOST OF THE WORK . . . .

Frank Pomin's (Pomin's Lodge) as seen from the lakeshore in the summer of 1914, one year after it was built. Cabins were uncompleted (see extreme left of photograph) and the trees were just starting to grow back again after extensive logging on the site.

were raised in supplication. This fiery, controversial woman has been likened to Maude Adams in her magnetic appeal, but most Tahoe residents felt that here the similarity ended. They were also generally agreed that Aimee's pioneering attempts at evangelism in the majestic timber stands above Pomin's Lodge bordered on blasphemy. One writer considered that there was "sufficient religion in the waters, mountains and skies of Tahoe without a McPherson type of ambassador to preach it."[5]

Since the early 1860's this sheltered site, that later became Pomin's, offered some of the finest fishing grounds and shoreline timber sections to be found on Tahoe and for decades the famous "Georgetown Snag" lay 150 yards offshore, directly north of the present lodge. The "Snag" was a massive, dead sugar pine with its heavy uprooted base lying in 110 feet of water. Standing on end, the tree appeared to be anchored to the bottom, with six to eight feet of its upper section projecting out of the lake.

In the summer of 1879 the "Snag" left its mooring and moved farther away from shore. A boatman from McKinney's, bent on recovering the landmark, braved the gale then lashing the bay and towed it back to its original resting place. The oldest inhabitants of Tahoe reported in 1882 that it had been there as long as they could remember, serving over the years as a convenient "hitching post" for fishing boats.[6] Until its disappearance shortly after the turn of the century, the "Snag" often shifted when heavy winds struck, but never moved far from the spot where it was first discovered by white men.

In the early 1880's the Carson and Tahoe Lumber and Fluming Company sent their lumberjacks and equipment across the lake to fell, drag to the water and log-boom 60,000 feet of choice sugar pine each week from the dense forest land between what later became Pomin's and the point. In the early 1900's Governor Kirman's son from Nevada acquired the property and, in partnership with J. M. Short of Glenbrook, started a fox farm. The venture proved unsuccessful, and in the spring of 1913 Frank Pomin of the pioneer Glenbrook and Tahoe City families located Pomin's Lodge on a knoll to the east of Tahoma.[7]

A large, rustic-finished resort hotel, with its brood of cottages, the Lodge had been built by its owner with the able assistance of Pomin's horse, "Old Bill," who dragged lumber to the site. The Pomins advertised their new establishment as a "homelike resort, with comfortable quarters, a daily steamer stop and all outdoor activities, including hiking and riding on the bridle trails through the forest of pine, fir and incense cedar."[8]

Another link in the growing chain of dockside post offices at Tahoe was added when 26 families signed a petition requesting the action in June of 1914.[9] Later old Pomin's Lodge and boat harbor constituted May-Ah-Mee Lodge, part of a growing settlement that included Tahoma and an extensive subdivision development in the forest land to the south.

WELCOME AIMEE

Aimee Semple McPherson at the conclusion of a Four Square Gospel revival meeting near Pomin's Lodge in the summer of 1927.

Marie Henry

HELLMAN'S MAGNIFICENT MANSION

I. W. Hellman completed this stately three story summmer residence in 1913. Standing for nearly a half century it comprises the last extensive private holding on the California side of Tahoe.

Chapter Fourteen

SUGAR PINE POINT

GENERAL WILLIAM PHIPPS, the old Indian fighter, was being watched. Moreover, he knew it. That crawling sensation between his shoulder blades meant only one thing— danger! But from what source he could not tell. Without breaking the rhythm, he continued to swing his heavy, double-edged ax against the limbs of a fallen pine. Safety lay behind the walls of his half completed saw log cabin, but it stood some 50 yards distant. A sudden dash for it could mean his death. Behind him lay Tahoe, a bluer mirror of the cloudless blue sky. To the west the clearing ended in a maze of manzanita and scrub brush. Nothing moved.

Deliberately Phipps turned his back on the only point of ambush and began to trim slowly, so as not to arouse suspicion, in the direction of the cabin. The only sound was the ring of iron on knotted wood. On a wooden peg by the door frame hung his holstered six guns. A Sharps buffalo rifle was propped against a nearby pile of cordwood. Tense and fearful, he worked his way foot by foot down the length of pine. Perspiration salted his eyes. He blinked it away. "Steady," he cautioned himself, "just a little closer . . ."

Suddenly an explosion shattered the air and a musket ball whistled past his head, but Phipps was already running, crouched and dodging, the remaining steps to the enclosure. He dove behind the barricade of logs, dragging his pistols off the peg as he fell. Although trapped, he was safe for the moment.

A feather of white smoke drifted up from the edge of the undergrowth. Then there was only silence, long and ominous. As he lay staring through a chink in the logs, Phipps frowned. A white man wouldn't use a musket and the Washoe Indians were a friendly tribe. Then Phipps recalled John McKinney's story of the week before. At the time the general had thought the tale just another of John's tall ones, but now he was not so sure.

McKinney had said that, on finding a side of venison missing from his hanging shed next to the ice house, he formed his own one-man war party and started off after "One-eyed John," a renegade Paiute from Truckee Meadows. When McKinney finally tracked him down in the canyon, that "crazy black-sooted paint face," as John described him, had creased his arm with a hunting knife.

With a patience acquired from years of stalking the Plains Indians, Phipps remained a motionless part of the silence which reigned over the clearing. If it *is* that coward killer, he thought, at least I have two good eyes to his one. The minutes became a half hour. Two red digger ants scurried along the sleeve of his buckskin jacket and across the bridge of his nose, but the general continued to peer steadily at the tangled scrub. There was not a whisper of wind in all the stillness.

Then a leaf fluttered. In an instant Phipps leveled his revolver and emptied it, the staccato crack of shots encircling the tell-tale movement with deadly accuracy. A coughing yell preceded the loin-clouted figure that spun into the open, staggered a few steps, fell, clutched at the air and then collapsed. Slowly the general rose 'to his feet. He stretched his cramped, aching muscles and reached for his buffalo rifle. From ten paces he sent a lead slug through the twitching brown body and walked over to examine his attacker. He rolled the dead man over with the toe of his boot. A grimy leather patch covered one eye; the other stared unseeingly at the sky.

"Well, I'll be hornswoggled," muttered Phipps. "McKinney sure was right this time." Grabbing the Indian by the ankles he dragged his body into the brush. There he pulled off the beaded moccasins and picked up the powder horn and long-barreled breechloader. "Couldn't have hit the side of Burton's Canyon with this relic anyway," he reflected. The general knew the wolves would have the wretch that night and save him a burial job. Damnation, wasn't he at least two hours behind in his work as it was? He had a cabin to build. Phipps returned to the felled tree and picked up his ax.[1]

This incident was not extraordinary in the life of General William Phipps. Locally famous marksman, hunter and fisherman, he was the first recorded permanent settler on Tahoe's southwestern shore. A native of Kentucky and veteran of the Indian Wars, he had settled in Georgetown during the summer of 1854,[2] but the wilderness high country bordering the lake appealed to him more than any town and in the spring of 1860 he moved to the southeastern promontory of Upson (McKinney) Bay.

Besides his guns, knives, ax, a bedroll and buckskins, he had $200 in gold dust. This constituted Phipps' total personal property.[3] He established camp about one-half mile south of what later became Sugar Pine Point, adjoining a sand spit and deep pool at the mouth of a creek flowing into the lake, where he whipsawed logs and split cedar for his first log cabin. By 1864 Phipps had added a finger wharf, boathouse and Whitehall sailing hull.[4]

Among the general's contemporaries were John McKinney, George and John Hunsucker, Homer

BELLEVUE LANDING — DEAD AHEAD

Bellevue's Club House on June 28, 1891, as seen from the steamer TOD GOODWIN, *looking northwest toward Sugar Pine Point. Bellevue Hotel was located at the head of the pier just to the south of five guest cottages, three of which are shown in the picture.*

George D. Oliver

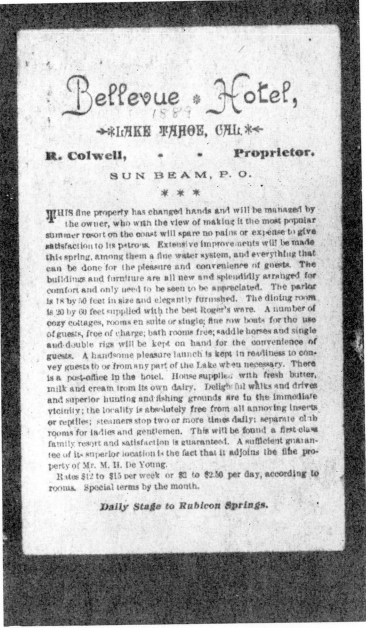

Bellevue ✳ Hotel,

➤✳LAKE TAHOE, CAL.✳◂

R. Colwell, ✳ ✳ **Proprietor.**

SUN BEAM, P. O.

✳ ✳ ✳

THIS fine property has changed hands and will be managed by the owner, who with the view of making it the most popular summer resort on the coast will spare no pains or expense to give satisfaction to its patrons. Extensive improvements will be made this spring, among them a fine water system, and everything that can be done for the pleasure and convenience of guests. The buildings and furniture are all new and splendidly arranged for comfort and only need to be seen to be appreciated. The parlor is 18 by 50 feet in size and elegantly furnished. The dining room is 20 by 60 feet supplied with the best Roger's ware. A number of cozy cottages, rooms en suite or single; fine row boats for the use of guests, free of charge; bath rooms free; saddle horses and single and double rigs will be kept on hand for the convenience of guests. A handsome pleasure launch is kept in readiness to convey guests to or from any part of the Lake when necessary. There is a post-office in the hotel. House supplied with fresh butter, milk and cream from its own dairy. Delightful walks and drives and superior hunting and fishing grounds are in the immediate vicinity; the locality is absolutely free from all annoying insects or reptiles; steamers stop two or more times daily; separate club rooms for ladies and gentlemen. This will be found a first-class family resort and satisfaction is guaranteed. A sufficient guarantee of its superior location is the fact that it adjoins the fine property of Mr. M. H. De Young.

Rates $12 to $15 per week or $2 to $2.50 per day, according to rooms. Special terms by the month.

Daily Stage to Rubicon Springs.

ELEGANT ACCOMMODATIONS
$2.00 A DAY

*Ralph Colwell's Bellevue Hotel
brochure published in 1889.*

Hattie Belle Colwell Almstaden

D. Burton, Lou and John Huntington, Ephraim "Yank" Clement and William "Billy" Lapham. With his neighbors, McKinney and George Hunsucker, he fished and hunted the heavily timbered back country of lakes and canyons. The mountain men netted silver and cutthroat trout in the stream Phipps had laid claim to under his 160-acre homestead right and trout spawn for rearing fingerlings was packed in moss and shipped over the Georgetown trail to lakes in the Coast Range.

In spite of Phipps' attempt to enforce a hands-off policy with the business end of his rifle, the magnificent stand of sugar pine on the point was being eyed covetously by loggers Nat Stein, Michel Spooner and George W. Wiggins from Tahoe City, Spooner's Station and Pine Grove. This trio of timber cruisers had been agile enough to elude the general's trained eye, and they reported the forest giants here to be the finest growing on the Pacific Coast.[5] As Augustus Colwell owned 203 acres on Sugar Pine the lumber contractors approached him and acquired timber rights to the land. The year was now 1878 and Sugar Pine would be systematically stripped of its marketable timber.

George D. Oliver

THE GENERAL'S OLD LOG AND SHAKER

A group of Carsonites seated at General William Phipps' original saw log barn and cabin built in 1862-63 and located in a clearing just north of General Creek's influx into Tahoe. Not to be confused with Phipps' second log cabin, constructed in 1870 and still standing on the Ehrman property today. Photograph taken in the summer of 1893 looking northwest.

Although the general resented this intrusion on his privacy, and roundly cursed the destruction of the trees, there was nothing he could do to prevent their exploitation. He did manage to keep the loggers off his own private preserve, which included the inlet of Phipps' Creek (General) and 600 yards of lakeshore.[6]

In May, 1883, the general was amazed to learn he was being sought by the law in the guise of the California Fish Commission. This agency was under pressure from the residents of Tahoe City to launch an investigation regarding the wholesale slaughter of native trout in the lake. It was rumored that the commission's efforts to stop this practice would be greatly advanced if the commissioners called on the general and cast an eye around his property, specifically at the point where his stream flowed into the lake. McKinney learned of the proposed visit and privately warned his friend. Phipps turned purple.

"I saved this hyar great country of ours from the clutches of the red man," he thundered, "and no politic-minded passel of blue noses is going to stop me from takin' a few measly spawnin' eggs that is rightfully mine."

The following week four of the commissioners visited Sugar Pine Point and were greeted by a sullen Phipps. While two of the men engaged the general in conversation the others wandered down to the creek outlet where, sure enough, they discovered more than 900 silver trout penned in a pool carefully screened over with willows. Caught red-handed, the old Indian fighter delivered himself of a fiery tirade, punctuated by blasts from his brace of Colt revolvers through the roof and sides of his cabin. Phipps' rugged display of individualism served only to antagonize his unwelcome guests. The general was given 48 hours to release the fish and advised that if the orders were not obeyed he would find himself a permanent fixture in the Truckee jail.[7]

From that day on the old plainsman changed and the mere mention of authority would send him into wrathful convulsions. On March 15, 1887, he died at Georgetown, leaving his name to General Creek, Phipps' Lake and the 9,300-foot mountain situated two and one-half miles south of Rubicon Peak.

One of his old cabins remained to become the scene of an incident that nearly ended the career of rancher Will Barton from Lake Valley.[8] In 1910 a posse of deputy sheriffs trailing an escaped convict from Carson surrounded Phipps' old abode, thinking they had cornered their quarry. They broke in with leveled guns only to discover Barton sleeping off a bout with distilled spirits.[9]

By 1882 a carriage and wagon road had been built along the lake from McKinney's to the Point, completing an "improved trail" to Tahoe City. The Point now became a favorite camping spot for Nevada outdoorsmen and its popularity prompted Captain W. W. "Billy" Lapham, former owner of Lapham's Hotel and Landing at south Stateline, to take an option on the land. Three years later Lapham purchased Phipps' original lakefront property and announced plans for a resort. Ground was broken two seasons later, when, in the fall of 1887, Lapham's plans materialized. West of the white sand beach, granite rock foundations were laid for a 120 x 34-foot, two and a half story luxury hotel.

In the spring of 1888 the establishment was completed. A large, ornate lobby, parlor, bar, billiard salon and several bedrooms occupied the ground floor. Directly in front of the building, and running for 100 feet out over the water, was a wharf for docking lake steamers and fishing boats. On the end of the pier a 30 x 20-foot clubhouse was constructed. It boasted a fireplace, eight rooms on the second floor for employees, a post office and saloon. Lapham described his new resort as a modest undertaking and called it Bellevue.

David Kaiser of the Ormsby House in Carson City joined Lapham as a partner and they added five single-room cottages directly north of the hotel, and more fishing skiffs.[10] During the same month, April of 1888, the Postmaster General authorized a mail receiving and departure point at Bellevue and it was named "Sunbeam" for the reflected sparkle of sunshine in the sandy shallow water. Kaiser was appointed postmaster.[11]

The new resort had a fine new horse livery to service what was described as an "excellent wagon road running all the way to the Central Pacific railroad at Truckee."[12] Bellevue's advertising brochure called vacationists' attention to "the most handsome new record on the lake, accommodating one hundred guests, with a fleet of unmatched fishing boats available, and a smooth stage road connecting with civilization."[13]

The gleaming white clubhouse with latticed verandas along three sides of the building, green shuttered windows and brick chimneys, outmoded Campbell's Custom House at Tahoe City and McKinney's Club House west around the Point. Oliver Roberts of the Arlington Hotel took over as manager the following season and "Fatty" Cohn was installed as the gentleman for laughs behind the polished rosewood bar.

With inspired foresight, Kaiser planted 40,000 fingerling trout in General Creek and visiting anglers who wished to take trout the easy way had only to stroll north a few hundred yards and, in a matter of minutes, return with a nice string.

Among the hotel's main attractions was a bevy of young ladies who wore wedding rings but whose husbands, if any, were not mentioned. By a crackling campfire on the beach these gay charmers and their admirers sang "Oft in the Stilly Night" and "Tim Finnegan's Wake" to a burnished summer moon. Across the dinner table they exchanged such hilarious stories as that of the Bar Harbor girl and the boatman: "He had suggested that the skiff be well-trimmed so she sewed two silk flowers 'round the gunwale."

In the fall of 1889 Bellevue was acquired by Wells Fargo Express Company, who sold to Ralph Colwell the following spring.[14] Colwell announced extensive improvements including a "fine water system, new furniture, a 20 x 60-foot dining room with the best Roger's ware, cozy cottages, free bath

875 POUNDS OF DEAD BLACK FURY AND FRIEND

The last recorded bear in the Tahoe region to be caught by the "pit-trap" method was photographed in the 1940's guarded by this comfortably unconcerned hunting dog.

Eleanor Swanson

rooms, saddle horses, single and double rigs, a handsome pleasure launch, and dairy." It was further noted by the management "a sufficient guarantee of its superior location is the fact that it adjoins the fine property of Mr. M. H. de Young." Rates were set at $12 to $15 per week or $2 to $2.50 per day, with special terms by the month.[15]

Ralph Colwell and his wife, Hattie Belle Colwell, operated the hotel four summer seasons. Then overnight Bellevue was gone from the Tahoe scene. On August 21, 1893, the hotel, cottages and part of the wharf disappeared when a conflagration leveled the resort to its foundations.[16] The only building of value to survive the fire was Bellevue's Club House on the water, and that would become Yank's Cascade House.[17]

In the years 1897 and 1898 Isaias William Hellman, a prominent Pacific Coast capitalist, with controlling interests in the Nevada National Bank and Farmers and Merchants Bank of San Francisco, started to buy up property on Sugar Pine Point. Fearing that the price of the land would skyrocket if he dealt with the owners, Hellman had enlisted the services of Joe Savage, a winter caretaker, as go-between. By 1900 Hellman obtained 1,016 acres from the Southern Pacific Company, the Bliss family, the Colwells and M. H. de Young. His property ran south to Chinquapin Cove and northwest around Sugar Pine Point. It included two miles of lake frontage. At Hellman's request, Walter Danforth Bliss, the noted architect, who had just completed plans for Tahoe Tavern, designed a sumptuous summer home. The foundations were laid in the summer of 1901 with Carl Leonard, Los Angeles contractor, in charge of construction. Completed in 1903 and situated north of the site of old Bellevue Hotel on a rise of ground facing eastward across the lake, the manor house was a magnificent accomplishment. Being listed as a "mansion" in the El Dorado County Court House records was the final accolade. On the property now stood a large, stately, gabled and turreted three-story building, with outlying servants' quarters, a tennis court, boathouses and water tower. The tower was supplied by a ditch and flume from General Creek. The main house, set well back from the lake, was ringed by what would become a beautiful grove of cedar and pine, including a 4-foot through juniper tree described by naturalist John Muir as "the largest and finest in the Sierra."[18]

Tons of topsoil had been brought from the back country to surface what was originally little more than a sand hill. Granite, quarried for the massive foundations of the home, had also been used to build the outsized chimneys. Much of the materials and interior finishings such as plaster, cement, plumbing, hand-wrought fixtures and finished lumber had been moved in by the steamer *Tahoe* from the railroad pier at Tahoe Tavern.

Joe Savage constructed and continued to maintain the flume that furnished water to the house. In addition, he took care of the new electric power plant that rivaled Tallac Hotel's in capacity and construction, and eliminated the original kerosene lamps. From Hellman's Paso Robles ranch came carriages and horses, harness, stable boys and grooms. Milk cows were also brought in from the ranch to stock the dairy. Flower gardens circled the main house, a vegetable garden was started to supply the kitchen and a sweep of meticulously maintained vivid green lawn ran from the top of the hill beneath the pines and cedars to the water's edge. When completed, Hellman's was the finest High Sierra summer home in California. By the summer of 1913 I. W. Hellman's estate totaled 2,021 acres and ran deep into the mountains to the west.[19]

Today the old pilings of Bellevue's wharf remain, bleaching in the summer sunshine, and a new growth of pine marks the site of the former hotel and cottages. To the north the Hellman mansion still stands in well-tended magnificence after half a century. Originally the seasonal residence of Mr. and Mrs. Sidney Ehrman (nee Florence Hellman) of San Francisco, it is now part of the California State Park system.[20]

C. O. Valentine

THE BAY AND RUBICONS

Second growth and scrub brush rims the crescent beach and Point at Meeks Bay in the early summer of 1912. Pilings (shoreline center) remain as last evidence of the C. & T. L. & F. Company's logging operations.

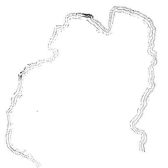

Chapter Fifteen

MEEKS BAY

Micks, Meigs, Meegs and "Buttermilk Bay" are known names and spellings foisted upon this wide, sweeping curve of fine sand beach that runs in a white crescent for nearly half a mile toward Sugar Pine Point to the north and Rubicon Bay to the south.[1] The shoreline is backed by meadowland and lodge pole pine. Timber stands reach westward up the canyon that forms a gateway to the Tallant Lakes and wilderness country beyond.

Today this beautiful, protected setting constitutes Meeks Bay.

Early records indicate that Meeks and Company cut 25 tons of wild hay from the surrounding flatlands during the fall of 1862.[2] This placed the name "Meeks" upon the location, and all future spellings of the word appear merely as corruptions of the original.

Attempts to place those early mountain men, Stephen and Joseph Meek, at this specific location in the Sierra Nevada have failed, although the brothers claimed to have scouted the Truckee Canyon in the 1830's and are known to have crossed what later became Donner Pass.[3]

For generations the native Washoe Indians used the beach bordering on the bay for their summer encampments and excellent hunting could be had in the great forest at their backs. The lake offered matchless fishing as did the snow water stream running through the meadow and across the beach.

The first white men of record to discover the bay were John Calhoun "Cock-Eye" Johnson, of Johnson Pass fame, and an anonymous *Placerville Herald* correspondent. In the summer of 1853, these two venturesome explorers from Hangtown made their way to the lake by breaking trail up Rubicon Gorge, traveling over the divide south of what is now Lost Corner Mountain and dropping down the present Meeks Canyon and Creek to the bay. Here Johnson and his companion were welcomed by a "friendly band of Digger Indians, some seventy strong."[4] They were amazed to find the sheltered cove "alive with speckled trout." A "venerable and blind octogenarian" regaled them with a legendary tale of the lake's formation and the trail blazers added some equally fantastic embroidery of their own, upon returning to Placerville.[5]

In the spring of 1878, George Thomas and James Andrew Murphy, winter residents of Coloma and native Californians, settled on the grassy flatland surrounding Meeks Bay. As boys they had worked for a rancher, C. W. Lusk, who ran stock in the fertile bottomland beneath Rubicon Peaks to the south, on land later to be known as Rubicon Park. Slowly the brothers acquired a small herd of milk cows and then entered into business for themselves, driving their cattle each summer to Meeks, where they had built a cabin and corrals.[6]

The Central Pacific owned this choice timberland and grazing property, having added it to their extensive railroad grants some ten years before. George and Jim Murphy now kept one thought uppermost in their minds—save enough money so they could purchase the holding outright. Finally

$250 was scraped together by the young cattlemen. Although they considered the figure ridiculously low for 640 forested acres, the two hardworking six-footers submitted their bid anyway, only to learn that Duane L. Bliss, representing the Carson and Tahoe Lumber and Fluming Company, had bought the land a few days before for the same amount.

Their disappointment flared into resentment when shortly thereafter the steamer *Meteor*, towing a 104-foot cordwood barge, churned into the bay and nosed up on the beach. A crew of French-Canadian lumberjacks swarmed off the carriers and started felling sugar pine "practically into the Murphy's corrals."[7] This unforeseen turn of events occurred so suddenly that the youthful ranchers didn't even have a chance to move their dairy cows. After a hurried conference they decided the matter had to be brought to D. L. Bliss's personal attention. James Murphy immediately slapped saddle to his cow pony and spurred south down the trail. Upon reaching Eagle Point he urged his horse into the water, and rider and mount swam across the entrance to Emerald Bay. Many hours later the dust-covered horseman arrived at Glenbrook, where he presented his problem to Bliss.

The lumberman listened quietly and, when Murphy had finished, he assured the anxious youngster that all he wanted from the property was the timber. Then Bliss promised voluntarily that, upon completion of his logging operations at the bay, the Murphys could have the cut-over land for the original purchase price. Jim Murphy's face brightened. He waved his thanks, mounted his lathered cow pony and headed back in the direction from which he had come. George would be waiting impatiently for an answer—and the news was good.[7]

The sheltered bay now became the hub of the C. and T. L. and F. Company's western shore operations. Sugar Pine Point, Meeks Canyon and the Rubicons fed saw logs to the lake where they were V-boomed in the quiet water of the bay and towed by steam tugs to Glenbrook's mills.

Heavy stands of pine in the rugged back country to the southwest had to be moved out; so a mile-long chute was built that snaked down Lonely Gulch from highline camps and dropped logs directly into Rubicon Bay.

By the summer of 1884 most of the choice timber surrounding Meeks had been logged off. Duane L. Bliss then kept his promise to the Murphys, transferring title to the 640 acres on August 20 of the same year. Payment in the amount of $250 was made in gold eagles.[8]

For the next 35 years George and James Murphy ran dairy cows and beef cattle in the meadows surrounding the bay, and when their sister Frances married Luke Morgan from Georgetown, California, they took him in as a partner. This led to an expansion of their activities at Tahoe and, in the summer of 1892, the three men leased McKinney's Resort from the Westhoff family.[9]

The early 1900's found Meeks Bay to be still unimproved. The old wood wharf and several shacks, built from lumber barged across Tahoe from Glenbrook, were falling into decay. Corrals that held 60 to 70 head of cattle stood where the present store is located and the Washoe Indians had moved their summer campgrounds from Meeks to McKinney's, where tourists and daily handouts made life easier.

At the new location they squatted cross-legged near the hotel and at meal times purchased a 25-

C. O. Valentine

ONE SQUARE MILE OF WHITE SAND BEACH AND MEADOWLAND . . . . $250.00 IN GOLD EAGLES

*Looking northwest across Meeks Bay from the Rim of the Lake's dirt road in July, 1914,
four decades before it became the "million dollar strip." The big timber
was gone and no one believed that this isolated, mile high stretch
of shoreline could ever be successfully exploited.*

cent ticket that entitled bucks, squaws and children to a community dinner. Leftovers from the kitchen were stacked on a huge tin plate and hungry-eyed Washoes sat in a circle around this delectable offering, fingering, grabbing and spearing succulent items of gastronomical delight—fish heads, steer entrails, ham bones, and raw vegetable tops.

The resort business at McKinney's kept Morgan and the Murphys so well occupied that they offered Meeks "wilderness beach and meadowland" to Howard and Ben Callender of Homewood during the summer of 1907 for $5,000. At the time this appeared to be a staggering sum to the Callenders, even had the mile square acreage not been cut over.

They turned the opportunity down.[10]

In the spring of 1909 Arnold P. Luneman, El Dorado County ranch hand, went to work for the Murphys, driving his rig daily from McKinney's to Meeks, where he handled what amounted to a three-man job, corralling, milking and pasturing over half a hundred head of cows.[11]

But development of the bay as a campground could not be postponed indefinitely. It was too choice a location for stock grazing and dairy ranching alone.

During the summer of 1919 Oswald V. Kehlet and his family camped on Meeks Bay's shoreline. Having previously stayed at McKinney's, they were convinced that the western side of Tahoe, and Meeks magnificent bay in particular, would be the logical choice for a commercial development. Kehlet and his oldest son, George, opened negotiations with the Murphy brothers. A price was finally agreed upon that came to approximately seven times the amount asked for the acreage 12 years before, and it is reported several other anxious buyers waited expectantly in hopes that the transaction might fall through, thus allowing them a chance to bid.[12]

The first building constructed by the Kehlets was a log cabin store, built shortly after they purchased the land. In 1921 they cleared their property adjoining the beach, opened a public campground and, over the years, gradually added tents, cabins and other improvements. On May 9, 1929, a post office was officially established at the bay and a dance hall, completed that year, became the Kehlet family's largest major improvement.[13]

West across present Highway 89 is Meadow Park, another summer settlement offering accommodations for the High Sierra vacationer. The land was originally purchased from the Murphys by Dr. L. F. Herrick of Berkeley, California, and during the last half century it has been both a dairy ranch and silver fox farm. It is now owned by Mrs. I. H. Henderson, Dr. Herrick's daughter.[14]

To the northeast of Meeks Bay stands Chinquapin Lodge, a private estate owned by the John S. Drum family of San Francisco. The large Tyrolean-style mansion was built in the summer of 1923 by Matt Green, Tahoe City contractor, and the Alpine setting inspired some interesting architectural innovations.[15] Boulders lie against horizontally laid sapling pine on the heavy shake roof and the exterior of the balconied house is rustic. Several outlying guest chalets front on the cove and, like the main building, are set in a grove of fir and pine, with "Honeymoon Cottage" located on the point toward Meeks Bay. Subdivision of Chinquapin has now allowed the Hillyer Brown and Hart families to build there and other private summer homes are following.

John Drum, Sr.'s, interest in Californiana was manifest in the interior treatment of the many-roomed lodge as well as around the grounds. A native of Bardstown, Kentucky, he traveled west early in life, settling first in the mining town of Aurora, California, and then moving on to the "Bay City." His collection of relics dating from the '49er and Bonanza eras is one of the finest at Tahoe. Massive andirons, forged originally for Phoebe Hearst's "Wyntoon Castle" at McCloud, California, set off the outdoor fireplace that is pyramided from immense granite boulders. On the east porch four large bronze plaques depict "Crossing the Plains," "San Francisco Harbor in 1849," "Gold Mining" and the "California Grizzly."

At the impressive western entrance to the lodge two hand-carved hardwood grizzly bears stand guard, the same life-sized animals that looked down from above the gates of San Francisco's famous Woodward Gardens during the 1870's. Near the Drum's entrance hang outdoor lamps of heroic dimensions, hand fashioned from horseshoes out of William C. Ralston's stables in San Francisco and Belmont—iron that clattered over the cobblestones of the "City by the Golden Gate" nearly a century ago.[16]

In addition, worn ox yokes that crossed the plains with the Argonauts swing from massive crossbeams supporting the lakefront porch, and a large scale relief map traces the topography of the Lake Tahoe region in exact detail.

Another early day memento stood for years at the end of the Drum's pier. Here the carved wooden figure of a "safe voyage mermaid" looked out across the waters of Tahoe. Originally she had proudly graced the bowsprit of a grain schooner windjamming around the Horn between California and England during the 1880's. When the vessel burned at her moorings in Port Chicago, California, a saloon-keeper salvaged the figure, which was later acquired by Drum. Brought to the lake, it was christened "Sue Smith" for a Stockton columnist. The meticulously hand-carved head featured jet black hair, set off by a brilliant red rose, and a fan, yellow decollete dress, and impressive bosom, highlighted the torso. The presence of the tantalizing, if startling, harpy will be sorely missed by marine travelers on Tahoe, as it was recently donated by John Drum, Jr., to Brayton Wilbur of San Francisco.[17]

By 1940 Meeks had grown into a thriving summer settlement with George Kehlet, Captain Fred O. Kehlet and their sons actively participating in the management of the resort. Although the mid-1950's brought a mass influx of vacationists to the bay, reminders of the fading and nearly forgotten early days still existed.

On the stock range to the west, Arnold Luneman still ran cattle during the season upon land owned by the heirs of the Murphy brothers and along the shoreline Washoe Indian stone arrowheads were frequently discovered, buried in the deep sand of the beach. The children, and children's children of the Murphys carry on the tradition of their pioneer forebears – returning year after year as summer residents of Meeks Bay.[18]

A Tahoe adage holds that natives of the region need not feel obliged to attend a "Laker's" funeral if the deceased has committed the unpardonable sin of passing away in such ideal climate before the age of 80 years. George and James Murphy appear to have subscribed heartily to this view, for they lived to the venerable ages of 93 and 91 years, respectively. When these pioneer Californians both joined "the great majority" in the year 1941 they carried with them the proud knowledge that they had contributed materially toward a way of life that spanned nearly a century of Lake Tahoe's early development.

FROST'S RUBICON PARK LODGE

High lake level in the spring of 1900 nearly inundated A. J. Frost's gleaming white hotel and outbuildings. The barn (right background), was the first structure to be built at Rubicon Park. Photograph taken looking west.

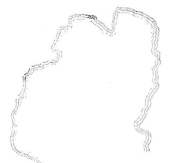

Chapter Sixteen

RUBICON PARK AND BAY

"The natural untouched wilderness of Rubicon stands as a primitive throwback to the times before man walked the country, and all the surrounding mountains are weeping like some vast amphitheater of waterfalls."

This passage, written in 1880, aptly described the remoteness of Rubicon, as neither road nor settlement existed at the time. The only sign of civilization was a cattleman, C. W. Lusk, who, assisted by young George and James Murphy, ran his stock in the meadowland west of Rubicon Bay.[1]

Five years later A. L. Frost, resident of Sacramento County, pre-empted land at the Bay, and by 1887 his holdings totaled 630 acres.[2]

In the year 1889, the *Sacramento Union* reported that a 20-acre tract of land fronting on the Bay, and including one-half mile of white sand beach, was to be developed under the name "Waterniche" by Dr. S. S. Southworth of Sacramento City.

Southworth's plans failed to materialize, but from the idea grew A. L. Frost's Rubicon Park Tract, sometimes known as "Frost's Homestead." Frost catered to outdoorsmen who wished to leave all semblance of civilization behind. Assisted by his daughter Josephine and son John "Jack" Frost, he first operated a summer campground. Their only link with the outside world was a small 30-foot long finger pier where the lake steamers docked occasionally but by the mid-1890's the Frosts had added two clapboard shacks, a storehouse, and barn. Corrals for their milk cows and riding horses were constructed in the meadow to the north.

Following the launching of the steamer *Tahoe* in 1896, a 200-foot pier was built out into deep water, and plans for a hotel were projected. By the turn of the century Rubicon Park Lodge had become a reality. The hotel was the usual two and one-half story structure, with the second floor partitioned into 12 small rooms and accommodations for additional guests were available off the downstairs lobby and in several cottages and tents on the grounds. Corrals had been removed, and the storehouse and other shacks to the south of the main building rebuilt. A combination barn and stable stood to the west of the establishment.[3]

Josephine "Josie" Frost was now married to Horatio T. Harper, a Standard Oil Company executive. When A. L. Frost died in 1904, the Harpers took over the operation of the resort and in 1905 the Western Company, controlled by the Harpers, acquired the land, hotel and other improvements. Included in the purchase were a launch, ten fishing skiffs, furniture, two pianos, machinery and livestock. The company now had 1,100 acres bordering Rubicon Bay.[4]

Various lessees, including Gus Casper, who assumed the management in 1910, ran Rubicon Lodge during the next seven years. The steamers *Tahoe* and *Nevada* made scheduled stops to discharge mail and passengers and return vacationers to Tallac or Tahoe City.[5] In 1912 the owners of the Lodge added

RUBICON — VALHALLA FOR THE VACATIONER

Amos L. Frost's Rubicon Park Tract, finger pier, corrals and guest cottages on a crowded weekend in the summer of 1895. Photograph taken from the crow's nest of the LILY VAN looking southwest.

BATHERS AND BOATS BENEATH THE RUBICON PEAKS

Rubicon Park Lodge (Hotel) and cottages in the spring of 1908, viewed from the resort's pier. Looking toward the western Sierra Range with the box camera set up just north of the spot where the photograph (above) was taken.

400 acres but the resort was losing its popularity and by the following summer it began to fade from the Tahoe scene.

Frank Pomin, who was building his new Pomin's Lodge on McKinney Bay, purchased several cabins from the Harpers and moved the structures by barge to his new location. The Young brothers from Bijou bought the hotel furniture. By the fall of 1915 Rubicon Park Lodge was gone, although several of the outbuildings stood until the 1920's.[6] The greater part of the land was sold, however a small parcel of the original Frost property was retained by Horatio T. Harper's descendants with adjoining land purchased by the Davies, Fletchers, Alexanders, Hotles, Hinmans, Else Schilling, Pennoyers, Metcalfs, Wieslanders, and Marian Huntington, among others.

During the decline of Rubicon Lodge the George Newhall family of San Francisco bought 273 acres two miles north of the Lodge on Rubicon Bay.[7] Here on a knoll above the lake they built a three and one-half story mansion, adding a large boathouse and pier on their lake frontage. In 1926 they increased their holdings to 350 acres and, 19 years later, sold the property to Fred Kilner and the Williams family who tore down the stately home during the summer of 1949.[8]

Subsequently the old Newhall estate became a flourishing subdivision with dozens of modern summer homes flanking the eastern end of Lonely Gulch above the waters of Tahoe.

The one unchanging aspect of this southwest section of the lake is the startling contrast between the vivid green shoal water and the deep blue depths offshore. Here a marine dividing line zigzags and serpentines between Rubicon Point and the southern approach to Meeks Bay in a breath-taking panoramic strike of color.

CLARET ON THE TABLE AND BRILLIANT SUNSHINE

Reception Day, July 10, 1909, at Rubicon Park Lodge. Captain Ernest Pomin, second man from the right, his crew from the steamer TAHOE, *lake residents and hotel guests. In the distance to the north lies Meeks Bay's south point.*

Author's collection

GRANITE GREMLIN ON A PEDESTAL

Balancing Rock, at D. L. Bliss State Park, west of Rubicon Point. View taken in July, 1912, facing north down the canyon toward Tahoe. Note the size of the rock as compared to the man.

Chapter Seventeen

RUBICON POINT

"SOME ENTERPRISING YANKEE should barrel the water here and furnish it to the trade for bluing solution." So quipped a newsman from the *Sacramento Daily Record Union* on July 6, 1889, after viewing the Stygian depths of Rubicon Point's aquamarine waters.

This marine wonder of the Sierra Nevada lies on the southwestern shore of Tahoe beneath a frowning sheer of granite that rises some 600 feet above the lake's surface. Here the snow waters drop off vertically to a depth of more than 1400 feet and the coloration is comparable to that of Capri's Blue Grotto.

The waters off Rubicon constitute the deepest part of Tahoe nearest the shoreline and a combination of tremendous depth and subterranean mountain causes the blue-black color that is found at the Point. Consistency of the water appears to be that of liquid gelatine and for decades this replica of the face of Yosemite's Half Dome with water against it was considered "bottomless."[1]

Over the years steamer captains took a particular delight in grazing the Point's jagged outcropping although near panic often resulted among their passengers. There was no need for consternation as the largest ocean liner afloat could pass within a rowboat's length of Rubicon with safety.

In the early 1850's the few mountain men who penetrated to the southwestern shores of Tahoe avoided the high granite peaks to the east of what became the Tallant Lakes' Basin, in favor of easier routes. No attempt was made to run out a trail or usable road through this rugged mountainous high country land of craggy peaks and precipitous defiles as the terrain was both perilous and impracticable. Therefore it was compared to Caesar's crossing of the Rubicon, and this historical legend prompted the naming of the gorge, mountain range, point and bay.[2]

Pointed out to the marine sightseer, since their discovery in the 1860's, are various natural formations of granite on the face of Rubicon. As a boat rounds the Point heading south, Frog Rock is first seen followed by the Hen and Chickens (sometimes Baby Chick Rock). Next a quartet of massive split sections of granite, known as the Four Loaves of Bread, rise above the surface of the lake.

Still farther south and bordering the first ravine past the Point, is found the Sleeping Lady, a sharply defined profile of a woman's face that stares into the sky. Above the Lady stands an immense stone figure, commonly known as the Gladiator, with ponderous head and straight hanging robes, that peers south over Grecian Bend in somber reflection.[3] Above the Gladiator sits famous Old King Cole, also known variously over the decades as the Turk in Turban, Grinning Negro and Old Squaw. A generous smile splits the profile from ear to ear and a crown of dark granite serves as his headpiece.

Facing this replica of the "Little King" is a reclining figure that resembles an animal carved out of stone. It is generally called the Stone Seal.

Two more of Tahoe's white sand beaches lie to the north of Rubicon Point. In the 1880's this section was a part of the Carson and Tahoe Lumber and Fluming Company's far-flung lumbering empire at Tahoe and some 50 years later the descendants of Duane LeRoy and Elizabeth Tobey Bliss donated 957 acres at the Point to the State of California as a memorial park.

Known as the D. L. Bliss State Park, this recreational area with its 14,640 feet of shoreline runs from the north beaches of Rubicon Point south around Emerald Bay's Eagle Point. On the northern approach to the park, surrounded by giant pine and cedar that are now preserved for future generations, stands Tahoe's Balancing Rock, tons of granite resting precariously on a slender stone base.

Over the years Rubicon's sheltered shoreline was the favorite picnic spot for homeowners at Tahoe and guests of the lake resorts. "Bull head" breakfasts on the white sand in the early 1900's gave way to lamb chop luncheons in the 1920's and 30's with white-hatted chefs dispensing the broiled delicacies from a glowing barbecue pit.

Today the solitude and remoteness of Rubicon Point is gone and vacationers line the beaches during the summer season with only the natural beauty of the Point remaining unchanged.

SO DEEP A ROWBOAT'S LENGTH SUFFICED

The steamer TAHOE *passing over Rubicon Point's 1411-foot depth only a pebble's toss offshore. To the left center of the photograph: Freel and Job's peaks and Luther Pass. Tallac and Tahoe Mountain are behind the vessel. Looking southeast.*

Author's collection

Chapter Eighteen

EMERALD BAY

★

"T HE WINTER before last I was on top of my kitchen throwin' snow from the roof four feet to the level above my head. Suddenly I heard something a-crackling away up there—." Captain Richard Barter, the "Hermit of Emerald Bay," pointed excitedly toward the summit of Granite Mountain that rose a sheer 3,000 feet above him and a visiting reporter.[1] Barter continued, "Looking up I saw everything a-breaking loose from their fastenings and coming down the mountain hoppity-jump. Yes sir, *everything* . . . pine trees, big boulders, snow and all, a-coming down together. They was making right for me and I thought Old Gabriel called me sure enough so I just dropped my shovel and waited. But sir, my time hadn't come yet for up yonder," he gesticulated toward an overhanging granite ridge, "it struck that point and slewed off, clearing me by about ten feet, and plunged right into the bay, sending the water up hundreds of feet."[2]

It was a sunlit August day of the year 1870 and Barter was in an expansive mood. That morning the San Francisco newspaperman and his boatman, Peter, had arrived at Ben Holladay, Jr.'s, wharf after rowing 16 miles down the lake from Tahoe City to call upon "Captain Dick." Barter welcomed them with a loaded derringer in each hand. Reassured by a display of friendliness in the form of a quart bottle of whiskey, the "Hermit" mellowed and entertained his visitors with stories of his life at Emerald Bay.

Richard Barter told his guests that he had come to the lake seven years before as caretaker for the famous overland stagecoach magnate, Ben Holladay. Holladay, then widely known as the "Croesus of the Coast" and "Napoleon of the Plains," had pre-empted the land surrounding Eagle Bay (Emerald) and also the island.[3] During the summer of 1863 he turned the property over to his son, Ben, Jr.

A two-story, five-room summer residence was built near the lakeshore, northwest of Eagle Falls. Holladay called it "The Cottage" and it was the first private "villa" to be constructed at Lake Tahoe. Nearby Barter occupied what he termed an "elegant new house." Rock-bordered paths, watercourses and stone dikes were laid out around the grounds, and "Willow Walk" led to the large boathouse and finger wharf, where several small skiffs and a Whitehall boat were moored. Old English seaman Barter appeared to thrive in his wilderness refuge and seven seasons had passed uneventfully for the self-styled shellback.

On the night of January 26, 1870, Barter declared, his luck nearly ran out. He had received a stern warning from the elements that, unknown to him, would serve as a prelude to ultimate disaster. The newsman pieced the story together.

Earlier in the day "Captain Dick" had rowed from the bay to Tahoe City and then immediately made for William Pomin's Tahoe House saloon. Here he lifted a booted foot onto the brass rail, leaned

CAPTAIN DICK AND THE ISLAND COTTAGE

Richard Barter, the "Hermit of Emerald Bay," on Ben Holladay's wharf, August 28, 1870, looking northeast toward Coquette (Emerald) Isle.

comfortably across the hardwood and regaled the bar's habitues with progressively taller stories during the rare intervals when he was not throwing back his head and tossing off shot glasses brimming with liquor. Over the years, easy-going Barter had become known as a salty, seafaring character, who combined a prodigious alcoholic intake with an enviable capacity. On this particular evening he was running true to form. By eight o'clock Captain Dick felt he had imbibed so freely that he'd better leave while he could still navigate. He reeled out of the saloon and stumbled down the wharf. From force of long habit Barter was able to climb unsteadily aboard his outsized dinghy and head in the general direction of Holladay's. Seven miles out and some two miles off Sugar Pine Point, a lashing line squall struck down Meek's Canyon. It caught the boat's starboard beam and before his befuddled senses could react, the craft heeled hard to port and capsized, tossing its owner into the icy waters of Tahoe. Half drowned by the high sea that was running, Barter somehow managed to reach his boat. It floated with gunwales awash. In the blackness he finally righted the hull and clawed his way aboard.

Recognizing that his one chance for survival would be to remain submerged in the near-freezing water, he stayed below the surface with only his nose exposed to the sub-zero air. Previously he had exercised considerable foresight by placing a demijohn of whiskey forward and by a quirk of circumstance it now floated within arm's reach. Uncorking the jug, he drew liberal lashings of alcohol into his numbed body and repeatedly cried out to the elements, "Richard Barter never surrenders."

As the half-light of early morning scattered the shadows on the western shore, Barter bailed some of the water from the foundering boat with his now empty jug. It was a slow process and thin sheets of ice coated his hands and face upon exposure to the biting wind and driving spray. Steadily growing weaker, Captain Dick managed to wrap himself in his soggy blankets. Then he started sculling for Emerald Bay. Several hours later he reached his landing, crawled on hands and knees down the wharf and collapsed on the bed in his cottage. The 65-year-old salt lay in a stupor for days, eating what he could reach. His toes had frozen, become gangrenous, and he amputated them with a carving knife. Miraculously Barter rallied but he was unable to leave his cabin for eleven weeks.[4]

The chronicler of this story reported that he watched fascinated as Captain Dick reached into a bureau drawer at Holladay's cottage and pulled out a box. Barter displayed its contents with a proud flourish as positive proof of his harrowing experience. "Them's my toes," he chortled.[5]

During his months of confinement he was able to build and rig a scale model of a steam frigate, seven feet in length, with every line, block and halyard in working order. He placed a clock mechanism in the hold to turn the propeller. Miniature boatswains, marines, sailors and officers made up the 225 hand-carved figures he painstakingly fashioned, and then painted in different color combinations. There were even two Negro cooks in the galley and Barter had armed the marines with Lilliputian cutlasses and pistols. To accomplish this time-consuming job he tied a cushion to each leg and "shoved around on his knees."

In addition to constructing the miniature man-o'-war that winter, Barter also built a four-ton "plunger." He rigged and launched the hull without help and christened her *Nancy*.[6]

Captain Dick had shown his callers around Holladay's and upon viewing the cascading waterfall they considered it to be "one of the lions of the place." Their host had another interpretation. To him it was "Old Gabriel's Voice." Barter next took the correspondent and his boatman to a cave in the side of the mountain where he had stored lumber to make his coffin, "with hinged doors to retire to, so his Marster shouldn't find him dead and smellin' bad in his own house."[7]

The scribe concluded his story of Richard Barter: "When we left, the old man hated to see us go as he didn't know when he would see anybody again and his last words to us were that he would probably answer Gabriel's call . . . shortly."

Before his premonition came true three years later, the old hermit was to battle many another storm on Tahoe. Barter's nearly fatal brush with eternity prompted him to change his plans and choose the island for his final resting place. First he built the "Island Cottage" on the south side near the water's edge. Then he excavated a tomb upon the island's summit. Over this solid rock sarcophagus he erected a miniature Gothic chapel, placing a small wooden cross on its sharply angled roof. Barter let it be known that he should be buried there if his body was ever found lashed to his sailboat, or washed up on the shore of Tahoe.

Captain Dick never tired of telling his infrequent visitors about the bay. In the snow and rock avalanche of 1868 two four-foot-through sugar pines had been driven like pilings into the bottom of

SHE WAS A THREE-MASTED MAN-OF-WAR—7 FEET LONG WITH 225 IN CREW

*Old shellback Barter, on the steps of his "elegant new cottage" at Holladay's
in Emerald Bay, with his dogs and hand-carved ship.
Summer of 1872, one year before his drowning at Rubicon Point.*

BURY ME HERE ON MY ROCKY ISLAND

Captain Richard Barter's Gothic chapel, near the summit of Emerald Isle, looking southeast toward the head of Emerald Bay, in July, 1872.

the bay some 200 yards offshore near the island. He always pointed these out to show what *could* have happened to him.

When questioned as to how he found the grizzlies in that remote spot, old mountain man Barter invariably replied, "I never lost none of them brutes, so I don't go out of my way to find any."

The entrance to the bay often came up for discussion and Barter made it clear the inlet was less than 200 yards across. He insisted that it took careful navigation to sail over the sand bar covered with only five to six feet of water when the lake was low. Most people left Holladay's amazed at that recluse living alone in the wilds of Tahoe.[8]

Captain Richard Barter's twelve years at Emerald Bay ended abruptly in 1873. On a gale-ridden night in mid-October, after an evening spent with convivial companions at Tom Rowland's Custom House (Al Tahoe), the 66-year-old deep water sailor was returning to the Bay when the *Nancy* was driven off course by another unexpected gale.[9] The waves broadsided his boat against the rocks at Rubicon Point, smashing the hull to kindling. Barter was drowned in over 1,400 feet of water and, ironically enough, Captain Dick's carefully laid plans for entombment on the island were thwarted, as his body was never recovered.[10]

The following day a search party found the splintered craft and one oar that had been snapped in half. The second sweep was not recovered until February 23, 1874, four months after the fatal accident. As this oar was undamaged, Lakers whispered that Barter had carried it down with him to his watery grave and released it after many months on the lake bottom.

A *Truckee Republican* newsman wrote with melancholy humor: ". . . Captain Richard Barter has drowned with the refreshing certainty that he can rise up bodily in his own identical petrified flesh when Gabriel's trumpet sounds announcing the Judgment Day." This would have pleased the old moss-back, as "Old Gabe" was his constant, if nebulous, companion.

The year before Barter's death a junketing reporter from the *Cincinnati Commercial* had unknow-ingly come closest to an epitaph for Barter when he reported Captain Dick's defense of the bottle and way of life: "Do ye think, comrade, that a man can spend his life upon this pond (Tahoe), among these snow steeples, and not have a spree now and then? Avast there with your jabber. There's too much ice water in the Sierrys for a man to be a temperance chap. Why 'Tahoe' is Injuyn for lager beer. It's put down that-a-way in the dictionary. I seed it myself. Who wants a dip across the lake in my Nancy? Trim a ship as ever rocked. Ho for Emerald Bay! Damn my eyes! Let's all drink . . . hurray!"

A legend still persists that on chilly autumn evenings, when a gray mist lies across the island, the ghost of Captain Richard Barter may vaguely be seen climbing slowly to the top of the rock in the hope that he will be able to pry open his sepulchre and find final rest in his granite tomb.

For a decade the antics of this eccentric salty character had cast their shadows across the natural magnificence of Emerald Bay.

Described as the "most beautiful inland harbor in the world," this land-locked oval of vari-colored water contains the only true island on Lake Tahoe. Sheer granite walls rise on the western and north-ern sides, towering upwards more than 2,600 feet to a sawtooth summit above the vivid greens and striking blues of the snow water. The southeast saddle of the bay is formed by a pine-covered lateral ridge tapering to the lake. At the head of the bay Eagle Falls cascades over the cliff, its tumbling waters fed from Eagle and Granite lakes, which lie high in the gorge toward Desolation Valley.[11] The stream drops down the rocks in a series of three successive waterfalls, two of which are over 75 feet high. Eagle is the only large cataract that leads directly into Tahoe and it winds through forested bottom-land before fanning out into the bay. High humor of the mid-1870's was offered by the *Placer County Directory* when its editor unbent and punned: "Eagle Falls is also known as 'The Lovers' because they fall out every day."

Near the head of Emerald Bay lies the island, a sparsely-timbered, brush-covered upthrust of granite rising some 150 feet above the water. During the last nine decades it has been known variously as Coquette, Fannette, Baranoff, Dead Man's, Hermit's, and Emerald Isle.

The key to its original name, Coquette, was discovered during the 1880's inside a weathered cham-pagne bottle hidden in a crevice on the island. A scribbled note, written during the summer of 1866, indicated that a party of young ladies and their escorts from Sacramento had disembarked from the sidewheel steamer *Governor Blaisdel* to picnic on the cone's rocky shoreline. One of the young damsels in the group was reported to have commented archly, "The island appears to be in the center of a bril-liant circle of admirers who, attracted by her beauty, still know she has a stony heart." The girl there-upon christened it Coquette. After failing in an attempt to find a way to the top, the men considered it properly named, "as surely the ways of this island, like those of an artful woman, are past finding out."[12]

The name Fannette is believed to be a corruption or misinterpretation of Coquette. Baranoff re-mains unexplained, and Dead Man's and Hermit's are names that may be traced directly to Captain Richard Barter.

In the year following Richard Barter's drowning, Captain "Jack Tar" Sweetser took over as care-taker at Holladay's. Like his predecessor he was the only all-year resident of the bay, with the excep-tion of a trapper named Armstrong who had built a cabin at the top of Eagle Falls on the old Indian trail leading to Rubicon Point.[13] Sweetser became a legendary part of Emerald Bay during 1877, with an assist from that famous "Jehu of the Sierra," Hank Monk. The sheltered oval, recorded as freezing only once previous to the winter of 1877-78, froze for a second time and Monk saw the chance to add new and equally fantastic laurels to his already colorful career.

A CROSS MARKED THE HERMIT'S UNOCCUPIED TOMB

For several decades Captain Dick's sepulchre remained on Emerald Isle as a prime tourist attraction. This view, taken in 1886 looking north, shows the chapel after it had fallen into disrepair.

He quietly spread the story around Carson that fishing had become a major winter industry at Tahoe. Hank insisted that miners, under the direction of Captain "Jack Tar," were driving shafts and winzes through the frozen bay, tunneling for the native cutthroat and silver trout with startling success commercially. Monk added more embroidery when he carefully explained that he had stock— not a working interest—in the claim, and he expected prompt and lucrative dividends. He estimated that nearly 100 tons of trout were imprisoned in the blue ice of Emerald and said "old Jack" and his associates planned to work straight through until spring, provided the cold weather held. The *Carson Appeal* bannered the yarn under the heading, "Trout Mining at Lake Bigler," declaring that the "finny tribe were fixed like bees in drops of amber."[14]

During the summer season of 1881 Emerald Bay became the favorite excursion spot on Tahoe for tourist and native Laker alike. Every weekend the steamers *Governor Stanford, Emerald I* and *Meteor* ferried crowds of vacationists to the bay from Campbell's Hot Springs, Tahoe City, McKinney's, Glenbrook and Tom Rowland's Station.[15]

Dr. and Mrs. Paul T. Kirby of Carson City noted the increased activity and bought 500 acres of land fronting on the northwest side of Emerald, including Holladay's "Coquette Island," Eagle Falls, the present site of Emerald Bay Resort, and other property running from the water's edge to the Indian trail.[16] By the spring of 1884, Kirby's Emerald Bay holding boasted a small hotel, several rough frame cottages, tents, and a steamer landing. For pleasure parties, Kirby offered a cruise on the lake in his sloop, the *Mollie Bawn*, and special trips on his fine racing yacht, the *Fleeter*, which also competed in lake contests. Mrs. Lucy N. Kirby started a vegetable garden to supply the resort's guests, and one lone cow, rafted across the lake from Glenbrook, constituted the flourishing dairy.[17]

Captain "Sailor Jack Tar" Sweetser, who had stayed on with the Kirbys, was again in the news. His black bear cub caught the fancy of tourists, who ran to the rail of the steamers as they docked to watch the round ball of fur perform. Sweetser was also commended for his "gentlemanly treatment" of all who stopped at what was still traditionally known as "The House of Holladay." Lucy Kirby assumed management of the resort after Dr. Kirby's death in 1889.

In the summer of 1890 a newsman discovered a "rustic hotel, dining room and cottages among alder, willow and poplar (sic) trees that formed a shaded grove." In addition he commented on the unusual opportunities for flirting with the school marms, a brand new piano, and—something that evidently struck him in the pit of the stomach—"lots of pie."[18]

Half a hundred guests were on hand, including "sketch artists and amateur photographers." Maiden Rock, near the resort's boathouse, and Parson's Rock (so named because it resembled a pulpit), were frequent subjects for the painter and camera student. Even a counterpart of the famous Buffalo lithia springs was discovered . . . "iron, salt, soda and lithia" and they were proudly pointed out as being "extremely medicinal."[19]

By 1895 all but 120 acres of the original Kirby holding had been sold to the William Henry Armstrong family, and the Armstrongs took a mortgage on the remaining land.[20] In the mid-1890's widower Russell Cowles Graves married Lucy Kirby, and they operated the resort until Mrs. Graves' death shortly after the turn of the century. Graves married again and he and his third wife ran Emerald Bay Camp for a decade.

Another seafaring Britisher had now taken the place of "Jack Tar" Sweetser. Also known as "Sailor Jack," he was actually Walter "Red" Comryn, late of Her Majesty's Navy. Sailor Jack invested in two acres of land on the west side of the bay, which included 300 feet of shoreline. His small, pie-shaped parcel lay just north of Parson's Rock. Here Comryn hauled out the schooner *Lily Van* and converted it into a cottage.[21]

Five seasons later "Sailor Jack" is said to have had an altercation with his wife, whereupon she immediately packed and flounced out of his life. In high dudgeon Comryn hurled his gold wedding ring into Eagle Lake, disposed of his property (including the *Lily Van*) to Comstock and Lawrence of Tallac for $600, and vowed he was through with "them females" forever. Dr. Hartland Law of San Francisco bought the two-acre strip some ten years later.[22]

The Russell Cowles Graves tenure at Emerald Bay Camp between 1907 and 1913 was highlighted by the efforts of their highstrung, bustling manager, Cuthbert. Cuthbert, a former dry goods clerk from Virginia City, operated the seasonal resort with frenzied inefficiency. It is said of Cuthbert that "fifteen guests would arrive and he was crowded." For a short period the place was known as "Cuthbert's Camp," and then the Graves, concerned about their own peace of mind and pocketbook, appointed a new manager, one Dunstall.[23]

In 1913, Tahoe's Rim of the Lake road circling Emerald Bay was completed. This had been one of the most difficult highway projects in the Sierra Nevada as the cut above the head of Emerald was made across the precipitous face of lower Maggie(s) Peaks. Besides being subject to rock avalanches the roadway had to be blasted from solid granite at many points. It took 50 cases of dynamite to break one granite boulder into four pieces, and regular steamer excursions were run to the bay so that tourists

---

"SWIFTEST SAILER IN THE SIERRA NEVADA"

Dr. Paul T. Kirby's broadbeamed FLETA (FLEETER) lying to on the northwest side of Emerald Isle in the summer of 1883. Dr. and Mrs. Kirby are in the after cockpit. In the background is the present site of Vikingsholm and (to the right, not shown) Kirby's Emerald Bay Resort which later became Armstrong's Milflores.

could watch, goggle-eyed, as thousands of tons of rock lifted into the air and thundered down the mountainside.[24] Nearly a quarter of a century later, on Christmas day, 1955, heavy rains loosened the precipitous slope of the mountain. A 1600-foot rock slide resulted that removed the highway, closing the road during the summer of 1956.

In 1914, 30 of the Kirbys' remaining acres were sold to Yosemite Valley's Nelson L. Salter. This included property at the site of the present Emerald Bay Resort. During the summer of 1916, Salter, Graves and Law completed the zigzag road leading down to the bay, and by 1918 Salter had expanded his resort into a full grown settlement. Spread around the grounds were two and three-room cottages, tents, a butcher shop, express depot and post office. A 34 by 64-foot dance pavilion had been built over the water alongside the steamer landing, and $12.00 a week was the going rate for two people.[25]

San Francisco's Potter School Camp for Boys was opened on the northwest point of the bay during the same year. Charles Bradley, school principal and educator from the Bay City, obtained the land from Walter Danforth Bliss and later the property reverted to the Bliss family.

At the head of Emerald Bay and bordering the lake road high on the mountain, a panoramic promontory was located and named Inspiration Point. Here in the early 1920's, Lakeview Lodge was built south of the dirt thoroughfare. It became known as a "gay spot" during the prohibition era with dusky waiters serving alcoholic concoctions of dubious origin but unquestionable effect. Totem poles and winged birds, props from the motion picture *Rose Marie*, now lure the tourist, and massive virgin pine and cedar ring the resort. Formerly run by Paul Craig, Lakeview was owned in 1957 by Robert E. Gruver.[26]

During the spring of 1947 Nelson Salter sold Emerald Bay Resort to Joseph Wheeler Watson and it was purchased by the State of California, Parks Division, in 1953. In order that his resort operation could continue, Watson leased it back from the State the following year.

The William Henry Armstrong family still owned 200 acres of Ben Holladay's original land sections at the head of the bay during the mid-1920's. This holding included the two and one-half acre Emerald Isle.

When the Armstrongs were approached, in the spring of 1928, by Mrs. Lora Josephine Moore Knight, former owner of Wychwood (Observatory Point), Lake Tahoe, Mrs. William H. Armstrong, her son, W. H. Armstrong, Jr., and daughter, Miss Jessie Armstrong, hesitated to sell.[27] They had held the horseshoe of land and island for over 40 years and the children had spent 27 summers at this beautiful location. Cottages, a clubhouse and wharf that still stood on the shore line, had long constituted a homelike mountain retreat for vacationists. Miss Armstrong described the spot as having a "safe harbor, beautiful white sand beach, wild flowers, pure, ice-cold water, matchless cliffs (later known as the 'back fence'), mammoth pine and cedar, waterfalls and an exquisite island." She named this Eden in the Sierra *Milflores*.[28]

Mrs. Knight is said to have finally offered $250,000 for the property, and, so the story goes, the Armstrongs then capitulated.[29] The way was now open for the heiress to proceed with the planning and construction of her imaginative *Vikingsholm*. Mrs. Knight decided to place the main castle in the center of a forest grove southwest of the Armstrong cottages (which she tore down) adjoining Eagle Creek's outlet. It would face northwest, with Emerald Isle lying directly ahead. Beyond the island

---

C. O. Valentine

BEYOND EAGLE FALLS LIES THE BAY

In the far distance past South Eagle Point and across Tahoe, rises Genoa Peak in Nevada's Carson Range of the Sierra Nevada. Eagle Creek (foreground) at the start of the falls, with Emerald Bay (center) photographed in early July, 1914, from the old road's log bridge.

the bay's inlet was clearly visible, and in the distance Lake Tahoe could be seen stretching in a 12-mile curve of aquamarine to Cave Rock on the Nevada shore.

This natural duplication of a Scandinavian fjord prompted Mrs. Knight to have architect Lennart Palme design a Viking's Castle.

Palme, in conjunction with contractor Matt Green, undertook the construction work, and ground was broken for the edifice during the last week of August, 1928. When completed in September of 1929, *Vikingsholm* was judged to be the finest example of Scandinavian architecture in North America.[30]

The mansion was built in the shape of a horseshoe with its northeast and southwest wings facing away from the bay. Architectural design, dating back some 1200 years, was faithfully reproduced in the massive stone structure. Hand-hewn timbers, intricate carvings, turrets and towers were carefully coordinated. The stone foundation and walls, formed of granite boulders, followed the exact construction pattern used in early Viking churches and palaces and many of the heavy exterior beam supports were joined without the use of nails or wooden pegs.[31]

Roof ridges saw-toothed above leaded glass windows at the southwest entrance to the flag-stoned courtyard, and sharply pointed "pike poles" (to ward off evil spirits) extended from the original split log roofs. Sod-covered lead sheathing topped the wings of the castle, upon which a carpet of grasses and native wild flowers grew, maintained a glistening green by sprinklers built into the roof. Nordic fireplaces, within the structure, terminated in brick "Crown chimneys," topped by weather vanes.

Mrs. Knight was one of the few true timber conservationists at Tahoe and before the castle was built she insisted that the foundation plan be laid out to skirt the giant trees. As a result the rock and mortar substructure right-angles around five and six foot thick pine and cedar that tower upwards of 180 feet into the air.

In order to authenticate the interior of *Vikingsholm*, Mrs. Knight, her architect and his wife (Mrs. Knight's niece) traveled to Norway, Finland and Sweden to purchase, or have copied, furniture hundreds of years old. This went into the Great Hall, South Tower, North Room, dining hall and bedrooms Most of the relatively few genuine antiques, which are difficult even for an expert to distinguish from the copies, may be found in the dining room. With the exception of the table, all of this furniture was purchased in Copenhagen. Mrs. Knight planned to obtain originals only, but a government ruling forbade the export of historically important antiques from the Scandinavian countries at the time. Many of the reproductions are exact even to the dates—1700's and 1800's—that correspond to the originals.

Rare hand-loomed Finnish weavings cover the living room walls. All are woven in harmonious pastel colors and the hand-hewn ceiling beams are painted to match. A story that still persists, is that Mrs. Knight had the South Tower built around a $30,000 Oriental rug, instead of having the rug woven to fit the enclosure. Be this fact or fiction, the heavy, closely-loomed treasure, fine as cashmere to the touch, is admittedly a museum piece.[32]

In the main entrance hall beside a page boy's complete suit of armor, stands the life-size, hand-carved wooden figure of a Finnish peasant girl, known as "Selma." When visitors step across the stone threshold, they are greeted by this startling multi-colored image that offers a circular clock for a face.

Craftsmen in Sacramento, California, were responsible for the detailed copies of heirlooms found in the living room. The work was so meticulously turned out that matched sets of the originals and

C. O. Valentine

HIGHLIGHTS AND SHADOW

Gnarled cedar and pine framing Emerald Bay, the Island and "Parson's Rock,"
(left of center), taken from a point high on Maggie's North Peak,
summer of 1913.

duplicates appear the same from the standpoint of measurement, coloration and aging of the wood.[33]

The third story of the castle consists of North Tower or "Tower Room." Massive columns frame this windowed sleeping porch. Here Mrs. Knight placed twin oak beds, exact duplications with the exception of being larger, of the Viking queen's bed found in the famous 1200-year-old Oslo Viking ship's "burial mound." Stylized horses heads set off the backboards. Architect Palme indicated that the original bed was only four feet six inches in length, venturing the thought that the Vikings must have slept in a sitting position so as to be on the alert against enemy attack.

Concessions to modern living (circa 1928) are the steam plant, which supplies heat to every room in the castle, and a stainless steel kitchen with adjoining butler's pantry. All hardware for the huge doors, leaded windows and drapery supports are handwrought. Attention to detail is also evidenced in the circle of small brass bells that formerly stood to the right of the front entrance door. The bells, purchased in Norway, revolved melodiously at a caller's touch.

Several luxurious guest houses are located throughout the grounds where hand-adzed beams and pastel blues, reds, and yellows, for interior color treatment, follow the pattern set in the castle itself. To the southwest of the main structure, Eagle Creek is backed up by a sand bar to form a quiet pool of water before flowing on into the bay. Upstream Mrs. Knight had her trout pond.

Nor did the island escape her attention. On its rocky summit she built a single-room stone "tea house" with a miniature fireplace and four small windows that overlook Emerald Bay. A temporary track is said to have been run up the southwestern side of the island to carry stone blocks to the top for use in building the structure, after they were barged over from the mainland.[34] The 16-foot square

A DESOLATE, FROZEN WASTE OF SNOW AND ICE

This mid-winter scene of Emerald Bay, taken in the 1930's when the secluded oval had frozen over and been blanketed by a heavy fall of snow, shows Mrs. Lora Knight's rock "tea house" on the island, Emerald Bay Camp, the open waters of Tahoe beyond the bay's inlet and a nor'easter sweeping in across the lake.

Eleanor Swanson

VIKINGSHOLM

Mrs. Lora Moore Knight's stone castle,
Vikingsholm, *the "finest example
of Scandinavian architecture in North America."
South Tower in foreground looking toward
Granite Peak.*

Jessie Armstrong

chalet lies slightly southwest and above the unoccupied and effaced tomb of Captain Richard Barter. A table and four wooden chairs constitute the spartan furnishings of the tea house. From the former site of Ben Holladay's Island Cottage and finger pier a series of winding rock steps lead up the south side of the island to the top.

During Mrs. Knight's occupancy of *Vikingsholm*, a whimsical and intriguing sight was occasionally seen. Accompanied by two of her 70-year-old female guests, Mrs. Knight would arrive at her pier. After carefully assisting the ladies into a rowboat, David, the uniformed butler, then seated himself at the oars. The dowagers, decked out in "chokers," light summer dresses and carrying parasols, reclined grandly in the stern while the stony-faced lackey applied himself vigorously to the sweeps, his dignity made ludicrous by the fact that he was lifted high above the water by the combined weight of his passengers.[35]

One season Mrs. Knight's privacy at her Emerald Bay retreat was repeatedly disturbed by an eccentric female tourist who wished to spend a few days on Emerald Isle. Finally Mrs. Knight gave her permission and graciously placed her chauffeur at the disposal of the excited woman. He loaded suitcases, canned goods and other paraphernalia aboard a skiff and rowed her to the island.

Upon landing and climbing to the summit, she was dismayed to find that the "castle of her dreams" was only a diminutive day shelter. Then the final blow fell. There were no rest room facilities! The distraught vacationist complained bitterly to the chauffeur, who resolved the crisis with gentlemanly reserve:

"Plumbing, madam?" he answered in an icy tone, "*that*, I am afraid, is up to you." In a matter of moments she and her belongings were back in the boat and headed for the mainland.[36]

Mrs. Knight channeled her substantial fortune into many worthwhile outlets, including the establishment of numerous scholarships without the donor's name being mentioned. She is also said to have co-sponsored the Charles Lindbergh "Spirit of St. Louis" transatlantic flight to Europe.

When Mrs. Lora Josephine Moore Knight died in 1945, it was reported that she had left $1,000 to each of the many servants at her St. Louis, Santa Barbara, and Lake Tahoe estates. This was considered by many to be little enough recompense for loyalty over the years, as some of her retainers had been in her employ for more than forty years. Then it was discovered that her bequest stipulated: "$1,000 for each *year* of service."

The girl from Galena, Illinois, who in later years literally built her "Castle in the Sky," had indeed displayed the benevolent manner even after death.[37]

CASCADE — FISH PRODUCER EXTRAORDINARY

This earliest known photograph of Cascade Lake, taken in 1886, shows Dr. Charles Brigham's boathouse (center) bordering "Fisherman's Cove" with Mount Tallac rising to the south. Native silvers and cutthroat were taken by the thousands each season in those days.

Chapter Nineteen

CASCADE LAKE

O N CASCADE's pebbled northeast beach, commercial fisherman Alonzo Zaletto put a shoulder to the stern of his small fishing skiff. As he glanced down the side of the craft he was startled to see a grisly object that resembled a human hand protruding from the fine washed gravel. After staring at it for a moment, he dropped to his knees for a closer look. Then the Italian began to dig carefully.

First he uncovered a blackened, withered arm, then a shoulder, and finally the body of an Indian woman. The corpse was dark mahogany in color, emaciated, and hideous in appearance. Further examination showed that the body had "turned to stone," and Zaletto found that the right breast and fingers of one hand were gone as though cut off cleanly by some sharp instrument.

All thought of fishing had now been erased from Zaletto's mind. He hurriedly wrapped the petrifaction in sail cloth and tied it securely with line from one of his old fishing nets. Half dragging, half carrying the surprisingly heavy load, he managed to move it back from the water. Then the Italian rounded up his burro, loaded the rock-like corpse onto an improvised litter and headed down the trail toward Tallac House.

A crowd had gathered by the time Zaletto reached the resort's stables. He proudly unwrapped his find and the group speculated on the weight of the body, whereupon Zaletto placed it on the hay scales. It was found to weigh more than 300 pounds.

In the group was a wealthy "patron of the arts" from San Francisco who immediately offered Zaletto $100 in gold for the fossilized female, explaining that he wished to present it to the Academy of Science in the Bay City. Alonzo, suddenly aware that his gruesome discovery was valuable, held out for $150 and received his price.

With the rambling assistance of an old Washoe Indian camped at the outlet of Taylor Creek, the petrified squaw's new owner learned its history. He was told that more than a century before the Pah-Utahs (Paiutes) and Washoes had met in pitched battle on the shores of Cascade Lake. It had been such a savage and bloodthirsty fight that even the squaws and children joined the hostilities. Fighting raged for days, with the normally peaceful Washoes emerging victorious. Following a tribal tradition, the dead were buried where they fell.

The wrinkled old patriarch was certain that this explained the fossilized squaw's presence in the gravel of Cascade.

After checking further with scientists and medical men it was determined that the human body could turn to stone if subjected to freezing water conditions.

Thus went the story of the "Mysterious Petrified Squaw of Cascade Lake" as chronicled in the *Truckee Republican* on September 19, 1880.

Harold A. Parker

REFLECTION

Early spring of 1909, looking southwest across the still surface of Cascade Lake toward White Cloud Falls and the cliffs leading up into Desolation Valley's primitive area. Maggie's South Peak (right) and Tallac Range (left).

GLACIAL TARN AND DISTANT "BIG BLUE"

Cascade as the lake appeared in the summer of 1914 from the southeast side. The slopes of Maggie's Peaks rise to the left. Beyond the pine tree (center) may be seen the old lake road.

Previous to 1873, Cascade Lake's mile long by one-half mile wide snow water basin was shown on the maps of the time simply as "Lake." In 1875 it became Silver Lake and a decade later this water-filled glacial amphitheater was given its present name—Cascade—after the cascading falls located at the lake's southwest end. This turbulence drops in 100-foot cataracts that reach higher toward the granite peaks of Tallac's range than Emerald Bay's Eagle Falls, and the stream is flanked by formidable cliffs that stairway into the high country.

Early settlers gave the name Snow or White Cloud to the falls because of their billowing brilliance which is apparent in early spring when the heavy runoff foams down the rocks into Cascade.

In the spring of 1882, Dr. Charles Brooks Brigham, internationally famous San Francisco surgeon, purchased a small acreage to the east of Cascade Lake.[1] Over the years he added to his holdings. A decade later Brigham's land encompassed Cascade, continued over the ridge to the southeast shore of Emerald Bay, then northeast to Eagle Point and south along Tahoe. Here it joined E. J. "Lucky" Baldwin's property in Tallac Meadows. On a bluff overlooking Tahoe, one-quarter of a mile west of the meadows, Dr. Brigham built a large one-story, four-bedroom summer home with steamer landing and circular inside pilings for mooring small craft. When he acquired Cascade Lake in the mid-1880's a stone cabin stood on the north end of the lake occupied by trapper-fisherman Jimmie Walker.[2] Near the original cabin Brigham built a shake-roofed boathouse and Tallac Hotel, which had been using the lake for its guests' fishing expeditions, continued the policy, even though the lake now belonged to Brigham.

From all indications Dr. Charles Brigham had a touch of the Spartan strain. His contention "that a jump into the waters of Cascade in late May was the most magnificent thing that could happen to

anybody in this world" was a literal ice-breaker. The good doctor did more than just prescribe—he followed his own advice, leaping into the freezing water and apparently liking it.

An untiring propagandist for swimming in the region, Brigham spent weeks one summer proving that Tahoe's and Cascade's waters averaged 10 degrees warmer than those of Monterey Bay on the California coast.

Like Emerald Bay and Tahoe, Cascade had been painted many times in the Bonanza period for Washoe nabobs. One of these Barons of the Comstock, newly elevated to dizzy monetary heights, and long on the gold eagles required to finance his silver mines, commissioned a Virginia City artist to paint Cascade in oils, paying the tidy sum of $2,000 for the finished canvas. This deep-rock miner later complained that it was "pooty" but missed showing the "distance and waterfall" that he was "damn sure presented itself to the eye." Further questioning of the brush and palette craftsman finally pried out the truth. The artist had only "visualized" Cascade Lake, going no farther than Clear Creek to gain his inspiration. His swiftly thought up excuse was that the "natural beauty of Cascade could never be captured on canvas anyway."

Cascade was recognized in the 1880's and 90's as a prime fishing location, rivaling Fallen Leaf and the Desolation Valley lakes. In the spring of 1892 Mr. and Mrs. M. J. Tillman from Sacramento took what then was considered slightly more than an average catch. On light rod and wet fly, during one afternoon of casting in the shallows of Cascade, they brought to net a total of 97 trout ranging up to two and one-half pounds each. Cutthroat were plentiful and Mrs. Melville Lawrence from Tallac boated a scarlet-gilled beauty weighing more than 20 pounds. The Brigham's summer home was frequently visited in the 1890's and 1900's by celebrities of the time. The noted chanteuse, Sybil Sanderson, was a guest who swung from a cross beam in the Brigham house and exercised her arms and coloratura voice, insisting that the "acoustics were better from that particular location."[3]

John Muir, the famous California naturalist, roamed the shores of Cascade with Dr. Brigham, Mark Twain enjoyed the medical man's hospitality, and the Governor of Nevada paid his respects and brought a brass band along to serenade the respected doctor.[4]

In 1896-97, the property to the northwest of the Brigham home was set aside for Dr. Brigham's brother-in-law, Harry Babcock. Here Babcock built his own house. This *bon vivant* of Tahoe is remembered by early lake residents as an exacting type of person who, every week during the summer season, ordered half a case of fresh eggs delivered at his pier by the steamer *Tahoe*. Upon their arrival he would carefully check each egg to see that none were broken, while the 169-foot vessel waited. When satisfied as to their condition he waved the vessel on. However, Babcock was always generous to the *Tahoe's* crew at the end of each season and a check awaited all members, from Captain Ernest Pomin to deckhands.[5] Babcock was also known for his "stable" of fast automobiles, ranging from one of the first Autocars through Packard tourings. He also owned and piloted the sleek black marine speedster *Pirate* on the waters of the lake.[6]

Dr. Brigham, like another Tahoe pioneer, Harry O. Comstock, bestowed the names of his daughters on two of the smaller lakes in the region. Comstock had named Gladys (Azure) and Velma lakes for his girls and Brigham gave the name Alice to a small tarn on the southwest end of Cascade. Katrine, for Katherine Brigham Ebright, was the name given to what is now Snow Lake.

Dr. Brigham came in for his share of ingratitude while splinting the broken arm of a Tallac fish-

C. O. Valentine

THE BILLOWING BRILLIANCE OF WHITE CLOUD FALLS
Cascade's feeder stream in the late spring of 1914, with the camera facing southwest.

erman. Lacking an office at the lake, Brigham had laid the protesting fisherman out on a table in his boathouse, administered an anesthetic and set the arm. As the victim emerged from the ether he sat up groggily and bit the doctor savagely in the hand, giving him an incipient case of lockjaw that lasted for several months thereafter. Such was Brigham's reward for answering an emergency courtesy call.[8]

At the time of Dr. Brigham's death in September, 1904, he owned 1,300 acres surrounding Cascade Lake. Today his youngest daughter Katherine Brigham Ebright and her sons Charles and Harold control some 790 acres, the balance of the original holdings having passed to the California State Park system.[9]

A fledgling student at Stanford University acted as caretaker for the Brighams during the summer of 1926. This tall, husky young man was an aspiring author who had come to the Ebrights from Fallen Leaf Lake. It is said that when a giant pine was uprooted by the wind and crashed through the Brigham home, carrying away two other trees and leveling the house in the process, the budding novelist, who was seated nearby and absorbed in a book, barely looked up. Thus John Steinbeck laid the groundwork for his earthy Americana to follow, and it is perhaps a fortunate thing for his reading public that Steinbeck buried himself in literature and ignored anything but a casual attempt at caretaking.[10] However, Steinbeck was impressed by a young Indian buck's diagnosis of an old Washoe tribesman's reported death. Upon hearing of the man's passing, he inspected the corpse where it lay on willow bark in Tallac Meadows, surrounded by mourning squaws. After this first-hand check-up, the Indian hotfooted it back to Steinbeck and solemnly reported that it was all a mistake. "Old buck not dead," was his frowning comment, "his skin too damn pliable."

In recent years Cascade's rugged setting, crystal water and backdrop of mountain peaks has often been the scene for some of Hollywood's more memorable wilderness pictures.

The film *Lightnin'*, starring Will Rogers, was taken here in the early 1930's and the stone fireplace of the cabin used in the moving picture version still stands on Cascade's western shore. *Rose Marie* followed in 1935, and in 1949 Dreiser's *American Tragedy*, which appeared under the title *A Place in the Sun*, proved conclusively that Cascade Lake's beauty could only be captured by the camera's eye, not the painter's brush.[11]

Chapter Twenty

FALLEN LEAF LAKE

A WASHOE INDIAN legend links the formation of Fallen Leaf with the plight of an Indian brave fleeing for his life from the Evil One. According to the story, the Good Spirit had pressed a leafy branch into the warrior's hands, telling him to drop part of it if he was pursued by the Demon. The branch, counseled the Good Spirit, contained magical powers and water would spring up wherever it was dropped.

The Indian started out and, upon reaching the south side of the Great Depression, was panic-stricken to see the Evil One in pursuit. He tried to pluck a leaf, but in his terror snapped off most of the branch instead. To his relief waters began to rise and almost immediately Tahoe (Big Water) lay between him and his pursuer.

Hurrying on up the canyon toward the spot where Fallen Leaf Lake now lies, the brave again glanced over his shoulder. The Fury had circled the newly-formed lake and was rapidly gaining on the young warrior. Fear gripped him anew. In his hand there remained one small twig with only four leaves. He plucked one leaf and threw it from him. With agonizing slowness it fell to the ground. Again water began to rise and "Doolaga" (Fallen Leaf) sprang into being.

With dread still clutching at his heart, he turned and raced on up the ravine, dropping the remaining leaves whenever the Evil Spirit threatened to overtake him. In his path Lily, Grass and Heather lakes rose up to protect him. The warrior crossed the wastes of Desolation Valley and, leaving the high peaks of the Sierra Nevada, found safety in the Great Valley (Sacramento) below.[1]

This fanciful account of Fallen Leaf Lake's formation was accepted for centuries by the native Washoe Indians as the true explanation of its origin.

The lake itself is believed to have been named for the Delaware chief, Falling Leaf, who guided Colonel Jack "Cock-Eye" Johnson during his Tahoe-Sierra explorations in the late 1840's and early 1850's.[2] Johnson and his trail-blazing party viewed the lake's brilliance for the first time from a point northwest of what is now Echo Summit.

Recognized as the largest of the region's Alpine lakes, Fallen Leaf, as it later became known, is located one and one-half miles from the southern shoreline of Tahoe. Shaped more like the bottom of a human foot than a leaf, it lies at an elevation of 6321 feet, only 90 feet above Lake Tahoe itself. Fallen Leaf Lake is three miles in length and averages less than a mile in width. The greatest measured depth is 418 feet.[3] To the west the slopes of Mount Tallac rise above this secluded glacial oval, and on the south, Angora Peak sweeps into the sky. Lake Valley lies to the east over a great lateral moraine, which in the early 1860's was surveyed as a possible route for the transcontinental railroad.

Before the turn of the century Fallen Leaf furnished some of the finest fishing to be found in the High Sierra. In July of 1880 the editor of the *Gold Hill News* made the trip to the lake from Tallac

Hotel. Later he reported, "I found trout by the hundreds lying at Fallen Leaf's only outlet, Taylor Creek. The big fish appeared to elbow the little fry aside in their rush for the bait, and with my two-bit rod and tackle I caught more silvers than I can safely tell my readers about." He added a husbandly afterthought: "Many more fish could have been brought to net if my wife hadn't talked so much."

Above the western shore of Fallen Leaf lies Floating Island Lake. Covering approximately five acres, this circular body of water at one time contained a 20-foot floating island that could be poled from place to place. Carpeted with grass and shrubs, it proved an excellent means of moving stealthily to the right fishing spots.[4]

When Tallac House was in its heyday, in the late 1890's, boatmen and skiffs were available on Fallen Leaf, and "Green Bay" was considered the prime fishing location, with a "trout a minute" practically guaranteed. "Lucky" Baldwin, of Tallac, owned most of the land sections encompassing the tarn and, although he insisted that the stands of pine on his hotel property never be touched by a logger's ax, he did not hesitate to cut saw logs from the mountain slopes surrounding Fallen Leaf Lake and run the timber through his steam-powered sawmill. A log chute, one of the longest and steepest in the Tahoe region, fed his staging yards.[5]

In the year 1896 William Whitman Price, professor at Stanford University and naturalist who had visited Fallen Leaf regularly during the summer seasons to study birds and fauna for the Smithsonian and similar institutions, opened a boys' summer camp in the canyon below Glen Alpine. This was Camp Agassiz, named for geologist Louis Agassiz, "Father of the Ice Age Concept."[6]

By 1905 an enthusiastic gathering of fathers, mothers, uncles and aunts had joined the boys and "Pop" Price, as he was familiarly known, decided to move down to the shores of Fallen Leaf and open a resort campground.

He took title to government land on the southwest end of the lake and transferred his camp to the new location. The resort, however, was run as a separate operation from the boys' camp. Price now had a growing clientele that equaled, and often exceeded, that of Glen Alpine.

In 1911 eleven faculty members from Stanford University acquired a quarter section of government land on a rise of ground above Price's resort. Here they laid out a subdivision and constructed summer cottages. Today this settlement is known as Stanford Camp tract, or Stanford Hill.[7]

By June of 1913 another resort campground run by an outdoorsman named Flugge, and bearing the high-sounding name Cathedral Park, had been started.[8] W. W. Price's retreat also expanded. He now offered a two-story lodge, dining hall, a boathouse and additional cabins and tents. Three years later the boys' camp was discontinued because of World War I, and in 1918 Price purchased additional land from the "Lucky" Baldwin estate and added housekeeping cabins. Mrs. Price took over the management in the early 1920's, after her husband's death, and combined the Charles A. Swisler and Blanchard properties with her Fallen Leaf Lodge operation.[9]

An old stagecoach and four had now been replaced by a hybrid five-seated gasoline burner aptly named the "Stan-ford." It carried a Ford engine in a Stanley Steamer body with Ruckstell 2-speed rear axle and jounced a load of passengers, mail and express daily from Tallac to the Lodge.[10]

The daughters of Mr. and Mrs. W. W. Price, Frances Park Street and Harriet Price Craven, now own and operate the Lodge. A one-way paved road has replaced the dusty wagon and stage thorough-

---

C. O. Valentine

FALLEN LEAF'S "ROCKY ROAD TO DUBLIN"

*Heading toward Fallen Leaf Lodge on the one-way thoroughfare
in late June, 1913, on what was little more than an improved trail.*

fare but it still follows the same winding course along the southeastern shore of the lake. In keeping with established tradition, the rustic Lodge is operated in a comfortable, family-style manner appropriate to the seclusion and natural beauty of its surroundings.

Author's collection

A FEATHERY PLUME EXPLODES INTO THE SIERRA SKY

Looking southeast in 1897 up timber stripped Tahoe Mountain as a saw log strikes Sawmill Flat's terminal pond at express train speed.

FORMED BY A FLUTTERING FALLING LEAF

Fallen Leaf Lake, known to the native Washoe Indians as "Doolaga," served as a high-country angler's paradise for "Lucky" Baldwin's Tallac House guests during the 1880's and '90's. This view, taken in the summer of 1910, looks northeast.

Author's collection

Chapter Twenty-one

GLEN ALPINE SPRINGS

Clinging red dust swirled from the iron-rimmed wheels of a creaking "sail top" and trailing supply wagon as the little caravan plodded through scrub oak on its slow, hot climb over the Sierra Nevada foothills toward the far blue mist of mountains ahead.

Reining the double span of mules from the high box was Nathan Gilmore, a young rancher from Ohio who had been caught up in the gold rush of 1849 and come west on the Central Overland Trail to California.[1] Settling in Mud Springs, below Hangtown, he acquired grazing land, married, and entered the livestock business.[2] Now, fourteen years later on a bright May morning in 1863, he and his group were starting on their annual cattle drive to summer pasturage in the high country south of Lake Tahoe.

Behind the vehicles his tightly-bunched herd of nearly 100 animals surged along the narrow road, urged on by two Mexican vaqueros sitting saddle on wiry cow ponies.

At Junction they joined the heterogeneous cavalcade of wayfarers, teamsters, and pack trains crowding the great Johnson Pass turnpike. Half the teams in California seemed to be moving to and from Washoe in a solid double line across the Snowy Range barrier. As 18-mule-span freighters lumbered through the Mud Springs contingent, Gilmore's cowhands were forced time and again to turn and close their frightened, bellowing animals. By late afternoon the deep-guttered streets of Placerville were behind, and men and animals fought their way against the living torrent higher toward the pungent-scented forest of cedar and resinous pine.

The following day Gilmore and his company reached the south fork of the American River that tumbled and boiled over rocks through a narrow ravine. Spurring their horses, the Mexicans urged the cattle through swift and dangerous cataracts. Some of the animals stampeded and slipped over the cliffs to the stream below, but the small band continued their tedious climb without pause, resting only at nightfall. On the sixth day they entered the gateway to the high country: Strawberry Station. Above lay Nevett's Summit, nearly a mile and a half above sea level,[3] and the herd stumbled on through a wasteland of boulders and polished rock guarded by great sentinel domes of granite. At Slippery Ford, Gilmore double-teamed his wagons, inching them over the wet, moss-covered rocks. Once again his party toiled upward. At sunset they arrived at the summit.

In the distance lay Tahoe, a vast inland sea stretching to the northern wall of the Sierra Nevada, its wind-rippled surface reflecting the brilliance of a western sky. To the east granite walls dropped to upper Lake Valley, shadowed now in the mountain twilight. Slowly the party started down the rocky defile.

At the base of the pass a flickering oil lamp hung from the drop-gate of Osgood's Toll House.[4] Out of the gathering dusk came the tollkeeper's request: "Five cents a head for the animals, if you please, and 'six bits' will go for the rest." They counted 74 head. More than a fourth of their herd lay dead on the road or drowned in the American River.

Gilmore pastured his stock on "Yank's" meadowland that night and set off again at sunup.[5] Even at that early hour, the highroad was crowded, and it took most of the forenoon for the party to reach the northwest turnoff that would take them over the ridge to Fallen Leaf Lake. Although dust-grimed and bone tired from their week of traveling, they moved faster now, heartened by what lay ahead— meadowland, snow-water streams and a chance to rest. For the next few days they camped on the south shore of Fallen Leaf, their cattle grazing in the bunch grass that bordered the lake.

One morning when Gilmore awoke, he found that his animals had strayed. Their tracks pointed west to unexplored country. He roused his vaqueros. They saddled up and spurred out of camp in hot pursuit. At the entrance to a canyon, Gilmore stopped, amazed. He had read of Switzerland's glacial glens, but never imagined such beauty as now lay before him. Sculptured walls of granite rose for thousands of feet above a rushing stream where cataracts roiled across the polished rock and pum- ice stone at the canyon's base. Nearly blocking the game trail were banks of elephant fronds. Huge tiger lilies flamed up, tier upon tier, in a profusion of greens and orange reds. Tamarack and sugar pine soared cleanly to the sky, unmarred by knots or limbs for more than 70 feet, in sharp contrast to the nearby gnarled and twisted cedars. Some of the trees were spiraled by lightning and burned by fire but continued to send out their branches above the sunlit carpet of bunch grass, maiden hair and lilies of the valley.

Nearly a mile up the canyon Gilmore and his men came upon an oval pond, its placid surface a

FORTY-NINER, FAMILY AND FRIENDS AT GLEN ALPINE

El Dorado Pioneer, Nathan Gilmore (center of group), in the summer of 1893 at the Springs that he discovered.

Dixwell Pierce

garden of water lilies. Another mile and some 300 feet higher they broke out into a small Alpine meadow, where Gilmore found his cattle grazing in waist-high wild grass. To his surprise, he saw that they had been drinking at a mineral spring bubbling from the rocks. Convinced by his first taste that the water was both fresh and palatable, Nathan Gilmore and his drivers returned to the shores of Fallen Leaf to move his family and their camp up canyon to the springs. His wife, Amanda Gray Gilmore, recalling a favorite passage in Sir Walter Scott's *Lady of the Lake,* named their discovery Glen Alpine Springs.[6]

Over the ensuing years Gilmore built a wagon road to the Springs, constructed a log cabin nearby and set up tents. The naturally carbonated mineral water contained iron and flowed at the rate of 200 gallons an hour. It was likened to "Congress water" and in the late 1870's he decided to bottle it commercially. By the year 1880 Glen Alpine Tonic Water had become famous throughout California and Nevada, being advertised as the "finest soda water found in the mountains of the Pacific Coast."[7] First a summer cattle pasturage and later a sheep range, Gilmore's mineral springs soon developed into a popular High Sierra resort.

Among the famous guests at the mountain retreat during its early development was the talented Madame Helena Modjeska, who had been playing to capacity audiences at Piper's Opera House in Virginia City. So enthusiastic was the actress over the beauty of Glen Alpine that the Gilmores named, in her honor, a nearby waterfall in the stream cascading down the canyon to Fallen Leaf Lake.[8]

Testifying to Glen Alpine's popularity is a reporter's description of his trip to the Springs in September of 1880: "With Hank Monk at the 'ribbons' we pulled up the wagon road from Tallac House in a carriage and two, passing Fallen Leaf on our right. A little over a mile further up the awe-inspiring canyon, we came to Lily Lake lying in a round cradle of granite, its aquamarine and emerald green glistening in the sunlight. The gorge was wet and heavy with Alpine flowers growing on either side of our steep route. Skirting Modjeska Falls we bumped to the end of the road where we found Glen Alpine Springs, sparkling like champagne. Soda water gushed, 'pure as a maiden's tear,' from the rocks, a source of amazement to all in the party. Everything would have been magnificent if it had not been for the density of the mosquitoes, which had bills one and one-half inches long, and unlimited persistence."[9]

The correspondent visited "Council Rock," where guests at the Springs held nightly campfire gatherings and before his party returned to Tallac they "drank once again of the curative liquid."[10]

In 1888 Nathan Gilmore's daughter, Susan, was married to George W. Pierce beneath the towering pines at Glen Alpine, where she later spent many summers managing the thriving resort business. Thirty-eight years after this marriage, Nathan Gilmore's grandson, Dixwell Pierce, was married in the same mountain region. He and his bride, Katherine Bradley, repeated their vows in the first wedding ceremony to be solemnized in the Chapel of St. Francis of the Mountains at Fallen Leaf, just two miles down Glen Alpine Canyon and, on September 2, 1949, Susan Pierce was married in the same chapel to Charles Stewart. The date was her parents' twenty-third wedding anniversary and it was sixty-one years after her grandparents' wedding at nearby Glen Alpine.[11]

In the early 1900's the illustrious California poet, Edwin Markham, described the region in words of nostalgic praise:

"There are many leafy roads and trails that run from Lake Tahoe into the mountains. The most traveled road is the one to the Glen Alpine region, seven miles south from the foot of Mount Tallac. Let us be up and away to it in the early dawn, so as to pause on the way at Fallen Leaf Lake before the magic crystal of its morning beauty is broken. On a high level lies Lily Lake, where fishermen, whose oars are 'lacquered in diamond,' are paddling among great golden lily bowls, upheld on broad salvers, green and garnet. Here are lilies with a tropic glory walled in by cold, gray granite bowlders.

Now another upward flight and we are at Glen Alpine, in the midst of the tall lilies and columbines of a mountain meadow. From this center, after sleeping under the stars, the travelers radiate into the higher mountains and lakes."[12]

Aided by his friend, I. B. "Bart" Richardson, who was also closely associated with Echo Lake and the south Tahoe region, Gilmore blazed trails to the many Alpine lakes dotting the upper canyon, the granite wilderness of Desolation Valley and the slopes of Mount Tallac. In the summer of 1887 he planted the first game fish—20 black bass—in a lake 8,000 feet above sea level, on the southwestern side of Tallac, that today—in honor of its discoverer—bears the name Gilmore.

Nor is this the only natural monument to the pioneering of Gilmore, Richardson and their families. Above Susie Lake, a memorial to the oldest daughter of Nathan and Amanda Gilmore, rises the sheer red wall of Mount Richardson.[13] Angora Peak and Lakes received their names from the herds of Angora goats that Gilmore pastured in the region.

On the side of the little Chapel of St. Francis of the Mountains, where two generations of the Gilmore family have exchanged their marriage vows, there is today a bronze plaque with this inscription:

"This tablet is in memory of Nathan Gilmore and I. B. Richardson, pioneers of the early Sixties, discoverers of Glen Alpine Springs, developers of the Fallen Leaf section. They were the first to stock the lakes in the region above Fallen Leaf."[14]

Another tangible reminder of the early days at Glen Alpine is the eleven-passenger tally-ho stage that was hauled up the steep Glen Alpine grade by four horses in the 1890's and 1900's. It has been purchased from Mrs. Mary Garcia, present owner of Glen Alpine, by Marjorie Johnson Springmeyer of Bijou. Today it is painted a bright maroon and yellow with cream-colored wheels. Padded horsehair upholsters the four seats, each of which accommodates three persons sitting abreast. Two privileged passengers may sit on the front seat with the "whip."[15]

The Gilmore family is gone from Glen Alpine Springs, but still untouched are the pines, firs and cedars, the gnarled junipers and quaking aspens. Now, as when Nathan Gilmore hunted his roving cattle, carpets of mountain flowers cover the meadows and mineral water gushes from the rocks "pure as a maiden's tear."

C. O. Valentine

**WHERE THE
SIERRA BRUSH THE SKY**
*View of Fallen Leaf Lake (below right)
and the great expanse of Tahoe, in the
far distance, from the vicinity of
Glen Alpine Springs
June 21, 1911.*

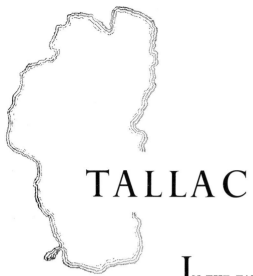

Chapter Twenty-two

TALLAC

★ IN THE FALL of 1873, Ephraim "Yank" Clement moved from his famous Yank's Station on the "Bonanza Road to Washoe" in Lake Valley, eight miles north to the shores of Lake Tahoe. He settled on beach and timberland property, homesteaded over a decade before, between Matthew C. Gardner's and Taylor Creek's outlet.[1]

Two seasons later it was reported that "Yank" had built and was operating a three-story hostelry. Cabin and tent accommodations were available along with a general merchandise store, horse livery, several barns, a saloon, and the sensation of the day, a dance floor mounted on springs. Not only did the undulating floor give the guests a feeling that they were floating on air; it made them dance "whether they knew how or not."[2]

The Fourth of July celebration that year at "Yank's" picnic grounds on the lakeshore was given extensive advance publicity in the Carson, Virginia, and Truckee papers. More than 300 holiday-mad excursionists attended, and the "oratory and brass-banding was handled on a scale of Independence Day splendor that should have caused the British Lion to shrivel up like a scorched boot and hide its diminished head."[3]

"Yank," described as tremendous and fierce to behold, was everywhere at once, supervising the allotment of hotel rooms and cabins, the serving of meals, dispensing of refreshments and chartering of boats with an unbiased friendliness and warmth. The spring-mounted dance floor creaked and swayed to the stomping of Lakers, Gold Hill nabobs and Washoe coquettes.

Down at the wharf the steamers *Governor Stanford*, *Emerald I* and *Truckee* shuttled between Glenbrook, the Hot Springs and Tahoe City, loaded to the waterline with frenzied and gay celebrationists. Overcrowding of the vessels was ingeniously avoided by towing sailing sloops, barges and rowboats in the wake of the wood-burners. Even Henry Burke's uncompleted 100-foot *Floating Palace*, jammed with more than 125 passengers, was hauled down the lake from the Truckee outlet dam to the accompaniment of popping champagne corks and unconfined revelry.[4]

A magnificent display of fireworks, personally touched off by "Yank," climaxed the day's festivities, and it was difficult for those on hand to realize they were actually celebrating on the 5th of July. The Fourth had fallen on a Sunday that year.

Only one serious casualty was reported among the hundreds of people attending. This resulted when a "fiend" from Silver City managed a little wholesale carving on a total stranger aboard the *Floating Palace*. The victim's only explanation for the attack was that his assailant had consumed the better part of a demijohn of "forty rod mountain red-eye." When his aggressor sobered up, he sheepishly admitted he had mistaken the object of his knife for a footpad who robbed him some weeks before in Carson. As the victim went to work two days later, the papers immediately lost interest in the affair.

"Yank" did a land-office business and even his fishing guides, headed by Portuguese boatman Martin Silvey, turned in the best catches of the season. The more sober patrons were rowed to the trouting grounds off Eagle Point and returned with boatloads of silversides. Repercussions from this great celebration rocked the Sierra for weeks, and those of the participants who could recall the least, were the ones who insisted they had had the best time.[5]

"Yank" was proud of the fact he charged "city prices" at his hotel for carriages, riding horses and boats. Board and lodging at the establishment came to $20 a week per person, which was high for the 1870's yet comparable to the rates posted by the acknowledged show places of Tahoe: Glenbrook House and Tahoe City's Grand Central.

A tall, shrewd-eyed stranger registered at "Yank's" in the summer of 1879 and, although no questions were asked, the newcomer was easily recognized as a personage. The cut of his broadcloth, the watch chain of gold nuggets that hung from a brocaded vest pocket, and his expensive boots bespoke importance. He marveled at the unspoiled timber stands surrounding the hotel, tramped the extensive beach and gazed out across the vast blue expanse of Tahoe. Then he left for the "Bay City." But on November 14, 1880, he was back. Elias Jackson "Lucky" Baldwin, Comstock Lode stock plunger, California real estate promoter and glamorous libertine, had decided to buy the hotel and land sections.[6] But first, "Yank" had to be convinced.

Finally, after some fast horse trading, at which Baldwin was an expert, "Yank" agreed to sell. Before he was through, Baldwin owned some 2,000 acres, one mile of which bordered on the lake. The balance, virgin timberland, stretched south to the shores of Fallen Leaf.

"My land acquisition," Baldwin announced, "will save this vast forest from the beauty-destroying ax of the woodsman so that the magnificent pines and cedars may be admired by generations to come."[7] His spoken word had substance, for today one of the last large stands of virgin timber bordering Tahoe may be seen on the former Baldwin tract.

"Yank's" now became Baldwin's Tallac House (Hotel Tallac), so named for the 9785-foot cross-

SPLENDIFEROUS—WAS YANK'S WORD FOR IT

Ephraim "Yank" Clement's 40-room "double record" after its completion in the late spring of 1875. Photograph was taken from a point near the lakeshore looking southwest.

BOOTJACKS WERE THROWN FROM THE SECOND STORY WINDOWS

In the summer of 1881 Yank's Hotel became "Lucky" Baldwin's Hotel Tallac. The hostelry was now on its way toward becoming a "genteel and tony resort."

BALDWIN'S TALLAC HOUSE NOW SPORTED A STEEPLE

By 1886, Tallac House (Hotel) had a pretentious steeple spire, gleaming white cottages ringed the establishment, Kenyon tents blossomed on the grounds and Tallac had become the place to go. Photograph taken from the new pier with Mount Tallac in the background.

Baldwin's Tallac House

LAKE TAHOE

* * July 4th, 1889 * *

M. Lawrence,
Proprietor.

SCHMIDT LABEL & LITH. CO., S. F.

Menu

Potage
Chicken Gumbo   Consommé

Releve
Chicken Salad   New Tomatoes

Relishes
Chow Chow   Queen Olives   Worcestershire Sauce   Mixed Pickles

Poisson
Baked Lake Tahoe Trout   Au Croquette, Pomme de Terre

Boiled
Leg of Spring Lamb, oyster sauce   Westphalia Ham, champagne sauce
Beef Tongue, sauce piquante

Entrees
Blanket of Sweet Breads, with mushrooms
Lamb Chops au petits pois   Stewed Terrapin à la Maryland
Banana Fritters, rum sauce

Roast
Prime Ribs of Nevada Beef   Stuffed Chicken à l'Anglaise
Spring Lamb, mint sauce   Young Suckling Pig, apple sauce

Cold Dishes
Dupée's Sugar-cured Ham   Pressed Corned Beef

Vegetables
Green Corn   Butter Beans   Asparagus, Italian sauce
Baked and Mashed Potatoes

Pudding
English Plum, Baldwin's brandy sauce

Pastry
Cocoanut and Apple Pie

Dessert
Assorted Cake   Nuts   Layer Raisins   Fruit
Banana Ice Cream   Vanilla Ice Cream
Eastern Cream Cheese   Tea and Coffee
Bonbons

Hattie Belle Almstaden

"A CUISINE EQUAL TO ANY AND EXCELLED BY NONE"

Eight-course spreads tickled the gourmet's palate and bulged both the fancy weskit and whalebone stay.

of-snow mountain to the southwest. During the 1881 season the Sharp Brothers, formerly proprietors of Ormsby House, Carson City, ran Tallac for Baldwin. The following summer Captain Gordon Southern of San Francisco managed the resort.

An authority of the times, listing the health and pleasure resorts of the Pacific Coast, described the hostelry as a "handsome white hotel building and cottages amid a splendid grove of pine, tamarack and poplars (sic). E. J. Baldwin has an extensive and complete improvement here—fine Hotel Tallac and cottages affording first class accommodations for 150 guests. Captain Gorgon (sic), the popular manager, and a throng of happy people met us at the landing."[8]

In the fall of 1882, George Lord Mortimer Comstock and Melville Lawrence arranged a ten-year lease with "Lucky" Baldwin, and the mutually beneficial arrangement continued for more than three decades.[9]

The *San Francisco Alta* reported on Hotel Tallac during July of the same year: "Tallac is rustic and comfortable as well as commodious, with a white sand beach running one-half mile west, yet the only signs of civilization are the hotel and wharf, so carefully have the natural beauties of the grounds been preserved." Over 100 noisy vacationists were now stopping at the hostelry or camping on the grounds. No charge was made for the bedroll and tent enthusiasts, except in the case of those who had horses to pasture.

Everybody was bartering something—lake trout for a bottle of "spirits" being one popular medium of exchange. Stealing wood from "Yank's" fence after dark seems to have been one of the chief diversions, although firewood in abundance was available for the gathering a few steps from the campground.[10] The evening dances turned into old fashioned hoedowns, alternated with loud and boisterous singing by the campers, who linked arms and nightly marched to the hotel on the hour. Annoyed guests

JOLLY JOKER BALDWIN AND TAHOE SCENES

Playing cards promoted the natural and man-made wonders of Lake Tahoe in 1900.

at the establishment retaliated by "hurling curses and throwing bootjacks from the second-story windows at the milling crowd below."[11]

In 1883, Lawrence and Comstock decided to improve both the resort and the caliber of their clientele. On the 40 acres immediately surrounding Hotel Tallac they built bridle paths and graveled roads. Promenade walks were laid out through the shady willow groves and beneath the pines. The wharf was rebuilt, and a pretentious steeple spire and outside veranda added to the hotel. Rates went up $2 a week, and guests were now given a second glance before being invited to register. The resort was indeed looking up. Another writer of the times visited Tallac House and wore out his quill pen describing the "towering firs, pines, mountain cedars, grassy sward, tamaracks and aspens." This time the beach was found to be "pebbly, and sloping gently from 'Tellec' (sic) Point."[12]

A popular outing was to take a sailboat from the wharf and tack along the shore to Cascade Canyon, where dandified vacationers scrambled ashore and hiked to Cascade Lake to view magnificent White Cloud Falls.[13]

Baldwin had built an improved trail to Cascade in 1881, connecting with the road turnoff south to Fallen Leaf and Glen Alpine Springs. Now he started a real estate development on his property in the vicinity of Taylor Creek's inlet into Tahoe. Building on the lots was restricted to private cottages, nothing commercial being permitted. Where the creek's waters fanned out west of Tallac Point, a large protected, shallow pool furnished an ideal setting for "swimming baths." Here bathhouses were constructed and it became fashionable for the more intrepid guests at Tallac House to shroud themselves in "night shirt" bathing suits and execute the nose-in-the-air dog-paddle.

The resort pirated, then garbled, Mark Twain's famous observation written some 25 years earlier: "To obtain the air the angels breathe, you must go to Tahoe." It was used with telling effect for decades in their brochure advertising.[14]

The hotel was particularly proud of its fishing boats, fishing guides, and the "limitless" trout in the lake. In those easy-money, bonanza days it was not uncommon for a competent guide to receive a gold eagle for his services, plus the trout his well-heeled customer could not use. Records in fish catches were being set at Tallac. Often in four hours of fishing two boats would bring in 80 to 90 silvers averaging two pounds apiece. A catch of 15 to 20 silversides in one hour's trolling was not too difficult even for the novice female angler. Trout were tallied by the hundreds each day during the season, as it was legal to take all the fish that could be boated with hook and line. An uprising was narrowly averted, however, when friendly tribesmen from the nearby Washoe encampment were forbidden to spear and net trout in streams flowing to the lake.

In addition to threatened retaliation by the Indians, something almost unbelievable to oldtimers at the lake, "high-fashion," now blossomed at Tallac. The *Truckee Republican*, always on the alert for social news, reported in July of 1883 that the guests of Tallac House were becoming "very tony." Young ladies at the resort were changing their dresses three and four times a day in order to add color to the afternoon and evening promenading. Formality had become a requisite at Baldwin's, and a minimum of one Saratoga trunk constituted the accepted repository for milady's wardrobe.

Life at the hotel continued in its carefree, unruffled way, until the *Tahoe Tattler* uncovered a "distressing incident" which it offered to an unsuspecting public under the heading: "Razors in the Air." The paper deplored the actions of one George White, a colored domestic, who upset the equilibrium of the genteel resort by endeavoring to carve up two of his fellow workers in the side hall of the establishment. Readers were reassured by the fact that "White had been subdued in good time."

The *Truckee Republican*, not to be outdone by that "scrap of tissue" at Tahoe City, gleefully discovered a character who proved Tallac was not the exclusive playground of the upper crust after all. An Indian belle was located near the hotel who "chewed nigger-head and was capable of spitting through

SARDINED INTO THE FRINGE TOP AND OFF FOR FALLEN LEAF

High-wheeler and mule team, with eleven guests and driver, at the western entrance to The Tallac in the summer of 1899.

the keyhole of a door at three yards without splattering the edges." The management of Tallac looked coldly down their noses, and canceled all advertising in the paper at once.

Now a distraction of a different nature caught the fancy of the more adventurous guests. The ascent of Mount Tallac was fast becoming a popular activity for the gentlemen and lady hikers, with "kind and gentle horses provided for the less robust." Reaching the pinnacle of this soaring granite peak was considered quite a feat of mountain climbing, whether it be achieved astride or afoot.

For those who wished entertainment with a minimum of personal effort, there was always the popular Tallac Glee Club. Three young dandies, complete with high celluloid collars, peg-bottom trousers, red and white blazers and straw "skimmers," comprised the group. They made the rounds of the lake resorts presenting "Finnegan's Wake," "John Brown's Body" and other popular tunes of the day, plus a final curtain call number, "What are the Wild Waves Saying?" This never failed to evoke thunderous applause.

Bathing had moved from the Taylor Creek pond to the beach in front of the hotel. It was now reported that a "full line of bathing suits were displayed, with an afternoon splash considered quite the proper caper." Promptly at 3:00 p.m. each day, the more daring of the young ladies at Tallac took over the lakeshore to display brightly colored balloon-like, below-the-knee creations set off by black or striped stockings and tightly-laced canvas galoshes. From vantage points on the wharf the younger blades clicked their heels, tipped their bowlers, twirled their mustaches and voiced boisterous, though proper, comments of appreciation. To the group of middle-aged women bystanders (those in their early 30's) such nonsense was strictly a vulgar exhibition. "Lucky" Baldwin, as consistent a pursuer of wide-eyed "femmes fatales" as he was of fiery horseflesh, seldom bestowed a second glance on this parade of charmers. The answer was found in his daytime activities, which consisted of bigger

and better promotions of his far-flung enterprises. Tallac House and his real estate development near Taylor Creek were only a small part of his over-all interests. He had sold a number of 100-foot lake frontage lots, running back a sixteenth of a mile in depth, at the going price of $300 each. Many of the "wiser heads" cautioned prospective buyers to wait until the prices came down within reason.

The summer of 1884 found "Yank" Clement and his wife, "Aunt Liddy," still residing at Tallac, apparently retired, but the oldest pioneer host and hostess at Tahoe were actually just marking time between resorts.[15]

Six seasons passed during which time Tallac's clientele and facilities steadily improved. In the spring of 1890 a new coated-stock brochure, printed in color, ushered in the Gay 90's at the hostelry and one inviting paragraph read: "Rail to Truckee, Stage to Tahoe, Steamer to Tallac and Trouting!" Barely six months later Baldwin, Comstock and Lawrence added their own large vessel to the growing fleet on Tahoe. Named for the resort, the *Tallac* was advertised as the "handsomest steamer on the Pacific Coast."[16] The hotel's pier was now a scheduled mail and Wells Fargo Express stop for lake steamers. Tallac was *the* place to go.

Baldwin was also planning a $200,000 railroad down the Truckee River Canyon to connect with the Southern Pacific (formerly Central Pacific) but the Bliss interests at Glenbrook were to build it themselves nine years later. Six-horse Concords and "mud wagons" continued to rattle tourists and guests directly to the ornate portico of Tallac House by way of the Clear Creek, Kingsbury, Luther, and Johnson Pass roads. Business was so good that another development was afoot.

It had been rumored for some time that Baldwin intended to construct a new hotel that would be the equal of any summer or winter establishment in America and a San Francisco newsman erroneously reported that "Lucky" had "burned a million brick" in the summer of 1896 with which to build his magnificent show place. Baldwin did not start on this enterprise until the fall of 1898.[17]

By the following summer the palatial three and one-half story edifice was completed. Known in grand simplicity as "The Tallac," it could accommodate over 100 guests, with quarters for another 150 people available in gleaming white cottages and the old Hotel Tallac. This new wonder of Lake Tahoe was situated in a grove of stately pine to the east of "Yank's" original structure and several hundred yards back from the lake. Lumber for its construction had been furnished by Baldwin's sawmill on the western shore of Fallen Leaf.[18]

A massive central tower crowned the roof of the main building and a covered porch ran the full length of the north entrance. Large picture windows on the lake side framed a dining room that could seat 100 people. A steam plant supplied heat to every room in the establishment. Hotel, outbuildings and grounds had an intricate system for piping water in from Fallen Leaf. The lighting plant was advertised as "turning night into day." Fountains arched above rocked-in pools throughout the gardens, and well-kept flower beds bordered the graveled walks and roadways. Even a long distance telephone was available for the active businessman in Tallac's lobby.

A fine string orchestra played during the day as well as in the evenings for dinner and dancing and the eight-course meal was served by colored waiters under the watchful eye of Maitre d' Joseph Cowen, formerly of San Francisco's Palace Hotel.[19] Two bars on the pier were presided over by white-coated, mustachioed barkeeps.

Author's collection

THE TALLAC
Splendid High Sierra "rory-tory" set in a magnificent grove of pine trees presented an irresistible appeal to the top-drawer summer vacationist. This view of Baldwin's new Tallac Hotel, completed in 1899, was taken in the spring of 1902 looking southwest at the establishment's north, or main, entrance.

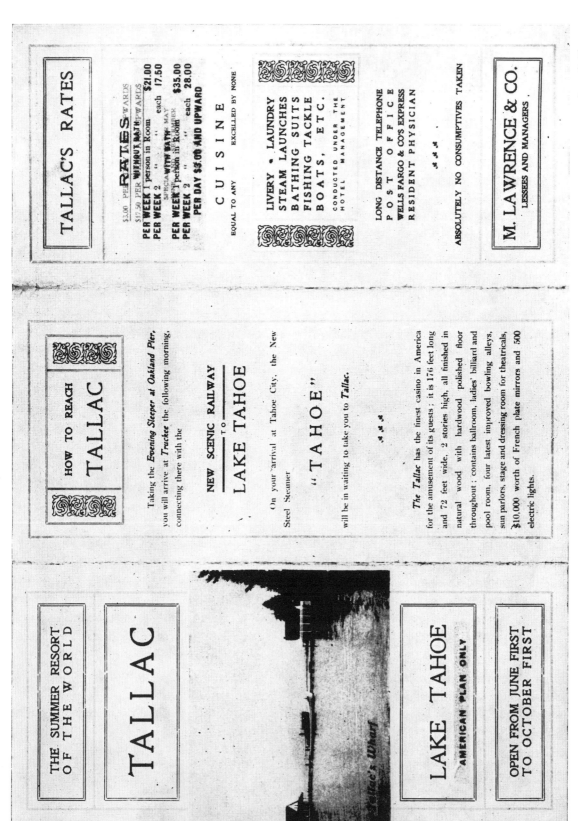

THE "& CO." WAS BALDWIN AND THE G. L. M. COMSTOCK FAMILY

Tallac's advertising brochure, brought out in color for the 1902 summer trade, offered unheard of conveniences and activities for the "rational enjoyment" of hotel guests.

On viewing this High Sierra magnificence wrought by Baldwin, Comstock and Lawrence, most people were inclined to feel that, self-styled or not, it was indeed one of the finest resort hotels in the world, "with a cuisine equal to any and excelled by none."[20]

The "greatest Casino in America and the marvel of the century" was constructed two years after the completion of The Tallac. East of the old pier and fronting directly on the water, it was 176 feet long and 72 feet wide. Three and one-half stories high, its exterior practically duplicated that of the hotel itself. Its managers proudly acclaimed the Casino as being "finished in natural wood with hardwood polished floor throughout, containing ballroom, ladies' billiard and pool room, four latest improved bowling alleys, sun parlors, stage and dressing room for theatricals" and containing "a magnificent display of French plate mirrors," carefully noted as "$10,000 worth."[21] As if this was not enough, 500 electric lights crowned this achievement in elegance.

Large vegetable gardens supplied the extensive kitchens. Two hundred dairy cows were milked in a modern dairy. Forty-five riding horses were now available, ranging in temperament from "gentle to fiery." Three hay barns and a large stable housed the animals, along with spring wagons, double open and hard-top buggies, several fringe-top carriages, and a Concord coach.

Pleasurable pastimes in the bracing mountain air were even more varied and numerous. According to Comstock and Lawrence, almost every "rational" sport was offered . . . croquet, swimming baths, fishing, trapshooting, rifle practice, lawn tennis, shuttlecock, horseback riding, canoeing, rowing, hiking, sailing and steamboating, in addition to "just plain promenading."[22] An expanding clientele prompted the addition of another bar to accommodate those who preferred to drink their vacation.

The Tallac was, in reality, the "Saratoga of the Pacific" that earlier Tahoe resorts had aimed for,

CASINO, CLUBHOUSES AND CROSS OF SNOW

Tallac's lakeshore buildings as seen from the bow of the steamer TAHOE *in the spring of 1904.*

Author's collection

Maillard Bennett

OFTEN A NEW HABILIMENT WON MILADY'S FAVORS

Elias J. "Lucky" Baldwin and friends at Tallac Meadow in the summer of 1905.

but left for Baldwin, Comstock and Lawrence to achieve. Rates were high, in keeping with Tallac's policy of maintaining a top-ranking resort. Many people considered the prices prohibitive and a popular yarn concerned the footpad who, in the process of holding up a traveler on the Kingsbury Grade, learned that the dejected vacationer had the misfortune to be returning from Tallac. With profuse apologies he pressed a silver dollar upon his intended victim and wished him Godspeed.[23]

In the summer of 1906, the height of Tallac's glory and popularity, a hotel brochure featured the amazing Mrs. Joseph Chanslor. With great admiration, and no little wonderment, the hotel's management pointed to the unparalleled feat of this female driver who coaxed her chain-driven Simplex from Sacramento over the Sierra to the resort. Outfitted in goggles, duster, gauntlets, veils, and with extra gasoline cans and spare Non-Skids, she made the solo run in the unbelievable time of eight hours. "Women! Goddam, what'll they be up to next?" moaned the clucking oldtimers at the hotel.

Additions to the resort continued. More trim white cottages, roomy and beautifully furnished, were constructed. Kenyon tents blossomed on the shore to the east of the main building. A new pier adjoined the casino, and the horse livery doubled to over 75 animals. Tallac's cuisine had now become so famous that the discovery of a "food scout" from the culinary department of New York's Waldorf Astoria, reconnoitering in Tallac's kitchen, only caused the management to wonder why he had taken so long to get there.[24]

Commercial fishermen and guides now numbered 35 and included Eric von Stroheim, later to gain fame as the monacled Prussian of motion pictures; Carl A. Bechdolt, present owner of Tahoe Inn; Guy Coburn, Chris Nielson, Solly McGraw, Bob Harkness, John Ernest Pomin, and Johnny Lang. John Woods was one of the bartenders, "Gimp" had charge of the livery stable, and hotel porters were Duffy and Fred Spriggs, who later operated Fred's Place on the Placerville road.[25]

The titular head of the Washoe tribe, "Indian Ben" James headed hunting and pack trips into the Desolation Valley area, and "night-frogging" with a line and piece of red flannel in the meadows west of Tallac had become the fad.[26] Captain Joe Pomin was about to take over the operation of the gasoline launch *Happy Day* with Joe Curry as engineer, and Captain Jack Clark piloted the double-ender cruise boat *Rosalie* out of Tallac's pier.[27]

Jim May, associate of Tex Rickard, who later mysteriously disappeared in South America, ran the gambling at the casino with Bill Trough as partner. Circular-wheeled slot machines with cast iron payoff cups lined the walls, and dice and roulette tables stood in the center of the room. Gambling was illegal, so a well-organized grapevine ran directly into the sheriff's office in Placerville. Hours before the law officer rode up to Tallac on horseback, the "word" had been received by May and all gambling equipment moved out and stored. The sheriff would be wined and dined and speeded on his way. As he disappeared down the road, slot machines and tables were already being carried back to the casino.[28] Some of the table games ran to high stakes, but old-timers cannot recall a time when the "T"-embossed chips, stacked on the roulette table, ever moved in any appreciable quantity into the pockets of Tallac's guests.

One night in the early 1900's William Fries and his son Frank arrived at the swank hostelry for a two-week vacation. Frank decided to try his luck at the tables and, surprisingly enough, his father urged him to do so, indicating that he was on his way to bed. Several hours later an urgent call was relayed from May in the casino to the hotel's comptroller. It seemed that young Fries was down several hundred dollars on the blackjack table and wanted more credit. What should be done? The manager roused Fries Sr. and put the question to him. How far did he wish his son to go? Fries pointed to the ceiling with his index finger, adjusted his stocking cap and slipped back under the covers.

The following morning one of the cashiers was posting guest charges when he came across a payout slip on which was scrawled an I.O.U. for $3,500 signed by young Fries in favor of May. Another

C. O. Valentine

THE WASHOE
INDIANS
CALLED IT
"GREAT
MOUNTAIN"

Mount Tallac, 9,785 feet,
with its famous cross of snow
showing high on the
northeastern slope.
Box camera study taken
in the early summer of 1913,
one year before the
original Tallac House
(center foreground)
burned.

rush call went out for the father, who finally sauntered into the hotel lobby and over to the teller's cage. He glanced at the charge, pulled a cigar out of his breast pocket and slowly lit it while young Harry O'Callaghan, the cashier, waited nervously. Suddenly a smile spread over Fries' face.

"That's fine," he said, "just fine. I always told my boy it was a sucker game, and now he's found out for himself. That's a damn sight better than piddling it away in lesser amounts and never learning a lesson."[29]

In the fall of 1908 the "Rose Cottage" built by Comstock and Lawrence burned to the ground. "Lucky" Baldwin's notorious "Love Nest" near the structure escaped. This sumptuously furnished double cottage, the scene of many of his nocturnal activities, might just as well have gone up in smoke also because "Old Lucky" was now 80 years of age. On March 1 of the following year, Elias Jackson Baldwin died, and it is said that "not a sob was heard nor a tear shed at his funeral."[30] The rugged individualist who, his associates wryly admitted, "loved most, after a sharp trade, to squeeze three girls at once," was gone from the scene.[31]

The curtain was slowly closing on famous Tallac. Baldwin's daughter, Anita M. Baldwin, took

over the estate and Melville Lawrence, along with G. L. M. Comstock's son Harry, continued to operate the hotel. Old Tallac House was leveled by fire in the early spring of 1914 and John Tait, the
famous San Francisco restaurateur, in partnership with Gustave Mann, managed The Tallac the following summer when Harry O. Comstock and Melville Lawrence gave up their lease.

To Mann is ascribed the profound statement, made just before he tried to jump across a water-
filled 12-foot ditch near the establishment: "If I can't make it in one yump, I'll make it in two."[32] Some
people felt that the caliber of Tallac's management had definitely tobogganed from its lofty plateau.

The Tallac operated as a resort into the early 1920's. Then it became merely a tabulation on the
El Dorado County assessment rolls: hotel, cottages, casino, boathouse, stable, power house and sawmill—value, $79,000.[33] In the summer of 1927 Anita Baldwin decided to demolish the buildings, and
one by one they were leveled and the salvage sold at give-away prices.[34] She wanted nothing of a commercial nature to remain on her lakeshore property and the grounds were ringed with "Keep Out"
signs. Old Tallac, its name already becoming a legend on the shores of Lake Tahoe, was gone and with
it an era of fantastic high living and memorable times in the Sierra Nevada.

Only the skeletons of weathered pilings today point to the sky at the water's edge and the crumbling
outline of the resort's foundations may be traced among the wild flowers and scrub brush, surrounded by
the same massive yellow pines that stand—as living monuments—to Elias Jackson "Lucky" Baldwin
who wanted them preserved for future generations.

GAS-BURNER AND GAD-ABOUTS

Pullman-Standard at the portico of The Tallac in the summer of 1906. Harry O. Comstock's partner, Melville Lawrence, is seated in the front seat with the driver.

Gladys Comstock Bennett

Gladys Comstock Bennett

FOUR ACES, BOYS—

Elias J. "Lucky" Baldwin demonstrates the "Baldwin Poker Touch" at Tallac in the summer of 1900.

TWO MEN IN A SKIFF

Melville Lawrence, proprietor of THE TALLAC, and "Lucky" Baldwin (holding bow oar) pose for their photograph in Tallac Meadows (Marsh) July of 1904, four years before Baldwin's death.

Gladys Comstock Bennett

Chapter Twenty-three

CASCADE HOUSE

OLD EPHRAIM "YANK" CLEMENT was a hard man to hold down. He had been "burned out three times, foreclosed on by mortgages, frozen out, and cycloned, yet here he was, after thirty years at the Lake, coming up with a new hotel, Cascade House, ready to receive guests." So reported a newsman admiringly in May of 1887.[1]

There was reason indeed for people to admire Clement's fortitude. He was an emigrant from the Gold Rush days of '49, friend of shoddy wayfarer, hopeful miner, and broadcloth banker alike, former owner of Yank's Station in Lake Valley and Yank's Hotel on Tahoe's lakeshore, and now acknowledged to be Tahoe's oldest pioneer host.

In 1886 he and his wife, Lydia Mark Clement, still owned 167 acres with 300 feet of beach frontage to the east of Baldwin's property.[2] Here they ranched for several years, although they still called Tallac House their real home, but the urge to open another hotel was too strong for "Yank" and "Liddy" to dismiss from their minds, even though half of their lakefront property was mortgaged to neighbors, Josiah H. Applegate and Mrs. Alice MacDonald.[3] During the fall of '86 the Clements built a pier, clubhouse and saloon over the water. One-eighth of a mile back from their sand beach they constructed a small two-story "record," calling it Cascade House.

Both "Yank" and "Aunt Liddy" still had a substantial local and California-Nevada following, consisting of vacationers less elite than those attracted to the Grand Central in Tahoe City and Baldwin's Tallac House. This was how the "Green Mountain Boy" wanted it.

"There ain't room hyar for the frilly-lace-petty and bowler-hatted trade, no sir," was his attitude toward the fancy nabobs who mistakingly reined up at his establishment expecting to be received with open arms.

On the Fourth of July, 1888, the Clements held one of their celebrated "crushers" for friends and the general public. Featured was an afternoon program on the lakeshore north of Cascade House calculated to leave participants and onlookers in a state of complete exhaustion. Included in the crowded schedule were rowing races between crack crews of striped-shirted, handlebar-mustached oarsmen, manning Whitehall boats, followed by paddling contests in which the younger fry squatted in wooden wash tubs and threw geysers of water into the air with their hands in an attempt to cross the finish line first.

In the meadowland, oldtimers squinted over the sights of Remington rifles and Colt sixguns, while "Yank" tossed red and green glass sphere targets into the air. A 75-yard footrace was run off for the boys, a walking match for the men. Pole vaulting and the high jump were open to all comers, seven feet being considered a creditable vault. Other tests of skill included a "go as you please" race, a "standing-jumping contest," a sack race, and a "three-legged 50-yard dash."

A log-rolling contest held in the shallows of the lake between Bliss's Glenbrook champion and Rube Saxton's challenger from Tahoe City, followed the pony race for the youngsters. The fast-stepping lumberjacks, outfitted in skin-tight underwear and britches, spun the two and one-half foot thick yellow pine log to a frothing draw when both men were simultaneously thrown into the water.

For a grand finale, "Yank" came up with a tug of war between the espoused and single men. He himself served as anchor man for the husbands and suffered the indignity of being dragged across the line to the accompaniment of loud catcalls from the bachelors. The holiday was a tremendous success and "Old Yank" was even more delighted than were the lucky winners of the flapping tom turkeys he had given as prizes.[4]

The life of Cascade House was short—but it was active. During the heavy winter of 1889-90 Cascade burned to the ground. Oldtimers shook their heads sympathetically and declared that "Yank" was "the best-liked host in the Sierra, all right, but damned if he wasn't the unluckiest." In June of 1890 "Yank" announced that "temporary accommodations would be put up immediately to house at least 20 guests."[5] But three seasons passed before he had his second Cascade House and then only because Bellevue Hotel on Sugar Pine Point was reduced to ashes. "Yank" purchased the undamaged two-story clubhouse, barged it across the lake and moved it to the site of his old hotel.[6]

Although the new hostelry was described as a "rickety structure that swayed like a reed in the wind" when the second story was used for dancing and "socials," it miraculously continued to stand. Every week-end during the season the *Meteor*, loaded to the gunwales with young couples from Glenbrook, Hobart and Bijou, pulled into "Yank's Landing." There they twirled to the music of a string band until the sun rose over the Carson Range.[7]

Clement was now in his early eighties and time was fast running out for him, but this did not prevent the twinkle-eyed mountain man from regaling his guests with tales of early Tahoe and the Bonanza days and he'd always slip in a tall story or two whenever he had an appreciative audience.

One of his favorites concerned the "fastest horseback ride ever to take place in the Sierra Nevada." Of course, "Yank" just happened to have been in the saddle.

"Why-y that mud wagon skedaddling Monk and Greely was ant-crawlin' 'longside my eagle flyin'," he'd begin.

"Flank-strapped to my mare was a sack of gold, an' wern't a renegade 'soot top' in the Sierry didn't know I had it. I seen 'em a comin' at the high of Big Hill (Echo Summit). So I laid rowel to 'Gertie,' an' wham! we leap off downgrade like a lightnin' zag; a rollin', flyin' cloud of fastness. We was flingin' rock, and air wuz shriekin' by like a tornado's rim. Couldn't even grab a breath. Jus' a suffocatin' from all that speed until old 'Gertie' winds out a full half mile past the grade bottom."

"Yank" would pause at this point in the yarn and pull hard at his pipe, a faraway look creeping into his watery eyes.

"It warn't a blue sky endin'. I slides off 'Gert,' feelin' kinda cool-like behind. Cripes! My coattails bin cut clean off from that consarned gale, just as tho' a herder'd took the trimmin' shears to me. Whut's more, my sackful of colored coin is gone—but so's them savages. Mebbe that evened the count."

"But wurst of all," he'd conclude, " 'Gertie' wern't the same from then on, and she's movin' nowhere less she's under a full gallop. So I sells her off to a whiskey drummer an' I hear she's a champeen' harness tracker now in Emer-villy."[8]

Old pioneer Ephraim "Yank" Clement passed away in the fall of 1895. He took with him vivid recollections of the far West's growth and a treasury of tall tales.

Shortly after his death, Lydia Mark Clement married a shiftless Tallac carpenter named Percival. It was reported as an unfortunate choice of husbands for the friendly, helpful "Aunt Liddy," as Percival's main interest in life was the amber liquid that pours from whiskey bottles. "Aunt Liddy" died mysteriously. Her body was discovered at the bottom of Cascade House's cellar steps, but Percival, emerging from an alcoholic bout, recalled nothing.[9]

Lydia Clement Percival was buried beside her first husband in Glenbrook's little white-fenced meadow cemetery. Their graves are unmarked, but they border the old Bonanza Road to Washoe over which thousands of travelers, who had shared the Clements' hospitality through the decades, passed on their way to the mines of Virginia City.[10]

California State Library

"CHAMPEEN LIAR OF THE SIERRY"

Ephraim "Yank" Clement shown on the old pier at "Yank's" Hotel in the summer of 1876, more than a decade before he built Cascade House one mile to the east. The photograph was taken looking west with Tallac (sometimes Aspen) Point on the left and Maggie's North Peak and Granite Mountain, above Emerald Bay, in the background.

CHIPMUNK CAMP — NEÉ RICHARDSON'S

Pine bough covered luxury on the site of Camp Richardson in the summer of 1873 with fishing, fresh air and food the prime requisites for this family group of vacationists.

Chapter Twenty-four

CAMP RICHARDSON

MATTHEW CULBERTSON GARDNER, native of Richmond, Virginia, and Carson Valley rancher and stock trader, acquired a large timber holding on the south end of Lake Tahoe during the summer of 1872.[1] It ran to several thousands of acres with the northern section adjoining a tract pre-empted by "Yank" Clement nearly a decade before. To meet homestead requirements of the day, Gardner paid the Federal Government 25 cents for each acre of land he had taken up. An additional $1 per acre was payable over the next 20 years.[2]

Gardner's initial operations consisted of felling and splitting fir and cedar close to the waters of Tahoe for cordwood and shakes. He cut sugar pine, tamarack and yellow pine for use as saw logs at the Glenbrook mills. Logs were chain-dragged to the water by oxen yoked in pairs, V-boomed and then taken in tow by the steam tugs *Governor Blaisdel*, *Emerald I* or *Truckee*. Gardner also used solid wood-wheeled lumber wagons in the backwoods. Here the felled trees were pyramided by bullwhackers and swampers who used stag oxen to inch the logs up an inclined lodgepole ramp onto the carriers.

Gardner appeared on the Tahoe scene coincidentally with the Carson and Tahoe Lumber and Fluming Company and Walter S. Hobart's Nevada Lumber Company. The Bliss-Yerington-Mills combine at Glenbrook started large-scale logging operations in 1873 and in May of 1875 Gardner obtained his first major contract from them. This called for the delivery of 60,000,000 feet of logs, 6,000,000 of which were to be furnished before the winter of 1875 with 12,000,000 feet to be supplied by Gardner every year thereafter to completion of the contract.[3]

A market for his cut was now assured. Gardner immediately began construction of a broad-gauge railroad to run from a trestle pier built out over the water at "Gardner's Camp," south along the west side of Lake Valley to a point near the base of Gardner Mountain (Twin Peaks). Two locomotives, duplicates of the engines used on the Virginia and Truckee Railroad, were purchased and unimaginatively named engines Number One and Two.[4]

Frank Craven, wagoner from Carson City, was commissioned to haul the first locomotive to the south end of Tahoe. He decided to move it up the steep zigzag of the Kingsbury Grade from Van Sickle's Station, then down canyon to Friday's (Small's) and along the lakeshore to the railhead. With Will James of Genoa "swamping" and several mule skinners making up the caravan, Engine Number One lumbered out of Carson City in the first week of August, 1875.

The locomotive had been cabled to two heavy-spoked freight wagons chained together and drawn by 24 head of horses and mules. From the eastern base of the Kingsbury, it took a full day to drag the ponderous load up-grade to the summit of Daggett Pass. The straining animals were split up at each hairpin curve, 12 pulling to the left of the leading wagon's tongue, and 12 to the right, in order to keep the top-heavy load from tipping over.[5]

Author's collection

HIGH-WHEELED SAW LOG CARRIER

Relic of early lumbering days
on display at Camp Richardson
in the summer of 1956.

Harvey Cole, Gardner's head bullwhacker (recalled as the horse handler who brought in Major Ormsby's body after the Paiute uprising and massacre near Pyramid Lake), met the group at summit and escorted them to the camp.[6] Sixty-pound standard-gauge rails had been spiked into place on the ties of the roadbed, and the line was ready for use. It turned to parallel the wagon, carriage and stage thoroughfare (present Highway 89) after running directly south from the pier. At the first meadow, beyond what is now Camp Richardson, a sharp curve in the track, known later as "Tip-Over," angled south again into upper Lake Valley.[7]

In addition to the locomotives a dozen logging "flats" were brought in from Carson, pulled by paired oxen, over the Clear Creek Grade to Glenbrook. Here the cars were loaded aboard cordwood barges and moved to the south end of the lake.[8] The *Pacific Tourist Guide* for 1882-83 noted optimistically: "The Gardner Railroad will be extended six to ten miles during the season of 1883." Actually the same rails were laid again and again into new sections of uncut forest land. It is reported that the equivalent of 40 miles of main and spur track was installed, torn up and reinstalled during the peak of Gardner's operations. Roundhouse and machine shops were located near the present entrance to Camp Richardson, the foundations remaining until recent years.[9]

During the early 1880's, an invitation from M. C. Gardner or his superintendent, O. A. Persing, to ride on one of the big locomotive's cow-catchers was an exciting privilege. Guests planted themselves on the front of the engine and, with engineer "Pop" Tait at the cab's controls, they hung on for dear life as the steam giant puffed out on the winding track, dragging the rattling tender and flat cars.[10]

In the year 1885 M. C. Gardner's railroad and lumbering project was suddenly concluded. Gardner's difficulties have been ascribed to overextending himself financially, and to contract misunderstandings concerning the delivery of saw logs, including allegations of "short measurement" of the log footages by purchasing inspectors. Whatever the reason, he was forced into bankruptcy and Lake Tahoe's first steam-powered standard-gauge railroad suspended operations. The line was abandoned and tracks and rolling stock sold.[11]

An erroneous report maintains that M. C. Gardner operated three mills in the vicinity of Gardner Mountain and that Rube Saxton of old Saxton's Mill was his partner. Aside from the early Robert Woodburn and legendary Heavenly Valley (Miller Creek) water-powered producers, mills then existing on the south end of Tahoe were two small units in the Kingsbury Grade-Daggett Pass region. An-

LOGGING . . . OLD METHOD

Saw logs being hauled up a lodgepole skid onto a lumber truck at one of M. C. Gardner's back country camps. Dust to the left of the carrier was raised by oxen stacking the logs. Photograph taken in the vicinity of Gardner Mountain, July of 1875.

other fantastic report credits Gardner with a daily output of 12,000 feet of lumber and as being in the lumber business twenty-one years.[12]

For some time E. J. "Lucky" Baldwin had been eyeing Gardner's holdings. When the railroad's operations ended he shrewdly offered Gardner $400 for all his land. Gardner accepted the proposition.[13]

He and his family then returned to their ranch in Carson Valley, Nevada, where Gardner entered into the cattle business in Smith and Eagle Valleys.

On the south end of Tahoe, resorts and private residences now sprang up. Within the next few years Clara Belle Gardner MacDonald purchased from Baldwin, for $3,000, a small acreage to the west of her family's former railroad pier.[14] When Will S. Tevis, Sr., of San Francisco offered $6,000 for the property at the turn of the century, Mrs. MacDonald sold out, and here the Tevises built an elaborate summer residence, with rock garden, fountained pools, graveled walks and rustic bridges.

Financial difficulties dissolved the Tevis fortune during the first World War and the George Popes, also of San Francisco, bought the home and lakeshore property from the bank. Named "Vatican Lodge," a whimsical peg to the name of Pope, this tract is still owned by the Pope family.[15] Among other Californians and Nevadans who owned summer homes on or near the lakeshore during the 1890's and early 1900's were the George P. and Melita J. Tallants, Mrs. Claire S. Heller, the Applegates and the Ralstons.[16]

In the spring of 1904 Joseph Parmeter purchased a 100 by 400 foot parcel of lakeshore land at the terminal point of Gardner's old railroad. This became "The Grove" under the management of John C. Copeland and his wife, Nellie, daughter of Parmeter. Copeland is remembered as a jovial character with a dedicated interest in strong distillations and a rare talent that elevated him to the position of "undisputed champion of the Lake's swear-masters."[17]

Old "J. C." (or "Cope") was said to have "appeared more as a hired hand who worked around the place instead of being its owner." Every so often he would be talked into going on the wagon, and 24 hours of complete abstinence was a triumphant record for "Cope." Frequently, Nellie Copeland would find her better-for-worse half reeling around the over-water saloon despite his most recent solemn pledge to leave alcohol alone. "Cope" invariably denied any deviation from the straight and narrow. Fixing a befuddled but accusing eye on the bartender and "brass-railers," he would insist, " 'Twarn't no fault of mine, *Missus* Copeland, they just *poured* it down me."[18]

The Copelands built summer cabins, put up tents, rebuilt the old pier and erected an over-water saloon. Nor did they overlook that essential of any seasonal resort—a dance pavilion. Theirs was a covered 40 x 20 foot affair partially built out over Tahoe, with its south end resting on a sandbar. The establishment was known as Copeland's Grove Hotel. In 1923 Nellie Copeland leveled a long, appraising look at fashionably elegant Tallac to the west and decided to advertise "The Grove" as "having no burdensome style—just a homelike summer retreat for folks weary of the city."[19]

Access to Parmeter's, and later to Copeland's, had been dependent upon a narrow 50-foot right-of-way following the old railbed north to the lake from the main road. This ran through property then owned by Harry O. Comstock and Melville Lawrence. In 1921 Alonzo LeRoy Richardson, who had been in charge of the stage livery as well as being general groundskeeper for Tahoe Tavern in 1907, leased the Lawrence and Comstock holdings. He built a small station on the main road and used this for his Placerville-Tallac stageline headquarters. "Al" Richardson actually started his stageline in 1909 and his locally famous, oversize, dachshund-slung Pierce Arrows served the south end of Tahoe for many years.

The same year Harley Lewright and his wife, May Copeland Lewright, daughter of J. C. Copeland, took over the operation of "Copeland's Grove." "Cope" and his son-in-law evidently spent a major portion of their time in the over-water bistro, for the next owner of the resort turned out to be none other than bartender Ziegler, who had been serving them for several seasons.[20]

The location now became known as "Ziegler's Grove," and remained a small parcel of lakeshore land while Richardson expanded on the surrounding acreage. In 1923 Richardson purchased the Lawrence and Comstock holdings, put up his first tourist cabins and served friendly notice on the Copeland family to move their tents and cabins.

Richardson then added his own pier 100 feet west of Copeland's and on June 17, 1927, transferred the post office from Tallac Hotel, which was then being demolished. Now Richardson offered a regular mail, express and freight steamer stop. Every year he added cabins, giving them distinctive names of engines and bus equipment that had served him over the years—Hall-Scott, Fageol, and Pierce Arrow among others.[21]

In the late 1920's and the 1930's "Rich," as he was familiarly known, built a new dining room and hotel on the north side of the highway and put up a general merchandise store, gasoline station and other buildings. The tragic death of Richardson's son "Bud," resulting from a duck hunting accident in the fall of 1953, and the subsequent passing of A. L. Richardson, left the ownership and operation of Camp Richardson to his widow, daughter "Sis" Richardson Knisley and son-in-law, Ray Knisley.

Chapter Twenty-five

ECHO LAKE*

"IT'S JUST LIKE advertising for a wife—pop the question once and you get more answers than you can attend to in a month." It was a sparkling, sunlit afternoon, the month was May, and the year 1866. That great Tahoe raconteur, Ramsdale Buoy, was speaking. The man who could "out-talk, out-fiddle, and out-drink any galoot in the Sierra" turned to his three tired, dust-covered companions from the Bay City standing beside him on the shoreline of Lower Echo. "Raise the dead!" he bellowed. His friends repeated the cry and a resounding chorus of echoes followed. The canorous sound bounced against the mountains, grew fainter and finally died away.

"Just like a pack of lovesick coyotes howling at the moon," Buoy grunted. "But if that's the best you can do, boys, I still give you Echo Lake."[1] With a sweeping gesture he pointed across the water. "If you'd follow west from here, past the upper lake into Devil's Basin, a man could own 75,000 acres of that granite waste and still not find enough soil to pasture a whip-o-will." The men chortled and slapped one another on the back. That joker Buoy sure did know the country, they agreed.[2]

That morning the party had left Jim "Poker" Taylor's ranch starting on their return trip to San Francisco by way of Johnson Pass and Placerville.[3] Arriving at Nevett's Summit, the driver reined up their "mud wagon and four" and they tramped through the yellow pine and tamarack forest to the shores of what was then known to the Washoe Indians as Osgood's Lake.[4]

Reluctantly Buoy turned away from the shimmering water and led his band of adventurers down the mountain to the waiting stage.

Echo Lake had been named.

Before the coming of the white man, Washoe Indians from Eagle Valley (Carson) camped on the shores of these two Alpine lakes during the summer and fall seasons. Proof that the Indians hunted this region is found in the arrow heads of obsidian discovered there.[5]

Six years after Buoy and his party named the lake, two brothers known as the "Lowery boys" built a cabin of hand-hewn logs on the extreme northwesterly island of Upper Echo. Here they seined native trout from the waters, selling the fish to wayfarers moving over the Johnson Pass road. They also trapped muskrat, white fox, mink and ermine. During the summer of 1884, Dr. Robert F. Rooney, general practitioner from Auburn, and James Henry Burnham, apothecary, gold buyer and real estate merchant from Folsom, purchased the cabin and a small fishing skiff from the Lowerys. Later they floated another cabin from the mainland across the water to the island, adding it to the original structure. It is reported that Rooney admitted he "couldn't hold a candle to Burnham when it came to fishing, but he damn well knew he could wipe his companion's eye with a shotgun when they were hunting mountain grouse."[6]

*Also Echo Lakes.

Glorene Dunlap Young

THREE SCHOOL MARMS AT LOWER ECHO

Visitors from Lakeside (seated to the left of the box-flume outlet) in the spring of 1894. Looking west toward Desolation Valley, Pyramid Peak and Crystal Range. Becker Peak to the left and Flagpole to the right.

A decade later the Charles Albert Swislers of Sacramento acquired both the island and cabin and later they became the property of the Nutting family.[7]

Activity at Echo was not restricted to that of the pioneer trapper, fisherman and hunter, however. In the late 1850's John Kirk, Placerville contractor, pre-empted the lands surrounding Echo.[8] In order to augment the waters of the South Fork of the American River, he planned to build reservoirs at Echo, Medley and Audrain and run the waters thus collected through a canal at Cedar Flat near the western summit of the Sierra. In 1872 he ran out a flume grade from Echo Lake and two years later the El Dorado Gravel and Deep Water Mining Company purchased the water rights and improvements from Kirk.

As Echo Lake lay on the eastern side of the summit, it was decided that a tunnel would provide the most practical way of dropping the water into the South Fork of the American. Work at the south end of the bore began late in the fall of 1874 and resumed on July 1, 1875, from both sides of the mountain. When completed, the tunnel extended 1,056 feet under the summit. Water was diverted into the cut on August 3, 1876. From a small rock-fill dam on the east end of Lower Echo, the lake water spilled into a four-foot wide box flume running for some 400 feet before entering the bore and emerging on the north side of the American River.[9] The dam raised the level of Lower Echo, connecting the two lakes.

By August 16, 1886, Echo Lake had become sufficiently important to warrant the establishment of a post office.[10]

It was not until the summer of 1897 that Hamden El Dorado Cagwin, later to become locally famous as the "Hermit of the Lake," settled at Lower Echo.[11] Described as a "genial, bushy-bearded backwoodsman," he built his cabin on the north side of the natural outlet in a secluded cluster of pine trees. A skillful hunter and fisherman, proven over the years by his activities in Carson and Hope valleys, Cagwin had located near Tahoe's south Stateline the previous season. His prowess in netting and hooking Tahoe's silver trout for the market prompted Charles Ramsey of Bijou to petition the State Legislature to pass a law preventing the wholesale destruction of trout in Lake Tahoe. Although the bill prohibiting commercial fishing was not passed until 1917, Cagwin evidently heeded Ramsey's admonitions, as he immediately moved his boats and nets to Echo and built his cabin.

Cagwin took a job as caretaker, maintaining the dam and flume for the water company. He also acted as guide and handyman for visitors and conducted a boating and fishing business. Whenever an emergency arose during the winter months, Cagwin, following in the footsteps of John "Snow Shoe" Thompson, carried the mail between Strawberry Valley and Carson City. His neighbors were "Zack" Darrington and Dan Phillips, who ran cattle in the vicinity of Phillips and Audrain Stations. I. B. Richardson and Charles Winstanley, who had settled on Echo Lake in 1886, were his summer cronies.

In the spring of 1916 a party of Washoes fishing at Echo discovered the hermit's lifeless body in the cabin he had built nearly two decades before. Surrounding him was his handiwork—hand-carved sections of driftwood and pine bark, stuffed wildcats and deer heads. Hamden El Dorado Cagwin was buried in old Hangtown's cemetery.[12]

On at least one occasion the waters from Echo Lake have caused considerable damage in Upper Lake Valley. During the spring thaw of 1911 the dam broke and unleashed some "two thousand acre feet of water," which followed the Echo Creek channel down the mountainside.[13] Osgood's Toll House, standing since the 1860's at the foot of Meyer's Grade, and located within 50 feet of the west side of the creek, was washed from its foundations by this deluge.

Today the Echoes form the southeastern link in a chain of glacial lakes that includes Fallen Leaf, Cascade, Aloha, Tamarack, Lake of the Woods, and dozens of other small bodies of water in the Desolation Valley primitive area. Standing at an altitude of over 7,400 feet, Upper and Lower Echo are natural stepping stones to the High Sierra wilderness country.[14]

Secluded in their setting, the Echoes offer summer and winter activities for the timberline vacationist and a community of summer homes has sprung up along their shorelines. Fittingly enough, little Cagwin Lake stands away from the larger lakes, above and to the west. It is an enduring reminder of the old hermit who chose to make his home in the region.

STAIRWAY INTO DESOLATION'S WILDERNESS COUNTRY

Lower and Upper Echo Lakes (center), Cagwin Lake (foreground) facing toward the Carson Range of the Sierra. Job's Peak, Job's Sister and Mount Freel are the high peaks in the distance.

Author's collection

SAW LOGS INTO THE UPPER TRUCKEE

Logging camp in Lake Valley, summer of 1890, showing eight horse team dragging sugar pine down the log chute into the river for flotation to Tahoe. Looking northwest near Meyers.

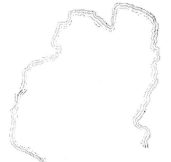

Chapter Twenty-six

LAKE VALLEY

"O<small>N THE NORTH RISE</small> the lofty mountains of Wasson Peak, and following the east side of the lake with the eye, one sees the divide of the Johnson Pass road to Eagle Valley. Moving south on the shoreline is found the Indian Cave with its legendary romance. Next comes Daggett Pass, used by the emigrants, northeast of Lake Valley, then Luther Pass, directly to the east over the divide."[1]

George H. Goddard, head of Seneca Hunt Marlette's California State Boundary survey party, was detailing a report on the "Valley of Bigler" and the vast lake which spread out below him. The date was September 14, 1855. From Goddard's vantage point, a granite knob high on the Johnson Pass Trail, he could obtain a sweeping panoramic view of sapphire water and the surrounding Sierra Nevada.

Goddard continued with the earliest known comprehensive report of the Tahoe region:

"The high peaks to be seen on the northwest are near the Truckee Pass (Donner), but the western outlet of the lake is a myth, still unauthenticated. The 120th meridian divides the lake about equally, California to the West and Utah Territory (Nevada) to the east, but the northern extremity of the lake is known by report only and its length is mere conjecture.[2] It could hardly exceed 20 miles in length and 6 miles in breadth, however, although it has been called 40 and even 50 miles from one end to the other.[3]

"The surrounding mountains are three and perhaps four thousand feet above the lake, which is a deep blue and perfectly fresh. The bases of the high mountain ranges are of white granite sand, forming beautiful beaches, and dense pine forests at other points run from the water's edge to the summit. The lake is stocked with salmon trout and in certain seasons of the year it is fished by the Pai-Utahs (Paiutes) and the Washoes. Directly below a satampy (swampy) flat lies, through which Lake Creek (Upper Truckee River) slowly meanders, gathering up all the streams in its tortuous course that flow from the south and southeast. Five miles of sandy deposits from the river are building out into the lake on the southern end, and the water level is evidently subsiding."[4]

Goddard then described the floor of Lake Valley: "It is comprised of granitic sand and banks of pebbles sorted by action of the waters, with the ground literally covered with wild strawberry vines and sunflowers." The surveyor added, "Trout are plentiful in the mouth of Lake Valley's stream and Bigler itself, but we did not take any because it was not the season, although we shot numerous duck in the meadowland."[5] Goddard mentioned "Hawley's Hill" on the far southwestern side of the valley and referred to the sheer mountainside drop from summit (Johnson Pass) to Lake Valley as "Johnson Hill."[6]

The white man's discovery of Lake Valley is credited to John Calhoun "Cock-Eye" Johnson, of Johnson's Ranch above Hangtown (Placerville).[7] Early in 1848, while searching for a shorter, lower and more direct route over the Central Sierra than the Kit Carson Pass, he found this natural am-

LAKE TAHOE—1855

*Earliest known view of Tahoe (Bigler)
sketched for Hutchings' California
Magazine. Looking north from
a point on the Johnson Trail near
summit. Lake Valley, center
foreground.*

Bancroft Library

phitheater between the eastern and western ranges of mountains. Emigrants camped with their pack trains in Lake Valley during the summer of 1852 and the rescue, that same winter, of a snowbound overland party prompted the following description: "The valley is a Siberia of snow wilderness and dreariness, flanked by granitic, towering rock."[8]

On January 6, 1853, John Adams and his partner, Borland, carrying the mails west out of Salt Lake City, were halted by a flood in Lake Valley when they attempted to push on over the Sierra. They had to return through the heavy snows to Ragtown in Carson Valley, after being on the trail since November of 1852.

This was the valley where the young wagon captain, Elias Jackson Baldwin, fed, watered and rested his stock during the summer of 1853. Later he would gain national recognition as "Lucky" Baldwin.

In the spring of 1854 Asa Hershel Hawley, a native of Vermont who traveled the Overland Trail to Mormon Station in 1851 and then settled in old Hangtown, followed the Johnson cut-off back into Lake Valley, where he established a trading post. Hawley later wrote: "I was the only white man near the lake with the exception of another trader and trapper (Martin Smith) located some four miles north toward Lake Bigler."[9] Hawley gave a pioneer's reaction to the Washoes found in the valley:

"The Indians would not allow white men to fish in the lake. They tried to drive me off, but I was not afraid of Indians, except their treachery. I consider all Indians to be treacherous and think the government ought to deal with them in a firm and steady hand." To document his opinion Hawley pointed out that "Williams and Company, with McMarlin, while returning from California with supplies packed on nine animals, were waylaid by Indians on top of Slippery Ford hill, and murdered."[10]

Hawley homesteaded 160 acres in Upper Lake Valley, bounded on the north by Smith's land. At the base of what became known the following year as "Hawley's Hill" he built his "2d Elkhorn House."[11] This was 1,000 feet south of the site where a wooden bridge would later span the Upper Truckee and here the trail started up the mountain toward Luther Pass.

"Hawley's Trail" from the valley to the summit of the western Sierra (Johnson Pass) described a horseshoe after it left the river. It ran a short distance south, then turned northwest and climbed up the mountainside above Lake Valley, rising nearly 1,000 feet in one and one-half miles. The base of the "Hawley Trail" or short-cut was two and one-third miles south of the original emigrant pack train and wagon road (Johnson Hill) which ascended directly up the mountain to summit.

Surveyor Sherman Day detailed Johnson Hill in his California Wagon Road report of September 20, 1855: "The route lies along a very steep, natural slope, through a thicket of manzanita chaparral, interspersed with large and small boulders of granite. The present road attains the summit by a length of only three-fourths of a mile, or 3,960 feet, which gives a grade of over 14½ degrees or about three and one-half to four times what it should be." (Actually the grade was more than 25%.)[12]

Day continued: "Two miles of road will be required to obtain the right grade, although most of the granite rocks need not be blasted, and the work can be done for $6,000 to $15,000 dollars." Appraising his estimate a century later it is evident that Day was well aware of the realignment difficulties involved. The surveyor originally estimated that the total vertical rise at this point was "about 1,000 feet" but he refigured it and came up with 1,100 feet. He also observed: "About a mile south of the present summit the top is supposed to be reached with 200 feet less altitude." Day was speaking of the Hawley short-cut.

On August 15, 1853, William Bartlett, writing in his Bartlett's Guide to California, had pointed out: "The length of the rise (of the Emigrant Grade) is seven-eighths of a mile with the ascent steep, crooked and stony." Bartlett's advice was a masterpiece of understatement. Emigrants that managed to haul through with their wagons from Eagle Valley over the Ridge Route above Tahoe, and reach this precipitous slide, must have indeed felt they were facing the handiwork of Satan. Oxen had to be unchained from their Conestogas and driven a short way up the face of the mountain. Block and tackle was cabled to a sturdy pine and secured by heavy rope to the wagon below. Then bullwhackers laid on the lash and the animals lumbered off down the mountain pulling the "sail-top" up and over granite boulders and through shoulder-high brush. This process was repeated again and again until "Cape Horn" was reached half way up the promontory, where the "road" leveled out.

Luther's Pass was surveyed in the winter of 1854 by El Dorado county surveyor Henderson. The trail's improvement, along with that of the West Carson Canyon road, helped to syphon traffic into Upper Lake Valley and stimulate the development of Hawley's Hill Trail. By 1857, the first easy elevation wagon road in the Central Sierra had been run out over the Hawley route, using a "tamarack bough and pendulum" to determine the gradient.[13]

In the summer of 1858, El Dorado County further improved the grade, but it remained a one-way road with several rocked-in turn-outs to allow stages and wagons to pass. Hawley's cut-off was now used almost exclusively until 1861. Then it was superseded by the old Emigrant Grade (Johnson's Hill) that had been realigned, widened and lengthened, and the Osgood (later Meyers) Grade.

George H. Goddard's report in the fall of 1855 to Marlette furnishes additional details on Lake Valley:

"We left camp, through Luther Pass into Lake Bigler Valley, continuing down the valley, passing and leaving to our left the trading post, now deserted, where the unsuspecting inmates were murdered in July last.[14] At this cabin the Johnson Pass road turns up the hill and crosses the ridge. We continued along the flats to Smith's Station, likewise deserted. The house that formerly stood here has been burned out like almost all the houses on the road. After halting for a couple of hours at Smith's, we continued along a low ridge of granite sand and pebbles slightly elevated above the flats and lying parallel with the base of the mountain to the east.[15] The whole country is so heavily timbered that we saw nothing of the lake and very little of the mountains; a large stream runs alongside of this ridge for several miles at the base of the mountains while the Truckee flows along on the northern side, winding through a large marsh flat which continues down to the lake.[16] At about four miles from Smith's, we arrived at the end of this singular ridge and crossed a large creek which falls into the Truckee.[17] The road then winds along over the spurs of the mountains to the east, crossing several small creeks all of which empty into the Truckee. At length we reached the point to leave the road for the lake.[18] We

BONESHAKERS . . . OLD AND NEW

A "drummer's" canvas-covered wagon and the last word in open touring gas-burners meet on the old Meyers Grade (Johnson Pass road) above Lake Valley (right foreground) in July of 1908. Looking northeast.

had been obliged thus to wind around the lake to avoid the swampy ground on its southern shore."

In the summer of 1856 John James from Mormon Station (Genoa), Nevada, led a pack-train party into Lake Valley. They carried some $700 in gold dust, panned from Gold Canyon, with which to purchase supplies in Placerville.[19] In the valley they met two Mexican packers who questioned James on the reason for his trip. Knowing that his group had the two men outnumbered, James proudly showed them their leather pouches of dust. The Mexicans then produced several large, old-fashioned pickle bottles, displaying handfuls of gleaming gold nuggets mixed with flakes of gold. James' Carson Valley party of rancher-miners were amazed to see a find of gold worth in their estimation tens of thousands of dollars. But all they could learn from the vaqueros was that their bonanza had been discovered southeast of Carson Pass in the vicinity of what is now Blue Lakes.

The following summer, on another trip through Lake Valley, James met the same Mexicans. Again the two men had a fabulous hoard of gold nuggets in their possession but John James and his companions were never able to determine where the great strike had been made.[20]

On December 29, 1856, a tragedy unfolded in Lake Valley that subsequently established the fame of John "Snowshoe" Thompson. Two weeks before, James Sisson, Asa Hawley's former partner at Six Mile House above Placerville, had started for Carson on a business trip. Alone, and caught in a blizzard above Slippery Ford, he managed to flounder through mounting snow drifts over Johnson Summit and down the trail to Hawley's deserted cabin at the foot of the short-cut.

Purely by accident, "Snowshoe" Thompson, who was guiding a party west from Genoa across the Sierra, stopped at the shack. Here he found Sisson, who had been lying in a stupor for 12 days, barely existing on raw flour. Sisson's boots were frozen to his feet and both legs were purple to the knees.

During his struggle to reach the cabin Sisson's matches became wet and it was not until four days later that he discovered a box of dry ones under a pile of hay tossed into one corner of the log hut.

By then the small fire he managed to kindle was of little help.

When Thompson found Sisson, he was lying face down on the rough pine floor, facing death from starvation and exposure. Sisson pointed weakly to an ax propped against the wall of the shelter, mumbling that he had intended to amputate his legs the next day.

Leaving his companions to care for the man, Thompson pushed over Luther Pass again on his homemade Norwegian type skis. At Daniel Woodford's he recruited five men (among them W. B. Wade, Harris, and Jacobs). He fabricated skis for them and they started back over eight feet of snow dragging a hand sled. By the time the rescue party arrived Sisson was delirious. They loaded him onto the carrier and began the long return trip across the eastern Sierra summit.

Pinned down in Hope Valley that night by another storm they managed to beat their way down the West Carson Canyon the following morning, reach Woodford's and move Sisson by wagon the remaining ten miles to Genoa. Dr. Daggett, the little settlement's only physician, decided that Sisson's legs would have to be amputated.[21] But no chloroform was available.

Although Thompson had been without sleep for three days, he started back across the Sierra at once. He arrived at Sacramento on January 9 and was back in Genoa on the 14th with the anaesthetic. Thanks to Thompson's incredible fortitude, Sisson's life was saved.[22]

"Snowshoe" Thompson's reputation as an able mountain man was now established. His winter trans-Sierra sleigh trips across the twin ranges above Lake Valley followed and on September 18, 1858, the Virginia City *Territorial Enterprise* ran its first issue with printing equipment carried, piece by piece, over Johnson and Luther passes by the brawny Scandinavian.

On July 12, 1857, a "former correspondent for the press of California," who had registered at Smith and Muir's hostelry in Lake Valley, noted: "The station is well kept with obliging proprietors and there is a respectable air about the place." The scribe urged people to "come over into these valleys and make friends of the inhabitants."[23]

Another dispatch from the way station chided the reading public for "not doing their duty to Crandall's line of stages." The note was discreetly signed "J.B.C." and its author turned out to be none other than Jarad B. Crandall, who personally was doing a little drum-thumping for his newly established Pioneer Stage Line.[24] Less than two years later a flood of gold seekers enroute to the Comstock would stampede through Lake Valley without any urging from transient newsmen or stage owners.[25]

By 1858 Martin Smith had taken out a patent on his land and in the summer of 1859 he sold the site of his station to Ephraim "Yank" Clement. It now became Yank's Station.[26]

It is also believed that Smith gave a small parcel of property, on which the old trading post of Gould and Company stood, to Neamiah "Nemi" Osgood, early El Dorado County settler.[27] Here Osgood located his toll house, where Osgood's Creek (Echo) flows into the Upper Truckee River. Osgood put up a tollgate that could be swung across the turnpike and collected from wayfarers traveling the Emigrant Ridge route and Daggett Pass trail, while Hawley levied tolls on those coming over Luther Pass. With the completion of a stage and wagon road crossing Daggett in the summer of 1860, Luther Pass and Hawley's cut-off became the longer route to Washoe and the improved "Johnson Hill" grade to the eastern summit once again served as the main artery of travel, with the "Osgood Trail cut-off" (later Meyers or Ogilby's) running from Osgood's Station directly south up the mountain to Summit, used as an alternate road.

D. D. Kingsbury and John McDonald, builders of the Kingsbury Grade, acquired quarter sections of land bordering their road, where it ran through Lake Valley.[28] They issued franchises to private individuals which gave them the right to collect tolls. Among these rancher-station keepers

C. O. Valentine

BEYOND THE VALLEY, TAHOE STRETCHED AWAY TO ITS NORTHERN RIM

Lake Valley (right of photograph) from the old Meyers' Grade road, Maggie's Peaks and Granite Mountain (upper left). Martis Peak and Mt. Rose in the far distance, 30 miles to the north.

were John Little, L. Dorr, S. Morten, P. McCormick, Jack Sargent Ellis, Fred Humphries, George N. Douglass, and Daniel Hate Holdridge, who had taken up land in the valley by 1860.[29]

On September 17, 1861, a post office was approved for Lake Valley and established at Woodburn's Mill. In December of 1863 the name was changed to "Taho" post office.[30] A debatable report places the first sawmill in Lake Valley on what is now Heavenly Valley Creek (Miller). Known as the Heavenly Valley Mill (sic) it is said to have been constructed in 1859, with the stream supplying water through a millrace to the large overshot wheel.[31]

Lumber was needed for rebuilding the way stations that were burned out in 1855, but previous to 1860 these trading posts and lodging establishments were constructed from saw logs felled and faced off on the spot.

During the summer of 1860, Robert Woodburn's water-powered sawmill was under construction at Trout Creek, some two miles north of Yank's Station on the Placerville-Carson "back road." Woodburn's supplied lumber for many of the hostelries, barns and stables now mushrooming on the Johnson Road. These included McCumbers, Hawthorne House, Pine Grove Station, and River House.[32]

Feed had to be supplied for the teams and pack trains moving over the thoroughfare to the mines of Washoe, and in the summer and fall of 1862, 400 tons of hay were cut in the valley's meadowland.[33] The early white settlers in the region could not count on help from the native Washoe Indians camping along the banks of Lake Creek (Upper Truckee), as they were reported as "inoffensive and willing to work, if all that was required meant thinking about it, allowing them to fish and hunt instead."[34]

A group of the "boys" from San Francisco, headed by adventurer Ramsdale Buoy, described the Hawley Grade and Lake Valley in an earthy manner after staging through in May of 1866. Buoy wrote:

"There is just room for a coach and team it (the Hawley Grade) is so narrow, with a sheer drop below us to the valley floor. Several long pulls from our bottle fortified us and we took off down the mountain toward the foot of the grade 1,500 feet below us.

" 'Shorty,' a member of the party, ventured the thought that if the stage should turn over here, nitroglycerin would be nothing to it, as you couldn't hold an inquest with a microscope. Our stage-driver didn't bat an eyelash, and we huddled in back of the conveyance, not daring to look down. Upon arriving safely at the bottom, some of the boys started back up the road to see what we actually *had* come over, but they didn't get very far in that altitude, and returned puffing and blowing."

The following day Buoy related that the party "traveled through a beautiful mountain park and meadow grove (Lake Valley) 12 miles to the lake. The portly anecdotist reminisced about "those good old days in the valley": "There stood the ruined cabin where the Stewart brothers were killed by Mickey Free and George Wilson. Brown had a cabin across the meadow, and Sam Higgins was down by the river." Ramsdale also recalled Captain Jim, Chief of the Washoe tribe, and the "hundreds of trout they used to spear and net." He chuckled at the recollection of the old judge (Seneca Dean) holding court in the valley to try a "Laker" on a stabbing charge. The trial had been in full session when suddenly a worried bailiff whispered in the judge's ear, "Bob Martin's sow's blundered into your Honor's garden and she's rootin' around turning it into a shambles."

"Is she now," the judge yelled, glaring up at his informant and tossing aside his papers. "Then damned if I don't make pork out of her." With that he vaulted through the open window of the courtroom "quicker'n hell."

Arriving at the lake, Buoy and his fellow travelers learned that Lake House had burned down several nights before. They moved east along the road and found accommodations at Almon M. Taylor's ranch (Bijou).[35]

In June of 1868 Martin Smith sold his remaining acreage to Samuel Alphonzo Nott of Nott's Station at "Junction" in Hope Valley.[36]

During the year 1870 the California Products of Agriculture census showed that 228 tons of hay had been baled in the Lake Valley Township and listed a creditable 100,600 pounds of butter as produced.[37] Five seasons later, C. F. McGlashan noted in his "Resources and Wonders of Tahoe" that Lake Valley annually turned out fourteen tons of butter and cheese with two cooper shops doing a capacity business in manufacturing butter firkins from the white fir of the region. Butter sold at the stiff price of 42 cents a pound and according to McGlashan was "in great demand for epicures." The productive season was June to November, during which time butter was kegged, eggs crocked, beef cattle fattened and hay baled. The valley was still mainly a "hay and dairy producing center, dotted with fertile ranches" and the Lake Valley ranchers contributed most of the 800 tons of hay cut along Tahoe's shoreline in 1875. That year hay brought the deflated price of $30.00 a ton in Carson.[38]

Ranching in Lake Valley, however, was now giving way to lumbering and the gigantic stands of tamarack, yellow and sugar pine were being cruised by representatives of the large lumber combines.[39] In the spring of 1876, Henry Marvin Yerington, of the Carson and Tahoe Lumber and Fluming Company sent Captain John W. Haynie into the valley to obtain timber leases for Yerington's companion organization, the El Dorado Wood and Flume Company.[40] Lower Lake Valley was now achieving the status of a major saw log producer, and by 1880 timber production had outstripped the dairying and haying industry, although one correspondent of the day reported admiringly: "The valley affords pasturage for 1,800 cows."[41]

During the fall of 1887, Messrs. Smart and Son were readying a winter logging camp with the expectation of banking 10,000,000 feet of saw logs and forest land leases were being snapped up, section by section. By 1888, lumbermen George Henry Dudley Meyers, Antonne Larson, John Hansen, A. M. Taylor, S. D. Weyant, George Washington Wiggins, Charles Siebeck, George Washington Chubbuck, and Matthew Culbertson Gardner had sold their land outright, given perpetual rights, or deeded timber holdings to the Glenbrook lumber and fluming group. In the vicinity of Sierra House alone, a grant of 1,720 acres was made to Bliss and Yerington.[42]

It was evident that the C. and T. L. and F. Company's lumbering empire was the one company on Lake Tahoe's shoreline that could successfully operate with widely scattered forest land holdings and still keep a step ahead of dwindling timber reserves. Lumber was king but a handful of ranchers in the valley stubbornly held out against offers of the lumber companies.

Notable among these settlers was the Celio family in upper Lake Valley, who owned much of the forested sections that ran from the site of Osgood's old toll house south to Luther Pass' western approach.[43]

The mid-1890's found lower Lake Valley stripped of its marketable timber and large scale logging in this region was over. However, other natural resources had not been depleted and the Upper Truckee River, where whitefish abounded, was still a favorite fishing stream for the Washoe Indian and the white man alike. The Washoes also continued their age-old practice of whisking the tops off sunflowers in the valley, gathering the seeds and grinding them into flour.[44]

After the turn of the century the Celios at last decided to cut the timber on their holdings in upper Lake Valley. A steam-powered sawmill was built in 1910 one mile north of Celio's Home Ranch. After the finished lumber had been graded it was hauled on wagons to Al Tahoe, Bijou and Lakeside for use in the expanding resort and summer home development. Double circular saws at the Celio's mill also supplied lumber to Echo Lake, Fallen Leaf, Camp Richardson and Glen Alpine. When the Tahoe market had become saturated the Celios delivered lumber by way of the Kingsbury Grade to Carson Valley.[45]

Today, ranching—mainly summer stock range and some lumbering—continues in Lake Valley, but a tremendous expansion in motel and hotel construction and other business enterprises stretching from south Stateline past the Tahoe "Y" (Tahoe Valley) indicates that upper Lake Valley will eventually be taken over. In spite of setbacks, such as the blaze that razed Al Tahoe in early June of 1956, the south end of Lake Tahoe is moving rapidly forward, with much of the activity centering around the new Heavenly Valley ski lift area.

In September of 1855, California's pioneer boundary surveyor, George H. Goddard, concluded his illuminating report on Lake Valley and the Tahoe region with an apologetic postscript that a century later still carries a wistful sincerity. His feeling for Lake Tahoe was expressed in a few self-effacing words:

"My poor attempts with pencil can give but a faint idea of the beauty of this spot and we can only hope to recall to those whose eyes have already beheld the scene, what must ever be one of memory's most pleasant pictures, while in those who have not yet seen it we hope to induce a desire to visit one of California's noblest lakes."[46]

GREAT-GRANDDAUGHTERS OF THE "BIG WATER'S" FIRST SETTLERS

Susie and Nettie, Washoe Indian squaws, near their summer campground in Lower Lake Valley. Photograph was taken on October 19, 1901, looking southwest at the Upper Truckee River and Western Sierra Nevada.

Glorene Dunlap Young

George D. Oliver

MYERS TO SUMMIT — A PUNISHING HAUL

The old Meyers Grade (Johnson Pass cut-off) was a series of switchbacks and obstructions when this picture was taken in the summer of 1891. Here a party of excursionists pause halfway up the mountainside while their drivers breathe the teams.

—slipping, sinking to their hips, struggling, falling. Half an hour later they were only black specks on the glaring whiteness. Then the men were lost to Yank's view. He was satisfied even though the small handful of gold coin they'd left at his station wouldn't pay for half of the food they had tucked away. Yank figured it this way: Wasn't he the host of the Sierry and wouldn't most of them be back? He turned toward his hotel and stamped down the snow steps to the entrance. He'd make up the loss some other time.

Eight years before this big winter the California Wagon Road Act of 1855 had provided for the Marlette-Day Central Sierra route survey that gave substance to a burned-out trapper's cabin at the foot of the Johnson Pass cut-off in Lake Valley. The log shack would be rebuilt a year later and develop into one of the most famous "home stations" on the Bonanza Road to Washoe and the old Central Overland Trail.

In the spring of 1851 Martin "Mart" Smith, a young broad-shouldered Pennsylvanian who bore the distinction of being Lake Valley's and the Tahoe region's first white settler, established his trading post in this back country wilderness.[1] Wayfarers, pack trains and even the emigrants' ox-drawn Conestoga wagons were passing over the Sierra Nevada by way of the Johnson cut-off, following feeder trails out of Eagle Valley (Carson City), Daggett's Ravine, from Mormon Station (Genoa) and Luther's Pass above Hope Valley. The travelers who took any one of these three routes had to move through Lake Valley on their way to Placerville, Sacramento City and the Coast.

Smith pre-empted land surrounding a broad, fertile meadow in what was to become Upper Lake Valley. Here, between the twin Sierra divides, he felled tamarack and built his log cabin. Lake Creek (Upper Truckee River) meandered through this loamy bottomland and awesome granite peaks towered more than 10,000 feet above sea level, their slopes thick with stands of pine and cedar. Smith hung out a crude, hand-carved sign that read: "Groceries—Meals at All Hours—and Lodging if Required."[2] During the winters of 1851 and 1852 he made the lonely, dangerous trek over Johnson Pass to Placerville, leaving behind a no-man's land of snow and ice.

In September, 1853, the *Placerville Herald* trumpeted the news of a gold strike under the heading, "Lake Valley Diggings." The *Herald* reported: "Gold has been found along the entire eastern base of the Carson-Sierra Range. Although it has long been known, it is now a fixed fact. A ditch has been constructed and miners are realizing $5.00 to $7.00 a day—proving that we are only beginning to know the extent of our gold fields."[3]

Two weeks later the *Herald* excitedly printed another account: "The gold find is now certain— Mr. Smith is going to arrange winter residence in the Valley and build a boat in the spring to explore the entire shore of the lake, which is more than 50 miles long, abounding in fishes of several varieties. It is a magnificent lake, formed from the crater of an extinct volcano, with amazing grottos. It (Tahoe) will become a world-renowned place . . ." The article closed with a space-filling appendage: "Lake Valley has strawberries in August."[4]

As no further mention of the "gold strike" was made after the eye-catching opening sentence, it is evident that Martin Smith, with the cooperative assistance of the *Herald*'s correspondent, had foisted a transparent hoax on the reading public of El Dorado County in an attempt to stimulate interest in the Tahoe region. Smith's drum-beating produced the desired effect. Miners, traders, then permanent settlers, trickled across the western Sierra and took up land near Smith's Station. Asa Hershel Hawley, Gould and Company, G. M. Duval, the Stewart brothers, George N. Douglass, Charles Scoffield, Michel Tagg, John Hulana—all established trading posts and "lodging cabins."[5]

In July of 1855, two murderous renegades, Mickey Free and George Wilson, hailing from the vicinity of Clarksville, California, slipped into the Valley. They killed the Stewarts in cold blood, set fire to many of the other trading posts, and burned Smith's Station to the ground.[6] The following year Smith took in Jim Muir as partner. Together they built a sizable hostelry on the site of Smith's old cabin and added a stable, corral and several outbuildings. In June of 1857, the first stage coach to cross the Sierra Nevada by way of the Johnson cut-off stopped at Smith and Muir's way station. A *Sacramento Union* correspondent accompanying the pioneer staging party reported: "We stayed in the Valley of Lake Bigler at the spacious hotel of Smith and Muir." With relish he wrote, "The natives gather around us in wonder and our hosts nearly refuse to believe the story of our trip. We made the mountains echo with cheers for the Pioneer Sierra Nevada Stage Company. Colonel Jarad Crandall's semi-weekly four-horse coach stage is a reality and two thorough braces and twelve horses will stock the line."[7]

Smith and Muir's was strategically located between Placerville and Carson Valley. It now became a logical stopover point and horse-change station for stages that ran on regular schedule during the spring, summer and fall months.

Among the handful of ranchers and trading post operators in Lake Valley, George N. Douglass appears to have prospered most. In April of 1858, Muir sold his half interest in the Station to Douglass, and a year later Smith and Douglass disposed of their holdings to Ephraim "Yank" Clement.[8] By the summer of 1859 Clement had the rudiments of a flourishing settlement. Through usage, the name had been changed to "Yank's Station."

The rush to Washoe had commenced and "Yank" and his wife, Lydia D. Mark Clement, watched in satisfaction as the dribble of traffic swelled to a deluge. The Clements expanded their facilities accordingly, and the old hotel was added to and renovated. It became a three-story, 14-room hostelry. A large combination horse-change stable and barn was built, across the road to the west. Corrals were enlarged to accommodate 200 head of livestock. Several private dwellings, two saloons, a general merchandise store, blacksmith shop, and cooperage were added. Opposite Yank's way station cattleman P. F. Powers built a stockyard, slaughter house and meat market.[9]

Wheelwrights, wagoners, traders, whiskey drummers, mechanics, hostlers, gamblers, and roustabouts made up the floating population of the station. Many stayed on to become permanent residents. Clement was grateful. He had made a good deal with Smith and Douglass and bought at the right time.

Several miles north of the habitation stood Woodburn's Mill and Mac's Sierra House. Osgood's Toll Station lay at the foot of Johnson Pass, one mile to the south. On Tahoe's shoreline, six miles away, Dean and Van Wagener's Lake (Bigler) House served the wayfarer.[10]

The immediate improvement of the trail up Daggett Ravine (later Kingsbury grade), and over the pass, prompted by the discovery of gold and silver at the end of the rainbow—the Comstock Lode —were the two major factors that made Yank's Station and the other Lake Valley lodgments grow.

Whenever Clement was asked how he received the nickname "Yank" he carefully explained: "There's none could pronounce Eph-raim ce-rect, so I'm handled with what marks my northern bringin' up."[11]

Mrs. Clement was well known to young and old as "Aunt Liddy." In contrast to her gregarious husband she was reserved, favoring black dresses and a tightly-flattened hairdo with severe part. In this Sierra outpost of civilization, hardworking, capable "Aunt Liddy" was a godsend. She ministered to the sick, acted as midwife, and answered all calls that concerned the unraveling of her widely-scattered neighbors' domestic problems.

Yank gained his measure of fame as a "teller of tall tales for timid people," and his reputation for being the "Champeen Liar of the Sierry" soon spread throughout the Tahoe region. As a '49er trail rider and mountain man, Yank's buckskins, long hair and moccasins were in occupational keeping, but he affected this mode of attire for many years after becoming a hotel keeper. Yank's reason made good business sense. "It dam' sure brings in them customers," he would say with a wink.

Edward Vischer, California historian and sketch artist of the 1860's, has handed down a vignette of Yank's Station that captures much of the famous hostelry's early day color and action:

"Our sketch (made in 1861) represents the peculiar movement brought about by the fall trade; the continued transit of California-bound western emigrants forming an almost uninterrupted caravan. All may find accommodations at worthy Yank's Station, a household word to the traveler, with associations more of the wayside inn than modern hotel description, a table always good and often supplied with bountiful gifts of the mountain and forest, and the delicious trout of neighboring Lake Bigler. A hearty welcome, above all, freely extended to the prevailing standard guest, the indefatigable but always jolly teamster, the restive, but not always prosperous miner, and, to the broken down wayfarer, the stirring stagedriver or expressman, the dashing merchant prince from Bay City (San Francisco), or the recruiting Washoe nabob, stopping their panting steeds for a breathing spell en route for some yachting rendezvous on the Lake."[12]

In December of 1861, William Morris Stewart, who was to become Nevada's first Senator and later the "father of American mining law," struggled on snowshoes from Carson over the Sierra; his destination San Francisco. Stewart was desperate. He needed $30,000 immediately to subsidize his mining and legal career. At dusk he reached Yank's. Although Clement had been all but eaten out of house and home, he rustled what food he could for the huge six-foot Nevadan. Another complication arose. The inn was crowded, and there was no bed for Stewart. Good naturedly he wrapped himself in his blankets and squeezed in among the sleepers on the floor. The next morning Yank warned Stewart not to attempt the trip over the western Sierra summit. The burly lawyer laughed and disappeared into a blinding snowstorm, bound for Johnson Pass. Over 40-foot snowdrifts and through one of the heaviest blizzards in the Tahoe region's history, he fought his way to Strawberry Station, then on to Placerville and Sacramento City. Finding the valley flooded, Stewart borrowed a rowboat, flagged down a river steamer and finally made it to San Francisco. After floating his loan, he was back at Yank's one week from the time he'd left.

The station was still snowbound. No one had come through—not even a sleigh had reached Johnson Pass. Yank, as amazed as though he were welcoming Stewart's ghost, threw his arms around him. Then Clement uncorked a bottle and both drank to the successful conclusion of the near-suicidal trip.

"Willie," Yank told the young giant, "if you can do *that*, you can dam' near make it to the 'Big Blue' all by yerself. But don't try no more shenanigans. Mebbe my payin' customers might try the same caper. I'll jus' tell 'em you came in from Deans. I've sweared to 'em all not even a werewolf could flip over the Sierry the other way. Don't make me no *liar* and a pauper besides." Stewart grinned understandingly and pushed on toward Daggett Pass.[13]

The summer of 1863 found Yank's Station once again caught up in the excitement of the stampede to the mines. Yank's stables had stalls for 40 horses, and he wished he had room for 400. Concord coaches, more realistically known as "Pitching Betsies," clattered in and out of the settlement at all hours of day and night. Braking to a stop in choking clouds of dust, they disgorged 12, 14 or more passengers from their leather-slung, swaying interiors, drivers' boxes, and "dickey seats." The famished wayfarers made for Yank's on the run, their mouths watering for one of "Aunt Liddy's" smoking hot meals. On the east side of the establishment, rows of "Kentuck" mules fed from portable cribs, with cargoes lashed to pack saddles. Their Mexican drivers lolled in the shade and spent the stopover time "under the solace of the cigarette or strumming the guitar." In sharp contrast to this picture of romantic idleness were the bearded teamsters' Washoe wagons with their splendid array of comfortably blanketed draft animals.[14] Dust-caked, masterfully profane muleskinners set the drags on their loaded carriers and stepped into Yank's saloon for a quick shot of "40 rod" whiskey, better known as a "high-country acclimator." Droves of sheep and cattle lunged down the main thoroughfare which served as the only street. They wheeled in all directions, holding up and disrupting traffic in Yank's "front yard."

Everyone was in a hurry. Stop at Yank's overnight, push on to the Comstock at dawn, unload the supplies that kept life throbbing at the mines, and then return to Sacramento City to start the cycle all over again. Would it last? No one really knew. Bummer, miner, nabob, gambler, women of the silk and the street, all were part of the milling throng that paused at Yank's Station and moved on.

Passage to and through the settlement took on an atmosphere of adventure and to some this had spine-chilling overtones.

One anecdote concerns the Wells Fargo fast freight making its western run over the Sierra Nevada. During a late fall in the mid-1860's, a canvas-covered freight wagon, drawn by three spans of horses, was hi-tailing it over Daggett Pass and rattling down the rutted canyon road toward Friday's Station and Yank's. Alongside the driver rode the "swamper" and at his feet lay the 5-foot horn used to scatter other traffic on the road. Inside the vehicle two passengers sat on top of the cargo—one was a grizzled Irishman from Virginia City, the other a corpulent Negro woman. Both were on their way to San Francisco. The main shipment consisted of two caskets containing, respectively, the last remains of a miner from Austin and a departed lady from the Washoe Hills.

The wind was rising as the horses and their macabre load passed Friday's and swung along the lake highway toward Yank's. Chill blasts moaned through the pines, creating a pall that shrouded the living and deceased inside the stage. Bounced and tossed, the two passengers waited grimly for the station stop. Since the fall of darkness the swamper had been toying with an idea. He now could not

ENOUGH FEED FOR 2000 ANIMALS

Yank's Station in the summer of 1865, with Washoe wagons and teams choking the rutted turnpike. Barns, stables and corrals (right of picture) housed hay, grain and animals. Station and outbuildings to left. Looking southwest toward Johnson Pass (Echo Summit).

resist the impulse that had grown into a whimsical compulsion. Carefully he parted the curtains and pushed his warning horn between the coffins.

"Isn't it awful to be dead?" murmured a ghostly voice.

White traveler and black turned startled faces toward each other as they heard the sepulchral tones.

"It is that, and mighty disrespectful to us dead to be tumbled about," a second and higher voice replied. Terror gripped the shaking passengers.

"There's an Irishman sitting on my neck," complained the first corpse.

"I've got a fat cook on my chest, and she weighs about 250 pounds," whined the high voice.

At this point the Wells Fargo flyer pulled up at Yank's Station. With a shriek that reverberated across the valley, the colored woman disappeared over the tailgate, closely followed by her companion from the Shamrock Isle.

After a stiff drink or two at the bar, the bug-eyed son of Erin managed to screw up enough courage to board the westbound express once again. But the Negro woman resolutely sat herself down on the steps of Yank's hostelry. *She* would wait for the morning stage.[15]

Unlike several other way stations bordering Lake Tahoe, Yank's could not boast of a natural wonder. Lack of an attraction such as Glenbrook's Shakespeare Cliff, Rocky Point House's "Lady of the Lake" and Campbell's Hot Springs was finally remedied in the summer of 1872. Near the station Ephraim Clement discovered a singular freak of nature. It was growing in the fork of a stunted tamarack. Yank immediately named the arboreal contortion "Nick of the Woods," pointing out that it resembled the features of a hoary-headed old sinner wedged sufferingly into the crotch of the tree for eternity. Clement proudly showed the large burl to all who indicated the slightest interest. Many viewers publicly stated that it looked as though an artist had carved the head. Privately they expressed the opinion old "Nick of the Woods" was the spitting image of "mine host" himself. But Yank was elated. At last he, too, had a tourist attraction.[16]

After the main route of travel shifted to the Central Pacific Railroad, Ephraim and Lydia Clement stayed on as owner-proprietors of the station for five more years. During the last few seasons that the Clements ran Yank's Station, an El Dorado County hotel keeper had been dickering to buy the establishment. The man was George Henry Dudley Meyers, native of Hanover, Germany, and owner of Six Mile House above Placerville during the period of heavy teaming to the mines.

On June 27, 1873, Meyers purchased the famous way station along with several quarter sections of land adjoining. Yank and "Aunt Liddy" then moved to their lakeshore property on Tahoe, located to the west of M. C. Gardner's Camp (Camp Richardson). Here they built a 40-room summer "record."[17]

Meyers and his family engaged in dairying and the cattle business. They also sold timber rights on their land to the logging and cordwood contractors who were now accumulating choice forest preserves in Lake Valley. By the summer of 1886, Meyers' astute handling of his business ventures had paid off handsomely and his holdings totaled 1,440 acres.[18]

Their rancher neighbors included William and Mary Lyons, William D. Rantz, Samuel Elliott Kyburz, Charles Abraham Lukens, Ruben Watson Jewell, Carlo Guisseppi Celio, Asa Hershel Hawley, William Alpha Green, Henry and Charles Dixon, Charles Warren Winstanley, Timothy Guy Barton, Himan Dana Barton, and Hiram "Hy" Barton.[19]

A story is told about William Lyons, who, in the late fall of 1884, questioned an old Washoe Indian, known as "One-Eyed" John, on the possibilities of a heavy snowfall that winter. The red men were supposed to be infallible weather prophets, and "One-Eyed" John looked long and hard at the sky for a few minutes. Then he turned to Lyons. "I can't tell for sure right now, Mr. Bill," he replied thoughtfully. "Better able to tell you next spring."[20]

William Lyons' wife Mary had an experience of a different nature with a young Indian buck who daily stole the single egg laid by her hen. The savage topped his thievery with impudence and, finally, with threats. Although she had never held a gun before, Mrs. Lyons went to the house and reached into the bureau drawer where her husband kept his service revolver. Then she returned to the yard, leveled the gun at the Indian and raised the barrel, firing into the air. The buck took to his heels across the meadow, splashed through the river and panted up to Lyons, who was cutting stove wood in the forest.

"Hey, Mr. Bill, what's the matter your squaw? She shoot," he blurted out.

"Well, Sam," replied Lyons, "take your choice, a hole in the head or no egg a day. Which do you want?" After considering a moment, the buck got the point. He never stole the precious egg or bothered Mrs. Lyons again.[21]

Yank had inaugurated the custom of holding an annual "Grand Ball" at the Station and George Meyers held to the tradition. The celebration was always an all-night affair. From miles around cowmen and their families arrived in buckboards and spring wagons for the great event. During the summer, horse races were held on weekends, and the settlement, which now sported four bars, did a land-office business. A half mile gravel and sagebrush racetrack had been laid out southeast up the valley, with the starting line in front of Meyers Hotel (old Yank's Station). "Hy" Barton's racehorses were usually the favorites and seldom disappointed the smart money boys—or anyone else for that matter.

In the 1880's the frontier gambler was still a stock character with his carefully creased hat, puffed-out hair, fancy gold-chained weskit and carefully manicured nails.

George Meyers learned to tolerate anything that walked on two or four legs or rode on four wheels —wagon loads of chickens, butter firkins stacked on freighter wagons, lean pigs to be fattened on skim milk for the market, shingle and cordwood carriers, fruit peddlers, cattle and sheep.[22]

After 30 years at old Yank's Station, the Meyers sold to the Celio family, who settled in Lake Valley during the spring of 1873. Celio's Incorporated Lumber Company was formed in 1905 and five years later the corporation built a steam-powered sawmill on property owned by the Celios some five miles to the south of the station. They also built another mill on the slopes of Gardner Mountain bordering the old back road to Fallen Leaf. For 47 years the Celios continued in the lumber business.[23]

On November 25, 1938, Meyers was swept by a fire. It destroyed the old hotel and store which had catered to travelers for more than 70 years.

The site of the original hostelry on the east side of Highway 50 is marked by a Pony Express plaque, and a small cluster of old and new buildings constitute the settlement of Meyers today. Across the road and north of the fireplace marking the site of old Yank's Station stands Osgood's Toll House, moved from the foot of the Meyers grade to its present location by the Celios.[24] The toll house constitutes one of the last proud reminders of the staging and bonanza days when the flood of humanity and animals, enroute to the Comstock, paused at its drop gate to pay for the right of passage over what is now Echo Summit.

Chapter Twenty-eight

SIERRA HOUSE

★ Tнıck sтΑνds of tamarack, bordering the west Kingsbury Grade, blurred to a black wall as darkness closed around the creaking, swaying coach. "Hank" Monk, "master whip of the Sierra," was running late out of Carson after being delayed on the summit of Daggett Pass by a broken wheel spoke. Now he was urging his six-in-hand along at a gallop toward Sierra House. The biting cold of late fall hung in the air and the famous Jehu gulped burning swallows from a half empty liquor bottle clutched in his gloved left hand, while hunching deeper into the tobacco stained collar of his great coat.

Between drinks Monk cursed the luck that had put him at least an hour behind schedule. Impatiently he looked forward to the station stop ahead. As his "mud wagon" rounded the last turn leading to the crossing at Cold Creek, Monk noticed a break in the timber ahead and the bright light of a rising moon brought the shadow of a moving figure into sharp relief. Instinctively Hank tightened on the multiple reins and an idea flashed through his mind. If this *were* a road agent, he thought, he'd capitalize on his reputation, which was based as much upon his drinking ability as it was on his prowess in handling a triple span of horses.

Monk leaned around the side of the careening four-wheeler and called sharply to his passengers. Then he upended the bottle, spilling its contents generously over the leathers and himself. Simultaneously he came up on the "ribbons" with his right hand and fell sideways onto the cushion. As his team slowed to a walk, Hank reached for a heavy iron spanner beneath his feet.

The anticipated "Hands up" penetrated to the travelers and a hooded figure leaped to the off-leader. Running swiftly past the swing and wheelers, the highwayman stopped short opposite Monk, leveled his sawed-off shotgun, then disposed of the stagedriver with a contemptuous glance. He reached for the handle of the coach door and, holding his gun high, ordered the passengers out.

Still pretending to be in a drunken stupor, Hank stealthily raised his improvised truncheon. Swinging heavily he brought it down on the flour sack covering the road agent's head. The desperado crumpled to the turnpike, his gun spinning beneath the wheels of the coach.

Monk swung down from his high box and picked up the weapon. Ignoring the body spread-eagled in the dust, he turned to his shaken passengers and shouted, "You and the bullion's safe alright, but that miserable bastard cost me my last drink." Astonished silence greeted this unexpected comment. Hank climbed back to the seat, clicked to his skittish team and rolled away toward Sierra House.[1]

Legend contends that the notorious road agents, Black Bart and Jack Bell, stayed at Sierra House during the peak of their plunderous activity, which centered on the dark green strong boxes of the Wells Fargo Express. This is coinage of fancy as these renegades never operated as far east as Lake Valley. However, "Long Haired" Sam Brown, the infamous coward-killer from Washoe, spent many a night in

Rose Chubbuck Dodson

HAUNT OF THE "SILENT TERROR" AND "LONG-HAIRED" SAM BROWN

Sierra House and Saloon in July of 1884, showing the Chubbuck family and loggers in front of the hostelry.

the Sierra House saloon challenging every defenseless customer who walked through the door. Brown's specialty was the unprotected. When the mood struck him—which was often—Brown would knife or shoot any man he could intimidate with his bluster and bragging, preferably when his intended victim's back was turned. He generally climaxed outright murder by wiping a bloody bowie knife on his buckskins or blowing smoke casually out of the barrel of his revolver. Then "Long Haired" would bellow, "What's one more?" This swaggering bully of the Comstock is said to have sported 20 notches on the butt of his gun and bragged that he maintained his own "private cemetery." "Fighting" Sam Brown, as he was also known, met death in July of 1861. A load of buckshot in the chest finished him off as he blubbered and cowered in front of Henry Van Sickle's shotgun. The now famous coroner's verdict serves as a fitting epitaph for this lethal butcher: "Samuel Brown has come to his death from a just dispensation of an all wise providence. It served him right."[2]

James Stewart, with his brace of six-guns, dubbed the "Silent Terror," was another unwelcome patron of Sierra House during the early 1860's.[3]

Many of the famous drivers gloving the reins on James McClean's Pioneer Stage Line made regular stops at the hostelry—"Curly Bill" Gerhart, "Big John" Littlefield, Johnny Bruso, Billy Hodges, Charlie Watson, Ned Blair, Charles "Coon Hollow" Saddle, "Newt" Spencer and Jacob "Big Jake" Putman. "Baldy" Green was another whip and he held the all-time record for being stopped by the greatest number of road agents. Hank Monk was the best known, although he was not generally considered to be the most skillful.[4]

To Robert Garwood Dean goes the distinction of building the original Sierra House. Early in the winter of 1858, Dean left Genoa, Nevada, striking southwest toward the summit divide of the Eastern Sierra Range. He camped the first night on 15 feet of ridge ice, running with his Norwegian skis into Lake Valley the following morning. He was looking for land on which to build a way station, when he came upon a pine-studded clearing, located some two and one-half miles southeast of Tahoe, that bordered the old Emigrant Ridge route and Daggett Ravine trail. Dean decided this would be his location.[5]

He was impressed by the fact that the extensive meadow overlooked a small stream (Cold Creek). In addition only two to three feet of snow lay on the ground.

The young woodsman rolled pine saplings together to mark his pre-emption and the following spring "hewed the logs and whipsawed the lumber" for a two-story hostelry. Dean completed Sierra House in the summer of 1859. Several months later he sold out to William Mac(k) of Sacramento and

HERE THE GIANT PINES
STILL STAND

*Ox teams and lumberjacks at
Sierra House in the summer of 1885.
Facing west on the Placerville-
Carson back road. The barn
(far left) was the only building
remaining in 1957.*

Author's collection

joined William W. Lapham and his uncle, Judge Seneca Dean who were building Lake Bigler House on the south shore of Tahoe.[6]

William Mack added to what he now also called "Mac's Station." By the summer of 1861 the main building consisted of five rooms downstairs with additional accommodations on the second floor. Mack converted the north end of the station into a saloon. Then he built a covered porch running the full length of the establishment, which fronted on the new Placerville-Carson Valley "back road."

Three hundred head of cattle could be pastured on the surrounding bottomland and double stalls in the stables took care of the relays of horses used by the stage and express companies. Mack constructed four large barns and a stock corral on the meadow's edge. Business couldn't have been better.

In September of 1862 the *Sacramento Union* reported: "William Mack is improving the place (Sierra House) very fast." The hostelry was now a familiar sight to the stagedrivers and teamsters when their animals forded Trout Creek going east or sloshed through Miller Creek (Heavenly Valley) and Cold Creek, headed west after leaving Lapham's Stateline Hotel.

On August 11, 1866, William Mack placed the following advertisement in the *Sacramento Union*: "The well known Sierra House in Lake Valley, on the route to Virginia City, is for sale. The dairy ranch is excellent and a surrounding acreage allows 300 tons of hay to be cut on the mowing land."[7] Mack had foreseen the competitive threat of the Central Pacific Railroad, which would reach Lake Station (Reno) the following year. The surge of traffic rumbling past Sierra House was about to vanish.

A. G. Tryon was running the inn at the time and he bought Mack out in 1867. Tryon ranched at Sierra House until the summer of 1871 and then sold to Haskin Calvin Swain, a 50-year-old farmer and native of Virginia.

The station now became a principal layover stop for fruit peddlers who were crossing with their wagons to Carson and Virginia cities. Swain raised hay in the meadowland, and ran his cattle into High Meadow to the east. Sierra House was still considered a "half way station" and Swain could count on a dozen or so guests each week during the summer months.

When Swain acquired Sierra House it was little changed from the time William Mack made his improvements. The new owner covered the log station with bark trim, sealing the interior with tongue and groove. To the rear of the building Swain added two L-shaped, one-story clapboard annexes. These served as extra guest bedrooms as well as sleeping quarters for the Chinese cook. Here also were dining room, kitchen and storeroom.

Author's collection

OXEN-POWERED SHORTLINE

*George Washington Chubbuck's
loaded flatcar headed northwest
downgrade toward
Bijou in the summer of 1884.
Chubbuck and children on top of the
chained logs. Trout Creek to the
right of the picture.*

Swain is said to have pre-empted additional land until his holdings totaled 2,000 acres. He sold the timber rights to Thomas B. Rowland of Rowland's Station and other loggers in the vicinity. Assisted by his son Charles Stevens Swain, he augmented his station business with dairying. The milk house was located to the northwest of the main buildings and a large water wheel, supplied by a diversion ditch from Cold Creek, turned the four-foot square butter churn. Butter was transferred from the box to white fir firkins, salted down and sold in Carson Valley during the fall months.

A. B. Sieger, Swain's son-in-law and former mine superintendent at Gold Hill, joined the Swain family. This touched off a dispute concerning the ranch's operation and Haskin Swain sold his holdings to S. D. Weyant and W. A. Chittenden, Lake Valley lumbermen, in the spring of 1884.[8]

The new owners leased Sierra House to George Washington Chubbuck, who moved his family over from McCumber's Ranch. James Henry "Hank" Martin, former partner in Lake House with R. G. and Judge Seneca Dean, purchased the way station in 1891 and in turn leased to dairyman Robert Lucius Bence in the late 1890's. Bence was still operating the ranch and station in 1905, and during December of 1912, Chris Johnson, Sr., a pioneer Laker known as "Old 7% Chris," obtained Sierra House by foreclosing on an $800 note.[9]

Johnson died early in 1913 without having resided at the station. His son Knox Johnson lived here for several seasons and then passed the ranch, on a rental basis, to the Robert Dixons. After Mrs. Dixon's death in 1918 it was again leased, this time to the Ray Smiths. Today the location of old Sierra House and the surrounding land sections are a part of Mrs. Stella Knox Johnson's holdings.[10]

During Henry Martin's tenure at the station he remodeled the buildings and made additions. The wings on the original structure were said to have been removed and a dining room, kitchen and divided pantry built to the north of the main house. Still farther north Martin constructed his own four-room residence. Martin continued to make extensive changes to the old way station, and photographic evidence shows the original Sierra House to have been either cut in half or replaced entirely by one of the annexes. The sign that stood over the front entrance and read "Sierra House and Saloon" was shortened to read "Sierra House" and the covered porch and green shutters on the windows were removed. The white picket fence, considered very "tony" for its day, was left standing.

In the early 1910's supernatural happenings were reported at the hostelry. Louis Filmore, a Washoe Indian employed by the Knox Johnsons, insisted that he often saw ghosts sweeping through the rooms of Sierra House in the late fall months after the place had been vacated. According to Filmore, the spectral visitors rattled windows and slammed doors at all times of day and night and interfered with his caretaking chores.[11]

Other strange occurrences were recorded. One Wolf, employed as a handyman and woodcutter around the ranch, added a macabre touch to daily life at Sierra House by talking to himself most of the time. Familiarly known as "Wolfy," he was considered somewhat muddled in his thinking. One gusty afternoon in April of 1914, Knox Johnson heard a cowbell jangling wildly on the road outside the house. He thought nothing of it until he suddenly remembered that none of his belled stock was grazing in the vicinity. Peering through the half open door Johnson was startled to see "Wolfy" sneaking from tree to tree in the gathering dusk. A brass cowbell hung by its rawhide strap from Wolfy's neck. When Johnson confronted him Wolfy gave a simple explanation: "I like to hear it ring."[12]

One night Johnson heard a light tapping on the front door of the way station. Upon opening it he saw a woman standing in the shadows, her face covered by a cape. She motioned toward her lathered horse and requested lodging. Johnson offered her food, then showed her to the guest room. The next morning when he saw her face in the daylight, it was so horribly disfigured he could not believe it to be the face of a human being. The woman mounted her jade without a word of thanks and left as mysteriously as she had come.[13] Several days later Johnson was idly thumbing through a Placerville newspaper when his eyes were drawn to a hideously familiar face. Above was the caption: "The Whipped Murderess of Hangtown." The article went on to describe how one of her poison victims had managed to beat her about the face with a riding crop before he died an agonizing death. Johnson was particularly impressed by the concluding sentence, "This female fiend escaped from custody last week and is now being sought by the law." Thereafter Knox Johnson kept a shotgun handy in the front hallway.[14]

During the 1930's and 40's the sagging remains of Sierra House gradually fell in, and one by one barns and other outbuildings collapsed under the heavy winter snows.

In 1953, the last remaining section of the famous way station was leveled and its sidings and support timbers were burned in the spring of 1955.

Southeast from the site of the former hostelry stands the last of the original structures, a 30-foot square stable. Carved alongside the door is the date, 1881, but the building probably dates back another decade, as over-width, 24-inch planking from Woodburn's Mill sheathes the south wall.

To the right of the dirt road going north, a 4 by 4-inch board juts from a scarred yellow pine, some 25 feet above the ground. Recalled in 1876 as "just high enough to clear the tops of the stages and wagons as they passed underneath," it was originally used as a cross-arm for loading bales of hay.[15]

Today the forest land surrounding this quiet mountain meadow frames Mount Tallac to the west and here are found some of the most impressive pine trees in the Tahoe region.

Behind the present wooden fence that borders the former Emigrant and Bonanza thoroughfare, a small grove of quaking aspen, encircled by bunch grass, marks the grave of old Sierra House.

TOURISTS AND TROUTING

Van Wagener's Hotel and Fishery as sketched by William Vischer on April 30, 1861. Left background: Lake (Bigler) House (Van Wagener's) with commercial fishermen's log cabin on lakeshore, boats, and nets. Looking southwest toward Mt. Tallac.

Chapter Twenty-nine

AL TAHOE

"A<small>T</small> L<small>AKE</small> H<small>OUSE</small>, a tolerably good sized shanty at the foot of the grade, we found a large party assembled taking their ease as best they could in such a place, without much to eat and but little to drink except old fashioned tarantula juice warranted to kill at 40 paces." J. Ross Browne, sage chronicler of Washoe, was describing the explosive commotion he found at Tahoe's first lakeshore hotel during the fall of 1860. Browne continued:

"One hundred maddened gold seekers of a night, on their way to the mines, are milling around presided over by their host, R. G. Dean, who bustles about in a constant state of nervous excitement, doing more scolding and general hotel work in the brief span of half an hour than any man I ever saw. Worn out with his run of customers and with no place to stow 'em and little if any standing room the scene presents a bedlam of disorganized confusion. It seems as though all are cussin' at the proprietor for not keeping enough provisions and how could he when they eat him clean out every day with some of 'em never paying and never intending to."

Browne stated emphatically that he was not sorry to get clear of Lake House, with its filth and troubles, but he admitted to being forewarned that it furnished the worst food on the road to Washoe. In this, at least, he was not disappointed.[1]

On a dog-leg of the old Johnson Pass emigrant road and fronting on the water one-half mile northeast of Lake Stream's (Upper Truckee) influx into Tahoe, construction of Lake Bigler House was begun in the spring of 1859.[2]

Earlier in the year Judge Seneca Dean of Genoa, Nevada, and William W. Lapham, former proprietor of Calaveras Mammoth Grove Hotel, pre-empted 320 acres on the far south shore of the lake. Seneca Dean's nephew, Robert Garwood Dean, joined the two men and the way station was completed by late fall of '59. Besides bearing the distinction of being the initial "record" on the shoreline of Tahoe, its conflict of names would confuse the historian for nearly a century. It was to be known variously as Lake Bigler House, Lake House, Van Wagener's Hotel and Dean and Martin's Station, until Thomas B. Rowland firmly established the name Rowland's Lake House and Station.

Originally the hotel was a relatively large eight-room, two and one-half story hewn log structure, set on a rise of ground several hundred yards back from the lake, in a grove of yellow pine.

The partners expected a run-out of the road projected by the California Wagon Road Act of 1855. They also logically, if mistakenly, believed that the Central Pacific would lay its transcontinental rails over the Sierra Nevada by way of Lake Valley and pass close by their station.

However, the discovery of the Comstock Lode in 1859 was the major reason for Dean and Lapham's hotel gamble and the attendant construction of Kingsbury and McDonald's Daggett Pass toll road into Carson Valley brought traffic sweeping past their doors in an unexpected flood tide.

LAKE TAHOE'S FIRST SHORELINE HOSTELRY

Lake (Bigler) House (Van Wagener's) as it appeared in the fall of 1865 looking southwest toward the lake and Upper Truckee River Meadow. Robert Garwood Dean (standing to the left of the riding horse), Judge Seneca Dean and family in the entrance way.

In the spring of 1860, Lapham, recognizing that greater monetary rewards lay in owning a hotel outright, sold his interest in Lake House to William Van Wagener, a native of Albany, New York, and pre-empted land two and one-half miles to the east. Here he built Lapham's Hotel.[3]

Van Wagener and the Deans now extended their log hotel on the south side, adding 20 rooms, a wall-papered lobby and pine-bark saloon. The enlarged log and mortar structure offered two white-painted entrance ways on the east side, brick chimneys on either end of the establishment, long thin shakes for roofing and a hollowed-out saw log watering trough, placed in front of a narrow porch where rough-hewn benches were secured to the building.

By the summer of 1860, the headlong rush to the mines was approaching fantastic proportions and the owners of Lake House reaped the harvest. The partners were strongly sympathetic to the Union cause and they took a dim view of "Honest John" Bigler's name that, for nearly ten years, had "besmirched the waters of the native Washoes' *Tahoe*." As California's ex-governor Bigler leaned closer and closer toward the Confederacy, the three men decided that the appellation *Bigler* would have to be changed. After assuring themselves that Tahoe meant "Big Water," by sounding out some of the more intelligent Washoes, they declared the lake's name to be Tahoe. They also "obtained a post office under the name Tahoe (Lake Valley Post Office) and a small town at the outlet of the lake sprang up and they persuaded the residents to call it 'Tahoe City'." Their feeling was that "Old John" would have to look to other means for immortality, as the waters of the lake were too pure to bear the name Bigler.[4]

William H. Brewer, a member of the Whitney Survey party and pioneer California historian, wrote on August 22, 1863, that he and his group camped in a pine grove adjoining Lake House and only a few rods from the lake. Brewer mentioned "the large log hotel" and the "prevalence of teamsters, pleasure seekers and 'gentlemen at large' on their way to the mines." Brewer advised that the hotel was "fine and well managed," a definite improvement over J. Ross Browne's findings three years before. He considered "the lake itself to be *the* feature of the place" and then quoted a conversation he overheard between two teamsters who had sidled up to the Lake House bar. According to Brewer, the first teamster ordered a shot glass of whiskey and then turned to the second muleskinner.

Number One: "A good many people here."

Number Two: "Yes."

First Teamster: "What are they doing?"

Second Teamster: "Nothing."

First: "Nothing at all?"

Second: "Why, yes. In the City we would call it 'bumming' (the California word for doing nothing, Brewer carefully noted) but here they call it pleasure." Both then took a drink and "depart(ed) for their more practical and useful avocations."[5]

In the fall of the same year a Conestoga wagon was rafted across Lake Tahoe from the beach below Lake House—destination, Centerville, in the heart of the mushrooming, turbulent Red, White and Blue Mining District. This was the first recorded barge tow on Tahoe, with the sailing vessel *Iron Duke* presumably doing the towing.

On September 3, 1864, Jesus Maria Estudillo, pioneer from San Leandro, California, penned a highlight of his Sierra-Lake Valley crossing in his diary:

"As we proceeded a little further I caught sight of the renowned Lake Bigler. Would that I had the Geoffry Crayon (a pseudonym of Washington Irving) to describe this wonderful lake.—I can't say much of the house (Lake House) and vicinity, as we got here in the afternoon about dark."

September 8, Thursday. "I have been able to have a better look at the place today, but this only from the house and when out in the water this morning, but the impression it has made on me will be as lasting as monumental brass. Such scenery and such beautiful water are enough to enchant the pleasure looking individual. There was a shooting match here today for a silver cup, won by the proprietor of the house, Mr. Dean. We will leave tomorrow and go to Glenbrook and then to Carson."[6]

Ramsdale Buoy, drum-beater for the Tahoe region in the 1860's, wrote in May of 1866 that "Lake House burned a few days previous to his party's arrival and they were therefore forced to find accommodations at Jim Taylor's Ranch house (Bijou) nearby."[7] Robert Garwood and "Judge" Seneca Dean

BUNG-STARTERS, BEER
SPIGOTS AND
BARLEYCORN BOTTLES
LAY IN THE WATER

*Tom Rowland's Custom House Saloon,
over-water general merchandise store
and station buildings
in the summer of 1876.*

now owned the property, having bought out Henry "Hank" Martin the previous year, three years after Martin acquired Van Wagener's one-third interest. The Deans decided against rebuilding. Instead they accepted an offer for their land submitted by Thomas Benton Rowland, a tall, angular, bewhiskered six-footer, former owner of Strawberry House (Station) on the Johnson Pass road between Slippery Ford and Kyburz.[8] Rowland took title to the land sections that today constitute Al Tahoe and added 33 acres in the vicinity of Taylor's Landing.

Tom Rowland shortly started construction of a new way station on the site of old Lake House. When completed in the spring of 1868, it was described as a "small place with only eight bedrooms." Six additional "sleeping rooms" were to be added within the next two years. Rowland also turned his hand to rounding out the little settlement. Half a dozen clapboard shacks and whitewashed houses were built, along with Charles Parrish's blacksmith shop and ox-shoeing stall. The Davis Brothers, from Carson and Glenbrook, fabricated a false front merchandise store down by the water and a smoke house and milk houses were put up to the west.[9]

Rowland's most ambitious project, soon to become the main attraction at his station, was a large, enclosed two and one-half story dance pavilion and saloon, completed in July of 1870. This structure allowed Thomas Rowland to inaugurate his custom of holding annual dances and "socials." His guest list read like a "Who's Who" of the Sierra Nevada and the sending out of invitations, in itself, was a major undertaking.

Rowland's Great Ball in August of 1870 had the makings of a "smash affair." Jim "Doc" Benton, owner of Benton's Stage Line in Carson City, placed additional four-in-hands on the run over Kings Canyon and Clear Creek grades to take care of the increase in business. The steamers *Governor Blaisdel, Truckee* and *Emerald I* were pressed into service to ferry guests from Tahoe City, Glenbrook, McKinney's and Campbell's Hot Springs. As the woodburners pulled into Rowland's wharf, jammed with shouting party-goers, a Carson correspondent discovered that nearly all of the 94 "regulars" attending were unmarried, thus promising a "crackling time." Devil-may-care stags and unattached young ladies dustered in aboard Concords, "mud wagons," fringe tops and spring wagons. Even a Washoe "sail-top" was commandeered for the exciting occasion.

Dancing to the music of Church and Jones string and organ quartet, brought over the mountains from Sacramento City, got under way at 8:30 in the evening and continued without let-up until 6:00 in the morning. Then, with the sun at their backs, all able-bodied males who could crawl, stagger, or be carried, joined the ladies who had clambered back on the steamers for an excursion around the lake.

Party crashers had arrived at the ball from Reno, Gold Hill and Virginia City. Two determined couples, with invitations, even made the long, spine-cracking trip from Placerville and stayed for a full week—recuperating. Another coach, crammed with merrymakers, started from Carson but, unfamiliar with the Sierra routes, missed the celebration entirely after driving all night. They, however, arrived on the summit of Luther Pass in time to watch a golden and scarlet sunrise over Tahoe. Although some of the stags, in various stages of intoxication, had to be routed out of the boiler rooms of the steamers the day following Rowland's "overwhelming crusher," the only reported casualty turned out to be "Doc" Benton's finest buggy horse that sickened and passed out of the picture while returning a group to Eagle Valley.[10]

The male participants unanimously agreed that the Great Ball had been a "thoroughly wet and highly successful affair" and the abstemious young ladies added their praises.

Tom Rowland bolstered his way station business by giving an amiable back of his hand to other resorts on the lake who claimed their locations to be the best fish producers. On a warm summer's day in 1872, Rowland arrived unheralded in Carson City, riding proudly atop one of his high-wheeled wood wagons that was literally awash with Tahoe silversides.

When weighed in at the public square, they tipped the scales at 1,052 pounds. "Old Tom" was sold out within the hour at "two-bits" a pound. He then announced that the proceeds would be devoted to providing additional facilities for the pleasure and comfort of his Tahoe guests—obvious proof of his natural flair for advertising Rowland's Station.

Several years later this attribute, combined with what the El Dorado and Alpine county voters termed "his virtues and great ability," won Rowland a seat for two terms in the California legislature as the first assemblyman to act for both counties.[11]

Rowland's prowess as a fisherman continued to bolster his local fame. In 1873, he brought to net a 23¾-pound native cutthroat which was displayed grandly in the window of Carson's Ormsby House. Autumn of 1881 found Tom Rowland setting another angling record. Goaded by reports that an upstart Tahoe City laker had caught 50 fish on a single "jerk line" in one day's trolling, Tom rowed out from his wharf before breakfast one morning and brought in four silvers totaling ten pounds. This was only the curtain-raiser. After four more hours of fishing he hauled in 65 trout with an aggregate weight of 108 pounds, thus cracking the one-man angling record then existing at Tahoe.

Another early pioneer also contributed to the growth of Rowland's Station. The man was Adelman Hargrave "Harry" Goodrich, a school teacher who came from New York to the lake in 1876. After first settling on the old Charles P. Young ranch, one mile up the Kingsbury Grade, he moved with his family to Rowland's settlement, where Goodrich and his wife taught at the little school house on the shortcut between Sierra House and the Station.

The region was still backwoods wilderness country. This was proven when Goodrich's son Don found himself pursued by a bloodthirsty Indian, said to be the legendary "One-Eyed Dick." The Washoe was swinging wildly with a butcher knife and Don had taken to his heels with whistling passes of cold steel coming uncomfortably close to his head. Upon reaching his cabin he managed to barricade himself behind the door and escape with his life. Goodrich went on to become Justice of the Peace and School Trustee at Al Tahoe.[12]

With the pinching off of traffic on the Bonanza Road, Rowland's Station became dependent upon business from cattlemen, loggers and woodcutters, commercial fishermen, and summer vacationists.

Picnics, and more picnics, were high points of the summer season for the young people. On September 18, 1878, a special outing was planned with entertainment to be furnished by the Reno Opera

Author's collection

ROTTING LOG WAY AND TALLAC RANGE

Meadowland between old Rowland's Station
and the Upper Truckee River's
influx into Tahoe.
Late spring of 1907 with the
camera facing west.

House Troupe. Flora and Fannie Rowland brought the jelly and silver cakes, Emmy Barton and the Davis children the coconut pies, Adda Averill, Cora and Rose Chubbuck three mince delicacies, O. W. Dickey the Dutch cheese and gallon crock of fresh milk from Barton's dairy, Charlie, Lena and Minnie Lyons elected to bring cookies, tea cakes, bread and butter, and Josie, Della and Mary Small furnished two mouth-watering gold cakes. They chose the sand beach at Lake Stream's outlet into Tahoe— splashed in the water, gorged themselves on food and applauded the shrill coloratura, deep bass and strong tenor that constituted the Opera House Troupe, until the sun was low on the western mountains.

By the year 1876, Rowland's Custom House Saloon had been built on pilings over the water and the lake floor, outside the bar, fast became a dumping place for chairs, brass bung-starters, beer keg spigots, bottles and silver and gold pieces, all tossed carelessly out of the windows by carousing lumberjacks and ranchers who frequented the establishment.[13] Augustus Colwell, from McKinney Bay, now ran the Davis Brothers' merchandise store in the settlement. He was followed by proprietors Anthony W. Ramsey and Samuel Brown from Placerville.

Rowland's holdings, as of this year, totaled 600 acres.[14]

Alexander Wilkshire Roop, a native of Ohio, was recognized as the finest cooper in the valley, and he turned out butter firkins and kegs for the trade at Rowland's. Unfortunately Roop was the unluckiest sailor on the lake, having seen the keel of his hull more often than the deck.

During 1876, Dan DeQuille had written in *The Big Bonanza:* "Old Lake House, though built of good pine logs, and warm and substantial, is giving way to more stylish structures." Contrarily, the

Pacific Tourist Guide advised its readers seven years later that "it (Rowland's) is the first place of resort on the lake."

Crofut's *New Overland Tourist and Pacific Coast Guide* mentions "Rowland's sawmills (sic) with their great annual cut." Mills, however, were non-existent at the settlement as it was only a staging location for logs and cordwood. Logging wagons, drawn by 16 to 18 laboring oxen, hauled timber down to the logging ramps on the lake where the tremendous loads were skidded into the water and rafted by steam tug to Glenbrook.

An eye witness described Rowland's in the same year as a "pleasant village composed of hotels, stores and farm houses, with a fine grove of pines, near the east end of the lake (sic) surrounded by extensive grazing land occupied by dairymen." He further observed: "The meadows are full of ducks and geese during the fall and winter months; and twice a week the stage leaves Rowland's for Placerville."[15]

Horse racing at the station was a favorite week-end diversion. A one-mile course, running along the lakeshore toward Taylor's Landing, was the scene of many spirited grudge matches until a fatality on the Fourth of July in the late 1880's put an end to this sport. Dan Tapem and John Dunlap had laid spurs to their mustangs and crossed the starting line together when Tapem's horse shied and broadsided him at full gallop into the first big pine west of the station. Tapem was killed instantly and the enthusiasm for racing at Rowland's passed with him.[16]

Thomas Benton Rowland died on August 29, 1883, and his widow, Mrs. Sophronia Dow Rowland, took over active management of the hotel, leasing out some 230 acres of meadowland to dairymen.

Fencing contained the cattle and a log corduroy road skirted the meadow to the south. Twelve wooden bridges were crossed and numerous stock gates opened before the road turn-off was reached that led to what is now the Tahoe Valley Y. The main thoroughfare continued on to Gardner's Camp and Tallac and this stretch, between the station and Baldwin's Tallac House, is recalled as "one continuous opening and closing of barriers."[17] It skirted the bottomland south of the Upper Truckee River's outlet, passing William D. Barton's ranch and milkhouse, that later would be known as Meadowedge.[18] At the time this meadow and sagebrush acreage was called "The Bank Land," but not for the reason most people supposed.

In 1889, two years after the Bliss and Yerington interests from Glenbrook had installed their Lake Valley Railroad, they drove double rows of pilings to hold back the sand at the influx of the Upper Truckee River. Then saw logs were floated down stream at high water and the timber "banked" at the outlet. Hence the name "Bank Land." Here the "go-devil" barge became a familiar sight in the shallow water where it was used to retrieve sunken logs. After the "sinkers" were winched to the surface, "dogs" were dug into the bark to hold them and they were then moved to the mills.[19] The year 1886 found the villagers at Rowland's moving to Bijou, where large scale lumbering operations and a railroad offered better business opportunities.

During the winter of 1889-90, heavy snows blanketed Rowland's settlement. The dance hall and saloon buckled and collapsed. Tom Rowland's old station was on its way out.[20]

The Samuel Elliott Kyburz family now dairyed in the meadow south of the station and Robert Bence ran the hotel for Mrs. Rowland. She had mortgaged 400 acres of her property to rancher S. Y. Halsey and difficult times lay ahead for the Rowland family.

Al Tahoe officially came into being in the year 1907, when "Al" Sprague built the original Al Tahoe Hotel. He had tacked his nickname to "Tahoe" and come up with the name "Al Tahoe" that identifies the resort today. Lumber for the inn, located one-half mile west of present Highway 50, was barged in and moved to the site by George Anderson, Edmund Hunkin and crews from the steamers *Meteor* and *Nevada*.[21]

A post office was established at Al Tahoe on August 11, 1908, seven months after the Al Tahoe Development Company took over the former Rowland properties. W. J. Wallace headed up the partnership which assumed management of the Al Tahoe Hotel and Water Company. Al Tahoe's pier was extended northeast into deeper water to accommodate the deep-draft lake steamers, and Rowland's old hotel was finally torn down.

A six-room building adjoining the old landmark was sold to W. W. Price of Fallen Leaf Lodge, as was the over-water Custom House Saloon, which is now a part of the main dining room at Fallen Leaf.[22]

Mrs. Sophronia Dow Rowland and her family now moved to Bijou, ending nearly half a century of activity at Rowland's.

During the next two decades the ownership of Al Tahoe Hotel changed hands several times. Among the proprietors were the Kaufmans and Taggerts.

In the summer of 1924, Frank Globin from Marysville, California, purchased Al Tahoe along with the company that brought in water from isolated Star Lake located high in the Carson Range under Mount Freel. Frank and Mrs. Globin still owned and ran the old Al Tahoe Hotel, casino, cottages and cabins after nearly 35 years on Lake Tahoe although the new Globin establishment and small settlement, fronting on Highway 50, was nearly wiped out by fire in the spring of 1956.[23]

Bordering the former site of old Lake House, west of present Al Tahoe, stands a large Jeffery pine. Driven into its bark, some ten feet above the base of the giant tree, is a hand-forged iron hook upon which the three-foot stagecoach lanterns were hung 85 years ago to welcome travelers alighting from the Concords and "mud wagons."[24] Some one hundred feet farther west of this tree lies a dead pine, sectioned during the summer of 1955 by the owner of the property, Grover Irey. An examination of the cross-cuts disclosed powder and ball shot circled by 50 years of ring growth. According to early residents, the tree had been lying on the ground for 75 years, which would place the firing of the lead pellets 13 years before Captain John C. Fremont discovered Tahoe.[25]

If such is the actual sequence of years, the explorer or mountain man who passed through the untouched forest that surrounded the lake at the time may be considered the first white man to set eyes on Tahoe, although his name remains lost to Tahoe history.

Chapter Thirty

BIJOU

"THEM FRESH WATER SALTS is layin' to, waitin' on a wind out of Blackwood Creek Gorge, Meeks or Emerald. There's not even a nor'west zephyr out of Tay-ho Canyon to help 'em."

"Captain" Almon M. (Jim) Taylor was directing his comments at Ramsdale Buoy's group of shoddy traveling companions from San Francisco who were standing on the white sand beach adjoining Taylor's Landing.[1] An oarsman had been dispatched early that morning to Tahoe City on what was considered merely a shirt-off pull at the sweeps, although the distance was a good 19 miles. The man had been ordered to charter Homer D. Burton's schooner, the *Edith Batty*, but a dead calm on the blue mirror of the lake was obviously the reason for his delay.

Captain Jim continued, "If you see them waves runnin' out of Emerald Bay there's a chance she'll make the trip across in four hours, but old Blackwood Gorge is sure the lair of the west wind, all right, fillin' the sails to start 'em off."

The monotony of waiting was beginning to tell on Buoy's group. They began cursing their misfortune in not getting started on their Lake Tahoe cruise and Buoy was afraid the expedition would turn into a traveling riot. Toward sundown a puff of wind struck the water, grew in volume, and built up a surf that pounded against the shore. "She'll be a comin' now," Taylor exulted, jumping up and down on the sand, "sure as this here's a dazzlin' spring day in May of '66."

Buoy, assuming the cloak of marine spokesman, turned to his companions and pointed at the combers sweeping across from the western shore. "Just like a flock of sheep in a sweet potato patch, those white caps," he marveled, "and mighty welcome." But the would-be mariners had had enough. Though sail finally showed far out on the lake, the cruise was put off until the following morning.[2] Taylor motioned to his weary guests and they struck out across the beach toward his ranch house.

Almon M. Taylor was no newcomer to the Tahoe region. He and his wife, Elizabeth Mott Taylor, had applied for a patent on their 160-acre ranch the same month that Buoy's party arrived, after homesteading the property in 1861.[3]

To the north the Taylors were bordered by Van Wagener's and Dean's Lake House. Martin, Dorr and McDonald held the land to the east, Henry Martin and William Mac(k) that to the south, and on the west lay "vacant land."[4] A ranch house, barn, yoke of oxen and cattle constituted A. M. Taylor's improvements; value, $1,000, and he ran his stock in the surrounding meadowland, commercially fished the lake, cleared the acreage with his yoke of oxen, and furnished overnight accommodations for the wayfarer when the other stations on the road were crowded.

Feed for animals hauling supplies to the Comstock in the early 1860's was at a premium, and in the fall of 1862 Taylor leased the cutting rights at Long Meadow (Siebeck's) to Warren and M. Upton Company, who scythed and bailed some 50 tons of hay from the rich bottom land.

J. Taylor was pinpointed on the Lake Tahoe Topographical Map of 1874, and that year William D. Rantz and Charles Siebeck acquired part of the old Taylor homestead along with other surrounding properties. But it remained for the extensive logging operations, starting in the early 1880's, to develop Taylor's, later Bijou (meaning gem or jewel), into a flourishing lumber settlement.

During the 1870's Tom Rowland's Lake House was the staging point for log booms and cordwood barges. This changed with the completion of George Washington Chubbuck's tramline railroad terminating at "Taylor's Landing." Until 1880 nothing stood on the shoreline between Rowland's and Lapham's except a few commercial fishermen's log shacks. Then, in the spring of 1884, Chubbuck, late of Zephyr Cove, McCumbers, and, starting with this year, lessee of Sierra House, acquired the timber rights on approximately 1,200 acres of forest land in the vicinity of Taylor's old ranch.[5] Here Chubbuck constructed his logging railroad. He installed narrow gauge track. Bridges were built crossing Cold and Miller (Heavenly Valley) creeks. The line was extended three-quarters of a mile along Trout Creek past Sierra House to the southeast for a total of four miles. At the shoreline terminus Chubbuck built a log ramp where he rolled timber from his logging cars directly into the lake. What with sidehill cutting, bridging, and fill work to maintain an easy gradient into the back country, the railroad was a costly project.[6]

Chubbuck placed French-Canadian lumberjacks along the railroad right-of-way to fell the giant pines. More than a hundred Chinese and Portuguese cordwood cutters were hired to split and stack tamarack, fir and knotted saw logs. Lumber had to be clear for the square-sets at the Virginia City mines and 40 to 50 foot topped tree sections, along with other parts of a felled giant, were left to rot because of a knot or two.[7] As the cutting moved back into the canyons, logs were snaked out of the backwoods on ox-drawn, solid-wheeled logging wagons to staging points on the railroad.

WHERE THE LOG CHUTE MET THE RAILWAY

Saw logs being loaded aboard flatcars of the Lake Valley Railroad in August of 1888. Engine SANTA CRUZ *on the left headed toward Bijou. Yoked oxen are straddling the log way.*

Author's collection

A YEARLING HAD STRAYED
ONTO THE TRACK

Locomotive SANTA CRUZ *deadheading
crippled* ENGINE NUMBER THREE
*to the Bijou "pits" in the autumn
of 1891.*

G. D. Oliver

At first Chubbuck used eight and ten oxen yoked in pairs to move the pyramided and chained logs on his five flat cars, but this method proved slow and costly. In an attempt to speed up the movement of saw logs and pine slabs he purchased a second-hand miniature steam locomotive named *Old Morsby*. Built by the Vulcan Iron Works in San Francisco for the Sutro Tunnel Company at Dayton, Nevada, it was the monstrosity of the day. In place of a tender, a saddle tank was mounted on top of the engine. Diamond smokestack and square, oil-burning searchlight set off the squat, dumpy low wheeler. It appeared to be all gears and boiler. Small 14 by 6 inch cylinders furnished the propulsion power. Combined with low gearing, they turned the drive wheels furiously under maximum steam pressure to maintain an eight-mile speed on the upgrade.[8]

The little engine proved too heavy for the railbed and loaded logging cars secured by "link and pin" clattered, buckled and swayed down the uneven track. Chubbuck had no alternative—he demoted the ugly duckling to the job of steam winch and log loader and it was dragged back into the woods. This was his only attempt to use steam power in place of oxen on the road.[9]

Chubbuck was forced into bankruptcy as a result of outmoded lumbering methods and he had to yield his two square miles of timber leases and personal land holdings to their original owners, Henry Martin, A. M. Taylor, S. D. Weyant and Charles Siebeck, among others.

On August 6, 1886, the Carson and Tahoe Lumber and Fluming Company, for whom Chubbuck had been subcontracting, stepped in. From Siebeck they obtained the railroad right-of-way. It "granted them the right to haul saw logs and cordwood provided they removed the rolling stock and rails at the conclusion of lumbering operations."[10] The Company controlled more than 10,000 acres of timberland on the southeast side of Tahoe. All they needed now was a way to transport logs and cordwood to the lakeshore. Chubbuck's bankruptcy opened the door, but they had to move quickly. The rival Nevada Lumber Company, owned by Walter Scott Hobart, had already acquired 8,000 acres in the region.

The future of Taylor's old homestead was assured because large scale lumbering meant expansion. On October 19, 1886, Almon Taylor deeded two acres of his remaining lakeshore property, east of what would become the Bijou pier, to Charles H. Parrish; price, $125. This was pretty steep, Parrish figured, but he wanted that land. He was a coarse, bald-headed, hard-swearing Cornishman with a violent temper, known as the "I say . . ." man due to his habit of prefacing every sentence with the words.[11]

Here, he and his wife Elizabeth built a spacious, rambling one-story house with a saloon and

George D. Oliver

FOREST GIANTS HEADED FOR THE GLENBROOK MILLS

The C. & T. L. & F. Company's "flats" on the Lake Valley Line being loaded at a staging yard bordering Trout Creek. Looking east in the spring of 1893.

dance floor. He also put up a large barn and stable north of the main house. Parrish is said to have made his own whiskey, a powerful revulsion of the devil that could tie up the hardiest lumberjack in knots. He also rationed out the "bottled brand" to those who gagged on his corrosive homemade distillations. Parrish obtained the contract to carry mail to and from the steamers each day and a post office was located in the main building.[12]

In the spring of 1887, Anthony Wayne Ramsey, a 45-year-old native of Mississippi, and therefore called "Old Man," purchased a two-acre strip to the west of Parrish. He had been watching the growing business activity at Taylor's Landing (Bijou) and decided to move his stock of goods from his store at Rowland's to the new location. Here he built a house and saloon, and added a dance hall and several small outbuildings. His hotel became known as "Dashaway Hall" and a lean-to against the main building went under the name of "Cowboy's Inn."[13]

Mrs. Ramsey was a talented pianist and she played for dances held on weekends during the summer months. On special occasions C. M. "Fiddler" Taylor (no relation to A. M. Taylor) and his four-piece band were brought up from Genoa, and often the bass viol, violin, cornet and piano (or organ) were heard until sunup, with couples dancing the Virginia Reel, Schottische Glide and Mazurka. Stout, sideburned "Fiddler" did the calling for the reel.[14]

By the spring of 1888, the C. and T. L. and F. Company had laid seven and one-half miles of narrow gauge 35-pound rail. An 1,800-foot trestle, built with 6 by 6-inch timbers, secured longitudinally on pole logs, replaced Chubbuck's log ramp.[15] On this pier the rails were carried out into deep water. From the shoreline the track followed Chubbuck's old right-of-way for two miles, continuing up Lake Valley south of Sierra House and gradually bearing to the west toward Meyers. Along the line log chutes and logging wagons fed the sidings with timber and cordwood.

The Company now had a landing for their steamers and barges. Logging cars were run out to the end of the long pier, where logs were discharged directly into the water to be V-boomed and towed to the Glenbrook mills. William Seth Bliss was appointed superintendent of the new Lake Valley Railroad and, with the introduction of a proven formula, tested in Glenbrook operations for over a decade, the operation became financially successful.

Rolling stock was barged in from the parent lumbering settlement. This equipment included the little 10-ton Mogul locomotive *Santa Cruz*, purchased especially for the line, plus fifteen flat cars.[16] Rails on the barge were lined up with those on the trestle and the engine and cars moved onto the main track after the carrier had been warped to the end of the new pier by the steamer *Meteor*. The *Santa Cruz* was equipped with small 28-inch drivers and carried 10 by 14-inch inclined cylinders, which allowed her to maintain a 12-mile speed on the run.[17]

In spite of the commercial activity now overshadowing the natural beauty of the lake, a newsman from the *Truckee Republican*, visiting the settlement in the fall of 1888, was moved to remark that the "beach at Bijou was the longest and finest on the lake, formed of white granite sand without a pebble to mar its surface." Another correspondent, representing the *Carson City Appeal*, was amazed to discover a "wild man near Bijou, barefoot, with long black hair hanging to his chest, and clothed only in a loincloth, who managed to live by spearing fish and eating them raw." The newsman hinted that this "creature of nature was actually just a Reno journalist on his vacation."

In the following year a "senseless killing" was reported at Almon "Jim Poker" Taylor's ranch house. For no apparent reason other than the fact that his victim refused to sing "Finnegan's Wake" for him, Charles Leamon stabbed William "Bill" Scott with a bowie knife. Scott died before Dr. Brigham could be rushed over from Eagle Point. Nothing was ever mentioned about the law catching up with Leamon.[18]

Timber taken out of Lake Valley in 1888 jumped to 21,000,000 board feet. Lumberjacks, log

J. M. Nevis

BIJOU IN THE SUMMER
OF 1902

*View taken from the end of the
1800-foot railroad pier
showing Ramsey's "Dashaway Hall"
hotel (right) and Parrish's
"Bijou Hotel" (left).
Siebeck's house is in the grove
of pine (center).*

rollers and even cordwood splitters were now receiving wages running to $150 a month. Everybody seemed to be doing well with the exception of G. W. Chubbuck, who had kept only 80 acres of his once large holding and the hybrid prime mover *Old Morsby*, which was for sale at $300 with no takers.

The expanding Lake Valley Railroad operation called for additional rolling stock. In order to fill the need, *Engine Number Three* was barged over from Glenbrook, along with ten more flat cars, and the equipment placed in use during the spring of 1891. As locomotives on the line could not be turned at the Lake Valley Railroad terminus, backward-facing headlights were installed on the roof of the cabs. When the engines reached the end of the line the engineers turned to face the tender and made the return trip in reverse. Machine shop, roundhouse and the pits were located at the lake terminal on the present site of Conolley's.[19]

In 1891, crews on the woodburners and flats included John Eugene Dunlap, 29-year-old brakeman, a native of Illinois; Oliver Franklin Griffin from Georgetown, senior engineer on the road; James R. Vair, a 39-year-old Canadian who was later killed at Coyote Flat while braking on *Engine Number Three*, and John Sheehy, another brakeman.[20]

The C. and T. L. and F. Company obtained timber rights on Woodburn's, Barton's, Hill's and Jewell's sections amounting to nearly 6,000 acres. Seven hundred and fifty thousand feet of logs valued at $3,000 and 5,000 cords of wood, carried on the books at $8,750, had been yarded in 1890, in addition to that moved across the water to Glenbrook. All but 320 acres of the property the Company owned outright had been logged over and they were searching for new timber sections. F. D. Weyant's 1,600 acres and Charlie Siebeck's 1,705 acres were the next to go.

In the same year a tabulation of old Charlie Parrish's holdings showed that he had increased his investment. His hotel was now known as the "Bijou House." He also owned "Heritage House" west of the post office. An important find of the county tax collector was 30 gallons of whiskey, valued at $30.

The Lake Valley Railroad ran on schedule until one autumn afternoon in 1891. *Engine Number Three*, the new addition to the line, was making the final trip of the day downgrade from Meyers. Engineer Fred Johnson was at the throttle and the locomotive, pulling five loaded logging cars, was running out in front. Riding the chained saw logs were a crew of Chinese cordwood choppers, taking the easy route back to Bijou. John Dunlap was firing and Jim Vair, braking. Dave Fountain and Bill Watson were also aboard.

As the train neared Bijou, one of rancher "Hy" Barton's yearlings happened to stray onto the track and before Johnson could back off on the throttle they plowed into the animal. When the dust and steam cleared away the little locomotive was a wreck, its forward running trucks jammed into the firebox, and several cars derailed. Four Chinese were killed instantly and many more injured. One of the Chinese had been skewered by an iron brake rod and was screaming for somebody to shoot him. Vair was not seriously hurt, but Engineer Johnson sustained such crippling injuries that he would never pull throttle on a locomotive again.

It was reported that the Celestials who had escaped injury high-tailed it back to their camp, hurriedly picked up their belongings and never returned to the spot where their fellows met death. The steamer *Meteor*, captained by Ernest J. Pomin, churned across the water to pick up Dr. Charles Brigham. Then the dead Chinese were laid away in oblong white pine coffins and their bodies sent to San Francisco for shipment to China for burial.[21]

Battered *Engine Number Three* was returned to the Glenbrook machine shops after the worst recorded accident on any of Tahoe's railroads. Engine *Number One* replaced the *Number Three* on the line and John Dunlap moved up from fireman to engineer.[22]

There were subsequent fatalities. Johnny Jukes from Cosumnes River, working as "roller" on the end of the Bijou Pier, was crushed to death after a cable snapped and a log caught him on the chest as he was thrown into the water. Homer Wyatt, assigned the same location some weeks later, narrowly escaped with his life when he managed to dive into the lake and swim beneath the pier as tons of logs tumbled above him. Jim Vair, after surviving the ill-fated multiple death accident, when the heifer derailed the locomotive and cars, was killed a year later (1892). The engineer was making a "flying switch" or "hi-daddy," Vair being caught while pulling a securing pin between cars.[23]

ENGINE NUMBER THREE GOES TO SEA

A terrier on the bow of Bliss' EMERALD II *waits for the boat to dock at the end of Bijou's 1800-foot pier, where the lumber barge will be taken in tow. Right of the locomotive's tender (background) is Parrish's. Photograph taken looking southeast in the early spring of 1891.*

G. D. Oliver

As if this were not tragedy enough for the settlement, a mysterious disappearance was added to the list in the early 1890's. Orsamus W. Dickey, husband of Tom Rowland's oldest daughter Flora, vanished into the blue of Tahoe while rowing one spring afternoon. Headed for Glenbrook, he never arrived. Some speculated that Dickey committed suicide, but his wife maintained he had drowned accidentally. In any case, it was believed his body had joined those the lake had claimed and never given up.

Five years after the disappearance of Dickey, a resident of Bijou, drawn by the gold rush excitement in Alaska, shipped out from San Francisco on a windjammer and arrived in Juneau in the fall of 1898. As he stumbled down the snow-covered boardwalk to his hotel he bumped into an unshaven prospector wrapped in a greatcoat that hung to his booted ankles. A flash of recognition showed in the man's eyes and he turned his matted, bearded face away. The Tahoe goldseeker shouldered up to him and peered intently at a face that seemed strangely familiar. Suddenly he let out a yell, "My God, man," he stammered, "if you ain't Dickey! I'd recognize you anywhere, beard and all."

Dickey finally admitted his identity. "Just might as well go on home to Tahoe now," he added. "I didn't really think it could last." Upon his return his family generously chalked up his extended vacation to "just wanting a change of scene." The Dickeys then bought Will Tevis, Sr.'s houseboat, moved it back from the shoreline at Bijou and converted it into a house. This appeared to be a step in the right direction and several Bijou residents theorized that the barge had been hauled from the water lest Dickey might again succumb to wanderlust and up anchor some dark night.[24]

By the summer of 1897 the Lake Valley Railroad had increased its rail line to 11½ miles but timber reserves were down to a handful of scattered quarter sections. Preparations were now made to move the entire operation across the lake to Tahoe City.

May of 1898 found the C. and T. L. and F. Company tearing up the Bijou rails and yarding the equipment at the head of the 1,800-foot trestle. Five hundred and fifty tons of second-hand narrow gauge track were stacked adjoining the pits, 25 flat cars were lined up on the last section of right-of-way, and the *Santa Cruz* was being loaded aboard a 104-foot cordwood barge for its trip across Tahoe.[25] By the summer of 1899 all that was left to show that the Company had been at Bijou were a sagging roundhouse, a blacksmith shop, and mile upon mile of slashings, bark trim, graveyards of sentinel stumps and cutover land laced with rotting log chutes, cordwood camps, and discarded equipment. Many of Bliss and Yerington's crew moved to the new location at Tahoe City, including the John Dunlap family. Dunlap continued as engineer on the locomotives for Bliss over a 25-year period before returning to the south end in 1928.

Title to land sections surrounding Bijou could now be obtained by paying the back taxes or, at the most, $1.50 an acre. An era of resorts and summer home subdivisions was starting. In October of 1902, Charles P. Young, a storekeeper who had come over the mountains from Genoa, Nevada, during the 1870's, and settled on land bordering the west Kingsbury Grade, now bought the Parrish lakeshore property from Siebeck. The Parrishes had sold out at the close of the Lake Valley Railroad operation. In June of 1908, Wilton Richard Young and Charles Rowland Young, sons of Dr. Malon W. Young, joined with their grandfather, Charles P. Young to purchase more property. It ran from Arthur Hill's Stateline monument south to Widow Sophronia Dow Rowland's holdings, 33 acres of meadowland and lakeshore property in all.[26]

Author's collection

BIJOU HOTEL AND HERITAGE HOUSE

*Charles Halsey Parrish's hotel, ranch house and outbuildings in the late spring of 1901
on the site of what shortly became Young's Bijou and later Bal Bijou.
Mount Freel, Job's Peak and Job's Sister lie to the southeast.*

Philip C. Cohen purchased the old Ramsey acreage west of what had now become Young's Bijou. He sold to Annie and William F. Conolley, who opened Conolley's Bijou Inn as a resort hotel and campground. The Conolleys featured a "daily chicken dinner" and "floored tents," competing in undisguised hostility with the Young brothers.

The C. and T. L. and F. Company still held 11,081 acres of cutover land, most of which was sold for back taxes during the next decade. In 1924 the remaining property owned by the Bliss family totaled a mere 447 acres.[27] Within the next 25 years Chris Johnson, Sr., took over the majority of the Siebeck holdings, and Anna Conolley sold Conolley's Bijou to Clyde Beecher. Charles "Chuck" Johnson and partner, Neal Olson, later bought Young's Bijou (Bal Bijou).[28]

Bijou has developed into a thriving settlement with two major resort hotels, cabins, dance pavillion (largest on the lake), coffee shops, market, store and boat landings. An even more ambitious program is now being projected for pioneer Jim Taylor's old lakeshore holding.[29]

"WASHOE BILLY" NEVER HAD TO BE PAID TO POSE

William "Washoe Billy" Lancaster stands like a ramrod for this picture taken at the Indian encampment northeast of Bijou in August of 1899.

Chapter Thirty-one

LAKESIDE

AGROTESQUE FIGURE came loping across the rime ice, crouched low like a hunted animal. Covering its shoulders was a multicolored swatch of grimy blanket.

William W. "Billy" Lapham, owner of Lapham's Hotel and Landing, slowly brought his heavy rifle to shoulder and trained his sights on the strange intruder.[1] From Lapham's point of concealment on the shadowed porch of his way station, he could now make out a streaked brown face and bobbing top-knot. Washoe or Paiute buck, he decided. The Indian disappeared behind a snow hummock. When he again came into view, Lapham squinted, then squeezed off a shot—high and to the right of the runner.

The buck let out a terrified whoop, clawed his way into the air and swung his right arm wildly in a sweeping arc. He was clutching a scrap of white paper. Hotelkeeper Lapham stepped from his hiding place and motioned the red man on with the barrel of his gun. The cringing savage slunk up to Lapham, planted wolfskin wrapped feet in the snow and held out the note.

As he unfolded the communication with his free hand, Lapham eyed the interloper warily. The Indian's mouth was frozen in an idiotic grin that showed two snaggled rows of tobacco-stained teeth. His eyes rolled in their sockets. From a braided deerskin thong dangled the split shinbone of an ox. Faded blue pantaloons and a ragged cotton shirt crept up his legs and wrists. The buck's only attempt at words spilled out in an inarticulate gutteral. Lapham glanced at the message. How could an illiterate, addle-brained savage find a more thoroughly business-like way to open negotiations, he asked himself.

Writing wandered across the foolscap in a quill-pen scrawl:

"Fellow Sufferer," it began. "This Indian is a damn thief. He will steal anything he can lay his hands on. If he comes about your station break his head. Signed—A Friend."

Lapham peered at the renegade with renewed interest.

The smilingly obsequious buck was now jerking his head from side to side and pointing to his stomach. He groaned loudly and his face contorted dramatically in pain.

The innkeeper snorted in disgust, seized his rifle barrel in both hands and swung. As the gun stock caught the buttocks of the savage squarely, an unskinned leg of mutton, followed by a shower of pinon nuts and "jerky," dropped from the folds of his blanket to the frozen ground. Snatching up a part of his plunder, the buck straightened and streaked off across the ice field.

Lapham didn't bother to waste another bullet. Instead he watched the fleeing Indian until he was only a shadow on the fringe of the forest to the north. Then "Billy" Lapham returned to the porch, slumped wearily into a high-backed rocker and laid his gun across his knees.[2]

Now that the California-Nevada traffic had advanced from wagon and stage to railroad, the win-

THE STATE LINE RAN THROUGH LAPHAM'S DINING ROOM

W. W. "Billy" Lapham's Stateline Hotel operated by John Carney when this picture was taken in the summer of 1875. Mrs. Carney and her four daughters are on the south side of the porch. View looking west toward Tahoe across the Johnson Pass-Carson road.

ters at his hotel were profitless, white hells rudely punctuated by pilfering savages and relieved only by a few widely scattered neighbors. Lapham tilted his head and slowly closed one eye. Here it was— February of 1869—and he and his second wife, Caroline M. Lapham, had spent a full decade in this Lake Valley outpost of civilization. It was good business, he reflected, to sell his one-third interest in old Lake House to Seneca Dean and William Van Wagener, back in the spring of 1860, and pre-empt 160 acres of land to the northeast.[3] Hadn't it taken foresight to place his two frame houses and barns at the junction Y of the Placerville-Carson-Johnson Pass "back road" and the Lake House dog-leg cut-off? Certainly, he reassured himself, but who in God's green earth would have expected Huntington and his railroad runts to lay the Central's iron over Donner Pass instead of through Lake Valley? Damned if it didn't beat the devil. Sure he had jumped the other station owners with his hotel location, but they couldn't blame him because there wasn't enough business for any of them now.

Lapham pulled a curved stemmed brier from his pocket and tapped its thickly caked bowl on the porch railing. Nothing but a handful of muleheads like himself stayed in all winter these days, plus brown-skinned vultures like that god-damn Indian, he mused.

But he wasn't giving up—yet. Not an old New England seafaring salt like himself. No sir. Hadn't he been among the first to make commercial fishing on Tahoe a major industry? Hadn't he netted thousands of native silvers and land-locked salmon in the shallows of Boundary Bay, using one of the first 28-foot whaleboats placed on the lake?[4]

That was August of 1860, he recalled, and at the time he established what was now known to all lakers as Lapham's Fish Market and Landing. Lapham's mouth twisted. Hell, he wasn't even sure about the exact confines of his lands and, what was worse, only *suspected* that it lay part in California and part in Nevada.

Lt. Sam Mowry and Ed Beal had run out a thoroughly inaccurate boundary survey for the Army in February of 1860, and bedded down three *camels* in his horse change stable after driving them all the way from Fort Tejon. Lapham frowned. It had cost the Federal government $72,000 before Mowry and Beal finished giving California 27½ more square miles of land and lake than the state was entitled to.

This startling miscalculation, corrected in '63 by John Kidder and Butler Ives, was laid directly at the feet of the stoical camels by wags in Carson.[5] The persuasive argument was that sane men could be driven completely out of their right minds by those swinging gaited "ships of the desert." However, the twin-humped Bactrians were said to have been practical—able to go for days without water, carry upwards of 1,000-pound loads and scrape a living from sagebrush, bitter weeds and timberline scrub that would gag a mule.

Lieutenant Mowry had told Lapham that his beasts of burden showed particular partiality toward overlooking a wide expanse of scenery, climbing without urging to the top of any available mountain if left to their own devices, for no other apparent reason than to contemplate the other side.

Beal swore that the appearance of these shaggy, long-nosed Mongolian imports caused horses to rear in wild-eyed terror, cattle to stampede and mule teams to career down canyon at runaway speeds.

Even the hard-bitten Nevada miners were prompted, after seeing this product of nature's ingenious carelessness, to fling their hats into the air and loudly proclaim the arrival of Judgment Day. Lapham remembered that one of his cowpokes at the station had considered the mere mention of climbing astride a camel justifiable cause for an immediate gunfight.

But the actual California-Nevada boundary was the problem that had to be resolved, Lapham reflected. Now there was talk that a San Francisco engineer, Colonel Von Schmidt, would be awarded a contract to resurvey the line.

"I'll bet a bundle of fox furs Von Schmidt officially finds stateline straddles *my* hotel," Lapham muttered to himself.[6]

He rose to his feet and stretched. Then Lapham pushed open the pine entrance door to his hotel and stepped inside.

During the peak of operations, William Lapham had increased his holdings to 400 acres, buying the additional land from his neighbor, Almon M. Taylor. Lapham had also consolidated his shacks into a twelve-room hotel, placing a saloon at the south end of the building. Upstairs were additional sleeping quarters for his gregarious wife, Caroline M. Lapham, and himself. The conventional covered porch, fronting on the road, was set off with a picket fence and watering troughs. Across the turnpike stood a large combination barn and horse change station that serviced, day and night for some seven years, the freighter teams, express and stage lines.[7]

When hard times came in 1868-69, Lapham turned to "getting out saw logs and cordwood." He was reported, in the spring of 1871, as "fitting out his large hotel and planning to launch a 30-foot sailboat for his guests' pleasure." Although the sailing vessel failed to materialize, another enterprise, more ambitious than his original plan, was about to become a reality.

In March of 1872, Lapham contracted with Glenbrook's Captain Joseph Todman for construction of Tahoe's first large luxury steamer, the *Governor Stanford*. He logically concluded the lake needed a vessel that could carry, in addition to mail and freight, one hundred or more passengers. Besides serving the four other major resorts then bordering Tahoe, the new boat's schedule would allow for a noon hour stop at Lapham's Hotel and Landing, thereby bringing in additional business.[8]

Although Lapham still owned his hotel during the years, 1872, '73, and '74, he had again added to

HIGH SIERRA HOOP-DE-DO

Lake House guests, residents and neighbors off on a hay ride from Lakeside's historic barn and stable in the summer of 1896. Mr. and Mrs. E. B. Smith in the front seat of the hard-top buggy. Included in the group on the hay wagon: Mattie Hobe, Laura McFaul, the Heiberts, Joe Hall and Ed McFaul. Picture taken looking east.

his land holdings (total 712 acres) and run heavily into debt. A $10,000 loan from Mrs. Marion Hill of the Bay City was secured by a first mortgage on his hotel and ranch, with most of the money going into the building of the *Governor Stanford*.[9]

In an effort to pay off his obligations, "Captain Billy" attempted to augment his passenger, mail and express marine transportation business by rafting logs across the lake to Tahoe City. During the summer of 1873, his contract with the Truckee River Lumber Company called for laying 600,000 feet of logs at Tahoe's outlet at an agreed price of $5.50 per thousand. Even though Lapham cut timber from the land surrounding his hotel he was unable to meet delivery requirements.

Preoccupied with his marine and lumbering activities, he leased his hotel to John Carney during the spring of 1873.[10] Carney, former owner of the Crystal Mine in Placerville, had first moved with his wife and four children (a fifth had died in infancy) to Sacramento and entered the hay and grain business. Advised by his doctor to go into the Sierra Nevada and thus avoid the epidemic of malaria then sweeping the valley, Carney welcomed the opportunity to take a five-year lease on Lapham's hotel.[11]

The hostelry now became Carney's Stateline House (or Station). Von Schmidt's new boundary survey had been run out and Carney could now correctly boast that his establishment lay half in California and half in Nevada, with the dividing line between the two states running through his dining room.

H. H. Parkell took over as manager for Carney and the station's revenue was derived mainly from vacationists, fruit peddlers, dry goods and whiskey drummers, local "jacks" and cordwood splitters. For two winters Carney's youngsters attended Miss Banning's School at the foot of the Kingsbury Grade in Carson Valley, and as the summer seasons at the lake proved to be a moderate financial success, Carney and his wife were convinced their move to Tahoe had been a wise one. Then late in the Centennial year of 1876 a catastrophe leveled Carney's Station.[12]

One chill September evening a woman and her child, guests at the hotel, built a small pine knot fire in the upstairs fireplace. Sparks, fanned by a brisk draft down the chimney, ignited a hook rug and Carney's Stateline House burned to its granite block foundations. The Carney family moved to a saw log cabin adjoining the blackened ruins and in November of the same year tragedy struck again with savage swiftness.

A fruit peddler, friendly with the family, stopped at Carney's with his wagon load of perishables. He was the last to cross the Sierra before winter set in. The children welcomed him, only to learn that he was recovering from diphtheria.

All four of the youngsters were stricken. A lumberjack from Charles Siebeck's logging camp was dispatched immediately to bring Dr. Daggett over the mountain from Genoa. Daggett arrived too late. Two of the little girls, Catherine and Ellen, died within 24 hours. With a pathetic resignation, John Carney nailed two white pine coffins together while Mrs. Carney ripped up her wedding dress for lining the tiny caskets. They buried their daughters in the little cemetery on land that later would become a part of Young's Bijou.[13]

The peddler had triggered a plague that swept through Lake Valley, leaving heartbreak in its wake. John Carney had had enough. His station lease with Lapham had been automatically terminated when the hostelry burned so the family loaded their remaining belongings on a wagon and moved, permanently, to Carson City.[14]

"Captain Billy" Lapham was now faced with other problems. He had defaulted on his interest payments to Mrs. Marion Hill and even neglected to pay back any of the principal of the $10,000 loan. Mrs. Hill foreclosed and took over Lapham's land and the remaining outbuildings.

E. B. "Starvation" Smith, Mrs. Hill's brother, now stepped in and plans were made to rebuild. Smith had received the unflattering nickname "Starvation" because neighbors were positive that he

Glorene Dunlap Young

THROUGH TRAFFIC HALTED FOR 3 MONTHS THAT WINTER

Lakeside House in deep snow during February of 1897, taken from the highroad looking southwest. Marion, Bessie and Wilbur Cottrel are standing on the south porch.

would "starve to death before he made a success out of the place."[15] Not until the spring of 1892 did Smith construct the new hotel, Lakeside House (or Tavern), tearing down the old shacks still standing but leaving the famous barn and stable across the road from the site of old Lapham's Station.

Smith re-named the location Lakeside Park and the Smith-Hill holdings totaled 1,000 acres.[16]

By 1895, Lakeside had developed into a small settlement and bordering the hotel on the south side was a log "social hall," with tents and cabins scattered around the grounds. Several years later Smith built a new steamer pier to the north of Lapham's old landing and installed narrow gauge track that ran to its water terminus. When a post office was officially established on June 12, 1901, and the lake steamers made their regular stops, a handcar picked up the canvas mail sacks and freight, summer and winter.

For decades the site of Lakeside had been the Washoe Indians' favorite location for their "love feasts" or fandangos. Preparations were made weeks in advance each season and more than two hundred tribesmen, accompanied by their squaws, children, cayuses and dogs, descended upon the settlement. A handful of Paiutes and Digger Indians were also invited provided they were in good standing with the Washoe tribe.

The feast consisted of fish, flesh and choice offal from nearby slaughterhouses, washed down with "lightning whiskey" whenever it could be procured from the white man. This was considered gourmet fare by the cavorting red brothers. The few white settlers who attended and were asked to sample raw entrails and fish heads topped off with a spicy paste made from red ants, invariably fought down stomach convulsions and settled for the role of onlooker.[17]

At one of these tribal conclaves, "Captain Jim," titular head of the Washoes, was asked by an inquisitive white man to what tribe he belonged. His staccato reply in pidgin English, "Damfino, we Wash-oos all mixed up same like you palefaces," contained both a squelch and a point. It is reported that his questioner got the point and the conversation was ended.[18]

Today the Washoes' annual gathering at Lakeside is only a poignant memory.

As the old Lapham Hotel site and ranch was equally divided between the Hills and Smiths, one-half of the property reverted to Mrs. E. B. Smith upon her husband's passing in October of 1904. That Mrs. Smith faced the situation with businesslike aplomb is evident in her written statement made on January 31, 1938, when she was 89 years of age. She wrote: "When Mr. Smith died I had half the land, *so the only thing to do was for me to marry Mr. Hill*, a much younger man, who died in 1913."[19] The new Mrs. Hill also stated that her first husband, E. B. Smith, "put all of Lapham's old shacks together and built Lakeside House." This is not confirmed by photographic evidence, as the Lakeside hotel appears to have been built from the ground up.

In the summer of 1913, the Lakeside Park Company operated the hotel and campground. Guy C. Smith had the property in 1917 and it later was taken over by Kimball and Bartlett. Durable Mrs. Hill outlasted young and old in her family. She was still listed as proprietress in 1938, shortly before her death.

Lakeside, in the middle 1950's, became a choice summer and winter residential subdivision with recreation grounds and an extensive community beach.

Here on the southern stateline, which was resurveyed in 1899 for the fourth time and finally established 2,000 feet northeast of old Lapham's Hotel and Lakeside House, now stand neon-lighted gaming casinos, jammed sidewall to sidewall, where music blares out across Highway 50, 24 hours a day during the hectic summer season. The clatter, whirr and grind of the solid banks of chromed slot machines, the spin of roulette wheels and monotonous drone of croupiers at the green felt covered gaming tables, punctuate the steady murmur of surging pleasure seekers.

Glorene Dunlap Young

A STUFFED WILDCAT GUARDS
THE MAIL SACK

*Mail rests on Lakeside Park's handcar
awaiting the arrival of the steamer
TAHOE. Photograph taken looking east
from the end of the pier
on July 9, 1902.*

COFFEE BREAK FOR
TEAMSTERS

*Lakeside was a regular stop for wagoners
who still moved over the old road
to Carson Valley.
Here a 12-horse shingle team
is reined up north
of the hotel in November, 1898.*

Author's collection

TWINS AT THE MONUMENT

*Marian and Bessie Cottrel clasping hands
beneath "Rustic Bower" at
Von Schmidt's south state line
California-Nevada granite marker
in July, 1900. E. B. Smith standing
to the left. This photograph,
looking northwest, shows Lake House
straddling the line between
the two states.*

Glorene Dunlap Young

Gleaming rows of high-stacked silver dollars and vari-colored chips back the tables offering the wealth of Croesus *if*—and there lies the quickly-resolved question.

Entertainment is furnished by top revues and star-studded talent. Name bands and smaller combinations blast throughout the night and early morning, while loudspeakers and brilliantly lighted marquees frantically bid for the transient trade. The famous and the insignificant, the rich and the impoverished, are inoculated with the needle of chance. Rubbing excited elbows with the gaudily jeweled, be-furred busty blond and her paunchy, middle-aged cigar-chomping escort, is bleary-eyed Eustace O'Grundy, morning cleanup man from Hamburger Heaven down the line.

This is the new bonanza—the alluring gateway to financial heights or the threadbare pocket—Lady Luck in her tinsel and finery—a dazzling syncrasy of the Silver State. Here is both incubator and hothouse that spawns an ageless fascination, the lure of plenty for pennies, with the silent, grim-faced press of eager players seemingly hypnotized by the machines and tables.

Kansas corn-fed beef steaks for a round silver dollar, jumbo Alaska crab, free merchandise and automobiles for the lucky winners are some of the "loss leaders" that pin down the nickel stretcher who turns thumbs down on the 20-cent coke with a sneer and elbows his way through the clot of humanity packed two deep at the dice table, yelling, "Ten dollars on the come line!"

The backdrop and cast have changed, but the motivating drive is the same as that which lured the hard-rock miner who passed over this very road to grub furiously in the heat and sterile wastes under Sun Mountain barely two generations ago.

The tense, pale player of today and the grimy sweat and dust-caked wayfarer of yesterday are brothers under the skin—their bond, the same nerve-jarring hopefulness—the same pulse-jumping winning streak—the same despairing loss frustration actioned by an urgent, fervent prayer—*please*, Goddess of Fortune, wash a blackamoor white for *once* and smile on me.

George D. Oliver

SUBSIDIARY FEEDER FOR THE COMSTOCK

Peter Van Sickle's sawmill, bark trim refuse pile and steam boiler, at "Peter's Flat" on the eastern slope of the Kingsbury Grade between Edgewood (Friday's Station) and "Overlook Point," as it looked in the summer of 1897.

Chapter Thirty-two

EDGEWOOD

★

SHORTLY BEFORE MIDNIGHT on April 28, 1860, a lone rider swept north along the partially completed lakeshore leg of the Johnson Pass-Kingsbury cut-off and clattered up to Friday's Station. Behind him jagged streaks of forked lightning flashed through the rain-sodden, storm-whipped forest wilderness. Drunken thunder rolled down the canyons and rumbled out across the turbulent blackness of Tahoe. The horseman swung down, soaking wet, bone tired, snow slush dripping from his gaunt face and slippery buckskins. "Friday" Burke, Jim Small and relief rider "Pony Bob" Haslem broke from the shelter of the log station, swinging sputtering oil lamps. "It's Upson," cried Burke. They threw their arms around him and pounded him on the back.

Hostler Kirk reined a fresh roan mustang into the flickering circle of light and, as the skittish mount wheeled and reared, the padlocked leather mochila was hurriedly transferred. Haslem, muffled in a great coat with a tight-fitting wool cap pulled down over his ears, laid a gloved hand on Upson's shoulder, "Bad?" he questioned. The wiry 120-pounder shrugged:

"There's heavy drifts above Slippery Ford—no sign of the 'pike' over Nevett's or around Cape Horn—and Yank's is swimming a foot deep in water." Upson caught the bleached flour sack that Burke tossed. He wiped his face. Overhead pinpoints of stars were beginning to glitter in the broken sky and a vagrant shaft of moonlight slithered across the swaying pine trees.

"Pony Bob" turned and vaulted into the racing saddle. Laying spurs lightly to his quivering mount, he pounded away into the night toward Daggett Pass and Carson.

The first Pony Express rider to cross the Sierra by way of the new Kingsbury Grade was on his way east![1]

Barely a month earlier Martin K. "Friday" Burke and James Washington Small had pre-empted 320 acres of meadow and forest land on the southeast shore of Tahoe, one and one-half miles east of the present southern Nevada-California boundary.[2] Blood-stirring events led them to this land acquisition. A silver miracle—the Comstock Lode—had exploded upon the world in 1859 and the lower, shorter "Daggett Ravine" Pass road leading to Washoe was being rushed to completion. It was to replace the Luther and Carson arterials.

The partners had chosen their location wisely. At this point Eagle Valley's Emigrant Ridge road left the lake, running two to three miles above Tahoe along the Carson Range to Walton's Summit (Spooner).[3] Several hundred yards north of their projected cabin site was "Trail Junction" connecting with the pack trail leading eastward over Daggett. An improved Washoe Indian game path wound to the north along the lakeshore toward Cave Rock and Walton's Landing (Glenbrook). Meadowland stretched to the lake and a small stream (Friday's Creek) and spring were available to supply water.

"NEITHER RAIN NOR SLEET . . ."

*Mail carrier crossing the
Central Sierra over the Johnson Trail
in the late 1850's.*

Bancroft Library

Here Burke and Small felled sugar pine for a log station and split the hearts of cedar into shakes for the roof.

David Demmen Kingsbury and his partner, John McDonald, who earlier contracted sections of the Johnson Pass route above Placerville, had already spent eight months on construction of the Kingsbury Grade. Dirt wagons, teamsters, horse and mule-drawn scrapers, chain drags, graders, and a crew of laborers continued to push the road toward completion in spite of the heavy winter of 1859 which laid snow 6 feet deep on the flats. Scarcity of labor and near-prohibitive provision costs were problems, but not insurmountable, for the new turnpike was finished in August of 1860. Burke and Small obtained the franchise to operate the western section of the Kingsbury as a toll road and other stations would form links in the chain of hostelries over the pass from Friday's to Van Sickle's Station.[4] The spring of 1860 saw momentous events unfolding in which Friday's Station would play an important role, From the Eastern States came the distant rumblings of a country torn by turmoil. There was talk of the South seceding from the Union and the States were drifting toward war. To the owners of Friday's this faraway surge of tumult seemed no more than a ripple, a remote something beyond the blue sweep of horizon, thousands of miles from the snow water and balsam-scented air of Tahoe.

An endless procession of men, vehicles, animals and materials now flooded and choked the Great Road leading to Washoe. In the short span of a few months, Burke and his partner found themselves caught up in a chaotic swirl of business. Along with Lapham's "Fish Market" and Dean's Lake House Fisheries to the southwest, Burke and Small became the first commercial fishermen on the lake. Using the name "Burke and Company" they spread a half mile of seine nets along the shoreline of Boundary Bay.[5] Daily they took thousands of native silverside and cutthroat trout from the sandy shallows, finding a ready market on the crowded road for their choice catch. Hunting parties set out from "Friday's" to track down deer and bear in the surrounding forest and venison and bear steaks were also sold to the wayfarers.

With the coming of the Pony Express and rerouting of James McClean's Pioneer Stage Line, Wells Fargo Express and other traffic over the Kingsbury, Burke and Small's became a "home station."[6] The accommodations of a one-room log cabin were augmented by the addition of a two-and-one-half story frame hostelry and outbuildings. A large dining room, rambling kitchen, storeroom and huge woodshed were built and Friday's could now house 25 lodgers in the main building and an equal number of teamsters and stage drivers in the outlying cabins.

Their combination horse-change stable and hay barn, one of the largest in the West at the time, was hurriedly erected with lumber run out in Woodburn's Lake Valley sawmill. Twenty-four stalls, 12 to each side, were provided in this 120-foot long by 30-foot high structure and large swinging doors permitted entry, one behind the other, of a coach and six and loaded 20-ton Washoe wagon with "back action" combination. Running water from the spring was piped to the stable and main building through 10-inch crudely hollowed-out logs.[7]

Several months before this expansion at Friday's and barely four weeks after the first run of the "Pony" over Luther Pass, one of the most famous Express riders, "Pony Bob" Haslem, made his headquarters at the Station. Haslem's leg in the Central Overland system took him east across the desolate wastes of Utah Territory (Nevada) to Fort Churchill and return, a round trip distance of 150 miles.

Trouble was brewing in the white alkali dust and barren reaches of Washoe during that first week in May, 1860. The Paiutes, smouldering under the white man's atrocities, finally retaliated.

Williams Station, some 25 miles east of present-day Dayton, Nevada, then a station on the line of the "Pony," was burned out. Five men, a woman, and a child died in the fire or were shot by savages who besieged the outpost. Panic swept Carson and Six Mile Canyon. In Virginia City the news was shouted—"5,000 redskins have taken up bows, guns, tomahawks, and are going on the warpath." Virginia's citizens quickly braced to meet the threat to their existence. A motley crew of volunteers were hastily rounded up, the mines were shut down and Six Mile barricaded. A thousand voices thundered, "Teach the murderous Paiutes a lesson"—and a pitiful raggle-taggle band of 125 men, calling themselves an "army," galloped their horses down the mountain into the heat of the sagebrush country. On May 12, 1860, they rode into an ambush near Pyramid Lake and were cut to ribbons by the battle-wise Paiutes and their allies. Seventy-six whites were killed. Twenty-eight returned, some riding but most walking, routed and defeated, the mutilated bodies of their companions left behind on the battlefield. Not until early June did the Sierra Battalion, from Downieville, team up with Captain Storey's "Virginia Rifles." Then this force of 750 trained men drove the Paiutes "pell-mell into the utmost reaches of the wastes in the Battle of Pinnacle Mount."[8]

Into this inferno of death Haslem had ridden from the mountain fortress sanctuary of Friday's Station, on the morning of May 6, 1860, to blaze a trail of courage and hard riding that would remain the most memorable in Pony Express history.

Haslem spurred up from the Station over Daggett Pass and down the serpentine course of the Kingsbury, cut into the eastern scarp of the Sierra. Turning north from Van Sickle's at the base of the grade, he roweled his mount into Genoa, then moved east to Reed's Station on the Carson River. Here no relief mount was available, as all the horses had been appropriated by Major William Ormsby's brigade for the Battle of Pyramid Lake. Haslem fed his flagging mustang and hightailed it 15 miles farther down river to Bucklands (later Fort Churchill). The country was alive with paint-smeared savages, yet the "Phantom of the Desert" streaked through. Bucklands was the terminal point of Haslem's regular run but his relief rider, Johnson Richardson, would not take to the road. W. C. Marley, superintendent at the station, tried to talk him into making the ride, gave up, and turned to Haslem. "Bob," he said, "I'll give you $50 if you make the ride." "I'll go at once," was Haslem's answer.

After adjusting his "seven-shooter Spencer rifle and Colt's revolver," he was off. "Pony Bob" threaded the lonely and dangerous 35 miles to the Sink of the Carson without a horse change and pushed across alkali bottom and sand hills another 30 miles. He couldn't find water anywhere along the route. Arriving at Sand Springs, Haslem changed horses and set out for Cold Springs (Williams Station) 37 miles farther east. Here he switched to a fresh mount and spurred on to Smith's Creek, 30 additional

David Wallace Park

HOME STATION
FOR THE PONY EXPRESS

*Friday's Station in the summer of 1896,
after it had been purchased by the
John Wales Averill family and
renamed Edgewood. Looking southwest.
Averill is seated on the ranch wagon.*

miles along the Central Overland route. Bob then offered the following terse statement: "Here I was relieved by J. G. Kelley. I had ridden 190 miles, stopping only to eat and change horses."

This, for a run that stands on the records as "the fastest along the entire Pony Express route of 2,000 miles" is modest enough.[9]

Haslem lay over at Smith's Creek for nine hours and then started back toward Friday's carrying the westbound mail. Arriving at Cold Springs he was stunned to find the station had been attacked by Indians and that keeper John Williams and his group had been killed and their bodies partially devoured by wolves. The Paiutes had taken all the horses. As he watered his tiring mustang he deliberated.

How could a single horseman now expect to get through, he asked himself. Weren't the renegades as thick as corn stalks in a field? Still he had no choice. He had to go on. Swinging into the saddle again, he started for Sand Springs in the growing darkness, through sagebrush in places high enough to conceal a horse. Ambush, he thought, but nothing barred his path as he streaked down the road.

It was a spine-chilling ride. All along the way he was keyed for a fight—tensed for the yell, the scream, the whooping war cry and the attack. When he finally galloped into Sand Springs without incident he was amazed. Haslem advised the station keeper to join him on his sprint to the Sink of the Carson, and his acceptance of "Pony Bob's" suggestion probably saved his life, as Smith's Creek was attacked the following morning.

Arriving at the Sink of the Carson, Haslem and the Sand Springs station keeper found the men armed and ready for a fight as some 50 brown-skinned warriors were reconnoitering. After resting an hour Bob pushed on alone, arriving at Buckland's only three and one-half hours behind schedule. By now he resembled a ghost rider, for he was doubled over with fatigue and red-eyed from the powdered alkali dust that covered him from hat to boots.

Marley and a stable boy led a pawing sorrel into the road at Buckland's and "Pony Bob's" bonus was upped to $100 by the station keeper when he learned of the Cold Springs tragedy. Once again Haslem booted a fresh pony into the blackness ahead, pounding along his regular route toward Friday's. After winding up the eastern Sierra barrier he finally crossed the last bridge and dismounted at his home station.

"Pony Bob" Haslem had pushed 380 miles behind the flying hoofs of his mustangs, and he was only a few hours behind schedule. Fast, steady riding, a cool head and unbelievable luck had combined to see him through.

Haslem was not through setting records. On May 13 of the following year he carried the news of Lincoln's election, riding 120 miles in 8 hours and 10 minutes on the Sink of the Carson-Carson City east-west run. It took 13 horse changes to accomplish the feat. He was reportedly attacked by Indians, receiving a shattered jaw from an arrow and a left arm injury, but existing "Pony" speed and endurance records were again broken.[10]

Adolph Sutro presented the accolade to the "Express" when he wrote of his stagecoach trip down the Kingsbury to Friday's Station during an April storm: "Flakes of snow and pellets of hail blew into the faces of the party, stinging and blinding. Trees tossed in the gale. The wind howled, bending and snapping branches. On the very summit (Daggett Pass) we met a lonely rider dashing along at a tremendous rate. We wondered what could possibly drive him to go through that blizzard—it was the Pony Express!"

Young Samuel Clemens (Mark Twain), headed west on the Central Overland stage, also wrote admiringly: "Here he comes. Every neck is stretched further and every eye strained wider. Away across the endless dead level of the prairie a black speck appears against the sky. It becomes a horse and rider, rising and falling—sweeping towards us, nearer and nearer—then the flutter of hoofs comes faintly to the ear—another instant a whoop and a hurrah from our upper deck, a wave of the rider's hand—and man and horse burst past our excited faces and go swinging away like a belated fragment of a storm."[11]

Although the Pony Express was a losing financial gamble, its romance fired the public's imagination. Fast, reliable travel linking the east and west over the Central Route had become a reality. Along with the other hostelries on the Great Road, Friday's Station prospered and expanded. Tolls collected by Burke and Small ran to the fantastic high of $1,500 a day at the crest of the summer traffic. Mule- and horse-drawn graders, rollers and water carts were constantly at work leveling the turnpike and settling the dust from Friday's drop toll gate up the canyon and over Daggett Pass. In the years 1861, 1862, 1863 the traffic doubled, then tripled.

As one of the principal "home stations" between Placerville and Carson, Burke and Small's continued to do a turn-away business. The parched, blinding length of the great Central American Desert stretched from Salt Lake City to the base of the eastern Sierra Nevada and was known as the "Sinkhole of Mormon Deseret." The location of Friday's Station, therefore, made it the last "mountain oasis" for travelers going east, and the first keen foretaste of high altitude lake and forest country for those pressing west.

In May, 1861, an eyewitness reported conditions on the expanding arterial: "Between the end of Swan's Toll House (Slippery Ford) and the beginning of the Kingsbury is a few miles of bad road on which little work has been done. It is to be improved this summer. From this spot Kingsbury's road extends to Carson Valley, leading down the east side of the west summit, crossing Lake Valley and passing (Friday's) over the east summit, a distance of 22 miles."[12]

Settlers other than Burke and Small had scrambled for land bordering on the new turnpike. Frank Powers, father of P. F. "Cy" Powers, pre-empted 160 acres to the north of Friday's after selling his butcher shop at Yank's Station. By 1864 Powers' livestock ranch in lower Lake Valley had become one of the largest stock ranches in the Tahoe region, with a fenced-in home and barn, slaughter house, wagons, sleighs, Spanish horses, sheep, hogs, fowl and stock cattle. Powers' barn was filled with 3,000 pounds of barley, 2,000 pounds of hay, and hides hung on the drying racks.[13] His neighbors included M. B. and Robert Clark, whose quarter section adjoined the Kingsbury Grade; S. Duckworth, who ranched on 160 acres near the road, and Donald D. Cameron and his brother Rob, who took over 300 acres three miles up the grade for cordwood cutting. The Clark brothers dragged saw logs over summit to the mill at Peter's Flat and sold liquor to travelers in their roadside saloon.

During the summer of 1864 the Pioneer Stage Company listed 50 tons of hay, 40 tons of barley, 44 horses and sets of harness, all located at Friday's.[14] On the eastern approach to the Kingsbury, J. W. Haines (Haines' Canyon) had sold land to William M. Cary, where he built a grist mill having "two runs of first Clap burn stones" fed by a flume and tail race.[15]

Although the Kingsbury cut-off served the masses moving over the Sierra for scarcely three years, Friday's remained as a key station on the still shorter, lower Butler Ives or "lakeshore turnpike" that was opened to traffic in 1863.[16] This new arterial syphoned off the east and westbound traffic just as the Kingsbury before it had dried up the Luther and Carson Pass travel.

With business reduced to a trickle in the summer of 1868, due to the completion of the Central Pacific, Burke and Small decided to divide their land interests but it was the summer of 1871 before they followed through with their plans. Burke then deeded the site of Friday's Station to Small. This included 400 surrounding acres running from Lake Tahoe across the meadow and flanking the Kingsbury Grade. Burke took the remaining 520 acres stretching north from Friday's Creek to Round Mound and including one and one-half miles of lake front.

In July of the following year Jim Small and his wife sold 280 acres of their land, located one mile up the grade, to Charles P. Young from Genoa—price, $350.[17]

Friday's Station, now more commonly called "Small's" or the "Old Friday Ranch," was erroneously described as the "only white settlement to be found after leaving Glenbrook traveling south on the lakeshore road, with a checkerboard of wheat, barley fields and orchards adjoining the road on either side."[18]

A junketing correspondent from Carson City, stopping at the way station during August of 1875, noted that "Big Jim" Small was operating his own "Buttermilk Bonanza Ranch" and offering the "finest hunting, fishing and general well-being to be found in the Tahoe region."

Small was not averse to entangling himself in harmless tall tales but he returned from his hunting trips with little evidence to substantiate his boasts. On one such expedition with his dogs and rifle the "Honorable Legislator" tracked down and killed a grizzly that far exceeded (according to his statement) even his own expectations of size and ferocity. He had encountered the brute two miles north of Daggett Pass, Small later told his skeptical friends, adding: "That grizzly devil ran 1400 pounds and his track exceeded the size of a Westphalia ham!" When his incredulous audience asked for the evidence Small patiently explained he'd given the hide to a traveling fruit peddler who wanted something soft and durable as a canopy for his wagon.

The *Carson City Appeal* investigated the story and advised its readers: " 'Old Wash' (Small) is the one who started all that grizzly hullabaloo just so the 'boys' would have an excuse to go off on a little tear into the mountains to drink up any available kegs of whiskey they might *just happen* to have dragged along." The paper pointed out: "This monstrous bear has been seen in five different places at once and claimed in each instance to be none other than 'Old Brin' with his two toes missing, the scourge of the Sierra for some twenty years." Therefore, the paper concluded, "under the leadership of Jim Small they are just calling a riot on Brin's name."[19]

"Old Wash" was adept at fabricating other phenomena. The *Appeal* cited an example: " 'Big Jim' tells us that he has seen a mermaid in the lake with a fine chest development, beautiful white mustache one and one-half inches long, and of a most amenable nature. As some of the lady guests staying at Small's had their underpinnings stolen from the clothesline in the meadow on that particular day, he is sure beyond a doubt that the loss was the doing of the fresh-water nymph, as he recognized one of the missing petticoats that she had decked herself out in."[20] This high humor of the day served as crackling publicity for Small's Buttermilk Farm and its owner.

In 1885, J. G. "Doc" Small took over active management of the ranch from his brother Jim.

"Doc" was the serious-minded member of the family. When his oldest daughter Josie eloped with pioneer Lake Valley resident William Henry Lyons' son, Charlie Lyons, a small earthquake shook the ranch, as "Doc" had indicated his whole-hearted opposition to the match. He is said to have "blasphemed the mountains" when he discovered the "outrage," and it took the combined efforts of both families to cool the irate father down.[21]

Three years after the "Doc" Small family settled at "Small's" they sold 130 acres of their land to the John Wales Averills. Averill, who named the site Edgewood, also operated the Lake Valley Meat Market in conjunction with a dairy, and still found time to grow the largest rhubarb in the Tahoe region.

William "Bill" Hanlon was Averill's regular driver. In order to make his rounds of customers, who were spread all along the lakeshore from Glenbrook to Tallac, Hanlon shook himself out of the hayloft at three o'clock each morning, loaded the meat wagon and started out on his deliveries before sunrise. One morning, early in the fall of 1890, Wales Averill took over the reins of his canvas-covered high-wheeler and, whipping up his span of mares, started off at a fast clip for Tom Rowland's Station. He was due in Genoa at noon, which left him little time for this one local delivery. In his haste he careened off the road into an irrigation ditch, nearly overturning the vehicle.

Fannie Rowland had ordered a side of beef and she met him at the Station. He climbed down, reached over the tailgate and found only empty space. Without a word to Miss Rowland, Averill swung back onto the leathers and wheeled his team down the lakeshore road at a gallop. Three miles north he located 250 pounds of meat floating in the watercourse he and his wagon had crossed in a flying leap shortly before. That was the last time John Wales took over from his man Hanlon.[22]

After Averill's death in 1897, his widow put the land up for sale. The following year it was purchased by David Brooks Park of Mottsville, Nevada, and the Averills returned to Carson Valley to live.

The Parks retained the name Edgewood. In 1957 a reduced acreage on both sides of Highway 50 was owned by D. B. Park's son, David Wallace Park.

Although the exterior of old Friday's Station has been modernized and the wing that formerly stood to the west, removed, the ridge pole, rafters and hand-hewn interior walls and floor are intact. The massive Wells Fargo and Pioneer Stage Lines' barn was torn down by David Wallace Park in the 1940's, but one of the log cabins that served as a blacksmith shop nearly 100 years ago still stands to the east of the main building.[23]

This historically important link in the Pony Express and Bonanza Road to Washoe route is situated one-sixteenth of a mile east of the present highway but it is seldom remembered as the old "home station" of courageous "Pony Bob" Haslem, the Pioneer Stage Lines, and Wells Fargo Express. The original turnpike may easily be traced where it ran north through the upper meadow from Stateline past the Station, and dog-legged across Friday's Creek on a rough hewn log bridge to join the Kingsbury Grade's western approach.

The Kingsbury-Daggett Pass cut-off into Carson Valley is one of the most magnificent drives in the Sierra Nevada. With the exception of several realignments on the steeper pitches of the switchbacks, where the dirt road climbs up the eastern Carson Range, the cut-off remains practically unchanged after nearly a century of travel. From the 7,375-foot summit the breath-catching drop of Haines' Canyon falls in an almost vertical tumble to the valley. Following the tortuous road as it hairpins down the crumbling granite mountainside the traveler comes first to the small flat where J. B. Campbell's mill stood. The next large meadow was the site of Peter Van Sickle's wayside station and sawmill (Peter's Flat) during the freighting days. Farther down the mountain "Overlook Point" affords a sweeping panorama of Carson Valley, stretching north and south with its square and oblong patchwork of dark green alfalfa fields and brownish yellow haystacks. Scattered farmhouses border the rich bottomland and encircle the towns of Minden and Gardnerville. Here a strange hush brings a feeling of intense solitude. Far across the contour of the valley rise the bare rolling "Painted Hills," lifting into the purple haze of the Pine Nut Mountains. To the south, sparsely forested, great upthrusts of the Sierra chain climb from the valley floor in a devil's toboggan 6,500 feet to the wind-swept rocky summits of Mount Freel, Job's Peak and Job's Sister.

EDGEWOOD—1958

Trim and beautifully maintained by the Park family, historic Friday's Station stands proudly today, substantially unchanged since its construction nearly one hundred years ago. Photograph taken looking northwest.

Author's collection

HERE THE "PONY" WAS SHOD

Saw log structure that served as a blacksmith shop in the days of the Pony Express, Wells Fargo and Pioneer Stage Lines, lies to the east of old Friday's Station.

Author's collection

Chapter Thirty-three

HOBART

"GENERAL MARLETTE and myself dissolved our saw log and cordwood partnership at Crystal Bay day before yesterday, Mrs. Burke, as the timber's mostly gone, so I'm aiming to go into business for myself and get out more wood for Hobart at Incline."[1]

Gilman Nathaniel Folsom was standing, hat in hand, talking to the Widow Burke on the porch of her log house that stood a pebble's throw from the lakeshore road. Earlier on that bone-chilling fall afternoon in 1888 he had cruised the thick stands of tamarack, yellow and sugar pine lying between the foot of the Kingsbury Grade and Daggett Pass. Now he was certain that "Burke's land" constituted one of the last private parcels of choice forest growth remaining on the southeast shore of Tahoe. Mrs. Burke wanted to sell, and if his purchase price met with her approval he'd be back in business.

"Much of your 520 acres is meadowland, Mrs. Burke," Folsom reminded her, "so I've figured it out carefully and $750 gold, payable over three years, is the best offer I can make." Inwardly he was taut as a bowstring for he knew that his future was riding on the Widow Burke's decision.

"Well," Mrs. Burke replied tonelessly, her eyes lifting to the meadow and the trees beyond, "now that Martin's gone I've no use for the tall pine. Talk is that you're a fair minded man with a word that's good, so I'll accept your offer."

Folsom was elated. "I'll bring the papers over for your signature when I move my crew in next week," he informed Mrs. Burke briskly. Then he replaced his hat and turned to leave.

The widow, however, had more to say. Still gazing thoughtfully out across land that would soon ring and whirr to ax and saw, she continued:

"Yes, I've no more use for it now, but I've seen much happen here in thirty years, Mr. Folsom. Take that young Walter Hobart, for instance—I remember when he struck it rich on the Comstock to become a millionaire at 21;[2] and even the very day he took up more than 7800 acres stretching from Glenbrook south past Cave Rock right to the border of my north forty.[3] Bought it the way I'd buy a dozen eggs from neighbor Small—didn't think twice. And now Hobart, Bliss, and Yerington's El Dorado Wood and Flume Company, they've near hemmed me in.[4] Yes, there's nothing here for me any more. It's your land now, Mr. Folsom."

The next spring Folsom moved in with his men and equipment, and began to fell pine and cord slab-wood, to meet his contract agreements with Hobart. Soon a small lumbering settlement sprang up a half mile north of Old Friday's Station where the head of the meadow bordered the main road. The little community consisted of a handful of clapboard houses, log cabins and tents to house the lumbermen and their families. There was also a combination store and post office, a blacksmith shop, cook house presided over by "Chinese Joe," a slaughterhouse, recreation hall and saloon. Across the turnpike to the west two barns were built. The largest, called "Big Barn," rivaled Wells Fargo's structure

A GOODLY SPRINKLING OF "BEAVERS"

Lumber and cordwood "stackers" preparing to move a loaded hand car into Hobart Meadow. Cordwood and pine slabs are stacked on the pier for barging to Incline. View taken looking northwest across Tahoe in the summer of 1889.

at "Friday's" with support timbers 60 feet long and 24- to 30-inch sidings supplied by the How(e) and Montrose sawmill on the Kingsbury Grade.[5] Two hundred tons of hay could be stored in the loft and the stalls accommodated 48 work horses and mules. A shed and corral adjoined to the north, furnishing quarters for the draft oxen. The smaller barn, which continued to stand 70 years later, held the riding horses and rigs, and the names of the animals could still be seen lettered on their stalls.[6]

Instead of naming the settlement "Folsom," Folsom called it "Hobart," a compliment to the man on whose patronage the success of the venture largely depended.

Two log chutes were built from highline west through the meadow to the lakeshore, one running a distance of half a mile, the other dropping three and one-half miles to the water. At Folsom's pier, a crew of loaders stacked the cordwood and assembled log booms for towing to Incline.[7] Folsom also built a water-powered shingle mill, fed by "Hobart's Ditch," up the canyon northeast of the Kingsbury Grade. Frank Powers' son, "Cy," supplied meat to the settlement and ran his cattle on the old Powers' ranch south of Small's. However, his tenure as butcher was terminated abruptly in the 1890's. Powers was killed when his horses panicked and his meat wagon hurtled out of control.[8]

G. N. Folsom's wife, Priscilla, was the first school teacher at the settlement. Her class of 1889-90 included Emma Frances Jewell, later postmistress at Hobart, whose family had a two-acre ranch there;[9] Arthur and Elliott Ramsey, sons of Charles Ramsey, Bijou; Bessie Vair, daughter of engineer James Vair; and the McFaul children from Marla Bay. From time to time a Washoe Indian boy or two would pop up in the class. Eva McClaskey, daughter of logger Sam McClaskey, followed Mrs. Folsom as teacher, then Maggie Park of the Carson Valley Park family and, later, Annie Brockliss.[10]

E. H. "Starvation" Smith, whose land adjoined on the south (Lakeside), drove his "fringe top" to Folsom's pier daily to pick up guests at what was then Sapphire Bay.

By the year 1893 Folsom had increased his land holdings to 610 acres. Thirty work horses, 40 draft oxen, 50 hogs, wagons and machinery constituted the equipment and livestock, and his lumbering activity was at its peak. The old Emigrant Road, running back of the settlement near Chimney Rock and continuing along the ridges above Tahoe to Spooner Station and Summit Camp, was now used for logging. In a small meadow above Hobart a rusting hay press lay where it had been abandoned by the emigrants in '49. Dan Jones was reputed to be the greatest ox driver at Hobart and his bullwhacking ability included a voice that boomed like thunder.[11]

By the year 1896 G. N. Folsom's operations had been reduced to cordwood cutting, and he moved his camps farther and farther back into the decreasing timber stands. He and his son, E. B. Folsom, were now hard-pressed to meet their obligations, and their working stock had been cut to 18 horses. Their main asset was 300 cords of wood valued at $600.[12]

Six years before, the C. and T. L. and F. Company had acquired Walter Scott Hobart's Nevada Lumber Company holdings on the south end of Tahoe. This amounted to nearly 8,000 acres, and they added 10,100 acres of their own. A small, though hard-working, operator such as Folsom had very little chance of success against the combine's competition.

Harry James, of Genoa, recalls driving to Hobart with his father, John James, in the summer of 1897. The Folsoms owed them $4,000 for hay and grain deliveries. Gilman Folsom met them at the gate and, when pressed for payment, said, "I'd gladly pay if I were in Carson City," to which John James unhesitatingly replied, "There's no time like the present, let's go!" Without batting an eyelash, Folsom accepted and they immediately drove into Carson. There he drew the money out of the bank in gold and paid his debt. Two days later Gilman Nathaniel Folsom went into bankruptcy. Unknowingly, the James family had contributed to his financial collapse.[13]

THE BLACK LOAM WAS A RICH PRODUCER

Indigenous crops grew fantastically in the fertile soil and rarefied air. Here, northwest of Hobart, oxen are pulling a wheel plow in the summer of 1892.

Folsom's land was now taken over by the bank in Carson and cordwood operations were closed down. Robert L. Bence leased meadowland here the following year and ran dairy cattle. Later Richard Kirman purchased a part of the holding. From the Kirmans it passed to the Chris' Rabe family, who farmed and ranched at the location and furnished lodging for fruit peddlers on their way to Carson in the mid 1900's.[14] Now the land, reduced to a quarter section, is owned by William Rabe, the son of Elizabeth and Chris Rabe, who uses the meadowland as a summer range for his cattle, wintering the herd in Carson Valley near Gardnerville, Nevada.

Part of the old Rabe holding constituted Sky Harbor Airport, the first airstrip to border Lake Tahoe, and Tahoe Village, a modern hotel and gaming casino, adjoined Highway 50, above the airfield.[15]

A LOG AND TREE STUMP FENCE BORDERED THE GREAT ROAD

Looking north in 1889 at the settlement of Hobart with "Big Barn" (left) and the combination store and post office across the lakeshore turnpike; now Highway 50. G. N. Folsom family in front of store.

The Nevada State Museum

Chapter Thirty-four

MARLA BAY

$\star$

WHEN SEEN from the air, small, secluded Marla Bay's contour resembles an Indian's profile. To the south lies Edgewood, and on the north, Zephyr Cove. Round Hill, alternately known over the years as Folsom's Knob and Peak, Round Mountain and Mound, here rises some 700 feet above the lake.

In the spring of 1864, John Marley, a native of England, pre-empted 160 acres surrounding the bay.[1] At the time the Lake Bigler Toll Road ran in a dog-leg above the present highway and here Marley built a log cabin facing the turnpike. On a small stretch of meadowland to the west running to the water, he raised timothy hay, scythe-cut his crop and baled it with a crude hand press. Marley also planted potatoes and other vegetables, obtaining fantastic prices for his high altitude "whoppers" from travelers passing over the Golden Road.

Rancher Marley bore the doubtful distinction of being listed on the first tax rolls of Douglas(s) County, Nevada, with a personal property valuation of $25. This assesesment covered one wagon. As no horses, mules, oxen, milk cows, or beef cattle were itemized, the intriguing question is posed—did Marley haul his own wagon?[2]

On November 19, 1870, Captain Augustus W. Pray of Glenbrook bought Marley's ranch for back taxes. Although an account of this pioneer's life after he left the bay is lost to history, John Marley's name remains on the cove—shortened over the years to Marla.[3]

Pray felled the choice timber in the surrounding forest land and left the stunted growth for cordwood cutting. In 1884, the Glenbrook lumberman sold the land to William McFaul, who brought his family over from Zephyr Cove the following spring.[4]

The McFauls were wood contractors who dropped and split trees during the winter months. One of their larger contracts is said to have been the clearing of Al Tahoe's present site.[5] During the summer months they pastured a herd of milk cows in the meadowland at the bay, hung sides of ham in their smokehouse, crocked eggs and kegged butter for the fall market in Washoe. The McFauls added a two-story house of battened construction with three rooms downstairs. Two barns, built out of "shoot poles," and a milk house, were put up northwest of the main home.[6]

Settlement hopping Joe M. Short of Carson City, Glenbrook and Brockway Hot Springs took over the McFaul ranch in 1890, but the McFaul family were back again in 1893.[7] During the 1890's William McFaul reportedly sold Round Mound to Heinrich "Dutch Fred" Dangberg of Minden, Nevada. A story still persists that Dangberg's son Fred lost the holding, now worth in excess of $100,000, to McFaul in a game of stud poker—the land against a $50 pot of gold eagles. Here fact is probably confused with fiction.[8]

For more than two decades the McFauls stacked cordwood on their wharf at the bay, loading the pine slabs aboard barges headed for Glenbrook. Upon William McFaul's death in 1912 the property was purchased by the Cogel family.[9]

In 1922, Norman DeVaux, recalled as builder and promoter of the DeVaux automobile, bought the quarter section surrounding Marla Bay and acquired additional land, bringing his total to 396 acres.[10] DeVaux built a private lodge on the north slope of Round Mound, and added bathhouses and a large boathouse on the shoreline of the sheltered cove. In the rocked enclosure he kept his express cruiser *Myrno III (Reverie)* and fast mahogany runabout the *Apache II*.[11]

After the 1929 depression, Arthur K. Bourne of the Singer Sewing Machine family took over DeVaux's property and by 1936 Bourne had nearly doubled his holdings.[12]

The lodge is now operated as a commercial summer establishment under the name Round Hill Resort and the Bourne's built other lakefront homes to the north.

HIGH NOON AT HIGHLINE

Logging by the "new method" (donkey engine with a dollbeer) and lumberjacks in the backwoods above Marla Bay. Summer of 1894.

Author's collection

Chapter Thirty-five

ZEPHYR COVE

Eᴀʀʟʏ sᴇᴛᴛʟᴇʀs attribute the naming of Zephyr Cove to prevailing winds that sweep across the lake from Emerald Bay Gorge and the Rubicon Peaks, often building up a heavy chop on the waters of the bay.

The Cove lies between Round Mound to the south and Cave Rock on the north, running in a crescent of fine sandy beach and bordering the old lakeshore road.[1]

In the spring of 1862 Andrew Boynton Gardinier, a French-Canadian who had traveled the Central Overland route in the 1850's from Massachusetts, homesteaded 160 acres bordering on the Cove. At the time, the nearest settlement was Friday's Station, four miles to the south, although John Ridinger had pre-empted 255 acres to the north.[2]

During the summer and fall of 1862 Gardinier built a pretentious hostelry fronting on the Lake Tahoe Wagon Toll Road, then being pushed to completion by Butler Ives.[3]

The hostelry was constructed in the form of a T, and its exterior finished in pine bark.[4] Total value of the quarter section of land, hotel, furnishings and outbuildings, which included a barn, came to $5,270.[5]

In the summer of 1863 Zephyr Cove House was visited by a correspondent from the *Carson City Appeal* who described it as "offering one of the better lodging places on the shortest route to the mines, and fronting on the most beautiful of Lake Bigler's bays." Obviously, the newsman was a loyal product of Nevada Territory, as the few mariners who had visited Emerald Bay on the California side of the lake agreed that it surpassed Zephyr Cove in grandeur.

On August 26 of the same year it was reported "300 laborers are working on the 14 miles of new road on the lake's eastern shore. It will average 20 feet in width, with a nominal rise of eight feet in every hundred when completed in September and open up another route (to Virginia City) three miles shorter, and 300 feet lower than the Kingsbury."[6] During October of 1865, the *San Francisco Alta* "discovered a commodious house, set among tall pines that ran to the water's edge, located upon a nearly level fall of ground at the foot of the Cove." The paper's correspondent was particularly impressed with Zephyr Cove hotel's modest rates of $12 per week.[7]

Like the other way stations lining the road, it had been spawned by the mass migration to Washoe. Travelers were diverted to the new lakeshore turnpike, and Gardner (he had now dropped the two i's in his name) prospered.

Over the great road flowed the lifeblood of the Comstock. Those wayfarers fortunate enough to secure accommodations at Zephyr Cove House paused for a night's lodging. If the "record" was full, they rolled up in their blankets under the teamsters' wagons or in Zephyr Meadow. In the morning

C. O. Valentine

"THIS EDEN OF BIGLER—VESTIGE OF A BYGONE ERA"

A correspondent from Carson so described Zephyr in the summer of 1871 and this photograph taken four decades later, showing the steamer
Tahoe *docking at the Cove and headed for Glenbrook, found it still unchanged.*

they would be caught up again in the endless stream of traffic sweeping north to Upper Glenbrook Meadow, Spooner's Station, and down Clear Creek or King's Canyon.

By 1869 travel on the toll road had dwindled to a few vehicles, and Gardner found himself unable even to pay his taxes. Captain A. W. Pray, who had been eyeing the timber stands surrounding the Cove for several years, now stepped in. He needed an additional source of saw logs for his mill at Glenbrook, and the accessible beach would allow him to bring his *Governor Blaisdel* in to pick up log rafts. In November of 1870 Pray took title to Gardner's 160 acres, including Zephyr Cove House.

Another correspondent from Carson, who made the trip to Lake Valley by spring wagon the following summer, was startled to discover that the Cove had turned into a ghost settlement. Birds nested in the "old hotel" and chipmunks scurried through the outbuildings. He reported sadly: "this 'Eden of Bigler' is now a vestige of a by-gone era"; bygone being all of three years previous.[8]

Two and one-half decades of large scale lumbering was now about to begin at Tahoe with a timber El Dorado in sight equal to many of the better producing mines at the Comstock Lode.

In the Centennial year of 1876 George Washington Chubbuck and his wife, Mary Lovell, brought their children overland from Vineland, New Jersey. Upon reaching Truckee they traveled to Tahoe City by wagon and boarded the sidewheel steamer *Governor Blaisdel* for Glenbrook. Arrangements had been made with Pray to establish residence at Zephyr Cove House, where Chubbuck would subcontract cordwood. From the lumbering settlement they were taken by rowboat six miles to the bay, there to be greeted by a large earthenware pot of red kidney beans. This constituted the Chubbucks' first dinner at Lake Tahoe.[9]

Albert Town Wakeman, his wife, and daughter Nellie were the only other family living at the Cove. They had located in a cabin down by the water's edge, and would later become proprietors of Saint's Rest on Clear Creek Grade.[10]

The Chubbucks and Wakemans cut the high timothy grass in the flatland surrounding the Cove, corded wood on the shoreline of the bay, and dragged logs to the water's edge for V-booming and rafting to Glenbrook by the steamers *Blaisdel, Meteor* and *Truckee.* A single Jersey cow constituted the Chubbucks' dairy, and one of the boys tended the toll gate, in front of old Logan House, walking the nine-mile round trip each day. A high point of the summer season for the youngsters at Zephyr was the arrival of produce wagons loaded with fresh fruit from the Valley towns and headed for Carson and Virginia City.[11]

After several years at the Cove, Chubbuck acquired timberland in the vicinity of Sierra House, and moved his family 5½ miles south to McCumber's Ranch.[12] The McFauls followed the Chubbucks as tenants at Zephyr Cove House. Two log chutes were run from a "pot-hole" on the mountain slopes above the bay, through the meadow to the water, and William McFaul, with his brothers Robert and George, continued in the logging and cordwood business, supplying Pray and the C. and T. L. and F. Company. Joseph Allen, the McFaul's youngest son, was born at the Cove in December, 1884, and the following year the family moved to Marla Bay. The Locksters, dairy people from Norway, now took over at Zephyr. In 1887 they returned to their native country.[13]

On April 10, 1889, the *Daily Nevada Tribune* reported: "A new Lake Tahoe town at Zephyr Cove has been christened Folsom, having a store and numerous buildings . . . and logging has been resumed."[14]

Actually, Gilman N. Folsom, after whom the "town" was named, had established the settlement of "Hobart" during the summer of this year on M. K. "Friday" Burke's former holding, and Folsom's Zephyr Cove location was only one of his many wood camps.

Any phenomenon that purported to link the Virginia City mines with Lake Tahoe was always caught up by the Nevada and California newspapers, and in June of 1890 the *Carson City Appeal* un-

UP KING'S CANYON TO THE LAKE OF THE SKY

Zephyr Cove was the end of the line for Gelatt's mud-wagons in the summer of 1868.

covered a miracle. Their reporter had learned from a French-Canadian cordwood cutter at the Cove that earlier in the month Tahoe rose four inches in a one-half hour period. As it was a calm day and no rainfall was reported around the lake, wags in Carson immediately attributed this amazing happening to "those miners in the Comstock who were getting tired of being on the receiving end of all that underground water flowing into the sumps, and who now pumped it back into Tahoe through subterranean fissures."[15]

In the early 1890's the Carson and Tahoe Lumber and Fluming Company acquired Zephyr Cove from the Walter Scott Hobart estate, and it became a part of George Whittell's extensive land holdings in 1938.[16] However, summer homes built on other privately owned land south of the present Zephyr Cove resort ring the bay, and "Conference Point" (Zephyr Cove Point) is also the location of a growing settlement.

ZEPHYR COVE.

Velma Comstock Eden

NAMED FOR THE STRONG AFTERNOON WINDS

Looking south toward Zephyr Cove in the summer of 1882 some 15 years after Zephyr Cove House (left of center) had ceased to serve the mass migration to Washoe. Trees have since disappeared from the island (right) which is now nearly covered at high water.

Chapter Thirty-six

CAVE ROCK

RISING LIKE a clenched fist, a jagged promontory known as Cave Rock thrusts up from the eastern shore of Lake Tahoe between Glenbrook and Zephyr Cove. Indian folklore romanticizes Cave Rock as the natural fortress where Paiutes and Washoes fought pitched battles for control of the "Big Water" and its surrounding forested hunting grounds.[1] It has been the mysterious source of numerous Washoe fantasies dealing with the formation of Tahoe and the ancestors of early Indian tribes living on its shoreline,[2] and in the fall of 1855 pioneer surveyor George H. Goddard described the rock as a "Legendary Cave."

The first detailed report of the Rock by white men contains statements almost as imaginative as the Washoe Indian legends.

During the summer of 1853 John Calhoun "Cock-Eye" Johnson and a *Placerville Herald* correspondent penetrated to the western shore of the lake by way of Rubicon River Gorge, arriving at what is now Meeks Bay, where they encountered a friendly band of Indians encamped on the beach. The chief of the tribe managed to communicate to them the fact that they were the first white men to reach those parts.

Directly opposite and some nine miles across the water on the eastern shore, the two men clearly observed a pyramidal mass of rock, pierced by what appeared to be a cave. Around the campfire that night a blind, wizened old patriarch "poured forth from his shriveled lips the ancient legend of his tribe, concerning the rock and water prison of the Demons."[3] After generously estimating the lake as sixty miles long by ten to twenty miles wide, the explorers decided to make the trip to the "Spirit's Cave." Two or three hollowed out log canoes, constructed from pine that grew on the extreme north border of the lake, were pulled up on the sand, and the men had to purchase one outright, as the "Grand Chief" of the tribe was certain they would not return.[4] Johnson and his companion persuaded two Indian bucks to go along by promising them a blanket apiece.

Up to this point in the story the Placerville correspondent's description is plausible. From then on a more masterful piece of overstatement would be difficult to find. According to his account, a great domelike rock was found, half way across Tahoe, "upon which one of the Indians jumped with a wild

---

C. O. Valentine

THE ROCK AND ITS SHADOW

*Low water in October of 1910; facing north with Cave Rock
in the foreground. Dead Man's Point
and snow-covered Mount Rose Range in the distance.*

"PRISON OF THE GENII"

Looking north along the old lakeshore road in the summer of 1892 at the legendary cave.

Author's Collection

cry." The depth of the water here was noted as "breast high on the sloping sides of the boulder and two feet deep on the top."

When the explorers "reached the Prison of the Genii," the narrator indicated that they "paddled into a mysterious grotto nearly two hundred feet wide upon the surface of the water, and more than two hundred feet high, full of icicles, stalactites, and resounding with low moaning sounds, such as they supposed would be made by a fall of water within an immense cavern." It was said that "the bottom could not be seen, but a small tin cup on the end of a forty-foot line was clearly visible in the water."[5]

As there is no great boulder rising from the fifteen hundred foot depth of Tahoe, which they supposedly crossed, and the cave in the rock opens high on the southern face, originally not more than thirty feet wide, it is evident that the imagination of the correspondent was put to colorful use. Another fact ignored almost entirely in the newsman's report, was their overwater trip. Had they accomplished this near-miraculous marine feat—9 miles each way across Tahoe's unpredictable waters in a dugout, surely more mention would have been made of the fact.

It is obvious that the trip to the Cave was never made, but the *Herald* newsman's articles, written over a century ago, nevertheless do have certain facts stitched in along with the embroidery. The Washoe Indian interpretation of the region's origin suggests that this may have been based upon early tribal memory.

Johnson and his companion were told that a vast, fertile plain through which flowed the mighty Tro-ko-nene River, occupied what was later to become the lake's basin and that a great tidal wave swept in from the Western sea, inundating the tableland. After the water subsided, volcanic action followed. The plain started to rise and mountains began to form. During this period, the legend avers, the Washoes' ancestors were conquered by a cruel and warlike tribe and the god of the world, aware of

C. O. Valentine

INSIDE THE CAVE

This view was taken from the Cave in the Rock looking south toward Rocky Point, Round Mound, Lake Valley and the South Carson Range in the summer of 1909. Two tunnels now carry Highway 50's traffic through Cave Rock.

ONE MILE OF ROAD—$40,000

*The road circling the Rock
in July, 1908,
looking north along the
hand-hewn granite buttressed turnpike.*

C. O. Valentine

their misfortune, fashioned a cavern on the eastern side of what became "Big Water." Into this cave he hurled the enemies of the Washoes' peace-loving forebears and imprisoned them when the water of the lake rose.

The blind centenarian who described these happenings concluded his story of the Rock: "And from that day to this their wailings and pent-up moanings have been heard, increasing in terror and intensity at that season of the year when the waters of the lake are increased."[6]

A decade later the Lake Bigler Toll Road to Carson City circled Cave Rock. It was used for more than half a century before the present 200-foot tunnel was blasted through the granite, destroying much of the original cave. At the time of its construction, this section of the Johnson Pass lakeshore turnpike constituted the greatest single expenditure for road building between Placerville and Washoe. Including extension of the right-of-way around the rock, the 100-foot trestle bridge and the hand-chiseled stone buttresses, the one mile of road improvement cost $40,000. Originally the old Indian trail ran above the rock, and this steeper but more direct route was widened to accommodate wagon traffic after 1863. The cut-off was maintained into the 1890's for use whenever the bridge was under repair.[7]

Harold A. Parker

TAHOE'S LADY OF THE LAKE

*A perfect profile, down to the eyelashes, of Tahoe's "Lady" photographed on May 16, 1909.
The start of the Gorilla Profile may be seen in the upper
left hand corner, and hewn granite block construction shores up the road on the bridge approaches.
Mount Tallac and the Rubicon Peaks rise in the background.*

The earliest settler to take up land near Cave Rock was William Hamilton of Carson Valley, who, in May of 1864, pre-empted 160 acres described as being "approximately half way between Spooner and Friday's Station on the Bigler Toll Road." Here he built a way station on "Rocky Point," known as the Rocky Point House, where he ranched and serviced the traffic on the turnpike.[8]

In March of 1865 a towering 90-foot flagpole was placed on top of Cave Rock and a large Old Glory run up that could be seen from all points on the lake. Feeling for the Union cause was running high among the pioneer lake settlers with the country still divided and struggling in the final grip of Civil War. It was noted that several weeks after the proud raising of the Stars and Stripes above the waters of Tahoe, "some dastardly wretch tore down the noble flag." An angry group of mountain men immediately assembled with their hunting dogs and rifles, and "a search was being made for the fiend." Undoubtedly someone with strong Confederate sympathies had found his way to the shores of Lake Tahoe.[9]

Today the early road construction at Cave Rock may be clearly seen to the west of the tunnel. It has changed little over the years. Although placed seven years before the completion of the Central Pacific, quarried granite blocks that carried the old highroad around the Rock's face are still in place.

To the north and south the landmarks of Rocky Point and Sierra Rocks flank the location. When a boat is brought in close to shore on the north side, one of Tahoe's more famous natural wonders becomes visible to the passengers.[10] Outlined on Cave Rock is the 50-foot profile of the "Lady of the Lake," complete in detail down to the eyelashes. Above the features of Tahoe's "Lady," and rising on the upper curve of the Rock, is the "Gorilla Profile," a somewhat startling example of beauty and the beast combined—an anomaly in the history of natural rock profiles.

This granite mass drops away in a vertical sweep nearly 400 feet to the translucent lake water below, and from the stone wall bordering the old bridge the aspect is that of a vast ocean stretching away to the distant Sierra Nevada in the west.

C. O. Valentine

A VAST MOUNTAIN OCEAN STRETCHING TO THE DISTANT SIERRA NEVADA

Panorama of Tahoe, taken in the late spring of 1912, looking southwest beyond the steamer TAHOE *(center) to Tallac's cross of snow and Emerald Bay. Summit of Cave Rock (right of picture).*

Chapter Thirty-seven

LOGAN HOUSE

"Say, Stewart, you ain't throwing a shadow in this Justice of the Peace business. Why not come up to Bigler and manage my new Logan House?" Robert Logan, Carson Valley rancher, was standing on the court house steps at Genoa, Nevada, talking to Wellington Stewart. The day was July 8 of the year 1863 and Stewart had just certified the transfer of 640 acres of lake property from George E. Pierson, Washoe mining man, to Logan.[1]

"Might just do that, Rob," Stewart answered.

"Could even work out a partnership," continued Logan. "Think it over, anyhow." He turned down the steps, mounted his horse and spurred north out of town along the dusty road toward Clear Creek Canyon.

"Yes, sir, might just do that," Stewart repeated to himself. He pushed through the high oak door into the court house. The Elliott boys and Michel Spooner were due in to see him about a flume dispute, otherwise he'd stage up to the lake that afternoon and look over Logan's new holding.

Robert Logan's mare settled into a fast trot and he sat the saddle easily. The midday sun was bright on the desert land and the pungent odor of sagebrush sharp in the air. To the west rose the steepness of the Carson-Sierra Nevada, covered with thick stands of pine and cedar.

Logan took deep, satisfying breaths. "Well," he thought, "I finally have that one mile square section." It was choice land—lakefront and timber. Captain A. W. Pray's ranch bordered his acreage to the north but there wasn't a settler to the east or south until you reached Gardinier's Zephyr Cove House.

The price had been steep, he reflected, $1,500.[2] However, a well-run hostelry would return that amount in short order. Travel over the new Lake Bigler Toll Road that swept past his proposed site for Logan House was fantastic. How could his venture help but pay out? Logan reined his horse onto the Jack's Valley cut-off and disappeared into the canyon.

By the summer of 1864 Logan's large two-story hostelry had opened its doors and was doing a brisk business.[3] Logan House stood on a bluff above the lakeshore, one and one-half miles south of Glenbrook House, and its outlook was so promising that Wellington Stewart left Genoa to enter into the suggested partnership. The owner-proprietors advertised rates of $15 a week, $6 less than the stylish way station at the head of Glenbrook meadow, and they catered primarily to the wagoner and foot traveler.[4]

It seemed that Logan and Stewart were two of a handful of opportunists who had correctly read the handwriting on the wall. Instead of following the headlong rush to the mines and gambling on making a "strike," they had chosen what appeared to offer a surer return for their efforts. The part-

USUALLY HORSES OR MULES WERE TRACE-CHAINED AHEAD OF THE OXEN

Saw log carrier and seven span headed downgrade to the Glenbrook mills in the summer of 1888. Photograph taken on a logging road east of Logan House.

ners let it be known that "fine meals, fishing and sailing skiffs" were available, along with "magnificent views of Bigler from Rocky Point, Cave and Sierra Rocks, nearby."[5]

Surprisingly enough, Logan House failed to prosper and at the conclusion of the season's operation the county assessor posted the establishment for delinquent taxes. Stewart arranged a first mortgage with his personal friend, Robert Lyon, nearby landowner, but this only carried them over until the fall of 1866.[6]

That same year all the Douglas County tax collector found at Logan House were "a house and barn, value $6,000," several hundred dollars worth of furniture and other personal property, and "one hog" listed in his ledger at $15. Logan and Stewart now had sold off all but 160 acres of their holding, and this was noted unimpressively as "one lot of sand."[7]

The prospect for Logan House and its owners was anything but promising. In December of 1867 one E. R. Cox obtained possessory title to the land and improvements. He was actually acting for Henry Marvin Yerington of the Glenbrook lumbering combine, who had purchased the acreage for its timber.

Yerington acknowledged ownership in 1870 and several years later Logan House was closed and boarded up.[8] The place gradually fell in on its foundations, without even the benefit of a conflagration to erase the crumbling structure. It is remembered as a "ghost hotel" where youngsters from Glenbrook played in the middle 1880's.[9] By the following decade Logan House was gone.

Today the shoreline below the bluff where Logan House once stood is known as "Logan Shoals." This constitutes the last public memento to Robert Logan and his partner, Wellington Stewart, who unsuccessfully entered the hotel business there during the peak years of the Golden Road.

Velma Comstock Eden

NATURE'S PORTRAIT OF ENGLAND'S IMMORTAL BARD

*Looking southeast at
Shakespeare Rock,
from Glenbrook Meadow,
through depleted timber
stands in the
summer of 1881.
The small, light-colored
profile of Shakespeare
is discernible near the center
of the rock,
facing right in the picture.*

Chapter Thirty-eight

SHAKESPEARE ROCK

"The beard is just a trifle longer than pictures of the famous bard, but the forehead, nose, and even eyes, are so near a duplication that it should be easily recognized by the most careless viewer." Thus was one of Tahoe's earliest landmarks, Shakespeare Cliff, described by a traveler in the spring of 1868.[1]

Since 1863 this lofty granite eminence has been pointed out to steamer passengers and guests at Glenbrook. One of these was Dan DeQuille, keen-witted scribe of the *Territorial Enterprise*, whose usually facile pen failed him in describing the unusual likeness of the great playwright. After spending the better part of an hour locating the poet's profile from the meadow south of Glenbrook's Lake House, DeQuille wrote, "All who visit the Lake desire first of all to see this rock. Like many other things of the kind, there is much in the position from which it is viewed, and not a little in the imaginative powers of the person viewing it."[2]

The wife of Reverend J. A. Benton from Massachusetts had discovered the curious formation in the summer of 1862. She was sketching mountain scenery when her attention was drawn to a small, deep stain on the side of the bluff lying above the little lumbering and resort settlement. As she concentrated her gaze the features materialized. She called to her companions and pointed out the portrait half way up the face of the cliff. After much squinting and craning of necks one of the party remarked that the picture on the rock resembled the original Chandos portrait of Shakespeare.

Public fancy was caught immediately by this identification of the natural portrait, produced by lichen growth, oxidation and erosion, with the immortal bard of Stratford on Avon. It was even reported that a resident of Carson City conceived the profile to be divine and that he visited the location frequently, seeking absolution of his sins.

One of the first tourist fatalities to occur at Tahoe took place on the cliff. A weekend group of excursionists from Washoe, including two prominent young people from Carson City, Carrie Rice and William Cramer, attempted to explore the 75-foot cavern in the rock. Instead of taking the safer route that led up the gorge, they tried to reach the cave by forming a human chain on the face of the rock. Half way across Miss Rice lost her footing and slipped toward the edge, dragging Cramer along with her. The others flattened themselves against the cliff in terror. As the two slid slowly toward the verge, Cramer grasped a projecting ledge but Miss Rice lost her grip on his hand at that very moment. With the words, "We must go, Will. There is no hope for us," she fell to her death on the boulders below.[3] The accident shocked Glenbrook and Carson. Cramer, as leader of the group, was censured and visitors were warned against making the climb for years afterward.

It remained for Sam Davis, Washoe pundit and editor of the *Carson Daily Appeal*, to change from the tragic to the ridiculous. He stopped overnight at Lake Shore House after staging to Tahoe in the fall of 1880. The following morning he took his stance near the little Glenbrook cemetery and gave his undivided attention to the famous profile. After a thorough scrutiny Sam acknowledged the profile's existence but declared he had been startled to discover the head of an Indian chief, decked out in full war regalia, also clearly discernible to the east of Shakespeare. Then he added thoughtfully, ". . . discernible only if you like Indians."

Davis concluded his article with the observation that "people spend hours studying out the profile of the great Bard of Avon, but it is not as plain as usual this season, because the house painter who goes up every spring to retouch the eyes and lay on a fresh beard fell off his scaffold at Glenbrook House in the canyon and is unfortunately laid up for a long spell. There is sadness at the Lake and a rejuvenated profile will be missed very much."

Sam's arid humor was, surprisingly enough, based on fact, as today, three quarters of a century later, both an Indian head and Shakespeare's profile may be seen on the face of the rock. Contrary to the dictum of Dan DeQuille, it takes very little imagination but a powerful amount of concentration to see them clearly.[4]

Velma Comstock Eden

CHASM IN THE ROCK

A rare photograph of the little known and seldom explored chasm in Shakespeare Rock (Cliff) where Miss Carrie Rice fell to her death in the late 1870's. Entrance (lower right) shows pine trees on the slope beyond.

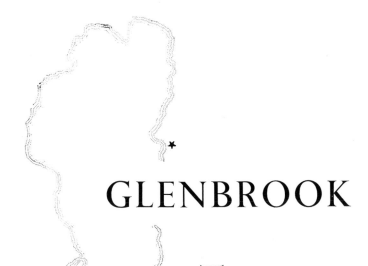

Chapter Thirty-nine

GLENBROOK

THE MUFFLED ROAR of Captain Augustus W. Pray's cannon shattered the warm afternoon air and resounded across Glenbrook Bay. House and shop windows rattled in protest. Up from the shoreline of the little lumbering settlement soared the shrill scream of mill and steamer whistles. It was the Fourth of July, 1875, and another celebration had joined in commemorating the Independence Day festivities.

Near the center of town bright twin ribbons of iron stretched northward toward Lower Pray Meadow. A squat, compact little locomotive straddled the terminal end of the narrow gauge track, its brass work gleaming in the sunlight. Steam popped in white plumes from the engine's safety valve and a black cabbage head of smoke funneled out of its balloon stack.

Lashed to the cowcatcher and enormous coal oil searchlight were two huge American flags that fluttered lazily from their standards and three flat cars, with railroad ties stacked aboard for seats, were coupled behind a tender piled high with pine slabs. The miniature train was aswirl with red, white and blue streamers, bunting and arching serpentine.

Again the howitzer rumbled, belching out a rolling cloud of grayish smoke that curled and spiraled through the cedar and yellow pine ringing the bluff above the water.

Milling around the small locomotive was a crowd of Lakers, Carsonites and Virginia City notables, and parents held their children high in the air, then stood on tiptoe to obtain a better view. Someone in the surging throng shouted: "Hurrah for the new *Glenbrook*." Others caught up the cry and it swelled into a chorus. A champagne bottle, swung from the beribboned speaker's platform adjoining the track, exploded against the boiler of the engine.

Duane LeRoy Bliss, president of the new Lake Tahoe Railroad, beckoned to a cluster of bowler-hatted dignitaries and their wives and they scrambled for the improvised seats on the logging cars. The cheering grew louder, nearly drowning out engineer Frank Johnson's three short warning blasts of the whistle.

Johnson cracked open the locomotive's brass throttle. Her drivers spun furiously for a moment and then the little *Glenbrook* pulled slowly away down the track on her inaugural trip up the mountain to Summit Camp.

Spewing ash and cinders and with her forty-inch drive wheels rapidly picking up speed, the engine and cars rocked out along the rails. Shouts from the crowd at the settlement faded, then died away as the passengers were carried toward the mouth of the canyon. Into the cut at Lower Pray and across the first trestle the iron caravan pounded, then on through Devil's Gate to the head of Upper Pray Meadow. Here the roadbed turned abruptly southeast on a horseshoe trestle before starting up the zigzag carved out of the mountainside. Acting fireman Ed Veazie tripped the circular firebox door and fed slabs of

Will M. Bliss

**BONANZA INN
ON THE GOLDEN ROAD**

*Glen Brook House (Hotel)
and outbuildings originally located
one-half mile east of Tahoe
at the head of Glenbrook Meadow.
Photograph taken in the
summer of 1866 looking
southwest at Shakespeare Rock.*

pitch pine into the crackling inferno. Couplings clanged as Johnson hauled back on the throttle, and the train buckled into the grade leading toward the first switchback.

Upon reaching the V-turn, locomotive and cars passed the switch on a 300-foot track extension while brakeman Pat McCarty swung to the ties and threw the switch for the upgrade track. Reversing direction, the train backed northwest up one and one-quarter miles of rail past the second switchback, then out on another track continuation running through a granite cut that opened on a 40-foot high dead-end trestle.

The passengers were now at the front of the train, with the engine snorting at their backs. It was a spine-chilling sensation. There, perched above the steep mountainside, the guests had their first view of Lake Tahoe since leaving Glenbrook Bay. Five hundred feet below, the deep blue waters of the lake stretched away in a shimmering arc to the western shore.

A Carson correspondent, accompanying the distinguished group, later wrote, "One shuddered to look down on the sheer side of the cliff, with that awesome beauty of snow water below, and it was necessary to fasten one's eyes on the heavens in order to regain some semblance of equilibrium."[1]

After the entourage had been allowed ample time to exclaim over the magnificence spread out below them, the switch at the second turn was thrown and once again the locomotive and cars clattered upgrade. They were now headed in a southeasterly direction, laboring toward the top of Slaughterhouse Canyon, high on the mountain.

Climbing steadily at ten miles per hour through the thinned out stands of fir and sugar pine, the *Glenbrook* pointed toward a narrow divide that would broaden into Spooner Meadow.[2] Passing to the south of Michel(e) Spooner's Station and sawmill, the train rattled across another curving trestle. Now less than half a mile from Summit Camp and at an altitude of over 7,000 feet, the puffing engine plunged into a tunnel. A choking swirl of smoke engulfed the passengers, until the train emerged and ground to a stop at the eastern terminus of the line.

The proud little eight and three-quarter mile Lake Tahoe Railroad was an operating reality at last and residents of the Silver State could now point with pride to another great accomplishment. A new era of expansion that would furnish the sinews for the Comstock Lode had been ushered in.[3]

Many of the pioneers at Glenbrook could scarcely believe that this miracle of development had taken place in the relatively short span of 15 years. To Captain Augustus W. Pray it seemed but yesterday that he and his three fellow land squatters had laid claim to that lush meadowland, bordered on the west by the waters of Lake Tahoe and surrounded north, south and east by dense forest wilderness.[4]

A stream running through the grassy mountain valley had suggested the name—Glen Brook—to the partners.[5]

Pray and his associates—N. E. Murdock, G. W. Warren and Rufus Walton—felled, barked and faced sugar pine to build a crude log cabin, splitting cedar for the shake roof. They harvested the wild hay that grew abundantly on the rich bottom land of the meadow and planted grain and vegetables. In the rarefied mountain air a yield of 60 bushels of wheat and 4 tons of timothy hay per acre was not unusual, while oats grew 7 and 8 feet high. The indigenous grass crop was so profuse that a horse-drawn reaper was brought over the Sierra from San Francisco to harvest it.[6]

Pray and his associates settled on the land during the spring of 1860.

By the following summer the bayshore was known as Walton's Landing and considered the eastern shore over-water terminus for the toll pack trail leading from Georgetown, California, to Upson Bay (McKinney's) on Tahoe. From here the haying schooner *Iron Duke*, or the sloop *Edith Batty*, transported trappers, gold seekers and other travelers across the waters to Walton's. At Glenbrook they continued their journey, following the old Clear Creek-Eagle Valley emigrant road to Carson.

The summer of 1861 saw the formation of the Lake Bigler (Tahoe) Lumber Company with two timber cruisers from Washoe City, Charles R. Barrett and Joseph D. Winters, joining Pray in the partnership.[7]

They constructed the first sawmill built on the shoreline of the lake, placing it on the southeast side of the bay. Known as Pray's Mill, its machinery consisted of a set of double circular saws, a muller, edger and shingle saws. The mill was operated by a 35-foot diameter overshot wheel, fed from a box flume paralleling Glenbrook Creek, that ran west one-half mile to the mill site. Undocumented records indicate that the machinery for the mill was purchased by Pray from the original Robert Woodburn sawmill in Lake Valley.[8]

Glenbrook's first lumbering operation produced 10,000 board feet a day in addition to shingles. Twelve mill hands were employed.[9] "Stag" oxen, yoked in pairs, hauled the finished lumber on high-bed logging wagons up Glenbrook Canyon to Summit, then down Clear Creek past Casta's and Kaskill's, Coyot's, Thomas G. Elliott's and Rufus Walton's mills into Carson.

The summer of 1861 also brought that "Secretary's Secretary," Samuel Clemens, to Tahoe.[10] He trudged to the lake with his companions, Thomas Nye and John Kinney, and they staked out a timber claim in the vicinity of Glenbrook with an eye toward ultimate riches. But the beauty of the vast emerald and sapphire lake and lure of the surrounding forests quickly dissipated the desire of Sam and his companions to prove up their holdings. Hard work became of secondary importance to the young gentlemen, and they spent cloudless days fishing and lazily boating on the lake. Clemens, later to gain fame under the pen name Mark Twain, described Tahoe glowingly in *Roughing It* as the "fairest picture the whole earth affords." He pictures his cruises on the crystal clear water as "comparable to floating high aloft in mid-nothingness, so empty and airy did the spaces seem below him." Sam termed their

California State Library

PRAY'S MILL STACK BLASPHEMED THE BLUE SKY

This earliest known photograph of Glenbrook, taken in the fall of 1869 looking toward South Point, shows Captain A. W. Pray's mill in full production with saw logs jamming the bay, sawdust dump (right of mill) and pine slabs stacked on the wharf. Tracks (foreground) lead from Goff and Morrill's MONITOR *mill (south) to the wagon road, and were used for lumber handcars.*

boat excursions "balloon voyages" and it appeared that the trio intended to stay on indefinitely, until a forest fire, inadvertently started by Clemens himself, pointed up the immediate necessity for their hasty return to Washoe.[11]

Tremendous building activity, mushrooming in the year 1859 with the discovery of the Comstock, had caused lumbering demands to skyrocket and in the summer of 1862 Pray obtained possessory title to several quarter sections of land held by his original associates, Warren, Murdock and Walton. Pray also bought out his other partners, Barrett and Winters, for $9,000, acquiring a total of nearly 700 acres surrounding Glenbrook and locating much of it with Sioux scrip.

On August 2, 1863, Joe D. Winters, Pray's former associate in the Lake Bigler Lumber Company, started another business enterprise. With Lou L. Colbath of Virginia City, he repurchased from Pray 45 acres of land situated one-half mile up the canyon. Here the two partners built the little settlement's first hotel, Glen Brook House.[12]

Opportunity was knocking. The King's Canyon, or Lake Bigler Toll Road, had been pushed to completion by August 6 of the same year, with H. F. Rea, Alfred Helm and Thomas E. Haydon financing the project. Butler Ives of Utah Territory (Nevada)-California boundary dispute fame, superintended construction of the turnpike which joined the Clear Creek road at Summit and then continued down Glenbrook Canyon and along the lakeshore to connect with Johnson's cut-off at Friday's Station.

Glen Brook House fronted on this main artery of travel. From the day its doors opened, the large two and one-half story wayside inn, with its cluster of outbuildings, made a pretentious bid for the staging and tourist trade moving past its porticoed entranceway. For the next decade the hostelry would be considered the finest and most luxurious on the lake. Discriminating guests, sojourning at Glen Brook House, paid the admittedly stiff rate of $21.00 per week, three meals a day included, but it was said that only the most penurious complained.[13]

A steam-powered mill, constructed by G. H. F. Goff and George H. Morrill on six acres of shoreline and timber land purchased from Pray and lying to the north of his sawmill, was completed in the fall of 1863. During the same year Pray rushed Lake Shore House to completion. This was the second hotel at Glenbrook, located several hundred feet back from the water at the foot of the meadow.[14]

The success of Goff and Morrill's *Monitor* mill and the uncertain flow of water from Glenbrook Creek prompted Pray to spend $8,000 converting his producer to steam power. Pray accomplished this in the spring of 1864 and now all of Tahoe's eastern shore was experiencing an amazing boom that far exceeded expectations. Insatiable lumbering demands called for the accelerated operation of the mills. Towns were stretching out in the valleys to the east, railroads were being pushed to completion and lumber was commanding a premium price at the mines. Water- and steam-powered sawmills had moved higher up Clear Creek and King's Canyon with flumes, log chutes, and logging roads reaching farther and farther into the heavy timber stands.[15]

Winters and Colbath prudently leased Glen Brook House to a capable hotel man, A. S. Beatty, from the Mansion House in San Jose, California. Beatty immediately advised the press: "My hostelry will be renovated and made into the finest hotel on the Pacific Coast, with enchanting vistas, plenty of water and fishing for trout already available."

The *Alta California* insisted that Lake Tahoe was now as easy to reach as Calistoga and Santa Cruz. One could be at the "commodious Glen Brook House," the paper stated, "in twenty short hours from the Bay City (San Francisco) traveling by Pioneer Lines Concord stages via Latrobe, Placerville, and over Johnson's Pass to the resort." The fact that it took only three hours from Nevett's Summit (Echo) to reach Glenbrook, was considered nothing short of miraculous. Prospective vacationers were also told that "the new establishment, accommodating 100 people and costing $25,000, fronts on a fine new turnpike to Virginia and Carson cities, where genial host Beatty stands ready to see to every comfort."[16] Arriving guests, even before bothering to remove dusters and gauntlets, buttonholed their landlord and asked those old familiar questions: "Good time to fish, eh?" "What kind of bait, hey?" "Got any tackle?" or "How big do you take 'em?" It was further noted that their "bland host Beatty, optics smilingly atwinkle," replied to all, "Well, come in and take a drink, the trout won't run off before you do." They would follow his suggestion reluctantly, grumbling among themselves. However, 6:00 a.m. the following morning always found them in a body out on the lake with "rod, reel and line long enough to sound any lake but Bigler's."[17]

Captain Pray, recognizing the need for additional recreation on the lake, built a miniature excursion steamer, the *Governor Blaisdel*. Operating by the spring of 1864, it helped to bolster the lumbering settlement's claim that it was the "Saratoga of the Pacific."[18]

In spite of the turnaway business at Glen Brook House, Beatty only lasted two seasons. In the summer of 1866, Caldwell and Dr. Fonda took over as proprietors, offering a telegraph office and coaches from Friday's Station to this "beautiful mountain lake valley." They also boasted "the lake steamer leaves from the Glenbrook Landing for all points on Bigler."

On the Fourth of July, 1867, the *Territorial Enterprise* reported that the hotel had again changed hands, being taken over by a Mrs. Mogenberg. Bathhouses were placed on the lakeshore and Glenbrook was described as "the gathering place for the fashionable of the world, a veritable 'Saratoga of Nevada'," this time. One year later a junketing reporter from the *Cincinnati Commercial* wrote with

THE BAY'S SHORELINE WAS A BEEHIVE OF ACTIVITY

Two members of the fair sex perched on the summit of Shakespeare Cliff in August of 1876. Directly above the lady's flowered hat is Glenbrook's wharf, over-water store, and warehouse. Beyond the store's roof lies the new METEOR *behind its breakwater. Protective piling encloses the free floating logs in front of Mill Number Two (white smoke), loaded cordwood barges float to the west of Mill Number One with the Davis Mill and railroad beyond. Pray's mill (left foreground above water) and shingle mill. Looking northwest.*

Author's collection

cool disdain: "Glenbrook is a pleasant place, which it has a right to be, for it charges $5.75 currency or $4.00 gold a day."

The shuffling of owner-management was not restricted to Glen Brook House. On January 20, 1870, Goff and Morrill sold their *Monitor* mill to A. H. and Frank Davis for $4,000.[19] Five and one-quarter acres went with the sawmill instead of the original six, and it appeared the Davises were shorted until it was discovered that Augustus Saxton, from across the lake, had won the remaining three-quarters of an acre in an all-night poker game several days before.

On March 16, 1870, the then-fledgling mining magnates, William Sharon and Charles Bonner, along with the Bank of California's William Ralston, organized the Glenbrook Hotel Company.[20] Ralston and Bonner acquired and deeded 200 acres in the vicinity of the hotel to the company and the establishment again opened under new managers, the enthusiastic Colonel and Mrs. Horace M. Veazie.

Late in the same year, Ralston challenged Bill Sharon to a horse race from Carson to Glenbrook —one rider to go by way of the King's Canyon grade and the other up Clear Creek. Sharon drove his mount so hard that it went blind from the effort and he had to forfeit the contest to Ralston. At the hotel, all-night poker games played between the Barons of the Comstock and the San Francisco Bank Ring were commonplace. It usually took a double gold eagle to open and Tahoe's blue sky was the betting limit. The leather bound guest register in the lobby disclosed an occasional forthright approach to life, one entry in particular, "Wm. Sharon and lady," attesting to the informal mores of the times.

The lumbering boom continued. After Seneca H. Marlette, former surveyor general of California, had made an inspection tour of Glenbrook and vicinity, he reported: "Twenty-five miles of V-flumes now run down Clear Creek and King's canyons and lumber operations are proceeding into the inexhaustible timber stands above the lake."

On December 2, 1871, Amaziah H. and Frank Davis sold the Davis Mill to George C. Thaxter and M. D. Hatch of Carson.[21] The new partners began their association with what at first appeared to be a definite financial loss. A circular blade flew apart as it bit into a one and one-half inch cannon ball embedded in a saw log. Early history of the region, no matter how fragmentary, was always seized upon eagerly, and dismay over the loss of a blade costing $400 was mitigated by Thaxter and Hatch's certainty as to the cannon ball's origin. They excitedly advised the press it could be none other than a shot fired from Captain John C. Fremont's mountain howitzer when he, Christopher "Kit" Carson and their party passed through the region 27 years earlier.[22]

A swing route of travel, attracting Lakers, "Comstockers" and tourists alike, was now in operation. Travelers staged by coach and six from Truckee by way of the Martis Valley road, to Campbell's Hot Springs (Brockway) where the little steamer *Truckee* ferried them to Glenbrook. From there, one of Jim "Doc" Benton's "four-in-hands" rattled them over Summit to Carson and Virginia cities. Those wishing to reverse the trip went from Carson to Glenbrook over the King's Canyon Toll Road, stopping at Swift's Station, two and one-half miles from Summit, before moving on past Spooner's and down to Glenbrook.

The Clear Creek Grade, formerly Rufus Walton's Toll Road, was used as an alternate route. On this road a horse change stop was usually made at the "White House," or Anson J. Pedroli's Ranch located at Big Meadow. Then the winding climb continued toward Summit, with another layover at Saint's Rest, one mile east of the 7200-foot divide. This small wayside inn sported a saloon run by owner Al Wakeman and his daughter, Nellie.[23] Stage passengers were given time to view the sweep of Carson Valley lying 2,400 feet below, before staging on over the mountain to Glenbrook, where Ben Holladay's steamer *Emerald* waited at the dock to transport them across the lake to Tahoe City. From there Cardwell's stages whisked the tourists down the canyon to Truckee, connecting with the Central Pacific for Reno, with the return to Carson made on the new Virginia and Truckee Railroad.

Many Glenbrook residents were apprehensive about the lake's drying up as the water level was six feet lower than that recorded in 1859, barely 12 years before. But another part of Tahoe that was "drying up" particularly pleased them. Their water route, by way of the Hot Springs, appreciably reduced the mule-drawn freighter hauls through the rival town of Tahoe City, and the "City" was now cheerfully reported by Glenbrookers to be devoid of activity. This rivalry reached a high degree of vituperation. The story used in combinations of Truckee and Bodie, Esmeralda and Aurora, applied equally well in describing the feelings of Tahoe's two largest settlements. It is said that a Tahoe City father overheard his small daughter saying sadly in her prayers, "Good bye, God, I'm going to Glenbrook." The populace of Glenbrook stoutly denied this aspersion, declaring that what the child obviously had said was "Good! By God I'm going to Glenbrook."[24]

With the summer of 1872, the proprietors again lined up to bid for the management of Glen Brook House. Augustus Saxton, formerly of Saxton's Mill across the lake, obtained the lease and advertised the fact that "gay, lovely times now existed, with a dance every night." Guests were reported "accumulating flesh at the astonishing rate of two pounds a day, and expecting to return to Carson and Virginia cities at the conclusion of their vacation in the shape of the elephant."[25]

The curtain was now rising on large scale lumbering, with production and expansion at the Glenbrook mills inextricably tied to the fortunes of the Comstock. During the summer of the same year, Duane LeRoy Bliss,[26] a former member of the Virginia City branch of the Bank of California, and Henry Marvin Yerington, construction superintendent for the Virginia and Truckee Railroad, formed a partnership with Darius Ogden Mills, president of the Bank of California. In 1873 the Carson and Tahoe Lumber and Fluming Company was incorporated with Duane L. Bliss as president and general manager. Yerington, Mills and James A. Rigby were the three other stockholders.[27] They were now in a position to add to their already extensive holdings and broaden the scope of their operations.

Equipment and manpower required for the success of this far-reaching, imaginative program was considered nearly impossible to assemble. The company needed cordwood and logging wagons, draft animals, pack mules, log chutes, V and box-type flumes; barges for hauling cordwood, steam tugs to tow the barges and log booms; back country and lakeshore logging camps; breakwaters, wharfs, marine ways; a narrow gauge railway with locomotives, lumber cars and companion rolling stock; maintenance repair shops and a roundhouse; saw and planing mills; a small army of Maine mill hands and French-Canadian lumberjacks; Chinese cordwood cutters, splitters and loaders; engineers, firemen, brakemen, oilers, teamsters, swampers, flumesmen, muleskinners, blacksmiths, foremen and cooks. All this had to be set up over a mile high in the backwoods country of Tahoe.

In addition, bunk houses, mess halls, stores, accommodations for employees' families, a social hall, saloon—in short, everything that constituted a flourishing town—would be needed, and needed immediately. Most important of all, was a tremendous, steady supply of running water.

Fortunately, Captain A. W. Pray, by now honored as Glenbrook's earliest settler, already had the nucleus of such a settlement. He numbered among his properties a horse livery, 30 cottages, a meat market and a new two-story building built on pilings over the water. This structure was run as a general merchandise store, with a meeting hall and dance floor on the second story.

The C. & T. L. & F. Company moved into Glenbrook in the spring of 1873. It purchased five and one-half acres of lakeshore and meadowland property from Pray, including his Lake Mill, adding this to the 7,000 acres of timber land it already owned or controlled.

One year before, Bliss and Yerington had bought the Summit or Elliott brothers' mill from Thomas and John Elliott.[28] Now they acquired, rebuilt and lengthened the Summit Fluming Company's V-flume running from a point near the head of Clear Creek down the canyon to a large terminal yard one mile south of Carson City. In addition, the combine bought Michel(e) Spooner's Lower Mill plus his

SMOKE, FIRE AND SPRAY

This photograph, taken in the summer of 1878, just north of Deadman's Point, Glenbrook, has caught the action of a saw log striking Lake Tahoe, leaving a rocket's trail of smoke and fire on the greased logway after streaking down the mountainside. Looking east.

Will M. Bliss

New Mill to the south, and the old Knox sawmill east of Spooner Station. They also built another steam-powered unit 300 yards south of the former Davis Mill, calling it Lake Mill Number One.

Now the C. & T. L. & F. Company was ready to proceed. From highline, giant pine logs were dragged by horse, mule and ox teams to the water's edge where the terrain permitted, and on precipitous slopes saw logs were fed into the heads of dry chutes that had their inner surfaces adzed and greased. The logs flashed down the carriers toward the water, picking up speed rapidly and leaving a trail of fire and smoke as they plunged into the lake.[29]

Five and six tons of pine were rolled up lodge pole ramps and positioned on creaking logging wagons by oxen or donkey engine cable drags. Oxen, yoked in pairs on the tongues of the vehicles, steadied the load. Ahead of the "stags," ten to twelve horses or mules were hitched on chain traces. A whistling crack of the bullwhacker's lash and the animals strained into the load, moving out through

"KEEP YOUR SEAT, HORACE, I'LL GET YOU THAR ON TIME"

An event that Mark Twain anticipated but loudly deplored materialized in the Spring of 1878 . . . Hank Monk sanctioned the publication of his Schottische.

the thick dust of backwoods roads pulling the top-heavy wagons that rolled on solid, 50-inch diameter wooden wheels built from log sections and banded with hand-forged iron rims.

In the coves and bays of Tahoe the logs were chained in V-booms and towed by company-operated steam tugs to the Glenbrook mills. The new 80-foot iron-hulled *Meteor*, a steam tug designed to be the fastest of its type in the country, was now under construction for the company on the eastern seaboard. It would be placed in service by August of 1876.[30]

Colonel and Mrs. Horace Veazie returned as proprietors of Glen Brook House in the summer of 1876, and the hostelry now offered a billiard parlor, barber shop, ten pin alley and a hand-carved cherry wood bar for the serving of "alcoholic stimulants." The Veazies held dances for the Carson, Gold Hill and Virginia City nabobs, advertising "hotel accommodations that furnished guests the homelike style they were accustomed to."

There was a flare-up of public indignation when it became known that "John Chinaman" choppers, employed in the company's wood camps, were spearing, seining and trapping spawning trout at the stream outlets of Logan House and Glenbrook Creeks, then selling the fish to white men. Everybody loudly deplored the slaughter, although nobody did anything more than talk about it.

Water and more water was the insistent demand. A dirt-fill dam had been constructed several years earlier on the west side of Marlette basin that fed a five-mile V-flume bringing water and cordwood down North Canyon to Summit Camp. Augmenting the Marlette supply was another feeder flume originating in the vicinity of Genoa Peak and running five and one-half miles north to the receiving ponds at Summit Camp.[31]

Along with the tremendous water carrier project, costing $10,000 to $15,000 a mile to build, materialized another bold engineering scheme—the Lake Tahoe Railroad. A survey line was run along the lakeshore at Glenbrook and through Upper Pray Meadow to the steep face of the mountain.[32] Here a 2 per cent grade would be maintained on the railroad's climb into the switchbacks and on to Summit Camp. Included in the eight and three-quarter miles of road were ten trestles and a 270-foot tunnel bore.

Four crews of Chinese laborers were put to work in the fall of 1874, filling and grading the right-of-way. Over half of the C. & T. L. & F. Company's men from the mills moved slowly upgrade the following spring, laying ties and spiking track into place. A mule-drawn flat car carrying rails and equipment supplied the workmen, following on the newly-laid line as it progressed up the mountain.

When completed, the terminus of the railroad was 910 feet above the lake, or 7,140 feet above sea level, with a total rise of 105 feet per mile. Including the tunnel and trestles, the project had cost $30,000 per mile to construct and it would average $3,000 a month in operation and maintenance costs alone during its twenty-three years of service. Construction superintendents from the Central and Union Pacific, who came to admire the work of Bliss and Yerington, praised it as "an engineering achievement of precision rail construction and ingenuity."

Baldwin Locomotive Works supplied the first two engines, powerful little Mogul locomotives weighing ten tons each and equipped with six 40-inch drivers, 13-inch by 16-inch cylinders and balloon (diamond) smokestacks.[33] An iron cowcatcher was carried well forward of each boiler on small running wheels. Above were huge square oil-burning headlights ornamented with gold scrollwork. Each engine could pull 70 tons of lumber or cordwood at a maximum speed of ten miles per hour on the upgrade, allowing an 11 to 12-ton loading per car. One locomotive was therefore limited to six cars stacked with 36 cords of wood, or five cars of lumber.[34]

Forty-five logging cars were purchased with the engines, and the rolling stock was shipped overland to the Carson City yards of the Virginia and Truckee Railroad. Here the equipment was partially disassembled, loaded on double-teamed logging wagons and hauled up the Clear Creek grade to the company's shops at Glenbrook.

BALLOON STACKER HEADED NORTHWEST

ENGINE NUMBER TWO *on the main track, back of Lake Mill Number One, in July, 1882.*

The first engine was named the *Tahoe*, the second *Glenbrook*. A third locomotive, *Number Three*, was added in the spring of 1884, and several years later *Engine Number Four*.[35]

During 1875, Lake Mill Number Two was built to the south of Number One. At the same time the company closed their other mills with the exception of Summit Mill.

Two and one-half miles of spur, siding and "double passing track" had been added to the railroad, and the network of flumes and log chutes completed by the summer of 1876.[36]

In the short space of three years the booming little metropolis became Nevada's leading lumbering town with an anticipated season's production exceeding 21,700,000 board feet. Glenbrook's citizens had to concede that they really didn't know their own capabilities, particularly when the thousands of cords of wood and two million shingles on hand at Davis and Noteware's mill, two and one-half miles north of the bay, were taken into consideration.

Then tragedy stepped in to dampen the enthusiasm of the Glenbrookers. The general merchandise store, subleased from Joseph M. Short by James A. Rigby and A. Childers, became the scene of a fatality. The store's location on pilings over deep water constituted a man-made hazard and early one morning Childers fell through a hole in the floor into the water. As his body was never recovered, people in the town thought this an ill omen indeed, and when the store later burned many considered it "only fittin'."[37]

Pray at once erected another building in the same place and Rigby took over the lease, bringing in Fred C. and George W. Davis as partners. The Davises had leased their Glenbrook mill back to Thaxter in April of 1877 and it was nearly impossible to keep track of the times the property had passed back and forth between the two parties.[38]

Fire struck again during the same year, this time leveling one of the company's boarding houses that quartered 28 loggers. The fire had broken out in mid-morning and there were no casualties. However, a tourist seeing the sights from the Lake Tahoe Railroad (on a pass obtained through the courtesy of Duane L. Bliss) was not so fortunate. He had apparently become dizzy from the height at the second switchback, fallen from one of the cars and been crushed to death beneath the wheels. The only other recorded accident on the Tahoe line occurred several years later when Patrick McCarty, brakeman on the road, was pinned between two lumber cars at Station Five. McCarty recovered.

While mishaps and personal injuries appeared to be routine, all were not without benefit to Glenbrook. The disastrous fire that swept through Virginia City in 1876 called for an immediate acceleration in lumber production. Added to this unforeseen demand for rebuilding purposes was the day after day requirement of the mines themselves. Cordwood by the carload was fed into the massive fireboxes of the steam-driven Cornish pumps used to lift the scalding water from the mine sumps. In addition 14-inch by 14-inch timbers were required for the "square sets" that replaced the ore extracted. It was said that the Comstock could not exist 24 hours without lumber and cordwood. Glenbrook was there to supply it.

Nationally famous figures were now being drawn to Glenbrook and the Comstock, both full fledged factors in the nation's economy. General William Tecumseh Sherman passed through the lake settlement in 1875 and President Ulysses S. Grant was feted at Glenbrook shortly thereafter.

On October 27, 1879, President Rutherford B. Hayes and his party were reported as taking a "four-in-hand" to Glenbrook after welcoming ceremonies at Carson and Virginia cities. Arriving at the lake, they inspected the mills, then boarded the *Meteor* for a cruise on Tahoe as guests of Duane L. Bliss.

The legendary Hank Monk was handling the "ribbons" when President Hayes and his group pulled up Clear Creek Grade toward the lake. At a steep pitch in the road, the President leaned out of the coach and called to Monk: "Pretty steep right here, will we have to walk?" Old Hank is supposed to have taken his cue and replied, "Keep your seat, Mister Hayes, I'll get you thar." This was noted as being "good for a general laugh all around" as it was reminiscent of the famous Horace Greeley-Hank Monk story of 1859, which by then had become a matter of history.[39]

Henry James "Hank" Monk is part and parcel of the Glenbrook story for he spent the last 15 years of his colorful career as "master whip" on James "Doc" Benton's Carson City-Glenbrook stage line.[40]

Monk's trademarks were a battered Stetson, a travel-worn corduroy shirt, trousers stained with tobacco juice, the stump of a black cheroot jutting from clenched teeth and an insatiable thirst for strong distillations. Hank Monk has been called the worst and the best stage driver to rein a team across the Sierra Nevada mountains, he has been jeered and revered, credited with nonchalance and valor, skillfulness and outright stupidity.

His admirers, and there were many, insisted that in his prime he could turn a six-horse team in a city street at full gallop with every line apparently loose, and that he was as much a part of the route he traveled as perfume is to the rose, Bokers bitters to the cocktail or salt to scrambled eggs.

Major William Banning, a recognized stage driver in his own right and co-author of *Six Horses*, considered Monk "no better and no worse than the crack drivers of his day," adding that he was "a cool, careful hand behind the multiple reins and deft and fast when the occasion warranted."[41] Another of Monk's volunteer press agents offered a contrary opinion. "He (Monk) drank so much hard spirits that he often forgot what he was doing when it came to the incidental tasks connected with staging, and fed whiskey to his horses and watered himself on numerous occasions, thus becoming accidentally sober enough to handle the inebriated team."

William D. Keyser, who drove alongside Hank Monk and later took over Benton's Carson-Glen-

LEATHER SLUNG LUXURY POISED FOR CARSON

Keyser and Elrod's Carson-Lake Tahoe stage, with ten passengers squeezed aboard, sags on its thoroughbraces as driver R. E. Elrod prepares to "duster" the group up Glenbrook Canyon, over Summit and down Clear Creek Grade to the valley. Among the people standing: Mr. and Mrs. Stevens, proprietors at the time of Lake Shore House (which later became the south wing of Glenbrook Inn), Bob Ward (Glenbrook's barber), Belle Calhoun, Frank Jellerson, Miss Amanda Jellerson and J. M. Short. Barber shop and shoemaker's shack are shown in the right foreground of the picture. Looking southeast in the late 1880's.

brook run with his brother-in-law, E. R. Elrod, recalled Monk as "only a middling driver compared to competent Knights of the Lash such as Nels Flack, Charles Emery, John Sickle, "Si" Hawley and Bill Blackmore, but he kept their company, had the 'breaks' and gained their fame."[42]

The pros and cons of Monk's driving ability will be argued by stagecoach historians for generations to come, but the undisputed fact remains—Hank Monk, from the standpoint of national prominence, was head and shoulders above his fellow Jehus during the 1860's and '70's. This resulted from a quirk of fate, a mischance that rippled a wave of laughter across the country on July 18, 1859—the episode, a stagecoach trip starring Hank Monk and Horace Greeley, with Greeley, the illustrious New York journalist and presidential aspirant, placed in a comical and unfavorable light as a direct result.

The incident that brought about Monk's claim to fame is best described in the words of Mark Twain, who devoted several pages in *Roughing It* to a satirical embellishment of what by then had become a tired old chestnut.

Twain reported that he was sitting the "box" with a driver of the Central Overland Stage when the man said:

"I can tell you a most laughable thing indeed, if you would like to listen to it. Horace Greeley went over this road once. When he was leaving Carson City he told the driver, Hank Monk, that he had an engagement to lecture at Placerville and was very anxious to go through quick. Hank Monk cracked the whip and started off at an awful pace. The coach bounced up and down in such a terrific way that it jolted the buttons all off of Horace's coat, and finally shot his head clean through the roof of the stage, and then he yelled at Hank Monk and begged him to go easier—said he warn't in as much of a hurry as he was awhile ago. But Hank Monk said, 'Keep your seat, Horace, and I'll get you there on time'—and you bet you he did, too, what was left of him."

At no time did Mark Twain consider this even a passable anecdote. The famous American humorist insisted that he had been forced to listen to the deathless, bald-headed incident four hundred and eighty-one or eighty-two times, to his knowledge, during his six years of stage travel between California and Nevada.

Twain ticked off a partial list of those who had inflicted this nauseating old saw upon him—the driver of the stage as he left Julesburg on the Platte, a Denver man well posted in the affairs of Colorado, a cavalry sergeant from Fort Bridger, a soft-spoken Mormon preacher from Salt Lake City, and a poor wanderer who had lain down to die ten miles out of Ragtown on the verge of the desert.

The trembling, emaciated stranger had been lifted into the stagecoach, made comfortable on mailsacks and given a drink of brandy. In an endeavor to show his appreciation he finally raised his feeble voice: "Gentlemen," he began, "you have saved my life and though I can never be able to repay you for it, I feel that I can at least make one hour of your long journey lighter. I can tell you a most laughable thing indeed, if you would like to listen to it. Horace Greeley——"

Mark Twain hurriedly broke in at this point and begged that he tell them anything but that worn fable for a change—even the George Washington and his little hatchet story.

Then Twain admitted guiltily, "We were saved. But not so the invalid. In trying to retain the anecdote in his system, he strained himself and died in our arms."

Mark was not through punishing Monk and Greeley with his caustic pen: ". . . I know that no passenger or driver on the Overland ever corked that anecdote in, when a stranger was by, and survived. . . . Drivers always told it, conductors told it, landlords told it, chance passengers told it, the very Chinamen and vagrant Indians recounted it. I have had the same driver tell it to me two or three times in the same afternoon. It has come to me in all the multitude of tongues that Babel bequeathed to earth, and flavored with whiskey, brandy, beer, cologne, sozsodent, tobacco, garlic, onions, grasshoppers—everything that has a fragrance to it through all the long list of things that are gorged or

Jeanette Pomin Watson

A MEADOW OF WILDFLOWERS . . . THEN THE SCHOOL

Many sons and daughters of Lake Tahoe's first settlers are among this group of youngsters. From left to right: Adeline Madatoll, Jeanette Pomin, Ida Pomin, Gertrude Barnes, Eva Short, unidentified, Edith Lester, a little girl visitor, Teacher Mabel French (Fairchild), Olivene Spooner, Jetora Watkins, Chester Pray, Frank Short, Wilbur Watkins, unidentified, the McPherson brothers, Maggie Pomin, Jennie Barnes, Joe Short, Jr., Ernest H. Pomin and Frank Pomin. Photograph taken in the late fall of 1887 looking north.

guzzled by the sons of men. I never have smelt any anecdote so often as I have smelt that one; never have smelt any anecdote that smelt so variegated as that one. I have even heard that it is in the Talmud. I have seen it in print in nine different foreign languages; I have been told that it is employed in the inquisition in Rome; and I now learn with regret that it is going to be set to music. I do not think that such things are right."[43]

Such is Hank Monk's place in the sunlight of the West's early development as seen through the superbly jaundiced eyes of Mark Twain. Anecdotes sprouted and when they had been carefully watered with exaggeration and grown into thriving tall tales they were usually attributed to Monk. Some were fact, many were pure fiction, most were fantastic. These opaque fables are a part of the Glenbrook-Tahoe story.

The redundant tale is told of an old gentleman and his niece being rattled down Glenbrook Canyon by Monk for a stay at Lake Shore House. Hank's four-in-hand slid in loose gravel on a turnout and overturned, tossing his two passengers into a clump of bushes and catapulting Monk onto the turnpike. While Hank was in the process of picking himself up and seeing to his horses a high-pitched male voice called from the scrub brush: "Where's my niece?" Monk testily yelled back: "Damn your *valise,* you aught to be mighty thankful your neck ain't broken."[44]

It has been said when Monk neared a stage station on the run, he would cast the "ribbons" to the four winds, let out a yell that would chill a Kiowa Indian and the horses would bolt for the hostelry, but that Hank "knew his teams and they would stop at the station all right."

In one instance a double-edged axe was discovered resting on the floor of the driver's box by a squeamish male passenger. Finally the traveler screwed up enough courage to question Hank on its use. Wishing to put a stop to his inquisitor without tossing direct offense, Monk replied:

"Well, sir, I don't often tell the use I make of that hatchet, but as you seem to be a sensible man and one I can trust with the secret, I'll tell you. The fact is there have been a good many accidents occur on this line; limbs have been broken and other injuries from the overturning of coaches, for which the company has had to pay heavy damages. Now in order to avoid any such after-claps, when an accident occurs and passengers have legs and arms broken or are otherwise seriously injured, I end the matter by knocking them on the head with this hatchet and putting them out of their misery at once."

The old gentleman was speechless for the remainder of his trip. He clung grimly to the rail iron of the seat with a horrified expression on his face, marveling at the wickedness of stageline corporations generally and his driver in particular.[45]

Another time Hank was entertaining a group of young female passengers, on the run up Clear Creek to Glenbrook, with a lurid account of the Mormon successor to Brigham Young. As they approached the settlement one of the wide-eyed girls inquired of Monk whether they would be likely to actually see the "wicked personage."

Monk squinted ahead and then cried excitedly: "Egad, woman, I do believe that's him now." He pointed with his whip stock toward Lake Shore House where bewhiskered proprietor W. A. B. Cobb was innocently standing, smiling and chatting with a group of middle-aged lady guests. "So help me, if that ain't the old reprobate and his wives with 'im," added Hank, his voice heavy with censure.

Upon being handed down from the vehicle, the young ladies blushingly swept past the bowing innkeeper and his "harem" into the hotel lobby, and for the duration of their stay every polite advance of the "Mormon wives" was treated with icy disdain.[46]

Hank Monk was not above carrying a practical joke literally to the feet of the barons of the Comstock. One evening he discovered a pair of muddy boots placed neatly outside the door of William "Bill" Sharon, who was sojourning at Glen Brook House. Hank energetically bent to and put a mirrorlike polish on *one* of the boots, leaving the other in its former shoddy condition. Their owner, rushing for an early appointment with D. L. Bliss the following morning, had no choice but to throw on the strange appearing footgear and clump through the settlement presenting, according to an eyewitness, "a rather ridiculous appearance when his pedal extremities were compared to his otherwise impeccable broadcloth."[47]

On another occasion Thomas Oliver, of the pioneer Carson Valley family, fell into the Clear Creek V-flume, and was sailing grandly down the watercourse with his hands and feet up in the air, when Monk passed on the upgrade pull with the afternoon stage. Oliver waved wildly for help but Hank casually pointed out the helpless figure flashing by to his passengers, commenting dryly: "That's old Tom Oliver, balmy as a blue jay, does that for exercise every day." When Oliver later ran into Monk he upbraided him for not trying to assist him out of the flume. "Assist you?" retorted Monk, "hell, I knew you'd get out—*eventually*—or at worst end up in the cordwood dump where you dad-gum belong."

At still another time Oliver was standing at the turn-off of the Clear Creek Grade inspecting a long, thin early-day steam boiler. Monk reined up his team and pointed to his friend who was now squinting through one end of the iron tube: "That thar's superintendent Oliver looking through his telescope. Marvelous invention—he can see clean up the canyon with it and follow every turn of the Clear Creek flume to summit."[48]

Another story, attributed to Hank Monk, has to do with the time he and his messenger, Bill Slade from Pike, were boxed in Glenbrook Creek Canyon by highwaymen. Monk was recounting the yarn several years later to a group of his passengers after stopping his stage at the head of the canyon to

ENGINE NUMBER FOUR IN A SEA OF SLAB WOOD

This little known locomotive on the Lake Tahoe Line at Glenbrook operated into the early 1890's only. Engineer Bob Dorne in the cab and the crew are loading pine slabs on the wood burner's tender. Glenbrook Bay and South Point (left center) looking southwest.

show them the scene of the encounter: "Here we was," drawled Monk in a serious, thoughtful manner, "just about dusk with steep hills on all sides of us, as nice a trap as could be sprung. Bullets from the guns of them bandits was whizzin' around our haids and I tell Bill to keep firin' back so's I can unloose the horses. I got back safe to him and together we kept those desperado's off for nigh on two hours." Monk's passengers were listening in respectful silence.

"But all the time our ammunition is getting lower and lower. I yelled to Bill to save his shots until he was sure of a hit, and the firing was not quite so plentiful from then on. By this time they was a passel dead among them Dick Turpins—about sixteen strewn around—mebbe seventeen, I don't recall exactly. At last," here Monk's voice dropped to a whisper, "we run clean out of powder." He paused reflectively, reliving the horror of that moment. Finally one of the male passengers could stand the suspense no longer.

"And did you escape?" he asked breathlessly.

Monk swallowed hard and his listeners thought they detected a trace of moisture in his averted eyes.

"No," he replied in a voice choked with emotion, "they buried me and Bill under a tall yaller pine over yonder. You can still see our graves to this very day."[49]

Imposing upon the credulity of the public appears to have brought a particular delight to Monk and his fellow whipsters. Problems of stagecoach travel in the Bonanza days included the transportation of Saratoga trunks, the scourge of all drivers and the particular abomination of Monk. Described as "three-decker bandboxes—about as long and wide as a first class spring mattress," they presented a problem of loading that would tax the ingenuity of a professional mule train packer.

One story, recalled as the "Saratoga anecdote," concerns Monk's handling of this problem. He had deposited a young lady on the porch of Lake Shore House at Glenbrook. Not so her trunk. It would come, insisted Hank, on tomorrow's coach. But the next day she was again disappointed as mail and express had taken up all the freight space. The lady stormed in vain. It would come, explained Monk patiently, on the morning stage. After several days of the same thing the female guest's distraction was pitiful to see. Even Hank appeared to be touched. "Well, Miss," he said, "I'll promise to bring your trunk tomorrow without fail. But tell me, what *part* of your trunk would you like to have first?" "What part?" she replied incredulously. "Well, Miss," he explained slowly, "I figured this morning that the only way I could manage that trunk of yours would be to saw it into three parts, and bring one section up on each of my next three trips. I had two men on the ends of a cross-cut all yesterday." The young lady is said to have turned a deep purple and fainted dead away. It is reported, however, that when Hank Monk delivered the trunk the next day she managed to survive the shock of seeing it in one piece.[50]

Hank's bouts with the bottle are legend and he was chronicled, in 1879, as pulling up to the Veazie House at Glenbrook with the afternoon stage, "so full of liquor he couldn't stand when hostlers unstrapped him from the 'box,' but he could sure drive alright."[51]

By the year 1881, Monk was considered by his detractors to be "an old dissipated driver with a worn-out heart," although they grudgingly admitted he could outrun the wind when a tight schedule had to be met. Two years later the famous Knight of the Lash was "done in from tippin' the rosy and the pack of lies told about him." On February 28, 1883, Greeley's nemesis died. He was buried in Carson City's Lone Mountain Cemetery.

Now Hank Monk was eulogized and a nostalgic mist swirled around his grave. An epitaph was conjured up for Hank that extolled his virtues in saccharine phrases:

"Sacred to the memory of Hank Monk, the whitest, biggest-hearted and best stage driver of the West, who was kind to all, thought ill of none. He lived in a strange era, and was a hero, and the wheels of his coach are now ringing on golden streets."

ON THE FALSE FRONT STOOD MAINE'S PROUD MOTTO

Frank Jellerson's Dirigo Hotel, photographed on the Fourth of July, 1887. The camera is facing northeast and clearly shows the mountains stripped of timber. Location: southeast of Glenbrook's present golf course Club House. Jellerson is the third man from the right, standing on the porch.

Monk's stained brownstone monument in Carson bears no such inscription; its simple epitaph: IN MEMORY OF HANK MONK, died FEBRUARY 28, 1888 (sic). FIFTY YEARS."[52]

Viewing the wonders of Glenbrook and Lake Tahoe during Hank Monk's time was not the exclusive privilege of the famous. In the same month as President Hayes' visit (October, 1879) two convicts escaped from the Carson City State Prison. The red-faced authorities reported: "Our elusive quarry is sojourning near Glenbrook without a care in the world with no one to bother them but the wild animals."[53]

James "Doc" Benton's stages ran daily between Carson City and the lumbering town throughout the summer season and on weekends as many as four open coaches and "mud wagons" made the trip each way.

In July of 1881, R. E. Wood, editor of the *Tahoe Tattler*, pontificated from a seat on the porch of Tahoe City's Grand Central Hotel and described Glenbrook as a "thrifty little place, but not the foremost lumbering town in Nevada and large city on the bay that people had been led to believe it was by those Carson City sheets." Wood's statement was loudly derided by Glenbrook residents and when they suggested that he make a personal inspection of their settlement he reluctantly consented. After carefully snooping around the town he discovered "two small hotels, a store, genteel saloon, railroad, machine shops, several sawmills, a livery stable, and an express and post office."

Wood found that most of the Glenbrookers now called that old horse killer, "Doc" Benton, a respectful "Doctor," Doc's salvation being pegged to row upon row of evil looking bottles in Davis' store bearing the labels "Dr. Benton's Miraculous Rheumatism Cure—Good for Horses, Humans and

Mules Alike." Wood was told the "kill or cure liniment" outsold its nearest competitor, Ye Old Mustang Oil, six to one.

"Hog wash," commented the unimpressed editor, who boarded the steamer *Meteor* in a huff and returned post haste to his "metropolis" across the lake.

The ingenious V-flume came in for its share of attention when it was found that the watercourse could float other things besides cordwood and lumber. A young couple from San Francisco, attempting to ride a makeshift "flume-boat" of eight by eight timbers down the carrier, successfully negotiated the steepest drop, only to be thrown off, at the first curve, onto a pile of bark trim. Helped to their feet by flumemen working nearby, they received a rainbow-tinted tongue lashing and were advised not to try the stunt again if they valued their lives.

A four-legged beast of burden didn't get off so easily. Under the dubious guidance of an old Negro named Bailey, the animal, along with three other pack mules, was being urged across one of 14 bridges that spanned the Clear Creek flume. Suddenly the mule lost its footing and slipped into the fast-moving water. Heavily loaded with cordwood, the beast floated down current on its back, sandwiched between 14-inch by 14-inch timbers on their way to the Carson terminal yard. Eventually the lumber in the wake of the thrashing animal overtook him at Pedroli's Meadow and crushed him to death. As the flume belonged to the C. & T. L. & F. Company, Bailey approached Duane L. Bliss and demanded reimbursement.

"How much do you consider your loss amounts to?" Bliss inquired.

The old darkey shuffled his feet nervously and peered at the ceiling.

"Eighty dollahs, Mistah Duane," he finally answered.

"Eighty dollars?" Bliss replied in amazement. "Why, Bailey, I was told that you paid eighty dollars for all *four* of your mules."

The Negro hung his head. "Yah suh, Mistah Duane, but mah remainin' animals is thin as barrel staves from livin' off scrub sage, and very *sparity*, very *sparity*. But that fine 'plendiferous mule that's now carrying wood for 'Old Gabe' was worth all three of them 'cause I fattened him on oats and timothy."

Bliss snorted and settled for $25.[54]

By now, Glenbrook had one of the first telephone lines on the Pacific Coast. A private wire in the new Bliss summer home connected with Carson, and Joseph M. Short, the town's leading merchant, who lived next door, was invited over one day by Duane Bliss to view the modern marvel. While Short was admiring the oblong box with its crank and gooseneck speaker, it suddenly came to life, ringing loudly. Short sprang away as though struck by a red hot poker, but his host urged him to take down the receiver. Joe gingerly picked it up and peeked into the mouthpiece. Then he "ee-awed" and "he-hawed" into the wrong end until rescued from his novel predicament.[55]

Lake Mills One and Two were operating on a ten-hour daily schedule and the summer population had grown impressively. All was not work, however, at the little lumbering settlement. Captain D. W. Avery, master aboard W. W. "Billy" Lapham's *Governor Stanford*, ferried excursionists to Emerald Bay and Carnelian at the going rate of $1.50 per passenger, returning them to Pray's Hall in the evening for "sociable country dancing to the strains of the Davis family's music."[56]

Spooner Meadow was another popular spot for parties, caterers from Carson City supplying the elegant midnight repast, while the younger Glenbrookers tripped the toe on the green-carpeted meadowland until the sun showed over the mountains.

Captain Joseph A. Todman, the town's hitherto intransigent bachelor, finally weakened and advertised for a wife through a San Francisco matrimonial bureau. A girl, generally meeting his specifications, was found and the marital knot tied securely at Tahoe City. After the wedding, Todman

**HEADED UPGRADE
ON HORSESHOE TRESTLE**

ENGINE NUMBER ONE (TAHOE) *at the head
of Upper Pray Meadow, climbing
southeast on its way to the first switchback
and Summit Camp with a maximum load
on five lumber cars. June 25, 1891.*

G. D. Oliver

brought his young bride across the lake on his steamer, the *Tod Goodwin,* and as the wedding party passed Deadman's Point the "boys" at Glenbrook saluted the couple with a resounding broadside from Pray's cannon.

It was reported that "more wadding and black powder than 'Old Betsy' had ever held" was rammed into the famous field piece for the momentous occasion. According to one observer the tremendous blast "put a permanent bulge in the howitzer's barrel and the resulting concussion demolished every front window in Lake Shore House." The appreciative Captain, in a rare moment of generosity, insisted that he be allowed to pay for the damage. The subsequent shivaree also had its lively moments. Several of the town's more inventive "blades," led by Johnny Griffin, poured a can of red pepper down the chimney of the bridal cottage and stuffed it with sailcloth in an attempt to smoke out the newlyweds.[57]

Lumber production was at its peak in the mid-1880's and the mills were beehives of activity. Three-quarters of a mile of piers, breakwaters, over-water spur track and buildings stretched along the shoreline of Glenbrook Bay. Free floating logs lay behind circular piling enclosures and chained log booms choked the shallows of the cove. Massive barges, 104 feet long by 30 feet wide, loaded to capacity with 180 cords of wood, moved through the pine bark and sawdust littered water to discharge their cargo after steam tugs had warped them into the docks.

Two-ton saw logs were dragged up the inclined ramps and transferred to the vertical saw racks by slings, lines and levers and a screaming, high-pitched whine from the double circular saws and planers struck the ears when the blades bit into the wood. Special furnaces fired the great accumulation of sawdust, and fifty cords of slashing and refuse wood were burned every day in the 100 foot long pit dug for the purpose. A Carson newsman advised: "The roaring fire and live coals on the outer edge of the pit keep the Glenbrook people 'so pious' as it is a constant reminder of some future location where they might be headed." He added, "The Blisses would give the tailings away if they could, as it costs them $200 a month just to maintain the blazing, leaping inferno in the dump." Along with the sharp crack of the finished lumber dropping onto the flatcars, could be heard the clang and whistle blasts of the little locomotives pulling out every two hours for Summit Camp and shrouding the bay and the mountains was a huge drifting pall of dense gray smoke rising from the mill stacks.[58]

On October 11, 1887, the company's Number Two Mill, built twelve years before, burned to its brick foundations. Flatcars stacked with lumber and standing on the rail siding adjoining the mill, exploded into flames, then smouldered to skeletons of charred wood and twisted iron. One of the company's large wood barges was moored at the wharf in front of the mill. As Chinese "stackers" hurriedly chopped the securing lines in two, pine slabs that had been loaded on the flat decking that morning at Camp Bijou, ignited and blazed up in a sheet of fire. The evening sky reflected the red-orange glow of the holocaust as the flaming carrier floated out into the bay, contributing to the fiery scene of destruction that was visible from all points on the lake.[59]

As Carson and Tahoe City were not directly concerned, they reported the loss philosophically and immediately acted as self-appointed spokesmen for Glenbrook. They agreed that "even though the company was not carrying enough insurance to cover the loss, it could well afford it, and the end of the season was at hand anyway."

The *Carson Appeal* pointed its editorial finger at the smoking ruins and commented libelously, "It is worth noting that if a mill or other structure at the lake has to burn, it often conveniently does so just before the winter snows set in."[60]

To meet production schedules the C. & T. L. & F. Company now ran its Number One Mill 24 hours a day and one of the more optimistic signs at Glenbrook was a proposed system of "electric lighting" that would turn the "night into day."

Frank Stephens Jellerson, assisted by his sister, Amanda Jane, was operating the 18-room Jellerson Hotel, built in 1882 and located in a grove of poplar trees several hundred yards south of the present golf course. In June, 1890, the Jellersons constructed Dirego Hotel (House) nearby, borrowing the name from the motto of the State of Maine.

The one-story establishment contained post office, saloon and restaurant, with Frank Jellerson postmaster. A touch of High Sierra style was evident when Jellerson climbed to the driver's seat of his gleaming carriage, and, sitting grandly behind two meticulously curried white horses, drove down to the steamer wharf to meet his arriving guests. Lap robes, proclaiming "Jellerson House" in bright scarlet letters, were provided for the comfort of the arrivees.[61]

"Miss Amanda" had become an institution in the little settlement.

UPSTAIRS WAS A MEETING HALL

The C. & T. L. & F. Company's over-water store originally built by Augustus W. Pray and leased over the years by J. A. Rigby, the Davises, J. M. Short and others. Looking northwest in the summer of 1892 with C. T. "Bud" Bliss' spring wagon in the foreground.

George D. Oliver

George D. Oliver

ONE UP — ONE DOWN

The Mogul locomotive NUMBER TWO (GLENBROOK) on the right, passing the NUMBER ONE (TAHOE) above the second switchback high on the side of Slaughter House Canyon. Lake Tahoe Line's NUMBER TWO is on its way upgrade to Summit Camp with a load of 14 x 14-inch mine timbers. The NUMBER ONE is backing down empty on passing track toward Glenbrook. Late October of 1893, looking northwest.

With a keen sense of humor and an amazing amount of patience, she dispensed advice on illness, family troubles and anything else that involved the Glenbrookers' welfare.[62]

Besides the Blisses and Jellersons, other families in the lumbering town were the Pomins, Shorts, Barnes, Quills, Prays, Watkins, Armstrongs, Todmans, Griffins, Davises, Notewares, Scoffields, Kleins and Tobriners. The millworkers had their own "protective organization" and its members were known as "Knights of the Golden Sawdust." Hands wigwagging on nose and ears were a part of the group's special signals, and initiations for a new "Knight" ranged from a "walk" across the bark-covered water of the bay, to dropping gunnysacked "bodies" (actually cordwood) from the second story window of the over-water store, while blindfolded neophytes shuddered apprehensively as they awaited their turn—which never came.

Railroader Johnny Watson, in collusion with "Pete" Hawkins and Johnny Griffin, excitedly announced one May afternoon in the early 1890's that they had located a "fantastic gold strike" just north of the settlement. The "boys" immediately named it Chipmunk Flat Mine and planted an iron strongbox on the site of their discovery. Joe Galliano, the town barber, was talked into joining the Miners Union in order to participate equally with the trio. It is said that Galliano had already closed shop and elevated himself to a frock coat and stovepipe hat when he discovered that the mine's total production, carefully placed in the strongbox that curiosity prompted him to open, consisted of iron washers and rail spikes.[63]

Norman Scoffield ran the single saw at Lake Mill Number One, where he cut slab wood which the Blisses furnished to the Glenbrook families without charge. James McMahon, another mill hand, worked in the wood yard for the company. McMahon was given to the quaint practice of beating himself regularly with a whip stock and therefore considered "crazy as hell" though otherwise reported to be "intelligent, a great reader and hard worker." One morning, in the mid-1890's, his body was found face down on the lakeshore road at Glenbrook. It was then discovered that a heavy, tattered vest, which had been his constant companion for years, contained $3,000 in $20 gold pieces carefully sewn into the lining so they wouldn't jingle.[64]

Mable French (Fairchild) taught school in the little one-room schoolhouse north of Glenbrook Meadow, across the road from the cemetery. The Pomin youngsters, Jeanette, Ida, Maggie, Ernest and Frank, attended, along with Chester Pray, Adeline Madatoll, Gertrude Barnes, Olivene Spooner, Jetora and Wilbur Watkins, Jennie Barnes, Grace Jellerson, and Frank and Joe Short, Jr., with their sisters, Eva and Evelyn.[65]

Making "scissors" from pins carefully crossed and placed on the railroad tracks was an exciting diversion for the children, because there was always the *chance* that they might derail the train. South Point had unofficially become known as "Gilmore's," named for the settlement's delivery man, who carried two 5-gallon cans of milk balanced on a pole across his shoulders. As he made his daily house-to-house rounds, Gilmore always prefaced his morning greeting with "Well I guess we'll have another wind comin' round the point today." . . . Hence the naming of the promontory.

Gilmore also cut hay in the meadow behind the school and no matter how hot the day, the teacher always closed every window because Gilmore's profanity was loud, profuse and entirely too educational for anyone but an appreciative mule skinner.[66]

The record snowfall of 1889-90 worked a hardship on the winter residents at Glenbrook. Snow, 15 feet deep, lay on level ground, and drifts 35 to 40 feet high marooned the townspeople, forcing them to dig themselves out of second story windows or tunnel through the frozen white blanket that enveloped their front entrances. Coal oil lamps burned day and night. In the evenings the monotony was broken by dancing at Lake Shore House to the violin and piano of Jack Armstrong and Camille Spooner. Spooner, a recognized pianist, had written the popular "Lake Tahoe Schottische" (his family expected a girl and therefore foisted the name Camille on the unsuspecting newcomer when he arrived). The gatherings were often enlivened by some high-flying lumberjack who couldn't resist the melody and felt the urge to execute a jig, his dancing shoes being spiked boots that raked the polished floor.

During the summer of 1891 holiday horse racing along the bay's shoreline was a popular diversion with week-end dances affording additional recreation. A near riot was barely averted one Saturday evening in Pray's Social Hall when Jack Armstrong unintentionally skewered Mrs. Charles Ramsey's red wig with his violin bow while she was pirouetting past the band stand. Young Frank Short, who planned to attend the festivities, was in an even more embarrassing predicament, having been hospitalized earlier in the week after warming himself at his uncle's pot-bellied stove in the overwater store. This was not unusual, but Frank had neglected to remove a pocketful of phosphorus he was carrying and the result was disastrous. Lake Tahoe's finest home, the Duane L. Bliss two and one-half story mansion, still boasted the only *real* bathroom in the settlement, and fantastic excuses were thought up by tourists in order to obtain a glimpse of the modern wonder.[67]

In the mid-1890's Glenbrook still presented an outwardly prosperous appearance, however the tempo of business activity was slowing down. Extortionate claims on the rapidly diminishing stands of timber remaining in the Tahoe basin were linked to the whims of an unpredictable veining of silver and gold on the Comstock that was now running out or becoming inaccessible in the steaming, water-filled lower levels of the mines.

The main flume of the Carson and Tahoe Lumber and Fluming Company had a maximum capacity

GLENBROOK INN GREW LIKE TOPSY

The building on the left is old Jellerson Hotel, moved to the new location from the north end of the settlement. Lake Shore House, after a face lifting, stands to the right of the pier and the center section of the Inn includes the over-water store that stood on the spot where the photographer took this picture in the fall of 1913. Note the low lake level and size of the trees which now hide the hotel.

Author's collection

LUMBERING WAS
ONLY A STIRRING
RECOLLECTION

*Looking west across Glenbrook Meadow
and 14 miles of Tahoe
to the Western Sierra Nevada
in the early spring
of 1911.*

of half a million board feet of lumber a day, or 700 cords of wood. This output was now cut in half and then quartered as the demand from Virginia City fell off. In the fall of 1892, the company's North Wood Camp had been abandoned and two years later South Camp was closed down. This marked the conclusion of large-scale lumbering at Glenbrook.

By 1895 nearly 10,000 acres of timber land, owned outright by the company, had been stripped, along with 7,200 acres of forest reserve purchased from the Hobart estate. Additional timber leases amounting to over 30,000 acres were cut over. Barely 950 acres of usable pine stands remained.[68]

In the same year the Bliss family formed the Lake Tahoe Railway and Transportation Company and prepared to move its scope of operations across the lake to the California side. During the next three years the transportation company purchased from the parent firm the steamers *Meteor* and *Emerald Number Two*. They also built the 169-foot Queen of the Lake, the *Tahoe*.[69]

From Harry O. Comstock, representing the "Lucky" Baldwin interests, the Blisses bought the *Tallac*, renaming it *Nevada*.[70] In addition they acquired the track, locomotives, lumber cars and companion equipment of the Glenbrook and Lake Valley railroads, along with the maintenance and repair shops and other buildings at Glenbrook and Bijou they would need for the new operation.

From the Pacific Improvement Company they obtained 40 acres of land that would constitute the site of Tahoe Tavern, and 1,000 acres in the vicinity of Tahoe City, then owned by the Donner Lumber and Boom Company.

In the fall of 1898 materials and equipment ranging from scrap iron to locomotives were loaded aboard cordwood barges and towed by steam tug across the lake to Tahoe City.

Ahead lay another formidable work project—surveying of the railroad right-of-way down the Truckee Canyon and grading, cribbing, bridging, then laying the track. Tahoe Tavern was to be built, along with a quarter mile railroad trestle terminal pier extending out into the lake. Maintenance and repair shops, car barns and marine ways at Tahoe City were to be constructed. In conjunction the mail and excursion steamers would operate on an uninterrupted year around schedule.

It was a project to discourage even those vigorous builders of the Bonanza era, but the work was accomplished with characteristic thoroughness and dispatch.

During 28 years of logging activity, it is estimated that the Carson and Tahoe Lumber and Fluming Company took from the Tahoe basin more than 750,000,000 board feet of lumber and 500,000 cords of wood. Truly, in the words of Dan DeQuille, "The Comstock Lode was the tomb of the forests of Tahoe."[71]

The way was now open for Glenbrook to settle back and become Glenbrook Inn and Ranch, its lumbering days fading to colorful memories with a gracious, hospitable atmosphere and pleasurable way of life taking over at the bay.

Today only the faint shadow of the Bonanza days rests on Glenbrook's shoreline—apparent in its historic buildings, rapidly disappearing mill foundations and crumbling breakwaters.

C. O. Valentine

ONLY A FAINT SHADOW FROM THE BONANZA DAYS RESTS ON HER SHORELINE

This picture, taken from South Point in the summer of 1910, shows the D. L. Bliss home (right center), J. M. Short's house adjoining Glen-brook Inn, outbuildings, and the old pier with slab wood stacked on the end to supply the lake steamers' fireboxes.

Chapter Forty

SPOONER STATION AND SUMMIT CAMP

I T WAS A SULLEN, rain-sodden day in May of 1883. Storm clouds, pushing over the eastern sweep of the Sierra, were hurling torrential flash floods down Glenbrook and Clear Creek canyons. Washout threatened a trestled section of the C. and T. L. and F. Company's 12-mile flume where it crossed the ravine above Saint's Rest and by mid-morning a maintenance crew from Summit Camp had been called out on the double.

The downpour stretched into the afternoon and the men worked steadily to resecure the foot bracing beneath the watercourse. Engrossed in their job and chilled to the bone, they paid little attention as twisting, flopping, vari-colored objects began falling in their midst. One worker finally glanced up and at that moment a slippery trout caught him squarely across the face.

"Jumpin' Jehoshaphat, boys, it's a miracle!" he yelled, unable to believe his eyes. "Brook trout!" he added with a shout. Then he grabbed wildly for the slithering shapes that by now were dropping steadily from the stormy skies.

Before the amazed workers could gather their wits, they were engulfed by a mass of fish that seemed to be pouring out of the slate gray blanket sweeping the pine trees overhead.

Work was forgotten as the men sloshed, slipped and fell in their efforts to collect the flopping "brookies."

"Big Jim" Easton, foreman of the work gang, scrambled to the top of the V-flume to get a fix on the situation. It took him but a moment to discover the reason for this generous manna from heaven. The scarlet-bellied trout had been crowded into the far end of the last control pond at Summit Camp where they were then sucked into the flume's supply inlet, sliding down the flume until they reached the mechanism that normally deflected bark and other floating debris over the side of the watercourse.

Easton sent two of his men back on the run to Summit Camp to get buckets, baskets, and a wagon.

A shuttle brigade was formed from the trestle's base to the road up Clear Creek, and before darkness set in over 700 pounds of trout had been scooped up. It took a prodigious amount of talking to convince many in the group that this windfall had actually not been a gift from "Old Gabriel." Some of the more accomplished fishermen needled the rest, reminding them that they had always known it would take an act of the Almighty to put the normally elusive trout in *some* people's frying pans.[1]

Twenty years before the establishment of Summit Camp by the Bliss and Yerington interests, the California Wagon Road exploratory party, headed by surveyor Sherman Day, detailed the following report to Surveyor General Seneca Hunt Marlette:

"Passing along the valley at the eastern foot of the mountains, about six miles below the Mormon Station (Genoa) we turned in to the left and crossed a low pass lying to the southwest of the Eagle

A RIBBON OF WATER SNAKED DOWN CANYON TO CARSON

The C. & T. L. & F. Company's 12-mile V-flume passing through Devil's Gate in the summer of 1888. Clear Creek Canyon road (bottom) looking east toward Prison Hill and the North Pine Nut Mountains.

Ranch (Carson City). Over this pass leads the wagon road known as Johnson's Cut-off. The altitude appears to be less than any pass in the range east of Bigler. It lies opposite to the middle, apparently, of the east side of Bigler Lake, and opposite to the pass which we came through on the Georgetown exploration.[2]

"The ascent is smooth, though sandy. Grades could be improved by sidehill cutting. The descent from the pass to Bigler directly west is abrupt and precipitous, but the wagon road does not follow this line because of several rocky points that put out into the lake and swamps at the mouth of streams between the spurs. It winds along the western sides of the mountains (Carson Range above eastern shore of Tahoe) and goes, at points, to great altitudes, higher than that which we crossed the summit. Six or seven lofty spurs are climbed and descended and it would have been better to cross directly at any point at the south.

"This road was preferred before the West Carson Canyon route was improved, as a means of reaching Bigler Lake Valley, and the western portions of the Johnson Cut-off road, but it is now better to go by way of Luther Pass."[3]

The "low pass lying to the southwest of Eagle Ranch" described by Day became "Walton's Toll Road Summit" five years later, and the canyon, "Clear Creek."

During this period, water and steam-powered sawmill construction proceeded up the canyon. Anticipating a boom in timberland at Summit, Michel(e) E. Spooner and Simon Dubois, French-Canadian wood contractors, pre-empted "640 acres more or less" placed as "about three miles east of Lake Bigler, and about ten miles west of Carson City," calling their holding "Spooner Ranch."[4]

Samuel Haire and Samuel F. Gilcrest, cattlemen from Genoa, Nevada, also acquired a full section adjoining Spooner and Dubois' timber and meadowland. At the same time Thomas and John P. Elliott were forming the nucleus of Summit Fluming Company.

On April 26, 1860, Rufus Walton filed at Genoa for a toll road that would follow Clear Creek to Summit, then drop to the lake and run along the shore south to Yank's and Hawley's ranches in Lake Valley. Three months later Walton was allotted the franchise, but the judge granting the toll right stipulated that it would be subject to the "determination of the Utah Territory-California boundary line."[5] As of that year, no one had the slightest idea where the division lay and many considered all of Lake Bigler and Lake Valley to be within the confines of the Territory.

In January of 1863, Haire and Gilcrest sold 500 acres of their timberland to the Elliott brothers. It lay on both sides of the Walton Toll Road near the source of Clear Creek and payment was made in lumber from their "Summit Mill" one mile to the west.

Before the year was out the Lake Bigler (Tahoe) Toll Road Company took over Walton's Toll Road and traffic to Washoe began moving down Clear Creek and the newly completed Kings Canyon turnpike.[6]

Spooner, with another partner, Carl,[7] was now operating a shingle mill on a quarter section of land south of the road between the Elliotts' mill and Glenbrook. Under the name Michel(e) Spooner and Company (the Company being Carl and Dubois), Spooner Station was built near the present junction of Highways 50 and 28.

The little settlement consisted of a hotel, saloon, several workmen's shacks and a combination stable and barn. Corrals bordered Spooner Meadow to the north, and here the partners kept their yoke oxen, pasturing milk cows and draft horses in the fertile meadowland.

G. W. Kenison's blacksmith shop and ox-shoeing stall was located east of the ox enclosure. Here the Pioneer Stage Lines also had their own large two-story barn where 120 tons of hay, wheat and barley were stored for their relays of blooded horses.[8] To the southeast of Spooner's, Oliver Lockie and Company acquired a 400-acre "timber ranch" where they established cordwood and saw log camps.

George D. Oliver

TIMBERS FOR THE BIG BONANZA'S SQUARE-SETS

Summit Camp terminus of the Lake Tahoe Railroad in May, 1892, with a work crew unloading mine timbers onto inclined ramps above the V-flume. Spooner Station one mile to the west.

Eleven yoke of oxen and several "lumber trucks" constituted their livestock and logging equipment.

Spooner and Dubois agreed to let the Elliott brothers erect a sawmill on their ranch and allow them to "cut as much pine timber as they wanted anywhere on the land, and make roads, provided they did not run sawdust upon, or injure the meadowlands." Payment for the timber and mill construction privileges was to be 50,000 feet of finished lumber at $3.00 per thousand for clear, and $1.50 a thousand for common.[9]

The Elliotts were also buying up a 16½-foot right-of-way for their V-flume which was to start several years later at George Schaeffer's old sawmill and run four and one-half miles down Clear Creek. The flume would be jointly owned by John and Thomas Elliott, Henry Marvin Yerington, John Lockie, Michel(e) Spooner, Simon Dubois and Will Fairburn. Other holdings included in the seven-man partnership, operated under the name Summit Fluming Company, would be the Clear Creek Toll Road, Summit Lake (now Spooner Lake), North and East Canyon flumes and "ditch extensions."[10]

By the summer of 1870 Spooner and Lockie controlled 1,840 acres at Summit, running a shingle mill and sawmill on their lands. James H. Rigby had the old "Knox" mill (also known as "the California Bank's") to the east with 640 acres of standing timber. Michel(e) Spooner's brother Louis and Simon Dubois both owned half sections at Summit and the Elliotts held nearly 2,500 acres.[11] In this same year, Wells Fargo Express Company listed Spooner Station as a regular stop, and Western Union strung its telegraph line through the settlement. Fighting had broken out in Clear Creek Canyon between the Chinese cordwood cutters and French-Canadian lumberjacks. Reported as "a disturbance resulting from the late massacre of French in China," it was quickly quelled.[12]

Two years later, W. T. "Buck" Davis, George Gillson and the Foster family moved into the thriving settlement where Freeman Foster built a livery stable and Gillson and Davis put up a general merchandise store and mill.

In 1873 Spooner and Lockie added a new mill one-half mile south of the Station and Michel(e) Spooner, who could neither read nor write but took pride in signing his name with an X, was quoted as "doing just fine in the lumbering, ranching and way station business."

Al J. Wakeman's daughter Nellie, of Saint's Rest, one mile east of Summit, had unfortunately acquired from the teamsters a taste for liquor during the hectic days of staging and teaming to Washoe. She became the female lush of the region and such a steady customer of Spooner's Saloon that bartender McHugh could not bring himself to lock the door in her face, even when she insisted on bringing the Wakeman's only milk cow in with her.[13]

Land boundaries were so loosely described in the recorder's office at Genoa that many ranchers and lumbermen never really knew what their actual acreage was or where their exact boundary lines ran. It was not uncommon in those days to find descriptions as vague as the following in the assessor's register:

"From a point adjoining Old Lady Mott's, running to a blazed pine, south eighteen chains, north over the ridge to a granite slab, then east to a marked stump, and west in the direction of Lake Bigler; 640 acres more or less."

Early in March of 1873, Patton replaced Lockie as Spooner's partner at the new mill and they sold their holdings several months later to the recently organized Carson and Tahoe Lumber and Fluming Company.[14] At the same time the Elliott brothers, Dubois, Gillson, Fairburn and Lockie disposed of their land and interests in Summit Fluming Company to the Glenbrook combine.

CAPACITY — 750 CORDS OF WOOD A DAY

Gang boss "Big Jim" Easton (next to man with camera case on left) and "pushers" at Summit Camp's cordwood feeder flume. Looking west toward Tahoe in the summer of 1892.

George D. Oliver

George D. Oliver

FRESH AIR FRINGE TOP

William D. Keyser's leather-slung stage that ran daily during the season in the 1890's, between Carson City and Glenbrook over the Clear Creek turnpike. Stops were made enroute at Bath's, the White House, Pedroli's Meadow, Saint's Rest and Spooner's Station. Photograph taken at Carson City in the spring of 1893.

In 1875 old Eagle Valley Pass became Summit Camp with the eastern terminus of the Lake Tahoe Railroad, loggers' shacks, terminal ponds, cordwood and lumber flumes, located one mile above Spooner Station.

Michel(e) Spooner held his ranch and Station over the next two decades, gradually selling off property to meet mounting obligations. In 1896-97 his holdings had dropped to 140 acres and he was practically bankrupt. Several years later this well known Tahoe pioneer who was to leave his name on "Spooner Summit" died penniless in the Ormsby County poor house.[15]

At the turn of the century, a few sagging buildings, dilapidated corrals and an old water-powered sawmill to the northwest, above Spooner Lake, were the only vestiges of the once flourishing settlement. A one-story clapboard house, where the office of Wells Fargo Express serviced the trade into the 1880's, held the last thing of value at Spooner's. In one corner of the room stood a heavy iron safe, covered with cobwebs, broken window glass and dust. The Douglas County assessor continued to levy a yearly tax of 69 cents on the strongbox and this amount was regularly paid by Wells Fargo for several years.[16] Eventually the safe disappeared and along with it the final pulsebeat of Spooner Station.

HERE THE RAILROAD MET THE FLUME

Partial view of the unloading ramps at Summit Camp (Summit Lumber Ranch) where lumber and cordwood began the 12 mile V-flume trip down Clear Creek to Carson Valley. Looking northwest in early spring of 1882.

Grahame Hardy

Charles Haine

HIDDEN HIGH IN THE CARSON RANGE ABOVE TAHOE

Air view of Marlette Lake taken in January of 1955 at approximately 11,000 feet showing box flume (right of center) that fed from the west side of the man-made lake running north to the tunnel entrance (not shown).

Chapter Forty-one

MARLETTE LAKE

IN PIONEER DAYS a legend persisted around Carson and Virginia cities. It was said the wastes of Washoe were so barren that wild animals, including the formidable grizzly, gazed eastward from the heights of the Carson Range, sniffed the acrid air and quickly turned west again into the sanctuary of Tahoe's forests.

As an indirect result of this allegory, Marlette Lake came into being. This artificial body of water lies in a mountain depression 1800 feet above the northeastern shore of Tahoe. Covering 300 acres to a maximum depth of 50 feet, it is set back one mile from a near perpendicular drop to the waters of Tahoe. Marlette runs north and south for one and three-quarter miles and is three-quarters of a mile wide. Known originally as Goodwin Lake, it was renamed in the 1860's after Seneca Hunt Marlette, Surveyor General of California in 1855 and early developer of the Tahoe region.[1]

The significance of the whole Marlette basin, as well as other sources of water on the eastern slopes of the Sierra Nevada, did not long escape the shrewd eyes of the engineers and financiers of barren, brawling Virginia City. Here, clustered on the sides of Gold and Six Mile canyons under Sun Peak (Mount Davidson) were the drones as well as the workers of society. Across the Washoe Sink from the Carson Sierra Range, Virginia City existed in all its glory because it was on top of one of the world's great mineral deposits—the Comstock Lode.

Virginia City was renowned as a thirsty place but it was parched with another thirst that all the forty-rod whiskey in the West could not quench. Each day the intricate processes of extracting gold and silver from the deep-mined rock required water by the millions of gallons. There was also the problem of domestic water supply for myriad uses in a city whose population fluctuated between 25,000 and 40,000 people. They had to bathe, cook, and, legends to the contrary, even drink water. Because the local supply, the springs of Mount Davidson, could not keep up with the demand, another source had to be tapped—the creeks and lakes on the eastern wall of the Sierra.

The first major engineering answer to the problem came in 1872. Although this project did not affect Marlette Lake, it touched off a chain reaction that was followed three years later by the transmission of Marlette's waters to Virginia City.

After extensive investigation surveys were run out in the spring of 1872 by engineer H. Schussler, a reorganized Virginia and Gold Hill Water Company found what it wanted in the course of Franktown Creek (Hobart), a stream flowing north through Little Valley into Washoe Lake.[2]

The company's engineers constructed a diversion dam high above the valley, hitting upon an almost incredible method of carrying water to the mines. This was a combination box flume and pressure pipe installation, at the time the most elaborate ever attempted. Wrought iron pipe was designed to withstand the tremendous pressure of water dropping nearly two thousand feet from Hobart Creek to

Bert Watson

LAKE HOUSE AND DOUBLE-ENDER— SUMMER OF 1882

Flumekeeper's cabin at Marlette Lake still standing in 1957. Northeast across the lake is Marlette Peak in the Carson-Sierra Nevada Range. Marlette's dam and outlet (not shown) lies to the left of the picture.

Lakeview Station on the Washoe-Eagle Valley saddle. Risdon Iron Works in San Francisco prefabricated the pipe to fit a predetermined course on the curving, mountainous terrain. Twelve inches in diameter and varying from one-sixteenth to five-sixteenths of an inch in thickness, depending on the water pressure encountered, the pipe was made up in 26-foot lengths. It weighed a total of 700 tons, and when installed stretched for seven miles.[3]

Fourteen air relief valves and sixteen massive sediment blow-off valves were required. There were 1,524 fitted joints secured by a similar number of metal connector rings. One million rivets were used and thirty-five tons of lead poured for caulking.

Thirteen deep canyons and gulches lay in the course of the pipeline but, in spite of the adverse conditions of altitude and terrain, a two and one-half foot trench was dug in the spring of 1873, the first pipe section laid on June 11, and the aqueduct completed by the 25th of July, only six weeks after ground was broken for the project.

This was the world's longest and highest inverted syphon with a pressure of 865 pounds per square inch at its lowest point, Lakeview Station.[4]

A tremendous celebration rocked Virginia City when the valves were opened and the letting of water into the pipeline was announced by smoke signals high on the mountain tops. Whistles at the mines were tied down and cannon fire roared across the city. A torchlight parade that evening with bonfires and fireworks, accompanied by the whoops and yells of the assembled citizens, unmistakably showed that the populace recognized water to be the lifeblood of the gold and silver mining operations.[5]

So well did these so-called "visionaries" build, that today the citizens of Virginia City still utilize snow water flumed and piped directly from the Tahoe Region.

Only one flaw was said to have been found in the entire 38,300 feet of pipeline and this was a pencil-sized hole that grew in a matter of minutes into a 2 to 3-inch escape-way for a jet of water spurting 200 feet into the air. It was reported the pressure was so great that it turned a man's fingernails down as though he had held them against a spinning emery wheel.[6]

In the meantime, Marlette Lake had not been overlooked. In order to augment the water supply for their lumbering enterprises, Duane L. Bliss and H. M. Yerington of Glenbrook placed a dirt fill and stone dam across the head of Marlette Basin in the summer of 1873.[7] The collected water was conveyed by six miles of V-flume running southward from the reservoir to Summit Camp, one mile east of Spooner Station. Here three small retaining ponds fed the twelve miles of trestled V-flume winding down Clear Creek Canyon to an extensive terminal yard in the valley south of Carson City.

However, the two million gallons of water supplied daily to Virginia City by the Hobart Creek Dam was not enough to meet the increasing demands of the Comstock and in 1876 the Virginia and Gold Hill Water Company arranged with Bliss and Yerington to draw from Marlette Lake. To increase the lake's available water supply, the dirt and masonry dam was raised eleven feet to a height of 37 feet, thus nearly doubling the capacity and providing for the storage of two billion gallons.[8] Moreover, a second pipeline from the Hobart Creek diversion dam to Virginia City, paralleling the line laid in 1873, was found to be necessary.

A covered box flume was constructed from Marlette's western outlet north along the Carson Range, 1800 feet above Lake Tahoe. The flume, with a 20 by 20-inch trough, ran four and one-half miles around the mountain rim to the west portal of a 4,000-foot tunnel blasted through solid granite under the Sierra summit.[9]

John Debo Galloway

SNOW WATER CARRIER
THAT FED THE COMSTOCK

A portion of Marlette's box-flume where it crosses a granite sheer some 1800 feet above Sand Harbor, several miles south of its entrance into the 4000-foot tunnel bore at West Portal's "Red House." Looking northeast.

On the east side of the divide another box flume picked up the water from the tunnel and carried it nearly three miles to junction with the Hobart Creek system. The Marlette water, in turn, was augmented by another feeder flume high on the northern slope of the Tahoe basin. This waterway was dug and blasted along the mountain slopes and ran more than eight miles before reaching the west portal of the tunnel.

By this complex system the supply of water now available to Virginia and Gold Hill had been raised to 6,600,000 gallons every twenty-four hours. The network of flumes and piping extended over thirty-two miles and represented an investment of $3,500,000. Yet such was the insatiable demand of the mines that in 1887 still a third pressure pipeline and additional flumes became necessary, and these boosted the total to twenty-one miles of piping and forty-six miles of fluming.[10]

Seldom assailed by twinges of modesty, the contemporary chroniclers of the Comstock and Tahoe region acknowledged this engineering feat for what it was, a miraculous achievement of the Silver State. Nevertheless, it was overshadowed by the tens of millions of dollars worth of bullion stamped from the ore that was spewing out of the shafts beneath Virginia City.

Myron Angel in his *History of Nevada* reported Marlette Lake as 7,700 feet above sea level, venturing the statement that it was the "highest lake in the world supplying water to a major city." If it was not the highest, he concluded, it was at least the "purest."

Not all observers of this man-made wonder were equally impressed. It is recorded that in the summer of 1880 a traveler, curious about the many improvements being made on nature in the Sierra, was directed to the Marlette tunnel by a logger at Camp Hobart on the northeast shore of Tahoe. The explorer-excursionist left his horse at the west portal and struggled through the long bore, his way lighted only by a sputtering candle. He emerged wet to the skin and thoroughly disgusted after falling into the flume, twisting his ankle and crawling the last few hundred yards on his hands and knees. Somehow he managed to limp back over the summit to his horse and spur the animal down the trail. When the battered adventurer stormed through the camp, a wild gleam in his eye, the helpful logger had mysteriously disappeared.[11]

Because of its importance as a water source, Marlette Lake figured in the perennial newspaper duels which were characteristic of the West's early days. In 1885 eastern brook trout were planted in the lake by Captain J. B. Overton with little initial success, since they were taken for their spawn, then much in demand for stocking the surrounding Alpine lake area.[12] The fish were also considered a great delicacy and their numbers decreased rapidly.

These circumstances inspired the article "Short of Brains" by the editor of the *Truckee Republican*, who harbored little love for his colleagues in Carson. He took acid pen in hand and scratched out his explanation of the lake's sudden depopulation in trout: "It is rumored that the Carson City staff of pencil pushers require vast quantities of brain food after drawing so heavily upon their imaginations when writing about Tahoe's wonders, and this undoubtedly explains the disappearance of the Marlette brook trout."

Brook trout, as well as the fulminations of newspaper editors, come and go according to time's vagaries, and such vicissitudes sharply contrast with the ageless serenity and permanence of the Sierra

C. O. Valentine

LIFEBLOOD FOR THE LODE

*Marlette Lake's snow waters supplied Virginia City for more than
three-quarters of a century. This panoramic view, taken from the southeast side of the lake,
shows Incline Mountain (center) and the Mount Rose range in the distance,
early in the summer of 1909. Marlette's outlet is hidden
from view by the pine tree in the foreground.*

Nevada. This changelessness appears to be shared in this instance by the product of man as the Marlette Lake flume, after nearly three-quarters of a century of use, still remains a visible scar high on the east Carson Range above Lake Tahoe, where the eye can follow its course for several miles.

In the winter of 1948 man's ingenuity was challenged in Marlette's sub-zero wilderness back country. Jack Ferguson, flumekeeper and lone resident at the lake, decided to construct a 40-foot sailing yacht on top of the mountain. Lumber for the hull was laboriously hauled in and Ferguson spent five years building the hand-pegged, heavy-beamed vessel. Upon completion of the project, he was confronted with a problem analogous to that of the amateur builder who constructed a boat in his basement and then had to remove the side of his house in order to get his handiwork out.

Consideration was given to waiting for the winter snows, skidding or sledging the craft from 8,000 feet to Tahoe, then shipping it from there to the ocean. But the problem resolved itself when a truck and trailer combination proved anything was possible by moving the heavy load to Spooner Junction in the remarkably short period of one hour. Ferguson completed and rigged his boat in Sacramento and sailed it to the South Seas, providing probably the first and last example of an ocean-going vessel constructed on a Sierra Nevada summit.[13]

Although silence now lies across Marlette's waters, the mark of the strong, enterprising builders stands against the mountains as a reminder of one of the great accomplishments of the Bonanza era.

Author's collection

HEWN GRANITE HELD BACK THE SNOW WATER

37 feet of rock dam at Marlette Lake impounded enough water to supply thirsty Virginia City. Photograph taken in the fall of 1940 looking east.

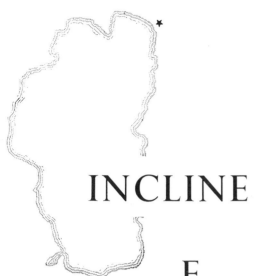

Chapter Forty-two

INCLINE

FAR UP THE precipitous mountainside two heavily loaded lumber cars on the "Great Tramline of Tahoe" crawled toward Incline Summit. It was a bleak, cold morning in early October, 1880, and Captain John Bear Overton, general manager of the Sierra Nevada Wood and Lumber Company, was standing at the base of the nearly vertical 4,000-foot-long lift. Two weeks earlier he had placed this prodigious steam-powered cable railway in operation. Now he was watching the trams as they moved slowly upward to their junction with the V-flume at the top, listening with an engineer's trained ear to the whir of the endless cable as it circled the lower 12-foot iron bull wheel and clacked along over the idlers.

Suddenly Overton saw the black dots hesitate as though pinned to the promontory. They were now some 3,000 feet up the narrow gauge track. He froze for a moment, then sprinted toward the printing telegraph shack to warn the steam engine tender at summit. But he was too late. The two lumber carriers on the north track had already reversed direction and started backwards down the mountain. Slowly at first, then picking up momentum with incredible rapidity, they broke away down the rails. Faster and faster they hurtled downward. Now flaming streaks of fire showed under the trucks and clouds of billowing smoke streamed out behind. Loaders and mill hands scattered on a dead run as the lumber-stacked trams whistled across the lower trestle. With an ear-splitting crash the cars tore into the thick stand of sugar pine at the tramline's base, and timbers flew in every direction, splintering into kindling wood. Both cars were demolished. A two-by-four board was driven like a lance through one of the trees, piercing it 20 feet from the ground and imbedding itself so deeply that it supported its own 10 feet of length, the free end whipping in great swinging arcs.

Bark on the surrounding pines was "gouged and raked as though fired upon by grapeshot" and the Great Tramline's base was a shambles.

After making certain that none of his mill crew had been aboard on the disastrous downgrade breakaway, Overton ordered an investigation. The accident was finally traced to an overwinding of a clutch brake.

Thus ended what an admiring newsman later described as "the fastest recorded run on wheels in America."[1]

In the summer of 1878, two years before the tramline disaster, Walter Scott Hobart organized the Sierra Nevada Wood and Lumber Company, appointing Captain Overton, then superintendent of the Virginia and Gold Hill Water Company, as his general manager. Timber sections were purchased or leased on the far northeastern side of Tahoe and along the southeast shoreline of the lake at prices ranging from $2.50 to $12.50 an acre.

By October of 1880, Hobart and Overton completed a steam-powered sawmill one-half mile from the lakeshore on what is now Mill Creek. It lay one and one-half miles east of the present Rim of the Lake-Mount Rose highway junction and average production was 40,000 board feet of lumber a day. The initial logging took place north of Carnelian Bay, with the first cut run through the mill's circular saws as railroad ties and flume timbers.[2]

A wagon road that followed the old emigrant route was also completed. From Franktown in Washoe Valley it wound up canyon through Little Valley, crossed the divide at over 8,000 feet, then zigzagged down the western side of the Carson Range above Tahoe, past the west portal of the Virginia and Gold Hill Water Company's water tunnel to Incline at Mill Creek.[3] When an enthusiastic reporter observed, "the trip over this new road is second only to a visit to Yosemite," stanch lake supporters protested indignantly. "Yosemite?" they questioned, "why we buried the equal of that furrow a million years ago in the middle of our bottomless lake."

In conjunction with the mill, the S. N. W. and L. Company embarked on an ambitious project—the construction of the Great Incline of the Sierra Nevada. A double track narrow gauge tramline, 18 feet in over-all width, was engineered by Captain Overton to run straight up the side of the mountain east of the mill. Cross ties spiked to a solid log bed carried the rails on which the lumber and cordwood cars were to operate, with the cars canted at an angle so that a near level inclination could be maintained on the steep grade. From the staging yard adjoining the mill, a spur track feeder line ran southeast one-eighth of a mile to join the tramline near its base. Here the carriers were loaded for the trip up the 4,000-foot-long, 1400-foot vertical lift to the V-flume running below the granite outcropping that anchored the top of the structure. Three-quarters of the way up the mountain, an eight-foot rise in every twelve was encountered, giving a near 67 per cent track gradient.[4]

Alpine funicular and cable car railways of the time actually furnished the pattern for the tramline, although Overton took full credit for the design and construction of the project. The machinery and equipment consisted of more than 8,000 feet of inch and one-eighth endless wire cable fed around two massive twelve-foot diameter, eight-spoked bull wheels. The wheel at summit was driven by a gigantic sprocket and gear turned with a 40-horsepower steam engine embedded into a granite walled powerhouse. Ten-by-twenty-inch timbers were butted to solid rock and secured with iron rods and ring bolts to support the weight of the terminal wheels with the cable ambiguously described as "running over the top of the cars and hitched on top of the hind ends."[5]

Twelve combination cordwood and lumber cars were used by the company, each car holding one and one-half cords of wood, or a comparable load of lumber. A maximum of 300 cords of wood, or its equivalent, could be carried up grade to the V-flume each day, with twenty minutes time elapsing during their climb up the mountain.[6] The tramway was engineered so that two carriers could be pulled up the steep ascent while the "empties" descended on the adjoining track, their weight assisting the overloaded steam engine.

Water from the Virginia and Gold Hill Company's north flume supplied the company's flume, which it paralleled. At the point where cordwood and lumber were discharged into the watercourse, heavy gauge iron plate was faced onto the planks of the V-flume to prevent damage to the structure One and one-half miles south of the tramway's summit lay the west portal of the water tunnel, through whose 4,000-foot length the flume ran.[7] A printing telegraph line, strung on poles, climbed up the side of the steep mountainside adjoining the south side of the track leading to the steam plant and watchman's house at the top.

In the spring of 1881 the company surveyed and installed a rail bed that led south from the mill two miles. It curved around the eastern crescent of Crystal Bay to Sand Harbor at the base of 8,800-foot-high Incline Mountain.[8] Another two miles of thirty-pound narrow gauge track continued west along the lakeshore.

SKY TRAMWAY
TO TIMBERLINE

*The Sierra Nevada Wood and
Lumber Company's great
Incline Tramway,
with a length of 4000 feet and
vertical lift of 1400 feet,
that carried cordwood and lumber
on the first leg of its journey
to the Washoe mines.
Photograph taken from Mill Creek
mill in the summer of 1882
looking east.*

Bancroft Library

Logging roads, V-flumes and dry chutes were extended back into the heavily timbered canyons that led toward Slide Mountain and the summit divide east of Mount Rose. Horses, mules and oxen drag-chained the logs to the chutes, with wagons and sledges used to haul cordwood to the flumes.

From the company's land sections on south Tahoe, logs were assembled in V-booms and rafted nearly 20 miles by the steamer *Niagara* to an elbow of land that formed Sand Harbor. Here the logs were cable-dragged by teams of yoked oxen out of the water up inclined ramps onto logging cars, or stacked in a staging yard with a "tripod" loader.[9]

Little Engine Number One, squat, mushroom funneled, with saddle tank, four thirty-eight inch drivewheels and square cab occupying almost half of the locomotive's length, labored north to the sawmill. Before unloading its logs at Mill Creek the train passed through a deep cut beneath Incline's tramway. One engine and thirty cars constituted the rolling stock on the line, with several of the carriers side-tracked at Sand Harbor for loading.

The S. N. W. and L. Company had a starting crew of 60 workmen. By the fall of 1881 the mill-hands, lumberjacks and cordwood splitters numbered 250. The ingenuity of the company, demonstrated by its construction of the Great Incline, caught the traveling public's fancy. Lake steamers ran special excursions from Tahoe City, Tallac House, McKinney's, Campbell's Hot Springs and Glenbrook so that sightseers might crane their necks and view the modern marvel.

Walter Scott Hobart now controlled more than 10,000 acres of timberland, including his Nevada Lumber Company holdings at the south end of Tahoe.[10] He ordered Overton to take everything worth felling along the shoreline and back up the slopes to the northwest of his sawmill, and extended his activities to the boundaries of Flood, Fair, Mackay and O'Brien's Pacific Wood, Lumber and Fluming Company.[11]

On January 12, 1884, the remote settlement was declared both an election precinct and a fourth class post office. Gilman N. Folsom was appointed postmaster. Tahoe City and Glenbrook residents now reluctantly conceded that the little mill town was looking up. During the severe winter of the same year, one full mile of the company's V-flume, where it trestled across Little Valley, was flattened by unprecedented winds that toppled the 50- to 70-foot-high structure as though it were built of match sticks. Rebuilding was accomplished in a matter of eight days, something of a record even in the Bonanza days when work projects were often completed seemingly overnight.[12]

A reporter from Washoe who visited Incline in July of 1891 found many of the old log chutes falling into decay, but the logging roads and feeder flumes were still in use, winding down canyon and mountain slope to the miniature railway. Charlie Blethen, first engineer on the Hobart Line, still cracked throttle on Engine Number One between Sand Harbor and Mill Creek and the engine was reported as being clean and shiny as a newly-minted Carson City dollar. A second locomotive, the Number Two, had been added two seasons before with engineer "Pall" Messenger at the controls. "Camp Hobart" now had a planing mill operating in conjunction with the sawmill. Captain Overton was also receiving assistance from Absalom Spencer, who took over as superintendent during the winter months.[13] In November of 1894 the company sold the majority of its holdings on the southeast shore of Tahoe to Bliss and Yerington's C. and T. L. and F. Company. Twenty-one hundred acres of partially cut-over timberland went for $4.00 an acre, 440 for a total of $1,000, and 160 additional acres were knocked down for a flat price of $50. Ten more land sections totaling nearly 7,000 acres were sold for $3,500.[14]

Several years earlier, a substantial holding of virgin forestland northwest of Truckee had been cruised by Hobart and in 1892 he started to buy up land in the region. The summer of 1896 found the company concluding its operations at Incline, with mill machinery, rolling stock, rail iron and other equipment moved, lock, stock and barrel, across the lake on wood barges to "Bay City" on the first leg of its journey over the Martis Valley cut-off to the new location, Hobart Mills.[15]

By the fall of 1897 nothing remained at Incline but stripped forest land, the deep scars of logging roads, and a maze of crumbling flumes and rotting log chutes. At the site of the abandoned mills, high stacks of bark trim and blackening sawdust piles rose like monstrous ant hills. An estimate of the total production, from the start of operations in 1879 through 1896, at which time the timber reserves were depleted, approximated 200,000,000 board feet of lumber and over a million cords of wood.[16] Most of this cut went underground to shore up the galleries of the Comstock Lode, some vanished into the fire boxes of the Cornish steam pumps that cleared the mine sumps of water at Virginia City, and thousands of cords of wood disappeared through the balloon stacks of the Central Pacific and Virginia and Truckee railroads' locomotives.

The tremendous vertical scars on Incline Mountain have been caused over the last 80 years by the washing out and overflow of Marlette Lake's box flume where it winds along the mountainside some 1800 feet above Tahoe. Today these slides may be clearly seen from the western side of the lake. In the 1890's steamer captains on Tahoe took a particular delight in advising naive passengers that the "more intelligent and fun-loving brown and black bears of the region left their hibernation haunts at the top of the mountain in the early spring and slid down the steep declivity to its base, thus causing the slides." This tall tale still circulates and the scars are often referred to as the "Bear Slides."[17] Two and one-half miles north, the path of Incline's Great Tramway of the Sierra Nevada can be followed up the steep slope, tie by tie, through heavy manzanita and other scrub brush that has grown up and hidden the old rail bed. One of the massive bull wheels, which carried the endless cable at the base of the lift, now backs Mrs. Harry O. Comstock's barbecue pit at Brockway, and the other wheel is still in place at Summit. In the water near Tahoe City's old machine shops, rusts a section of the original cable that was salvaged by the Bliss interests in 1901 for use in drydocking their steamers.

The recollections of Tahoe pioneers add colorful touches to the picture of Incline's heyday: rides on the cowcatcher of Walter Scott Hobart, Sr.'s, miniature locomotive, the Number One, with Hobart clutching a guitar in one hand and, with the other, passing around a brightly colored five-pound box of chocolates, while the engine puffed and swayed along the track toward Sand Harbor; family trips by spring wagon from Franktown and Carson City to Incline following the '49ers' route over the 8,000-foot summit divide, the spindle wheeler bulging with the personal belongings for a two months stay at the lake, splashing through snow-water freshets, dragging upwards across deep sand, and behind the wagon a milk cow tied to the tailgate; gold "double eagles" running into the thousands of dollars counted into a large, worn satchel and for years lugged faithfully by an old wrinkle-faced Chinaman to the paymaster at Hobart's Mill Creek sawmill until the day a single gold piece was missed, whereupon the trusted Oriental was summarily fired.[18]

The story of Incline would be incomplete without the inclusion of Walter Scott Hobart, Jr., the "Slapdash Sage of Sand Harbor." Reared in the grand manner, young Hobart exploded meteorically upon the Harvard University scene around the turn of the century, reportedly sporting the finest coach and four the good old Crimson had seen in decades.

Walter was destined to go the way of all flesh because of his insatiable appetite for alcoholic spirits, fine food and sparkling women. Early in life his girth increased until his weight hovered around 280 pounds and it became difficult to determine where his neck left off and his shoulders began. Known as the "Prince Fortunas" of his day, he was endowed with a rugged constitution, a complete disregard for convention, a whimsical sense of humor and the financial means to assure tolerance for his idiosyncracies.

As the years edged into the 1920's, he spent his summers at Sand Harbor, where he had the misfortune to put out an eye on a piece of barbed wire. Hobart rushed to Reno, unattended, in an unsuccessful attempt to save it. His accident was brushed off as an incident by Hobart and did little to dampen his enthusiasm for high living. On days when he thought that he might have lost a pound or two, and provided he had a sufficiently large audience of friends, he would grab the nearest cat or dog and stuff the animal into the back of his voluminous pants, roaring that this feat proved he had reduced to a point bordering on starvation.[19]

Privacy at Sand Harbor was a "must" and Hobart delighted in ringing his estate with carefully

George D. Oliver

HOBART'S HUFFING IRON HORSES

ENGINES NUMBER ONE and Two running on the S. N. W. and L. Company's Sand Harbor-Mill Creek line in July of 1891. Engineers Charlie Blethen and "Pall" Messenger in the cabs. Looking southeast.

lettered signs such as "Pixies and other Indians Stay Out." His bald head bothered him as much as his over-weight and he usually crowned what he termed his "Daytona Beach" with a battered felt fedora crushed down over his ears.

In the early 1920's travel to and from the Harbor was by boat, and at the start of each season an extravagantly outfitted water caravan, loaded down with meats, liquors, canned goods, Chinese servants and guests, disembarked at the isolated boat house under Incline Mountain. Hobart maintained a small army of mechanics and boatmen who puttered constantly with his fleet of boats. These hulls included the picture-window cruiser *Quit-Cha-Kiddin'*, the fast runabout *Orange Blossom*, the general utility hull *Garazebio* and various and sundry rowboats and fishing skiffs with personalized names such as *Adenoid, Tonsil, Ya-Ya*, and *S. A.*[20]

Practically every electrical contrivance then known to man was carefully installed aboard the larger vessels during the season and Hobart's crew of mechanics would work feverishly to put the equipment in top operating condition. This was usually accomplished just as the first chill winds of fall arrived when the boats had to be hauled out for winter storage. In the following spring the cycle of marine improvements would start all over again.

It has been said the cooking range aboard the *Quit-Cha-Kiddin'* could handle meals for at least 40 people and that the anchor, stowed forward on the bow, was sizeable enough to hold the *S.S. Leviathan*.

Hobart once had occasion to cast a jaundiced eye on an acquaintance named Mary Eyre. With characteristic deviltry he named the outhouse after the object of his disfavor and thenceforth with a grand flourish directed his guests to the "Mary Eyre."

Two foundling pigs also wriggled their way into the spotlight when Hobart bestowed the names Carrie and Georgie upon them, after his good friends, Carrie Newhall and Georgiana Drum. With incomprehensible humor he thereafter insisted that "Carrie had spots on the Canadian side of her fanny, but Georgie would stand for no nonsense." This was accepted as "just another Hobartism" by his guests, who wondered vaguely what in hell he was driving at.[21]

Walter Hobart was extremely proud of his fast hull, the *Orange Blossom*, and the main marine event of each season was his grudge race with either George Newhall or Norman DeVaux. The stake was usually $1,000, and the course a 30-mile triangle around the lake. DeVaux, driving his *Apache II*, and Newhall, looking like a jack-in-the-box in his *Apache I*, raced Hobart's Liberty powered speedster. Walter took particular delight in defeating Newhall and when the happy event occurred he framed the check and crowed over the fact that he had "twisted the tail of a banker for once."[22]

"Bill," as his intimates called him, could always be counted upon to remain unperturbed in any crisis. The story is told of a hysterical employee who ran into his office with the news that Hobart Mills was on fire. Hobart swung slowly around in his swivel chair and eyed his agitated informant gravely for several moments. Before turning back to his desk he said quietly, "Well, then, why in hell don't you go back and put it out?"[23]

In the year 1938 "Captain" George Whittell, multi-millionaire San Francisco and Burlingame real estate magnate, purchased 14,623 acres of lakefront and back country forest land from the Hobart and Bliss estates. Of these acres, 452 border Lake Tahoe, and the land stretches from the east side of Crystal Bay south to Zephyr Cove. However, Whittell was unable to acquire, for inclusion in his eleven-mile holding, several parcels of property—Secret Harbor, Glenbrook Inn and Ranch and the settlement at Cave Rock.[24]

On a jagged, rocky promontory directly above the lake and some two miles south of Sand Harbor Whittell built his legendary $300,000 Thunderbird Lodge. Constructed of faced granite blocks, with leaded windows and sharply angled slate roof, it is reminiscent of a medieval French chateau. To the east of the lodge an artificial waterfall cascades over the rocks at the turn of a valve. Everything on the grounds appears to be of stone—the guest chalets, caretaker's house, 100-foot boathouse blasted out of solid rock, and the winding rock pathways. Massive iron doors close off the four-car garage, and handwrought iron thunderbirds ornament the three-story castle and surrounding lodges.

At the extreme southwest end of the point a granite watchtower looks out across the lake. To the north of the chateau stands the bombshelter-like boathouse. Inside, on its electrically operated cradle, lies an $87,500 torpedo-shaped mahogany express cruiser, designed by marine architect John Hacker. This 56-foot cabinet worker's dream, with its stainless steel tear-drop superstructure, is so infrequently used that its appearance on Tahoe is apparitional.[25]

Many are the stories, some fact, most fiction, of "Whittell's Castle" and its elusive owner. These include gossamer tales of his $100,000 losses at the Tahoe gaming casinos; of lions, a tiger, and a baby elephant flown to the lake and allowed to roam the grounds behind a ten-foot electrified fence, and of a barrage of searchlights that suddenly turn night into day if an intruder is suspected of being on the grounds. A loudspeaker system is said to extend a startling reception to the inquisite marine traveler by blaring a recording of "I'll Be Glad When You're Dead, You Rascal You" out across the lake.

It has been rumored that until the last few years champagne parties featuring chorines from nearby bistros lasted around the clock, that the castle grounds were enlivened by sprightly, full blown nudes leaping from rock to rock pursued by eager males, and that savage packs of police dogs and ex-pugilists patrolled the property to keep out the unwelcome. No evidence supports this scandalmongery.

One certainty exists. The forbidding, mysterious castle, which has become Tahoe's counterpart of "Wuthering Heights" on a dark, storm-clouded day, will continue to hold its cloistered secrets well.

TRIPOD LOG LOADER AT THE HARBOR

In the sheltered waters of Tahoe's Sand Harbor, beneath Incline Mountain, saw logs are being pyramided on a logging wagon for transportation to Hobart's Mill Creek saw mill, November of 1880, one year before the narrow gauge railway went into operation.

Author's collection

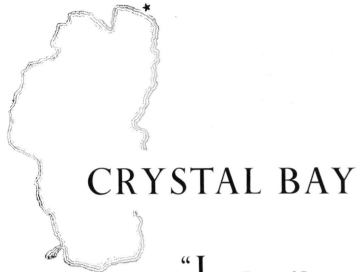

Chapter Forty-three

CRYSTAL BAY

"J AMES FAIR and I were to ride in one of the flume boats and James Flood and Hereford in the other. There were at least fifty lumberjacks standing around and Fair suggested we take a third man with us. One of the group, a red-faced carpenter somewhat the worse for alcohol, turned out to be the only one to volunteer. Three of the workmen immediately caught up the first boat and held it over the V-flume. They told us to jump in the second it touched the swift moving water and then hang on to our hats. The signal had already been given by then and we leaped aboard and were off like the wind." H. J. Ramsdell, *New York Tribune* correspondent, was reporting on the "wildest ride ever undertaken by man in the Sierra Nevada mountains."

Earlier on that crisp autumn day in September of 1875, Ramsdell and his distinguished hosts had been driven to the top of the world's longest V-flume. The watercourse started nearly 9,000 feet above sea level and some 3,500 feet higher than Truckee Meadows, Pleasant and Steamboat valleys. From this awe-inspiring vantage point the barren mountains of Nevada stretched to the far horizon, appearing to be part of a gigantic relief map. To the east rose the desolate Virginia Range. Lake Tahoe's forested north rim lay to the south.

The flume ride had been an impulse of James Fair and Jim Flood (titans of the Comstock and co-owners, with Mackay and O'Brien, of the Pacific Wood, Lumber and Fluming Company), who challenged Ramsdell and their superintendent, J. B. Hereford, to make the trip down the terrifying lumber and cordwood carrier. Ramsdell later explained, "They didn't actually *tell* us to go, they just *dared* us to, and I figured if men worth 25 or 30 million dollars would risk their necks, I could take a chance on mine that wasn't worth quite half as much."

Once the challenge was taken up, Flood and Fair ordered the construction of two V-shaped boats to fit the flume. When completed, the carriers resembled swine troughs more than any known means of transportation, but the die had been cast, and the quartet, plus the carpenter, took off down the slope. Ramsdell continued his description of the hair-raising trip:

"The grade at the upper mill was a near perpendicular drop and the terrors of that ride I have never been able to completely block out. An outing on the cowcatcher of a locomotive down a straight track is really exhilarating because you know that the brakes can be applied or the power of the engine shut off. But a ride down a flume—well—that's another story. There is no element of safety, no controlled slow or fast, you cannot stop or lessen speed, there is little or nothing to hang on to and you are at the mercy of the rushing water pushing you faster and faster.

"I tried to grab my hat and hold on as well as possible, which turned out to be not very well as my bowler went skimming off into the awful void below us. I now bunched up in a knot with my eyes closed, clenching my fists until the knuckles showed white, and my prayers came out in a rush of words. I was waiting tensely for eternity. The florid-faced carpenter was in the front of the boat, crouching on the boards, Fair came next and I brought up the rear.

"The water that barreled over the stern quickly filled the craft, creeping up my legs and soaking me as though I had plunged into the surf. I was of great service in keeping the water that broke over the end board off of Fair but that was evened up by the geyser that sluiced in over the bow, and Fair's broad shoulders helped there.

"I can only compare it to riding down an old fashioned eaves trough at an angle of 45 degrees, hanging in mid-air without support of roof or house and thus shot a distance of fifteen miles. I was flabbergasted that we could travel faster than the schedule of any train of the day and average a mile every two minutes.

"All of a sudden it felt like the whole bottom of the boat had dropped out from under me and we were again tearing down a steep grade with the water flying up so heavily that when I opened my eyes I couldn't see anything.

"Here we were on two slats no wider than a chair, ranging in the air from twenty to seventy feet, and all because Flood and Fair had *dared* us to join them in this wild ride.

"When we came to an easier gradient, I finally could look ahead and see the terrible, but beautiful, vision of the trestle stretching ahead like a winding chalk mark, small, narrow and fragile, with all of us suspended in nothingness on this spider web structure.

"Suddenly I felt the boat hit an obstruction and the carpenter was catapulted into the flume ahead. Fair was thrown forward on his face and I fell on Fair's back. In a matter of seconds he had the carpenter by the scruff of the neck, successfully dragging him back into the boat, but Fair crushed his fingers between the hull and the flume doing it.

"It was only ten minutes, but it seemed like an hour before we reached the worst part of the flume. I looked over quickly and thought the only possible way to get to the bottom was to fall and that's just about what we did. The breath was knocked out of my lungs and I was sure suffocation would set in on the spot. I've been in 80 mile winds on mountain summits but it was nothing compared to this. The water was foaming over Fair's face like ocean white caps. I didn't know whether it would be possible for me to survive the journey but I had to again see how fast we were going, even if it was my last look.

"One quick glance over Fair's shoulder convinced me that we were headed for everlasting oblivion, but I still wished to be certain of the speed in which we were approaching it. Huddling close to the multimillionaire I looked toward the mountains. Everything passed in a blur of motion, each object was gone before I could see what it was. I felt light as a feather even though I knew I weighed 200 pounds.

"Flood and Hereford, in the meantime, had been slowly creeping up on us, due evidently to the fact that their flume-boat carried a lighter load than ours. They also had a full velocity of water at their backs. Suddenly they struck our stern with a rending crash that threw them on their faces and engulfed them in a sheet of water.

"The boats, jammed together, swept across the terminal line at Huffaker's in a cloud of spray and we were dragged from our seats by the loggers who had been waiting for us at the bottom of the watercourse.

"Barely able to stand, I leaned heavily on Fair, and the five of us presented a white-faced, bedraggled sight. We wrung out our clothes and water cascaded to the ground. After squirting out a mouthful of water, Fair swore that we had traveled more than a mile a minute at times, adding that he would never again place himself on an equality with lumber and cordwood. Flood fixed him with a scornful eye and vowed we had gone at speeds *exceeding* one hundred miles an hour, insisting that he wouldn't make the trip again for all the gold and silver in the Consolidated-Virginia mine. Hereford pounded his ears, shook himself like a wet water spaniel, and snorted: 'I'm sorry I ever built the damn flume in the first place!'

"The carpenter stood, and shook, and said nothing.

"All I knew was that we had gone at a speed that annihilated space, that we were lucky to be alive, that I had accepted my last challenge, and that V-flumes were made for but one thing—the transportation of lumber and cordwood."[1]

Such were the diversions offered by the Pacific Wood, Lumber and Fluming Company's 15-mile

**EVERLASTING
OBLIVION
LAY DIRECTLY
AHEAD**

*This spirited lithograph
that appeared
in Vischer's* VIEWS
*during the 1870's
was inspired by the
Flood and Fair flume
fiasco and ably
expressed
the derring-do
of the era.*

LOGWAYS GROOVED THE DENUDED MOUNTAINSIDES

Marlette and Folsom's saw log and cordwood operation north of Crystal Bay near the present Mt. Rose highway. The camera is looking east in the summer of 1881.

V-flume built in 1874 by those barons of the Comstock Lode, James Flood, William S. O'Brien, James G. Fair and John W. Mackay.

Five years later, and some ten air miles distant, southeast over the divide from the "Comstock Big Four's" flume, a group of lumberjacks employed by the rival Sierra Nevada Wood and Lumber Company, had engaged superintendent Seneca Hunt Marlette in conversation on the subject of cats. "You mean them mountain climbers is going to take along a bag full of cats when they try for the top of old Wasson Peak?" asked one of the fallers incredulously.[2]

"Read for yourself," suggested Marlette, handing French-Canadian Pierre DuBois a crumpled copy

HIGHLINE CAMP LIFE WAS CONSTANT IN ITS MONOTONY

Marlette and Folsom's "East Canyon Camp" with log sections positioned in the "horse railway" ready for dragging to Lake Tahoe, lying some 1700 feet below. Fall of 1883.

of the *Reno Evening Gazette*. DuBois' lips pursed as he smoothed it out on a pine stump and studied it carefully. After several minutes of intense scrutiny he handed the sheet back.

"Sacre-bleu, Mister Marlette, you know I can no read print. What she say?"

The men, standing on the shoreline of Crystal Bay near Marlette and Folsom's wood camp Number One, now began to display a keen interest.

"Plans call for releasing the cats one by one on the way up this 13,000-foot mountain," Marlette read, "and it is said that the electricity in the air will sustain these felines."

"Felines?" questioned one of the lumberjacks importantly. "How's about them cats and climbers? Who's going to keep 'em alive?"

"We'll have to wait on that one," chuckled Marlette. He tossed the paper to another of the bearded lumbermen and changed the subject. "Rafe's in with our beef cattle out of Colfax. Says he lost half the herd this trip over Donner and that don't leave many on the hoof for the slaughter house. That *is* important." Marlette turned and struck off down the trail toward the corrals in North Meadow.

The men crowded around the paper, their exclamations attesting to the fact that any trifle of news, no matter how inconsequential, served to break the boredom of life in the logging camps of Marlette and Folsom.

Several weeks passed and finally another issue of the *Gazette* was brought over the mountain to Crystal Bay. The daring climbers had scaled the icy summit of old Wasson Peak. Breathtaking panoramas, including a view for hundreds of miles, were described in glowing detail. A step-by-step account filled the equivalent of half a page in the Reno paper. One of the lumberjacks who could read made a careful search of the article—sentence by sentence—but not a single, solitary word could be found that even hinted at the fate of the bag full of cats. To the "boys" this was a sneaky trick and a sad disappointment.

The widely accepted belief that Crystal Bay originally received its name because of the clarity of its waters is logical but unfounded. In the late 1860's, George Iweis Crystal, a lumberman from Douglas County, Nevada, filed with the United States Land Office for extensive timber sections on the northwest shore of the bay. Crystal left his name on the stretch of white sand beach and rocky promontory running east in a seven-mile horseshoe from north Stateline (Boundary Point) to Sand Harbor.

A decade later Seneca Hunt Marlette, former surveyor general of California and later county surveyor in Nevada, entered into a partnership with Gilman Nathaniel Folsom[3] of Washoe City, Nevada. The lumbermen intended to supply saw logs and cordwood from timberland surrounding Crystal Bay to Walter Scott Hobart's Mill Creek mill.

Marlette and Folsom originally operated a wood camp, obtaining their first major contract in July of 1881. During the summer and fall of that year they cut 40,000 cords of wood for Hobart, following this with 30,000 cords a year later and 60,000 cords in 1883.[4] By then the partners had a year-round operation and a crew of 150 French-Canadian lumberjacks and 225 Chinese woodcutters were dropping and splitting the heavy stands of pine.

Although Marlette and Folsom had access to some of the finest timber in the Tahoe basin, the problem of getting it out was difficult until Hobart constructed his "Great Tramline of the Sierra." Roads to Truckee and Reno were non-existent and the old emigrant trail over the Carson Range to Franktown in Washoe was impractical for wagon hauls. Prevailing winds out of the south and southwest built up heavy combers on the lake's unprotected northern shoreline, discouraging the loading of cordwood barges and the assembling of log booms.[5]

In February of 1884, the partners banked 3,500,000 feet of logs during the four-month period of heavy snows at the lake. They expected to chute and drag from highline another 1,000,000 feet before the spring thaw set in.[6]

It was planned to grade and widen the trail from Crystal Bay to Campbell's Hot Springs (Brockway) with the financial help of Truckee's businessmen. In return Marlette and Folsom would guarantee to give their trade exclusively to the railroad town. The trail improvement failed to materialize.[7]

As a result, life at the camps was reported as constant in its monotony. On weekends the boys sometimes rode horse or mule to Reno—even then a gambler's paradise. In the mid-1880's, 31 games of chance were operating full blast and listed by a correspondent of the day as "seven games of stud poker, two wheel games, one Rouge et Noir, one Ichi-Ban, six Faro layouts, one Rondo, two Autan, four Chuck-a-Luck, one Arabian Pool, and six pin ball games." Everybody was making money in a hurry and losing it even faster.

In the fall of 1888, Gilman N. Folsom dissolved his partnership with Marlette and moved his base of operations to Hobart on the southeastern shore of the lake, where he continued to "get out logs and cordwood for the Sierra Nevada Wood and Lumber Company."[9]

Captain John Bear Overton, superintendent of Hobart's Incline operation, and Seneca Marlette then took over at Crystal Bay but timber reserves were fast being depleted. By the summer of 1895 the mountainsides surrounding the bay were stripped clean and, after usable equipment was removed to the new Hobart Mills northwest of Truckee, the camps were abandoned.[10]

Today, to the north of Crystal Bay, 50 square miles of second growth pine carpets the slopes. Unfortunately the pine and cedar giants that once covered this region are gone, only their rotting five and six foot high winter cut stumps remaining as skeletal reminders of the unrestricted logging methods employed by the early lumber companies.

On the bay's rocky western shoreline, Lake Tahoe's equivalent of Italy's Amalfi Drive winds to north Stateline Point. The road passes private residences perched high above steep drops to the deep blue waters beneath, and the northern beaches provide some of the choicest summer home locations to be found on Tahoe.

Chapter Forty-four

BROCKWAY HOTEL AND HOT SPRINGS

"THIS END OF THE LAKE will eventually become the most desirable spot for persons in the pursuit of pleasure" was the prophecy voiced by William H. Brewer in August of 1863. In retrospect, this becomes a remarkable example of advance perception when it is recalled that the north Tahoe country, traveled by Brewer and his Whitney survey party nearly one hundred years ago, was an undeveloped wilderness.[1]

Early records indicate that William Wallace and Lambo Company harvested 25 tons of wild hay near the present location of Brockway in the fall of 1862.[2]

Eighteen air miles away the Central Pacific was soon to blast its tunnels and run ribbons of steel over Donner Summit, sparking a demand for lumber and cordwood to complete its imaginative project.[3]

During the summer of 1867 citizens in the wide open "hell on wheels" railroad town of Truckee agitated for a new wagon road to follow Middle Martis Creek and pass the deserted settlements of the Red, White, and Blue Mining District that had flared up and sputtered out barely six years before.[4] At summit divide, between Martis Peak and Mount Pluto, the proposed thoroughfare would lead down the northwest slope of the Tahoe range to the lakeshore and follow the shoreline for three miles to the natural hot springs.

July of 1869 found promotion of this Truckee-Tahoe arterial still in the talking stage, but it was to receive immediate practical attention. William "Billy" Campbell and George Schaeffer, stage and mill owners, respectively, from Truckee, privately began construction of the road with a crew of laborers, mule and horse-drawn graders and dump wagons. One month later the road was completed. Campbell now took title to 63 acres surrounding the hot springs and his workmen erected a 20-foot square bathing house over the principal attraction, a mineral spring that boiled out of a large granite rock at the water's edge.

By the end of August, 1869, Campbell had framed and roofed several additional cottages and it was reported that "everything was fixed fine at Campbell's Hot Springs, and in readiness to receive guests."[5] Then a major tragedy cast its shadow over the new development. Five men, employed at the Springs to build the breakwater—James Cain, Isaac Stein, William Riddle, James Henley and Charles Anderson, were returning from Tahoe City by sailboat on the night of September 8, 1869, when their overloaded craft capsized off of Chinquapin (Observatory) Point. All were drowned. This was Tahoe's greatest single marine disaster and, although it was explained that "all were drunk after an election," this did little to quiet the fears of the mystified and frightened Lakers as none of the bodies were recovered.[6]

Spring of the following year found "Billy" Campbell with a new partner. Henry Burke, from Tahoe City and Truckee, builder of the ill-fated lake steamer *Floating Palace*, had decided to try his

SOME DETECTED A FAINT TASTE OF GUNPOWDER

William "Billy" Campbell's Hot Springs viewed from the southeast in the summer of 1872. Boat sheds and bathhouse (center), the little steamer TRUCKEE at the finger pier and two-year-old hotel (right) are shown.

luck in the resort business. The two men completed what was termed a "commodious 40 by 60 foot hotel, two and one-half stories high with wide veranda fronting on the lake." Two more cottages were added to give a total of five twin-roomed outbuildings. These were available for families who wished to stay at the Hot Springs over extended periods during the summer season.

The *Truckee Republican* pointed with pride to Campbell's Hot Springs, advising its readers that "another of Tahoe's wonders has been opened to the elite from the lumbering and railroad town, as well as the traveler and vacationer, all without calling for public subscription or county assessment for the connecting road."

The *Nevada State Register*, not to be outdone by that "Truckee sheet," listed the advantages to be found at the hotel itself:

"Campbell's bathing house is over the principal hot spring and is both restful and medicinal with the waters bubbling out of a flat rock that slopes gently to the margin of the lake." The reporter from the Silver State was particularly impressed by the springs, "which continued to rise for a distance of 200 feet along the shoreline." He also discovered that when the water was cool it had a "faint taste comparable to gunpowder." Another feature that struck his fancy were the cottages "neatly papered and lighted by windows."

In May of 1871, Campbell's partner, Burke, opened the season by rattling his four-in-hand stage from the Central Pacific depot in Truckee over the Martis Valley road to the wharf at the Hot Springs. Here he connected with what was described as the "stanch steam propeller *Truckee*." The little wood-burner fired up and transported Burke's passengers across the northeast side of the lake to Glenbrook, where they climbed aboard "Doc" Benton's "mud wagon" and headed for Carson and Virginia cities.

Placer County's tax collector was less enthusiastic than the newspapers over the "magnificent development at the Hot Springs." All he could find was a house and barn. With a naive use of the double-entendre he described the hotel as a "house of entertainment, value $1,000, adjoining the California-Nevada line on Lake Bigler."[7]

But Burton, the Hot Spring's assistant manager, took anything but a dim view of the resort. He drew the hotel guests' attention to the spacious front lobby fitted out with a desk of solid walnut, pointed to the well-stocked bar adjoining, and proudly showed them the horsehair stuffed furniture in the comfortable parlor. Burton explained that the second floor had been partitioned into 11 rooms, and that each room was furnished with new brass beds and oak chairs. He dismissed all questions concerning the third floor with the remark, "it is naturally heated in the summer season."

As the Upper Truckee River (then Lake Creek) flowed into Tahoe on the south end and the Hot Springs were located on the far northern side of the lake, the hotel was considered to be at the "foot of Bigler" during the 1870's and 1880's. This conception was understandable but another idea was not so easily explained. Despite repeated State and Federal surveys indicating that the Springs were in California, Nevada claimed it was located one-quarter of a mile on its side of the line at "Carnelian Point." It was indeed a moot question and debate on this misconception would flare up from time to time over the next 20 years.

C. A. Richardson of Truckee leased the Hot Springs in the spring of 1874 and a new wagon road was pushed through to Tahoe City by way of Observatory Point.[8] This gave Campbell and Burke the incentive to extend their stageline past the settlement at the Truckee River outlet to McKinney's Landing. Thirty-five horses and eleven coaches constituted the livery. Depending on their purse, genteel ladies and their escorts could now take buckboard or coach and four over the dust-clouded Martis Creek road from Truckee, tonic themselves with the warm mineral waters of the Springs, and luxuriate in the swimming baths that boiled up on the lakeshore. The return trip was made around the lake to Tahoe City and down the canyon to the railroad town.

REVITALIZING RETREAT
FOR THE NEUROTIC NABOB

*The Hot Springs when it was managed by
Reverend R. A. Ricker
in the summer of 1875.
The wharf had been extended,
an over-water storehouse added
and trees planted in front of the hotel.
Looking northeast.*

Another proprietor took over the hotel's operation the following season. Reverend R. A. Ricker had arrived on the Hot Springs scene. The stout-hearted clergyman felled trees, blasted granite boulders to clear the grounds, and saved souls from eternal hellfire, all with the same driving energy. Seemingly inexhaustible in his efforts, he combined improvement of the resort's physical appearance with the spiritual counseling of his guests. A large stable, wharf extension and storehouse were constructed, with Reverend Ricker personally assuming most of the heavy labor. Loading platforms, leading from the stage and freighting road to the pier, were spiked together for use in moving merchandise from wagons to carrier barges and steamers. Ricker even found time to contract cordwood for the Virginia City mines and pine slabs for the fireboxes of the lake steamers. Overlooking nothing in the way of revenue, he arranged for Davis and Scott, who were running a shingle mill two miles north of the Springs at Mink Harbor, to ship their seasonal production of cedar shakes from his wharf to Glenbrook. In May of 1875 it was reported Davis and Scott expected to run through 1,000,000 shingles that season.

With a hundred and one material things to accomplish, the good minister still found time to discourse on the evils in the world, and to suggest corrective measures. Suffragettes and school marms, who comprised the majority of the hotel's guests, listened attentively and then headed for the relaxing swimming baths. It was considered proper for the strictest church members to drive to the Springs on Sunday as a sermon indoors or out always awaited them. With this determined emphasis on the gospel, it is little wonder the gayer blades at the resort bitterly complained that there wasn't a red-headed girl to be found at the Springs; in fact, no young ladies worth sparking, even under the romantic spell of Tahoe's full moon.

The hard-driving clergyman could not stay out of the news. He was against woman suffrage and no end of heated discussions ensued, with feminists from San Jose and San Francisco forcefully asserting their views far into the night.

But a more vital local issue directly affecting the status of the Hot Springs was in the making. In August of 1872 Colonel Von Schmidt had undertaken a state-financed boundary line survey between California and Nevada, originating at the Oregon line. Completed in 1874 at a cost of $42,500, it obviously favored California. The Silver State's citizens immediately bellowed in protest, declaring that they had a God-given right to the water and Nevada was not going to lose a half-mile strip of both land and water because of some politically controlled rod and transit no-good.

The *Truckee Republican*, in July of 1873, unwittingly joined the Nevada faction which considered the Hot Springs a rightful part of their state. A granite boundary marker was discovered by the *Republican's* correspondent one-half mile *west* of the resort, "proving conclusively" where the division line lay between the two states. Nevada's loud protests went unheeded, however, and another slice of her western territory dropped into California's lap.

Nor was all sweetness and light at the Hot Springs itself. In the fall of 1875, Mrs. W. H. Virden, wife of the *Gold Hill News'* manager, experienced an unfortunate accident that did little to assure a good press for the resort. She was badly scalded while moving from the shower to the steam bath when the boards covering one of the mineral springs broke away, plunging her into eight feet of near-boiling water. Luckily, Mrs. Virden caught herself on the rim of the pool and was pulled out before being "parboiled beyond recognition," as her husband angrily put it. Reverend Ricker was not allowed to forget this unwelcome incident, and some of the kindlier items printed by the *News* about the "miraculous Hot Springs" and its owner stated flatly that the clergyman-proprietor was actually a "combination of the church consorting with Pluto's burning waters from the underworld."

Another ever-present problem was the furious rivalry between Tahoe City and the Springs for the tourist and freighting trade out of Truckee to the west and Carson to the east. The Hot Springs appeared to have the edge over its competitor since the Martis Valley short-cut was not a toll road like Tahoe City's turnpike. Both routes were an average two and one-half hour haul for freighting

DRESSED IN WHITE AND EXTENDED

Campbell had added eight rooms to his hotel by the summer of 1878 and the hot mineral springs were now famous throughout California and Nevada. View taken from the end of the breakwater.

California State Library

Gladys Comstock Bennett

WAS MILADY WITH THE BUMBERSHOOT STANDING IN NEVADA?

Colonel Von Schmidt's north stateline marker placed to the east of the Hot Springs in 1872 by the surveyor sparked a bitter debate over the true California-Nevada boundary.

wagons and the road leading directly to the north end of Tahoe was generally preferred by teamsters.

During the winter months snow closed the two routes but horse-drawn sleighs and mail carriers on snowshoes maintained contact with the Springs. It had taken a crew of laborers eight days to open the 14 miles of road through Martis Valley to the lake in the spring of 1875, and by the middle of June drifts still lay six feet deep on the summit divide.

Steamers on the lake also had a bad time that winter. A swirling blizzard struck in January of the year and threatened the Hot Springs breakwater behind which the little *Truckee* was moored. As the wind and waves increased in intensity, a section of rocked-in wharf pounded out. Acting Captain "Billy" Campbell, fearing that the vessel would be thrown upon the rocks, fired up the boiler and beat his way through six-foot combers to the shelter of Agate Bay. That night the remainder of the pier was demolished by the storm.

In the summer of 1877 the excursion steamer *Niagara* scheduled a night cruise once a week to the Hot Springs. Professor James W. Varney's Brass Band was featured and as Varney's traveling musicians were a familiar and well-received attraction at Truckee, Reno, and Virginia City, where they played for social gatherings, the *Niagara* was always jammed at departure time with admirers of the mutton-chopped, shako-hatted Professor. For $1.00 the celebrants could enjoy both the cruise and a gala evening at the Springs, where guests and the band went ashore. Here the revelers danced the Parisienne Quadrille, the Glide, the Waltz Quadrille (denounced from the pulpit as "hugging to music"), the Lancers, and the Newport.[9]

The actual geographical determination of the Hot Springs continued to be a hotly contested issue with many "reliable" spokesmen of the times insisting that Campbell's was definitely situated one-half mile within the State of Nevada. It appeared that this verbal tug-of-war would never be ended.

On July 27, 1881, the *Tahoe Tattler* soberly reported a fracas that occurred in the Hot Springs bar:

"In a little difficulty over a game of poker last evening one Lawn, a teamster in the employ of Marlette and Folsom, Crystal Bay, was severely cut in back of the hand by a knife in the hands of Johnny Hogan, a fireman on the narrow gauge railroad of the Sierra Nevada Wood and Lumber Company. Both parties were in a state of intoxication and came up on the excursion steamer to Tahoe (Tahoe City) where the hand of the wounded man was taken care of as well as could be, and this morning he left on the *Governor Stanford* enroute to Carson (via Glenbrook). He will probably lose the use of the hand."

At the conclusion of the 1881 season the financial solvency of the Springs hit a new low. The sheriff padlocked the hotel for nonpayment of taxes and the understatement of the year was that the resort "had done rather poorly."

In the summer of 1883, A. J. Bayley, proprietor of the Grand Central at Tahoe City, leased the resort from Campbell and placed his son, A. A. Bayley, in charge. The establishment's name was lengthened to "Carnelian Hot Sulphur Springs," thereby adding another element of confusion as to its location. Carnelian Bay (originally spelled Cornelian) had been so noted on the maps of the Tahoe region for decades. Now vacationers bound for Carnelian Bay, 3½ miles to the west, were often let off at the Springs and vice versa. In May of the same year the Postmaster General was asked to consider the establishment of a post office under the name "Carnelian Hot Sulphur Springs." He rejected the request and substituted "Carnelian," a move that only compounded the muddle. In spite of this perplexing duplication of names, a post office was sanctioned and established at the Hot Springs on June 15, 1883, with the official name "Carnelian."[10] Local postmasters and mail clerks on the steamers wrung their hands in frustration, dividing correspondence and packages addressed to Carnelian Bay and simply "Carnelian" into two piles and hoping for the best.

GUESTS AND THE FOUR STARRED *MAMIE*

Visitors from Tallac on a marine outing in the summer of 1900 stop off at the Hot Springs. Left to right: Nancy and Harry O'Fallon, Captain Joe Pomin, Nellie Staples Dow Comstock Alverson, Emma Lawrence, Harry Oswald Comstock. Extreme right: Colonel and Mrs. Northam. John Ernest Pomin hiding behind the slab wood in the MAMIE *Photographer, Frank Brockway Alverson.*

Confusion was not limited to that occasioned by the resort's change of names. The pattern of proprietorship also became perplexing. In the summer of 1884 Sisson Wallace and Company took over the management from Bayley. They were quickly followed, during the next few seasons, by Stuart McKay, A. V. Bradley and others. Fortunately the Springs were ideally situated at Tahoe and the resort managed to survive good and bad management alike.

The story is told of Joe Short, one of the many lessees of the hotel, who was beating a hasty retreat from the sheriff at the end of an unprofitable season. He began to remove the post office boxes and a concerned bystander called his attention to the fact that they belonged to Uncle Sam. "Uncle Sam?" questioned the bankrupt proprietor blankly, "don't think I know him." He continued to cart off government property. When Short had loaded the last mailbox on to his wagon he climbed to the seat. Then he called apologetically over his shoulder to the disturbed onlooker: "Say, son, if you see your Uncle Sam, tell him I'll sure make it up to him sometime."[11]

The 1887 season concluded with a "Grand Picnic" held on the lakeshore. George Irwin, of Irwin Stage Lines, Truckee, was in charge and "Deaf Bob," "Doc" Benton, Al Nichols, Will Keyser and other famous Sierra Nevada "whips" dustered the guests in from all points around Tahoe. Irwin put on a great show for the group that attended. Foot races, including a barrel race for the "gents," Washoe and Paiute Indian wrestling matches and chicken shooting were featured. Two hundred pound ox heads were buried in the live coals of barbecue pits dug especially for the occasion, and the roasted delicacy served on white pine boards. Everybody agreed it was a "crusher" and, at the conclusion of the festivities, George Irwin was given a rousing "three cheers and a tiger."

In the spring of 1893, directors of the Lake Tahoe and Chautauqua Improvement Company, in Reno, leveled an appraising eye on the beauty and natural advantages found at the Springs. A new Washoe County road was in the promotion stage, planned to run along the northern end of the lake. A great sanitarium, summer resort and home location for the Lake Tahoe Chautauqua assembly were envisioned. In addition, an extensive real estate development was also being considered, and glossy brochures stimulated interest in this "superb property overlooking the 'Lake of the Sky,' and lying within the State of Nevada."[12]

Boiling sulphur and cold mineral springs were rediscovered, bubbling up in quantity, the cold iron spring being considered the most medicinal. As though this was not enough, clear non-mineral water was reported to be available near by. To this statement the enthusiastic promoters might logically have added: "billions of gallons of it, and all from the lake itself."

It was also found that one of the 112 degree springs required only the addition of a little salt and pepper, and, presto, "one had a superior quality of soup." After borrowing extensively from Mark Twain's memorable word pictures of Tahoe, the brochure praised the "thirty room, three story, $17,000 hotel that stood on the property along with the five cottages, large swimming and plunge baths, two story stable, 100 foot pier, and acres of available land."[13] All were pointed up in glowing terms. Finally the promoters promised that an electric railway, to match the best in Switzerland, would soon become a reality. Naturally its terminus would be at the Hot Springs. All this fanfare failed to evoke the desired results, and nothing further was heard of the project.[14]

In 1899 the Hot Springs was reported as "falling into a state of disrepair with the buildings needing attention, and only the remnants of a road leading into the old resort."[15]

A year later, however, Frank Brockway Alverson and his wife, Nellie Staples Dow Comstock Alverson, purchased the hotel and surrounding property for $3,500 and moved in as owner-managers. Alverson bestowed his middle name on the resort and it became Brockway Hot Springs. He was an aggressive salesman, grouping "livery, launches and laundry services" in his advertising pamphlets and tossing in fishing boats, tackle, parasols, cushions, bait and even "free swimming suits" as bonus amenities. A further touch of the modern approach lay in Alverson's slogan: "Top of the Map, Top of the List," and decks of playing cards which showed the many and varied scenes that could be viewed around Lake Tahoe were sold to the guests.

"Gentle saddle horses," presumably for the weak-hearted, were listed as available in a modern stable. Much was made of the tally-ho coach that met incoming guests at Truckee and the fact that it could be hired for group picnics and moonlight rides.

Brockway now accommodated 75 guests. Natural hot water from the springs was piped to each hotel room, to the kitchen and cottages. A vegetable garden on the premises supplied the resort's table, and milk, cream and butter were furnished by Alverson's dairy.

A brochure stated: "The handsome new hostelry features launches and steamers that are bright and cozy and bait aplenty is available with fish biting accommodatingly." Rates started at $2.50 per person per day and were less by the week.

Although the Alversons revived the resort's popularity, they found it necessary to call upon Lawrence and Comstock of Tallac to assist financially. In the spring of 1909 they were forced into bankruptcy because of further reverses. In order to protect their mortgage, Melville Lawrence and Harry Oswald Comstock bid for the hotel and hot springs at public auction on the Auburn, California, court house steps. As they were the only bidders on hand for the sale, their offer of $9,000 was accepted.

Lawrence and Comstock were still operating Tallac and the purchase of Brockway Hot Springs was considered a "protective investment." The death of Tallac's owner, Elias J. "Lucky" Baldwin, in March of the same year was another factor that affected their decision. During the ensuing four years

various managers were employed to operate Brockway. Included among these men were Harry O'Callaghan (later comptroller of the resort) and David Chambers, who, within the decade, bought McKinney's from the Westhoff family. The Alversons also returned to manage the Springs for one season.

Early in the summer of 1914, Lawrence and Comstock left Tallac. Lawrence moved to Brockway, ostensibly to retire, and Comstock took over the company ranch at Meyers, where he ran cattle.

Upon young Harry's return from a 30-day stock drive, he rode on horseback around the lake to inspect the Brockway operation. Here he found that "Uncle Mel" Lawrence had taken an active interest in the management and the resort was prospering. "Perhaps it would be wise to move the family over if Mel is this serious about the hotel business again," Comstock is said to have exclaimed. The Harry O. Comstock family immediately left the south end of Tahoe, joining Lawrence in the development of Brockway and the extensive land interests, which included holdings at present north Stateline.[16]

Vacationists and health seekers were now being advised about the resort's merits with pleonastic, high-sounding verbiage such as was foisted upon the reading public by George Wharton James: "The invalid or neurasthenic, the physically overworked or mentally overtaxed, who are benefited by baths in natural hot springs find at Brockways (sic) that rest, care and natural stimulation that will restore them to health."[17]

The Brockway casino and dining room were built in 1917, and after the present post office building was moved farther west, space was available for a swimming pool. This would later be constructed above the lake and supplied with naturally heated water from the hot springs.[18]

Brockway became a club during the early 1920's and a golf course was added, adjoining the site of what is now King's Beach. Harry Comstock took Robert P. Sherman of Los Angeles in as a partner at this time, Melville Lawrence having joined the "great majority." Comstock and Sherman added cottages, built the swimming pool and subdivided much of the property, selling land and memberships under the name Brockway-Tahoe Club. The Brockway Water Company was organized to take care of the new development and in the late 1920's Comstock purchased Robert Sherman's interest. Above the resort at north Stateline a gaming and entertainment mecca had been born.[19]

Harry Comstock had now made his name and that of Brockway Hot Springs famous throughout the Sierra Nevada. The respected and well-informed Tahoe pioneer was known as "Mr. Tahoe," a reflection of the high esteem in which he was held by lake residents.

He personally supervised the many improvements at the hotel, golf course and water company and also set aside valuable time to participate in matters that were vital to the conservation, development and promotion of the entire Lake Tahoe region.

With the passing of Harry O. Comstock on March 4, 1954, his daughter, Gladys Comstock Bennett, and son-in-law, Maillard Bennett, became owner-managers of the 85-year-old resort.[21]

Two classic passages from the pen of Mark Twain are recalled as favorites of "Mr. Tahoe." They eloquently express the same refreshing strength of feeling and admiration, the identical twinkle-eyed humor that Harry Comstock himself demonstrated when he enthused about the Lake of the Sky—a lake that had been an integral part of his life for more than half a century. Wrote Mark Twain in "Roughing It":

C. O. Valentine

THIS GREAT INLAND SEA THAT IS TAHOE

Panoramic view of the lake, taken in the spring of 1909 looking south.
The snow-covered Tallac Range is behind Brockway Hotel, and continuing northwest the Rubicons,
Desolation Valley, Burton(s) Pass and Mount Ellis. Steamer
TAHOE *and Brockway launch at the pier.*

"At last the lake burst upon us—a noble sheet of blue water lifted six thousand three hundred feet above the level of the sea, and walled in by a rim of snowclad mountain peaks that towered aloft full three thousand feet higher still! It was a vast oval, and one would have to use up eighty or a hundred good miles in traveling around it. As it lay there with the shadows of the mountains brilliantly photographed upon its still surface I thought it must surely be the fairest picture the whole earth affords."

Twain further assured the skeptical: "Three months of camp life on Lake Tahoe would restore an Egyptian mummy to his pristine vigor and give him an appetite like an alligator." After pondering, he added thoughtfully, "I do not mean the oldest and driest mummies, of course, but the fresher ones." The inimitable counselor concluded: "The air up there in the clouds is very pure and fine, bracing and delicious. And why shouldn't it be?—it is the same the angels breathe."

"TOP OF THE MAP, TOP OF THE LIST"

Frank Brockway Alverson's Brockway Hot Springs as it appeared in the spring of 1908, with the pencil beamed HAPPY DAY, *skippered by Captain Joe Pomin (center foreground). Photograph taken looking north at "Lookout Mountain."*

Author's collection

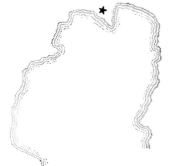

Chapter Forty-five

KING'S BEACH

J AMES STEWART, the "Silent Terror," brought his fist down on Griff's bar with a resounding crack that rattled the shot glasses and overturned an uncorked whiskey bottle, spurting liquor in a beaded froth down the front of his companion's buckskins.[1] Drunkenly, Stewart turned and started toward the door of the log saloon. Half way across the room his befuddled eye caught the clumsy movement of his drinking partner, who was reaching for a shotgun propped butt down on the brass rail. Stewart pawed for his revolver, spun around and aimed, in one flashing motion. As he squeezed the trigger, the ten-gauge "scatter gun" exploded simultaneously.

Lead pellets dug into Stewart's greatcoat, and he staggered backward. At the bar the man holding the shotgun fell forward on one knee, then slowly slumped to the rough floor. Stewart's bullet had driven through his throat, traveled upward and killed him instantly. On this fateful September day in 1872 the most feared gunman in the Tahoe region tried to stand but his legs buckled and he dropped in a heap. Barkeep Hagen peered cautiously out from behind the bar as several onlookers approached the two bodies. Finding Stewart still breathing, they picked him up, carried him into the back room and laid him on the bed. His heavy coat, torn and riddled by shot, was pulled off and a towel thrown over his bloody face. Although Stewart was badly shot up, he was not seriously wounded. Nothing could have been more disappointing to the small gathering.

Out in the corral Griffin, owner of the station, had just laid saddle to his mare "Hippy" when the shooting occurred. He rushed back into the saloon. Seeing the dead logger on the floor he let out a yell, "How about Stewart? Is the son-of-a-bitch dead, too?" Everybody tried to answer at once. Griffin collared his bartender and headed for the back room, elbowing the gaping bystanders out of the way. Seeing Stewart on the bed, he shook his employee and demanded, "Is the bastard finished, Rube?" Stewart's eyelids fluttered, then blinked open. He struggled to a sitting position and, exerting a super-human effort, swayed to his feet. With a bellow he threw himself at Griffin, swinging a looping, crushing right that landed squarely on the amazed proprietor's mouth, splitting his upper and lower lips and knocking out his front teeth.

Griffin turned and bolted out of the room, unaware that he had just taken his first step up the ladder to local fame. From then on he would be known as the only man to survive an "attack" by the cold-blooded killer of the Sierra.[2]

At the intersection of the present Tahoe-Truckee-Martis Valley road, where it joins the lake road on Griff's Creek, originally stood Wiggins' Station. Built in 1864 by wood contractor George W. Wiggins, it became known as the "logger's headquarters" and by the year 1872 it had been taken over by John Griffin, a well-educated lumberman from the Truckee Basin who cut saw logs and cordwood on the mountainous slopes of north Lake Tahoe.

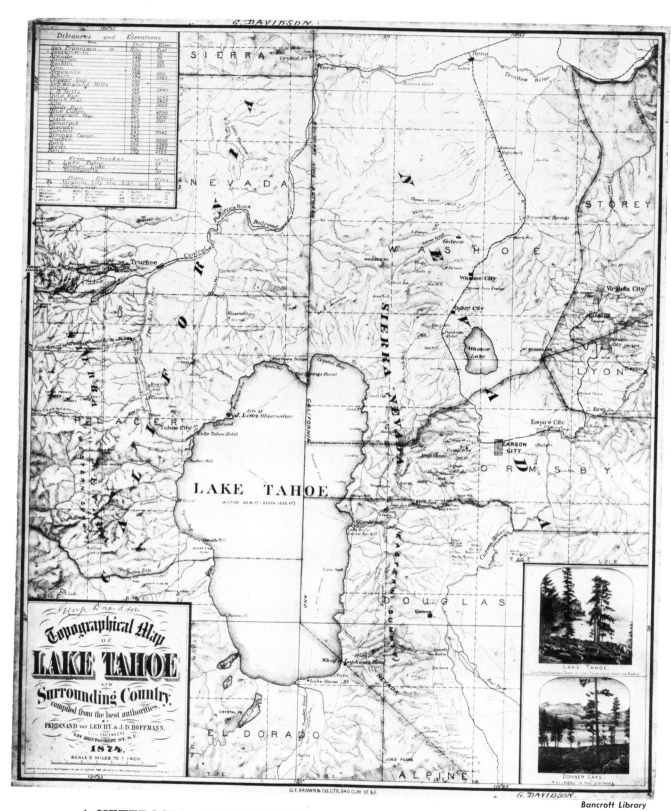

A HETEROCLITICAL TOPOGRAPHICAL WAS BETTER THAN NONE

Von Leicht and Hoffmann's map of Lake Tahoe, compiled in 1874, was the first comprehensive, if somewhat gar-
bled, detail on the "Big Blue." What would become King's Beach lies just northwest of the Hot Springs Hotel.

The establishment has been described as a "large log cabin, fronting on the thoroughfare with quarters in the rear for 'Griff' and his family, corrals for his draft oxen and other stock, and several outlying shacks for the workmen." On the eastern side Griff Creek (named for Griffin) opened into the lake.[3]

To this gentleman logger a well-phrased sentence was a ponderous one. Consequently, in his dealings with the average timber buyers from Truckee and Reno he was often completely misunderstood.

In one instance a hard-headed logger questioned "Griff" on the price of 30,000 feet of felled sugar pine. Griffin studied the prospective purchaser carefully and replied loftily, "After perusing your request, my man, it is highly possible that the going rate, as determined by the market at this specific time, will be acceptable provided you can procure the full cash amount required." The baffled woodsman turned to another lumberjack standing nearby and muttered, "That's 'Griff' for ya'. He jus' don't want to sell a dam' thing." Shaking his head in bewilderment he mounted his horse and started back up the road to Truckee.[4]

As Griffin's star ascended, speeded by his encounter with Jim Stewart, he became progressively more assured of his prowess as a "gun fighter." This conviction of "Griff's" was obviously not based on experience and believed only by himself, but he was always careful that no recognized desperados were present when he made his boasts. Then he would throw out his chest, display a mouthful of false teeth and roar dramatically, "Some day I'll rifle a man clean through his chest, then leap on my mare 'Hippy' and ride away like the wind, one hundred miles or more!"[5]

Robert Montgomery Watson, mountain man and trail blazer from Tahoe City, often witnessed these outbursts. Later, in a jocular manner, he told his son Rob that "if good old 'Griff', by some startling miscalculation, ever did make good his boast, his well-fed and barrel-shaped horse 'Hippy' would be lucky to carry the old gentleman ten miles before dropping in her tracks—provided Griffin wasn't shaking so hard that mounting the animal was impossible in the first place."[6]

"Griff" never did carry out what amounted to harmless threats and good entertainment for dull days. One winter night while reining a four-horse team furiously over the mountain to Truckee, his sleigh careened off the icy road and the following day a search party found him and his animals frozen to death in the snow.[7]

In the late 1890's Frank Brockway Alverson, of Brockway Hot Springs, acquired the land surrounding Griff Creek, including the shoreland and back country that is now King's Beach. During the year 1925 Joe King, from Truckee and Tahoe City, obtained the property west of the creek from Robert Sherman, partner at the time of Harry O. Comstock and representative of the Brockway Water Company. King gave his name to the location and developed it into a flourishing town of motels, theaters, markets, stores, cafes and homes.

Legend has it that Joe King acquired the land after an all-night poker game with Sherman, but the only verification from King is that he "used to be a 'passable' card player."[8]

Southern Pacific

WINTER'S FINERY DRESSES TAHOE'S SHORELINE

Looking southwest at Agate Bay and Flick's Point from Tahoe Vista across the snow covered shallows of Tahoe. Winter of 1934.

Chapter Forty-six

TAHOE VISTA

A GROUP of loungers in front of the Tahoe Vista Hotel could not restrain low whistles at the sight emerging from the tonneau of the cream-colored Packard "Four" touring car. First came a broad-brimmed, multi-flowered hat, then a vividly rouged and powdered face framed by blonde, corkscrew curls, followed by a lowcut lace dress and pair of high heeled patent leather shoes with rhinestone buckles. The wasp-waisted, bosomy creature carefully removed her white suede gloves.

"Sam, hand the parasol," she commanded in a throaty voice. Her colored chauffeur reached across the divided front seat, grasped a bright red "bumbershoot," swung it out and snapped it open in one sweeping movement. Lifting her dress daintily to reveal a well-rounded calf, she minced up the front steps of the hotel and disappeared inside.

"Hot diggity-dig, if that ain't something!" exclaimed one of the younger peg-trousered blades as he and his spellbound companions stared at the closing door.

Ten minutes later she reappeared, swept across the porch and down the steps, leaving a strong scent of French perfume in her wake. Sam reached for the parasol, closing it carefully. He assisted her onto the running board and into the rear seat, a flash of silk stocking rewarding the bug-eyed group watching every movement. Then the box door was slammed shut. The intriguing face appeared again for a moment from behind the isinglass side curtain. "Goddam it, Sam, we got the lot" carried clearly to the ears of the startled watchers who froze in shocked amazement.

Sam grinned, then hustled around to the front of the car. Freeing the crank from its leather keeper he pulled up sharply. A wheezing cough followed and the engine thundered into action. After rehanging the handle he vaulted over the false door into the driver's seat, released the outside spring-action brake and, with a grinding of gears, clutched off in a swirl of dust toward Tahoe City.

It was July 18, 1911, and Cherry de St. Maurice, notorious "madam" from Sacramento and owner of the finest "parlor house" on the Pacific Coast, had just bought herself the first lot in Tahoe Vista's new subdivision.[1]

Fifty years before Cherry de St. Maurice's bid for respectability through the acquisition of summer home property at Tahoe Vista, the northwest shore of Tahoe was an undeveloped forest and meadowland wilderness. What had originally been a Washoe and Paiute Indian trail leading from Martis Valley east over the divide to the lake became, in the years 1849-52, a branch of the Emigrant Trail.[2]

Consideration for reopening the "road" was given by Placer County surveyor Thomas A. Young in 1856, when he and his party traveled the route, but nothing was done to put it into shape.[3]

In the summer of 1865 D. H. Wright, wood contractor from Douglas County, Nevada, established Pine Grove Station at the present site of Tahoe Vista. Here Wright built a large log cabin, with hewn beams, rough plank flooring and conventional hand-split cedar shakes.[4] His cordwood camps

Tevis Paine

TAHOE — IN A FIT OF FREAKISH WRATH

Giant combers pounding Tahoe Vista's Casino in the fall of 1913, shortly after its completion. View shows present Highway 89 (right center) with several tents surrounding Tahoe Vista Hotel (not shown) on the hillside. Looking north.

fanned out up the mountain and with the completion of the Martis Valley-Hot Springs road in August of 1869, Wright was able to load lumber wagons in the summer and sledges during the winter, hauling logs and pine slabs over the pass to a ready market in the railroad town of Truckee.

When Walter Scott Hobart completed his Great Incline of the Sierra in 1879-80, Pine Grove Station became a marine terminal for saw logs chuted down from the high country near Martis Peak and the headwaters of Griff Creek. From here they were rafted into Crystal Bay and Hobart's Mill Creek sawmill.[5]

Although lumbering at Pine Grove continued through the late 1880's, extensive development of the land did not start until well after the turn of the century.

The Tahoe Development Company was formed in 1910 with Morris Brooks, president, and Charles W. Paine, secretary-manager. They purchased 1100 acres from Frank Brockway Alverson and finished lumber was hauled in by wagon from Truckee to build the Tahoe Vista Hotel.[6] This relatively large 80 by 30 foot lodge was another of the many lake establishments constructed by Tahoe City contractor Matt Green. Situated on a bluff overlooking the water, northwest of old Boiler Point, site of a steam-powered shingle mill in the 1880's, the hotel featured a massive stone fireplace which still stands today. It held six-foot logs that threw out enough heat to warm most of the 22 rooms in the building.[7]

On July 18, 1911, Tahoe Vista officially became a post office stop for the mail steamers, and building lots were laid out by the Tahoe Development Company in the same year, with Tahoe Vista Hotel becoming a vital part of the real estate promotion. In the spring of 1913 a casino was erected on the lakeshore below the main establishment. Two-thirds of its length extended out over the water and eight rooms on the second floor could accommodate additional guests.

The casino, or "social hall," fronted on Tahoe Vista's 200-foot L-shaped pier that had been extended out into deep water to allow docking of the 169-foot *Tahoe*. Diving from the second story windows into the lake was high sport for the hardier summer vacationists, and logically explained to timid onlookers "as fun, besides being the quickest way down."[8] Guests in the upstairs rooms reported that heavy blows out of the south built up ocean-size combers, giving them the feeling of being at sea on the bow of an ocean liner.

Eighty people could be accommodated at the resort when "Kenyon houses" and tents were spread throughout the grounds. Advertisements run in the summer of 1913 proudly listed the new "Tahoe Vista Inn" as "electric lighted and offering a dance floor second to none, with rates of $2.50 per day."[9]

Tahoe Vista was strictly a family retreat. Families from San Francisco, Stockton, Sacramento and Reno returned each year loaded down with valises, band boxes, suitcases and Saratoga trunks that contained everything from needle and thread to Irish frieze ulsters.

Although the hotel and casino were a financial success, the real estate venture did not show the expected results. A resident of Tahoe Vista ventured the thought that buyer resistance might be traced to the over-enthusiastic sale of the first lot as not until the property had been legally transferred was Miss Cherry de St. Maurice's true identity discovered. Word got around and prospective purchasers sometimes asked pointedly just what type of development was being promoted anyway? Another blunt condemnation of Tahoe Vista was recorded by a feminine correspondent in the late 1920's. "Many lots have been sold," she admitted, "but what's the good? It's too windy to build on them anyway."[10]

In the winter of 1922-23 the Tahoe Vista Hotel on the hill burned to the ground and the casino became the center of activity. Tahoe Vista continued as a mail stop for lake steamers until marine service was discontinued in May of 1941. Today the location serves as a hub for an expanding community that includes a general merchandise store, garage, remodeled casino, motels, summer homes and boat harbors. The adverse wind reported 25 years before appears to have blown nothing but good fortune across the sandy beaches of Tahoe Vista.

Tevis Paine

NEXT STOP—CARNELIAN BAY

Steamer TAHOE *making her regular mail and passenger stop at Tahoe Vista's pier during the summer of 1922. Photograph taken looking southwest toward Observatory Point (right background). Facade of Tahoe Vista Casino may be seen at the foot of the pier.*

SEVEN TONS WAS SOMETHING OF A RECORD

Bullwhacker Dave Gray (nearest wagon) with swamper Henry Keyser, their logging wagon and yoke of 12 oxen in the vicinity of Pig Pen Hill southwest of Agate Bay. Summer of 1885.

Chapter Forty-seven

AGATE BAY

Cub reporter Darling from the *Sacramento Union* stared in amazement at "seven hundred crazy people running around in the woods," and shook his head in disbelief. Earlier on that August day in 1863, he had crossed Donner Summit by freight wagon over the new Dutch Flat Wagon Road and, at Coburn's Station (Truckee), continued on horseback through Timi-lick Valley (Martis) to this "great silver strike."[1]

There was no question about it. This was the damndest flurry of mining excitement he had witnessed since the flareup at "Old Dry Diggin's" (Hangtown) in '49 and in patriotic deference to the Union cause the settlements had been named "The Red, White and Blue Mining District." Here hundreds of miners pitched camp during the summer of the same year near a draw appropriately known as "Monte Carlo Canyon." The largest "town" that the newsman could discover exploded into being practically overnight. Named Elizabethtown, for a Mrs. Elizabeth Gazley, it was located some seven miles northwest of Agate Bay over the Tahoe divide. To the east of Elizabethtown were Centerville, Modiosho, and Neptune City; all beehives of activity, but towns in name only.

One shrewd resident calling himself "Recorder of Claims" had thrown some saw logs together to form a crude lean-to against a granite outcropping where he struck a bonanza in fees when claims were staked out and tunnels driven in every direction. Assay certificates were produced ranging fantastically from $500 to $7,000 a ton for ore samples. Town lots soared to $200 each and word was passed around that "the richest ledges of silver yet found in the Sierra Nevada had been discovered."[2]

William Henry Brewer, a member of the Whitney survey party, also arrived at the mining district in August of 1863. He noted that the new excitement was just starting and that people were pouring in. Numerous prospecting holes were passed by him and his companions as they traveled west down the canyon where "a search, more or less, had been made for silver ore" but Brewer attributed the growth of this mushrooming metropolis to the "immense wealth of the Washoe mines being demonstrated and setting the people mad on the subject of silver."

His attention was first drawn to Centerville, where "notices of claims of town lots decorated trees, stakes, and stumps." He also commented ironically that "the town had as yet not been built." Brewer continued: "One cabin, hut I should say, with a brush roof is the sole representative of the *mansions* that are to be. Three miles below is Elizabethtown, a town of equal pretensions and more actual houses, boasting of two or three. We stopped at the main store, a shanty twelve feet square, made by driving stakes into the ground, siding two sides with split boards, and then covering with brush. Bacon, salt, pepper, tobacco, flour, and, more than all, poor whiskey, are kept.

"The miners have camps, generally some brush to keep off the sun and dew, but as often nothing. Some blankets lying beside the brook, a tin kettle, a tin cup, and bag of provisions, tell of the *home* of

SPAN OF FOUR ALONGSIDE THE GREASED LOG CHUTE

One of H. E. Casey's highline teams and two "skinners" above Sawmill Flat west of Agate Bay in July, 1893. Logs are loaded in the head of the chute, ready to move out downgrade.

MAHER OF MARTIS

Forest Ranger "Waddles" Maher (left) and friend in front of "Hotel de Chipmunk" atop 8665-foot Martis Peak in August of 1926. Looking south from the Station toward Tahoe.

George D. Oliver

some adventurous wandering man. We passed the town and camped some two miles beyond in Tim-i-lick Valley."[3]

Brewer did not mention Neptune City but the scribe from Sacramento pinpointed it as being five miles northwest of Agate Bay, considering it to be the "most promising of the mining settlements." Here he found "several drinking shops, eating houses, a baker and a butcher, with forty to fifty miners constituting the 'city's' population." He further stated "The Truckee River has been bridged on a line with the Dutch Flat Wagon Road, and connects with the camp following the old Emigrant Road to the shores of north Lake Bigler."[4]

The newsman left the Red, White, and Blue Mining District with an optimistic view regarding its prospects; however, Brewer, a noted chemist and geologist, recognized the "strike" for what it was —worthless.

Within a year the district was deserted. An eyewitness from the *Carson Appeal* wrote that the "diggings now resembled a tomb, just as though the miners had been scalped by savages, buried by a volcano or run for their lives" and the surrounding forest undergrowth was already beginning to close in on sagging shacks, slag heaps and crumbling shafts. The mining camps bordering Middle Martis Creek were finished, never to rise again.

During this period in the early 1860's, Agate Bay, also known at that time as Little Cornelian, sprang into life for a few short months supplying trout and wild hay to the camps. Stone from the mountainside north of the bay was used by the miners for their fireplaces and cabin foundations, but nothing was built at Agate in the way of a permanent settlement.[5]

Eight years prior to the "silver strike" George H. Goddard, a member of Marlette and Day's California Wagon Road and Boundary Survey party, had used the shore of the bay for signal fire markers to determine State and Territory boundary bearings. Here the expedition found "agate and crystals on the water's edge" and named the bay Agate.[6]

During the next two and one-half decades the sheltered inlet remained largely undeveloped, but the spring of 1881 saw extensive logging operations getting underway. Wagon roads and logging chutes were run deep into the canyons and up the mountains to the north and west. Systematic cutting proceeded up the slopes past what later became "Sawmill Flat" into the high country in the vicinity of Martis Peak. In this year H. E. Casey, logging contractor from Truckee, obtained a substantial saw log and cordwood contract from the Sierra Nevada Wood and Lumber Company at Incline. He assembled his V-booms and loaded his barges in the protected bay, towing them to Sand Harbor with the "one teakettle power" steam tug *Niagara*.[7]

Agate Bay had its last commercial spurt of the century in 1896-97 but, surprisingly enough, logs and cordwood played no part in the operation. The Walter Scott Hobart estate interests were moving all of their equipment from Mill Creek and the Great Incline Tramway to a new location, Hobart Mills, north of Truckee. General Manager John Bear Overton had decided it would be easier to haul the hundreds of tons of machinery over the Martis Creek grade 21 miles to the new site, rather than take it by way of the Truckee River Canyon.[8] Logger "Winnie" Smith from Tahoe City was awarded the contract. Locomotives, logging cars, trams and rail iron from the tramway and shoreline railroad, along with dismantled machinery out of the sawmill, were loaded aboard 104-foot cordwood barges at Incline. Then they were towed by steam tugs across the north end of Tahoe to Agate Bay, which by then had become known as "Bay City."[9] Shacks for the workmen, corrals for the horses and mules, unloading ramps and a wharf had been hurriedly built on the shore, where Smith and his crew skidded the equipment onto logging wagons and iron-runnered sledges for the long trip over the mountain to Hobart Mills. Again activity at the bay was limited to a few months and at the conclusion of the operation temporary buildings and ramps were removed.[10]

North of Agate Bay now stands the fire lookout ranger station high on Martis Peak. Here for 30 summer seasons after the turn of the century lived a locally famous character, Frank Maher, better known as "Waddles" due to his rolling gait. Visitors arriving at the rocky summit in the 1920's were greeted by a sign reading "Hotel de Chipmunk," for Maher's wind-buffeted station literally swarmed with chipmunks who came scampering at his whistle. He had named each of the little animals after famous personages, such as Theodore Roosevelt and Jack Dempsey, who signed the register over the years.

"Waddles" spent his winters in Carson City, climbing to Martis Peak's 8665-foot summit in March of each year to carry on his lonely observations until the first snows fell. Canned goods were his staple and wandering sheepherders furnished him goat's milk from time to time. When the mailman failed to make his once a month call, the tower's flag could be seen fluttering mournfully at half mast. Frank Maher's manner of dress was described as a "rather limp shirt, immediately followed by a pair of tattered trousers, hanging from his barrel-like form on wide suspenders, with chipmunks for accessories."[11]

During the mid-1930's Agate Bay again began to develop, this time on a more substantial basis. Summer homes and piers now ring the western shoreline and motels stand among the pines along its northern extremity.

Chapter Forty-eight

CARNELIAN BAY

T HE BLOATED, shapeless body of a man dressed in the remnants of a fine broadcloth suit and expensive high-heeled boots was found floating in the scalding water 3,000 feet below the streets of Virginia City. It presented anything but a welcome sight to the 3 a.m. shift of deep-rock miners coming on duty in the bowels of the Savage Mine. However, the men fished the corpse from the sump and an unsuccessful attempt was made to identify it. A check was made of the miners' union rolls but all the men were accounted for. Visitors could not enter the mine without a permit and it was impossible to reach the lower levels without being challenged. Where had the body come from?

To obtain the answer to this enigma, it is necessary to return to the hectic days of 1869-70. At that time the papers were headlining reports of violent stock market fluctuations and this near-panic had a direct bearing on the discovery of the man's body.

In the fall of 1869 a tired and jaded San Francisco stock speculator named William Meeker decided to take a vacation at Carnelian Bay. He had lost a fortune on California Street and was trying to regain his health. While placidly fishing a mile offshore, he noticed that his boat was drifting in a circle in the center of which was a mass of churning debris. The astonished Meeker was certain that there must be a hole in the bottom of the lake. He hastily put in to shore, where he selected a piece of wood on which he carved his initials, "W. M." Tying a line to the block, he then rowed cautiously back to the whirlpool and heaved the block into its vortex. The line paid out with a rush. Then the boat jerked and the rope broke, its end snaking down through the transparent water.

Meeker was convinced. After some moments of intense self-communion, he rowed back to shore, gathered his belongings and left for San Francisco.

There he sought out Colonel Clair, the most astute and unscrupulous trader on the exchange, and took him into his confidence. The two men pored over maps and survey reports and discovered that the level of Tahoe had dropped a foot since large-scale pumping began on the Comstock. That proved it. There was no time to lose. Meeker must go to Virginia City at once.

Disguised as a miner and armed with a recommendation from the colonel, he secured a job in the Savage as station tender at the sump. There he waited patiently for several days, and was finally elated to see his initialed piece of pine wood bobbing about on the steaming surface of the water. Meeker immediately left his job and hastened back to San Francisco by fast train for consultation with the colonel.

Within a week he was back at Carnelian Bay, where he hired carpenters to build a flat-bottomed boat with a small cabin enclosing a deck well—a fishing boat, he said. When the strange craft was completed, Meeker towed it to Tahoe City, where he loaded aboard a consignment of bulky and mysterious crates and packages. Colonel Clair came up unobtrusively from San Francisco to join him and

"HERE I'LL LIVE TO BE A CENTURY PLANT . . ."

Dr. Bourne's Hygienic Establishment, CASTLE KEEP, blanketed by heavy snows in January, 1874. The high bed of a light wagon provided winter storage for Bourne's skiff EVA (center foreground). This clapboard house became Carnelian Bay Hotel in 1876 and, 70 years later, The White House.

the two proceeded back to Carnelian Bay with their flatboat, which they anchored well offshore, ostensibly for a long spell of fishing and relaxation.

There, inside the cabin, they were able to go about their work unobserved. A slot in the roof threw sunlight upon an ingenious series of mirrors in which they were able to study the reflection of the lake floor at their leisure. They found the hole at last—a circular orifice about four feet in diameter. Then they dressed down the butt of a five-foot log to conical shape and secured it to a heavy chain which in turn was attached to a windlass inside the deckhouse. Carefully they lowered the log butt through the well and centered it in position above the hole. They lowered away again and the chain and log sank into the vortex. Suddenly the tension on the chain increased. The handles of the windlass flew out of control, whirled wildly for a few moments and then stopped dead.

The plug was in Lake Tahoe! But could it be pulled out again? Meeker and Clair strained on their windlass, but the stopper would not budge, so great was the pressure. Finally they bored a hole in the windlass shaft and by means of the slow leverage of crowbars, they were able to overpower the suction and lift the log. After a few hours of practice, Colonel Clair was satisfied. He left Meeker on board with instructions and went back to San Francisco.

During the next ten days the San Francisco exchanges were astonished to see the brokerage firm of Goodman and Crowley recklessly buying up stock in the worthless Savage Mine. Five—ten—fifteen —twenty—thirty-five thousand shares were snapped up by senior partner Joe Goodman in one lot after another. When he finally kited his bid for 50,000 shares, the selling stopped short. There was something afoot. The street was in a turmoil and the wires to Virginia City were hot with coded telegrams. All replies showed that the Savage was still full of water and that no new ore bodies had been struck. Colonel Clair, who was careful to sell small dribbles of stock during the excitement, circulated about town belittling the run and declaring that the stock would never yield a penny until the water was out of the shaft. Everybody listened with respect and the suspicious traders began selling again.

A week later came the unbelievable news that the pumps had cleared the Savage and several adjoining shafts as well. Prices began to skyrocket and Colonel Clair cleaned up a cool million.

Then, with the pumps idle and everybody overconfident, a tremendous flood of water struck the Savage again, overwhelming the terrified miners. Prices plummeted to the bottom. The colonel, who was selling short, cleaned up another million. He was very cool, very assured, and his reputation on the street, already great, grew fantastically. There followed a dizzying succession of rises and breaks in the Savage stock, with the colonel making fabulous fortunes at every turn. Meeker was at Tahoe, working steadily at the windlass, now lowering the plug to give the Savage a chance to drain, now raising it to send the baffled miners running for safety before the sudden surge of water.

Finally, one beautiful evening as the happy Meeker was about to crank the windlass and pull the plug out of the lake, a cheery hand clapped him on the shoulder. It was the colonel. He wanted to know how she was working, and Meeker assured him that she was working fine, just fine. The colonel told him that his share—a million dollars—was on deposit in the Nevada Bank. Meeker was stupefied with delight and gazed with rapture at the windlass.

"How big the moon looks over yonder!" exclaimed the colonel. Meeker turned obligingly to look. Something struck him on the head and he knew no more. The colonel tied a substantial weight to the body and lowered it into the well. For a few seconds he watched in the dim light as it whirled madly in narrowing circles. Then it sank like a rock. Colonel Clair rubbed his hands, turned to the windlass and let down the plug. And that was how the body of the elegantly dressed gentleman happened to get into the Savage sump.[1]

This brilliant tall tale, masterfully concocted by Washoe journalist Sam Davis, was undoubtedly prompted by the newspaper report of a strange occurrence that took place on Carnelian Bay in July of 1883.[2] Walter Coombs, head steward at the Brockway Hot Springs Hotel, and two other fishermen were trolling for trout several hundred yards offshore in 20 feet of crystal-clear water. Without warning, their boat began revolving in a circle, spinning faster and faster. Peering over the side, they discovered they were caught on the edge of a whirlpool and Coombs noticed what appeared to be a hole in the rocky bed of the lake bottom. The group immediately assumed that this must be the lake outlet rumored by fishermen to exist over the last two decades.

Tying a line to a gunny sack, they threw it into the revolving water and watched it sink into the middle of the whirlpool. Then the line was jerked from Coomb's hands. Both sack and line went straight to the bottom and disappeared in the 30-foot-wide aperture.

This phenomenon was construed as factual evidence that tremendous quantities of water were escaping from the lake and, in all probability, the source of the steaming waters plaguing the miners

in the sumps of the Comstock Lode.[3] But startling happenings at Carnelian over the years were not limited to the mysterious.

The bay had been named by the Whitney survey party in the summer of 1860 after a variety of chalcedony (semi-precious stones) they discovered lying in abundance along the pebbled beach. Originally known as "Cornelian Bay," it stretches north from Observatory Point to Manzanita Promontory.[4] Not until the 1880's was the spelling changed to "Carnelian." In the spring of 1871, the bay gained local prominence with the construction of "Dr. Bourne's Hygienic Establishment," a rival spa to William "Billy" Campbell's Hot Springs three and a half miles to the northeast.[5]

Dr. Bourne had formerly run health clinics in San Francisco and Sacramento, featuring "fresh vegetable juices and complete abstinence from stimulants."[6] Convinced that the rarefied, pure mountain air and "hot and cold mineral springs," found at Cornelian, were the answer to healthful living, he moved to the lake. Here Bourne could offer curing, bathing and fine fishing.

An assured location for catching the famous Tahoe Royal Silver trout was the influx of Boston Creek (Watson), and one of the doctor's first guests, Charles B. Turrill of San Francisco, proved it by bringing to net a seventeen and a half pounder on his initial boating trip to the spot.[7]

Dr. Bourne insisted that his patrons participate in healthful activities and constantly urged them to take long, invigorating walks, tempting them with the likelihood of finding red and yellow gem stones on the beach at the same time.[8] Some of the good doctor's patients could not walk, so they were told to "breathe deeply of the mountain air and rock diligently in their armchairs on the resort's front porch." In one instance a female healthseeker had heeded Bourne's suggestion to search for stones, only to rush back in a great state of agitation to report that, instead of finding anything of value, she had lost her $300 diamond ring.[9] Guests and patients who previously could not move without assistance, stampeded in a body toward the beach. This time no urging from Dr. Bourne was needed.

In the summer of 1873 the high-sounding name "Cornelian Springs Sanatoria" was adopted, and the aged and infirm flocked to the resort. Two seasons before, journalistic agitation had been stirred up concerning the "Springs" by those masters of satire, Dan DeQuille from the *Virginia City Territorial Enterprise* and Sam Davis, editor of the *Carson Morning Appeal*. They traded verbal punches over the name "Cornelian." DeQuille argued that the name of the bay stemmed from the "mineral or semi-precious gem, cornelian." Davis scoffed at this interpretation, advising his readers "that it was obviously named for the wild Cornelian cherry trees that dotted its shores." Both agreed, quite remarkably, that the bay was located on the northwest shore of Tahoe, failing at least to confuse it with Carnelian Hot Springs (Brockway) to the northeast.[10]

On June 27, 1874, it was reported that Dr. Bourne, by then known as the "Hermit of Carnelian Bay," was exerting his best efforts to foist the name "Lake Sanatoria" on Lake Tahoe. Fortunately for succeeding generations, this whimsy was ignored.

During the winter months, the doctor lived alone in his rambling log and clapboard house known as "Castle Keep," without a neighbor for miles. The *Truckee Republican* observed that he devoted his time to "literary penmanship and thermometrical pursuits," interpreted as meaning that in addi-

---

Author's collection

CARNELIAN STONES COVERED THE BEACH

This panoramic view of Carnelian Bay, taken from the south above what is now Highway 89,
shows "Flick's Point," sometimes "Manzanita" (center) Martis Peak
(left background), Tahoe Vista and King's Beach (right) in the summer of 1907.
Carnelian Bay Hotel, pier and outbuildings stand on the shoreline at the foot of Carnelian Meadow (far left).

C. O. Valentine

A DEEP-THROATED WHISTLE ANNOUNCED THE CARNELIAN LANDING

Looking northeast across Carnelian Bay from the shoreline south of Carnelian Bay Hotel at passengers on the pier waiting to board the steamer TAHOE *rounding the point. July 14, 1912.*

tion to writing he kept a detailed record of the region's snowfall, air and water temperatures, and rise and fall of Tahoe's lake level. This information was sent out each month to Truckee for publication, and Dr. Bourne's greatest hope was that he would, God willing, live to be a century plant on the shores of the bay.

By the spring of 1876 Cornelian Bay Hotel had become a regular stop for the *Governor Stanford*, and excursionists were reported combing the shoreline for cornelian stones and taking the water cure.[11] "Doc" Williamson, the well known dipsomaniac from Truckee, was also sojourning at the establishment, "enjoying a brief spell of delirium tremens." On the 4th of July of this year "Old Settler Bourne" (he had now been at the lake all of six years) notified the press that one Homer Young had been surprised by a hunter named Hammond and shot through the chest. It was explained that Hammond mistook Young for a deer while he and a friend were working up Cornelian Creek to divert water past their new log cabin. When the *Stanford* docked on the afternoon of the shooting, the boy's body was sent to the Hot Springs for transference to Truckee by wagon.

The bay continued as a popular spot for excursionists and anglers who came from all points on Tahoe to this choice fishing location. What was probably the largest flotilla of marine sightseers ever assembled at one time on the lake moved into the bay late in the summer of 1881. Sixteen rowboats, accompanied by the *Meteor* and the *Governor Stanford*, left the Custom House wharf and Pomin and Morgan's pier early in the morning. They were filled with parasol-shaded young ladies and bowler-hatted gentlemen plus a generous sprinkling of chaperones. The day was spent digging for "stones" and picnicking on the shore, and at sundown the entourage was taken in tow by the steamers and towed grandly back to Tahoe.

Rancher James Cleland acquired most of Dr. Bourne's holdings upon the "Old Settler's" death in the mid-1880's. Cleland had one of the first mechanical hay presses seen on the north end of the lake with which he baled timothy grass on his meadowland bordering Carnelian Creek. He also proudly announced in 1887 that he had grown carrots 5 inches in diameter, along with rutabagas and potatoes twice the size of those grown elsewhere and then astounded residents in the town of Truckee by producing these outsize wonders for all to admire.[12]

By the year 1889, Carnelian was listed as one of the lake's permanent settlements. Although it was more readily reached by steamer, a stage and wagon road running between Tahoe City and the Hot Springs passed through Carnelian; also a branch logging road from the divide above Martis Valley continued down the southern ridge to the bay.

Tahoe's second bona fide newspaper, the *Sierra Nevada Tourist*, appeared in the summer of 1891. Edited and published at Carnelian Bay by one Sisson, formerly of Reno, it consisted of five columns printed on thin, tinted stock. Like the *Tahoe Tattler*, brought out a decade before, this tissue sheet struggled for more than ten months and then publication was discontinued.

By the year 1896, the three Flick brothers—Joseph, Nicholas and William—had acquired most of the Carnelian Bay land fronting on the water. Their holdings included Dr. Bourne's old establishment, now known as Carnelian Bay Hotel, the post office, general store, cottages and wharf. Described as "eccentric pioneer characters who had a deep-seated distrust for banks and banking," they kept an iron strongbox known to have contained as high as $10,000 in gold at one time with which to pay off their creditors.[13]

But the Flicks will be recalled in Tahoe history for a coincidence of facts worthy of a Ripley's "Believe It or Not." All three were bachelors; all were born on Christmas day—William in 1841, Joseph in 1847 and Nicholas in 1851. William died first in April of 1929, and Joseph and Nicholas passed away on April 9 and 19, respectively, nine years later.[14]

The brothers had fished commercially on the lake until substantial profits were realized from the sale of their lakefront property in 1909-10. At this time the Carnelian Bay Improvement Company was formed, headed by J. Humiston of Tulare, California, and two Reno businessmen, F. O. Norton and L. P. Delano.[15] The new company embarked on an extensive subdivision program. A large hotel and inland harbor were projected, streets were laid out running down to the bay and summer cottages were constructed. Water from a mountain spring, 1700 feet above and west of the bay, was piped to each structure. "Gasoline buggies" now bounced over the dirt road to Tahoe City and a market and store at Carnelian made it almost self-sufficient. During the summer season the steamer *Tahoe* made a daily stop at the pier, and in winter the *Nevada* took over, dropping off mail and supplies.[16]

The Branch family now owned the way station, store and post office purchased from the Flick brothers. Orin Branch commercially fished the north shore of Tahoe, bringing in a record catch of 30 pounds of trout in one hour's trolling during the fall of 1914.[17]

Carnelian Bay now offers two stores, an inland boat harbor, marine livery and motels. Old Carnelian Bay Hotel and post office has become a recognized restaurant. It was here that Dr. Bourne originally settled with the hope of becoming a "century plant" on the curving sweep of Carnelian Bay.

CORDWOOD CARRIER AT CARNELIAN

Earliest known photograph of Carnelian Bay taken in the summer of 1878 and showing cordwood barge at finger pier with pine slabs stacked along the shoreline. Photographer's horse (center foreground).

Velma Comstock Eden

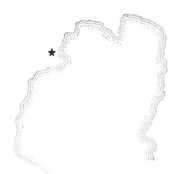

Chapter Forty-nine

DOLLAR'S POINT

As BEDRAGGLED cordwood cutter Griffin bellied up to the bar at J. B. Campbell's overwater Custom House, the group of brass rail-standers melted away as though his unwelcome presence heralded the arrival of a great plague. If this bothered "Old Griff" it was not noticeable. He pounded on the polished hardwood and called loudly for "three fingers of the usual."

After pouring and gulping his drink, Griff turned and lumbered over to Campbell's pot-bellied stove on the far side of the saloon. The men lining the bar slowly closed ranks. One of them squinted over his shoulder at the unsavory character and muttered, "That land squatter Griffin just don't believe in changing clothes mor'n once a year—says it's only for city folk." Then his voice rose in a shout, "Hoopin' Harry, just look at him now!"

With a detached air, Griffin had begun to pluck small crawling objects from the exposed parts of his anatomy, punctuating this plucking practice with violent scratchings and back rubbings against the flue of the squat stove.

The men watched Griff in fascinated amazement, but they held their distance and at times their noses. Then another customer spoke up, "Hey, Griffin, why don't you go on back to your lousy broken down shack on your lousy point?" Griff continued his bizarre efforts with the utmost unconcern. Some 15 minutes later he left his warm retreat and ambled out of the entrance-way.

Thus, in the late summer of 1872, did the "boys" at Tahoe City retaliate in their contempt and saddle the promontory northeast of town with the derogatory appellation—"Old Lousy."[1]

Originally the point that forms the southern extremity of Carnelian Bay had been called Chinquapin by the Washoe Indians.[2]

Shortly after the elbow of land was named in Griffin's dubious honor a third and more auspicious designation of the point was coined when James Lick, the San Francisco philanthropist, offered to appropriate $1,000,000 for the construction of a large observatory on the site.

Lick had been impressed by the clarity of the atmosphere and the comparatively light snowfall at the point during the winter months. An added incentive was the boost given by Duane L. Bliss and Henry M. Yerington of Glenbrook, who owned a half section of land at "Old Lousy" and generously agreed to donate 140 acres to James Lick if his plans materialized.

Lick's proposed gift of such a large sum of money for a telescope and astral dome in the confines of the State of California was bound to create a furor. A controversial storm immediately broke in the California and Nevada newspapers.

In December of 1873 the *San Francisco Bulletin* announced its unconditional sponsorship of the project, pointing out that: "Lick Observatory will be situated 300 feet above Tahoe on a beautiful peninsula of land with its own stately trees to form the nucleus of a magnificent park." The paper's cor-

VARIOUSLY — CHINQUAPIN, LOUSY, OBSERVATORY AND DOLLAR'S

On the wooded Point (center foreground) philanthropist James Lick planned to place an observatory in 1873, but the site was changed to Mt. Hamilton, California. This photograph was taken June 27, 1909, north of what is now Lake Forest. Looking northeast.

respondent continued: "The point known as 'Old Lousy' has a fine harbor, and 40,000 gallons of pure spring water is available every 24 hours—with Boston Creek (Watson) only two and one-half miles away, and another fine stream (Burton Creek) little more than a mile."

Ominous editorial thunder was rolling out of Nevada, however, and the *Virginia City Chronicle* pointed to Mount Davidson (then more commonly known as Sun Mountain or Peak) as being unquestionably the choice of any thinking astronomer. The *Chronicle* contended that the summit of their mountain was the logical location for the observatory, insisting, "it lacks the humidity which we are positive exists at Tahoe, and besides hadn't the point been named Lousy in the first place?"[3]

The San Francisco and Washoe papers continued to toss the plum around and at one time even jointly supported Donner Summit as a compromise location. Such an unprecedented harmony of editorial opinion, heretofore practically unheard of, confused the public. People felt better when the *Gold Hill News* issued a thumping denial: "The observatory belongs only upon a mountain in the Carson Range of our Silver State."

So went the editorial tug-of-war concerning the location of James Lick's observatory with claims and counterclaims being bandied back and forth. Ultimately the victory went—unexpectedly—to those who were backing a dark horse in the spirited competition. What was termed a "miserable goat hill in the Pacific Range" was finally chosen as the coveted site. Mount Hamilton, above the Santa Clara Valley in California, had won out. The bidding was over and residents of Tahoe, Truckee, Carson City and Virginia City swallowed the bitter pill. No further mention of "that Observatory" appeared in the regional newspapers, but its name remained on the Point.

Early lake residents recall that the location was thick with giant sugar pine and cedar, running to the water's edge. In 1884 the Glenbrook mills reached across Tahoe to Observatory and systematically timbered the 337 acres owned by the C. and T. L. and F. Company.[4] The promontory and surrounding waters continued to offer excellent hunting and fishing in spite of the commercial activity existing. In the late 1880's two young couples left Tahoe City in a skiff, catching 34 trout on the way to the Point and shooting mountain grouse when they arrived. While spitting the birds over a roaring fire that evening they gazed up at the Milky Way and counted the constellations in the clear sky. One of the youthful charmers observed with flattering directness that "the man in the moon was too far away to attract her, preferring the gentleman beside her to anything that remote and intangible."[5]

The D. L. Bliss interests took title to Observatory Point when they formed their Lake Tahoe Railway and Transportation Company in 1898, and upon the death of Duane L. Bliss in 1906 the land was turned over to his heirs. A decade later Mrs. Lora Moore Knight of St. Louis acquired the acreage. Here she built her first home on Tahoe, actually a cluster of chalets surrounding a main structure, which contained dining room, living room and kitchen. To this establishment Mrs. Knight gave the name Wychwood.[6]

In 1927 the property changed hands once more. It was purchased by Robert Stanley Dollar, Sr., San Francisco shipping magnate, who also added another tract of land to the west of Highway 28.

This secluded area, which includes the sheltered cove north of the Point, is considered one of the choicest residential sites on Lake Tahoe.

After the sale to Dollar, Mrs. Knight purchased the horseshoe sweep of land and the island at the southwest end of Emerald Bay. Here she erected her world-famous "Vikingsholm Castle" that was completed in 1929.[7]

Observatory Point, or Dollar's as it is more commonly known today, runs offshore to form a knife-like dividing line. Here the clear snow water of the lake drops from a shallow 25 to 40 feet on the south side to a depth of nearly 600 feet within 50 yards of the northern slope extension. In brilliant mid-morning sunlight, a marine viewer may see, through the glassy smooth surface waters of the lake, the subterranean mountainside falling away in a shamrock green sheer to merge and be lost in Tahoe's deep blue. Another natural wonder, the "Sunken Cliffs," is discernible on calm days beneath the water on the lake bottom in a direct line between the Point and Tahoe Tavern pier.

Although equal to any marine fairyland in the world, the cliff's amazing detail has largely escaped the notice of Tahoe's visitors. Hundreds of thousands of years ago, lava floes moved down from the slopes of Mount Pluto, high on the western rim of the basin, and fanned out along the present lake floor south of the Point. This underwater plateau is interrupted abruptly by two ledges, one-quarter of a mile apart. They serpentine far out into Tahoe and are like miniature Grand Canyons.

Faced off, polished and honeycombed over the centuries by the grinding action of sand and rocks agitated by the water, the lava has eroded into fantastic patterns of stony filigree. A few yards farther and the submarine formations assume a resemblance to amphitheaters flanked by broad, flat steps.

Along these lake floor water ridges, vast overhangs of volcanic rock conceal shadowy recesses that suddenly expand into submerged valleys, only to narrow again into perpendicular cliffs. "Footprints," spaced far apart in stately procession, are observable here on Tahoe's floor, as though some prehistoric mammoth walked the lava shelf ages before the lake's inception.

Shades of "Pop" Church, the old Tahoe-Truckee stage driver with the urge to christen every rock, cliff and road turn-out on the Truckee Canyon turnpike with such "handles" as Devil's Slide, Bluff and Rockpile—Church would have had an etymological field day at the "Sunken Cliffs," with so many features to be named.[8]

When traveling slowly in a boat across this fairyland of fantasy the lake bottom seems to be only an arm's length away instead of some forty feet below. This creates an illusion that the viewer is falling off a mountainside one moment and going aground the next, as submerged palisades appear to rush up and then drop breathtakingly away again. Here the symmetry and casual perfection of nature's artistry are dramatically preserved for all time, to be seen—and magnified—through the crystal transparency of Tahoe's waters.

UNDERWAY WITH THE STARTERS GUN

Ability to finish a race, not speed, was the prime consideration nearly half a century ago. Here a fleet of speedsters churn down the course on July 4, 1915. Observatory Point to the northeast.

C. O. Valentine

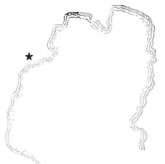

Chapter Fifty

LAKE FOREST

Homer D. Burton, proprietor of Burton's Island Farm and Hotel, rocked comfortably back and forth in a spindly wicker chair.[1] The porch upon which he was sitting ran the length of the establishment. Gingerbread trim and mid-Victorian scrollwork decorated the front of the pretentious two-story house, and pewter catches secured shuttered windows. "It's very tony," he had been told by his admiring guests, and he was in complete agreement.

His head was now buried in a three-day-old edition of the *Truckee Republican* and the last thing he wanted was to be disturbed. He flipped a page. The date in the upper left hand corner showed it to be June 14, 1884.

Past the island and across Tahoe a brilliance of color lay against the Carson Range of the Sierra.[2] Deep shadows pushed upwards from the motionless water toward high peaks and a flaming sky. The screen door opened quietly behind Burton, and his second wife, a tall Puritanical-appearing woman with flattened hair done up in a bun at the back of her head, called softly, "Homer, come to dinner."

"Yes, my dear," was the listless reply. Burton continued to rock. Five minutes passed and she called again.

"Mr. Burton, dinner is on the table." A flintiness had crept into her voice.

"Yes, my dear," came the detached response again.

Then there was silence, except for a sighing wheeze from the nodding head and the creaking of the chair. Several more minutes ticked slowly by. Suddenly a porch window banged open. Irish lace curtains were whipped aside and Mrs. Burton's face burst through. Her normally well-modulated voice rose in a shrill scream, "Burton, you old bald-headed son-of-a-bitch, come to dinner! Now!"

Homer erupted from his chair as though shot from a cannon and scurried into the house.[3]

This incident is recorded as one of the few times Homer Burton took orders instead of giving them. He was a consummate extrovert and had gained a reputation as the "tallest teller of tales" in the north Tahoe region. These products of his imagination, however, were veined with enough truth to make them seem credible even to the local residents who knew better. When foisted upon a gullible public they became established fact. During the summer of 1890 a valley newspaper referred to Burton as ". . . that old moss-back at Tahoe, one of the first white men to settle at the lake and now a resident for thirty years."[4]

There is no question that Burton knew the Tahoe country intimately, and such was his inventive genius that he could top any story going the rounds at a moment's notice, be it fact or fiction. His overseeing of the Island Farm allowed this verbiage vendor of the High Sierra ample leisure to troll for the flashing silver trout in the lake and hunt deer, brown bear and mountain lion through the dense pine forests. It also offered him the solitude of vast back country, where in his lonely trampings he could

Author's collection

TUGBOAT OR TERRA FIRMA?

Burton's "floating island" resembled a steam vessel when this photograph was taken, in the fall of 1911, from a bluff north of Tahoe City. The houses (left center) are part of the old wood camp, south of the mouth of Burton's Creek. Burton's home stood in the grove of aspen to the left of the Island. Beyond rise the slides on Incline Mountain.

fabricate, and sometimes experience, those extravagant happenings passed on to his guests during the long summer evenings.

The highest accolade in Homer Burton's book was to be ranked with those other "Forty-niner bah-stahd's"—Ephraim "Yank" Clement and Captain "Dick" Barter,[5] for when it came to the spinning of yarns created from unadulterated fiction, these three were recognized as expert craftsmen.

Old Burton ran a summer boarding house and campground. It was a favorite retreat for ailing ministers of the gospel who wished to soak up the high altitude sunshine and clear the fog of civilization from their tired minds.[6] They had chosen the right spot. Given 24 hours, host Burton could rekindle the spark of well-being in the most worn-out patron. He would start by recalling for them the early days at Tahoe when nothing stirred but the "wily Indian and fierce grizzly," carrying through year by year to the 1890's. His stories were spiced with colorful and explosive anecdotes, calculated to bolster the spirits of the timid and leave his listeners in such a state of mental exhaustion that no energy was left to think about their personal problems.

Burton's Island Farm could accommodate upwards of 30 guests and, as his property extended over 300 acres, he often magnanimously bestowed ten acres here and 20 acres there, to certain appreciative visitors. He is said to have told them that it was theirs to do with as they saw fit, provided no timber was cut and, most important of all, that they returned the land to him before leaving Island Farm. This double-edged humor usually appealed to all but the thickest heads.[7]

Anything that was the "biggest" always intrigued Homer. As a consequence, he spent a part of his summer and fall seasons developing and cultivating the "largest garden vegetables, highest buckwheat, and the most profuse timothy hay to be found in the Tahoe region." When Jim Cleland of Carnelian Bay claimed the same distinction, Burton went a step farther, insisting that his farm products were the finest in these "Yew-Nited States"; and people looked, admired, bought and agreed with him. One white turnip out of his well-tended garden ran a whopping 16½ inches in diameter, and buyers in

Truckee swore it wasn't possible even though they had seen it with their own eyes. His crop of oats grew to a height topping eight feet one season, and he vowed it would have gone another three feet if Burton Creek hadn't gone dry.

"It's the rich soil, snow water, mountain air, the Almighty's wish, and of course me," he would say modestly when questioned about his phenomenal successes.[8]

The old man enjoyed nothing more than to gather a group around his campfire on the shore, peer across the burning pine slabs past his shadowy island and regale his guests with tales of the olden days at the lake. Always included was the fantasy about Tahoe drying up during the summer of 1864.

"All that water slipped out through a slit in the bottom to Carson and Washoe Valleys," he would say thoughtfully, "and it sure watered down them farmers, you bet! Why, I collected over seventy-odd fifty-dollar slugs of silver melted up by old man Knox's miners at Squaw in '63," he would squeak dramatically in his high-pitched voice, "all, mind you, from the hulk of the schooner *Iron Duke*, and it's too bad more didn't sink on this here mountain ocean, 'cause if they had I could have bought up all the timber and grazing land from the 'Sierry' top to Sacramento City."[9]

Burton even reached back to the fall of 1859 to tell his incredulous listeners about the record haul of lake trout, never since equalled.

"Why I took 626 fish, all in a matter of four measly hours," he would insist. "Them boats was lined out in a solid string between my fishing grounds off of Chinquapin Point and the shore, taking them in as fast as I could pull my hooks. A couple of dinghies even swamped in flat water, they was so full of silversides, and but for that I would have had a count of mor'n a thousand."

Then he would add: "I plumb retired for two whole seasons after that as them fish, salted down in barrels, brought two bits a pound at the south end of the lake during the fall months."[10]

Burton could shift from a fish story to another of his favorites without so much as wasting a breath. He always claimed to have participated in quelling the Paiute uprising in Nevada during the spring of 1860, and been with Major William Ormsby as a member of his rag-tail brigade when over half of the volunteers were massacred at Pyramid Lake "before Captain Crook and his battalion from Virginia City chased them red savages into the Black Rock Desert."[11]

Burton contended that Ormsby's original contingent had been "sorely misdirected into a slaughter pen," when common judgment would have prevented their falling into the Paiute's trap.

"Why, even the marksmanship of that motley array of horse thieves, bar-standers and hard rock drillers was just too dam' awful," he would moan, holding his head in both hands. "I seen one stumpy Paiute buck wrapped in a bright red blanket hightail it through the mesquite toward a ridge and— would you believe it?—all five companies of men let go at him with six guns, Sharps rifles and a howitzer—Rumpf! Bang! Crack!—but that redskin just ducked and dodged up the hill skedaddling over the top without a bullet striking him."[12]

Questioned as to why he hadn't picked off the Indian himself, Burton's scornful answer was, "Chrize, I was too goddam taken up with standing off the whole Paiute war party while my sow-headed companions missed at target practice."

Everybody heartily agreed that "Old Burt" certainly could tell those long stories. He had the undisputed proof of one tale that he told and retold each season. Holding a letter personally signed by President Ulysses S. Grant, he would wave it wildly in front of an astonished group of his guests.

"This here says I caught, and had delivered, one cut-throat scarlet-gilled trout to the President of these here Yew-Nited States and, God bless 'im, he had it for Easter dinner, he did, all 29¾ pounds of the monster."[13]

It was difficult for anyone to slip a word in edgewise whenever the old pioneer launched on one of his story-telling extravaganzas, but many of his more persistent patrons sometimes stayed up most of the night cudgeling their memories for a tall one that would allow them at least an even start with Burton the following day. They should have been forewarned by past experience. The old master generally knocked them out in the initial round of any verbal bout.

Two of Tahoe's first sailing vessels, the gaff-rigged sloop *Edith Batty* and the smaller *Pride of the Lake*, were placed in service by Homer Burton in 1859-60.[14] Immediately he prefaced his name with the title "Captain." The windier the day, the more this fresh water salt liked it. Bets were often laid on the chances of his coming back from foolhardy expeditions into the teeth of Tahoe's infrequent, but deadly, east winds. A plunging white sail returning across the lake with the "Captain" miraculously tacking into the Island cove through the rolling combers always drew a crowd of excited spectators. When the tall, spare, soaking wet figure leaped to the wharf and shrilled "Chrize, the big blue's a gasser today," many a pocket was emptied of its silver.[15]

In the late 1880's Burton disposed of his Tahoe holdings to dairyman Antone Russi, an early day settler of Swiss extraction, and then retired to Sacramento where he became interested in breeding and racing thoroughbreds.

Russi, who was to leave his given name on Antone Meadows two miles west of the Island Farm, moved his large family into the old Burton home and pastured his cows on the surrounding bottomland. When Russi died suddenly in the 1890's under mysterious circumstances, his widow married Frank X. Walker, a relative of her deceased husband. Walker located his living quarters, corrals and milk house on the edge of the meadow where Tamarack Lodge was later built and managed the cattle business successfully for two decades. His stock wandered at will, even roaming the streets of Tahoe City, until a county ordinance ended this practice. When it also became illegal for a horse to wear a cowbell residents insisted that the authorities had gone too far and they were doubly convinced after Ripley's "Believe It or Not" spread this oddity across the nation.

Walker continued to prosper, leasing his range at various times to Bud Jones, "Red" Dixon and Louie Rossi. He committed financial suicide, however, when his family persuaded him to go into the sheep business and at the time of his death, in the 1930's, Walker was bankrupt.[16]

A part of the old Island Farm is now the Methodist Camp Grounds, where student groups vacation each year.

During the last three decades the settlement of Lake Forest has grown up west of Burton's former lakeshore establishment. It borders on the old dog-leg of Highway 28 between the Tahoe City Fish Hatchery and "Dollar Hill."[17] Although the road was recently rerouted farther to the west, an expanding colony of summer and winter residents support motels, a lumber yard, store and Italian inn, where the indomitable "Captain" Burton pre-empted land nearly 100 years ago.

Homer Burton's move away from Lake Tahoe did not mean that the "Lakers" had seen the last of him. Several seasons after selling his holdings, the spry old pioneer appeared at Tahoe City. It was a bright spring morning and he was decked out in a swallow-tailed coat, fancy vest and stovepipe hat. Such formal attire at the City presented an irresistible target for several youngsters in the town, who promptly belted him with snowballs, scoring a direct hit on his topper. Collared by an onlooker, the culprits were dragged before Burton to apologize. After carefully flicking the snow off his broadcloth with a gaudy handkerchief and resetting his hat at a jaunty angle, the old gentleman turned to the quaking fledglings, who cowered in fright, expecting a sound thrashing.

Aiming a trembling forefinger he began, "This unfortunate incident reminds me of a . . ." Checking himself, he bit his lip as though recalling an urgent appointment elsewhere and focused his attention on the man holding the young scalawags.

"Let loose of them little monsters," he piped. "Chrize sake, I was a boy once myself!"

Then "Captain" Homer D. Burton turned and stalked grandly away down the street.[18]

Chapter Fifty-one

THE GREAT BONANZA ROAD TO WASHOE

"**B**Y THIS TIME the station buildings were in sight and far down the canyon, winding in even grade around spur after spur outlined by low clinging clouds of red dust, we could see the Great Sierra Mule Train—that industrial gulf stream flowing from California plains over into arid Nevada, carrying thither materials for life and luxury. In a fast, perpetual caravan of heavy wagons drawn by teams of from 6 to 14 mules, all the supplies of many cities and villages were hauled across the Sierra at immense cost with such skill of driving and generalship of mules as the world has never seen before.

"Our trail descended toward the grade, quickly bringing us to a high bank, immediately overlooking the trains a few rods below the group of station buildings. . . . Close in front came a huge wagon piled high with cases of freight and drawn along by a team of 12 mules whose heavy breathing and drenched skins showed them hard worked and well tired out. The driver looked anxiously ahead at a soft spot in the road and on at the station, as if calculating whether his team had courage left to haul through.

"He called kindly to them, cracked his blacksnake whip, and altogether they strained bravely on. The great van rocked, settled a little on the near side, and stuck fast. With a look of despair, the driver got off and laid the lash freely among his team. They jumped and jerked, frantically tangled themselves up, sulked, and became stubborn, immovable.

"Meanwhile, a mile of teams behind, unable to pass on the narrow grade, came to an unwilling halt. About five wagons back I noticed a tall Pike, dressed in checked shirt and pantaloons tucked into jack boots. A soft felt hat, worn on the back of his head, displayed long locks of flaxen hair which hung freely about a florid pink countenance, noticeable for its pair of violent blue eyes and facial angle rendered acute by sharp long nose. This fellow watched the stoppage with impatience, and at last when it was more than he could bear, walked up to the other team with a look of wrath, absolutely devilish. One would have expected him to blow up with rage, yet withal his cut and manner were cool and soft in the extreme. In a bland, almost tender voice he said to the driver: 'My friend, perhaps I can help you,' and his gentle way of disentangling and patting the leaders as he headed them around in the right direction would have given him a high post under Mr. Birch.[1]

"He leisurely examined the embedded wheel and cast an eye along the road ahead. He then began in a rather excited manner to swear, pouring it out louder and more profane until he truly eclipsed the most horrible blasphemies I ever heard, piling them up thicker and more fiendish until it seemed as if the very earth must open up and engulf him. I noticed one mule after another gave a little squat, bringing their breasts hard against the collars and straining traces till only one old mule with ears back and dangling chain still held out. The Pike walked up and yelled one gigantic oath; her ears sprang forward,

Bancroft Library

A BOTTLE ALWAYS HELPED

*Four-horse sleighs passing on the Johnson
cut-off turnpike at "Cape Horn"
in the mid-1860's.
View sketched by W. H. Hilton in 1871
for Edward Vischer's* PICTORIAL.
*Looking south over Upper Lake Valley
with Stevens Peak in the background.*

she squatted in terror, and the iron linkings grated under her strain. He then stepped back and took the rein, every trembling mule looking out of the corner of its eye and listening at *qui vive.* With a peculiar air of deliberation and of child-like simplicity he said in every-day tones, 'Come up there, mules.' One quick strain, a slight rumble, and the wagon rolled on to Copples (Station).

"Our horses being stabled, we betook ourselves to the office which was, of course, barroom as well. As I entered, the unfortunate teamster was paying his liquid compliment to the florid Pike. Their glasses were filled. 'My respects,' said the little driver. The whiskey became lost to view and went eroding its way through the dust those poor fellows had swallowed. He added, 'Well, Bill, you can swear.' 'Swear?' repeated the Pike in incredulous questioning, 'Me swear?' as if the compliment were greater than his modest desert. 'No, I can't blaspheme worth a cuss. You just orter hear Pete Green. He can exhort the impitent mule. I've known a ten-mule team to renounce the flesh and haul 31,000 pounds through a foot of clay mud under one of his outpourings.' "[2]

Such was the atmosphere of the Great Bonanza Road during the mid-1860's.

Barely 15 years before it had been only a narrow, tortuous Indian trail winding over the Sierra Nevada and past Tahoe, through desolate, uncharted high wilderness country. The trail's first use by white men swirls with conjecture, but this probably occurred during the winter of 1844. From Council Grove on the Missouri, the Stevens-Townsend-Murphy overland party, guided by Caleb Greenwood, 81-year-old iron-sinewed mountain man, rolled west to the alkali wastes of the Humboldt Sink and on to the fork of the Salmon Trout River (Truckee) below Truckee Lake (Donner).

Here the emigrants divided, those on horseback "going by way of a stream draining northwest out of a great lake" (Tahoe). Upon reaching the headwaters, they made their way along the western shore and "passed over the hills to Sutter's Fort without difficulty."[3]

Nine months earlier, "Mountain Lake" (Bonpland-Tahoe) had been discovered by Captain John Charles Fremont and Charles Preuss from a peak above the Carson Pass trail. The Stevens-Townsend-Murphy splinter group from the main party were therefore the first white expedition of record to reach the shores of Lake Tahoe, discover its outlet and possibly pass over what became the Johnson Pass cut-off four years later.

Official credit for blazing the Hangtown (Placerville)-Carson Valley route by way of the South Fork of the American River goes to John Calhoun "Cock-Eye" Johnson, who opened up the "Johnson

Trail." It was reported on April 15, 1848, that the first mail from the Pacific Coast started overland on the "Central Route" and crossed the Snowy Mountains following "Johnson's cut-off."[4]

However, it remained for Major George Chorpenning, "Father of the Pony Express," and Absalom Woodward to run out the initial government contract pack train mail over the trail. This first "Jackass Post" left Placerville on May 1, 1851, striking over the Sierra Nevada leg of its 910-mile extent to Salt Lake City. It took 16 days for the party to slog across the western and eastern summits of the Central Sierra. Snow conditions were so bad that Chorpenning and his men often had to push ahead of their mules, beating down a path through the deep drifts with wooden mauls.[5]

They fought their way over the western summit, dropped down the precipitous mountainside into Lake Bigler Valley (Tahoe), forded Lake Stream (the Upper Truckee), surmounted Luther Pass and floundered through West Carson Canyon to Mormon Station (Genoa). On June 5, 1851, the party arrived in Salt Lake City. The first United States mail to reach the Great Basin by way of Johnson Pass and the Humboldt Sink cut-off had been delivered.[6]

On May 9, 1852, the *Sacramento Placer Times* proudly announced that "Colonel Johnson's newly discovered pass reduces the distance over the Sierra to less than 100 miles." In the summer of the same year Colonel L. A. Norton belittled the new route: "The Johnson cut-off is a mere bridle trail. Fallen trees are not even cut from the path. It is an unbroken forest, wild, inhabited by grizzlies, California lions and wild Indians. . . ." Norton had ascended from Carson Valley over "Dayit's Ravine" (Daggett's) to Lake Valley.[7] On August 13, 1853, William Bartlett of Placerville published, "from actual measurement and survey," his *Bartlett's Guide to California*, wherein he detailed the Johnson Pass route, mile by mile, from Eagle Valley Ranch (Carson) along the Carson Immigrant Ridge Road above Truckee Lake (Tahoe) and on to Placerville.[8]

Heavy snows during the winter months closed the passes, but the shorter Central Route had proven practical, with all-year passage becoming a reality in 1853-54.

At this time "Old Man" Jacob "Daddy" Dritt, George S. Murdoch and Frederick Aubrey Bishop, using basket-type Canadian snowshoes, stomped out a trail from Strawberry Valley to Woodford's in the dead of winter. These men were predecessors of John "Snowshoe" Thompson, Judge Child and George Pierce, who were to carry the mails regularly during the winter months in the 1850's, using Norwegian skis and horse-drawn sleighs.[9]

On May 6, 1854, Dritt and Bishop presented a bill to the California Senate requesting permission to open a toll road from the West Carson Canyon over Luther Pass to the Johnson Trail. The bill was tabled, but on April 28, 1855, the legislature passed the California Wagon Road Act, authorizing an expenditure "not to exceed $105,000 for the construction of a wagon road from Sacramento Valley to the eastern boundary of the State, with the Surveyor General to decide the most practical and economical route."[10]

The immediate result of this act was the formation of an exploratory survey party headed by Sherman Day, State Senator and prominent railroad engineer, acting for Surveyor General Seneca Hunt Marlette of California. Day first traversed the Georgetown-Lake Bigler-Washoe Valley route (Placer County Emigrant Road). Then he followed the Eagle Valley-Lake Bigler Emigrant Ridge Route along the eastern scarp of the Carson Range into Lake Valley and over the Johnson cut-off to Strawberry Valley. He decided that the Johnson Route was the most practical.[11]

George H. Goddard, described as "an able California engineer," now joined the Day and Marlette survey party, and left Placerville on August 26, accompanied by Day and six assistants. They traveled the Carson Pass-Hope Valley road into Carson Valley, returning by way of Luther Pass. Goddard and Day estimated that Luther Pass was 741 feet lower than the Carson Pass and, hence, more suitable for a wagon road.

On Admission Day the surveyors returned to Clear Lake (El Dorado County), where Day had established camp. Here they found that the rest of the party had been "living on squirrels and ground rats for several days." Goddard supplied them with provisions brought from Mormon Station. On September 13, Day started back to Placerville and Goddard's group again crossed Luther into Lake Valley to run out the boundary line between California and Utah Territory (Nevada). Goddard determined that the line bisected Tahoe itself.[12]

Meanwhile the California Legislature had failed to pass the Wagon Road appropriation. Thus the surveys were not backed financially. In June of the following year, however, the citizens of Placerville raised $5,500 toward the construction of a wagon road following the Day-Marlette survey, and the California Stage Company promised a coach line. On April 25, 1857, Sacramento, El Dorado and Yolo counties belatedly appropriated $40,000 for the Johnson route improvement. At last it appeared certain that the road would become a reality.[13]

When the initiative was passed to the counties in California who would benefit directly, a joint board of Wagon Road Directors became a necessity, and representative citizens were appointed to serve in this capacity. Jarad B. Crandall, partner in Crandall-Sunderland and Company's Placerville-Sacramento line of stages, placed a coach and four at the disposal of the directors and the possibility of crossing the Sierra Nevada over the Johnson cut-off by stage coach was about to be put to the test.[14]

On June 11, 1857, a party of 7 men reined out of Placerville at 2:45 in the morning—destination, Carson Valley.[15] Horse relays had been placed along the route ahead of the turnpike pioneers and western history was in the making. The stage arrived at Sportsman's Hall, 12 miles east of Placerville, in time for a 6:00 a.m. breakfast, served by proprietor John Blair.

This was the farthest point east to be reached by coach at that time, but the challenge of the Sierra still lay ahead. At 5:00 p.m. that afternoon the group rattled into Clear Creek Station, footing on Peavine Hill and the Brockliss Grade, where a fresh team was led into the traces. Here William D. Keyser and Theo. F. Tracy joined the men.[16]

The small cavalcade now moved on to Foster's Halt, some 6 miles west of Strawberry Valley, where they camped for the night. So far the trip had been uneventful. Up at 5:00 a.m. the next day, the stage coach road's vanguard pushed on to Slippery Ford, where their driver, Jarad Crandall, "had them across this major hurdle before they were even aware of it."

Excitement mounted as the team strained toward "Johnson Hill Summit," which was reached shortly before noon. To accompanying cheers, a bottle of wine was broken in front of the lead horses and the 7,400-foot divide christened Nevett's Summit in honor of James H. Nevett, chairman of the Wagon Road Directors.[17]

Then the stage clattered down the eastern slope of the western Sierra range and skidded into Smith's Station in Lake Valley, where the astonished proprietor, Martin "Mart" Smith, "threw his hat into the air to celebrate the momentous occasion."[18] Another change of horses and the party turned south into Upper Lake Valley again, forded Lake Creek and, careening over two- and three-foot granite boulders, pulled steeply up grade. After skirting "Marlette Meadow" (Grass Lake) they arrived at Luther Pass summit, where Crandall breathed his double span before dropping into the meadowland of Hope Valley surrounding Jim Green's "Junction Station" on the Carson Pass emigrant road.[19] The elated riders then threaded their way down West Carson Canyon to Cary's Mill (Woodford's), where Mrs. Daniel Woodford "provided a fine meal."[20]

Collis P. Huntington, James H. Nevett, J. M. B. Weatherwax, Asa Herschel Hawley, W. H. Smith and J. M. Dorsey, representing the El Dorado, Sacramento County and Utah Territory (Nevada) directors, joined the jubilant group. The newcomers had preceded the stage on horseback from Silver Creek Station on the Brockliss Grade. All slept in Woodford's haymow that night.

Saturday morning, June 13, 1857, the now sizable troop rode on 12 miles to Genoa, where they were welcomed by Mr. Taylor (described as a moderate Mormon with only two wives) and a cheering crowd of "fifty to sixty men."[21]

The "great feat had been accomplished" and the nine-passenger Pioneer coach, carrying 500 pounds of freight in addition to the road blazers, had "passed the crucial test and attained its objective without mishap." Including meal stops, it had taken the party 27½ hours to travel the circuitous 64½ miles from Placerville and surmount the twin summits of the Central Sierra ranges.[22] The Johnson Pass stage route was a reality and Placerville celebrated the news with a 100-gun salute.

As the "road" was little more than a mule trail, immediate steps were taken to improve it. Nevett and John Cary returned to Smith's in Lake Valley, and 48 hours after the initial stage crossing they were letting contracts to clear and grade the two-mile slope from Nevett's Summit (Echo) into the Valley, as well as the Slippery Ford Grade. Johnson, Vosburgh and Brockliss were the low bidders among some seven Johnnie-on-the-spot contractors who submitted estimates.[23]

Ten days later it was announced that a stage line from Placerville to Genoa had become a "fixed fact." Thereafter, a coach would start east every Monday morning, as Crandall and Sunderland had stocked the road, establishing horse change stations at Silver Creek, Strawberry Valley and Martin Smith's in Lake Valley. William Keyser was appointed station agent for Crandall's Pioneer Stage Line in Utah Territory and on September 7, 1857, he announced from Genoa that "stages would come down the new road into Lake Valley on the next trip over." He also stated that the hazardous pull over Slippery Ford "was receiving attention because it still required the lead horses with the 'fifth chain out' to get safely over."[24]

Earlier in the year President Pierce had approved the Great Federal Wagon Road bill appropriating $300,000 to improve the Central Overland route to the eastern boundary of California. This became a motivating force behind the County Wagon Road Directors, and the trickle of traffic, now diverted to the Johnson Pass cut-off as a result of their efforts, presaged what would shortly be called "the greatest movement of men, materials and animals ever known in the world's history."

This was triggered by an explosive June day in 1859. Discovery of the fantastically rich Comstock Lode at Virginia City was confirmed.[25] The stirring news resounded across America like a thunderclap. It brought an immediate tide of travel surging east again over the Sierra Nevada, flooding into Carson and rolling up Gold and Six Mile canyons to lap at the slopes of Sun Mountain (Mt. Davidson).

John "Snowshoe" Thompson and his partner, Judge John A. Child, appear to have anticipated the Comstock discovery. On January 12, 1859, they established the first winter passenger and freight service between Silver Springs and the West Carson Canyon over Johnson and Luther passes, using horse-drawn, three-seated sleighs instead of coaches.[26] A reasonable chance to maintain all-year service across the Central Sierra now existed.

With the electrifying news of the silver strike at Virginia, a crackling current of activity slithered along the length of the partially improved Johnson Pass road. Trading post operators and the general public scrambled for way station locations and toll rights.[27]

Dan DeQuille declared that "if all the toll road franchises applied for were granted, and the toll roads built, they would not only fill Nevada but hang far out into the desert like a fringe."[28] Shacks, clapboard shanties, hand-hewn log cabins, brush and canvas-covered shelters were hastily thrown up, dotting the highroad and bidding for trade with the growing throng of customers passing along the route. Barely three weeks after the Lode's discovery, a majority of the turnouts on the Johnson road harbored a rough board bench, platform or tent—anything that would allow a place to rest or the sale of food and liquor.

LEADERS TO TAIL GATE

Empty Washoe wagons dropping down the haul-over at Slippery Ford to Strawberry Station in early June of 1865. Looking eastward toward Johnson's Summit (Echo).

Improve the road! Build stations on the route! Shorten the miles to the mines! Speed up the flow of materials! These were the demands of the hour.

"One Hundred Men Wanted to Work Slippery Ford Hill," "Top Prices Paid for Kentucky Mules," and "Washoe Mines; Riding, Work, and Pack Mules for Sale," blared the ads in San Francisco and Valley town newspapers. Scrapers, drags, rollers, dirt wagons, water carts, tools, black powder and regiments of laborers were hurriedly rounded up. Horses and mules were pressed into service by the hundreds. Oxen hauled the heavy materials, bridge timbers, and chisled granite slabs used for shoring the rock fills.

The urgent cry continued. Level the cuts! Fill in the ravines! Straighten the crooked miles! Above the South Fork of the American River charges of giant powder were placed to blast out massive boulders in order to widen the sidehill cuts. Hairpin turns were eliminated wherever possible, turn-outs rocked in, wood and stone bridges built, water diversion ditches and culverts dug, roadbeds graded, smoothed, rolled and watered. The right-of-way was widened to 20 feet and at certain points passing roads were laid in, one above the other. Costs shot up.

Laborers cursed the dust and confusion. They had come to California to work the mines, they grumbled, not the turnpike leading to the Comstock.

But hundreds signed up to earn their stake and then moved on over the mountains. All had seen the loaded ore wagons lumbering downgrade from the diggings enroute to the Coast, and the men leaned on their shovels and watched enviously—hopefully—as 20, 30, often 40 pack mules singlefooted past, the animals swaybacked under sackfuls of silver-bearing quartz.

The "boys" talked of the gleaming silver bars they had seen in the windows of the Sacramento and San Francisco banks. Silver and gold was waiting for them in that devil's wasteland, they knew, locked beneath the barren mountainside that spawned Virginia, Gold Hill and Silver City. Each man was sure that overnight he, too, would become a Croesus.

On to Washoe! was the rallying cry. On to Sun Mountain and a smiling Goddess of Fortune! Let the laggards take the Donner, Henness or Carson Passes; Johnson's cut-off was the shortest route.

Hostelries, way stations, remount stables, inns and toll houses mushroomed. Two thousand or more hostlers, toll gate keepers, station masters, blacksmiths, grooms, stable boys, cooks and bartenders were drawn into the throbbing activity.

Six and Eight Mile House, Sportsman's Hall at Twelve Mile, Pacific House, "Dirty Mike's," Whitehall, Uncle Johnny Maze's Roadhouse, Saul Perrin's, McMurtry's, Sugar Loaf House, Dick Yarnold's, Old Mother Welty's, Foster's Halt, Champlain House, True's Place, Georgetown Junction House, San Francisco House, What Cheer House, Strawberry Station, Slippery Ford House, Hermit's, Sayle's Flat House, Geo. Swan's Upper Toll House, Snowslide House, Phillip's Station, Tom Audrain's, North American House, Sixty Mile, Hawley's Second Elkhorn House, Gould's, Winstanley's, Nemi Osgood's Toll House, Yank's Station, Sierra House, Hawthorne House, Pine Grove Station, Lake Bigler Hotel (Lake House), Miller House, Dixon's Place, McCumber's, Lapham's Stateline Hotel, Friday's Station, Rob's Station, Peter's Flat House, Van Sickle's . . . these were some of the way stations, numbering nearly 100, either contemplated, under construction, or completed by the spring of 1860.[29] They lined the throbbing arterial mile after mile, and "home stations," set 10 to 15 miles apart, and usually operated by families, offered the best meals and lodging.

Each owner of a toll franchise maintained and improved his section of the Great Highway. Some factions contended that the counties through which the road ran had done all the expensive spadework on the thoroughfare, only to hand it over to private individuals who reaped the benefits. The toll road operators fired back their rebuttal: "Who was taking the gamble that the Comstock Lode would continue to produce?" they asked. "Who was spending fantastic sums on road betterment in spite of the competitive talk about a transcontinental railroad? We are," they shouted. What if several of the way stations were collecting upwards of $1,000 a day in tolls? What if the better saloons on the road took in some $3,000 each night? Let the soreheads be damned!

As the great turnpike straightened out, widened and leveled, the number of animals trace-chained to the mammoth Washoe wagons increased to 14, 16 and 18 mules, horses, or combinations of both. Loads increased proportionately. Carson bound freighters that originally carried 3, 5 and 7 tons now hauled "back action" wagons and creaked along under 10, 12, and even 15 tons.[30]

The early spring of 1860 had been marked by a Paiute uprising in Carson Valley which culminated in the Battle of Pyramid Lake.[31] Traffic into Nevada Territory slowed to a halt, only to burst through again in mid-summer. April of the same year had found the road flanking the South Fork of the American River converted into a mud slough from the spring freshets. Freighters waited in line at "Berry's" on the western approach. More wagons were stopped at the foot of the West Carson Canyon on the eastern side of the Sierra. Given the word, they rolled out through this quagmire that stretched ahead mile after mile. In places slush and mud were so deep that a growing wall built up against the wagon bodies as they pushed forward until the struggling, slipping animals bogged to a standstill. All along the line the creeping caravan would then come to a halt until the stalled lead vehicle was winched aside so the wagons behind could take over the work of breaking through the mud ahead.

Teamsters were fortunate to haul one-third of a full load through the axle-high mire, and freight rates fluctuated wildly.

J. Ross Browne described the conditions found on the still uncompleted arterial: "The road from Placerville to Washoe is 5 feet deep by 130 miles long (sic) and composed mostly of mountains, snow and mud."[32]

"GOT ANY MORE STRAW — BERRY?"

Famous Strawberry Station, favorite teamster stop in the early 1860's, as it appeared on July 10, 1891. Camera is facing southeast toward Lover's Leap. Old Bonanza Road to Washoe in foreground.

In August of 1860, 353 wagons were counted crawling over the road on a single peak day of traffic. It was estimated that 50 more vehicles were loading and unloading at either end.

One million three hundred and fifty thousand dollars in tolls was collected that year in spite of adverse conditions of weather and the Indian troubles. A toll franchise was proving more profitable than a run-of-the-mill mine, despite the staggering overhead. Tolls taken in during the first year's operation alone often paid the expense of road construction and maintenance, allowing, in addition, a handsome override.

Franchise holders on the Great Road were not the only recipients of the gold and silver that was dispensed recklessly in the mad scramble to reach the mines. Teamster Stephen T. Gage, later city marshal of Placerville, paid $500 for a team of mules in Marysville and in 83 days of hauling freight to Virginia he cleared $10,400 in gold eagles.[33] Then he sold his equipment at triple its cost.

A report on the conditions found on the road and in Carson had been wired over F. A. Bee's newly completed telegraph (Bee's Grapevine) in April of 1860 after one of the heaviest winters recorded in the Sierra Nevada. The correspondent advised: "The road is in wretched condition. Time required between Placerville and Genoa is two days by stage, and three by any other mode of travel. Stage fare is $28, and horse hire $30 to $40. Meals and lodging are 75c each until Strawberry is reached (going east) and after that $1. The thirsty can obtain drinks for one bit each for 30 miles east of Placerville; after that, they are uniformly two bits.

"Provisions and other articles of prime necessity (at Carson City) have almost reached starvation prices. Flour, none in quantity for sale, 60c a pound; sugar, $1 a pound; liquors, $10 to $12 a gallon.

Hay sold today for $350 a ton; barley, corn, wheat, 30c a pound, and prices will not be materially reduced for a month."[34]

In 1861, 25,000 passengers were reported to have traveled on the Pioneer Lines stages to and from the mines and Jarad Crandall placed 12 Concords on the run to handle his increased business.[35]

Conflicting reports from newsmen, railway survey engineers and toll house keepers nevertheless document the fact that traffic and revenues on the Bonanza Road were reaching fantastic proportions.

From 50 teamsters, noted as "crossing on the new grade through 18 inches of snow" in November of 1859, the freight hauls into Nevada Territory during the summer and fall of 1862 had jumped to 30,000 tons, averaging $100 a ton in tolls. Passenger traffic soared to 56,500 people, at $30 each, bringing in $1,095,000. In addition, mails and express came to $125,000.[36]

George W. Swan, station keeper at Slippery Ford (Swan's Upper Toll House), estimated that 250 tons of freight, plus 200 stage passengers and 1,000 horses, mules and oxen passed his doors every 24 hours.

Swan was assessed $14,000 in taxes by El Dorado County in 1862, but he collected $75,000 in tolls during the same period. The gamble was paying off handsomely.

During the same year, Governor Nye of Nevada Territory tossed in his considered estimate. He calculated that freight charges alone would reach $5,000,000.

Theodore D. Judah, "Father of the Central Pacific," stepped up the tempo of his drum beating for the railroad when he asserted: "One-half a million will be realized from passenger fares on the Johnson road, and Wells Fargo will carry 200,000 pounds of bullion." He added that "120 tons of freight moves daily at 6 to 8 cents a pound, with this alone returning $5,250,000 each year."

High flown talk, reaching astronomical figures, continued. Incredible estimates on combined freight charges for the year 1863 were submitted. One authority contended that it could not be less than $12,000,000. On August 18 of the year William H. Brewer of the Whitney Survey party submitted a reliable report while stopping at Swan's. He listed 5,000 teams steadily employed in the Washoe trade (2,772 teams in one eight-week period alone), 14,652 mules and horses, and 1,400 freighters and stages. Another informant insisted that "15,000 mules and horses, and 3,000 men were utilized on the road."

Scarcity dictated the prices of food and feed. Hay and barley sold by the pound, instead of the ton, with 5 and 6 cents a pound the going rate during the previous summer of 1862. Often there was not enough feed at the way stations for the teamsters' animals. Straw was then substituted. Many wagoners carried their own grain, setting up canvas cribs on the sides of their freighters during stopovers. The larger operators often sent baled hay ahead to stations on the road, thus avoiding larcenous prices such as then found at Strawberry, one of the worst offenders.

This famous home station (and Strawberry Valley) is widely believed to have received its name from proprietor Irad Fuller Berry, but this misconception is a canard with no basis in fact. Berry neither named the valley and station nor were they named for him. The legend gained currency because of Berry's penurious reputation as a hard man with a "bit-piece." He is known to have substituted straw and chaff for grain when feeding the teamsters' animals at his station and resorted to the ruse of applying mucilage to the mules' mouths, upon which he planted a few kernels of ground barley to create the illusion of well-fed animals. Berry is even said to have filled his guests' pillows with hay instead of goose feathers and it is an established fact that wagoners stopping at his hostelry called out derisively: "Do you have any more straw—Berry?"[37]

This, however, has no bearing on the appellation Strawberry. The simple, unadorned truth of the matter is that Strawberry Valley and Station were named for the wild strawberry plants that grow there. An article in the *Placerville Herald*, dated August 6, 1853, indicates that a group of young ladies and their escorts made the trip from Placerville to the valley and found wild strawberries in profusion

—whereupon they called it Strawberry. William Bartlett's *Guide to California*, published on August 13 of the same year, also mentions "Strawberry Valley." This was five years before Berry even settled in the region.

And still the traffic on the Great Road increased. During three months of 1864, 6,667 "footmen," 883 horsemen, 3,164 passengers riding the "Pitching Betsies," 5,000 pack animals, 2,564 teams, 4,649 head of cattle and a daily freight haul of 320 tons passed through Tahoe's Lake Valley. Bonanza at Virginia City? Actually it lay in the freight charges and tolls on the Golden Road that nearly equaled the value of the ore spewing from the mines. Some considered the Comstock to be only a secondary producer.[38]

Although short cuts had been blasted out early in the road's improvement, there was no way to bypass the haulover at Slippery Ford. Here conditions were still so bad that the "whip" often shouted: "All out, saving the ladies, of course, God bless 'em—*and push!*" The famous, if mythical "Foot and Walker" stageline had not been entirely eliminated.[39]

Double teaming of wagons on the difficult pulls continued and many wagoners swore that the "Grand Highway" was still no better than an improved Indian trail.

It was now estimated that more than $500,000 had been spent filling, cutting and grading the toll sections of the road—averaging in cost $5,000 per mile. Maintenance on the right-of-way each year see-sawed between $2,000 and $3,000 a mile, depending upon the terrain. Transportation facilities were now valued at $5,000,000.

The Bonanza Road had become the "Appian Way of the West" and over it rolled the greatest concentration of humans, animals, merchandise, supplies and bullion ever assembled. Every creation of man and nature was represented in the cargo moving over the turnpike: hay, grain, firewood, liquor, building bricks, furniture, mining machinery, canned goods, Whitehall and whale boats for Tahoe, silks and finery, fresh fruits, marble and bric-a-brac for the newly affluent Washoe nabobs' mansions, pianos, stained glass, rosewood bar panels, chandeliers, drugs, kitchenware, brass beds, mattresses, blankets, linens, crocked eggs, vegetables, kegged butter, guns, gunpowder . . . the list was limitless. Everything needed to sustain a fluctuating population of 25,000 to 40,000 people was being dragged slowly and laboriously over the High Sierra.

The arterial formed a pulsating lifeline to a high desert community where men were burrowing like moles in the wastes of Six Mile and Gold canyons—tunneling into parched rock and powdered alkali that would not sustain a blade of grass.

This heterogeneous multi-tonnage of necessities and gim-cracks was piled aboard high-wheeled, deep, boxlike Missouri "sail tops," sun-dried stake wagons, solid-wheeled lumber carriers, massive mule-drawn Washoe freighters, with their two rear wagons chained pole to tail gate, and even the Argonauts' outmoded, unwieldly Conestogas.

Along with this creaking caravan moving up the mountain highway, plodded the "blanket brigade," mounted and on foot. An eyewitness described the amazing cavalcade:

"The motley train which stretched in an unbroken line from Sacramento to the mines calls to mind the grotesque march to Finchley. Old men and young, waifs from many nations who had drifted during the ten years to California gold fields, with every variety of dress and equipment, driving pack mules, burros, horses, and oxen, dusty, muddy, tired, and footsore—this oddly assorted company was knit together by a bond of common purpose. In the little stations on the route, Piedmontese and Cornishmen, Jews and Catholics, mechanics and scholars, honest men and rogues, snatched their food from the same rude board, splashed with all the stains which a medley of dishes could furnish, and slept at night in the same bed of straw, unwashed, unkept, stiff, bitten by fleas and bugs, and began their tedious march to the Valley of the Carson."

Another earthy writer of the day brings the homely picture into direct focus:

"The teamsters sit down . . . to the table . . . in patience; a few of the more elegant sort clean their teeth with their forks, and nearly all speared with this instrument small specimens from the dishes before them.

"The luxury of a dried apple, a square inch of pie, or even a pickle, amid the crash and spatter of thrown plates . . . beans swimming in fat, meats slimed with pale, ropy gravy, and over everything a faint Mongol odor . . . the teamsters stuffing and swallowing with a rapidity which could only have come from long practice . . . (in comparison) sharks and wolves may no longer be figured as types of prandial haste . . . a few tilted back chairs, their occupants drumming upon the bottom of their plates the newest tune of the road.

"In fifteen minutes the room is empty . . . grain is being fed to the mules, or—cigars lighted (as the men) linger around the bar."[40]

And still another typical scene in one of the way station saloons:

"The turning of the once white neck handkerchiefs inside out, producing the sudden effect of clean linen . . . much clearing of throats, loud and prolonged, and blowing of noses not heard on this globe ever . . . (the drivers then) stepping to the bar to partake of a 'dust cutter'."[41]

These were the teamsters—the grit-caked, bearded, weatherbeaten, able veterans with thousands of miles of Overland Trail bullwhacking experience behind them; the Bob Bences, "Gassy" Smiths, "Dusty" Rhodes, "Ollie" Gilises and Osgood Longs, who swore by and at their animals, a hardy crew whose blistering curses matched their man-killing jobs, men who yielded the palm of originality to no one. They were famous for the "longest whips and oaths in Creation" and it is claimed that their profanity would scorch a brake shoe or purple the hairy ears of a jackass. With their 20-foot buckskin lashes the drivers could flick a fly off a leader's ear or split a leaf squarely in two at ten paces.[42]

And their choice of animals? Not oxen. They were powerful but slow. Nor horses. The tremendous loads and hour after hour upgrade pulls would drop them in their traces. Only prime stock mules were good enough for teaming on the Bonanza Road. Two to four hundred dollars was the going price for a top draft mule and the price paid was reflected in his trappings. These rugged beasts sported an iron arch over their necks from which hung five or six tinkling brass bells. Great squares of glossy, combed bearskin—black, brown and grizzly—covered their collars, and their harness metal glistened in the sunlight.

The hard working teamster walked beside his animals, sat the wagon box, or, more often, rode the off-wheel mule. An ore team "skinner" usually chose the left hand wheel animal to ride so that he could check his distance when passing another team. He was satisfied if he only brushed another vehicle without running into it. A mere lifting of his three- to four-foot whipstock was the only signal a trained team needed to move out, turn, or stop.[43]

Another colorful segment coursing over the Silver Road were the drovers with their tightly bunched herds of sheep or wild-eyed Mexican steers that hurtled uncontrolled through the press of humanity and vehicles, sometimes overturning stage coaches in their concerted rushes. There were also the Chinese drivers urging on burros staggering under loads of firewood as they pressed forward toward a sun-baked, treeless region where anything combustible brought $70 or more a cord.

Pack trains were a common sight. Each animal was cinch laden with several hundred pounds of merchandise—everything from sacked flour to darning needles, weighing down the steadily plodding animals that, nevertheless, were considered so surefooted that they "could carry a barrel of whiskey across a stream on a log one foot in diameter."[44] A rider on a belled horse usually led the line of mules that followed the sound as they had been trained to do.

Everything with two or four legs either walked, was ridden, carried or pulled a load. Probably

the most unusual record was set when a flock of turkeys was successfully driven over Johnson Pass from Placerville to Virginia City.[45]

In one instance unroasted coffee left its mark for life on W. Smith, a teamster on the Bonanza route. Running out of feed for his animals at Pacific House, Smith slit open sacks of green coffee beans from his wagon's cargo and fed them to his mules. Fellow wagoners, admiring his resourcefulness, dubbed him "Coffee" Smith, considering this a costly if unique experiment in mule nutrition. "Coffee" resigned himself to the name and when Mrs. Blair at Sportsman's Hall respectfully asked of him, "Mr. Coffee, do you want any more hot biscuits?" he didn't bother to take issue. He took the biscuits instead.[46]

The queens of the Johnson road—those rumbling, swaying Concords careening in and out of the hordes of wayfarers and animals, were flashing, kaleidoscopic marvels of bright English vermilion and straw colored magnificence that tracked smartly behind matched spans of spirited horseflesh.[47]

On their high boxes, deft and poised, rode those "Knights of the Lash," variously called "Jehus," "whips," "whipsters" or "Charlies," and sometimes simply stagedrivers, but never *coachmen*.

Mark Twain immortalized this breed of stalwarts as "A hero (to his public), a great shining dignitary, the world's favorite son, the observed of nations," upon whose prophetic and seldom spoken word beggar and bonanza baron alike waited with admiring deference. Indeed, the driver was a glamorous symbol of leadership, the acknowledged head of this great parade.[48]

These cool-headed men were also proudly pointed out as "Kings of the Road," well able to be trusted with the destinies of their 15 to 20 passengers. The whips found some tokens of appreciation acceptable recompense for reining their human cargo safely through the hazards of the turnpike. A good cigar, a new light felt hat, a gold chronometer, even a shot glass of whiskey was received in quiet dignity. But a monetary tip was unacceptable and often considered a direct insult.

Normally the "Knight of the Ribbons" rode the box seat on the right hand side of the coach, holding the leaders (pointers), swing and wheel horses steady with multiple reins.

The high esteem in which this exclusive fraternity was held is clearly indicated in an article of the times:

"The fearless and sure Jehu safely guides the highest nettled horses, those untamed broncos of a Spanish sire and dam, with the lives of sometimes 19 passengers resting easily in the palm of his clenched hand, the flick of his whip, or the multiple reins. No matter how stormy the night, how dark or dreary, he seldom fails in his judgment or skill. How many errands he handles on the stage road; parcels purchased and carried, from cambric needle to grindstone. And the treasure he carries, bills he pays, and how honestly. Bank presidents, brokers and men in high station may embezzle, but not this Prince of the Ribbons. He is not overpaid for all this, but he had one consolation. There is none so high, none so rich, none so profane, none so religious, none so poorly dressed or richly clad but they all want to sit alongside the driver.

"Presidents, priests, editors, judges, Senators, my lady with the golden tresses and rich laces, all are troubled with the same weakness: 'Agent, give me a seat alongside the driver'."[49]

Schuyler Colfax, Speaker of the House of Congress, voiced the attitude of many when he an-

C. O. Valentine

HIGH-WHEELER AT HAIRPIN CURVE
Heading south on the Meyers Grade above Lake Valley in the summer of 1910,
spare tire, drop windshield and all.
The road had changed little since the floodtide of traffic passed over it in the 1860's.

nounced: "There is more talent required to drive a stage than to be a member of Congress." Some people, however, felt that Colfax was insulting the intelligence of the drivers in spite of his verbal bow.

The Concord stage and "mud wagon" symbolized the pinnacle of luxurious travel on the road, but the majority of the wayfarers were not fortunate enough to ride in such style. These hopeful pilgrims constituted the vast majority, those who had to content themselves with sitting saddle on donkeys, mules, and horses, or hitching a ride on the tailgate of some farmer's produce wagon, jaunting from valley and foothill to syphon vegetables and fruits through the great horn of plenty spilling into Washoe.

A sprinkling of the elite also traveled the Golconda route in buckboards, "Celerity" wagons, spring wagons, fringed topped carriages, single passenger sulkys and broughams—anything that had wheels under it, anything that would roll, was commandeered. Even a wheelbarrow and its trudging owner were discovered on the road.

Not all travelers on the Placerville-Carson route were impressed with this "macadamized," rolled and graded replica of the great Roman roads. One such passenger, recuperating from his trip at the Arlington Hotel in Carson City, penned his views with obvious distaste:

"Volleys of oaths urged the struggling mules up the steeper grades and the mountain walls echoed and re-echoed the incongruous sounds with startling effect. The descent to the valley led through (West) Carson Canyon, a precipitous gorge down which the stage slipped, pitching and creaking, while the grating shoe brake squeaked incessantly. The jolts and jars became a torture, and we left the coach with one accord and watched it rolling and swaying about among the rocks. The wheel horses, threshed about by the jerking, flaying pole, stagger and groan, and the leaders stop and look about them in amazement, wondering no doubt at the cool impudence which would locate a road in such a place. Yet a city in the desert must be built and sustained by supplies transported over this Sierran barrier."[50]

Another disgusted wayfarer wrote, after staging across the Central Overland route:

"A through ticket and fifteen inches of seat, with a fat man on one side, a poor widow on the other, a baby in your lap, a bandbox over your head, and three to four persons immediately in front, leaning against your knee, makes the picture . . ."[51]

Delays, hazards and accidents on the Bonanza Road were legion—and have become legend as well. If a teamster was forced to pull his wagon out of line it often took two or three hours, sometimes half a day, before he could nose his leaders back into the mule-to-tailgate procession. It is little wonder that 8 miles in one day was considered not merely good time for a loaded vehicle, but spectacularly good.

Flash floods that swept across the right-of-way overturned freighters, scattering their loads and carrying animals and vehicles down sheer canyon walls into the river. Runaways were reported, but infrequently, for the press of traffic boxed in the more skittish animals. On wind-swept, bare summits, stages were sometimes lifted and then blown over by fierce wintry blasts.[52]

Although much of the thoroughfare was kept sprinkled like a city street of the times, with water carts drawing from wooden tanks set alongside the road every mile or so, dry midsummer days brought hardships said by one red-eyed traveler to be comparable to struggling through snow up to one's knees, yet choked by an impenetrable blanket of talcum dust.

At the conclusion of each season broken and demolished stages, wagons and carts were discovered in every ravine and gulch.

In one instance three tons of loaded Concord coach slewed around a granite rock turnout on Hawley's narrow cut-off high above Lake Valley and toppled over the edge. The passengers were miraculously spared from a 1,000-foot drop by a heavy-limbed sugar pine that caught the stage and whipsawed the span of six to the rim of the precipice.

On another occasion a grizzly suddenly reared in front of the Pioneer Lines' afternoon express as the horses were stumbling over the granite rocks at Slippery Ford. The terrified animals bolted, snapping the traces and overturning the coach, while the bear, according to one news report, "watched this 'horseplay' with relish and then ambled off into the forest."

Hazards of the road were not limited to those caused by the elements and wild animals. Some were premeditations of men. Strangely enough, patriotism inspired one such peril. At 10 o'clock on the morning of June 30, 1864, a brace of coaches driven by Ned Blair and Charlie Watson were halted by six highwaymen with leveled shotguns near Somerset House, 14 miles above Placerville. Eight sacks of bullion and the dark green Wells Fargo strongbox from one of the stages were removed by the road agents. A gun battle later ensued at the way station and Deputy Sheriff Joseph Staples was killed and D. S. George and C. Raney of the sheriff's posse were badly wounded. Not until one of the gunmen was captured on September 29 of that year was it learned that a Confederate officer, Captain R. Henry Ingram, and his men, all Union standard bearers, had staged the holdup to obtain gold for use in recruiting soldiers for the Army in Gray.

The curve in the South Fork of the American River at the site of the robbery became known as "Bullion Bend" and a monument marks the spot today."[53]

These were the philosophically accepted hazards and hardships of the Great Road that for nearly eight years was indisputably the Main Street of the Far West, connecting the Golden and Silver States and "stretching out like a great snake dragging its slow length along."[54]

Greater wealth never passed over a boulevard as passed over this dirt and stone fill thoroughfare.

With the completion of the Central Pacific Railroad across Donner Pass to Lake Station (Reno) in 1868, traffic on the Bonanza turnpike was pinched off as quickly as it had rumbled into being. Way station owners on the route, who had brushed aside requests of the railroad interests to allow their rails passage across the Sierra Nevada by way of Johnson Pass and Lake Tahoe, were forced to bow out at last.

In the short space of a full to crescent moon what has been described as the greatest mass movement of men, wagons, materials, animals and bullion known to history faded from the scene.

"MAIN STREET OF THE FAR WEST"

Massive mule drawn Washoe freighting wagons headed upgrade above the South Fork of the American River on the Great Road between What Cheer House and Strawberry Station. Photograph taken during the summer of 1865.

Bancroft Library

The Saga of LAKE TAHOE

WAY STATIONS ON THE
BONANZA ROAD TO WASHOE   Section *I*

EARLY MARINE HISTORY OF LAKE TAHOE   Section *II*

Marine Activity . . . The Gay '90's Into the Atomic 1950's

FISHING FACTS AND FANCY   Section *III*

FACTS OF LAKE TAHOE   Section *IV*

C. O. Valentine

BENEATH THE CRAGS . . . THE STATION

Phillips Station (center) camp grounds and old barn (left) as it looked in the summer of 1912. Between the photographer and the saw log cabin lies the Great Road (now Highway 50). Looking west.

WAY STATIONS ON THE BONANZA ROAD TO WASHOE*

Phillips Station

Joseph Wells Davis Phillips, native of London, England, who came around the Horn to California in 1850, homesteaded 160 acres on the Johnson Pass road nine years later.[1] Although Phillips was primarily a cattle man, the heavy traffic to the mines prompted him to erect a 2½-story way station, above Snowslide and Swan's Upper Toll House, one and one-half miles southwest of North American House. South of the mountain meadow where the present settlement of Vade now stands, Phillips built five large barns and the station became a Pony Express, freighter and stage stop during the early 1860's. In order to provide additional pasturage for his cattle he leased another 160 acres near Echo Lake.

In the early 1870's, John J. Sweeney took over as proprietor at Phillips Station. A condition of the agreement provided that he keep the hostelry open to furnish meals and a stopping place for the few teamsters and other travelers who still used the Johnson road. Sweeney, however, failed to take the terms of his lease seriously and concentrated instead on producing dairy products. Soon he discovered that those who did stop at the station appeared to time their arrival to coincide with his milking and churning. His dairy business suffered accordingly. Inasmuch as he knew nothing about putting together any sort of a regular meal, his unwanted patrons had to content themselves with the standard Sweeney menu: hard tack biscuits and cold beans.

Sweeney was well on his way toward establishing a reputation for furnishing the worst food of any "record" on the Pacific Coast when the Station burned in 1873, happily putting an end to his responsibilities.[2]

*Phillips Station to Friday's Station, inclusive.

Over the next two decades a sizable list of cattlemen leased the Phillips acreage, one of them being Levi Darrington, brother of "Zack" Darrington, who was closely linked with the development of Echo Lake.[3]

J. W. D. Phillips died in 1909 and the family establishment at Phillips Station burned two years later. The hotel, in what was known as The Grove, went down under the heavy snows of 1951-52, but the land is still owned by the granddaughters of Joseph Phillips, Mrs. Elaine Lyon and Mrs. Mehetable Jane Sickels, whose mother, Sierra Nevada "Vade" Phillips Clark Bryson, gave her nickname to the post office.[4]

[1] J. W. D. Phillips, 38 years, landlord, Lake Valley Precinct. Great Register of El Dorado County (1867).
[2] James E. Sweeney to Donald Page, Placerville, July 19, 1950.
[3] Refer Echo Lake chapter 25.
[4] Refer Rubicon Springs chapter 9.

Audrain's Station

On the evening of April 14, 1865, a small group of wayfarers were gathered around the telegraph instrument at Audrain's Station when it suddenly came to life and a message clicked over the wire. Station owner Thomas Audrain deciphered the dispatch and then jumped to his feet shouting: "Hooray, they've killed Abraham Lincoln; the dirty — — — —— should have been shot long ago!"

There was a stunned silence, and one of the party rose slowly to his feet, walked over to Audrain and, glaring down at him, remarked grimly: "That kind of talk calls for hanging." The others seized Audrain and were about to drop a noose over his head when someone thought of a better idea. After a hurried conference the men gathered up their belongings, set fire to the station and watched until it had burned to ashes. Then they sternly warned Audrain never to re-build, or they would string him up on the nearest tree, and walked on to North American House to spend the night.[1]

Thus, according to legend, ended the short life of Thomas Audrain's way station that had been built in the spring of 1860, halfway between Phillips Station and North American House, on the west side of the Johnson road going east. Here Zack Darrington ran a store in the early 1900's and it is now Audrain's Lodge, rebuilt decades later after tempers cooled and the warn-ing was forgotten.

[1] Historical file: El Dorado National Forest head-quarters, Placerville, California. Letter of January 18, 1933, Arnold Weber, Jr., Forester.

North American House

"Jesus Christ, Jack, is that the North America we studied about in geography?" shouted a young goldseeker riding the high box of John J. Sweeney's fruit wagon in the spring of 1870 as North American House came into view.[1] Such was one wayfarer's reaction when he first saw the station that had been built by the Coates family in 1859 on land granted to them by road-builders D. D. Kingsbury and John McDonald.[2]

An undocumented report indicates that the Coates sold to Hiram Denny in 1861 and that the hostelry then became Hiram Denny's Trad-ing Post.

The inn was located east of Audrain's and north of the present Echo Lake turnoff from Highway 50, where the "Mailbox" later stood. Eli Clark took over as proprietor in 1864 and '65.

[1] El Dorado Forest Service letter, August 13, 1919. R. H. Cross Library, Berkeley, California.
[2] Refer Edgewood chapter 32.

Sixty Mile House

"Well, boys, we're sixty mile' from George-town," is the observation that is said to have prompted the naming of this way station that lay between Johnson Summit and Osgood's Toll House, one mile downgrade traveling northeast toward Tahoe.

A one-story log structure built in 1861 on a small flat where timothy hay was cut during the summer and fall seasons, it stood on the left hand side of the old Osgood (Meyers) grade below the second turn from Summit; the turn being known as "Sixty Mile Bend." Celio's Dairy House in Upper Lake Valley was below and to the east.

The station fast became a popular stopping place because of the panoramic view it com-manded of Lake Tahoe and Lake Valley. George Wallenrodt was proprietor in 1867 and later Francis F. Harris.[1]

[1] Judge Peter J. Shields, Sacramento, October 18, 1955; El Dorado County Great Register (1867-92-94), Placerville, California.

Hawley's Second Elkhorn House

Established by Asa Hershel Hawley in Upper Lake Valley as a trappers' location and trading post during the summer of 1855, Hawley's stood south of the present bridge crossing of the Upper Truckee River (Highway 89) at the start of the Luther Pass Grade and the base of the old "Haw-ley Hill" or Hawley short cut.

Operated as a way station into the early 1860's it became Hawley and Company in 1870—3,000 acres with 75 cows, 12 horses and 125 beef cattle. (Refer Lake Valley and Bonanza Road to Washoe chapters 26 and 51.)

Osgood's Toll House

In the summer of 1859 Nehemiah "Nemi" Osgood, a native of New Hampshire, located his station where Echo Lake Creek now crosses High-way 89, one-tenth of a mile southeast of Highway 50, at the foot of what became Osgood's short cut the following year.[1] This route dropped directly north down the eastern scarp of the western Sierra by relatively easy grade and reduced the distance between Summit (now Echo) and Yank's Station (Meyers).

Osgood's Toll House, a small log structure, stood on the left-hand side of the road going northeast. Directly across the road was Osgood's family establishment.

Osgood's came into general use with the open-ing of the Kingsbury Grade (1860) and in 1866 Osgood was given the title of Superintendent of the Kingsbury-McDonald Toll Road. Jesse Rhodes Keefer, a 23-year-old farm hand from Ohio, along with Elija Powell, from Illinois, were listed as toll keepers at the station.[2]

[1] Refer Echo Lake chapter 25.
[2] Great Register of El Dorado County (1867-68).

On August 5, 1867, Osgood's witnessed the capture of highwaymen Hugh De Tell, Walton Sinclair and Faust, desperadoes who had been trailed over Johnson Pass by Undersheriff J. B. Hume (of Bullion Bend stage robbery fame) and his posse. Hume and his men ambushed the gunmen at Echo Creek Bridge and, when ordered to throw down their guns, the robbers fired instead, hitting Hume in the arm. The posse returned the fire, knocking Sinclair off his horse and killing Faust outright.

De Tell took cover beneath the bridge and escaped. He was caught several days later above Brockliss bridge and sentenced to San Quentin.[3]

There are several versions concerning the ultimate end of Osgood's Toll House, one that it was moved circa 1911 and made a part of old Yank's Station (Meyers), where it burned in 1939. Reliable authority, however, places the hand-hewn blockhouse that is now located on the northwest side of Meyers as the original station where it was moved by the Celio family after being washed from its foundations by flood waters from Echo Creek in the early 1910's.[4]

---

[3] *Historical Souvenir, El Dorado County, California,* Paolo Sioli, 1883.
[4] Norman Celio and Hazel Celio Taylor, October 26, 1955; also Benjamin Caesar Celio to Ralph King.

Smith's Station, Smith and Muir's, Smith and Douglass', Yank's Station, Meyers, Celio's

Refer Lake Valley chapter 26 and Yank's Station chapter 27.

Hiram Barton's Milk Ranch

Although Hiram "Hy" Barton's Ranch, situated in the first meadow north of Yank's (Meyers) with the Upper Truckee River running through the holding, was not strictly considered a way station in the 1860's, it supplied feed for the freighting teams and dairy products to the traveler, serving also as a lodging house when other establishments on the Lakeshore leg of the Johnson cut-off were filled to capacity. Homesteaded by cattleman Hiram Barton, who came to California in the 1850's, it served as his Lake Valley "Home Ranch" during the summer season. Barton was the father of two girls and seven boys and one of his sons, William Delos Barton, was still active in the cattle business in 1955 with his headquarters at the Tahoe Valley Y. "Hy" Barton is recalled for his boast: "I have seven sons of the Golden West with a Grizzly Bear pinned on their chest,"[1] and it is said that his two-fisted drinking at Rowland's Station Custom House sometimes required the use of a halter to get him out.[2] One of Hiram's brothers, Timothy Guy Barton, settled on meadowland to the northeast, his ranch later being acquired by Samuel Kyburz. Hiram Barton's holding was purchased by the J. Chester Scott family, formerly of Deer Park Springs.

---

[1] Mrs. Ouida Kyburz Barton, Tahoe Valley, October 14, 1955; also Mrs. Fannie Rowland Barton, Sacramento, October 2, 1955.
[2] Mrs. Frank Celio, Lake Valley, November 28, 1955.

Fountain Place

Five air miles northeast of Meyers, on an offshoot of the Placerville-Carson back road to South Stateline and at the headwaters of Trout Creek, a log station was built in 1860 by Garret Washington Fountain, a native of New York State.[1]

Fountain is recorded as taking up 160 acres of grazing and forest land here in 1859 where he ran beef cattle and milk cows. It is probable that he considered the route to the Washoe mines would cross the Carson Range at this point, and the Pony Express is said to have made one of its initial runs over the eastern Sierra by way of Fountain Place in 1860.[2]

Fountain was still shown as "hotelkeeper" at this location in 1882 although Patrick Hagen, native of Ireland and "milkman" from Placerville and Diamond Springs, is reported to have bought the property from Fountain in the 1870's. David Broderick Fountain, night watchman for the Bijou-Lake Valley Railroad in 1892-94, had the holding in 1905 and Daniel Hate Holdridge's family later took over, the ranch becoming known as "Tuck Holdridge's Range."[3]

---

[1] Great Register of El Dorado County (1867); also Assessment Rolls, El Dorado County Court House, Placerville (1860).
[2] Grant Merrill, Woodford's, October 28, 1955.
[3] Great Register of El Dorado County (1892-94), Assessment Rolls, 1905, Grant Merrill, Woodford's, October 28, 1955. "Holdridge, Daniel Hate, 25 years old, native of Illinois, farmer, White Oaks and Lake Valley." El Dorado County Court House, Great Register (1867).

SABBATH IN THE SIERRA

George Washington Chubbuck (fifth man from right), family and friends in front of McCumber's ranch house in the summer of 1883. Mrs. G. W. Chubbuck is standing, fifth from left, with her daughter Rose Chubbuck (Dodson) in back of her. Looking northeast across cut-over timberland.

Pine Grove House
(Station)

Seven-tenths of a mile south of Woodburn's Sawmill on the east side of the back road and one and one-half miles north of Yank's Station stood Pine Grove House.

Constructed and operated in the year 1863 by Samuel Milliser, native of Illinois, the holding was recorded in 1864 as consisting of one house, one barn, a span of horses, hogs, and one-half ton of hay, plus $150.00 worth of furniture.[1] Milliser had a total of 80 acres and in the late 1870's Himan Dana Barton ran Pine Grove Station, catering to the fruit peddlers and shingle teams who preferred the "back road" since there was less sand to haul through than encountered on the "Lakeshore Road."

The only remaining evidence of the way station's location are blazes on the trees near the spot where it stood and the cellar depression of the storehouse, across the road on the west side, now overgrown with scrub brush. Here lead water pipes were discovered and salvaged in 1908.[2]

Between the time Milliser left as owner-manager and Barton's tenure, two other Lake Valley residents ran the hostelry: John Montgomery Gillard, native of New York, in 1867, followed by James Battson McConaha, a southerner from Virginia.[3] The last owner was Robert Jones, and Pine Grove House is believed to have burned in 1888.

---

[1] El Dorado County records (1864).
[2] George Anderson, Bijou, October 29, 1955.
[3] El Dorado County records (1867-71).

Woodburn's

The second sawmill to be constructed in Lake Valley was erected by Robert Woodburn, a native of Ireland, who became a citizen of the United States "by virtue of his father being a '49'er miner."[1]

Said to have been built in the fall of 1860, it

---

[1] Common practice in 1850's and 1860's was the automatic naturalization of a son if his father had come to America as a miner.

was a small, crude structure when compared to the mills operating at Glenbrook two decades later.

Woodburn threw a dirt and rock fill dam across Trout Creek, one-quarter of a mile southwest of the present stone bridge that crosses the stream, faced the spillway with rough finished timbers and then diverted water into a ten-foot-wide millrace that ran west before turning to parallel Trout Creek and flow through the flume feeding the small overshot mill wheel.

The operation of Woodburn's sawmill's single blade, with its chattering vertical motion, became a curiosity of the day as saw logs were run through with a cut being taken the full width of the log. Thus outsize planks became the mark of Woodburn's lumber, and maximum output approximated 6,000 board feet a day.[2] The mill had cost $3,000 to construct but the equivalent of ten horsepower, produced by the wheel, made lumber production a tedious business. It is reported that Bob Woodburn would set a saw log on the rack, start the cutter and retire to a comfortable spot to read a week-old newspaper. Only after he had read it completely through was one 24, 36 or 40-inch board ready for the market.[3]

On June 1, 1870, the ninth census of El Dorado County showed: "Woodbine (sic), Robert, water powered sawmill, consisting of one unit and turning out sash and saw lumber with four men employed, $1600 in wages during the 8 months operation, eight oxen for dragging logs to the yard and 250 M of finished boards on hand along with $2,500 worth of logs."[4]

As the back road between Yank's Station and State Line did not cross Trout Creek at the present stone bridge during the 1860's, but followed the stream and passed Woodburn's, the mill was on the main road; however, it was not a public house or stopping place for teams or stage coaches, strictly a lumber settlement and later a post office location. Oxen and mule corrals, a blacksmith shop and loggers' shacks were located on the flat above and to the west of the sawmill and logging chutes and oxen drags ran from the high ground down to the mill on the river. One source indicates that the machinery from Woodburn's mill was purchased by Captain Augustus W. Pray in 1863 and moved to Glenbrook for installation in the first mill to operate on the shore of Lake Tahoe.[5] This statement is not supported by fact as Woodburn's producer continued to operate through the early 1890's.[6] In 1895 El Dorado County assessed Robert Woodburn's sawmill, oxen, horses, mules and buildings against him personally, although the C. & T. L. & F. Company had purchased or leased a majority of his timber holdings by this time.

---

[2] Increase in production to 10,000 feet of lumber per day in 1888. El Dorado Assessment Rolls, County Court House, Placerville, California.

[3] George Anderson, Bijou, October 29, 1955.

[4] Ninth Census (1870), El Dorado County, June 1, page 2. California State Library, Sacramento, California.

[5] *Early Engineering Works Contributory to the Comstock,* University of Nevada Bulletin XLI (June, 1947), John Debo Galloway.

[6] "My father, Thomas Rowland, drove me in a rig to Woodburn's Mill in the summer of 1877. It was operating then and continued to operate into the 1890's." Mrs. Fannie Rowland Barton, Sacramento, May 2, 1955.

Glorene Dunlap Young

OVER-WIDTH BOARDS WERE ROB'S SPECIALTY

Robert Woodburn's sawmill in Lake Valley on the back road between Yank's Station and Sierra House. Photograph taken in August of 1893, looking southeast, also shows the dam (right foreground) on Trout Creek that supplied water for the overshot wheel.

A few structures, with sidewalls built of Woodburn's double width boards, still stand in Lake Valley and include the old stable across the road from the original site of Sierra House and the barn and stable at Lakeside. Pioneer lakers used to examine buildings and then announce proudly, "Here's one made from old Rob's lumber."[7]

Robert Woodburn is remembered as a genial, industrious bachelor and the records of El Dorado County show 160 acres of land owned by "Robert Woodburn" in the year 1924, which would have made him 94 years of age at the time. This may have been Woodburn's son but no records substantiate the theory.[8]

Today the crumbling remains of Woodburn's mill, with part of the machinery intact, lie one and four-tenths miles southwest of Sierra House meadow, constituting the oldest existing remains of a mill in the Tahoe region.

[7] George D. Oliver, Carson City, September 14, 1954.
[8] El Dorado County Records, Placerville, California. Great Register, 1867; Tax Rolls, 1924.

Hawthorne House

Built by Loyet A. Hawthorne of Carson Valley in the summer of 1862, this two-story clapboard house stood on a ridge overlooking the western meadows of the Upper Truckee River, two miles northeast of Yank's and one-half mile east of Pine Grove House on the right-hand side of the Placerville-Carson road when traveling toward south Stateline.

In the spring of 1868, Dr. Obed Harvey purchased, and then dismantled, Hawthorne House, freighting it by Washoe wagon to his 4,000-acre ranch near the present town of Galt, California.[1] Loyet Hawthorne then moved to Meyers, where he later became Justice of the Peace.

Contrary to general belief, Hawthorne House was never known as "Harvey House" when it stood in Lake Valley, nor did Dr. Harvey live in the valley. Dr. Harvey's name has probably been confused with that of hotelkeeper Charles Wesley Harvey, who kept an inn in Lake Valley during the years 1863-68.[2] There is also no foundation for the story that the station burned in 1870.

Hawthorne House was still standing on the old Harvey Homestead at Galt in 1957, occupied by Miss Genevieve Harvey, Dr. Harvey's daughter. The old way station bears the distinction of being the last remaining hostelry that bordered the Lake Valley leg of the Great Bonanza Road to Washoe in the 1860's.[3]

[1] Dr. Obed Harvey traveled overland in the spring of 1850 to Placerville, where he practiced medicine as assistant to Dr. Asa Clark. A strong Republican, he was considered to have "more influence politically in his day than any man in Northern California." Harvey, who served two sessions in the State Senate, was the co-founder of Galt when the Western Pacific pushed through on May 15, 1869. He died in the year 1893. Miss Genevieve Harvey, Galt, May 5, 1955.
[2] Charles Wesley Harvey, 34, native of New York, Hotelkeeper, Lake Valley, 1867. Great Register, El Dorado County, 1867.
[3] The Pony Express stable and barn standing at old South Stateline (Van Sickle's in 1956) was not a way station and Osgood's Toll House at Meyers is a log blockhouse, not a hostelry.

River House

River House stood one mile northeast of Hawthorne House and three-tenths of a mile southwest of Sierra House on the banks of Trout Creek. Unimportant as a freighter and stage stop during the 1860's it was a small one-story frame building, built in 1862 on a flat where the road formerly crossed the stream.[1]

Lake Valley Post Office is erroneously shown as being located here in 1870 but the office was actually at Woodburn's.[2] William DeCastle ran River House in the mid-1860's followed by Irishman William Brannon.[3]

[1] George Anderson, Bijou, October 29, 1955.
[2] Wheeler's *Topographical Map of Lake Tahoe*, 1876-77.
[3] Great Register of El Dorado County, Placerville, California, 1867; also Assessment Records, 1869-70.

Sierra House

Refer chapter 28.

Miller House

Built in the spring of 1862 by John G. Miller, 23-year-old dairyman and native of Pennsylvania, it was situated on the banks of Miller Creek (Heavenly Valley) on a rise of ground above the stream. Miller House existed primarily for the travel to Washoe and during the heavy winters in the early 1860's it is reported that "a team would leave the roadhouse every 15 minutes to keep the snow packed down and the road open with eight stages passing the doors of Miller House every 24 hours during the height of the staging."[1]

After 1870, dairying became the staple at Miller House; cream was churned into butter and packed into kegs, covered with brine and hauled by wagon to the market in Carson Valley.[2] Miller House was located six-tenths of a mile southwest of Dixon's Place and one and one-quarter miles northeast of Sierra House. One side of Miller's barn was still standing in 1938, but it was gone by 1950. A burial plot to the east of the former location of the way station, and bordering on the creek, is believed to have held the body of the first white child to pass away at the lake.[3] In 1886 the range to the east was known as the "Miller Range" with 1200 acres included in Miller's holdings.

_____

[1] Miss Edna Smith, Folsom, February 21, 1938. R. H. Cross Library, Berkeley, California.
[2] Ibid.
[3] George Anderson, Bijou, October 29, 1955.

Dixon's House

Constructed by R. P. Rainey in the summer of 1861, this way station served as a hotel and lay-over trans-Sierra freighting team stop for six years and in 1867 it was sold to Mr. and Mrs. Harry Dixon of Placerville. Traveling east on the Placerville-Carson road toward State Line, Dixon's was the first place after Miller House.[1]

To the west of the hewn-log structure were two connected meadows known as Miller Meadows and the station bordered "Miller Creek." The main house was situated on the right-hand side of the road going northeast, midway up a slight hill, and Dixon's large barn and stable stood on the crest of the hill to the left of the road, with the back of the building pointing west toward Lake Tahoe. Rotting logs still mark the 80 by 38 foot structure and a small pine tree is growing up through the center of the ruins. The stable was divided, one side for horses and mules, the other for oxen, a necessary precaution to prevent the oxen from goring the other animals.[2]

Dixon's was also known as Log Cabin Number One and Freeman McComber's place stood one mile to the north. It is said that a solid line of wagons stretched for a full quarter of a mile north and south of Dixon's at the height of teaming,

their drivers hoping to obtain lodging for the night at the hostelry.[3]

In 1870 Dixon House was purchased by lumberman Charles Siebeck and at the conclusion of logging operations in Lake Valley the acreage reverted to the Dixons.[4] One of Harry Dixon's sons, James, is remembered as the "Gold Nugget Man from Placerville," a colorful character with gold nuggets pinned to a red flannel shirt and blue jeans tucked into high heeled boots.[5] Jim Dixon also claimed to be the first white child born in Lake Valley, but Frank Power's son "Cy" is generally conceded to have been the first.[6]

When the Robert Dixons ran the station in the summer of 1904, one of the high points of the season was Mrs. Dixon's housewarming (which included home-made ice cream, popcorn balls and cake), attended by friends and campers who bought milk and other dairy products from the Dixons during the summer months.[7]

Chris Johnson owned the property after the Dixons and Stella Knox Johnson had the land in 1957.[8]

_____

[1] George Anderson, Bijou, October 6, 1955. Also El Dorado County Court House Assessment Rolls: "H. G. Dixon, native of England, dairyman, Lake Valley, 1871."
[2] Ibid. George Anderson, Bijou.
[3] Mrs. L. J. Esper, October 3, 1938. Ralph H. Cross Library, Berkeley, California.
[4] Mrs. Edna P. Goodrich, Placerville, October 5, 1955.
[5] Ibid.
[6] Ibid. Others in the Dixon family: Elizabeth, Charlie, William, Fred, George, Henry and two half-brothers, Tilden and Lee Claybourne. Reference: George Anderson, Bijou, October 6, 1955.
[7] Mrs. Goodrich, Placerville.
[8] George Anderson, Bijou.

McCumber's

Freeman McCumber (McComber)[1] built this large two-story clapboard structure in the spring of 1864, locating it one mile south of William W. Lapham's Stateline Hotel on the back road to Yank's Station. Situated on the east side of the turnpike it was notable for its high stone chimney, five outbuildings and the largest log watering trough in Lake Valley.[2]

Although serving primarily as a home for McCumber, his wife, and sons George and Charles, it also became a stopping place for teamsters and

_____

[1] McCumber also spelled McComber; Freeman. Native of New York State, 36 years old, April 5, 1870, hotelkeeper. Great Register, El Dorado County, 1867-72.
[2] Photographic reference: McCumber's House in 1880's when Chubbucks had taken over.

other travelers on the road. Before moving to Lake Valley, Freeman McCumber owned and operated a flour mill at Hangtown Crossing, California, in the early 1850's.

Robert Lucius Bence, wagoner on the road in the 1860's and later dairyman in the Valley, recalled the McCumber ranch as being "on the slopes of Mount Freel, one and one-half miles from Lapham's, going south." In the year 1882, George Washington Chubbuck[3] moved his family from Zephyr Cove to McCumber's and logged the surrounding sections before going on to Sierra House two years later.[4]

McCumber had a dairy, ran beef cattle and cut cordwood on his wood land.[5] In 1918 his sons held only 30 acres of the original 240 acres that bordered Lapham's in the 1860's, and the site is now the location of the Langdon L. Charlesworth's summer home some 200 feet south of Ski Run Boulevard.

[3] See Bijou and Zephyr Cove chapters 30 and 34.
[4] See Sierra House chapter 28.
[5] Mrs. Rose Chubbuck Dodson, Carson City, September 28, 1954.

Lapham's Landing, Stateline Hotel, Carney's Station, Lakeside

Refer Lakeside chapter 31.

Friday's Station

Refer Edgewood chapter 32 for Friday's Station (Burke and Small's).

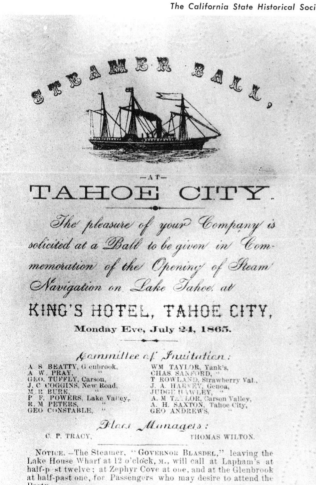

TAHOE'S AGE OF STEAM

Lake Tahoe's first Steamer Ball was held at Tahoe City nearly a century ago with an impressive list of pioneer Laker's making up the Committee of Invitation. "Blaisdel" is incorrectly spelled.

EARLY MARINE HISTORY OF LAKE TAHOE

The first boat of record on Lake Tahoe, aside from the Washoe Indians' dugouts and trappers' skiffs, was "Kelly and Rogers' 20-ton sailing yacht" reported in the *Daily California Chronicle* on February 6, 1856. It was noted that "lumber had already been sawn for the hull and the vessel was on the stocks bordering the shores of Bigler." Nothing further was heard about this hull and no evidence points to it even operating on the lake.[1]

Three years later, on February 4, 1859, one "Tennessee," writing from Virginia City to the *San Francisco Herald*, advised that another sailing craft was being built in the city for use on the lake. This boat was also mentioned in the *Nevada Journal* as a "Yacht for Bigler," completed that year by Messrs. Benton and Phillips. Dimensions were given. She would be 19½ feet in length, carry a beam of 6 feet and draw 23 inches. With native pride the correspondent pointed to Benton and Phillips as "pioneer architects and shipwrights, who even fabricated their own sails." The operational life of this boat is also clouded by conjecture but it is probable that it became Captain Howland's *Challenge*, which sailed on Tahoe into the early 1900's.

On August 6, 1860, teamster George F. "Little Dock" Gordinier freighted two 28-foot whaleboats over the crowded Johnson Pass road from Sacramento. One of the beamy hulls had been ordered by Lapham and Company of South Stateline, the other was for Rufus Walton at Glenbrook.[2] Hauling this unwieldy load through the heavy traffic spilling eastward across the Sierra Nevada stands as a creditable accomplishment

and it paved the way for the trickle of small craft that followed. This, however, was only a prelude.

Commercial sailing and steam vessels of more sizable dimensions now moved out upon the waters of the lake in rapid succession. Today their names are legend: Fish and Ferguson's *Iron Duke*, Burton's *Edith Batty* (*El Dorado*) and *Pride of the Lake*, Captain Augustus W. Pray's *Governor Blaisdel*, Captain Richard Barter's *Nancy*, Ben Holladay's *Emerald I*, Henry Burke's *Pavillion* (*Floating Palace*), Howland and Coy's little *Truckee*, William W. "Billy" Lapham's *Governor Stanford*, *Gazelle* and *Lily Van*, Captain Frederick Eliot(t)'s *Minnie Moody*, Captain Joseph A. Todman's *Niagara*, Duane L. Bliss' *Meteor*, John Washington McKinney's *Transit*, Ogden and Moody's *Lady of the Lake* (*Hi-Yah*), John Moody's *Bessie*, Dr. Kirby's *Fleeter* and *Mollie Bawn*, Captain Todman's *Tod Goodwin*, the C. & T. L. & F. Company's *Emerald II*, William Pomin's *Mamie*, "Lucky" Baldwin's *Tallac* (*Nevada*), Ralph Colwell's *Hattie Belle*, the Bliss family's *Tahoe*, "Queen of the Lake," and Tahoe's last packet boat, Brodehl's *Marian B.*

These were the more important commercial vessels launched (with the exception of the gasoline-powered Marian B.) previous to 1897, that set canvas or built up a head of steam on the lake.

---

[1] A possibility exists that this vessel may have been the *Edith Batty*. Refer to Lake Forest chapter 50.

[2] W. W. Lapham, later master aboard the *Governor Stanford* and *Lily Van*. See Lakeside chapter 31. For Rufus Walton refer to Glenbrook chapter 39.

Two ships, the *Caroline* and *Bellevue*, were reported on Tahoe in 1875 and 1888, respectively, but no record can be found to prove that they ever existed.[3] The rise of such misconceptions is understandable when it is recognized that in pioneer days the shore of the lake was a planning board on which newer and finer craft were constantly being projected.

Even Captain Joseph A. Todman, known as the "Fleet Builder of Tahoe," failed to follow through at times.[4] The *Carson Daily Appeal* reported on November 16, 1887, that Todman was constructing a new steamer to be launched in the spring of 1888, and the public was told that this masterful undertaking would overshadow all vessels that had ever operated on Tahoe, including the huge double-decked *Governor Stanford* and the fast, 20-knot *Meteor*. It was said that this collossus would be 130 feet long, have a beam of 25 feet and, at maximum steam pressure, log more than 21 knots. Her designer confidently estimated that she would be able to accommodate 200 or more passengers. Two spacious decks were planned, the lower one for handling carriages, freight and wagons, the upper for promenading.

Elegantly appointed staterooms and a dining salon with connecting galley were specified. This luxurious "steam propeller" would indeed be a floating palace, its enterprising builder boasted.

In the spring of 1888, however, Captain Todman quietly launched a new 104-foot cordwood barge that was immediately taken in tow by the *Emerald II* and nothing further was heard of Todman's "Great Eastern" for Lake Tahoe.

Despite such vagaries of boat construction, a sizable fleet of vessels materialized, ships that circled and crossed the waters of Tahoe carrying the hopes and heart-swelling ambitions of their captains and crewmen alike.

---

[3] For the phantom *Bellevue*, see *Sierra-Nevada Lakes*, George and Bliss Hinkle, p. 316. The *Caroline* is mentioned in the *Carson City Appeal*, June 8, 1875. The Hinkles, in one of their few misstatements, refer to the *Meteor* Number I and II, mention the *Tod Goodwin* as the *Tod Goodman* and confuse the "new" *Emerald* with the "old" *Emerald*. There was only one *Meteor* and the *Emeralds* were never known as I and II. They are referred to in this work as such only for purposes of distinguishing between the two hulls. Refer *Sierra-Nevada Lakes*, pp. 318 and 366.

[4] Captain J. A. Todman earned his title "Fleet builder of Tahoe." He built the *Niagara, Lily Van, Tod Goodwin,* and assisted George Middlemas in constructing the *Governor Stanford*. In addition Todman turned out numerous 104-foot cordwood barges.

IRON DUKE

"Leave them last four bales out of the hold and wedge 'em port side on the afterdeck, the wind's arisin' from the southwest and sails to be set," hallooed Al Fish, partner in Fish, Ferguson, Coggins and Smith Company, as he swung down from the after shrouds of the *Iron Duke*. He had been directing the loading of Tahoe's first multi-tonnage commercial hay and general cargo schooner, constructed by the partners during the spring of 1860 and launched on a narrow strip of shoreland in front of what would become, three years later, Tahoe City.[1] This 60-foot vessel was named after the famous Englishman, the Duke of Wellington, who defeated Napoleon at Waterloo, and she carried impressive canvas: a foresail and mainsail with flying jib and topsail on a forward bowsprit and jib boom. Her beam was 18 feet and her two masts, 42 and 48 feet high, were three feet through at deck level. A low guardrail ran part way around the gunwale and her crew almost literally had to "walk the plank" to board her.[2]

The *Iron Duke* was a double-ender designed to carry 125 tons of hay on each of her trips to the south shore of Tahoe. At the river's outlet she took aboard bales that were hand pressed from the company's land sections in Squaw Valley, along with those cut at the future site of Tahoe City. Meadowland at the present locations of Carnelian Bay, Tahoe Vista, Incline, Chambers' Lodge and Meeks Bay were also loading stops for the sturdy schooner. Passenger service on a "catch-as-catch-can" basis was offered by the *Iron Duke's* owners to travelers moving up the Truckee Gorge or over the Georgetown-Burton Pass Trail, bound for Walton's Landing (Glenbrook) and the Washoe mines.[3] However, passengers and excursion parties were a secondary consideration as hay was bringing $250 a ton at Lapham's Landing and Lake House Fisheries wharf during the first two years of the schooner's operation on Tahoe.

In May of 1866, an eye witness described "that old schooner with the steam engine aboard that was used in the lumbering business at Glen-

---

[1] Placer County Tax Rolls, Auburn, California (1860-63).

[2] Detail and scale measurement from photographic evidence. California State Library, California Section, Sacramento, California.

[3] "Fish and Ferguson's schooner of 125 tons burden is still plying about the lake, taking out excursion parties and bringing in full cargoes of hay." *Sacramento Union*, September 6, 1862.

brook."[4] Undoubtedly the *Iron Duke* was here confused with the wood-burning sidewheeler, *Governor Blaisdel*, as the *Duke* did not carry auxiliary power.

The sailing hull continued in the passenger, haying and general cargo business until 1867, at which time Ferguson, acting for the company, sold the vessel to Captain J. A. Todman for use as a combination lumber carrier and freighter on the lake.

At the close of another decade the large wind-jammer lay abandoned and rotting on Glenbrook's South Point, serving as a "playground for the children of the little lumbering settlement."[5] Here, in 1884, the *Iron Duke*, Tahoe's first high-tonnage commercial vessel, was scrapped and her timbers burned.[6]

---

[4] "A Cruise on a Mountain Sea," H. C. Watson, *Sacramento Union*, January 1, 1873.

[5] Walter Danforth Bliss, Glenbrook, August 26, 1955, and E. H. Pomin, Tahoe Pines, August 15, 1954.

[6] George D. Oliver, Carson City, September 18, 1954.

California State Library

THE *IRON DUKE* COULD HAVE SAILED THE SEVEN SEAS

This view, taken in the summer of 1873, shows the 60-foot, two-masted IRON DUKE *on the north side of Tahoe City's Custom House and Pier. The General Merchandise store, acquired by Davis and Noteware that year, stands at the head of the landing.*

EDITH BATTY

(El Dorado)

"I crossed Lake Bigler in a half open boat, captained by a sailor who indicated he had been operating on the lake for several years. Her sails were set by a crew of one."

So wrote a *Carson Appeal* reporter, signing himself "E. H.," on August 12, 1862. Although the pilot and vessel were unnamed, it is evident that "E. H." was referring to Homer D. Burton's sailing hull, the *Edith Batty*.[1] During the summer of 1860, Burton, owner of Burton's Island Farm, two miles north of Tahoe City, had placed this sizable windjammer on the lake. Christened the *Edith Batty* (presumably the maiden name

of his first wife) she was a slow-moving sloop, conventionally rigged with jib and mainsail, of seven tons burden and valued at $800.[2] Captain Thomas Jackson signed on as master aboard.[3]

The *Batty* was a commercial craft, carrying the first mails and supplies on an irregular schedule around Tahoe. It took a full week for the vessel to make the entire trip, with Jackson stopping overnight at trappers' cabins and small settlements along his circular route. Layover points

---

[1] The only other large sailing vessel of record on Tahoe at the time was the 125-ton *Iron Duke* and she does not fit the description.
[2] Placer County Tax Rolls, County Court House, Auburn, California (1860).
[3] Captain Thomas Jackson, native of Sweden, pioneer sailor and steamer pilot on Tahoe. Jackson retired to Bijou in 1892. El Dorado County Court House Records (1892-93).

California State Library

TAHOE'S FIRST WOOD-BURNER APPEARED LITTLE LONGER THAN HIS EXCELLENCY

The low-lying GOVERNOR BLAISDEL, *moored to the right of the Custom House, Tahoe City, in August, 1873, with the* GOVERNOR STANFORD *docked at the end of the wharf. Looking southwest.*

included General William Phipps' Sugar Pine Point, Meeks and Company at Meeks Bay, Ben Holladay's in Emerald Bay, Dean and Van Wagener's Hotel and Fisheries (Al Tahoe), Lapham's Hotel and Fish Market (Lakeside), Taylor's Ranch and Landing (Bijou) and Walton's Landing (Glenbrook).

In the spring of 1864, Captain Jackson moved to the wheelhouse of the new *Governor Blaisdel* and Richard Barter, the original "Hermit of Emerald Bay," acquired the *Batty* from Burton and continued to carry the mails when his job as caretaker at Holladay's permitted.

The *Batty* was also available for charter and a party of four adventurers from San Francisco, headed by Ramsdale Buoy, cruised on the vessel in May of 1866. Buoy described the boat as having "a neat little cabin, a centerboard extending six feet below the fixed keel and provision for rowing with long sweep oars when becalmed, which," he added thoughtfully, "appeared to be a majority of the time."

The "schooner," as the small craft was generously referred to, still carried a crew of one, said to be "an old seafaring salt with ample ocean experience." It was appended: "The longest experience at sea would not qualify a seaman necessarily for operation on these innocent looking waters, although the pilot appeared to be entirely familiar with the squalls and crosswinds frequently encountered on this inland ocean."[4]

Ramsdale Buoy unofficially renamed the boat *El Dorado*.[5]

An example of the vessel's ability to drag out a normally short cruise was painfully detailed. It had taken a full afternoon of tacking north and south before the group finally beat their way across the water from Taylor's Landing to Ben Holladay's in Emerald Bay. Upon leaving north Eagle Point at the bay's entrance the following morning, six hours passed before they docked at Tahoe City and the "creeping effects of the sun's rays, reflected on the water, became an agony of overexposure."

After Captain Dick Barter built his own four-ton "plunger," the *Nancy*, in the winter of 1870, the *Edith Batty* reverted to Burton, who moored the sloop at his Island Farm and used it for taking his guests on fishing and excursion junkets.[6]

The *Batty* was beached on the south side of the island during the fall of 1871 and, several seasons later, W. T. "Buck" Davis and George Gillson from Spooner Summit bought the hull. After refitting the vessel, they ferried merchandise and other supplies across the water from Tahoe City to Glenbrook. During the late 1870's the old hull was permanently removed from service and beached on the south shore of Glenbrook Bay.[7]

A legend persisted into the 1890's that the *Edith Batty* could still be seen on autumn days when the wind was fresh out of the south, tight hauled under her own white canvas and moving at a leisurely pace across the blue expanse of Tahoe. Thus was a recollection of the lake's first mail boat passed down through the decades.[8]

[4] "A Cruise on a Mountain Sea," Henry C. Watson, *Sacramento Union*, January 1, 1873.
[5] Ibid. *El Dorado*, Spanish for "Gilded One."
[6] Refer to Lake Forest chapter 50.
[7] George D. Oliver, Carson City, October 2, 1954.
[8] Ibid.

GOVERNOR BLAISDEL

On December 5, 1863, the *Gold Hill News* announced that a "steamer for Bigler" would be launched in the spring of 1864. Captain Augustus W. Pray of Glenbrook, who had constructed the lake's first shoreline sawmill two years previously, was marine architect, builder and owner. During the fall and winter months of '63 he had laid the keel, milled the sidings, steamed and bent the ribs, and sectioned the deck timbers. The boat's steam engine, fire box and boiler were purchased in San Francisco, then hauled to Tahoe by mule-drawn Washoe wagons over the Johnson Pass cut-off. Pray named the vessel for the Honorable H. G. Blaisdel, first Governor of Nevada, and, according to a Carson newsman, "she looked little longer than His Excellency, who stood nearly six feet six in his stocking feet."[1]

The *Blaisdel* was described as a "neat little ferry boat with an over-all length of 42 feet and monstrous beam of 24 feet." A shallow-draft side-wheeler, her design was similar to that of the famous *Monitor*, used by the Union forces against the *Merrimac* one year before the *Blaisdel*'s construction. Two paddle wheel guards rose above her low decking like covered half sections of a Ferris wheel. An iron smokestack on the port side lifted 20 feet into the air and her raised, boxlike pilot house was set well forward. Amidships a square wooden structure enclosed the engine room. The *Blaisdel* displaced approximately 38

[1] Governor H. G. Blaisdel of Nevada considered the vessel to be his "own private carrier" and it was always made available to ferry him and his party around the lake when he "wished to show off the wonders of Bigler." *Beyond the Mississippi*, Richardson, 1870.

"IT TOOK 24 OXEN 7 DAYS . . ."

Ben Holladay's steamer EMERALD, *lying in Glenbrook Bay in front of Lake Mill Number Two, after it had been sold to the C. & T. L. & F. Company. Photograph taken August 3, 1876, looking northeast from Pray's old mill. The* METEOR *may be seen to the left of the* EMERALD *behind the protective pilings of Mill Number Two.*

gross tons and her name was painted in impressively large block letters on the outboard sides of her paddle wheel enclosures.[2]

By June of 1864, the *Governor Blaisdel* was running on the lake, acclaimed as the "only vessel in the world to operate at such an altitude, on the highest body of fresh water known."[3] Captain Thomas Jackson was in the wheelhouse and Pray used the vessel primarily to raft log booms to his Glenbrook mill. The boat also doubled as a passenger and freight carrier.

Captain William Rice and engineer Jack Cameron took over operation of the miniature steamer in the summer of 1869, and in the spring of 1871 Pray's frame house, in a hayfield overlooking Glenbrook Bay, was the starting point for a party of excursionists from Carson City who embarked on the *Blaisdel*, ostensibly for a pleasure cruise. Their destination was Sugar Pine Point, where the boat was to pick up a log raft and tow it back to Pray's sawmill. At dawn, engineer Cameron fired up and the *Blaisdel* puffed out of the bay at 8:00 a.m. Four hours out and half way

across the lake, one of the young ladies in the party slipped while inspecting the machinery and her sweeping skirt caught in the walking beam's forward bushing. With each revolution of the engine her dress wound tighter around the shaft. She would have been crushed to death, according to the report, if it had not been for the quick thinking of the captain, who, with what was described as the "utmost mastery," shut off the power.

Upon reaching Sugar Pine Point early that evening, Captain Rice made fast to the chained log boom and immediately started back. Tahoe's mile-high waters remained calm as a millpond until 11:00 p.m. Then, without warning, gusts of wind screamed out of the southwest and within minutes the lake was a froth of whitecaps followed by mountainous waves that smashed at the wallowing steamer. The small vessel "rocked, creaked, plunged and groaned" as Jackson strug-

---

[2] Detailed from a photograph of the *Blaisdel* taken at Tahoe City in 1871.

[3] *Nevada Daily State Register,* August 14, 1864.

gled with the wheel in his efforts to turn the steamer's bow into each heavy sea. In three hours the *Blaisdel* logged a discouraging three miles. Streaks of lightning silhouetted the Carson-Sierra peaks and thunder rumbled across the turbulent water. Surging crests swept over the pilot house each time the overburdened craft dropped shudderingly into a trough.

Shakily whittling out "joss sticks" in the vessel's hold, and calling upon his ancestors to save his life, was a "Celestial" whose panic was transferred to the other passengers. "Cut the log raft loose, Captain," pleaded a hysterical woman passenger in the group that now huddled fearfully in the pilot house, but Rice shrugged off the request with the remark that "they would make port or else."

The storm subsided as quickly as it had come up and suddenly Glenbrook's South Point loomed ahead in the blackness. It was then 3 o'clock in the morning and the round trip had taken nearly nineteen hours. Not until all were safely ashore did they cease their prayers and then the thankful, water-soaked Carsonites knocked on the nearest available pine tree, vowing they would "never again go aboard a steam tug for a pleasure cruise if they lived until the year 1900."[4]

Weak boilers and excessive heads of steam were hazards of the day and the little *Blaisdel* had her troubles. On June 17, 1872, after nearly a decade of service, her boiler exploded as she was backing away from the Custom House wharf at Tahoe City. Her boatload of passengers were luckily all forward when the blast occurred. Even engineer Cameron had stepped into the pilot house to speak with the captain only seconds before she went up and no one was hurt, but the superstructure covering the engine room was reduced to kindling wood.[5] When a replacement boiler had been freighted in from San Francisco and installed, the "Old *Blaisdel*" continued to operate for another three years. She was then beached at Glenbrook, north of Pray's mill.

In the autumn of 1877, after twelve years of service during which the *Blaisdel* had carried thousands of tourists and towed hundreds of log booms around Lake Tahoe, the squat little sidewheeler, bearing the distinction of having been the first steam vessel to operate on the lake, broke up in a storm as she lay with her stern buried in the sand of Glenbrook Bay.[6]

EMERALD I

Punctuating the groan and creak of massive wheel and axle were the sharp, popping cracks of the bullwhacker's snakelike lashes as 24 oxen, yoked in pairs, strained into the ponderous load. Through clouds of drifting, powdery dust, swirling from the animals' hooves, moved two highbed logging wagons chained bumper to tongue. Roped to the carriers on a hewn log cradle was a steamer hull that rolled with sickening sway as it edged forward, foot by foot.

Ben Holladay's new tugboat, the *Emerald*, was on its way up the canyon to Tahoe.[1]

The caravan was three days out of Truckee, three snail-paced days and barely six miles lay behind the cursing drivers and swampers. Four more sun-ups on the rutted turnpike, that wound across and above the river, were ahead before the top-heavy load would reach the lake.

On Monday, July 11, 1869, the *Emerald* had arrived at Truckee, lashed to a Central Pacific flatcar, but it was July 18 before she lay on the shoreline of Tahoe below the City. Here the hull was completely fitted out, her machinery placed, and the boat repainted.[2] She was launched July 23.

The 55-foot *Emerald* did not resemble a tugboat. Her builders had incorporated a graceful upsweep into her design and provided a low hexagonal pilot house butting directly to 28 feet of cabin that reached nearly to her stern. Twenty-four square drop windows gave her the appearance of a railway parlor car of the day. Amidships, two mahogany doors, port and starboard, opened into the interior accommodations, and a boxlike raise eliminated the necessity for stooping when entering. Behind the wheelhouse and above the engine room a pencil-slim stack lifted straight into the sky.

On Sunday, following her launching, the *Emerald* was "fired up" and two round trips were made across the lake to pick up and return a large party from Virginia City, on hand at Glenbrook for the official trial run. According to a San Francisco newsman, "the *Emerald* was just what had been wanted for years to make it convenient to get around." The reporter added, "She is safe and strong in any kind of weather and makes 12 miles an hour."[3]

[4] *Carson Daily Appeal,* June 16, 1871.
[5] *Truckee Republican,* June 17, 1872.
[6] George D. Oliver, Carson City, September 26, 1954.

[1] Refer Emerald Bay chapter 18 for stage magnate Benjamin Holladay.
[2] *Alta California,* July 20, 1870.
[3] Ibid.

"A STANCH LITTLE DAISY OF A PROPELLER"

The miniature steamer TRUCKEE *lying to at Campbell's Hot Springs (Brockway) in the summer of 1873. Note her squat boiler, and stallion's head on the bow. Looking southwest.*

Captain Mackey had brought her to the lake, but Captain Fred Scott was placed in charge after her shakedown cruise. Navigation was sometimes haphazard in those early days of steam operation and on the night of July 28, 1871, the *Emerald* ran solidly aground south of Observatory Point, after crossing the lake from the eastern shore with a group of excursionists. Her passengers were badly shaken up and the boat's propeller was sheared off on the rocks. Led by Captain Scott, who failed to have an explanation for missing his destination by several miles, the marine travelers dismally waded ashore and footed it to the City. Here the steam tug *Truckee* was dispatched the following morning to tow the *Emerald* back to the Commons for repairs.[4]

Holladay's vessel now made scheduled tri-weekly trips across the north end of Tahoe for the "accommodation of passengers wishing to make the Tahoe City, Hot Springs, Glenbrook junket." On June 29, 1874, Duane L. Bliss and James Rigby of the C. & T. L. & F. Company purchased the small steamer from Holladay and used it to tow log booms to their Glenbrook mills, but it was reported as "running in regular service again" in the summer of 1875.

After being returned to towboat service the following year, the wooden vessel ran on the lake until the fall of 1881.[5] At this time her boiler was condemned and she was permanently removed from operation and beached on the south shore of Glenbrook Bay. The sailing days of Lake Tahoe's second steamer were over.

[4] *Truckee Republican*, July 29, 1871; see also *Placer County Directory and Guide to the Truckee Basin*, Bancroft Library, Berkeley.

[5] "Steamer *Emerald*, Tahoe City, Captain Todman, master; Cranmer, Queen and Lanigan, crew." McKinney's Hotel Register, November 7, 1875. "Ernest Pomine, Captain; J. Cranmer, engineer, Steamer *Emerald*." Ibid., June 16, 1876.

TRUCKEE

"She's mighty small pickin's for a steamer, but them two-foot-high by eight-foot-long block letters on her bow markin' out *Truckee* sure'll make 'em all sit up and take notice." Captain David Howland proudly pointed up his remark to partner Benjamin F. Coy by slapping the side of their new 40-foot pot-bellied hull. It boomed like a kettledrum.[1]

"Mebbe a mite of gold scrollwork above, and the head of a fiery stallion forward like will find her trimmer appearin'," suggested Coy. How-

land nodded his approval and they set to work with a burning iron.

On a sandspit, bordering the meadowland south of Rowland's Station, Howland and Coy had laid keel for their miniature wooden steamer during the summer of 1869. In August of the same year Coy staged to Sacramento City, boarded a river boat for San Francisco and purchased a small slow-turning 40-horsepower steam engine manufactured by John Lockhead of the Bay City. After arranging to freight the prime mover and companion equipment to the south end of Tahoe, Coy returned in order to rush the boat toward completion. Although a transient carpenter was hired to help speed the work it was evident that Ben Holladay's rival hull, the *Emerald*, would precede the partners' marine handiwork into the water.[2]

The *Emerald* beat them, but by June, 1870, the *Truckee's* squat, bottle-shaped boiler, steam engine and thin stack had been installed. A 15-foot open-sided boxlike structure covered the after cockpit and canvas was laid over the iron supports. Twenty feet of mast and a finger boom would later be mounted eight feet back of the bow to provide auxiliary power should the steam engine fail.

The little *Truckee*—so named because Howland and Coy's building site adjoined the Upper Truckee River's inlet into Tahoe—was launched on July 28, 1870, and her suspender-snapping owners found that their narrow 7½-foot beam hull could log eight knots running light.

Captain Howland alternated with his partner as master aboard and during Ben Coy's first week behind the wheel he, too, added "Captain" to his name and signed on A. Hiestand, who doubled as engineer and deckhand.

In the summer of 1871 the San Francisco *Alta California* reported: "Everybody can now be steamboated when they visit the lake," and Lakers went a step further when they admiringly called the little vessel "the strongest tugboat operating on the Big Blue." During the spring of 1872, Howland and Coy sold the *Truckee* to J. B. Campbell of Tahoe City and W. B. Camp-

[1] Captain David Howland, seaman from New Bedford, Massachusetts, pioneer fisherman and boatbuilder on Lake Tahoe, age 46. Benjamin F. Coy, fisherman, Lake Valley, native of New York, age 34 years. Great Register of El Dorado County, October 7, 1868. Coy's last name has been erroneously listed as McCoy and Cay in various references to Tahoe.

[2] "Rowland and McCoy (sic) building steamer . . ." *Sacramento Union*, July 20, 1870, also Mrs. Fannie Rowland Barton, Sacramento, May 14, 1954.

Author's collection

bell of the Hot Springs (Brockway),[3] and the new owners installed a larger boiler, renovated the hull and then announced that they were prepared to offer tourists "combination staging and boating trips on the Truckee, Tahoe, Hot Springs circle route." However, the following year found the stanch *Truckee* "still towing logs, carrying freight, transporting passengers, barging railroad ties, and rafting mining timbers around the lake."[4]

By the summer of 1875 the *Truckee* had graduated to "towing schooners and other boats on excursion trips" with Captain J. A. Todman the new master aboard, assisted by a crew composed of Jack Cranmer, W. C. Queen and Lanigan.[5]

In the fall of 1881 the third steamer to ply the waters of Lake Tahoe had made final port. The little *Truckee* lay at the breakwater alongside the Tahoe City Custom House, condemned as unseaworthy by hull and boiler inspectors. Here she was broken up for firewood.[6]

[3] "J. B. and W. B. Campbell were no relation." R. H. Watson, Lake Forest, September 14, 1956.
[4] *Truckee Republican,* December 3, 1873.
[5] McKinney's Register, Lake Tahoe (1875-76).
[6] "The *Truckee* broke up when beached at Glenbrook in 1879" (sic), *Sierra-Nevada Lakes,* George and Bliss Hinkle. "The little *Truckee* operated until the fall of 1881 before being permanently removed from service" George D. Oliver, Carson City, October 22, 1954.

GOVERNOR STANFORD

"We left Campbell's Hot Springs on the *Stanford* yesterday morning with Captain W. W. Lapham at the helm. Our original destination was to be Emerald Bay but unfortunately Lapham had to settle for the shorter trip to Glenbrook, otherwise we would have returned somewhere in the neighborhood of the Fourth of July."

This smudge of newsworthy abuse was offered by the editor of the *Truckee Republican* to his reading public on June 8, 1873, after a disappointing cruise on Tahoe's new marine wonder. Adding insult to insult, the correspondent continued: "I feel safe in saying that a trim sailboat running before the wind, yes, even a skiff manned by one oarsman, could easily outdistance this one teakettle-powered hull." Lapham's reaction to these derogatory, if truthful, barbs is unfortunately unrecorded.

In June, 1872, a reporter from the *Carson Appeal* had located "two small steamers on the lake, the *Emerald* and *Truckee,* along with several trim schooners."[1] The important news, however, was his discovery of a tremendous luxury side-wheeler under construction at Lapham's

[1] The "several trim schooners": *Edith Batty, Iron Duke,* and *Challenge.*

Landing. On October 1 of the same year the *Nevada Register* advised that the new vessel was being built by "Messrs. Middlemas and Bool of San Francisco for the account of Captain W. W. Lapham, owner of Lapham's Hotel at South Stateline." Captain J. A. Todman also participated in its construction.

The contract agreement called for completion of the hull within forty-three days after her keel was laid. She was 92 feet over-all, with a beam of 16½ feet, a draft of 4½ feet and "measurement of 64.18 tons."[2] A locomotive-type "balloon" spark catcher topped off 25 feet of smokestack to which an iron inspection ladder was riveted. Cabin space took up two-thirds of the lower deck and fixed windows, port and starboard, overlooked the water. In addition to the captain's stateroom behind the wheelhouse, her upper deck had accommodations for crew members between the crescent-shaped paddle wheel enclosures.

It was estimated that 125 passengers could be loaded aboard and a large, open decking forward, which ran to her sharply pointed bow, was provided for wagons and teams. This space could also be used for dancing during excursion cruises. Guard rails and outside superstructure trim were painted black and green and the completed hull was given three coats of white paint. A 75-horsepower steam engine furnished the propulsion power. Her builders anticipated that the "magnificent *Stanford*" would log ten to eleven knots under 180 pounds of steam pressure."[3]

On October 19, 1872, the *Governor Stanford's* machinery arrived at Tahoe City and three days later the boiler was hauled in from Truckee on a mule-drawn lumber wagon. From the City the equipment was barged to Lapham's Landing. December 6 saw the *Stanford*, proudly bearing the name of California's "Civil War" governor, skidded on greased ways into the waters of Boundary Bay and on the tenth of the month she made her trial run across the lake to Tahoe City.

The vessel had cost $15,000 to build. This price was considered high by some, but Lapham and his associates thought it reasonable enough for such a showboat. A crew of six manned the vessel: fireman, engineer, three deckhands, and a "mess steward," who turned out to be Mrs. Caroline Lapham.

Captain Lapham blandly believed that his new ship was the answer to the traveling public's demand for a palatial passenger, mail and freight carrier. During the summer of 1873, however,

the performance of the *Stanford* proved to be a bitter disappointment to its owners as well as other marine-minded Lakers. A maximum speed of seven knots was the best that could be coaxed from the under-powered vessel and after editorial goadings from the press Lapham finally ordered a new 10,000-pound 20-foot behemoth of a steam boiler from San Francisco, since experts claimed "he could not build up sufficient steam pressure with the old one." The outsize replacement tank arrived at the lake on October 20, 1874, appearing more like an up-ended hay silo than a boiler to the startled citizens of Tahoe City.

Lapham now met his critics head on with the statement that his "overhauled and repowered vessel would again be ready for service in May of 1875, capable of a fourteen-knot speed." He added: "My new *Stanford* will cruise easily at ten knots and therefore run the hundred mile trip (sic) around the lake in eight hours."[4] These declarations were taken as a personal challenge by the die-hard *Republican* editor. After the new boiler had been installed and the boat received its certificate from marine inspector C. C. Bemis, the Truckee newsman accepted another complimentary ticket and joined an excursion party aboard the vessel. This time he ungraciously described the *Stanford* as "suitable from the standpoint of speed," but now the "smokestack appeared to be too short, pouring out a cloud of sparks and cinders that enveloped the unfortunate passengers." He suggested that a "canvas be provided over the after deck to assure comfort

---

[2] "James McM. Shafter, San Francisco, owner; W. W. Lapham, master; George Middlemas, master builder." Official number of the hull, for which only one document was issued, 85253; enrollment number 242, May 13, 1873, San Francisco. Bureau of Marine Inspection and Navigation; Record Group 41, United States National Archives and Record Service, Washington, D. C., April 27, 1955. "Valuation of *Stanford*, $5,000"; signed, W. W. Lapham for James Shafter, December, 1873, Placer County Tax Records, Book X, Auburn, California.

[3] Dimensions of the original steam boiler, 16 x 5½ feet; dimensions of the pilot house, 12 x 8 feet; crew's quarters (upper deck), 15 x 8 feet. At first this was only a canvas-covered section aft of the stack, then it was converted into a cabin. A fence-like railing ran completely around the upper and lower decks, with the upper deck reached by approach stairs on the stern of the vessel. Paddle wheels worked in 10-foot-high wells. On her transom guard was emblazoned *Governor Stanford, Lapham's Landing*. Port and starboard on the paddle wheel enclosures was lettered the abbreviation "*Gov. Stanford*" and, underneath in a circle, the American eagle and U.S.M. (United States mail).

[4] Lapham's regular run around Tahoe, when he included the Hot Springs stop, came closer to 50 miles than 100.

and safety for the tourists." Lapham is said to have "colorfully aired his views on the public in general and newspapermen in particular."

As the steamer's mail contract stipulated that a schedule be followed, the steamer made regular tri-weekly cruises from Tahoe City to the Hot Springs, Glenbrook, Lapham's Landing and Rowland's Station, returning by way of McKinney's and McConnell's to the City. Although not considered a towboat, the *Stanford* occasionally moved saw logs to the river's outlet and towed barges and schooners.

On August 11, 1877, the little *Truckee* challenged the larger vessel to a mid-morning race from Tahoe City to Glenbrook. Amid catcalls and a flurry of side bets the two boats pulled away from the Custom House wharf, their departure signalized by ear-splitting whistle blasts. The *Truckee* led all the way and dropped anchor at Glenbrook a full mile ahead of the *Stanford*. Once again Lapham had to stomach the complaints of those who had backed his boat and hear his vessel called "a wash tub that would do better if sails were run up." But more ill luck was in store for "Captain Billy." On August 2, 1880, George Mullen, from Carson City, jumped or fell from the stern of the *Governor Stanford* while she was crossing the lake. Mullen's body was never recovered.

It was of little comfort to Lapham that the tragedy was listed as a suicide after evidence proved Mullen had tried to take his life three times previously. "Why would he have to pick *my* boat?" groaned Captain Billy.

This casualty probably induced Lapham to transfer command of the *Stanford* to Captain D. W. Avery, who was known as the "Ruler of the Lake's Navee." Avery took over at the start of the following season, and his misfortunes began almost at once. He had been master aboard barely a month when he met unseasonable weather while beating his way southwest from the Nevada shore toward McKinney's. Ten-foot waves were reported as "breaking over the pilot house of the tossing sidewheeler, the giant rollers shattering window glass and carrying away two lifeboats swung on davits above the afterdeck." After two and a half hours of being pounded by water Avery finally docked on the lee side of Tahoe. The *Stanford's* superstructure was a shambles but at least she still floated.

In July of 1881 Captain Joseph H. Pomin, W. H. Turner and L. A. Hawthorne purchased the *Stanford* from Lapham. Competition was

brisk among the lake steamers and the new owners were finally required to advertise "$1.00 per person cruises to any particular landing place on the lake." Cut rates threatened to finish off the *Stanford's* operational days at Tahoe and when the vessel carried through the middle of Tahoe City's pier in the fall of 1881 "making the Custom House an island," Pomin and his partners "figured they had had it."

The final blow came two summers later when Hillman and Furman, hull and boiler inspectors for the district, checked the *Stanford's* machinery and condemned her steam boiler.[5] In disgust her owners decided to remove the propulsion power that winter and convert the boat into a cordwood-carrying barge. The *Stanford's* mail contract was turned over to the *Niagara* and on October 31, 1883, the *Governor's* machinery was lifted out at Glenbrook.

On December 29, 1883, before the vessel could be placed in service as a wood carrier, a storm that swept the lake delivered a death thrust to the crippled show boat of Tahoe and she ground to pieces against the pilings of J. M. Short's over-water store at the lumbering settlement.[6]

[5] "Captain Joe Pomin was 'uppity' with Furman and Hillman which resulted in their condemning the *Stanford's* boiler." G. D. Oliver, September 16, 1954. "The *Stanford's* boiler was later used for heating purposes at Glenbrook, therefore proving it was still serviceable," Will M. Bliss, September 23, 1954.

[6] "The exact date that the *Stanford* broke up was December 29, 1883, for I was there." G. D. Oliver, Carson City, September 16, 1954. The vessel's document was surrendered at San Francisco June 19, 1884, and bears the endorsement, "Vessel broken up about April, 1884." United States National Archives and Record Service, Washington, D. C., April 27, 1955.

PAVILLION

(Floating Palace . . . Burke's Barge)

"But I'm telling you, boys, I only took the Central down to the Bay City to locate a steam engine for the *Pavillion*."

Henry Burke, co-owner of the massive new 100-foot vessel, was patiently trying to explain his absence from Tahoe City to a group of "toothpickers" in front of Pomin's Tahoe House.

"We wuz told different, Hank," nosed one of Burke's listeners. "There's a story floating 'round town says you wuz committed to an asylum while away on the jaunt, and you with a spankin' new missus and all—." His voice trailed off.

Burke reddened. "Sufferin' Crize, Luke," he

IT WAS HELL
WITHOUT AN ENGINE

The uncompleted PAVILLION
(BURKE'S BARGE) *off of Chinquapin
Point in the summer of 1874
waiting for a tow from the*
GOVERNOR STANFORD *(right center)
after a "trial run."
Note flat top and "carrier"
overhang.*

California State Library

flared, "nobody seems to believe me, not even my partners, Campbell and Wood, so I say to hell with it." He twisted on his heel and kicked his way through the heavy dust of Main Street, heading south toward the outlet. "Everything's gone wrong," he muttered under his breath, "Everything."[1]

Henry Burke was right. Everything *had* gone wrong yet his saga of disappointment and failure was actually only starting. Early in the spring of 1870 Burke had envisioned a grandiose marine leviathan and sketched it out on paper. Then, with the financial aid of J. B. Campbell and R. E. Wood from the City, he rounded up a crew of workmen who pieced together the vessel's 100-foot keel and steamed and bent the 30-foot strips of clear yellow pine for her frame. Sixteen "sumptious" staterooms, with seven by nine foot picture windows to overlook the water, were planned. An extensive promenade deck was part of Burke's design, and he promised the few towns-people who listened that "everything lacking in a vessel up until that time would be incorporated in his *Pavillion*." A few cynics at Tahoe City figured they had heard that one before.

Financial difficulties halted work on the boat during the fall of 1870 and talk of the new and glamorous *Governor Stanford* diverted the public's interest from Burke's hull that now lay only partially in frame.

In the summer of 1873, Burke finally acquired

a third, and this time active, partner, A. R. Shively, the Wells Fargo Express agent from Truckee. Sufficient money was scraped together to plank over the ship's skeleton and lay on a temporary decking. Appearing more like the prototype of a miniature, modern-day aircraft carrier than an excursion vessel, the uncompleted hull slipped down her icy ways at the Truckee outlet in December, 1873. A heavy curtain of snow was falling at the time but the optimistic owners broke a bottle of champagne over the bow and christened the boat in the presence of a handful of shivering spectators.

The ugly duckling miraculously floated, although enough green lumber had been used in her construction to erect a medium-sized settlement of houses. Costs had far exceeded estimates, however, and nothing remained with which to purchase machinery for propelling the unwieldy craft. Consequently, a corporation was formed in December, 1874, in order to raise funds to complete the white elephant. Known as the Lake Tahoe Transportation Company, it bore the Swiss-navy type distinction of being the first marine organization in the Sierra Nevada. Campbell and Wood dropped out and the company's officers now consisted of Henry Burke, A. R. Shively, John Moody, Pembroke Murray and Fred Pauson. Even with its new businesslike name, the corpo-

[1] Anecdote based upon the *Truckee Republican*, July 26, 1872, news item of Burke's trip to San Francisco.

USUALLY HER
WHITE SAILS
SHOWED AGAINST
THE BLUE

The MINNIE MOODY
*at the end of the
Custom House's outer
wharf in the spring of
1878. Looking south in
the direction of
Sugar Pine Point and the
Rubicon Range.*

Author's collection

MINNIE MOODY

Mrs. John F. Moody sat bolt upright in her hard-backed chair, a copy of the *Truckee Republican* fluttering to the floor at her feet. The color rose in Mrs. Moody's face and, with a determined air, she reached for a quill pen and foolscap lying on the marble top of her sitting room table.

"Dear Captain Eliot," she began. Then her eyes wandered to the newspaper beneath her feet and she snatched it up and scrutinized the startling article for the second time. It was datelined Tahoe City, July 9, 1876, and read: "Captain Fred Eliot, formerly of Truckee, today drydocked his *Minnie Moody* on the Tahoe City Commons for repairs to her bottom . . ." There was more but that was enough. Mrs. Moody's eyes flashed, she crumpled her first note and started afresh.

"*Mister* Eliot," she wrote, "when you so courteously suggested that I christen your sailing vessel it did not occur to me that my name, now gracing the sides of your craft, would be held up for public ridicule. Kindly strike the words *Minnie Moody* from your boat at once." Then she signed her name with a flourish and added . . . Proprietress, Truckee Hotel, California.[1] Eliot evidently failed to receive this letter as the name of his vessel was never changed.

Captain Eliot had constructed the *Minnie Moody* during the summer of 1874. She was a "plunger" type sailing vessel, 34 feet long with a 12-foot beam, a low, nearly flush deck cabin carried well forward, and a deep after cockpit that ran half the length of the boat. Twenty-four feet of mast stood ahead of the cabin and a boom of equal length extended out over the square transom.

The *Moody* could accommodate 30 passengers, if no one minded being "sardined," and when Eliot launched her on Donner Lake she had cost him $1,300 to complete.[2] After a successful trial run, in which she covered the three-mile length of Donner in 17 minutes, Eliot decided that such excellent performance called for spreading the *Minnie's* sails upon a larger body of water. On July 20, 1874, he removed the mast, spars and rigging, loaded the boat and equipment onto a lumber wagon and hauled the hull by ox-team through Martis Valley over summit to Campbell's Hot Springs.

ration failed to attract the capital necessary to complete the hull and in the spring of 1875 she still lay at the Truckee River outlet, fast becoming a museum piece.

Finally, the "Floating Palace," as she was now facetiously referred to, had her fleeting moment of glory. On the Fourth of July, 1875, a large group of holiday-happy celebrationists from Truckee staged into Tahoe City, expecting to board the *Governor Stanford*, which had been chartered for the occasion—but the usually reliable *Stanford* was laid up for repairs. Almost before the hundred or so young ladies and their escorts were aware of it, they had been herded aboard "Burke's Barge," the diminutive steam tug *Truckee* had the great hulk in tow, and the party was headed south down the lake toward Yank's Hotel, where the celebration of Independence Day was in full swing.[2]

Although the bewildered passengers found themselves aboard the equivalent of a wood scow with a high freeboard, instead of the palatial *Stanford*, Truckee's Brass Band, hired for the event, struck up a thunderous rendition of "Suwanee River," drowning out all protests.

It turned out to be a particularly fine day's outing—if somewhat hazy and difficult to recall—particularly for five stags in the party who indiscriminately swizzled claret, champagne and whiskey while reclining in a dinghy secured by a long painter from the stern of the *Pavillion*.

Five years later the *Pavillion* sank at the river's outlet, still only half completed, the victim of a violent winter storm.[3]

---

[2] Refer to Tallac Hotel chapter 22 for the Fourth of July celebration and more on the *Pavillion*.
[3] Refer Tahoe City chapter 4.

[1] Refer Tahoe City chapter 4 for John F. Moody.
[2] Placer County Records, Auburn, California, December, 1881. "Minnie Moody assessed on valuation of $150.00."

The citizens of Truckee were somewhat taken aback by the loss of "their boat to that large lake" but a newspiece in the *Republican* detailed the procurement of "new cushions" for the single-masted speedster and wished her captain good luck. It was believed that Eliot would shortly be back where he could be appreciated. However, Captain Eliot appeared to like what he found at Lake Tahoe as the *Minnie* was there to stay.

Captain James Powell took over the sailing vessel in 1879 for use as a commercial freight carrier and Tahoe City became her home port. Actually the true owners of the *Minnie Moody* were J. B. Campbell and Joe Forbes, proprietors of the Custom House at the City, and Powell's role was that of master aboard. Not one to overlook exploiting any and all possible sources of revenue, Powell advertised that he would "carry excursionists, fishing parties, and sail down the Truckee River if the price was right."[3]

On the afternoon of July 17, 1881, the *Minnie Moody* was recorded as sailing from the river outlet settlement headed for Crystal Bay and loaded with railroad iron for Captain J. B. Overton, of the Sierra Nevada Wood and Lumber Company.[4] Delivery of railroad equipment for the narrow gauge line at Incline did not stop the *Minnie* from doubling as a passenger carrier, and during the same year a reporter from the *Reno Gazette* wrote pridefully: "She (the *Minnie Moody*) is the largest and best outfitted sailboat on Lake Tahoe . . . you can always see her white sails in the distance and she takes out pleasure and fishing parties for two months during the summer."

Captain Powell's thirst for publicity induced him to eagerly accept a challenge from the *Dora*, a fast, privately-owned, smaller sailing ketch on Tahoe. From the start the broadbeamed *Minnie* was outclassed in speed and she lost the three-mile event by sixteen boat lengths, whereupon, it was reported, "the crew aboard immediately hauled to and went fishing."[5]

The life of the *Minnie Moody* came to an end in the winter of 1884 when she pounded to pieces on the beach in front of the Grand Central Hotel at Tahoe City.[6]

---

[3] *Truckee Republican*, July 20, 1880.
[4] Refer Incline chapter 42.
[5] *Tahoe Tattler*, "Jottings," July 11, 1881.
[6] George D. Oliver, Carson City, September 12, 1954.

THE MOURNFUL WHOOSH ONE-LUNGER

Tahoe's 83-foot NIAGARA *shown lying off of Incline, Crystal Bay, on July 28, 1880. This pine slab engulfer held the all-time record for slowness in steam travel on the lake. Four of the five people in the dinghy: Frank A. Titus, John W. Titus, Ernest Folsom and Mrs. Folsom.*

Author's collection

NIAGARA

"Mistah Georgie, Mistah Georgie," came the excited cry of the Chinese wood stackers' straw boss, Fong Loo. "Here come heap tired boat . . . hear . . . heap-tigh, heap tigh, heap tigh!" Young George D. Oliver, foreman of Glenbrook's Lake Mill Number Two, turned in the direction of Deadman's Point to listen as the mournful cough of the steamer *Niagara's* whooshing "one-lunger" carried faintly across the water.

"She's damn slow, that's for certain," commented Oliver.

"You thlink heap tigh 'agra mebbe make a landing by Clistmus, Mistah Georgie?" questioned Fong Loo. Then he doubled up with laughter and slapped his thighs.

Half an hour later the *Niagara* crawled into sight and Loo's crew of pine-slab loaders grinned and jabbered scornfully at the boat's barely perceptible progress through the calm water. This was a daily sight for Oliver and he knew that the wheezing woodburner would be another hour at least before she stood off the mill's breakwater and warped her raft of saw logs behind the protective row of circular pilings.[1]

In the spring of 1875 the *Niagara*, acclaimed previous to her launching as the "fastest greyhound on Pacific waters," had dropped down her ways into the shallows of Glenbrook Bay. The hull was constructed by Captain J. A. Todman from the lumbering settlement and financed by Clark and Cross of San Francisco.[2] Eighty-three feet over all with a beam of 10 feet, she drew 4 feet 6 inches of water. The *Niagara* had been built as a final rebuttal to the miniature sidewheeler *Governor Stanford* and a raised pilot house and 12-foot stack topped off this new "steam propeller." Unfortunately for her owners, the wooden hull's massive 50-horsepower slow-turning, single-cylinder steam engine was barely able to push the boat along at four and one-half knots on her trial cruise, prompting one witness to caustically remark: "The *Stanford's* performance is nothing short of sensational compared to that of Todman's latest handiwork."[3]

In the winter of 1876 her disappointed owners let the *Niagara* "go on the block" at a sheriff's sale in Tahoe City and it was purchased by A. L. and F. H. Fish, original owners of the schooner *Iron Duke*. Machinery, hull, "apparel," and furniture aboard went for $6,984.25 in gold and silver coin. Her new owners, who were used to

sail, reported: "We are completely satisfied with our moderate speed hull."[4]

On April 14, 1877, the vessel, overhauled and refitted for the coming season, was taken on a trial cruise with the ship-shuttling master, Captain D. W. Avery, in charge. A contemporary handbill advertised nightly excursions, Sundays excepted, to W. B. Campbell's Hot Springs (Brockway), J. W. McKinney's Sugar Pine Point (Chambers' Lodge), Yank's (Tallac), and T. B. Rowland's (Al Tahoe). The boat carried J. W. Varney's five-piece brass band and for $1.00 her passengers could enjoy a cruise on the lake and dance at ports of call.[5] Another advertisement, distributed by Sam Miller, tourist and ticket agent from San Francisco's Palace Hotel, informed the public that "overland passengers, tourists and pleasure seekers could view the grandeur of mountain scenery (and) cross the placid waters of the lake, from Tahoe City to Glenbrook, by the new and elegantly fitted up steamer *Niagara.*"

On June 22, 1880, the dependable if snail-paced *Niagara* again changed hands. This time she was acquired by J. B. Fargo, acting for Walter Scott Hobart of Incline, who demoted the vessel to the status of a towboat. Now the *Niagara* could be regularly seen plowing along on the Nevada side of the lake, pulling a chained log boom, her deck forward of the pilot house and aft of the cabin stacked eight to ten feet high with pine slabs to feed her firebox. With incongruous embellishment, a spike of buck antlers had been nailed above the wheelhouse and behind the guy-wired smokestack stood an iron towing bit and coil upon coil of securing line.

On special occasions the vessel was still used for excursion cruises, and the Fourth of July, 1880, found a "grand picnic party" crowded aboard consisting of members of the more lively Carson City social set whose presence practically guaranteed that the outing would be a "gasser."[6] With Captain Joe Pomin at the helm, the *Niagara* throbbed away from Glenbrook's wharf and headed for Emerald Bay, its flank speed of four and one-half knots going unnoticed by the cork

---

[1] George D. Oliver, Carson City, September 16, 1954.
[2] Todman was also a Tahoe City resident in the 1870's and 1880's.
[3] Captain Ernest J. Pomin to G. D. Oliver, July 4, 1896.
[4] C. & T. L. & F. Company's Land and Title Record, Will M. Bliss, San Francisco, September 12, 1953.
[5] Contemporary handbill, Glenbrook Inn and Ranch (1875).
[6] *Carson City Appeal*, July 5, 1880.

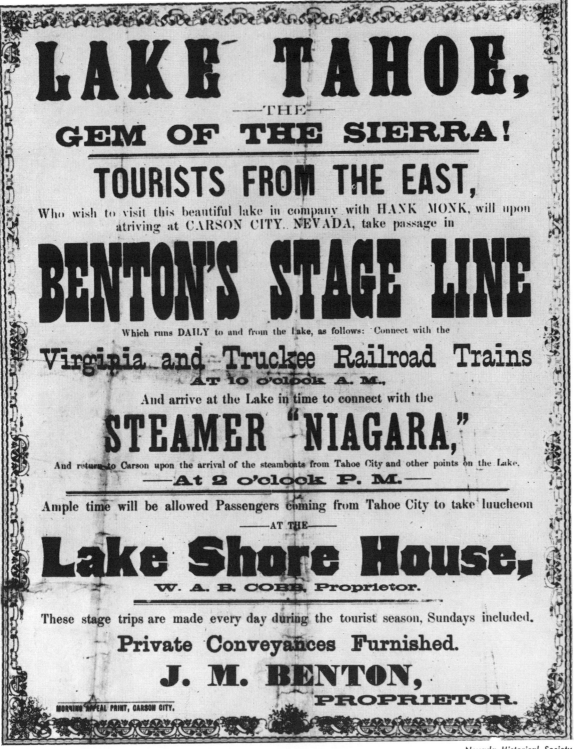

AN INVITATION TO HIGH LIVING AT TAHOE

Jim "Doc" Benton's Carson City to Glenbrook staging handbill wooed the traveling public in the summer of 1878 with a cruise aboard the NIAGARA.

STRIPPED FOR TOWBOAT SERVICE

The 80-foot Meteor, approaching Glenbrook's over-water store and pier in the summer of 1881. Captain Ernest John Pomin emerging from the pilot house and engineer Jack Cranmer on the after deck. Looking northwest with Dead Man's Point to the extreme right of picture.

popping, champagne swizzling merrymakers aboard. When the boat docked that evening, skyrockets were shot from the after deck and blazing pinwheels illuminated her from bow to stern, presenting a fitting Independence Day show of splendor.[7]

On June 29, 1887, the *Niagara* was erroneously reported in the *Truckee Republican* as "burning at the Custom House pier." Actually she was being refitted once again for passenger service with her "woodwork regrained, Brussels carpets laid in and additional accommodations made available for 35 passengers in her ten-windowed cabin."

The *Niagara* continued to operate throughout the 1890's,[8] but the new century found her lying gutted and stripped on the shoreline north of Tahoe City. Here, in 1905, logger Nat Stein broke up the "whoosh one-lunger's" remaining sections for firewood,[9] ending the life span of a hull that had held all records for slowness in marine transportation on Lake Tahoe.

---

[7] Ibid.
[8] *Sacramento Union,* June 15, 1890.
[9] Robert H. Watson, Lake Forest, September 17, 1956.

METEOR

"Why that slim iron slipper's going to sink like a rock if Bliss makes the mistake of launching the vessel instead of turning her into quarters for his millhands." This derisive prediction was tossed by the florid faced perspiring editor of the *Carson City Appeal* at his unperturbed stage driver as the scribe hoisted himself back onto the box of "Doc" Benton's mud wagon.

"I've crawled under, over, and around that thing, questioned riveter and pipefitter alike and we all agree she'll go down surer than hell thirty seconds after she hits the water," the newsman continued heatedly.

"You gonna print that, Sam?" drawled whipster Hank Monk as he shifted a quid of King George's Cut Plug to his left cheek and squirted a fine stream of tobacco juice past the rump of his off-wheel horse.

"You've got a bottle if I don't," replied Sam Davis.[1]

From their vantage point on top of the stage the two men now watched with keen interest as final preparations for launching the Pacific Coast's first iron-hulled steamer were concluded. Davis fished a pad of scratch paper from his back pocket, wet the end of a stubby carbon pencil and began to write: "August 27, 1876 . . . Glenbrook. . . . The largest, fastest inland waterway tug in the country was launched at noontime today from the steamer ways of Nevada's new lumbering settlement. W. R. Wichart, from San Francisco, designed the hull and she was constructed by Harlan, Hollingsworth and Company of Wilmington, Delaware. Prescott and Barth of the well-known Marysville Foundry in California built the powerful steam propulsion engines. The 80-foot hull, with a beam of 10 feet, was dismantled and shipped in numbered sections from the eastern seaboard to our metropolis of Carson City, where mule and ox teams then hauled each part upgrade to Glenbrook for reassembly. A 16-foot long by 52-inch diameter boiler, built by the Baldwin Locomotive Works, was installed. Strength of hull combined with graceful design and a powerful, compact prime mover would have given her an estimated speed of 18 knots had not this vessel, christened the *Meteor* by Mrs. Duane LeRoy Bliss, gone straight down. . . ."[2]

At this point Davis' jottings were interrupted by an excited outburst from Monk: "Thar she goes and, Cripes, if she don't look purty!" The Oracle of Washoe glanced up to see the narrow-beamed hull rapidly picking up speed down her tallowed ways.

"Bet the bottle she floats?" questioned Hank.

"The bottle goes," answered Davis firmly.

Seconds later the *Meteor's* stern dropped deep into the water and then floated out upon the surface of the lake. Hank Monk pulled out his saucer-sized gold watch, suspended from a heavy chain of gold nuggets, snapped open the lid and began to count off the seconds. Without a word Davis picked up his pencil again. Methodically he scratched out the words: "would have given," "had not" and "gone straight down." Then he substituted: "will undoubtedly give," capitalized the "t" in this, and added . . . "is a marvel of our day and after viewing the stirring, proud·lift of the *Meteor* as she cleanly cut the waters of

---

[1] Refer Glenbrook and Carnelian Bay chapters 39 and 48 for Hank Monk and Sam Davis.
[2] The *Meteor* carried two 10 x 12-inch high-pressure, noncondensing, direct-acting, inverted cylinders that developed 180 horsepower at 220 pounds steam pressure. The Bliss family's memorial plaque has a few minor inconsistencies: the vessel is noted as 70 feet instead of, correctly, 80 feet long; Booth, instead of Barth, is named as the partner of Prescott (Marysville Foundry), and Echart, instead of Wichart, as the designer of the hull. Refer In Memoriam Plaque, Brockway Hotel lobby, Lake Tahoe.

Tahoe, we as Nevadans may gloriously salute a masterpiece of engineering. . . ." Here he paused, glanced at Monk's timepiece and then at the *Meteor*, riding high in the water. With a resigned air Sam Davis concluded . . . "that will float for decades upon our noble lake."

"The bottle?" queried Hank Monk.

"The bottle is yours, you miserable, Greeley-punishing, horse-killing crystal gazer," retorted Davis grimly. "And I hope they plant you six feet under after you sniff the cork."[3]

Sam Davis' final version of his news story was prophetic, as the *Meteor* would confound her critics and operate reliably and safely on Lake Tahoe for sixty years.

The vessel was steamed up and taken on her trial run September 15, 1876. She recorded the amazing speed of 19½ knots at 190 pounds steam pressure and 20½ knots at 220 pounds, turning a Ziese two-bladed 54 inch diameter propeller. As her owners, the C. & T. L. & F. Company, planned to use the boat primarily for towing logs, a three-bladed wheel, more efficient under heavy lugging conditions, was obtained to replace the original propeller.[4]

The *Meteor's* superstructure consisted of an enclosed pilot house and engine room with crew and passenger quarters running to within 15 feet of the stern. Fifteen feet of open decking had been provided in the after cockpit and an iron railing ran completely around the raised sidings of the hull. A monstrous square kerosene-burning searchlight, comparable to those used on Glenbrook's locomotives, was mounted on top of the wheelhouse. Above the transom, on a 10-foot flagstaff, floated a gigantic Old Glory that could be seen halfway across the lake when the *Meteor* was underway. When used for private passenger service a removable top covered three-quarters of the cabin and decking.

An iron towing bit, secured to a tubular standard some 25 feet from the stern, allowed maximum maneuverability in swinging and controlling the tow. The contract price for a 100-foot wooden steamer approximated $15,000 in 1876 but the

Meteor's 80-foot hull had cost $18,000. Her proud owners considered the extra amount well worth spending for a fast iron ship. Laymen and engineers alike now made the trip to Tahoe to check the unbelievable performance of the vessel.

For twenty years after the *Meteor's* launching, Captain Ernest J. Pomin of Glenbrook was master. A reporter of the day described Pomin as a "nice gentleman and good sailor," and Jack Cranmer, engineer and fireman aboard, was termed a "genial gentleman who could outswear a bull-whacker or a gale of wind."

When Captain Ernest Pomin moved up to the bridge of the *Tahoe* in 1896, Captain Edmund Hunkin took over command of the *Meteor*. During Hunkin's tenure as master, which continued off and on until 1919, he gained a degree of local fame as the man who *really* knew every rock and shoal on Lake Tahoe. It is said that if his ship glanced off an underwater obstacle he was the first to call loudly to his startled crew: "See, there's one now." It is also reported that Hunkin would set the wheel in the general direction of his destination and then prop his feet up on the spokes with the morning paper in front of his eyes. Somehow he always managed to make port without going aground and the little matter of a smashed pier or two did not detract appreciably from his otherwise creditable record as a capable pilot.[5]

From 1876 to 1896 the *Meteor* steamed out across the lake, towing thousands of log booms from Bijou, Emerald Bay, Lonely Gulch, Meeks Bay, Sugar Pine Point, Observatory and Carnelian. Even under a heavy tow of 250,000 to 300,000 feet of saw logs, the vessel could hold her

---

[3] The anecdote is based upon the widely held belief at the time of the *Meteor's* launching that she would "go down like a rock, or if she floated, sink in the first storm encountered." George D. Oliver, Carson City, September 21, 1954, and H. O. Comstock, Brockway, July 4, 1952.

[4] Report of W. R. Wichart, San Francisco, after making the trial run on the *Meteor*, September 15, 1876.

[5] Stella Tong Watson and Ernest Henry Pomin, Tahoe City, August 16, 1954.

George D. Oliver

SHE WAS AMERICA'S FASTEST INLAND MARINE GREYHOUND

Looking south from the larboard side of the Meteor *at a loaded 104-foot cordwood barge under tow from Camp Bijou on August 10, 1891. Round Hill (Folsom's Knob) to left of the carrier. Frank S. Oliver standing beneath towline; destination—Glenbrook.*

GOING . . .

Near the center of Lake Tahoe the METEOR
*settles heavily in the water
after her seacocks were opened on the
afternoon of April 21, 1939.*

GOING . . .

*The 65-year-old vessel heels sharply
to port as water pours into her
hull. This picture was taken
looking directly east several minutes
after the first photograph.*

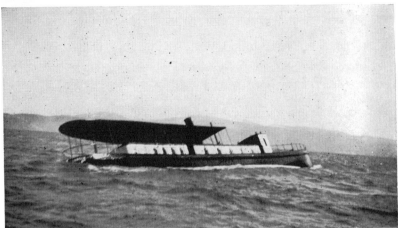

William F. Ham

own with many of the other steamers on Tahoe. Personages of the times . . . presidents, generals, members of the "Bank Ring" and rival "Barons of the Comstock" . . . accepted courtesy passes from Duane L. Bliss and relaxed on the *Meteor's* afterdeck.

After the *Meteor's* home port was transferred to Tahoe City in the late 1890's she continued to steam on through the decades as a commercial passenger boat during the summer and mail carrier in the winter. In order to afford large excursion parties the opportunity of cruising on Tahoe, a cordwood barge was often secured alongside the vessel. With canopy and deck chairs for their comfort, the entourage would move grandly out upon the water bound for Secret Harbor, Emerald Bay, Rubicon Point or other sheltered coves and inlets.

A social group from Carson City was noted as taking one of these outings in the summer of 1908. Families, composed of sedate oldsters and their not so sedate, screaming youngsters, participated. One six-year-old who had a habit of becoming violently seasick at the sight of a half filled wash tub insisted on going along although his mother warned him that he would "surely throw up his shoes if the lake got rough." When all were loaded aboard the barge, and the *Meteor's* whistle announced departure time, the tiny moppet raced up the gangplank at Glenbrook. With

precocious foresight he came barefooted, carrying a shoe in each hand.[6]

On another occasion a tragedy interrupted the scheduled mail run of the vessel. As Captain Hunkin was passing Idlewild he noticed a man balancing precariously on the *Meteor's* stern. Hunkin called to engineer Andrew Jackson Sumpter and requested that he immediately warn him to stay in the cockpit. As Sumpter ran aft he recognized the man as a quiet-spoken member of the crew, Frank Warner. Warner glanced over his shoulder and then dove into the boiling wake. Although the *Meteor* was turned at once and a thorough search made, Warner's body was never recovered.[7]

The night operation of Tahoe's fastest steamer was an unforgettable sight. Early residents of the lake recall the fascinating picture presented by the low-lying hull as she glided along the shore-line in the darkness. When she was running under a full head of steam, flaming sections of pine slabs, reported to have been "big as a man's fist," erupted from her stack, giving the *Meteor* the appearance of a giant Roman candle as she churned away into the blackness.[8]

The *Meteor* changed hands in the mid-1920's when the Bliss interests dissolved the Lake Tahoe

[6] Walter Danforth Bliss, Glenbrook, August 26, 1955.
[7] Jack Bell, Sparks, Nevada, September 1, 1955.
[8] E. H. Pomin, Tahoe Park, October 5, 1954.

Railway and Transportation Company. During the fall of 1928 she was hauled onto the marine ways at Tahoe City and her operating days terminated. A decade later William S. Bliss bought back the hull with the sentimental determination to provide her with a fitting resting place in the great deep of Tahoe.

Although the boat was not up for general sale when Bliss repurchased her, Norman Mayfield of Tahoe City was considering buying the vessel, converting her to diesel power and using her as a work boat, since her hull of Norwegian iron was as sound as the day she was launched in 1876. Some running gear, such as lights and bells, had been taken from the vessel but the *Meteor* was not stripped.[9] William Fenton Ham of Glenbrook, acting for W. S. Bliss, had the boat prepared for her final voyage on the lake. Two coats of white paint were laid onto the hull and then the suggestion, by Tahoe City residents, that this made her look like a "ghost ship," prompted the application of a third coat, this time black. The superstructure, with the exception of the after canopy, was left white.

On April 21, 1939, the *Meteor* was taken in tow by the *Gypsy* (ex *Nomad I*) piloted by W. E. Viljoen of Richardson's Camp with William Ham in charge. Bliss had given orders to sink the *Meteor* in a direct line halfway between Tahoe City and Glenbrook. Viljoen checked the navigational chart of the lake, located a mountain upthrust some five to six miles offshore, and on or near this subterranean peak he and Ham decided to drop the boat. When the *Meteor* reached blue water, Ham ordered her sea cocks opened; then the trip was continued until she began to settle heavily in the water. Approximately halfway across Tahoe the towline was thrown and the *Gypsy* stood by to watch the *Meteor's* last moments. A chill wind out of the south had blown up and a heavy sea was running. As water poured into the hull she heeled sharply to port, appearing to eyewitnesses as though she was about to roll completely over. Then she righted herself again, her bow rose slowly and the famous vessel sank beneath the waters of Tahoe.[10]

Sam Davis' original prediction had finally come true, but only after six decades, when, at the hands of her original owners, the *Meteor* was given the decent burial she deserved.

[9] William Fenton Ham, Glenbrook, October 4, 1955.
[10] Ibid; also W. E. Viljoen, Carmel, November 27, 1955.

LADY OF THE LAKE
(Hi-Yah)

"She will add to the many attractions at Grand Central and a moonlight ride, any time, will prove romantic and pleasant." So wrote a correspondent from the *Truckee Republican* in May of 1877, with a flower in the buttonhole touch, after attending the launching of the pint-sized steam launch, *Lady of the Lake*, at Tahoe City.

The little steamer, also known as the *Hi-Yah*, had been completed in San Francisco on April 28, 1877, for John Moody, of Truckee and Tahoe City, and R. L. Ogden of the Bay City.[1] Moved to the railroad town on the Central Pacific, the boat was skidded onto a logging wagon and hauled by ox team to the lake. The *Lady* had cost $2,000 to build, a princely sum at the time, and she was 26 feet long with an 8½-foot beam. Red and white striped canvas stretched above the large after cockpit of this "plunger type" craft and her prime mover was a 10-horsepower steam engine that pushed her along at 6½ knots. Captain W. C. Queen doubled as pilot and engineer.[2]

John Moody operated the diminutive steamer in conjunction with his Tahoe-Truckee stage lines, berthing her at the Custom House pier during the summer season. Winter storage consisted of pulling her out on the Commons alongside J. B. Campbell's barn, south and below the Grand Central Hotel.[3] Fishing and excursion parties were carried on the little kindling-wood burner into the late 1880's, when she was permanently removed from service.

[1] Ogden financed and Moody managed the operation of the *Lady*.
[2] Also erroneously given as Captain W. C. Owen, *Truckee Republican,* May 7, 1877.
[3] Two *Lady of the Lakes* operated on Tahoe. The second *Lady* was owned by the Callender brothers of Homewood and ran on the lake some 30 years later.

GONE . . . *The* METEOR'S *bow raises and she slips beneath the waters of Tahoe.*

William F. Ham

NEARLY FOUR HUNDRED POUNDS OF "COMMODORE" USUALLY SAT FORWARD

The steamer TOD GOODWIN *leaving Tahoe City in the summer of 1887 on its counter-clockwise 72-mile trip around Tahoe. Looking west with the Truckee River Canyon on the far left of picture. Commodore Todman is standing on the forward deck with the freight.*

TOD GOODWIN

"I'll lay you a gold eagle against a flagon of Old Monogram I take that toothpick of Bliss'," came "Commodore" Todman's taunting shout as the *Meteor*, with Captain Joe Pomin at the helm, slid alongside the *Tod Goodwin*.[1]

"That's a bet and there's more if you want it," Pomin yelled back.

This was the big day—July 12, 1888—the day of the grudge race between those two marine Titans of Tahoe; Bliss' *Meteor* and Todman's *Goodwin*.

Todman rang for full speed ahead and Pomin ducked back into his wheelhouse, where he signaled his engineer to get under way. The two boats vibrated, a white froth boiled from their sterns, their bows rose and they churned away toward Glenbrook. One mile out of Tahoe City the *Meteor* pulled into the lead, laying down an impenetrable curtain of billowing smoke, sparks, and fire-box ash that blanketed the deck of Todman's challenger. Thirty-eight minutes later

Captain Joe Pomin swept across the finish line, marked by Dead Man's Point. The *Meteor* had won by a good two and one-half miles.

Pomin swung his wheel hard over, circled and grandly administered the "coup de grace" by accompanying the *Goodwin* into her mooring at Glenbrook's landing. A cheering crowd had gathered at Joe Short's over-water store and as Pomin stepped dockside he announced with forthright aplomb: "I could have lain to at Campbell's Custom House another quarter hour and still waggled my stern at Tod's barrel stave all the way across."

Todman and his relief pilot, Captain Frank Holt, looking as though they had just emerged from a tunnel after a snorting wood burner had passed through, complained: "Anybody who'd lay down a solid cloud of smoke and cinders, forcing us to alter course three times, should feel obliged to *forfeit* the damn contest."

A verbal hassel ensued in which the spectators

---

[1] The name *Tod Goodwin* was a combination of Todman and his sister's married name, Goodwin.

joined enthusiastically, until the two captains and their crews adjourned to Pat Daly's saloon, where Todman reluctantly presented Captain Joe with a worn gold eagle and then was prodded into standing drinks all around.

On September 15, 1883, five years before the *Tod Goodwin's* defeat by the *Meteor*, J. A. Todman had laid keel for his new Oregon-pine steamer that would replace the old *Stanford* on Tahoe. He framed his vessel around ribs of angle-iron and carried her narrow 11-foot beam out to a length of 100 feet (94 feet at the waterline). She would be the slimmest ship of her size to operate on the lake and her draft ran to 5½ feet.

The *Goodwin* had a 12-foot hexagonal pilot house with conventional square drop windows. Engine room and crew's quarters butted to the wheelhouse. Spacious accommodations in her long cabin terminated in a 14-foot after deck. The *Goodwin's* smokestack, set at a rakish angle, topped off the superstructure. Todman installed the latest in propellers; a 54-inch wheel with its four blades bolted to the hub, so that damaged blades could be replaced without removing the propeller from the shaft. The engine was a double steam unit, similar to the *Meteor's*, weighing 7700 pounds and standing 6½ feet high with a bore of 12 inches and stroke of 14 inches.[2]

_____

[2] The *Goodwin* had 28 drop windows, 26 feet of engine room, a 10-foot smokestack, without spark catcher, and passenger cabin 26 feet long. A permanent canopy hairpinned around the deck from the pilot house and the vessel sported the highest flagstaff on Tahoe, the flag soaring 16 feet above the water. Lifeboats were carried over the passenger's quarters.

TALLAC AND THE *TOD GOODWIN*

"Commodore" Joseph A. Todman's 100-foot flagship, the Tod Goodwin, *docked at Hotel Tallac to pick up passengers, mail and freight on June 12, 1891. Looking southwest.*

George D. Oliver

On October 31, 1883, her machinery arrived at Tahoe City, hauled up the Truckee Canyon by ox and mule team. Here it was transferred to Glenbrook by cordwood barge. On December 18, 1883, nearly three months to the day after construction work had been started, the *Tod Goodwin* was completed . . . total cost, $15,000. W. W. "Billy" Lapham entered into a partnership with Todman and the mail contract from Lapham's *Governor Stanford* was taken over by the *Goodwin*. In April, 1884, the *Tod Goodwin* was officially placed in service with Captain Jack Holt as master aboard. The new steamer could accommodate 150 passengers and cruise at 13½ knots, making it the fastest packet vessel on Tahoe,[3] and, as a dockside post office had been established at Incline in Crystal Bay, the *Goodwin's* schedule called for a Glenbrook departure at 7 o'clock in the morning in order to include this and other stops. She steamed to the north end of Tahoe, then across Crystal Bay to Campbell's Hot Springs, southwest to Tahoe City and on to McKinney's wharf, Tallac House and Rowland's Landing on the south end of the lake. After another stop at Hobart's (Sky Harbor) the vessel returned to Glenbrook. A late afternoon round trip was then made to Tahoe City when business warranted.[4]

In the summer of 1887, Captain Pete Wherner replaced Holt as master aboard Todman's flagship, and Jack Cranmer moved from the *Meteor* to take over the engineer's berth. After a complete job of overhauling and repainting Wherner announced, "The *Tod Goodwin* is now ready for any and all competition." "Commodore" Todman, owner of several of the lake's steamers and now recognized as the "Fleet builder of Tahoe," transacted much of his business aboard the *Goodwin*.[5] This 350-pound giant of a man could usually be found squeezed into a deck chair between the pilot house and a towering pile of pine slabs stacked near the bow. Here he sat in comfort and unraveled the daily problems of his marine empire.

Todman still smarted under the defeat handed down by the *Meteor* and he cast an appraising eye in the direction of anything afloat that might conceivably redeem the reputation of his flagship. Nothing competitive showed on Tahoe's horizon until the spring of 1891 when "Lucky" Baldwin's *Tallac* took over the mail and express contract on the lake. Here at last was a worthy contestant, Todman decided. He issued his challenge.

In June of the year the two steamers moved away from the Tallac wharf on a counterclockwise run around the shoreline, after both captains had agreed to lay over for the same length of time at prearranged ports of call. The *Goodwin* forged into the lead as they left Campbell's Hot Springs and bettered the *Tallac's* time by 17 minutes for the complete trip. Todman was elated as the victory had neutralized his defeat at the hands of Bliss' record holder.

For the next five years the *Tod Goodwin* continued to churn around the lake carrying passengers and freight. During this period, R. J. Waters, veteran Tahoe photographer and purser aboard the ship during the summer season, said of Tahoe's largest steamer: "Hundreds of babbling, excited vacationists climb on every day or so. Loaded down with sketch books, cameras, folding chairs and vacant, awestruck looks, they push, shove and squeeze aboard at every scheduled landing."

In the summer of 1896, a new "Queen of the Lake," the magnificent *Tahoe*, outmoded the old *Goodwin* and, after twelve years of service, she was beached on the shoreline near Tallac, where her hull broke to pieces in the winter of 1898. Early in the following year Todman removed the steam engine and boiler from the smashed and twisted *Goodwin*, then sold her metal ribs for scrap. The last of Tahoe's large wooden steamers was gone from the scene.[6]

---

[3] The *Meteor* was the fastest hull on Tahoe, but it did not carry mail and passengers in regular service at the time.

[4] A revised schedule for the *Goodwin* called for leaving Tahoe City at 8:30 a.m., destination the Hot Springs and Incline, with a Glenbrook stop for lunch, then on to Rowland's, Tallac, McKinney's, Idlewild, and return to Tahoe City by 4:00 in the afternoon. Fare: $3.00 for the complete trip.

[5] "Tahoe City is the headquarters for Commodore J. A. Todman's fleet of boats." *Sacramento Union*, June 15, 1890.

[6] The *Tod Goodwin's* boiler stood for years on the old E. J. Baldwin property (Tallac) and the steam engine was still lying there in the summer of 1956.

LILY VAN

"Only last week I saw a monster cutthroat surface some six miles off Sugar Pine Point and if I can ever hook it you can bet it'll scale in at 80 pounds or better."

Captain "Billy" Lapham was sitting on the steps of Lake Shore House talking to a group of Glenbrook's "Knights of the Golden Sawdust."

THE *LILY VAN* WAS INDEED A CELEBRATED SCOW

Lapham's sailing barge, the LILY VAN, *shown (left of Pray's old mill in center foreground) during the summer of 1884, shortly after her launching, with her twin masts and deckhouse clearly visible. The* TOD GOODWIN *lies at the wharf (left foreground) and Glenbrook's Lake Mill Number Two beyond. Over-water store and warehouse is in back of the* LILY. *Looking northeast.*

He raised his right hand and shook an index finger at the boys. "Mark me, I'll begin on a big, beamy sailing vessel this winter and troll for that whopper in comfort. Come to think of it, I'd better price lumber right now." He rose hurriedly to his feet and started up the road toward Duane L. Bliss' large new mansion on the hill. When Lapham contracted with Captain Joe Todman later in the year 1883 to "carpenter up" a new sailing hull the boys suddenly realized he had not been merely talking.[1]

Lapham's celebrated scow was launched in the spring of 1884 and named the *Lily Van* in honor of Lily Van Sickle from Carson Valley.[2] The boat was an unwieldy, molasses-slow, two-masted, flat-bottomed sailing barge 80 feet in length, with a broad 25-foot beam. A large, square fishing well had been cut through the bottom of the boat and covered by a ten-windowed boxlike cabin which contained seven small staterooms and a sizable galley. Detachable, waist-high railings were run around the sides of the ark's flat decking as a

protection for strolling passengers, and looking aft from the ramlike bowsprit two masts could be seen fore and aft of the cabin. High on the after spar stood a crow's nest from which Lapham intended to scan the water and thus determine where the fish were rising. In order to nail down his chances of hooking the mammoth trout that plagued his imagination, Captain "Billy" ordered 1,000 feet of special 80-pound test line with cork floats to hold it at various depths. On one end was a length of wire leader and a formidable-looking hand-forged hook.[2]

During the time the *Lily* sailed under Lapham's flag it was generally reserved for his own private use. Occasionally he chartered her to private parties who wished to spend weekends "drift-sailing" upon the waters of the Big Blue and trolling for the giant trout that even Lapham had finally begun to realize only existed in the fumes

---

[1] Anecdote based on "Lapham's big fish story" as told by Ernest Henry Pomin, Tahoe City, October 2, 1954.

[2] E. H. Pomin, October 6, 1954.

EIGHT OF THE GAY "JOLLY NINE"

This poised and posed group of wasp-waisted, flower-hatted ladies and their three escorts, headed by Oscar Tally (on the right with flag), was taken on the shoreline at Tallac in July of 1899. The "J.N." emblem may be seen in the upper left-hand corner of the picture.

of his fancy. If there was no wind to fill the sails, arrangements for a tow could always be made with one of the smaller steam-powered vessels on the lake and, after his difficulties with the *Governor Stanford*, it is understandable why sail instead of mechanical propulsion power appealed to him now.

Beginning with the year 1889, nebulous and varying newspaper and "eyewitness" accounts of the *Lily Van's* operational life on Tahoe clouded the true story. In September of 1889, the *Truckee Republican* reported that the hull was discovered by Dr. Kirby and his wife, owners at the time of Emerald Bay Camp, and that it was "lying near shore in a half sunken condition, whereupon the Kirbys hauled it ashore and converted the scow into additional sleeping rooms." According to another story, the *Lily* was beached at Bijou by Orasmus W. Dickey, Thomas B. Rowland's son-in-law, "who remodeled it and made a house out of the old hulk." Actually Dickey had acquired Will Tevis Sr.'s houseboat, the *Mahala*, formerly anchored off Tallac.[3] Still another yarn is that the *Lily Van* was purchased by a gang of murderous cutthroats who utilized the boat's fishing well as a convenient deep-water "disposal dump" for the weighted bodies of their victims.

Indisputable evidence, however, points to Walter "Red" Comryn, a Scot who claimed to have been an officer in Her Majesty's Navy, acquiring the hull from Lapham in 1890 and using it as a fishing barge out of Tallac and Emerald Bay, but rumors concerning the location of the sluggish *Lily* continued. The *San Francisco Call* even mistakenly reported ". . . that schooner (*Lily Van*) wrecked in a storm on Tahoe in October, 1892."[4]

In the summer of 1895, title to the *Lily Van* was passed to Mrs. Walter Comryn, who transformed the sailing barge into a houseboat, complete with flowered chintz curtains. In 1896 the hull was towed to Taylor Creek's outlet, west of Tallac Hotel, where she was placed in service by the California Fish Commission as a floating station to obtain spawn from trout seined out of the lake.[5] One "Billy" Osborne is mentioned as owner at this time but county records show the hull was still the property of the Comryns. Early in the 1900's Walter Comryn purchased two acres of land on the northwest shore of Emerald Bay, adjoining Emerald Bay Camp. Here the elusive "now you see her now you don't" *Lily Van* was finally winched from the water, foundations were laid beneath the old barge and she became a bayshore home.[6]

A decade later Dr. Hartland Law of San Francisco bought the property and ownership of the pie-shaped parcel changed hands again during the 1940's and '50's. However, the remodeled sailing vessel continues to stand on the shoreline of Emerald Bay, the last physical record of a wooden hull still existing at Tahoe that plied the waters of the lake nearly three-quarters of a century ago.

------

[3] Lloyd Tevis, Sunnyside, August 12, 1955; also Mrs. Fannie Rowland Barton, Sacramento, May 5, 1955.
[4] *San Francisco Call,* October 9, 1892.
[5] El Dorado County Court House Records, Placerville, California, 1896.
[6] E. H. Pomin, October 6, 1954.

MAMIE

The sun had broken over the eastern Sierra, reaching into pockets of darkness that lay in the canyons and shafting its brilliance across a seemingly endless expanse of placid water. Not a ripple disturbed the mirrorlike smoothness of Tahoe on this early morning in June, 1898.

To the sizable group of Tallac House guests waiting on the wharf this was the moment that made rising in the darkness worth while. Boatmen and porters hurried about, making last-minute additions to the equipment they had loaded aboard the fleet of small fishing boats tied bow to stern in a semicircle. Cushions were tossed onto hard pine seats, gigantic fishing nets shaken out, hampers of food covered with starched linen, bait wells filled with flashing minnows, and wriggling angleworms packed into the damp sawdust of tobacco cans. Rods, reels, lines, extra leaders, Red Star spinners and cards of hooks had already been stowed aboard; now they were rechecked. Parasols, floppy hats, sun visors, fringed laprobes, stone crocks of sarsaparilla and ginger beer, jars of Dr. LeRoy's sunburn lotion and jugs of limewater completed the stores. Such activity seemed to indicate that a prolonged sea voyage was about to get under way.

Alongside the pilings, supporting Tallac's overwater boathouse and saloon, the little cigar-thin, forty-foot *Mamie* waited, smoke funneling from her aproned stack. Captain Joseph H. Pomin reached for the safety valve and a white head of steam swirled from the *Mamie's* tiny Babcock boiler. As his son Ernest stacked the last pine slab carefully amidship, the whistle piped. A mad scramble ensued. Wasp-waisted ladies were

John Ernest Pomin

CAPTAIN JOE AND THE CAPER-CUTTERS

Captain Joe Pomin (holding setting pole), the MAMIE and the "Jolly Nine" at Tallac Hotel's wharf and outer boathouse in August, 1900, upon their return from the "trouting grounds."

handed carefully aboard the fishing skiffs by their attentive escorts who then climbed in beside them. Fishing guides took their posts. An elite group clambered onto the bow and stern of the *Mamie* while a mustachioed barkeep hastily slid a case of Baldwin's Chicamauga sauterne, vintage of 1892, onto the after deck.[1]

The high-pitched whistle sounded again. Slowly the marine cavalcade pulled away from the wharf, the diminutive woodburner churning a froth of crystal as she took up the slack in her tow. Puffing like a toy locomotive, the *Mamie* moved grandly out into the lake, turned in a wide arc and headed toward South Eagle Point. Evenly spaced in her wake plowed her brood of fishing boats filled with excited, chattering anglers.

Upon arriving at the "trouting grounds," Captain Pomin dropped one boat at a time and then continued on with his own party in a slow troll toward Rubicon Point, popping the whistle each time a fish was caught. This event, re-enacted daily by the *Mamie* during the height of the season, became a symbol of the spirited living at Tallac in the "Gay '90's."

The miniature steamer had been built in San Francisco during the spring of 1887 for William Pomin of Tahoe City. Shipped to Truckee by rail, she was hauled up the canyon to the lake by one of Rube Saxton's logging wagons and launched on June 26.[2] Captain Frank Holt moved from the wheelhouse of the *Tod Goodwin*, taking over as master aboard, and the *Mamie* was placed in operation immediately as a passenger, freight and mail boat.

During the summer of 1887 the boat left Tahoe City regularly on her morning run to Carnelian Bay, Campbell's Hot Springs, and Incline, returning to the City at noontime. Here, at the Custom House wharf, she lay to for afternoon charter work on the calm, lee side of the lake. A news item described the pocket-size eight-foot-beam hull as a "neat and swift little daisy of a propeller, holding ten to twelve people and available to the discriminating."[3]

With the launching of the *Tallac* in the fall of 1890, the *Mamie's* scheduled run was turned over to the larger boat and Lawrence and Company of Tallac Hotel purchased Pomin's craft for use as a fishing and excursion vessel.

The proud little *Mamie* now became an essential part of swank Tallac's summer activities and she would be remembered for decades after her propeller had turned for the last time. Her tiny steam engine and miniature boiler were carried amidship with two-foot pine slabs stacked forward and aft of the funnel to feed her firebox. A large paddleboard-shaped top ran above her deck, and when she was under way, an oversize "Old Glory" fluttered from her high standard on the bow. The flag was carried here instead of above the stern so that it would not interfere with the fishermen reclining comfortably in the after cockpit.

The *Mamie's* covey of fishing boats were named by number: Mamie One, Two, Three, Four, and so on up to Twenty-five. When guests of Tallac House pursued the Tahoe silversides the boat towed a dinghy from a port outrigger spar. This allowed four-line fishing; two lines from the *Mamie* and two from the smaller boat.[4]

No one could mistake this queenly little vessel for others running on the lake during the same period. Four gold stars adorned her bow, port and starboard, and on her transom three stars were emblazoned in gold leaf over her name. Captain Joe Pomin had been given a permanent berth as master aboard the *Mamie* and for 15 years his name would be synonymous with that of Tallac's party boat. As she was able to cruise easily at 7 or 8 knots, trips to all points on the lake were made during the season. Champagne and caviar parties became the order of the day and young dandies and their ladies could always be assured of an exciting time whether they boarded the boat for a picnic junket or a moonlight cruise.

Pomin's steadiest customers at the famous hostelry were a gay party group calling themselves the "Jolly Nine." Its members even had their own flag made up with the letters "J. N." embroidered on a star-studded white silk background. As Captain Joe was not averse to downing a few tumblers of sparkling grape himself, given the proper occasion, he usually took his young son Ernest along as a standby pilot to assure the safe return of the wassailing revelers.[5]

The colorful little woodburner safely made hundreds of trips on the waters of Tahoe only to bow at last to an unexpected northeast wind that struck the lake during the winter of 1907. Curling white-capped combers snapped the *Mamie's* mooring lines and she pounded to pieces and sank at her berth alongside Tallac's old wharf.[6]

[1] John Ernest Pomin, Idlewild, Lake Tahoe, September 4, 1954.
[2] Ibid.
[3] *Sacramento Union*, June 15, 1890.
[4] J. E. Pomin, September 26, 1956.
[5] Ibid.
[6] Ibid.

DRY DOCKED WITH A LOG RAFT ASSIST

The second EMERALD *owned by the C. & T. L. & F. Company is here shown off of Glenbrook's South Point in August of 1888 with a V-boom in tow. Note floating logs (foreground) in front of Lake Mill Number Two. Looking west.*

EMERALD II

The steady throb of the *Emerald's* steam engine rattled the iron grating beneath Captain Ernest John Pomin's feet and he blinked his eyes sleepily. It was a Sunday in the last week of August, 1887, and behind the towboat on a close-haul tie moved 160,000 feet of log raft picked up early that morning at Camp Bijou after an emergency call had come through from George Oliver, foreman at Glenbrook's Lake Mill Number Two. Suddenly an ear-splitting blast snapped Pomin erect. The engine's monotonous beat faltered, then stopped abruptly. Moments later engineer Cranmer's face appeared at the door of the pilot house. "We've blown a cylinder head clean off, Ernie," he announced breathlessly. "I'll finish valving down." Cranmer turned and disappeared.

Pomin set the wheel, stepped out on deck and walked forward to the bow. They were several hundred yards off the Point and headed in the direction of Pray's Cove. "A few more minutes of power and we would have made it," Pomin muttered in disgust. Then he peered aft. The taut towline had slackened and dropped into

the water but the log raft was rapidly bearing down on the *Emerald*, its momentum assisted by a brisk wind out of the west.

Seconds later the stern of the boat was caught by the V-boom and the heavy tow lifted the hull and carried it forward. Captain Pomin jumped back into the wheelhouse and set his course for the sand beach ahead. Cranmer joined him and they exchanged glances as shallow water showed beneath them. "Brace yourself, Jack, we're going ashore," Pomin shouted. At that instant the bow of the *Emerald* plowed into the sand, lifted and furrowed its way up on the beach. Cranmer glanced over the side. They were high and dry. "I'll lay odds that's the first time a log raft has drydocked a vessel. You'd better break out the stack ladder, Jack, or we'll never get down without snapping a leg," commented Pomin dryly. As Cranmer lowered the steps Captain Pomin waved him ahead. "You first, Jack," he remarked with a smile. "Remember—captains and other dunderheads are always last."[1]

---

[1] Walter Danforth Bliss, Glenbrook, August 25, 1955. Captain E. J. Pomin, and Cranmer on occasion, operated the *Emerald II* as well as the *Meteor*.

This incident was recorded as one of the few times when the *Emerald's* performance had not been dependability itself.

The second *Emerald*, taking the name of Ben Holladay's wooden hulled steamer launched in 1869, was an iron vessel built by the Union Iron Works of San Francisco. She was shipped to the lake on the familiar "land route of the steamers."[2] On May 16, 1887, the *Carson Appeal* announced that a new steamer would be placed on Tahoe, adding that her builders were confident she would be "faster than the speedy *Meteor*" and, stripped to her decking, she was loaded onto two chained logging wagons at Carson City and laboriously dragged to Glenbrook by mule and ox team. Although she was 60 feet long, her narrow beam of nine feet had allowed the boat to pass through the tunnels and snowsheds at Donner Summit without difficulty.

After being jockeyed onto the lumbering settlement's marine ways, workmen outfitted her, and the new *Emerald* was launched on June 15, 1887.[3]

Glenbrook's marine workhorse was placed in service by her owners, Bliss and Yerington, delivering logs to the lumbering settlement's whirring circular saws. With the exception of the *Meteor*, the *Emerald* towed more V-booms during her lifetime than any other tugboat on Tahoe.

In 1898 the *Emerald's* home port was changed to Tahoe City, where she operated as a workboat until permanently removed from the water in 1935. Six years later she was sold for scrap and, with her bow blow-torched off, the hull was shipped back to Oakland, California, ending nearly a half-century of service on Lake Tahoe.

---

[2] The "land route of the steamers" was considered to be Carson City to Glenbrook by way of Clear Creek and Spooner's.

[3] Accounts of the *Emerald's* shipment to Tahoe vary. "The hull was hauled to the Tahoe City Commons by Rube Saxton's logging wagon up the Truckee River Canyon and launched early in the summer of 1887." Ernest Henry Pomin, September 5, 1954. "New steamer (*Emerald*) launched at Glenbrook on June 15, 1887." *Carson City Appeal*, June 18, 1887. "New steamer *Emerald* launched at Glenbrook and now operating." *Truckee Republican*, June 16, 1887.

THE PROUD LITTLE *HATTIE BELLE*

Ralph Colwell's steam launch, the HATTIE BELLE, docked at Moana Villa in the fall of 1898. Clubhouse over the water on the left of picture and resort cottages to the right. Looking southeast in the direction of Sugar Pine Point.

Hattie Belle Colwell Almstaden

HATTIE BELLE

In June, 1890, a 38-foot-long steam launch slipped down the ways into the water at Tahoe City. Built in San Francisco for Ralph Cowell, owner of Bellevue Hotel on Sugar Pine Point, the wooden hull had been shipped by rail to Truckee and moved by mule team up the Truckee Canyon to the Tahoe Commons. Before the launching the first name of Colwell's wife, *Hattie Belle*, was lettered on the bow.

This new "single propeller," following in the wake of the little *Truckee* and operating during the same period as the *Mamie*, carried a squat, upright boiler and the highest stack of any vessel approaching her size on the lake. Her designer had laid a clean, seaworthy rise into her bow and the boat was acclaimed as "the most modern marine accomplishment seen in decades." Twelve large drop windows framed a 14-foot cabin, and her steam engine and boiler were installed nearly amidships. A high wafer-like canopy on pipe supports covered the *Hattie Belle's* large after cockpit that ended in a fantailed stern with a long overhang. Fifteen passengers could be accommodated comfortably, as this trim-looking launch had a generous beam of 8½ feet.

In the summer of 1893 the home port of the *Hattie Belle* was changed to Moana Villa, where she operated for some 30 years, carrying guests of the resort and Rubicon Springs Hotel on excursion cruises and fishing trips around Tahoe. During the early 1920's she was removed from service on the lake.[1]

---

[1] Mrs. Hattie Belle Colwell Almstaden, Placerville, October 6, 1955.

NEVADA

(Tallac)

A rifle bullet whistled across the water and cracked through the glass of the *Nevada's* pilot house. Captain Joseph H. Pomin lunged to the floor. Two more reports followed and more glass tinkled around Pomin as lead slugs nicked the steering wheel and buried themselves in the window frame.

"Lucky I'm backing away from *that* damn dock," muttered Pomin as he rose slowly to his feet and peered warily around the half-open door of the wheelhouse. What he saw made him chuckle in spite of his dangerous predicament.

Jumping up and down on the east end of Tahoe City's Custom House pier, and waving a gun wildly in one hand, was Charlie Ferris. It appeared as though he were about to leap into the water and swim out after the boat.

"Come back and fight, you snivelin' coward," screamed Ferris, his voice carrying clearly across the water. Pomin didn't bother to answer. He shrugged and rang for full speed ahead, spinning the wheel hard aport at the same time. The *Nevada* shuddered and swung slowly around. Pomin corrected the wheel and pointed the vessel's bow toward McKinney's. After making certain that he was out of gunshot range he inspected the damage. New window glass, that was about all, he decided. But that crazy Ferris, what in hell had gotten into him?

Captain Joe reconstructed the circumstances of their meeting earlier that afternoon. He and his brother Fred had been standing at Campbell's bar having a quiet drink when Ferris walked in. An argument started when Ferris accused Fred of picking up his change; then Ferris made the mistake of getting fighting mad. When Charlie swung on Fred, he had naturally stepped in to help his brother. Finding a billiard cue handy he laid Ferris out on the floor with a simple warning tap on the head. That was about it, Pomin reflected, and he figured it didn't call for gunplay.

McKinney's pier lay directly ahead now and, ringing for slow ahead, Pomin dismissed Ferris from his mind. It was a Wednesday evening and he'd bet a two-bit piece Jim Murphy was serving venison stew for dinner. His eyes sparkled. He'd have a "charge" or two with Luke Morgan at the bar and then eat. After all the best part of the day lay ahead . . . and he was still alive to enjoy it.[1]

This was the summer of 1908 and Captain Joe had taken over as master aboard the *Nevada* several weeks before, having lost the *Mamie* the previous winter. The *Nevada* was a steel hull and considered a good command, purchased originally by Elias J. "Lucky" Baldwin and Lawrence and Company of Tallac House.[2] Built at Buffalo, New York, during the spring of 1890, the 60-foot steamer was shipped by rail to Truckee and moved by logging wagon and "back-action truck"

---

[1] Pomin-Ferris affray is based on a description by Ernest H. Pomin and Robert H. Watson, Tahoe City, May 22, 1954.

[2] Lawrence and Company, the "Company" being Mrs. G. L. M. Comstock, wife of M. Lawrence's former partner, whose lease interest in Tallac was later acquired by her son, Harry O. Comstock.

to Tahoe City. In the fall of the same year the new vessel was launched on log ways from the Commons after being christened *Tallac*.

In March of 1891, a correspondent from the *Carson City Appeal*, cruising on the snowbound lake aboard the *Meteor* with a group of Nevada legislators, noted that "they passed the little mail steamer *Tallac* off of Bellevue Hotel" (Sugar Pine Point), and during September, 1891, the *Tallac* was reported by her owners to have "burned to the water's edge along with a part of the Tallac House pier."[3] Damage is said to have totaled $4,000 and the metal hull was towed to Tahoe City and hauled out again on the hewn saw log ways for repairs.[4] Here workmen from the Union

Iron Works, San Francisco, not only renovated the *Tallac*, but extended her length 25 feet.[5]

After being reworked and sectioned out to 85 feet she was launched again in the spring of 1892 and grandly advertised in Tallac Hotel's brochure as the "handsomest steamer on the Pacific Coast." Ample evidence supported this claim and the "Lucky" Baldwin touch was found throughout the vessel. Her cabins were finished in rare woods

[3] G. D. Oliver, Carson City, September 18, 1954.
[4] R. H. Watson, Tahoe City, August 26, 1954; also El Dorado Tax Rolls, Placerville, California.
[5] E. H. Pomin and R. H. Watson, Tahoe City, May 22, 1954. The vessel originally measured 60 feet and her length in 1940 was 85 feet, hence the footage added must have been 25 feet.

THE MARINE SURREY WITH THE FRINGE ON TOP

E. J. "Lucky" Baldwin's 60-foot TALLAC *at Armstrong's "Milflores," Emerald Bay, in July of 1891, previous to her being lengthened 25 feet. Looking northwest at the "back fence" (Granite Peak—Mountain).*

George D. Oliver

BALDWIN'S SHOWBOAT . . . SECTIONED OUT TO 85 FEET

The TALLAC *(later* NEVADA*) headed south after picking up passengers and mail at Tahoe City on July 16, 1893. View taken looking north-west at what later became the Tahoe Tavern grounds with Truckee Canyon in the background.*

Glorene Dunlap Young

WINTER AND
THE WEEKLY MAIL

*The NEVADA arriving at Lakeside Pier
in February, 1903.
Looking northwest up the lake.*

. . . teak, cherry, ash and black walnut, and her staterooms' plush seats were appointed in silk brocade. Black-sided above the waterline when delivered, she was now repainted a gleaming white with massive pennant and flag standards, fore and aft, topping off the mahogany trim of her superstructure. Behind her hexagonal pilot house

lay the engine room and two lifeboats swung on davits ahead of the conventional stack.

A large open cockpit on the after deck was covered by a top that ran to the stern in a jaunty upsweep.

Her narrow 11-foot beam and clean lines had allowed the vessel's original builders to guarantee

NOW SHE WAS THE *NEVADA*

The old TALLAC after she had been purchased by the Bliss, Lake Tahoe Railway and Transportation Company and re-named NEVADA. View taken in Emerald Bay looking northeast toward the island in August, 1905.

Author's collection

RUBICON POINT AND THE MARINE TOURIST

The steamer Nevada pausing at Rubicon's deep to allow passengers aboard a chance to view the "Blue Grotto" coloration of the water. June 14, 1912, with Sugar Pine Point to the north (center background), Mount Watson and Pluto in the far distance.

a speed of 12 knots and "double steam engines" produced 25 more horsepower than the slow-turning twin-cylinder Goliath in the 100-foot *Tod Goodwin*. Nor had passenger safety been overlooked. The *Tallac* was equipped with two watertight compartments, one in the bow and the other in the stern, and her boilers were of the "latest safety tube, non-explosive type."[6]

Another feature of the hull was the graceful and seaworthy lift of the bow, seldom found in vessels of the times. Although narrow of beam after being lengthened, the *Tallac* rode comfortably in a bad chop. She did, however, tend to roll in heavy weather despite the addition of bilge keels.

As the boat was licensed for only 40 passengers she was automatically placed in the "luxury class." The steamer operated for five years under the Tallac House flag and during the summer season made a daily run around the lake carrying passengers, Wells Fargo express, freight and mail. In 1895, Melville Lawrence of Tallac casually listed the vessel "as about 20 tons, with 70 h.p. (sic), value $4,000."[7]

Late in the spring of 1896 the C. & T. L. & F. Company purchased the *Tallac* from Harry O. Comstock, who represented "Lucky" Baldwin in the transaction. Her new owners renamed her *Nevada* and Captain Edmund Hunkin alternated in his command between the new vessel and the *Meteor*. Two years later the Bliss family added the *Nevada* to their Lake Tahoe Railway and Transportation Company marine fleet at Tahoe City.[8] For more than 35 years the vessel carried mail under government contract during the winter months and operated as a passenger and mail

THE SPIT AND POLISH "CAPPY JOE"

Captain Joseph H. Pomin in his best Sunday "bib and tucker" taken on the Tallac House grounds in July, 1906.

John Ernest Pomin

relief boat in the summer. A company circular, brought out in 1909, advertised: "The *Nevada* is available for charter at the rate of $1.50 per person, provided a minimum of $35.00 per day is guaranteed."

Her crew, which now included burly Pete Hawkins, engineer, and purser Frank Evans, under the command of Captain Joe Pomin, inspired some colorful anecdotes. Evans took a particular delight in waiting until most of the passengers had moved to the bow. Then he would stride importantly forward clutching a one and one-half

[6] Tallac House brochure, 1893; also El Dorado County Tax Rolls, 1895.
[7] El Dorado County Tax Rolls, 1895.
[8] The "fleet": *Tahoe*, *Meteor*, and *Emerald II*.

Jeanette Pomin Watson

SLENDER AS A CORSETED COURTESAN

The NEVADA leaving Homewood pier in the summer of 1912 headed north toward Idlewild (Tahoe Pines).

G. D. Oliver

UP CLEAR CREEK AND OVER SUMMIT

It took the combined pulling power of 18 horses and mules to move the TAHOE's firebox up and over the 7140-foot "Spooner Summit" to Glenbrook in the fall of 1895. Here the firebox (upper left) is shown half way up the old Clear Creek grade after crossing a bridge spanning the V-flume above Pedroli's Meadow. Looking north in the direction of present Highway 50.

inch pipe, bent at a 90 degree angle and, assuming a serious expression, carefully sight through the contraption as the *Nevada* neared Sugar Pine or Rubicon points. Invariably someone would ask what he was looking for and Evans' reply: "I'm just checking around the promontory to see if it's all clear on the other side" never failed to bring hearty buffs from the marine-minded aboard.[9]

Another story concerns the proverbial little old lady who carefully handed aboard an assortment of empty bottles insisting that "she wanted to take home some samples of the emerald green and deep blue water."[10]

During her lifetime the *Nevada* encountered her share of heavy weather. On September 20, 1920, she battled one of the severest blows ever recorded on the lake, striking the height of the gale on the Glenbrook, Brockway, Tahoe City leg of her run. A five-gallon milk can, full of cream, had been lashed to the forward deck at Glenbrook and it is reported that the cream churned to butter before the vessel made home port. An eye-witness swore the *Nevada* rolled so badly that water feathered down the smokestack and hissed in the firebox and that even the crew were certain the boat would fail to right herself after each long, sickening lunge as three- to four-foot walls of green water crashed over her forward decking and battered at the pilot house. Relief pilot Captain Hunkin had ordered all his passengers below when the storm screamed down on them. Hatches were battened down and doors locked. One honeymooning couple ignored his command and were nearly swept into the lake before they could be dragged inside and taken to the boiler room to dry out.

Hunkin is reported as "chewing on the ends of his handle-bar mustachios and humming in a low monotone, a sign to his crew that he was greatly disturbed." When they finally arrived at Tahoe City, everybody aboard, with the exception of the captain, had become deathly seasick and the unanimous cry was "I hope we never see Tahoe again."[11]

In October, 1940, after the *Nevada* had been removed from service and lain idle at Tahoe City for several seasons, she was prepared for her last trip on the waters of the lake. Her stripped hull was towed out across Tahoe in the direction of Dead Man's Point by Captain Henry Wehrman, and several miles from the Nevada side her seacocks were opened. Then the vessel's superstructure was drenched with gasoline and ignited. As flame and smoke rose into the air it marked an end to the 50-year-old vessel to those watching from the Nevada and California shoreline.[12]

[9] Jack Bell, Sparks, Nevada, September 1, 1955.
[10] Ibid.
[11] Ibid.
[12] Jeanette Pomin Watson, Tahoe City, September 27, 1956. William F. Ham, Glenbrook, October 24, 1955, and E. H. Pomin, Tahoe City, May 22, 1954.

TAHOE

Glenbrook Bay shimmered like silver foil under the direct sunlight on that memorable morning of June 24, 1896. In a hollow, several hundred feet north of Lake Shore House, a majestic new vessel lay cradled on her launching ways. Workers, resembling a cluster of drones around a queen bee, swarmed up the support timbers and along the remaining scaffolding. Shouted orders and the muffled thud of mauls and sledges on securing blocks rose into the still air.

The bow of the ship rested against a raised platform. Beneath her keel, narrow gauge track dropped to the sandy beach and ran out into the water. John T. Scott, superintendent of construction, and H. P. Freer, designer of the hull, bustled about under the long, slim vessel, intent on their final inspection, and Knute Dahl, master machinist in charge of machinery installation,

George D. Oliver

STEAM MAKER FOR THE "QUEEN"

The TAHOE'S *firebox loaded onto a freighter's truck in the Virginia and Truckee Railroad yards, Carson City, on September 28, 1895. William D. Keyser, pioneer stage driver, in front of the load and Rube Saxton, Tahoe logger, on top.*

CHAMPAGNE FOAMED AND A SHOUT WENT UP, "SHE'S AWAY!"

The day was June 24, the year 1896, and the proud TAHOE, *decked out with flags and bunting, slid down her ways into the waters of the lake. Looking southwest with Bliss' store and warehouse (center of picture), Lake Shore House on the far left and Glenbrook's South Point in the distance.*

G. D. Oliver

A MARINE PARAGON
TAKES ON HER STEEL PLATES

The TAHOE *in frame on the lakeshore
at Glenbrook, October 24, 1895.*

was deep in the engine room checking over the maze of piping, valves, and fittings.

From across the lake the *Meteor* churned into the wharf in front of the company's over-water store and debarked a throng of invited guests. Among the passengers was Robert Forsyth, chief engineer of San Francisco's Union Iron Works, who had conducted speed trials on the battleship *Oregon* several weeks before. Now he was at Glenbrook to make certain that Hull Number 42, the official designation for Tahoe's new flagship, logged her expected 18½ knots.[1]

Excitement mounted as people arrived by stagecoach, carriage and on horseback, then moved in eager little groups toward the speaker's platform. Young ladies in puffed-shouldered dresses and straw "skimmers" balanced on the toes of their high-buttoned shoes to flutter handkerchiefs at friends while their escorts fanned themselves with bowlers.

Lakers from all points around Tahoe, notables from Reno, Carson, Virginia City, Sacramento and San Francisco were on hand to celebrate the launching of Tahoe's new "Queen of the Lake."

The penetrating high-altitude sunshine was becoming unbearable and a sea of parasols blossomed as if by magic. On the improvised speaker's stand, which was festooned with the national colors, stood Duane L. Bliss, the grand old man of Glenbrook. Beside him was his daughter Hope, two of his sons, Charles Tobey and William Seth Bliss, and his brother-in-law, Walter D. Tobey. Seated on Bliss' right was his wife Elizabeth. As owners of the impressive new ship, the Bliss family were understandably concerned with every detail of the ceremony.

Across the bow of the vessel lay a large wreath of Nevada wild flowers: vivid blue lupine, scarlet sword's tongue and pink Alpine lilies-of-the-valley. Above the speaker's stand, plumed masses of yellow and orange goldenrod and white lilacs had been placed. From the wreath ran red, white and blue streamers, their ends tightly wound around the christening bottle of champagne. Miss Hope Bliss was given the red ribbon, Miss Ada Tobey the blue, and the tiny fingers of William Seth Bliss' two-year-old son, Master Will, who was resplendent in a white satin coat, clutched the white one.

Duane L. Bliss glanced at his gold timepiece. It was three minutes before noon. He raised his right hand and a hush fell over the expectant crowd of well-wishers. After a few crisp sentences of welcome he stepped back to a seat beside his wife. Then the bottle flashed in a swinging arc, and champagne foamed off the bow. Miss Tobey exclaimed: "I name thee . . ." her voice faltered. "Ta-hoe," piped up young Master Will. ". . . of Glenbrook," Miss Hope Bliss added, ". . . and may fortune attend thee."[2]

The tension was broken, a shout went up, "She's away!" and those ashore and aboard cheered lustily.

Imperceptibly at first, then swiftly gathering momentum, the stately *Tahoe* slid down the ways, her superstructure and rigging so decked out with bunting and flags that she presented the appear-

[1] Although the *Tahoe* was not completely outfitted until July 22, 1896, speed trials were conducted shortly after her launching.

[2] The *Tahoe* launching story is based upon an unidentified newsclipping dated June 24, 1896. George D. Oliver, Carson City, September 6, 1954.

ance of a vessel under full canvas. Pray's brass cannon boomed a salute, the signal for the steamers *Meteor*, *Emerald II*, and *Tallac* to tie down their whistles. The settlement's locomotives and sawmills added to the din with blasts that screamed across the bay. While the spectators shouted themselves hoarse the stern of the big vessel dropped deep into the water, lifted, and floated smoothly out upon the lake. After being towed to her mooring alongside the pier, the *Tahoe* was opened for inspection and guests crowded aboard for a buffet luncheon and toasts to the success of the largest, most luxurious ship to float on the Lake of the Sky.

Well might the townspeople of Glenbrook feel proud. It had taken months of effort to build into reality this marine accomplishment that now rode gracefully on the waters of Tahoe. Less than a year before she had been put together in San Francisco, and then disassembled, after which the heterogeneous puzzle of related sections was shipped on the Southern Pacific and Virginia and Truckee railroads to Carson City, where they were loaded aboard sturdy lumber wagons and hauled by horse and mule teams over the old Clear Creek grade to Glenbrook. The firebox and boiler were the heaviest parts, and it required the combined efforts of 18 animals to drag each of these sections up canyon to summit.

During the fall of 1895, mule-drawn scrapers cleared the construction site on Glenbrook's lakeshore, and a marine ways was built. The *Tahoe's* keel was laid December 25, 1895, but work ground to a halt with the winter snows. Early in the spring of 1896 riveters again began work on the hull, and on June 22 she was ready for her launching, which took place two days later. On July 22 the *Tahoe* was placed in service.

To lake residents the specifications and other engineering details of the vessel read like a fairy tale. The hull displaced 154 tons. She had an over-all length of 168 feet 9 inches, an extreme beam of 17 feet 10 inches, and a draft of 6 feet. Several feet below the waterline, two bilge

keels, 80 feet long by 18 inches wide, had been installed port and starboard to minimize the ship's roll in heavy seas.[3] One locomotive-type boiler, 8 feet in diameter and over 16 feet long, fed twin steam engines that furnished the propulsion power, each having three compound expansion, high-pressure cylinders 18 inches in diameter with a common stroke of 12 inches. A total of 1200 horsepower could be developed at 180 pounds steam pressure. Two three-bladed manganese-bronze propellers turned at a maximum speed of 353 revolutions per minute.[4]

The *Tahoe's* hull was divided into eight watertight compartments, making it virtually impossible for the ship to sink. This would create a sense of security for the 200 passengers who could be carried on the boat's decks and amidships. A sloping, cream-colored stack set off the *Tahoe's* gleaming white hull. Highly polished brass work and mahogany trim ornamented her superstructure. The vessel's 100-foot deckhouse was built in three sections, with the ladies' cabin "handsomely fitted out in primavera paneling relieved with teak and mahogany." Seats were richly upholstered in crimson plush and carpeting was of the finest Brussels. The gentlemen's smoking lounge, sumptuously finished in Spanish cedar panels, boasted lounge chairs upholstered in the choicest morocco. Above the *Tahoe's* sweeping deck a cabin overhang, beaded with a tassled fringe, extended from the pilot house to the stern. Below deck was the dining room, accommodating 30 people. Forward of the dining room baggage was stored. A combination windlass and hydraulic crane, installed directly above near the bow,

[3] "Bilge keels were installed on the *Tahoe* before her launching." E. H. Pomin, Tahoe Park, June 2, 1954. "The *Tahoe* was out of commission during a regular run only once in her lifetime when she lost steam in Emerald Bay due to a clogged stack and was held at the dock 5 hours." *Tahoe Tattler*, 1939 edition, Placer County Library, Tahoe City.

[4] The *Tahoe's* underwater streamlining and her narrow beam allowed this clean running ship to carry a high (7' 6") pitch and low (4' 10") diameter propeller with a minimum of slippage.

C. O. Valentine

SHE GLIDES IN MAJESTY

The steamer TAHOE *leaving Tahoe Tavern railroad pier on July 14, 1912. Note the cargo and mail sacks on the forward deck and passengers on the after "sun lounge." Looking west with Tahoe Tavern showing above the stern of the vessel.*

NOT A BREATH OF AIR STIRRED

The TAHOE docking at McKinney's wharf and Clubhouse on June 21, 1914. Looking nearly due north at snow-covered Mount Watson in the distance. Idlewild to the left of the tree.

MAIL SACKS—STEAMER TRUNKS AND FREIGHT

Captain Ernest John Pomin (upper left-hand corner) preparing to back the steamer TAHOE away from the Tahoe Tavern railroad pier on her around-the-lake trip, July 9, 1912. Tavern Casino (center foreground) looking west.

handled the heavy cargo.[5] For night operation, an electric searchlight of 4000 candlepower had been mounted on the pilot house and the *Tahoe* carried a "modern system of electric lights and bells." Hot and cold running water was supplied to the lavatories, which sported white marble fixtures. Steam heat was provided throughout the ship. The center section of the deck house, like the hull itself, was built of steel, and here her boiler, firebox, engines and auxiliary equipment were bolted in place.

On the main deck some 30 feet of space was available for freight and express.

When excursion parties were carried this area would be used for dancing. In addition there was a main salon, large galley, crew's quarters and raised pilot house.[6] Interstate Commerce regulations required that a chart room be provided and this was located on the upper deck directly aft of the wheelhouse. As navigational charts were not needed on the lake, the Bliss family converted the cabin into a private stateroom.

Command of the vessel was assigned to Captain Ernest John Pomin. The original crew of six included purser Frank S. Oliver, a steward, two deckhands, a fireman and an engineer. Starting with the year 1901 the *Tahoe* left the new Tahoe Tavern railroad pier every morning at 9:10 during the summer season, taking eight hours, with frequent stopovers, to make the "seventy-three mile" trip around the lake.

Passengers, mail, freight, and express were loaded aboard the narrow-gauge train at the end of the trestle pier and the steamer then made regular and call stops at all major landings, returning to the Tavern at 5:00 p.m. Over the years many old-timers served in the crew aboard the *Tahoe* . . . William Lindsey, second engineer; Peter "Pit" Hawkins, fireman; Bert Watson, engineer; Ernest H. Pomin, engineer and relief pilot; Sam Neff, purser; Jack Bell, engineer, and many others.

Stories are told of the *Tahoe* running "blind"

[5] Interior detail of the *Tahoe* is taken from a news article supplied by the late George D. Oliver (see footnote 2).

[6] "The original pilot house was raised some 3 feet several years after the vessel was placed in service." Will M. Bliss, Glenbrook, September 9, 1954.

through driving snowstorms and of gigantic waves breaking high against the pilot house windows, forcing Captain Pomin to turn the 169-foot vessel and run for her mooring. In contrast there are recollections of calm, moonlit summer nights with dancing aboard and stops at McKinney's and Tallac House, where passengers disembarked at the over-water club houses.

Over the years the *Tahoe* became an established link in the lake's lifeline, presenting a stirring picture as she steamed on her daily run with her deep-throated whistle announcing each landing and departure.

Captain Ernest John Pomin continued as master aboard until his untimely death in 1919,[7] and his dedicated service to the Bliss family for nearly 45 years stands unmatched in Tahoe's marine history. Captain Edmund Hunkin followed Pomin,

piloting the vessel from 1919 until his death on January 9, 1932. Then Captain Henry Rose took over in the wheelhouse and George Mawdsly replaced Rose during the last few months of the *Tahoe's* operation on the lake.

Numerous anecdotes concerning the *Tahoe* brighten the memories of the lake's old-timers. Former crew member Jack Bell recalls with amazement the general apathy of excursionists

[7] "Captain Ernest John Pomin's death was accidental. On the morning of December 8, 1919, he was boarding the *Nevada* at Tahoe City and, as he failed to return home for lunch, an investigation was made. Footprints in the fresh snow led up the gangplank; none returned. His body was discovered in approximately 5 feet of water and an autopsy indicated he had struck his head on the side of the boat, resulting in his death. There was no water in his lungs. Captain Pomin's watch had stopped at 8:10 that morning and he died at the age of 71 years." E. H. Pomin, August 4, 1954.

C. O. Valentine

SKIRTING THE NEVADA SHORELINE

The TAHOE *steaming toward Glenbrook on its around-the-lake cruise in the late spring of 1915. Beyond the vessel, to the southwest, rise Rubicon's snow-covered peaks.*

aboard the vessel when it came to interpreting "announcer" Sam Neff's comments over the loudspeaker.

"Why, Neff could tell those people *anything*," Bell reports incredulously, "and they would just sit there nodding and gazing blankly out across the water. A standard 'leg-pull' was to advise them that 'Jack Bell's grandfather lost his umbrella right here,' as we steamed past Rubicon Point, and, would you believe it, they all would cluck and shake their heads just as though Neff had announced that the lake had dried up."[8]

With the coming of improved highways, to and around the lake, and the loss of the remunerative mail contract in 1934 to the *Marian B.*, the operation of the "Queen" came to an end. High overhead was another factor that contributed to the decommissioning of the *Tahoe*, for even after she had been converted from a wood-burner to oil, running expenses averaged $125 a day. For more than five years the *Tahoe* lay dockside at Tahoe City, the paint peeling from her funnels

and stack, rust eating into her streaked sides and souvenir hunters stripping what they could carry. Offers for the famous vessel were based only on the value of her weight in steel scrap.

William Seth Bliss, concerned at the disintegration of the lake's flagship after it had proudly circled Tahoe for so many decades under his family's ownership, bought her back in the fall of 1940 from the Lake Tahoe Development Company, who had taken over the Bliss interests on the west side of Tahoe in the mid-1920's. William F. Ham of Glenbrook was delegated to prepare her for sinking and given orders regarding the location on the lake where she should be scuttled.

On the afternoon of August 29, 1940, Walter Scott Hobart's former cruiser, the *Quit-Cha-Kiddin,*' piloted by Lloyd Saxon of Richardson's Camp, arrived at the Tahoe City machine shop pier to take the *Tahoe* in tow. With unfortunate relevance, the escort boat's name reflected the dismal atmosphere of the occasion. Last-minute

[8] Jack Bell, Sparks, Nevada, September 1, 1955.

CONDEMNED TO HER WATERY GRAVE

The proud Queen of the Lake under tow of Hobart's old QUIT-CHA-KIDDIN', *leaving Tahoe City's machine shop wharf at dusk on August 29, 1940, for her last trip on the waters of Tahoe.*

C. W. Vernon

petitions from the school children of the City had been handed to William Bliss, asking that some way be found to save the historic vessel, but no solution could be worked out.[9]

The *Tahoe* had not been completely stripped, as it is generally believed, and her generators and engines could have been placed in operation within a matter of hours. It is true that the pilot house wheel, running lights, brass door hinges, and bronze bell with "Tahoe, 1896" engraved on its side, were trucked to Glenbrook, but other usable equipment, including hundreds of feet of new chain and a 500-pound anchor, were still aboard.

At twilight, the *Tahoe* was towed slowly away from her mooring and the time had come for her to join the *Meteor*. Ham instructed Saxon to head toward Dead Man's Point (Glenbrook's north point) across the lake. Several small boats followed but they turned back as darkness fell. A barge tow was tried but found to be unworkable and straight line towing was resumed. Twenty minutes before midnight, Ham boarded the *Tahoe*. First he made his way forward and paid out the auxiliary anchor and 85 to 90 feet of chain over the bow to prevent her going aground if they moved into shallow water in the darkness, then he climbed down into the engine room and "opened every valve he could find that would let water in and air out."[10] After the seacocks and main injection valves on the engines had been backed off Ham again boarded the *Quit-Cha-Kiddin'* and the doomed vessel's funeral march across the lake continued. Half an hour later the towline began to tighten like a bowstring and it became almost impossible to maintain steerageway.

The searchlight from the escort boat picked out the steamer as she settled deeper in the water and Ham estimated they were still several miles off of Glenbrook and at a depth approximating 500 feet.[11] Here the escort boat backed water and the line was removed from the *Tahoe*. The steamer's bow gradually began to lift, rising higher and higher until her anchor and chain were completely out of water . . . swinging and clanging against the steel hull. Dynamite had been brought along but it was obvious to Ham that he would not have to use it.

Now the bow of the *Tahoe* pointed almost vertically into the blackness and the hull hung in this position, transfixed, for long, agonizing seconds. Then a rusted, airtight compartment forward ruptured, and with a hissing of air the ship

slid beneath the waters of Tahoe.[12] The time was 3:00 a.m.

Saxon continued to play the searchlight on the boiling froth marking the spot where the *Tahoe* had gone down. A muffled explosion carried up from the depths and suddenly the *Tahoe's* after flag standard flashed back into the beam of light and soared to a height of 30 to 40 feet. Unbelievably, the flag unfurled, clearly showing the name *Tahoe* for an instant, and then dropped back to the surface of the water. A few moments later the pilot house section emerged, having broken loose from the vessel hundreds of feet down. Nothing else appeared.[13] The *Tahoe* was at rest in the lake which she had crossed and circled thousands of times in nearly half a century of operation.[14]

Lakers, upon hearing the scarcely believable news that the ship was gone, shook their heads in dismay and swore that her sinking had been a sacrilege. They were even more convinced of it the following day when the *Tahoe's* flag floated into Glenbrook and washed up on the shoreline near the point where she had been launched.[15]

As though this singular incident was not sufficient proof to the lake residents that the historic hull should never have been sunk, a section of superstructure drifted back past her old berth at Tahoe City and up on the rocks . . . final evidence to many old-timers that the *Tahoe* was more than just steel and wood.[16] The famous vessel was gone and a legend had been started on its way.

[9] "Tahoe City residents wished to make a marine museum out of her. I offered $1,000 for the vessel." A. L. Richardson, Richardson's Camp, July 4, 1952.

[10] William Fenton Ham, Glenbrook, October 24, 1955.

[11] Ibid.

[12] Ibid.

[13] George Anderson, Bijou, October 27, 1955.

[14] Many and varied are the reports on the *Tahoe's* sinking and the one contained in this work is based on eyewitness accounts. One story has the ship "groaning as if in pain, accompanied by an eerie cry of agony nearly human"; another is that being "unsinkable" she had to be dynamited; still another that she was sunk in shallow water "where she may be seen on calm days and her bell heard tolling." All this is pure fiction. "She slid beneath the waters quietly." W. F. Ham and George Anderson, October 24, 1955. "We were further inside Glenbrook Bay than the Point and in 400 to 500 feet of water." Lloyd Saxon, March 19, 1955. "The boiler probably exploded and the buoyant oil tank amidships evidently broke loose." W. F. Ham, Glenbrook, October 24, 1955.

[15] A story told by early Tahoe residents; possibly factual.

[16] "It (the superstructure) drifted in between the entrance way of the driven pilings that served as a breakwater for the *Tahoe*." Eleanor "Swanee" Swanson, Tahoe City, August 3, 1953. Photographic proof of the superstructure section exists.

D. M. Brodehl

TAHOE'S
LAST MAIL PACKET

The MARIAN B. *arriving at Tahoe City in early June of 1940, one year before she vanished on the waters of the lake.*

MARIAN B.

The days of the mail packets on Lake Tahoe ended with the tragic loss of the *Marian B.*[1]

In the year 1934, Daniel Martin Brodehl, who had previously operated the mail and cargo vessel *Tahoe* out of Seattle, underbid the Lake Tahoe Development Company and obtained the United States mail franchise for all points on the lake.[2] Captain Brodehl's vessel was a conventional cruiser-type hull with raised cabins and open after cockpit. Forty-two feet long, with a beam of 10½ feet, the *Marian B.* could carry 18 passengers comfortably. Although her twin automobile engine conversions did not furnish sufficient power to raise her forward when she was fully loaded, ample flare had been built into her bow and she was a dry-running ship, even in heavy seas. Marine minded skeptics at the lake termed her "unseaworthy" when compared to the larger vessels that preceded her, but the *Marian B.* operated satisfactorily for 7 years on a winter and summer schedule.

On May 18, 1941, while she was bucking a late spring storm on her return trip across the lake from Glenbrook to her home port at Tahoe City, she disintegrated off the eastern shore.[3] Charred wreckage, found later, indicated that an explo-sion had taken place. This was believed to have been caused by faulty gasoline lead lines although the boat had passed marine inspection shortly before her disappearance.

Three persons were aboard at the time the *Marian B.* vanished: pilot Arthur Daniel Brodehl, son of D. M. Brodehl; 10-year-old Donald Brodehl, and mail clerk Everett Dolan. On the morning of the fatality, a relief clerk had arrived to take over Dolan's duties and Dolan was making his last scheduled trip. Both Dolan and Brodehl's son were wearing life preservers and their bodies floated ashore near Homewood the following day. The body of Arthur Brodehl was never recovered.

So, in disaster, went the last of the mail boats to join in the vast graveyard of Tahoe's 1,500-foot deep—the *Meteor*, *Nevada*, and *Tahoe*.

---

[1] "The *Marian B.* was not named for a member of the Brodehl family; it carried the name of her original owner, Mrs. Marian Bernhard." Mrs. Rebecca Shontz, Tahoe City, September 19, 1956.

[2] The marine mail contract at Tahoe is reported to have brought in between $14,000 and $18,000 a year.

[3] Storm waves on Lake Tahoe reach incredible heights. At times the 169-foot steamer *Tahoe* drove into heavy seas that battered her pilot house, some 25 feet above the water, and forced the ship to turn and run for her home port. Following seas that rolled aboard over her stern, normally 8 feet above the water, were reported. Ernest Henry Pomin, Tahoe Park, September 8, 1954.

MARINE ACTIVITY . . . .
THE GAY '90's INTO THE ATOMIC 1950's

In the mid-1890's a flotilla of raised bow double-enders, arrow nosed, pencil beamed, tassel tops, high windowed marine barouches, low-lying fantailed speedsters and palatial, multi-crewed yachts, made their debut on Tahoe. Designed by barrelmaker and qualified marine architect alike they were powered with slow-turning gasoline burning monstrosities, storage batteries and naphthene "coughers."

The long list includes those acknowledged early day show boats of the lake: Frederick Kohl's 60-foot *Idlewild*, built by San Francisco's Twigg and Son in 1906 and captained by John Ernest Pomin, acquired by Herbert Fleishhacker, Sr., in the 1920's and returned to the East Bay for use as a commercial fishing boat two decades later; J. F. Elliott's 50-foot double-ender, the *Miduena* (My Lady), constructed by the Michigan Yacht and Power Boat Company previous to 1910, later owned by I. W. Hellman, and, in 1928, E. J. Hall of Hall-Scott Motors, who shipped the cruiser to the Oakland Estuary; William Saunders Tevis, Sr.'s, magnificent 72-foot, $60,000 twin-screw *Consuelo*, a product of Twigg's yards in 1909, purchased by George Newhall in 1915, and burning in Newhall's Rubicon Bay boathouse five years later. The *Consuelo* was replaced by Newhall's palatial 70-foot, Twigg-built *Rubicon*—sold in 1941 and moved to Clear Lake.

The Tevis family also had a brood of smaller hulls, the fast *Arrow*, nearly 43 feet in length with a toothpick beam of 6 feet, the 24-foot *Chinquapin*, a seaworthy bottom which originally plied between San Francisco Bay and the Farallon Islands, and the houseboat *Mahala*, rivaling Lapham's *Lily Van* and launched at Tallac with the blessings of a brocaded, black-bearded Spanish bishop, brother of King Emanuel of Spain, who became entangled in the launching lines and was ignominiously dragged to the water's edge after young Lloyd Tevis prematurely started the "ark" down the ways.

Charles Wieland's 28-foot cabin hull was the silent marvel of the early 1890's. Moored at Bellevue Hotel on Sugar Pine Point, she was powered with a formidable set of electric batteries that required a recharging plant ashore nearly half the size of the boat itself. The William Bissell family at Sunnyside owned another electrically propelled hybrid named the *Corona*, 22

feet long and quiet as a drifting cloud. It ran on the lake in the 1910's and was followed by the Bissells' *Checog* (Washoe Indian for skunk), so named because the fumes from her slow-turning gasoline engine nearly asphyxiated the passengers.

Harry Babcock's sleek, black-sided 42-foot *Pirate*, built several years before the turn of the century, joined other pleasure launches that moved around the lake fifty years ago. Purchased and placed in commission again by John Drum, Jr., she was running in 1956. Add to these boats "Lucky" Baldwin's many-windowed excursion and fishing cruiser, the *Happy Day*, skippered by "Cappy Joe" Pomin; Thomas' 35-foot enclosed cabin double-ender, the *Wild Goose*, with the jaunty mast forward, acquired by Tallac House, then Tahoe Tavern, and the *Rosalie*, another of Baldwin's launches, resembling the *Happy Day*, with Captain Clark in the wheelhouse.

Phillip King Brown's 19-foot, open cockpit "one-lunger" was another famous old-timer. Purchased in 1900, she bore three names in her lifetime—the first unrecorded, the second *Drinkwater* (because she is reported to have shipped half the lake when barely under way), and the third, *Friendship*, a sentimental addendum bestowed upon the hull when she was loaned by the Browns to the Raymond family one season.

Isaias W. Hellman's *Florence*, named for his daughter and puffing out of Sugar Pine Point in the 1900's, was followed by Elsie Brougher's original *Elsie*, William Kent's 28-foot *Marin* (with the 3-cylinder Union Gas cast iron monster), Tahoe Tavern's commercial marine flyer *Catalina*, Harold Ebright's tiny hull, the *Wren*, last reported on Fallen Leaf Lake, Schmidel's *Taha-na* (with a Hicks 2-cylinder "make and break" ignition power plant), a broad-beamed, awning covered, 26-foot marine phaeton; Gordon Blanding's *Chipmunk*, and Harry Herod's *Menina*, the last named a 40-foot commercial passenger boat running out of Bijou.

Captain George Hotchkiss' ill-starred bucket, the *Aileen*, was still another commercial hull. Launched in 1909 at McKinney's, she was notable for her 2-inch planks that were boiled in oil, a reversible propeller and a near disastrous encounter with Captain Joe Pomin's automobile ferry on a dark night off of Sugar Pine Point. Others were the fishing and cruise launches *Will-Till*, *Wildwood of Brockway* and *Brockway*, backfiring out of the Hot Springs in the late 1900's with the 26-foot *Brockway* joining the Callender Brothers commercial fleet at Homewood in 1913 that originally consisted of the 22-foot *Lady of the Lake* (said to have moved through the water 25 feet for every revolution of her clublike propeller), and the *Firefly*, a 26-foot metal hull with an Elmore engine, operating in 1912, and boasting the only self-starter on Tahoe at the time, so low lying that its progress down the lake in a moderate chop resembled a submerging submarine.

Dr. Hartland Law's fast-moving power boats, the *Bluebird* and *Skylark*, were cutting a swath on Tahoe at this time as were the *Thelma*, *Nyack*, Tahoe Vista's 22-foot *Colleen* and the survey boats, *Rip Van Winkle* and *Mount Rose*.

Senator George Nixon's *Pronto I* was also in the marine spotlight. Seaworthy, and good for a "phenomenal 16 miles per hour," she was later purchased by the Charles Merrill family, who replaced her with the *Pronto II* in the late 1920's. Designed by Bruce Merrill, and built by Stephens Brothers of Stockton, the *Pronto II* was a trim teak and mahogany, twin-screw 42-foot day cruiser that was lost when the Merrills' overwater boathouse collapsed in a winter storm.

Norman DeVaux owned the Luders-built 52-foot *Myrno III*, a fast express cruiser that was first placed in operation during the mid-1920's. Narrow beamed and multi-cabined, the vessel was acquired in 1930 by Arthur K. Bourne, who renamed her the *Reverie* and turned her over to the Coast Guard Auxiliary on Lake Tahoe in 1956. Another large express "commuter" comparable to the *Myrno III*, was George Pope's twin-engined *Sheik* with its meticulously maintained decking and highly varnished superstructure whose owner provided rubber-soled "sneakers" for his guests in order to protect her mirror-like finish.

Nelson Salter, of Emerald Bay, owned the 38-foot *Shamrock*. Built in 1913 as a cruise boat, it was still running on the lake in 1957, operated by Robert Pomin. Perry, of Tahoe City's "Merc," had the *Solicitor*, and Harry S. Williamson, the *Standard*, both used for carrying supplies around Tahoe. Photographer Arthur Pillsbury owned the *Annie*, a small 24-foot open cockpit hull, from which he took many of his panoramic box camera studies of the lake.

The *Nomad I*, a 30-foot party boat with a candlestick beam of 6 feet, churned out of Meeks Bay Camp with Jack Hale in the pilot house. It was renamed the *Gypsy* and moved to Fallen Leaf Lake in the early 1940's, to be followed on Tahoe by the 47-foot *Nomad II*, built in 1907 and still plying the waters of Tahoe as a passenger carrier during the mid-1950's.

Jim Moffitt launched a "sport runabout" in 1915 that, along with Carol Skinner's *Florence M* and J. P. Obexer's *Hobo*, set the stage for the high speed planing hulls to come. Moffitt's marine slipper, bearing the name *Alice*, was the sensation of her day as she carried "that amazing steering wheel, just like an automobile." The Ortman family also had a flashy, low freeboard sportster painted black, comparable to the *Pirate*, and some 30 feet in length, recalled as always "shipshape and well maintained."

The Clinton Walker family acquired the 25-foot launch *Dorothy* in 1915, which is reported to have borne two other names previously—the *Mary II* and *Ellen*. They renamed her the *Hesperus* and Brooks Walker was usually found behind the wheel.

Adolph Mueller originally owned the *Viking*, a 36-foot double-ender with stream-lined, for its day, superstructure and a mast carried well forward. The vessel was later purchased by Harry Poett and it still crossed the lake regularly in the mid-1950's.

Among boatman Chris Nielson's "fleet" at Sunnyside Bay was a formidable old 19-foot tub, the *Kemah*, that he used for general salvage work and fishing parties.

William Wallace Mein placed the clean-running 36-foot *Viva* in service during the summer of 1919. A V-bottom day cruiser, designed and built by New York marine architect William Hand, she operated for a quarter of a century under the Meins' flag before being sold to James Lloyd of Reno and renamed the *Prospector*.

Other gasoline powered eye-catchers on the lake in the 1920's included George Kelham's *Sierra*, Mrs. Lora Moore Knight's *Amanda* (later named the *Walkure* (Valkyrie), and Ralph Graves' 28-foot custom Stephens canvas-topped beauty that reportedly attained a speed of 25 miles an hour. Running out of Emerald Bay Resort, she was considered the fastest thing afloat on the south end of Tahoe for years and ran until an explosion put an end to her career in 1941.

Walter Scott Hobart's long line of medium speed bottoms included the *Quit-Cha-Kiddin'*, a

PHOTO FINISH — EARLY MARINE STYLE

Jake Obexer's toothpick beamed runabout HOBO *and Carol Skinner's racy* FLORENCE N. *jockey for the lead with a burst of speed off the Tahoe Tavern railroad pier in the early 1910's. Looking southeast with the Kingsbury Grade and Daggett Pass beyond the* FLORENCE N.'s *bow.*

44-foot top-heavy marine equivalent of a Concord coach, sporting massive picture windows and a luxurious interior, with keel stabilizers to compensate for her narrow beam. She became a "shoreline home" at Camp Richardson in the early 1950's. Hobart also had the *Garizibio*, $8,000 worth of Kneass-built supply and pleasure launch, named for a fast-starting alcoholic punch invented by the "Slapdash Sage of Sand Harbor."

J. P. Obexer, of Homewood, had a diversified array of work boats and fast hulls in his personal "stable" over the decades: the 6-h.p. *Dorothy*, 28-foot *Olive*, twin-screwed *Red Wing*, the *Wasp*, *Hobo* and the *Osprey*, the last named originally built for W. S. Ray of Bijou.

Leland Stanford Scott owned the 36-foot *Skipalong*, a Consolidated lapstrake cruiser that was sold to Maxwell Milton in the early 1930's. The *Skipalong* survived a mid-section encounter with Edwin Letts Oliver's Gar Wood (one of the many *Hey-There's*) in 1935 and still churns around the lake as a commercial passenger carrier out of Emerald Bay.

One of the most spectacular of Tahoe's glamor boats, built previous to 1950, was launched on July 14, 1940. Designed and built by naval architect John Hacker of Detroit, Michigan, for "Captain" George Whittell, it was aptly named the *Thunderbird*. This marine "futura" reportedly cost $87,500 to complete and originally carried four engines totaling 1600 h.p. Fifty-six feet in length, the *Thunderbird* is quadruple mahogany planked, with her underside copper sheathed. Her streamlined, cigar-shaped lines are set off by a series of tear-drop, stainless steel cabins with interior accommodations custom tailored to her owner's specifications. Even a chrome-plated, electrically operated anchor retracts into her bow. In 1957 the *Thunderbird* was still stored in her special rock and steel boathouse at Whittell's "Thunderbird Castle" on the northeast side of Tahoe.

The early 1920's ushered in the speedboat era on Lake Tahoe with hulls and performance inappreciably improved by many stock and custom runabouts of the mid-1950's. One of the first 40-

mile-an-hour boats to leave a flat wake on the lake was George Newhall's Hacker-designed *Apache I*, with a cockpit aft of the engine that placed driver and passenger high in the air without benefit of windshield protection. This mahogany bottom was running at the same time as Walter Scott Hobart, Jr.'s *Orange Blossom* (named for his favorite "eye-opener" of gin and orange juice), a 30-foot, open cockpit, Kneass-built job originally carrying a Van Blerk engine that was replaced with a 450 h.p. Liberty "12" to compete with Norman DeVaux's *Apache II*, powered with a Hall-Scott "super-compressed" 250 h.p. power plant. The *Apache II* was a 28-foot Kneass-constructed mahogany, twin-place runabout (sister ship of the needle-beamed *Mohawk* owned by Hall-Scott Motors) and the Hobart-DeVaux yearly race around a 30-mile triangular course on the lake became the feature of many summer seasons during the 1920's.

Other custom built Hacker hulls and stock Belle Isle Bearcats from Detroit followed: Ester Ehrman's (Mrs. Claude Lazard) *Cherokee*, John

Drum, Sr.'s *Pueblo*, Elsie Brougher's *Elsie B.*— with Miss Ehrman's Belle Isle a consistent winner in her racing class, the victories being assisted by blasts from an oxygen flask into the carburetors of its LM-6A engine at the crucial moment. Another Belle Isle, the *Paiute*, was owned by Al Richardson of Camp Richardson and raced, in the late 1920's and early 1930's, by his daughter, "Sis" Richardson (Knisely).

Queens of the runabouts were the de luxe, streamlined Hall-Scott powered 30-foot Belle Isles with angled windshields, rounded decking and triple cockpits. Bert C. Scott's *Comanche* and Herbert Fleishhacker, Sr.'s *Washoe* were the only two of this type on Tahoe. A custom built, closed cabin, V-bottom, day cruiser of comparable lines was the Sydney Ehrman's 32-foot eye-catcher, the *Comet*. In addition to the stock and custom runabouts from the planning boards of Hacker and Belle Isle, there were the round bottom, copper fastened Honduras mahogany 26-footers built by Stephens Brothers of Stockton, California, precision crafted and powered with

NO TRIMMER DOUBLE-ENDER SAILED ON TAHOE

Tahoe Tavern's WILD GOOSE *heading south down the lake to Rubicon with a picnic party in the summer of 1917. Tahoe Tavern Casino (center) and the Tavern to the left. Looking west.*

C. O. Valentine

IT TOOK NERVE, MUSCLE AND A WELL PADDED POSTERIOR
TO HANDLE THIS STREAK OF SPRAY

Harry Hush Magee (right) piloting his Liberty powered single-step hydroplane, the LUCKY STRIKE II, *in which he shattered existing Lake Tahoe and Pacific Coast marine records during the mid-1920's with speeds exceeding 85 miles per hour. Mechanic E. R. "Petie" Coyle is in the cockpit with Magee.*

6-cylinder Scripps engines. Owners of these durable hulls included Edwin Letts Oliver, Herbert Fleishhacker, Sr., Carol Skinner, Gustave Knecht and Charles Townsend. Gar Wood boats followed with J. P. "Jake" Obexer distributing and servicing the "Gars."

Competition in the late 1920's and '30's sharpened with claims and counter claims, scuttlebutt and outright slander circulating concerning the "Big Three" at the lake; Hall-Scott representing Hacker and Belle Isle, Roy Stephens acting for his own boatbuilding concern, and Obexer thumping for Gar Wood. Rumors were spread that the Hall-Scott engines would drop through the bottom of their mahogany hulls. The company retaliated by assuring the marine minded that Obexer's Scripps power plants were throwing con-rods and that a 6-year-old could put his fist through the "thin" mahogany sidings of "those cheaply constructed Gars." Stephens products were dismissed as "too slow to bother with."

Actually all the craft and engines gave over-all satisfactory service.

From Obexer's marine ways came Charles Kendrick's *Navajo*, a black-sided, red-bottomed flash of color, driven by his son Marron; Randolph Walker, Sr.'s line of *Ranjacs*, competing in friendly rivalry with brother-in-law Edwin Letts Oliver's *Hey There's* and *Letts-Go's*, Robert Stanley Dollar's *President*, William Wallace Mein's *Checog*, and Brooks Walker's *Sergeant* (both with enclosed forward cockpits), Jim and Robert Stack's *Jim Jr.*, the Metcalf family's *Tecalote*, Obexer's own *Miss Tahoe's*, and many others.

Keeping pace with the "Gars" were the early Chris-Crafts, such as Leon Roos' *Whoopee* and a newer model, Frank Fuller's 28-foot *Water Wagon*.

Step-hydroplanes were also pounding into the picture during the mid-1920's with antitypes of today's 180-mile-an-hour "rooster-tailers" roaring and careening around the lake during the Lake Tahoe Yacht Club Regattas. Racing boats lying on the bottom of their boathouse wells on the morning of race days, with sea-cocks mysteriously open, steel grindings discovered in carburetor intakes, or ball bearings rattling around combustion chambers, were not uncommon "below-the-belt" occurrences in the dog-eat-dog struggle for the checkered flag.

Harry Hush Magee's 26-foot Liberty powered single-step hydroplane, the *Lucky Strike II*, was an 80-mile-an-hour "plus" streak of spray that shattered existing speed records on Lake Tahoe in 1925. (The *Lucky*, with Magee driving, gained national recognition in 1926 when she flashed over the San Francisco-Stockton run in 2 hours, 9 minutes and 34 seconds, averaging 75.02 miles per hour.)

Magee, along with Brooks Walker and, several years later, Louis Fageol (in his small, high-speed *So Long*), actually pioneered the fast hydro hulls on Tahoe, opening the door for those other lead-footed, hard-driving marine sportsmen who followed over the next three decades: Stanley Dollar, Jr., Morlan Visel and Danny Arena among others.

Hard on the heels of Harry Magee's *Lucky Strike II* was Brooks Walker in his *Psyche*, a Hall-Scott aviation conversion powered hydroplane which regularly battled it out for lead position with Magee's *Little Lucky*, another step-hydro built by Kneass. Twenty feet in length and, driven by Bill Magee, it was kicked along by the first supercharged power plant on Tahoe, a 151 Miller engine.

When the *Lucky Strike II* dropped out from under Harry Magee and his mechanic, "Petie" Coyle, after an exhibition performance off the San Francisco Marina, Magee purchased the tricky four-step, Liberty powered hydroplane *Flash* that saw one season of racing on Lake Tahoe.

Bill and Bud Oliver's Star conversion powered "crackerbox," one of their "Let's Go" line, was another single-step hull entered in the lower horsepower class which turned in a creditable performance.

Herbert Fleishhacker, Jr.'s Nunes-built Liberty powered *Mabee Not I* (repowered and owned in 1956 by George Ehmann) and the Kneass-

MAHOGANY QUEEN OF THE V-BOTTOMS

Leland Stanford Scott (driving), with Joe deSaules riding as mechanic, warms up during the early 1930's for a Lake Tahoe Yacht Club Regatta championship race in his 55-mile-an-hour, Packard powered BABY SKIPALONG. *The former Gold Cup contender is now owned by Stanley Dollar, Jr.*

built twin Liberty engined *Mabee Not II* were, respectively, hydroplane and 36-foot V-bottom contenders in the late 1920's and early '30's. The tempo of speed was also increased with the appearance of Stanley Barbee's hybrid multi-step twin Liberty, *Saxon, Jr.*, a combination runabout and racing boat, turning outboard propellers through V-drives and driven on Tahoe by Fred Main; Stanley Dollar, Jr.'s International racer, the miniature *Uncle Sam*, and, pressing the hydroplanes, the fast V-bottomed Liberty powered custom Gar Woods; Kenneth Pope's *Challenger* and later her sister ship owned by Arthur K. Bourne of Round Mound.

Leading the V-bottom contingent was Leland Scott's meticulously maintained 275 h.p. Gold Cup mahogany bullet, the *Baby Skipalong* (ex-*Greenwich Folly*), purchased by Stanley Dollar, Jr., and still racing and winning in her class after a quarter of a century of competition on Tahoe;

also Dollar's 33-foot aluminum torpedo, the *Mercury* ("*Merc*"), originally carrying a Curtis Conqueror 12-cylinder engine, which was replaced with an Allison conversion in the early 1950's.

The late 1940's and early 1950's found speeds running well over the 100-mile-an-hour mark, with Allison conversion powered three-point suspension hulls screaming around the race courses on Tahoe. Stanley Dollar, Jr.'s *Skipalong of California*, winner of the Harmsworth trophy, his *Short Snorter* that followed; Morlan Visel's *Hurricane IV* (later owned and driven by Bill Stead); Henry J. Kaiser's *Hawaii Kai's*, among others, and Phil Murphy's *Breathless*, were some of the Gold Cup contenders that competed on the lake.

From this marine potpourri of trial, error and accomplishment came the modern day hulls that now flash across the waters of Lake Tahoe during the summer season.

A "ROOSTER TAIL" CLIMBS INTO THE TAHOE SKY

The HURRICANE IV *driven by owner, Morlan Visel, accelerates down the straight-away in Tahoe's Mile High Race at a speed in excess of 140 miles an hour. Photograph taken in August of 1953.*

Sierra Boat Co.

FISHING FACTS AND FANCY

The earliest record of commercial fishing by white men on Lake Tahoe dates back to 1859 when the "Fishery" was established on the southeast shore of the lake, north of Lake Bigler House. Here thousands of native silver trout were hooked, netted and speared in the shallows of Tahoe and Lake Stream (Upper Truckee River) with Italian and Portuguese fishermen, employed by the pioneer settlers, utilizing small punts, skiffs and even high-peaked gondolas with distinguishing candelabra crosses on their sterns. The catch of Tahoe's first fishing fleet was sold to the travelers plodding over the great road to the Comstock, and wagon loads of silversides were teamed into Carson and Virginia cities to be sold in the streets.[1]

Taking of trout became a major industry, with William W. Lapham's "Fish Market Landing" and Burke and Small's Friday's Station, to the north, joining in the piscatorial bonanza. By 1862 Burke and Company were using a half-mile seine to take tons of Tahoe trout daily from the waters of Boundary Bay between what is now Bijou and Round Hill.

William H. Brewer, writing in his *Up and Down California*, noted in August of 1863: "I was amazed to find that the lake abounded in the largest trout in the world, a species native to the region (salmo clarkii), often twenty pounds in weight and sometimes thirty pounds." Brewer was referring to the giant Tahoe cutthroat; however, he neglected to mention the lake's native silvers.

For centuries Washoe Indians had been using nets, weirs, baskets and spears to catch the lake's finny denizens for their own use, but when the white settler arrived fishing was placed on a strictly commercial basis.

In 1864 the Virginia City *Evening News* announced: "It is forbidden by law for the whites to take fish (from Tahoe) between October 15 and April 1 and during the open season fishing will be confined to hook and line." This regulation was particularly notable for its lack of enforcement, but at least an attempt had been made to halt the wholesale slaughter of thousands of spawning trout as they moved up the lake's affluents. The *News* caustically pointed out that Indians were allowed to take fish all year around by any means they saw fit. A case in point was Lapham's Fish Market Landing, where the sale of trout brought an average of $4,000 per month throughout the year, with the Washoe Indian fronting for the hotelkeeper.

A general apathy toward the eventual extermination of Tahoe's trout was widespread in the 1860's and this continued for more than half a century. Most Lakers were convinced that the supply was inexhaustible, and only a few failed to subscribe to this optimistic view. Among the minority were Pringle and Hurley of Tahoe City's "Lake Fishery" and Comer's Fish Ranch on the Truckee River. In 1872, after four years in the business, Pringle and Hurley had 30,000 fingerlings in their rearing ponds and they boosted the total to 57,000 trout the following season, with fish ranging in size from five inches to two pounds. Eggs were taken in June, July and August and, after they had hatched and the trout reached one pound size, they were turned into the commercial fishing ponds.[2] Suckers and white

---
[1] Refer Al Tahoe and Edgewood chapters 29 and 32.

443

fish, seined from the lake, were cut up and fed to the trout and the sight of the flashing silvers boiling after the "chub" was considered well worth the admission price of 25 cents.

On May 6, 1872, a patriotic group of French commercial fishermen at Tahoe shipped 20 specimens to San Francisco for exhibition at the French National Fair, where 17 of these beauties brought $1,500 at auction.[3]

The largest trout recorded as caught up until that time was a native cutthroat brought to net by Charles Johnson of Johnson's Ranch on the south end of Tahoe. It tipped the scales at 29½ pounds.[4] On April 20, 1873, Ben F. Coy of Rowland's Station took two cutthroat weighing 16 and 22 pounds, following this up with a three-

"WON'T BITE"

Ephraim "Yank" Clement and "Aunt Liddy"
near Yank's Hotel wharf
during the summer of 1876 in calm,
unproductive waters.

[2] Growth of fingerling out is dependent upon the temperature of the water and feed. One pound a year is exceptional growth.

[3] *Truckee Republican,* May 6, 1872.

[4] A 31½-pound cutthroat was taken at Tallac in 1911 to set a new lake record. Tallac Brochure, 1911.

[5] "Resources and Wonders of Lake Tahoe," *Sacramento Union,* May 29, 1875, C. F. McGlashan. Benjamin F. Coy, not McCoy, is correct. Refer Early Marine History of Lake Tahoe section.

ONLY A "FAIR TO MIDDLIN'" CATCH

Eighty silversides in four hours of fishing strung up for display on the shoreline in front of Tallac House during the summer of 1902. Captain John Ernest Pomin to right of picture.

hour catch of silvers on hook and line that aggregated 148 pounds.[5] Trout retailed for 15 cents a pound in Truckee during the summer of 1873 and the industry showed such promise that a cannery was established at Wadsworth on the Truckee River below Reno.

In the summer of 1875, C. F. McGlashan from Truckee listed six varieties of fish in Lake Tahoe: the native silver and cutthroat, landlocked salmon, Great Lake's white fish (actually native), Royal Silver and German Brown. During the same year W. F. Edwards, compiler of a Placer County tourist guide, generalized on four varieties, the "silver, red, black and crossbreed in the order of their importance."

Such was the demand for Tahoe trout during the late 1870's that tons of fish were shipped east and west out of Truckee in ice cars. Menus at San Francisco's Russ, Lick, Palace and Baldwin hotels and the Palmer House in Chicago featured the popular delicacy. Shipments of silvers increased. During the year 1880, 70,000 pounds of trout moved down the toll road from Tahoe City to the railroad town and wagon loads ranging from 1,000 pounds to a ton continued to find a ready market in Washoe, sold out in a few hours to the highest bidders. In 1881 the *Tahoe Tattler* sagely advised its readers: "Fishing has been going on at the lake for over 20 years and the supply is inexhaustible if trout are taken by hook and line only." The *Tattler's* editor announced: . . . "Any one person catching over 50 trout in one day will be given the paper free for one month."

This generous offer evidently spurred the local "trouters" to new angling heights, as recorded catches during the summer of 1881 were fantastic. Messrs. Stetson and Dean caught 198 trout in six days that tipped the scales at 300 pounds. The Honorable A. B. Dibble from Grass Valley boated 23 fish in three hours of trolling—total weight, 43 pounds. J. Ballard of San Francisco landed 33 silvers in two hours before breakfast one morning under the expert guidance of Tahoe City's well-known fishing guide, Captain H. L. Mayo, and William Pomin's catch of 25 "pogies," the same day, was barely considered newsworthy. The *Tattler* discovered that the northwest side of Tahoe had become a leading fish producer. It reported: "Mr. Branch, the fisherman, caught 300 trout in five days last week." Then the paper noted a week later that "600 fish were brought to boat in seven days."

Finally two hard-working fishermen outdistanced their rivals when they set an all-season record—65 trout in four hours, aggregating 115 pounds in weight. The scribe from the *Tattler* personally vouched for the catch as he had been called upon to transport half the boatload to the Grand Central Hotel, "after which he couldn't straighten up for a week."

Female anglers were also making headlines. A Miss Carrie Stebbens appeared to be queen of the feminine rod and reel enthusiasts, as she experienced little difficulty in bringing 17 beauties back to Tahoe City after trolling with "flasher and line." Fishing guides Mayo and Hurley, along with Pomin and Morgan, were consistent producers, each man regularly averaging 75 pounds daily during the summer season.

Such a state of excitement prevailed that a zealous "trouter" over-extended himself one morning, in his efforts to capture the fish pool at Tahoe House, with a wild cast that tipped him off balance and plumeted him into the swirling waters beneath the gates of Von Schmidt's dam. Luckily Hurley saw him disappear and fished the half-drowned neophyte out with an oar.

The "Great Sweepstakes of 1881" took place in August of the year. Ten young ladies and their escorts brought 112 fish to boat in a three-hour period with the winning "high line" among the group taking 25 of the combined total using a single hook only.

True sportsmen, however, were working the Truckee River with four-ounce rods and hand-tied flies. In spite of the shambles the lumbering interests had made of the pools and fast water, a seven-pound salmon was recorded as being caught by one such "purist" in the summer of 1882.

Ben Coy's lake record of a 29½-pound cutthroat stood for two decades although unauthenticated mammoths weighing in at 45, 50 and even 70 pounds were claimed as caught.

On the eastern side of the lake Jim "Doc" Benton from Carson was recognized as one of the better fish producers and as he was owner of Benton's Stage Lines, running between Carson City and Glenbrook, he had ample opportunity to concentrate on his hobby during the season. An Irish friend of "Doc's" could always be counted upon to sound the trumpet call to early spring fishing and the announcement invariably coincided with Benton's immediate need for stage passengers. The man from Dublin would pass the word: "The wathers thick with 'em, and they jostle each other in the streams and loch," thereby triggering a near stampede to Tahoe, with "Old

SIXTY-THREE TWO-POUNDERS
ON FOUR-OUNCE RODS

*Oscar Tally (right) and friend in Tallac Meadow
during the summer of 1903 displaying
a morning's catch.*

Doc's" self-appointed press agent riding the box
with him "on the house."

Under the headline "Fancy Fishing," the *Carson Morning Appeal* touted Benton's ability with
both rod and "jerk line," indicating that the versatile stage operator had brought to net three
scarlet-gilled cutthroat in one evening's fishing,
each of which weighed 17 pounds or better. The
Appeal advised its readers that "a full description of the fish and a suitable recording of Doc's
pride would be impossible as it would fill at least
six pages and crowd out all paid advertising."

During the summer of 1880 the *Appeal's* editor
was constantly bothered with requests concerning
the proper procedure for "planting trout." In
order to put a stop to this persistent questioning
from amateur "fish farmers" upon a subject that
the baffled newsman knew nothing about, he
finally fabricated an article calculated to silence
these would-be fingerling raisers once and for all.
With studied maliciousness he wrote: "I under-
stand from good authority that the best way to

plant trout is tail down and pretty well watered
to insure success, with soft moist soil, the moister
the better, and mark me, see that the worms don't
get to them or you are done."

On the west side of the lake it remained for a
British tourist, one Sir Edward Dalles, to really
show the local fishermen the most expeditious
way to deplete Tahoe's trout population. Again
the *Carson Appeal* reported the incident. It was
a June evening in 1881 and Dalles left the wharf
at Tahoe City in one of Morgan and Pomin's
large Whitehall boats after equipping himself
with "an electric hook and line." He returned
shortly before midnight, gunwales awash with
nearly 1,000 pounds of lake trout. The populace
of the City were astounded when inspection of the
apparatus showed it to consist of "100 feet of
insulated wire line, three large gang hooks, a
small light on the end and a crude, hand-operated
battery." Morgan, who had guided Dalles, veri-
fied the fact that the fish crowded around the
submerged light by the hundreds, whereupon
Dalles "just pulled his hooks to the surface
through the milling mass, hauling one or more
trout in each time he retrieved the line." Tahoe
residents sourly commented upon the unsports-
manlike conduct of "that beef-eater who hadn't
even used bait."

Although this mass slaughter of the native
silvers came under the heading of "sport," early
records point up the important part that strictly
commercial fishing played in the demise of Tahoe's natural heritage. In the summer of 1875,
C. F. McGlashan of Truckee had estimated that
20 to 25 market fishermen were working the lake,
averaging 45 to 60 pounds of fish each day on
deep line. In 1880, 70,000 pounds of whitefish
had been taken during the month of July alone
and in February of 1882, 20,000 pounds of silvers
were boxed and shipped to the market. During
the five years, 1900 to 1905, 115,357 pounds of
trout passed through the Tahoe Tavern express
office, 58,667 pounds of this total being brought
to net in 1900. The year 1900 also saw the
Truckee River yielding 96,000 pounds and it is
estimated that an additional 10,000 pounds of
trout were used by the resorts each summer
season.[6]

In May, 1895, the Fish Commission (forerunner of California's Fish and Game Commission) had decided upon an experiment in trout

[6] For additional facts on Lake Tahoe trout refer *California, Volume IX, Outdoor Heritage,* Harold Child
Bruant, page 221.

Millard Bennett

"OLD JASPER" FINALLY BOWED TO A FLY ROD

E. W. S. Woods of Stockton, California, holding the 25-pound 5-ounce Tahoe trout he caught on light tackle June 1, 1909, off Brockway Hot Springs Hotel. The fish measured 25½ inches in length and took one hour and 35 minutes to bring to net. Woods is standing at the west entrance to the resort.

Author's collection

CROWN PRINCE OF THE CUTTHROATS

*Chris Nielson, locally famous Tahoe
fishing guide, with his 29½-pound cutthroat
that only missed the record by ounces.*

planting that stirred up a heated debate, one that continues to this day. Available in their rearing ponds at Sisson hatchery, Mount Shasta, were 65,000 Great Lakes mackinaw fingerlings, voracious feeders that ran to more than 30 pounds when full grown and distinguished by a forked tail. Transported to Tahoe in five-gallon metal containers, they were packed on horseback into the Tallant Lakes' basin above Meeks Bay and planted.[7]

Native Tahoe residents report that for over a decade nothing was seen of these trout but gradually cutthroat were becoming scarcer on the south and southwest side of the lake and some of those caught showed signs of having been attacked, with their heads and tails lacerated and sides running blood. Still no one appeared to know the reason for this.

In the summer of 1920, Ben Callender from Homewood hooked a strange looking six-pounder in Stony Ridge Lake, one of the upper Tallant

group. As the fish was unfamiliar to him and other residents, the head was sent to the University of California for examination. It proved to be a mackinaw.

By then the "cannibalistic trout" had gained a secure foothold in Tahoe, having migrated from the Tallants down Meeks Creek into the lake. It is said that the cutthroat were now doomed and as the mackinaw moved northward up the lake the last stand of the scarlet-gilled trout became the fishing grounds off of Brockway and in Crystal Bay. Finally these deeps were also taken over by the "naturalized citizens of the lake" (which besides the mackinaw included Rainbow, German Brown and cross-breeds) and the native silvers, cutthroat and Royal Silver trout became practically nonexistent.[8]

It is generally conceded that the mackinaw assisted in putting an end to Tahoe's native trout, but the sluggish if palatable fish was not entirely responsible for the wholesale drying up of the prime fishing in this world-famous lake.

Years of unrestricted commercial fishing, inadequate replanting methods (including the placement of trout fingerlings in Tahoe that were not large enough to survive) and the blocking off of feeder streams into the lake, up which the trout normally migrated to spawn, are other sound reasons for the nearly complete destruction of Tahoe's trout population. Many fishing experts minimize the part the mackinaw played in destroying the lake's native fish, logically contending that all large trout are equally cannibalistic.

In a belated effort to halt the extermination of Tahoe's trout the California Fish Commission placed 900,000 fry in the lake during the fall of 1903. Plants had been made in previous years by the Commission, however, quantities were limited and few survived. After 1911 the catchable

[7] Tallant Lakes (named for George Tallant of Tallac) was decided upon for the "Mackinaw experiment" after Lake Tahoe's resort owners, headed by Harry O. Comstock, contested the plan to plant them in Tahoe.

[8] Silver trout, the planted Rainbow, German Brown (Von Behr trout of Europe), and the early-day whitefish, are the shallow water fish, normally found in depths up to 120 feet. The native cutthroat was readily recognized by its dark olive colored body, large black speckled spots on its sides and dash of scarlet under its gills; sometimes known as the "black speckled trout." Except during the spawning season when the affluents of Tahoe were black with their fins, the cutthroat was a deep water fish. The Royal Silver trout (Salmo Regalis) was another native of Tahoe found in deep water along the eastern shoreline of the lake. Their spotting was inconspicuous, a white underside and beautiful steel blue coloration on their back marking the fish. Seldom did they run over 9 pounds in weight.

John Ernest Pomin

NEARLY HALF HIS WEIGHT IN MACKINAW

Robert Pomin standing beside a record 32¾-pound Mackinaw caught by his uncle, John Ernest Pomin, off Idlewild during the winter of 1926. The fish was 40 inches long and took 50 minutes to land.

limit was reduced from 100 pounds per day per fisherman to 50 pounds, but market fishermen, Indians and whites alike, sent out 22,000 pounds in 1911, half of the catch coming from Tallac.

Amidst this pillage of Tahoe's natural resource, isolated cases of the true sportsman angler were sometimes found. Archibald Treat's article in the *Pacific Coast Magazine* for June, 1904, entitled "Trolling with Rod in Shallow Water on Lake Tahoe," gives a picture of the fishing paradise found at the lake in those days. Treat, using a steel salmon rod and small Red Star flasher, Kentucky reel and 80 to 100 yards of number 21 Cutty Hunk line with nine feet of gut leader, repeatedly brought to boat Royal Blue Silvers ranging to 9½ pounds each. The fishing locale was Brockway Hot Springs and Crystal Bay, where, in the same year, ten boats would often return to the pier with an average catch of 20 fish per boat after four hours of fishing.

In the heyday of fishing at Lake Tahoe it was contended that only a single variety of trout were natives of the lake, one recognized authority advising that the male cutthroat, female "pogie," Silver and Royal Silver were one and the same thing. The difference in appearance was attributed to varying local conditions, the skipping of spawning seasons and cross-breeding. Another interesting theory concerns the origin of fish in Tahoe. It is not improbable that the "natives" in the lake were originally land-locked salmon that migrated up the rivers, streams, and finally rivulets into the high country (Desolation Valley Wilderness Area in the vicinity of Mount Tallac) where they found their way, after heavy winters that raised the Alpine tarns' levels, into lakes that spilled into the Tahoe basin as well as down the western scarp of the Sierra Nevada.

The mysterious and unpredictable Tahoe minnow is one of the attractions of the lake. By the hundreds they move inshore during the springtime, spending the summer and early fall months floating and feeding in the shallow waters near the protection of piers and breakwaters. When a group of these wary 4 and 5-inch fingerlings venture out into deeper water, they keep a sharp lookout for the large rainbows and silversides that consider the minnow a choice, if elusive, meal.

The presence of a 4 or 5 pounder is immediately transferred to the minnows even though the larger trout may be several hundred yards away. Then the fry wheel like a regiment in formation and make for the safety of the piers.

When a hungry rainbow levels on a school of these small fish, the transparent water turns into a marine battleground, with the big trout driving in from deep water at tremendous speed, turning and twisting with lightning rapidity, and thrusting at the skittering minnows streaking across the top of the water.

A big trout may often carry completely out of the water in his headlong rush, throwing spray and slapping back on the surface of the lake as he doubles on his quarry like a cat after a mouse. Contrarily, a large fish may float in the center, and slightly below a school of minnows and the closely packed smaller fish appear to sense the fact that, at the moment, they are not the target for an attack. When this happens they continue their surface feeding just as though the voracious trout were not present.

If a top-line fisherman is fortunate enough to be on the end of a pier when the large trout makes his flashing thrust through the water after the minnows and has his hook baited with one of the fry, his chances of hooking a Tahoe beauty are excellent. The big fish will often mistake the fisherman's hooked minnow for one of the laggards in the group he is chasing and take it before he realizes his mistake. Native Tahoe minnows never grow larger than 4 to 5 inches in length and appear to be small varicolored rainbows upon examination. When they disappear into the great deep of the lake in the late fall they are not seen again until the following season. Where they migrate no one has been able to determine.

For decades the California State Fish and Game Commission's Tallac Hatchery operated at Taylor Creek on the south end of Tahoe. It was established in 1882 and here spawn from Maine and Vermont (mostly Eastern Brook) and eggs from the lake trout were cultivated. Although Tallac's hatchery has been closed down, another is operating one mile north of Tahoe City on the lake highway.

In 1917 the California Legislature finally took action to halt the destruction of trout in the state. They banned commercial fishing in lakes and streams but, unfortunately, it came too late and the restocking of Tahoe became a problem that is not satisfactorily solved today. California and Nevada state laws applying to Lake Tahoe were standardized in the mid-1950's with fishing once again opened on an all year around basis.

Despite the 12 months season, Tahoe's trout population is slowly coming back. Rainbow,

Mackinaw, Silver, German Brown and cross-breeds are taken regularly. An experimental plant of Kokanee land-locked salmon, with a life cycle of only four years, was tried in the early 1950's but the fact that they were generally unseen during the summer months and when seen found to be difficult to catch, has contributed to their lack of popularity among fishermen. Cutthroat fingerling are now being tried.

Proper planting, regulations protecting spawning fish and their spawning grounds, and feed in the lake, may once again bring Lake Tahoe to the forefront as an angler's utopia; however, it appears that the emphasis is still being placed on stocking the 120 or more high country lakes in the region with relatively small sub-catchable plants going into Tahoe.

The answer to Lake Tahoe's year-around popularity is an abundance of trout in the lake. When this is clearly recognized and action taken, Tahoe will be assured of an unprecedented surge of activity.

TAME DEER AND TAHOE TROUT

John Ernest Pomin, Captain Joe Pomin and Henry Soll (left to right) with "Mary" the Soll family's domesticated deer and record mackinaw taken on the shoreline of the Sydney Ehrman estate in the 1920's. Looking east.

Mrs. Annie Soll

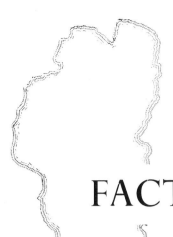

FACTS OF LAKE TAHOE

FORMATION OF LAKE TAHOE

For the purpose of simplicity, Lake Tahoe's formation may be divided into four main periods: earth deformation, volcanic, glacial and conservation.

In the first stage higher portions of the tremendous upthrust constituting the original mountain block, which eventually became the Sierra Nevada, were broken up by a vast disturbance. Mammoth trough-like depressions and fractures were formed that ran in a north-south direction, east of the original crest and extending approximately from Honey Lake to the Mono region. This faulting of the massive and symmetrical range left the northern portions with a double, serrated crest; the older western summit of the Cretaceous period and the later Tertiary, or eastern ridge.

During the second period, violent volcanic action poured huge masses of lava into the trough and formed a broken lateral ridge, practically connecting the two crests of the fractured Sierra and damming up the southern half of the trough. The waters collected behind the barrier eventually rose hundreds of feet above the present lake level, escaping northward through a channel between

Mount Pluto and the western summit. A recurring series of eruptions blocked this outlet and the rising waters forced a new channel.

The third period brought an extensive ice pack, known as the Lake Valley Glacier, originating in the Silver Mountain region at the south end of the depression. This filled the blocked trough, pushing great masses of rock ahead of it in its slow march to the north. At the same time glaciers from the west left large moraines in the Truckee River Canyon, causing the lake to rise once again and the river to seek another channel. Feeder glaciers in the present Fallen Leaf, Cascade, Emerald Bay and Rubicon Peaks area joined the main body of ice in what would become Lake Tahoe.

Geologist Joseph LeConte, writing in the 1870's, considered that the Tahoe basin was filled with a giant "mer de glace" during the Age of Ice. Said to be 50 miles long by 15 miles in width, it was believed to have attained a depth of 2,000 feet. LeConte determined that the glacier spilled over the present Mount Rose-Slide Mountain rim to the plains of Nevada and that an offshoot escaped down the Truckee River Canyon. This

---

C. O. Valentine

"GIVE ME MEN TO MATCH MY MOUNTAINS"

Looking north from the summit of Mount Tallac in June of 1911 with box camera mounted on a tripod.
Cascade Lake and Emerald Bay are below (foreground), Rubicon Point is in sunshine (center),
Meeks Point and Sugar Pine Point are to the left and Tahoe City lies beyond.
Twenty-two miles of Lake Tahoe stretches to the northern rim
of the Carson Range in the far distance.

theory has since been re-examined and it is now generally believed that the great southern glacier extended only into the basin that now constitutes Tahoe.

With the coming of a warmer climate the tongues of ice that had gouged out Fallen Leaf and Cascade lakes and dammed their outlets with detritus, melted to form small bodies of water flanked by high lateral enclosure ridges. The Emerald Bay glacier pack extended farther into the Tahoe oval which explains its present day connection with the main body of water. Great icebergs were formed in the lake and, as the sea of ice receded, Tahoe again rose, spilling down the present Truckee Canyon and once again cutting its way through the gorge.[1]

The man-made development of Tahoe took place in 1870 when Colonel Von Schmidt constructed his cribbed and rock-filled dam at the natural outlet. This raised the maximum water level of the lake six feet above the normal rim, determined as 6,223 feet, and provided additional water storage for irrigation, log flotation and power facilities in California and Nevada.

Throughout most of its extent the Sierra Nevada range is formed with a single crest. At the upper end of Hope Valley, however, the mountain chain divides into two branches—the western Sierra Nevada and the Carson range to the east. Between these two upthrusts lies Lake Tahoe. On the south and southwest, the mountains rise steeply 3,500 to 4,000 feet above the lake. Here the terrain furnishes dozens of examples of true Alpine high country tarns cut and polished during the glacier period. The Carson range, or eastern scarp of the Sierra, lifts in a precipitous wall of granite 5,000 to 6,000 feet above Carson and Washoe valleys. On the western approach to summit, however, the slope is relatively gradual, ascending to more than 10,000 feet above sea level in approximately 75 miles.[2]

---

[1] For a concise account of Lake Tahoe's formation refer to *Sierra-Nevada Lakes,* George and Bliss Hinkle, 1940, pp. 252-253. See also Waldemar Lindgren, *The Tertiary Gravels of the Sierra Nevada of California,* U. S. Geological Survey, Professional Paper 73 (1911), G. D. Louderback, *"Lake Tahoe, California-Nevada,"* *Journal of Geography* (1911), J. A. Reid, *The Geomorphogeny of the Sierra Nevada Northeast of Lake Tahoe,* University of California Publications, Bulletin of the Department of Geological Science, Vol. VI (1911), pp. 89-161, and Joseph LeConte, *"On Some Ancient Glaciers of the Sierra,"* *American Journal of Science,* 3 Series, Vol. X (1875), pp. 126-39.

[2] *Early Engineering Works Contributory to the Comstock,* John Debo Galloway, University of Nevada Bulletin XLI, June, 1947.

COLORS OF THE "BIG BLUE"

Brilliant blues, vivid greens, intense ultramarines, magnificent deep indigos, delicate shadings of purple, violet and cobalt: these and other combinations of the chromatic colors and tints may be seen in the crystal purity of Tahoe's snow water.

The surface viewer, when looking down into the great deep of the lake, sees a blue-blackness that changes gradually to ultramarine as the eye moves toward the horizon, and a cloudless, quiet day on Tahoe is comparable to resting in an inverted vault of blue sky. However, when clouds blot out the sun and drift across the lake its surface quickly changes to a mirror of gray or dull silver.

Shallow water, underlain with white sand, is a striking apple or emerald green. Close inshore the green fades away until it appears that the achromatic water is non-existent and it is difficult to determine where the water ends and the beach begins.

Tahoe's waters strongly reflect the moods above it: pastel blues and pinks on crisp autumn evenings, blazing scarlets and deep orange spreads of color preceding summer sundowns, and striking yellows and golds fanning out across the lake at sunrise.

The purity of Lake Tahoe's waters, its great depth, the clarity of the atmosphere at more than 6,200 feet, all combine with a reflective sky to give the lake its varied and intense colors.

Described in 1865 as the "brightest gem in the mountain coronet of those twin Queens, the Golden and Silver States," Tahoe is fittingly known today as the "Lake of the Sky," with its contrasting ring of sparkling emerald green surrounding a heart of deep blue.

WATER TEMPERATURES OF LAKE TAHOE

The surface water temperature of Tahoe fluctuates with the changing conditions of sun, wind, snow and rain, but the main body of water, below 750 feet, remains nearly constant at 41.5 to 39.2 degrees winter and summer, dropping less than two degrees between 800 and 1,645 feet. Sixty-eight degrees is the average surface temperature of Tahoe in the hottest weather. Shallow and isolated sections of the lake often range higher, with the surface water rising four degrees on a cloudless summer day. It is said that a "shoreward current" travels from north to south on the lake and that this accounts for the water being several degrees warmer in the vicinity of Bijou, Al Tahoe and Camp Richardson.[1]

Other sample temperature checks have been made; for example, the surface water in Emerald Bay in the late summer of 1940 was found to be 68 degrees with the temperature at 22 feet, 62 degrees.[2]

During the winter time the surface water drops to an average 50 degrees.

----

[1] *Historical Souvenir, El Dorado County, California,* Paolo Sioli, Oakland, 1883.
[2] Brian Curtis, Tallac Fish Hatchery, August 2, 1940.

HOW IS THIS VAST STORAGE BASIN FILLED?

More than 70 feeder creeks, streams, and rivers empty into Lake Tahoe. The largest is the Upper Truckee River, on the south end of the lake, originally known as Lake Creek (1855-60), and Lake Valley Creek (1860-85). Its headwaters start high in the vicinity of Little Round Top, Stevens Peak and Round Lake, with another feeder running out of Luther Pass' Grass Lake.

On the western slopes of Tahoe: Cascade, Eagle, Lonely Gulch, Meeks (Mick's, 1873-77), General (Phipps, 1863-75, and Sugar Pine, 1876-88), McKinney's (Burton's, 1863-74), Quail, Madden, Blackwood, Ward, Bliss, Burton, Dollar (Slim Jim, 1875-90), Watson (Gordon's, 1877), Carnelian Canyon Creek (Kuhleborn, 1874-79, and Cornelian, 1880), feed into the main body of water.

The northern affluents are Griff (Griffin's, 1876), First, Second, Third, and Incline (White Cliff, 1877-78).

Tributaries draining into the lake from the eastern, or Carson Range of the Sierra, are Mill, Harbor, Tunnel, Marlette (Secret Harbor, 1876), Bliss, Glenbrook (Glen Brook, 1861-70), Lincoln, North and South Logan House, Zephyr (Severy Cove, 1882), Small's (Friday's, 1876-77).

From the southern watershed flow Heavenly Valley (Miller, 1863-80), Cold, Trout, the Upper Truckee, Taylor, and Spring.[1]

As the watershed surrounding Tahoe exceeds 500 square miles, it serves as an immense storage basin for the snow and ice pack that builds up during the winter months. Heavy winters pile the drifts 40 to 50 feet deep in the canyons on the south and west sides of Lake Tahoe and record snowfalls have seen 16 or more feet fall on level ground during January and February.

The winter of 1867 was one of the heaviest known. Although accurate measurements of snow depths for that year are unavailable, a comparison may be made with the winter of 1889-90 when 14 feet of snow was recorded on the flats south of Tahoe City. Rainfall records in Sacramento show 20 per cent more precipitation during the winter of 1867 than in 1889-90, which would indicate that nearly 17 feet of snow lay on the western shoreline in 1867. During a "mild winter" in the early 1900's a snow measurement rod, 20 feet long, failed to reach solid ground through the pack in Ward Creek.[2]

When the spring thaw comes every valley, canyon, ravine and gully becomes a gentle flowing brook, then a leaping cataract and, finally, a raging torrent, pouring water and debris into Tahoe.

Contrary to general belief, there are no major springs in the lake that affect its level, therefore most of Tahoe's water is snow runoff.

Not to be overlooked as a major contribution to the increase in lake level, is the snow, rain and sleet deposited directly into Tahoe itself.

----

[1] Spring Creek flows into Taylor Creek and Heavenly Valley and Cold creeks join Trout Creek.
[2] Robert H. Watson, October 9, 1955.

THE REASON TAHOE DOES NOT FREEZE OVER

Although air temperatures at the lake may remain far below zero for days at a time, the main body of water does not freeze. Shallow, or detached sections of Tahoe, have been known to freeze during extreme winters and ice occasionally forms around the shoreline, but it is broken up and scattered by heavy winter winds.

Hot springs, such as those found at Brockway, have been offered as an explanation but these springs do not appreciably affect the water temperature even in the vicinity of their issuance into the lake.

Scientific studies give the following logical explanation for the mass of water in Tahoe remaining in a liquid state: First is the great depth and quantity of water with its constant surface to depth and depth to surface movement; secondly, the high specific heat of the billions of gallons in Tahoe which makes it impossible to bring the mass down to the freezing point, and, lastly, the agitation of the water by strong winds that sweep its surface during the winter months.[1]

[1] *The Lake of the Sky,* George Wharton James, Boston, 1915. Observation of Joseph LeConte.

HAS A SWIMMER EVER CROSSED THE LAKE?

Previous to the 1880's bathing in the shallows of Tahoe was indulged in but swimming in the lake was another matter entirely. Strangely enough, Tahoe's waters were considered incapable of supporting a swimmer and Lakers sagely advised tourists that logs, after a few days in this snow water that lacked buoyancy, upended and sank. Tahoe residents, therefore, concluded that those who attempted such a foolhardy stunt as swimming would plummet to the bottom of the lake like a rock. An unidentified dare-devil finally took the plunge in the early 1880's and he is said to have "amazed all and sundry when he managed to thrash around on the surface and stay afloat."[1]

Since that time, five long distance swimmers of record have conquered Lake Tahoe's width and one of these its length. The first, Mrs. Myrtle Huddleston, who had previously set a world's endurance record by staying afloat 83½ hours, entered the water at Deadman's Point, north of Glenbrook, shortly before 8 o'clock on Sunday morning, August 24, 1931. She was smeared with ten pounds of grease to minimize the effects of Tahoe's chill waters. Winds blowing from the southwest set up a surface tidal action when Mrs. Huddleston was half way across and the waves carried her off course toward Observatory Point. But at 6:55 Monday morning she fought her way to Tahoe Tavern pier and claimed the $700 in prize money that had been offered. Mrs. Huddleston was forced to swim in a southwesterly direction to reach her objective and she covered more than 20 miles in all. During the night she was temporarily separated from her escort boat. After having gone without nourishment for the entire trip, she lost 12 pounds. The swim had taken 23 hours and 53 minutes to accomplish.

Mrs. Huddleston's crossing of Tahoe was considered a remarkable feat of endurance when conditions of water, temperature, altitude and wind were taken into consideration.

The first man of record to conquer the width of Tahoe was William Long, a 27-year-old life-guard and long distance swimmer from Van Nuys, California. Long stroked across the lake in 12 hours and it was estimated that he actually swam a distance of 17 miles as winds also carried him off course.

In 1954 a young girl and a 44-year-old man negotiated the width of Tahoe. This brought the successful crossings to four, although dozens of swimmers had tried and failed.

The summer and fall of 1955 found long distance swimmers setting records at Tahoe that were formerly considered impossible. At 7 o'clock on the morning of August 8, 1955, Fred Rogers from South San Francisco waded into the water near Cave Rock. He struck out for Meeks Bay, some nine miles across the lake to the west, arriving there at 1:46 in the afternoon. His time of 6 hours and 46 minutes was the fastest on record although he did not cross the widest section of Tahoe (Glenbrook to Tahoe Pines) which would have added three miles.[2] Rogers had attempted to swim the "impossible" length of the lake earlier in the year, along with other internationally known swimmers, but it remained unconquered.

Encouraged by his successful crossing of the lake, Rogers decided to again try the north-south distance. On Sunday, August 28, 1955, he entered the waters of Tahoe at King's Beach. Jose Cortinas, who had negotiated the Catalina Channel both ways, also started with Rogers. It was 11:30 in the morning.

Maintaining a steady pace the two men stroked their way down the middle of Tahoe with Rogers gradually pulling ahead. He arrived at the El Dorado Campground beach on the south end shortly after 6:30 Monday morning, and became the first swimmer to cover Tahoe's 21.6-mile length. He had been in the water 19 hours and 6 minutes.[3] Cortinas landed near Stateline Beach after traveling nearly the same distance as Rogers but actually not swimming the full length of Lake Tahoe.

The "impossible feat" had been accomplished.

[1] Harry O. Comstock, Brockway, July 4, 1952.
[2] *Truckee Sierra Sun,* August 11, 1955.
[3] *Lake Tahoe News,* September 1, 1955.

THE REASON BODIES ARE NOT RECOVERED FROM TAHOE

Between the years 1860 and 1874 early records indicate that a total of 14 people were drowned in the lake. None of the bodies were recovered when the drownings occurred in deep water and in practically every instance "excessive alcoholism" was blamed for the loss of life.

The worst recorded marine disaster took place on the night of September 8, 1869, when five workmen from Campbell's Hot Springs (Brockway) disappeared after their sailboat capsized in stormy weather between Tahoe City and Observatory Point as they were returning from an evening of "bucking the tiger" in Truckee.[1] Captain Richard Barter, the Hermit of Emerald Bay also sailed to his death on a winter's night in 1873 while crossing from Rowland's Station to his home at Ben Holladay's in Emerald Bay.[2] Other casualties were successful suicide attempts and drownings in shallow water.

Many curious stories circulated in the 1870's and 1880's concerning the ultimate fate of those who disappeared in the depths of Tahoe. In 1872 the *San Francisco Bulletin* solemnly assured its readers: "A corpse remains suspended and motionless (in Tahoe) at a depth of 200 feet and over, frozen stiff as though encased in a block of ice, and the great pressures encountered in the vast deep of the lake reduce an adult's body to that of a child's stature, exercising a clamping effect that holds the person in a viselike grip, preventing its rise to the surface."

Discarding conjecture and the fanciful, a sound, proven reason why bodies do not return to the surface of the lake is that corpses sinking into snow water, only a few degrees above freezing, do not decompose, as would normally be the case in warmer waters. Thus gases are not formed which would cause them to inflate and rise to the surface. It is conceivable that bodies are preserved in the watery abyss of Lake Tahoe much in the same manner as prehistoric mammals are found in massive ice floes after thousands of years of entrapment.

[1] *Resources and Wonders of Tahoe, Sacramento Union,* May 29, 1875. C. F. McGlashan.
[2] Refer Emerald Bay chapter 18.

IS THE LAKE BOTTOMLESS?

A legend still persists, originally fostered by the native Washoe Indians and handed down for centuries, that Tahoe is bottomless. This follows the familiar pattern set for many large fresh water lakes throughout the world: Tanganyika, Titicaca, Crater, Nyasa and the Caspian Sea among others. Lake Tahoe, like these lakes, has been sounded at its greatest depth.

On the Fourth of July, 1875, when C. F. McGlashan of Truckee and Charles Burkhalter of the United States Observatory found Tahoe's maximum depth to be 1,645 feet, they used a leaded champagne bottle and fishing line for their calculations. It is notable that this was the same depth as that determined by the United States Coast and Geodetic Survey in 1922, although as late as August, 1939, the "greatest depth" of Tahoe was shown on official maps as 1,592 feet.

In spite of McGlashan and Burkhalter's factual findings the *Carson Appeal* reported in August of 1880: "D. L. Bliss, of Glenbrook, ran the nose of his steamer *Meteor* against a rocky shoreline on the western side of Tahoe (Rubicon Point), dropped a line from the stern and it went 3,000 feet without bottom being sounded."

The Great Tahoe Deep lies four miles southwest of north Stateline Point and one mile west of the California-Nevada state line. This places the absolute bottom of Tahoe 92 feet below the level of the capital of Nevada, Carson City, lying in the valley directly east of Lake Tahoe.[1]

[1] This calculation is based upon lake level at 6228 feet, Carson City at 4675 feet and the depth of Tahoe, 1645 feet.

CLARITY OF THE ATMOSPHERE

It should be recalled that you are nearly 1,000 feet higher than a mile above sea level when you look into the distance at that "grassy knoll" across the far reach of Tahoe. Grassy knoll? It would take an acclimated hiker hours to gain the top after hard, steady climbing. That carpet of dark green shrubbery stretching to summit? In reality it is a heavy stand of pine, cedar, and fir, some of which tower upwards of 180 feet into the High Sierra sky.[1]

What is the average guess as to the dimensions of Lake Tahoe? Often five to six miles in length and several miles in width, although the lake is nearly 22 miles long with a breadth of close to 13 miles.

When seen from the south end of the lake those "smooth foothills" to the northwest are actually Mount Watson and Pluto, both over 8,500 feet above the sea. Stand on the bluff at Tahoe City and view that sandy trio of "hummocks" to the southeast. They are Job's Peak, Job's Sister and

[1] Trees in the Tahoe region include the Western Yellow, Jeffery, Sugar and Tamarack pine along with two other conifers, the White fir and Incense cedar. At higher altitudes the Red fir and Western hemlock are found.

Mount Freel, all three more than a vertical mile above the lake itself and over two miles above sea level.

On a calm day the distance between Glenbrook and Tahoe City appears to be not more than a few minutes run by power boat. It would take a full hour for a medium speed outboard to reach the halfway point, however, and then the farther shore would appear to be the same distance away as when you started. An inexperienced oarsman may believe he is only a few hundred yards off shore when actually a half hour trip lies ahead before he will reach land.

The crystal clarity of Tahoe's atmosphere is so pronounced that often trees, houses, canyons and high mountain meadows on the Nevada shore appear to be focused in a powerful telescope when the sun drops behind the western Sierra, with minuteness of detail standing out in bold relief.

At night Tahoe reaches to the sky and stars, pinpointing the heavens, almost seem to brush the water.

WEATHER ON LAKE TAHOE

"The calm changes to weather flaws that come tearing through the mountain canyons, slapping at the lake to create flurries and gusts of wind that arrive in an instant and go as quickly. One Laker told me she can be as treacherous a body of water as may be found in the entire world, the wind blowing from all points of the compass at the same time."

One "Jibenonasa" from Georgetown so advised the *Placerville Recorder* in the summer of 1866, after making his way to Tahoe by way of Blackwood Creek Canyon, sailing on the lake and leaving with a healthy respect for its variable moods.

Henry R. Miquels, early day California and Nevada newsman, reported a decade later: "Truly no man knows whence the wind comes or whither it goes. One moment there comes a puff from the south, the next there is a no less decided breeze from the east; in a twinkling there comes at cats-paw from the nor'west, in the same second the water surface seems glown in two or three directions simultaneously." Miquels further discovered "whirlwinds no small boat could withstand, a snow squall that came from the north, described a horseshoe and flew off at a tangent, and the questionable case of a "boatman who had been

blown clean off a raft while trying to navigate with a setting pole near shore."

Tahoe can also be the quiet, calm dilettante resting without a ripple to disturb her stillness day after day. At such times the lake is dazzling in her brightness, the surface smooth and polished, and the clearly discernible curve of the earth stretches away across the placid deep blue in an endless arc. Generally the summer and fall months at Tahoe offer a cloudless, brilliant sky, quiet water and penetrating sunshine.

Thunderstorms strike infrequently, but when they do they are often preceded by terraced pyramids of white-topped clouds, their altitudinous bases black with the threat of rainwater, bringing a sombre hush that lies upon the mountains. Then a breeze fans out across the water, tracing serpentine patterns, followed by swirling gusts that burst with a sudden intensity, slashing at the flatness of the lake's surface and driving across the extent of Tahoe to leave in their wake a sawtooth of snow water froth that tumbles boiling breakers on the farther shore.

On Tahoe a combination of roiling water, dead calm and storm waves may occur at various points on the lake at one and the same time. Often a flat surface, intersprinkled with isolated circles of wind disturbance, is evident when not a breath of air may be felt. Crosswinds frequently come from three or four different directions at once, whipping the water into a turbulent white-crested cross-chop. It is also true that a marine traveler may experience wind in his face, while following the oval perimeter of the shoreline, without it once blowing at his back.

A serrated ridge of water on the horizon usually means that surging combers will erase the calm of the lake within minutes. If a boat from the western side of Tahoe is caught on the mid-eastern shore in an "up the lake blow" a logical course to follow is south along the shoreline to the far end, making the turn close in past Camp Richardson and the entrance to Emerald Bay, into the smooth water on the western, or lee side. Starting east across Tahoe under these southwest wind conditions may find the mariner leaving a dead calm at Tahoe City only to encounter three and four foot rollers in the center of the lake and even heavier water at Deadman's Point and Glenbrook.

The distance between crests of storm waves on Lake Tahoe has been estimated at more than 40 feet with 10 to 12 foot troughs following sustained, high-velocity winter blows.

Prevailing winds are out of the south and southwest, moving north up the lake, therefore, the western shore is considered the lee side and normally navigable by even the smallest of craft unless an east wind strikes. When this occurs, and a "Washoe Zephyr" funnels out of Nevada, the waters at Incline, Glenbrook, Zephyr Cove, Bijou and Al Tahoe experience a flat calm and Carnelian Bay, Tahoe City, Homewood, Meeks and Emerald Bay receive the full brunt of the northeaster. A north or east wind is the exception; however, a prudent boatman restricts his travel to the east side of the lake in the mornings, when the waters are usually calm, and keeps to the west and south sides after the afternoon winds strike the Nevada shoreline.

Tahoe's waters agitate so suddenly that lake residents in the 1870's thought gigantic subterranean geysers existed in the Great Deep. The reason for these flash turmoils of water is found in the fact that Tahoe lies cradled on the summit of the Sierra Nevada, vulnerable to winds that blast over the nine to nearly eleven thousand foot mountain ranges, sweep down the deep canyons and fan out across the water.

In 1873 the *Sacramento Union* aptly described the weather conditions encountered on the lake: "Smiling and lovely as she looks, Tahoe has fits of anger when even an old salt would prefer the wilds of the Atlantic to braving her freakish wrath."

Charles Goodwin, in his *Comstock Club*, placed these words in the twinkle of an Irishman's brogue when he spoke of the Big Blue:

"Her natural face is bluer than that of a stock sharp in a falling market, but when the wind comes a wooin' and she dons her foamy lace, powders her face with spray, and fastens upon her swellin' breast a thousand diamonds of sunlight, O but she is a winsome looking beauty to be sure!"

DIMENSIONS, DEPTHS & OUTLET OF TAHOE ... ANYBODY'S GUESS

Tahoe's first recorded discoverer, Captain John Charles Fremont, came closer to a true determination of the lake's actual length than a full dozen pioneers, explorers, surveyors and resort owners would for decades to come. Fremont estimated the lake to be 15 miles in length, missing its actual north-south measurement by over 7 miles. However, he viewed this vast body of water in mid-winter from a point some 16 air miles distant. When his calculation is compared to the fantastic measurements submitted as fact over the next half century, which ran as high as 65 miles in length, Fremont's estimate may be considered reasonably accurate.

It was a stubborn and erroneous conviction of Fremont's, for some 40 years, that the outlet of Tahoe issued from the south end of the lake even though the lake's actual outlet had been discovered barely nine months after Fremont first viewed what he called "Mountain Lake." A horseback party of six young men and women from the Stevens-Townsend-Murphy emigrant group had broken off from the main company at what is now Donner Creek's influx into the Truckee River. They traveled "up the stream draining northerly out of the mountains" (Fremont's Salmon Trout River—Truckee) following its northeast side. Daniel Murphy is said to have been the first to reach the lake's outlet, and he and the others became the first white people to set foot on the shores of Lake Tahoe.[1]

William Morris Stewart, who went on to become Nevada's great lawyer and senator, was the seventh white person of record to locate the outlet. During the summer of 1850 Stewart left Nevada City to prospect up the North Fork of the American River. From its headwaters he crossed a ridge and then dropped down to the lake, where he "followed the shore with great difficulty" to the head of the Truckee River.

June of 1853 found John C. "Cock-Eye" Johnson and an unnamed *Placerville Herald* correspondent moving up the Rubicon River Gorge and striking east over the Sierra past Lost Corner Mountain to what is now Meeks Bay. Upon viewing Tahoe spread out before them they generously estimated it to be 60 miles in length by 20 miles across.[2]

During the summer of 1856, Asa Hershel Hawley, James Green and John "Snowshoe" Thompson carried a small skiff, built by Hawley, to the lake and while Green and Thompson rowed on a course paralleling the shore, Hawley paced off a half mile on land to determine their rate of speed. The three would-be mariners then proceeded to circumnavigate the lake, becoming the first white men to do so, and came up with the startling calculation that it was 150 miles around, more than twice its actual circumference. The trio passed Tahoe's outlet, but Hawley later ad-

[1] Refer Lake Valley chapter 26.
[2] See Meeks Bay chapter 15.

mitted that he and his companions did not realize it was the head of the Truckee River.[3]

In August of 1856, a Placer County survey party, headed by Thomas Young, moved up the Truckee River after crossing the western Sierra by way of Squaw Valley. Young described the lake's outlet in detail before traveling north around Tahoe and over the Carson Range.[4]

During the fall of 1860, Lieutenant S. Mowry, in the course of running a government survey to determine the California-Utah Territory (Nevada) boundary, reached the astonishing conclusion that Tahoe was 40 miles in length. He compounded his error by placing the division line, running through the lake, one and one-half miles farther into California than it was later proven to be.

In June of 1863, Butler Ives of Nevada and John Kidder of California, after a joint survey, repudiated Mowry's fantastic findings when they determined that the length of Tahoe was 26 miles. Von Leicht and Hoffmann's *Topographical Map of Lake Tahoe and Surrounding Country*, published in 1874, shows the length correctly as 21.6 miles but places the width as only 10½ miles. Depth is noted as 1,525 feet and the altitude of Tahoe above the sea, 6,202 feet.

On July Fourth, 1875, C. F. McGlashan and Charles Burkhalter took 35 evenly spaced soundings between Campbell's Hot Springs (Brockway) and Emerald Bay. Their most important discovery was that Tahoe's maximum depth was 1,645 feet. In addition they found a variance of only 245 feet in the water's depth for 18 miles down the center, the soundings running between 1,400 feet and 1,645 feet.

In the summer of 1881, R. E. Wood, editor of the *Tahoe Tattler*, bracketed the lake as 26 miles in length and 12½ miles in width, hitting the width nearly exactly and placing the maximum depth at 1,506 feet.

So went the see-saw of Tahoe's length, width and depth, with the final official measurements showing the lake to be the second deepest body of water in North America (Crater Lake is first) as well as the largest Alpine lake in the world from the standpoint of elevation, dimensions, depth and volume of water impounded.

Tahoe is a vast marine amphitheatre with 193 square miles of surface area that averages, including shallows and bays, a remarkable 980 feet in depth. Its perpendicular drop-offs occur so suddenly that a boat may be in 25 feet of water one moment and in 1,400 feet the next. At nor-

mal high water level the lake is 6,229.1 feet above sea level, although shoreline rocks show that it has reached 6,231.49 feet. The natural rim level, below which water may not legally be drawn, is 6,223 feet, but factions are now at work in both California and Nevada to change this ruling.

At the northern stateline point soundings show a descent of 1,500 feet one-half mile offshore. A five-mile shelf runs along the southwest side of Tahoe varying in depth from 4 to 22 feet, with a granitic sand underwater floor extending well out into the lake, caused by deposits from the Upper Truckee and shoreline erosion. On the northwest side of Tahoe, in the vicinity of Tahoe City, a six-mile shelf follows the shore, averaging several miles in width, with depths running to 120 feet. Beyond these shelves lies the Great Deep of Tahoe, flanked by massive sections of sheer rock that constitute the perpendicular underwater walls of the subterranean canyons. In many places they drop 800 feet straight down and even incline in over the vertical, running for miles north and south through the lake.

Three separate shelves are generally recognized: the first a shallow sand and gravel margin banding the shoreline up to 160 feet in depth; the second, an "introductory deep" running to 700 and 800 feet; and, lastly, the tremendous bottom basin or Big Deep of Tahoe which drops off from 800 to 1,645 feet and accounts for three-quarters or more of the billions of gallons of water in Tahoe.

[3] Asa H. Hawley, "Lake Tahoe," Bancroft MS, University of California.

[4] Refer Squaw Valley chapter 1.

CONTROVERSY IN THE NAMING OF LAKE TAHOE

On a blustery St. Valentine's Day, February 14, 1844, an exploration party headed by Captain John Charles Fremont and guided by Christopher "Kit" Carson, struggled through the heavy snows in upper Hope Valley toward a pass that the Paiute Indians had indicated would lead them over the Sierra Nevada into the Valley of the Sacramento. Fremont, representing the United States Topographical Engineers, had been searching for the mythical Buenaventura River and Mary's Lake. Now he, Carson and the remnants of their original group of 39 men were caught in the Great Snowy Range in mid-winter. Two weeks had been spent in breaking trail through the mounting snowdrifts. Their Indian guides and bearers had deserted. Provisions were running low and in order to survive they must scale the formidable barrier rising ahead.

As the men neared the first summit divide, Fremont and his topographer, Charles Preuss, struck northwest toward "the highest peak to the right of the Pass" to take observations.[1] Upon gaining the top they looked north across what would become known, a decade later, as Luther Pass and Lake Valley. In the distance, some 16 miles away, they were astonished to see a vast expanse of blue water. Fremont later wrote, "We had a beautiful view of a mountain lake at our feet, about 15 miles in length, and so entirely surrounded by mountains that we could not discover an outlet."[2]

On February 21, one week later, Fremont and his party viewed the lake for the second time. The pathfinder observed: "Immediately above the eastern mountains was repeated a cloud-formed mass of purple ranges, bordered with bright yellow gold; the peaks shot up into a narrow line of crimson cloud, above which the air was filled with a greenish orange; and over all was the singular beauty of the blue sky. Passing along a ridge which commanded the lake (Tahoe) on our right—we began to discover an outlet through a chasm on the west."[3]

Fremont was now between Twin Lakes and Little Round Top due south of Tahoe, and the "chasm on the west" that he judged to be the stream leading out of the lake was actually the canyon of the South Fork of the American River, which heads at Audrain Lake, less than a mile, airline distance, from the Upper Truckee River.

Although the explorer erred in identifying the lake's outlet, not realizing that it was actually on the west side of Tahoe and the headwaters of the Salmon Trout River (Truckee) which he had located and named several weeks before, he did establish a number of "firsts." The initial winter crossing of the Central Sierra Nevada mountains by white men had been made, the first peak in the Sierra surmounted, Lake Tahoe discovered and the Kit Carson Pass route, over which a floodtide of '49'ers would move, had been run out.

Now the lake acquired the first of the numerous and conflicting names placed upon its waters by white men. Fremont called it Lake Bonpland, after Aimé Jacques Alexandre Bonpland, the eminent French botanist who accompanied Baron Alexander von Humboldt on his western exploration.

Charles Preuss' narrative maps of the expedition, however, show Tahoe as "Mountain Lake" and it was generally known as such until 1852. Fremont also substituted "Mountain Lake" for Bonpland in his reports of 1845-46, but the name Bonpland was placed upon the maps published in Europe for the French emigrants.

Gold region maps variously record Tahoe as "Fremont's Lake" and Mountain Lake (or Lakes), with several early cartographers failing to place the lake at all. On the United States Exploring Map of Upper California (1849), Tahoe is shown but not named and its outlet is designated as the South Fork of the American River.

W. M. Eddy, surveyor general of California, identified Tahoe as Lake Bigler on March 15, 1853, showing its full extent as lying on the eastern scarp of the Sierra in Utah Territory (Nevada).

The name Bigler had become unofficially entrenched during the previous year. California's third governor, John Bigler, who held office between 1852 and 1858, personally led a rescue party into Lake Valley in the winter of 1852 to bring out a snowbound group of emigrants. Upon their arrival in Hangtown (Placerville), Bigler was feted by a gathering of dignitaries, who it is said gracefully (many insisted disgracefully) named the lake "Bigler" in his honor.[4]

William Bartlett's *Emigrant Guide to California*, published in August of 1853, mentioned Truckee Lake and Bigler, applying both names to Tahoe.[5] J. H. Coulten's *Map of California*, distributed in 1855, lists Bigler but shows the lake as being two-thirds in Utah Territory and one-

---

[1] Stevens Peak (10,100 feet) is generally accepted as the mountain climbed by Fremont and Preuss; however, Red Mountain (9950 feet) is a more logical choice as (a) it is the first high peak to the right of the pass going west, (b) it is only a mile and one-quarter airline distance from the pass, whereas Stevens Peak is two and three-quarters airline miles, (c) an altitude differential of only 150 feet exists between the two peaks, (d) heavy mid-winter snow conditions existed at the time Fremont and Preuss climbed the peak. This practically rules out a round trip distance of nearly 6 miles to Stevens Peak when it was only 2½ miles round trip to Red Mountain. Mount Freel, Job's Peak and Job's Sister have also been claimed as vantage points from which the explorers first viewed Tahoe. As they lie in a group some 6 miles north of the West Carson Canyon, they do not fit Fremont's description.

[2] *The Exploring Expedition to the Rocky Mountains, Oregon and California*, John Charles Fremont, Buffalo, 1852, p. 334.

[3] Ibid., p. 336.

[4] Refer *Sierra-Nevada Lakes*, George and Bliss Hinkle, p. 267.

[5] *Placerville Herald*, August 13, 1853.

third in California, completely reversing the final division between the Territory and State.

The confusion was compounded by Baker's *Map of the Mining Regions* (1855) that showed a complete stranger, "Maheon Lake" on the actual location of Tahoe itself, and Milleson's *Map of the Southern and Middle Mines* (1854) continued to use "Mountain Lake" in the old Fremont-Preuss tradition.

With the outbreak of the Civil War, on April 12, 1861, former Governor John Bigler's name, as applied to Tahoe, once again became the subject for debate. He was recognized as an ardent Democrat and Southern sympathizer, supposedly having worked for a "Pacific Confederacy." The pro-Union papers raised the cry of "change from this Secesh appellation" and "no Copperhead names on our landmarks for us." Another faction of Unionists, bucking the Democratic "100 Drinks Legislature" of California, were now agitating to change the name of Tahoe to the fanciful "Tula Tulia," which they stoutly declared was the true Indian designation. Nothing came of this.[6]

Still another chronicler of the times, Edward Vischer, referred to Tahoe as "Big Truckee Lake" following the lead of Bartlett's *Guide*, published nearly a decade previously. But in spite of bitter opposition the name Lake Bigler remained in the foreground.

William Henry Knight, map maker for the United States Department of the Interior, now stepped into the picture. He had been gathering data for a General Land Office Map of the Pacific States and Knight issued instructions to the map's draughtsman, V. Wakenreuder, to omit the name of the lake until a more suitable one could be found.

In February, 1862, Knight invited Dr. Henry DeGroot, ace writer on the old *Evening Bulletin* and at the time correspondent for the *Sacramento Union*, to join him at the Bancroft Publishing House in San Francisco, for a review of the partially completed map. DeGroot remarked that the name Lake Bigler was missing. Knight replied that many were dissatisfied with the name and that it would be a good chance to substitute another one. Several were suggested—Washington, Lincoln and Fremont among others. Knight finally asked DeGroot for an Indian word, whereupon DeGroot consulted his notebook and found "tahoe," which, he said, meant "big water," "high water," or "water in a high place." The euphonious Indian appellation was decided upon and

Knight requested that the Land Office in Washington, D. C., use the name on all future maps and publications.

With the support of the press of California the name Tahoe gained immediate public support and the hotly contested debate that ensued made excellent newspaper copy. However, the Legislature of what was now Nevada Territory, considered it high handed indeed for California to proceed without consulting them and fuel was added to the verbal conflagration.[7]

In June of 1863, the *Nevada Washoe Times*, under the headline "What's in a Name," lamely insisted that it would be sensible to change Bigler to Sierra Lake, if it were not for the fact that a small sheet of water near the Downieville Buttes (California) had already been given the name. On May 28 of the same year the *Sacramento Union* also promoted "Sierra Lake" along with "Te-ho." In their opinion either was more acceptable than Bigler. "Largo Bergler" was actually a name that would be even more fitting, the paper declared, "as it would stand as a punishing illusion to the bibulous habits of 'Honest John' Bigler when he was Governor of the State."

The *Washoe Times* responded in agreement, "If a lake of beer is discovered Bigler will obviously be more suitable, but until that time arrives the native designation should be accepted."

Late in the summer of the same year the eminent Unitarian pastor from New York, Reverend Thomas Starr King, visited the lake, where he gained the inspiration for one of his most famous sermons, "Living Waters from Lake Tahoe." The good minister stanchly defended the name Tahoe: "It stems from the Washoe Indian 'Tache' (Much Water) plus 'Dao' (Deep or Blue Water) and is the name that should rest upon its waters."

In spite of the widespread denunciation of Bigler as applied to the lake, the Democratic California Legislature passed an act on February 10, 1870, that officially legalized the appellation, and stated "the lake shall hereinafter be known as Bigler."[8] However, the name Tahoe was firmly, if unofficially, linked to this great body of water through usage and the battle of words continued.

Surprisingly enough, Mark Twain was one of the few who vented his spleen against "Tahoe."

---

[6] *Sierra-Nevada Lakes,* George and Bliss Hinkle, p. 268.

[7] Ibid., pp. 268-270; also *Tahoe Tattler,* 2d edition, July 5, 1935.

[8] California Statutes, 1869-70.

Undoubtedly he was prejudiced because of his unflattering opinion of Indian lore, Indians generally and Digger Indians in particular. In his *Innocents Abroad* he calls down "sorrow and misfortune" on the heads of those who still promoted the use of this "unmusical cognomen" which, he declared, could never do justice to the lake's varied wonders and magnificent setting. His final thrust chides the attempts at defining the word "Tahoe."

"People say that Tahoe means 'Silver Lake'—'Limpid Water'—'Falling Leaf.' Bosh! It means grasshopper soup, the favorite dish of the Digger tribe—and of the Pi-utes as well."

On January 29, 1870, the Placerville *Mountain Democrat* stated flatly, "Tahoe was a renegade Indian who led a band of his murderous followers in pillaging forays on the whites. Was this therefore a logical choice for the naming of those beautiful waters?" it asked.[9]

Several days later the *Sacramento Union* quoted "Captain Jim," Chief of the Washoe tribe, when he rumbled: "Ta-ho mean Big Water, not Big-Ler," and a scribe from the *Truckee Republican* ventured the thought that Tahoe was probably the idiomatic Indian word for whiskey—"Big Water."

Nevada's *Daily State Register* joined with Mark Twain and the *Mountain Democrat* when it leveled a devastating salvo of editorial grape-shot at the name "Tahoe." The paper scornfully advised the public, "Tahoe was nothing but a thieving, conniving, mean, treacherous Indian, so bad in fact that he was actually outlawed by his own miserable tribe of Washoes, while Bigler is the name of a man who actually saved an early emigrant party in Lake Valley from those same thieving Indians. That was, and is, all that Tahoe signifies," the *Register* added.

It was getting so bad that even the Lakers and Washoeites were entirely confused on the issue. One of the junior legislators in Carson City went so far as to draw up a bill to change the name of Nevada's part of the lake. Things had really reached a ludicrous level.

In 1875, the *Carson Appeal* wheeled up its biggest guns and touched off a broadside, "Tahoe means an Indian squaw in mourning with burgundy pitch trimmed with chimney soot in her hair and the other parts of her physical economy in proportionate cleanliness." The *Appeal* had evidently exhumed Mark Twain's diatribe and added several new touches of its own. In May of 1877, the paper was still at it. "Not anybody, living or dead, knows what Tahoe means," they complained. "It is mock gibberish."

Naming of the lake had even become a political issue as shown by the *Appeal's* complaint, "Every time we allude to Bigler all the Sharon newspapers within 200 miles of Carson rise up to howl that we have sold out to Democracy."[10] The *Appeal* insisted, "California legalized the name in 1870—and this therefore proves we are absolutely right."

On August 12, 1881, the *Reno Gazette* belatedly tossed its editorial hat into the ring on the Tahoe question when it advised darkly: "Tahoe has an obscene meaning in Cosumnes Digger Indian jargon, from which it was taken," concluding in a complete about-face, "Tahoe is considered the aboriginal, appropriate, non-personal, legal, non-political and legitimate name and is so carried on the official maps."[11]

W. F. Edwards, Truckee publisher, questioned the native origin of the name when he complained in the year 1883, "If Tahoe is an Indian word, it must be an importation from the lingo of an extinct tribe in Massachusetts, or some other eastern state. Certainly the Washoes of the present day claim that they have no knowledge of its meaning."

John Charles Fremont, in 1844, had heard "Tah-ve" from the friendly Washoe Indians defined as "snow." Henry DeGroot, who listened attentively to the Washoes and Paiutes, interpreted "Tah-oo-ee" as meaning "much water" and "Tah-oo" as simply "water." Other spellings of the word were given as "Taa-joe," "Ta-ho," "Ta-jo," and even "Pah-hoe." To complicate matters further a Nevada newsman voiced the opinion that "Ta-au" in Washoe dialect was pronounced "Was-soo" and sometimes even "Da-au" with the word meaning "lake."

Clear water, deep water, big water, snow water, and fish lake were additional fist shaking translations argued back and forth with every interpretation actually the opinion of some white man.[12]

One of the more logical explanations of how the word Tahoe came to be applied to the lake is that Spanish explorers preceded Fremont in the

9 No documentary evidence points to a Washoe Indian named Tahoe, previous to or at this time.

10 Referring to the Democratic party, not democracy.

11 The *Reno Gazette* erred; Tahoe was not the legal name of the lake at the time.

12 *Sierra-Nevada Lakes*, George and Bliss Hinkle, p. 271.

discovery of this body of water, possibly in the early 1800's, and noting its obvious resemblance to a deep chasm filled with water gave it the Spanish name, "Tajo," pronounced "Ta-ho."

As "Tajo" is variously translated "cleft," "incision" and "cut," in addition to chasm, it is conjectured that "Tajo" could have entered the Washoe Indian vocabulary as easily as other Spanish words have entered native languages.[13]

Pronunciation of the word Tahoe has also been the source of heated debate for nearly a century. Pioneer Lakers pronounce "Ta-hoe" as "Tay-hoe," and the true mark of the early lake resident is the inflection he or she gives the word. One venerable gentleman, who had lived 80 years in the Tahoe region, insisted that they always used to say "Tay-ho" and "Tellec," but it had been finally changed to "Tahoe" and "Tallac."[14] Another old-timer with a background of seven and one-half decades at the lake indicated that "Tay-ho" was the accepted pronunciation until the steamer *Tahoe* was launched in 1896, at which time the pronunciation was changed to "Ta-hoe."

Editor R. E. Wood, writing in the *Tahoe Tattler* during the summer of 1881, added an element of confusion to the accepted version of Tahoe's early day pronunciation. He chided his readers, "Only the Washoe Indians say 'Tay-hoe,' the white men say, and correctly so, 'Ta-hoe'."

On August 21, 1886, the *Truckee Republican* wrestled masterfully with the problem. Taking a resigned, tongue-in-cheek attitude, the paper summarized a conversation overheard between a group of vacationers "deep in a discussion of our great lake."

The First Tourist: "I think Taw-who is magnificent."

The Second Tourist: "Tay-hoe's sunsets are simply gorgeous!"

The Third Tourist: "Never such beautiful colors as at T-hoo."

The Fourth: "They say a body of a person drowned never rises in Tay-how."

The Fifth: "Never ate finer trout than caught in Taw-o."

The Sixth: "I'm bringing my wife and daughter up to Tay-ho-ee."

The Seventh: Taw-whoo is it."

And finally the reporter: "Ta-hoe is fine, but leave out the tourists and their pronunciations."

It is an acknowledged fact that native Lake Tahoe pioneers still consider it nothing short of blasphemy to pronounce the word other than

"Tay-hoe," R. E. Woods admonitions to the contrary.

The generally accepted interpretation of Tahoe today is "Big Water" and, in spite of the eminent Mark Twain's views, Tahoe symbolizes the epitome of magnificence found in those high country reaches of the world wherever blue sky, towering mountain peaks and snow water combine.

Rather appropriately, a Mrs. Sigouney once said, when referring to Indian appellations, "Their names are on your waters and you may not wash them off."

This holds true today with the name Tahoe, although it took a full 75 years from the passing of the statute legalizing Lake Bigler, before the California Legislature solemnly convened and rescinded the act.[15]

The new statute read, "The lake known as Bigler shall hereinafter be known as Lake Tahoe." A spirited issue had at last been laid to rest.

[13] Ibid.
[14] George Davidson Oliver, Carson City, October 2, 1954, speaking of his father-in-law, William Keyser.
[15] Rescinded July 18, 1945.

COMPARISON STATISTICS OF LAKE TAHOE

(1) The lake is as long as the English Channel is wide, with the width of Tahoe being half again as wide as San Francisco Bay.

(2) With a surface area of only 193 square miles (70 of which are in Nevada) Lake Tahoe contains 122,160,280 acre-feet of water, or over 30,000,000 more acre-feet than the combined capacities of ten of the largest man-made reservoirs in the United States.[1]

(3) The Panama Canal averages 700 feet in width and 50 feet in depth, yet such a canal could be filled by Tahoe's water and extend completely around the earth at the equator, with enough remaining in the lake to fill another channel of the same width and depth runing from San Francisco to New York.[2]

(4) The State of California would be completely covered to a depth of 14½ inches with one dispersion of Lake Tahoe's water, and Texans can pride themselves on the fact that their extensive Lone Star State could only be covered to a depth of 8½ inches.[3]

[1] *Lake Tahoe and Vicinity* map, E. R. Smith, 1947.
[2] Ibid.; also refer to *Sierra-Nevada Lakes,* George and Bliss Hinkle, 1949, p. 253.
[3] Ibid.

(5) On an average, 1,400,000 tons of water evaporates from the surface of Tahoe every 24 hours, yet this drops the lake level only one-tenth of an inch. The total evaporation averages more per day than the water released through the Truckee River dam outlet; for example, the maximum flow through the gates at a lake level of 6,227.56 feet amounts to 1,464 cubic feet per second.[4] If the water that evaporates from the lake every 24 hours could be recovered, it would supply the daily requirements of a population exceeding 3,500,000 people.

(5) Lake Mead is backed up 227 miles by Hoover Dam into the Grand Canyon of the Colorado and is considered one of the largest man-made lakes in the world. Tahoe contains nearly four times the maximum capacity of Lake Mead.[5]

---

[4] Arthur Frodenburg, Tahoe City, June 14, 1954.
[5] *Lake Tahoe and Vicinity* map, E. R. Smith.

MOUNTAIN PEAKS, PASSES AND VALLEYS SURROUNDING TAHOE

FREEL PEAK (10,900 feet)

Named for pioneer miner and cattle rancher James Washington Freel, native of Illinois and White Oaks, '49'er resident. Freel ran his stock along the slopes east of Lake Valley and into Gold Valley. In 1855 the name "Job's Peaks" was given to the group of three mountains that became Job's Peak, Job's Sister and Freel, and in 1876-77 "Freel" was applied to the westerly peak on the United States Army Corps of Engineers *Topographical Map of Lake Tahoe*. Freel, or Freel's Peak, is the highest in the Tahoe region, lying seven air miles southeast of the lake. In the spring the number 27 may be clearly seen on the lake side of the mountain, formed by the melting snow.

JOB'S SISTER (10,820 feet)

The second of the original "Job's Peaks" group and changed on the Wheeler Survey map of 1876-77 to Job's Sister. In the 1860's the peak was also known as Sand Mountain due to its barren, brownish yellow summit. It is located between Freel and Job's Peak with Freel to the west.

JOB'S PEAK (10,637 feet)

Said to have been named for Moses Job, early Mormon settler who ran a store at what later became Sheridan at the eastern base of the mountain in Carson Valley. The peak is the fourth highest in the Tahoe range and its summit lies three miles directly east of Freel. "Survey flag will be placed by Mr. Mott (Mottsville) on Job's East Peak in September." George H. Goddard, September 20, 1855.

MONUMENT PEAK (10,085 feet)

Known as "Monumental Peak" in the 1860's and early '70's, it was a location point for Kidder and Ives boundary survey. Its summit lies four miles east of Tahoe straddling the former California-Nevada state line. The name comes from its use as a survey "monument marker."

RED (LAKE) PEAK (9,950 feet)

One and one-quarter air miles directly north of Carson Pass summit and an equal distance south of Stevens Peak. Important because Fremont wrote in February, 1844: ". . . we climbed the first mountain to the right of the Pass."

STEVENS PEAK (10,100 feet)

Nearly due south of Tahoe's Lake Valley, 16 air miles, and above Hope and Faith valleys. Famous as the mountain Fremont and Preuss are supposed to have climbed when they discovered Tahoe. Named for James M. Stevens, county supervisor, who operated a stage station in Hope Valley during the 1860's.

PYRAMID PEAK (10,020 feet)

Landmark in the late 1840's and '50's for the emigrant and exploratory parties. In 1873 it was considered the highest peak this side of Lassen Buttes; however, Freel's is nearly 900 feet higher. Ten miles southwest of Tahoe and named for its pyramidal shape, Pyramid overlooks Devil's Basin in Desolation Valley and the Placerville road to the south. First climbed by William Brewer of the Whitney Survey, August 20, 1863, from Swan's Upper Toll House, near Slippery Ford.

JACK'S PEAK (9,910 feet)

The name is attributed to Hardin Green Jacks, native of Missouri and Placerville miner; also to the settler who located Jack's Valley, near Carson. Its summit overlooks Lake Aloha, Heather, LeConte and Clyde lakes in Desolation Valley. Six and one-half air miles southwest of Tahoe.

TAHOE MOUNTAIN (7,300 feet)

Directly above the southeast shoreline of Fallen Leaf Lake, it is reported to have been named by E. J. "Lucky" Baldwin, who purchased the surrounding lands in the early 1880's.

TWIN PEAKS (GARDNER MOUNTAIN) (7,086 feet)

Originally Gardner Mountain after M. C. Gardner, early day lumberman at the south end of Tahoe. Later re-named Twin Peaks because of its double summits.

ECHO PEAK (8,900 feet)

Named by the Wheeler Survey in 1877 and located directly north of Upper Echo Lake, northwest of Flagpole Peak and six air miles from Tahoe.

MOUNT TALLAC (9,785 feet)

Tallac is the most famous peak in the Tahoe region due to its cross of snow showing high on the northeastern slope in the spring and early summer of the year. Known as Crystal Peak in 1874 and Tallac Peak on the U. S. Geographical map of 1876-77. The *Carson City Appeal* in 1875 indicated that the name "Tellec" was a native Washoe Indian word meaning "Great Mountain," and it is also believed that "Tellec" means "Large Mountain" in the Washoe dialect. A more common acceptance of the name is that it stems from A. L. Taylor, first white settler at Bijou, with the Indians corrupting Taylor to Tallac. A William Tallick is shown in the Douglas(s) County, Nevada, register of 1862 and possibly his name may have been applied to the mountain. Tallac's summit is 3½ air miles from the south shore of Tahoe.

TELL'S PEAK (9,125 feet)

Named for Swiss settler Ciperano Massiminio Padrini, better known as William "Bill" Tell, pioneer merchant in Garden Valley, El Dorado County. The peak overlooks Rubicon River and the Desolation Valley area. Eight air miles directly west of Emerald Bay.

KEITH'S DOME (8,450 feet)

Above Lucille, Margery, Triangle and Lost lakes. Two air miles southwest of Fallen Leaf Lake. Named for pioneer W. F. Keith.

RALSTON'S PEAK (9,300 feet)

Named for William Ralston, Bank of California and bonanza king. Overlooking Upper Echo, Cagwin, Saucer and Ralston lakes. Eight miles southwest of Tahoe, with Phillips and Audrain lakes to the south.

ANGORA PEAK (8,625 feet)

Located on the extreme southern end of Fallen Leaf Lake, it overlooks Angora Lakes and Glen Alpine Springs. It was named for the Angora sheep that pioneer Nathan Gilmore pastured in the vicinity.

DICK'S PEAK (10,015 feet)

Named in 1868 for Captain "Dick" Barter, the Hermit of Emerald Bay. It rises above Alta Morris, Half Moon and Dick lakes in Desolation Valley Primitive Area. Five and one-half air miles southwest of Tahoe.

MAGGIE'S PEAK(S) (8,725 feet)

Variously known as "Round Buttons," "Squaw Tits" and "Maggie's Mountains," previous to the turn of the century, the twin peaks lie directly above the head of Emerald Bay and were pointed out and described to "men only" on early steamer runs around the lake.

GRANITE PEAK (8,824 feet)

Known as Bald Eagle Mountain in the 1860's and early '70's, it is located to the west of Eagle Falls above Emerald Bay. Its southeastern slope was the scene of a snow and rock avalanche in the winter of 1868 comparable to Slide Mountains, and later (1955) Maggie's Peak's.

PHIPPS PEAK (9,300 feet)

Southwest of Rubicon Peaks and west of Emerald Bay, five air miles from Tahoe. Named for General William Phipps, who settled at the influx of the creek on Sugar Pine Point in 1860. Phipps left his name on the stream (General) and the lake (Phipps). The peak is above the headwaters of Stony Ridge, Crag, Shadow, Cliff, Hidden and Lake Genevieve that form the Tallant Lake chain to the south.

RUBICON PEAKS (9,193 feet)

Termed "Gray Ridge" in the 1860's, it was placed as "Rubicon Peak" in the Wheeler Survey of 1876-77 and became known as the "Rubicon Mountains" in the 1880's. This chain of peaks parallels the lake on the southwest shore with Rubicon Point, Bay and Grecian Bend (Bay) on the eastern slope and the Tallant Lakes on the western side. Described as "a craggy mass surrounded by pure white hair" in the 1880's, the peaks were named "in jesting analogy to Caesar's crossing of the Rubicon" due to their rugged terrain. Refer *Place Names of California,* Gudde, and *The Dictionary of California Land Names,* P. T. Hanna.

LOST CORNER MOUNTAIN (8,279 feet)

Headwaters of General Creek, five air miles from the western shore of Tahoe. Above and north of Lost and Duck lakes and southeast of Sourdough Hill and Richardson Lake.

SUGAR PINE PEAK (8,230 feet)

Named after Sugar Pine Point to the east, it rises

between Meeks Bay and Chambers Lodge. Known as "Napoleon's Hat" in the 1870's, as the peak's cleft summit resembled "the cocked hat of an officer of the line." Two and one-half air miles from Tahoe.

ELLIS PEAK (8,745 feet)

Ellis overlooks Bear Lake to the southwest, Buck Lake to the southeast and lies at the head of Madden Creek's watershed. Named for Jack "Jock" Sargent Ellis, disgruntled miner who established a dairy and cattle ranch south of Burton's Pass in 1863 on the McKinney-Rubicon Springs-Georgetown road.

BARKER PEAK (8,186 feet)

Known in the 1860's as Liberty Bell Mountain due to its resemblance to the historic Bell of Independence in Philadelphia. The summit is located three and one-half miles west of Homewood and constitutes the head of Blackwood Creek's watershed. Named for rancher William Andrew Barker, who also gave his name to the meadow and pass.

TWIN PEAKS (8,887 feet)

Three and one-half air miles west of Tahoe Pines at the headwaters of Blackwood Creek and north of Barker Pass and Peak, this prominence was named "Union Peaks" in 1866 by Ramsdale Buoy, as he considered them "like two connected pyramids." Today they are unofficially known as the "Little Matterhorn."

GRIZZLY BEAR PEAK (8,286 feet)

Northeast of Ward Peak and known variously as the "Bear's Profile" and "Sleeping Bear" in 1874-79, the mountain was pointed out from the steamers in the 1870's as the "first natural wonder" at Tahoe after leaving Tahoe City going south. Four air miles from the lake, west of Tahoe Pines. Also unofficially "Rabbit Rock" today, as it resembles the profile of a rabbit's nose and ears.

STANFORD ROCK (8,502 feet)

Named for California's "Civil War Governor," Leland Stanford, in the 1860's, it is not to be confused with Eagle Rock at the foot of Blackwood Creek Canyon that overhangs Highway 89. Stanford Rock is located between Ward and Blackwood creeks, two miles from the western shore of Tahoe.

WARD PEAK (8,644 feet)

Known as "Old Hat" Peak in 1874, it rises above the headwaters of Ward, Bear and Five Lakes creeks. Its summit is west of Sunnyside Bay, five air miles from Tahoe. The peak derived its name from early settlers Ward Rush or J. Ward, pioneer Tahoe City residents (1864).

SQUAW PEAK (8,900 feet)

Squaw Peak, called Sugar Loaf in 1876, stands above the southwest side of Squaw Valley and was skirted by the Placer County Emigrant road in the early 1850's. It lies between Granite Chief and Ward Peak, six and one-half air miles northwest of Tahoe City. Climbing its slopes is one of the greatest chair lifts in the world and here the 1960 Winter Olympics have been scheduled.

GRANITE CHIEF (9,020 feet)

Named for its barren granite composition, the peak stands one and three-quarter miles northwest of Squaw Peak, with Needle Peak directly west. Granite Chief lies at the headwaters of Squaw Creek and Five Lakes Creek.

NEEDLE PEAK (8,976 feet)

This thin upthrust of rock rises at the headwaters of the North Fork of the American River, eight and three-quarter air miles from Tahoe, northwest of Tahoe City.

TINKER(S) KNOB (8,945 feet)

The "Knob" is above the head of Deep Creek that leads into the Truckee River to the northeast below Big Chief Camp. Nine air miles from Tahoe.

FIR CRAGS, THUNDER CLIFF, TWIN CRAGS (7,000-8,200 feet)

Promontories above Rampart and the Truckee River (northeast side). Fir Crags is the Tahoe City ski jump hill and Thunder Cliff the headwaters of Burton Creek.

MOUNT WATSON (8,500 feet)

Named for Lake Tahoe pioneer Robert Montgomery Watson, it lies above Carnelian Bay on the northwest end of the lake and constitutes the headwaters of Watson Creek with Watson Lake on its northeastern slope.

MOUNT PLUTO (8,700 feet)

One of the last active volcanoes in the Tahoe region, it derives its name from Pluto, mythical god of the underworld. The mountain is directly north of Mount Watson, one and one-half air miles, and west of Agate Bay.

DEVIL'S PLAYGROUND (7,674 feet)

A volcanic rockpile between Pluto and Watson mountains. There is also a Devil's Playground on the Truckee River between Tahoe City and Squaw Creek.

LOOKOUT MOUNTAIN (8,084 feet)

Northwest of Mount Pluto overlooking Truckee and the Truckee River Canyon, south of Martis Valley and above Saw Mill Flat to the east. Four airline miles from Tahoe.

MARTIS PEAK (8,665 feet)

Located on the northern rim of the western Sierra range and named for one Martis, rancher in the valley bearing his name, that lies east of Truckee. An unpaved road leads to the fire lookout station on its summit. Four air miles from the lake.

STATELINE POINT (6,980 feet)

This steep promontory overlooks Brockway and Kings Beach and was known as "Boundary Point" in the 1870's. Here Von Schmidt placed his north boundary marker dividing California and Nevada in 1874. A fire lookout station on the summit is reached by a road that leaves Highway 89, one-half mile north of the present Stateline.

MOUNT ROSE (10,800 feet)

The third highest peak in the Tahoe region, Mount Rose lies on the extreme north end of Tahoe, seven and one-half miles from the lake. Known as Mount Wassoon and Wassan in 1855, it became Boundary Rocks in 1863, Bald Mountain in 1874, Mt. Washoe and Rose Peak in the 1880's and '90's, also Rose Mountain. Its present name, Mount Rose, honors Rose Hickman, said to have been the first woman to scale the peak in the 1880's. A United States Observatory and A. T. & T. relay station are located near its summit.

ROSE KNOB (9,491 feet)

Shown as "Rose Knuckle" on the State Boundary Survey Map of 1889, it is the lower peak on the south flank of Mount Rose, two miles airline distance directly north from the northwest elbow of Crystal Bay and Stateline Point.

SLIDE MOUNTAIN (9,720 feet)

In 1864 the mountain's eastern face was denuded by an avalanche, hence the name. It lies east of the Mount Rose grade in Nevada, Galena Creek to the north and Washoe Valley and Lake to the east. Site of the Reno Ski Bowl.

MARLETTE PEAK (8,845 feet)

Named for Seneca Hunt Marlette, Surveyor General of California in 1855 and later Nevada engineer, it is part of the watershed supplying Marlette Lake and Hobart Creek on the northeast side of Tahoe, one and one-quarter air miles from the lake.

INCLINE MOUNTAIN (8,500 feet)

Known as "White Cliff" in 1874, it became Incline in the early 1880's, named after the Great Incline Tramway of the Sierra Nevada. One mile east of Tahoe.

SNOW VALLEY PEAK (9,774 feet)

On the northeast side of the Tahoe rim (Carson Range), it forms the watershed for Marlette Lake on the eastern side, with its runoff also leading south into North Canyon Creek. Three air miles from Tahoe.

SHAKESPEARE ROCK (CLIFF) (6,746 feet)

The famous promontory directly south of Glenbrook Meadow where a profile resembling William Shakespeare was discovered on the face of the cliff in the early 1860's.

DUANE L. BLISS PEAK (8,729 feet)

Named for the senior member of the Bliss family, the peak is located west of Jack's Valley and Carson Valley, and three air miles east of Glenbrook.

GENOA PEAK (9,173 feet)

At the mountain's eastern base stands Genoa, the first settlement in Nevada, which was named for the birthplace of Columbus. The peak is situated three and one-half air miles east of Cave Rock.

CAVE ROCK (6,612 feet)

A serrated upthrust of rock rising from the southeastern side of Tahoe between Zephyr Cove and Glenbrook. Famous for its "Lady of the Lake" profile and named for the small 30-foot cave that originally stood on its southern face.

SOUTH CAMP PEAK (8,821 feet)

In 1876 the south wood camp of the Carson and Tahoe Lumber and Fluming Company was located on the west slope of the peak, hence the name. Its summit lies at the head of North Logan House Creek, two and one-quarter air miles southeast of Glenbrook.

ROUND HILL (MOUND) (6,583 feet)

Known as Folsom Peak until the 1900's, it was originally named for pioneer G. L. Folsom who timbered the adjoining land in the 1880's and '90's. It rises on the southeast shore of Tahoe between the west Kingsbury Grade approach and Zephyr Cove, with Castle Rock to the east.

KINGS CANYON GRADE

Completed as a wagon and stagecoach road by engineer Butler Ives in November of 1863; financed by H. E. Rea, Alfred Helm and Thomas Hayden, it became the Lake Bigler Toll Road. Distances on this road: Summit Camp to the site of old Swift's Station, 2.7 miles; Summit to John S. Heidenreich's ranch and toll house, 8.8

miles; Summit to John Quill ranch, 9.6 miles; Summit to Carson City, 11.8 miles. Refer to Glenbrook, Spooner Station and Summit Camp chapters 39 and 40.

KINGSBURY GRADE AND DAGGETT(S) PASS
(7,375 feet)

Originally "Daggett's Pass Ravine Trail," named for Charles D. Daggett, whose toll house stood at the foot of Haine's Canyon (later Haine's and Henry Van Sickle's). Operated as a toll pack train trail previous to 1859. With the discovery of the Comstock Lode, David Demmon Kingsbury and John M. McDonald completed an 8½-mile road from Friday's Station to Daggett's Toll House, in August of 1860. The Placerville, Humboldt and Salt Lake Company's magnetic telegraph line followed this route. Today it is Highway 19 (Nevada). Refer Edgewood chapter 32.

MOUNT ROSE PASS (8,933 feet)

Northern and highest pass leading to Tahoe, it drops down Galena Creek on the north side of the Sierra to Reno, and on the south the route approaches summit from Incline, Lake Tahoe.

KIT CARSON PASS (8,600 feet)

Named for Christopher "Kit" Carson, who broke trail over the route in February of 1844 with Fremont. Jonathan Holmes proved the practicability of the road for emigrant travel in the summer of 1848, and in the spring of 1849 Jefferson Hunt, Captain of a Mormon Battalion and later founder of San Bernardino, took the first wagon over the pass, opening it up for the Argonauts.

LUTHER(S) PASS (7,740 feet)

Named for Ira M. Luther, pioneer Sacramento settler who was the first man to cross with a wagon and team over this route in the summer of 1854. The pass was used extensively as a connecting trail and then a road between Lake Valley and Hope Valley in 1850-60 on the

Placerville-Carson Valley route to the mines. It was supplanted by the shorter Kingsbury Grade (Daggett Pass) in 1860-61. Refer Lake Valley chapter 26.

HOPE, FAITH AND CHARITY VALLEYS
(6,800-7,600 feet)

Hope Valley was named by members of the Mormon Battalion returning to Salt Lake City in the summer of 1849. As it was the first major valley after crossing the Carson Pass going east, the Mormons called it Hope, due to the abundance of water and grass found there. Faith and Charity valleys were named by a survey party in 1868.

HAWLEY GRADE (6,383-7,383 feet)

Refer Lake Valley chapter 26.

CLEAR CREEK GRADE (7,143 feet)

Refer Glenbrook, Spooner Station and Summit Camp chapters 39 and 40.

JOHNSON PASS (ECHO SUMMIT) (7,383 feet)

Refer Lake Valley and Bonanza Road to Washoe chapters 26 and 51.

BURTON(S) PASS (7,108 feet)

Refer Rubicon Springs and Chambers' Lodge chapters 9 and 10.

TRUCKEE CANYON ROAD

Refer Truckee River Canyon chapter 2 and Tahoe City chapter 4.

PLACER COUNTY EMIGRANT ROAD

Refer Squaw Valley chapter 1.

MARTIS CREEK ROAD

Refer Brockway Hot Springs chapter 44 and Agate Bay chapter 47.

BIBLIOGRAPHY

Angel, Myron: *History of Nevada,* Oakland, 1881.

Bancroft, Hubert Howe:

History of California, San Francisco, 1884–90.

History of Nevada, Colorado and Wyoming, San Francisco, 1890.

Scrapbooks MSS, 1860–64, Bancroft Library.

Banning, Captain William and George Hugh: *Six Horses,* New York, 1930.

Boggs, M. H.: *My Playhouse Was a Concord Coach.*

Brewer, William H: *Up and Down California,* 1860–64.

Browne, J. Ross: *A Peep at Washoe,* Harpers Magazine, December, 1860; February, 1861.

Clemens, Samuel L. (Mark Twain): *Roughing It* and *Innocents Abroad,* Hartford, American Publishing Company, 1872.

Davis, Sam: *History of Nevada,* Reno, 1930.

Day, Sherman: *Report on the Immigrant Wagon Road Explorations.* Annual report of the Surveyor General of California, 1855.

Directories: W. F. Edwards, *Tourists' Guide and Directory of the Truckee Basin,* Truckee, 1883.

Drury, Wells: *An Editor on the Comstock Lode.*

Fremont, John Charles: *The Exploring Expedition in the Rocky Mountains, Oregon and California,* 1852.

Galloway, John Debo: *Early Engineering Works Contributory to the Comstock.* University of Nevada Bulletin, Geological and Mining Series, Number 45, June, 1947.

Glasscock, C. B.: *Lucky Baldwin.*

Goddard, George H: *Report of a survey of a portion of the eastern boundary of California, and a reconnaissance of the old Carson and Johnson immigrant roads over the Sierra Nevada.* Annual report of the Surveyor General of the State of California, 1856, Assembly document Number 5.

Hafen, LeRoy R.: *The Overland Mail*

Hittell, Theodore H.: *History of California,* San Francisco, 1885.

King, Clarence: *Mountaineering in the Sierra Nevada,* 1872.

LeConte, Joseph: *On Some Ancient Glaciers of the Sierra.* American Journal of Science, Series 3, Volume X, 1872.

Lillard, Richard D.: *Desert Challenge.*

Lord, Eliot: *Comstock Mining and Miners.*

Lyman, George H.: *The Saga of the Comstock Lode,* New York, 1934.

Maps:

Metsker's Map of El Dorado County, California, Seattle, Washington.

Topographical Map of the Lake Tahoe Region, U. S. Geographical Survey Expeditions of 1876–77.

Topographical Map of Lake Tahoe and Surrounding Country, Ferdinand Von Leicht and J. D. Hoffmann, 1874.

Eddy's Official Map, 1854.

Maps of the Pacific States, Bancroft, 1862.

Geological Survey, United States Department of Interior. *Truckee and Carson City Quadrangles; Markleeville and Pyramid Peak* sheets, 1889.

MacDonald, Claire: *Lake Tahoe,* private printing, 1929.

Mack, Effie Mona: *History of Nevada,* Glendale, 1936.

McKeon, Owen F.: *The Railroads and Steamers of Lake Tahoe,* San Mateo, 1946.

Morgan, Dale: *The Humboldt.*

Newspapers:

Alta California and *California Star,* San Francisco.

Alta Telegraph, San Francisco.

Carson City Morning Appeal, Carson City, Nevada.

Carson City Daily State Register.

Gold Hill News, Gold Hill, Nevada.

Marysville Appeal, Marysville, California.

Placerville Republican, Placerville, California.

Pony Express Courier, Placerville, California.

Reno Evening Gazette.

Sacramento Union and *Sacramento Bee.*

San Francisco Bulletin.

San Francisco Herald.

San Francisco Chronicle.

San Francisco Examiner.

Tahoe Tattler, Tahoe City, Lake Tahoe, California, 1881, and new *Tahoe Tattler,* 1930's-40's, Tahoe City Library.

Truckee Republican, Truckee, California.

Truckee Tribune, Truckee, California.

Territorial Enterprise, Virginia City, Nevada.

Washoe Times, Nevada.

Periodicals:

Harpers Weekly.

The Golden Bear Magazine.

Hutchings' Illustrated California Magazine, San Francisco.

Overland Monthly.

Society of California Pioneers Quarterly.

Sunset Magazine.

Richardson, Albert D.: *Beyond the Mississippi* (1857-67), Hartford, 1867.

Root, Frank A., and William Elsey Connelley: *The Overland Stage to California,* Topeka, 1901.

Shinn, Charles H.: *Story of the Mine,* 1896.

Sioli, Paolo: *Historical Souvenir, El Dorado County,* Oakland, 1883.

Stewart, George R.: *The Opening of the California Trail,* University of California Press.

Stewart, William M.: *Reminiscences of Senator William M. Stewart of Nevada,* New York, 1908.

Tevis, Rev. A. H.: *Beyond the Sierras,* 1877.

Thompson and West: *History of Placer County, California,* Oakland, 1882, and *History of Nevada County, California,* 1881.

Tuthill, Franklin: *The History of California,* H. H. Bancroft and Company, 1866.

Upton, Charles Elmer: *Pioneers of El Dorado,* Placerville, 1906.

Vischer, Edward:

Sketches of the Washoe Mining Region, San Francisco, 1862.

Vischer's Pictorial of California, San Francisco, 1870.

Ward, Henry C.: *Stage Coach Days in California.* California Historical Society Quarterly, XIII.

Watson, Henry C.: "A Cruise on a Mountain Sea," *Sacramento Union,* March 17, 1873.

Wiltsee, E. A.: *Pioneer Miner and Pack Mule Express.*

Wren, Thomas: *A History of the State of Nevada,* Lewis Publishing Company, 1904.

Wright, William (Dan DeQuille): *The Big Bonanza,* Hartford, 1876.

CHAPTER NOTES

Chapter 1—Squaw Valley

1. Western Utah Camps: In the 1850's Nevada was known as Utah Territory, then Nevada Territory upon passage of the Organic Act by Congress, March 2, 1861, and Nevada when the territory was admitted as a State on October 31, 1864. E. A. Grosch is referring to mining camps in Six Mile and Gold canyons that later became Virginia City, Gold Hill, Silver City, et al. Lake Tahoe: Named Bigler in 1852 after California's third governor, John Bigler. See Facts of Tahoe section.
2. Truckee Lake, now Donner Lake. See Truckee River Canyon chapter.
3. Sun Mountain: Now Mount Davidson, with its summit above and west of Virginia City, Nevada.
4. El Dorado, town of: Originally Mud Springs, California.
5. Ibid.
6. It is generally agreed among Comstock Lode historians that Richard Bucke had limited, if any, knowledge of the Grosch brothers' great discovery. He never attempted to locate the fallen pine tree marked with a cross. For the life and history of Ethan Allen and Hosea Ballou Grosch of Reading, Pennsylvania, see: Angel, Myron, *History of Nevada,* pp. 52-53; *The Story of the Mine,* Shinn, pp. 25-26; Bucke, Richard M., *Twenty Five Years Ago,* Overland Monthly, Vol. I, 6—1883, p. 560; Lyman, George D., *The Saga of the Comstock Lode,* Chap. IV; Davis, *Nevada,* Vol. I, pp. 385-386; Wilson, Rufus R., *Out of the West,* p. 193.
7. Fork House: Junction of Michigan Bluff, Yankee Jim's, and Iowa Flat roads. See *Historic Spots in California,* Rensch and Hoover (Stanford Press), 1948.
8. Other passes: To the north, Truckee (Donner), Beckwith's (Beckwourth's), Henness, Wasson, Nightingill's, Noble's (Fredonyer's), Madeline's (Smoke Creek) and Lassen's. To the south, Daggett's (Kingsbury), Luther's, Eagle Valley (Clear Creek), Johnson's (Echo), Carson, De-Groot's, Walker, Ebbett's, Mono (Tioga), Sonora.
9. Thomas A. Young, brilliant young surveyor, joined the California Volunteers in 1862, rose to captain, met untimely death December 2, 1864, from "dropsy of the brain." *History of Placer County, California.* Oakland, 1882. Besides Young the party included David Orr, James Herrick, George Haycock, A. G. Cook, James Gest and Capt. W. C. Gray. Placer County Records, County Court House, Auburn, California.
10. Thomas A. Young report September, 1856, to supervisors of Placer County. California State Library, Sacramento. Also see *History of Placer County, California,* 1882.
11. Ibid. Meadowland: Tahoe City, Lake Forest, Carnelian Bay, Tahoe Vista, Griff Creek, Incline.
12. Shortest, but including near impassable grades at Squaw Valley going west and Incline going east.
13. *History of Placer County, California,* Thompson and West, 1882.
14. Ibid.
15. Robert Howard Watson, Tahoe City, September 27, 1955.
16. Fish, Ira Almirin, from White Oaks Township, El Dorado County; originally from Ohio, occupation farmer. Ferguson, William Sinclair, from Mountain Township, El Dorado County; native of Kentucky; occupation, farmer. (Great Register, El Dorado County, 1867.) Smith and Coggins: See Book of Records No. X, Placer County Court House, Auburn, California.
17. Keiser, John, miner, Georgetown; native of Germany; in 1871 owned Webber House in Truckee. *Sierra-Nevada Lakes,* p. 292, George and Bliss Hinkle. Knox, Shannon, native of Pennsylvania. Georgetown carpenter by trade. (Great Register, El Dorado County, Placerville, 1867.)
18. *Up and Down California,* William H. Brewer, August 28, 1863, p. 446. Brewer estimated 600 miners. Number has been given variously as 1,000 to 1,200, but this has no basis in fact.
19. Ibid. Also see p. 744, *Up and Down California.*
20. Ibid.
21. Hal Johnson of the *Berkeley Daily Gazette,* November 6, 1954.
22. The miners: Ward Rush, Ward Creek; Richard Ashmore Madden, Madden Creek; Hampton Craig Blackwood, Blackwood Creek; John Washington McKinney, McKinney Creek; Homer D. Burton, Burton Creek; Jack S. "Jock" Ellis, Mount Ellis (Great Registers, El Dorado and Placer Counties, 1867).
23. *Truckee Republican,* June 9, 1864.
24. Tax roll, Placer County, December, 1872.
25. Ibid.
26. *Tourists' Guide and Directory of the Truckee Basin,* W. F. Edwards, Truckee, 1883.
27. Squaw Valley: 6,200 feet above sea level, 1½ miles wide by 1¾ miles long. Needle, Granite Chief, Silver and Squaw Peaks ranging to over 9,000 feet, surround the valley (U. S. Geological Survey Topographical Map, California-Nevada Truckee Quadrangle Edition, 1940-1951).

Chapter 2—Truckee River Canyon

1. Brickell and Krueger were the first lumbermen to timber the Upper Truckee River Gorge, starting in the early 1860's. Brickell also entered into partnership with one Guysendorfer in 1867. They built and operated their water-powered sawmill south of Truckee and across the river. It adjoined the mill of Joseph Gray and George Schaeffer. Placer County Court House tax rolls, Auburn, California, 1864-69. Refer also to *Sierra-Nevada Lakes,* George and Bliss Hinkle, pp. 246, 287.
2. Obvious overstatement. The equivalent of 360 miles per hour was never reached by logs running down a logway. See Tahoe Pines Chapter 7 and Glenbrook Chapter 39 for additional log chute and V-flume data.

3. *The Big Bonanza,* Dan DeQuille (William Wright), Hartford, 1876, p. 175.

4. C. A. Bragg and G. N. Folsom are credited with being the first loggers to construct the dual log chute used in the Sierra Nevada. "In the spring of 1864 they built a two-mile logway that ran down the Carson Range, east of Lake Tahoe, to Washoe City, Nevada." George D. Oliver, Carson City, September 28, 1954. *Diary of Gilman N. Folsom,* Ellis Folsom, Carson City, Nevada.

5. "An average of 40 pounds of tallow per mile of chute used each day during peak of activity." Augustus H. Saxton, as told to George D. Oliver, G. D. Oliver to author, September 28, 1954.

6. For additional details and "natural wonders" of the Truckee River Gorge see Tahoe City Chapter 4. Eagle Rock (Cliff) is often mistaken for the legendary Lover's Leap of the region. This is not borne out by the Washoe Indians' early folklore. See Tahoe Pines Chapter 7.

7. Charlie (Charley) Smith to Mrs. Ethel Joslyn Vernon. Edited by author, Tahoe City, August 21, 1954. A horizontal and vertical profile of Chief "No-Name" are visible but the horizontal profile is the clearest.

8. *The Old California Trail,* J. C. Altrocchi, p. 295.

9. Captain Fremont crossed the "Truckee Pass" or "North Pass" (Donner) in December of 1845. Refer Facts of Lake Tahoe section for Carson Pass route.

10. *Illustrated History of Plumas, Lassen, and Sierra Counties* (San Francisco, 1882), p. 99.

11. *Sierra-Nevada Lakes,* George and Bliss Hinkle, p. 53. For the death and burial of Truckee see the *San Francisco Alta,* May 10, 1875.

12. Ibid.

13. Ibid, pp. 246, 247, 287.

14. *Alta California,* August 22, 1870, p. 2.

Chapter 3—Deer Park Springs

1. Robert H. Watson, Clarksville, February 7, 1956.

2. Ibid.

3. *California the Wonderful,* Edwin Markham, pp. 300-301.

4. See Chapter One.

5. R. H. Watson, Clarksville, February 7, 1956.

6. Ibid.

7. Stella Tong Watson, Tahoe City, October 8, 1955.

8. Ibid. Post office discontinued at Deer Park Springs, March 31, 1929. Post Office Records, Washington, D. C.

9. Ibid. Refer Chapter 5.

10. Refer Chapters 10 and 24.

11. Stella Tong Watson, Tahoe City, October 8, 1955.

12. Carl Andrew Bechdolt, Sr., Tahoe City, September 14, 1955. Mail brought in by snowshoes or sleigh as narrow gauge train did not operate during the winter months. (Author's note.)

13. R. H. Watson, Clarksville, February 7, 1956. Also Mrs. Edward Grover Chandler, Berkeley, May 4, 1956.

14. Dr. Clark Burnham, Jr., Piedmont, May 1, 1956. Also R. H. Watson, Clarksville, February 7, 1956.

Chapter 4—Tahoe City

1. Alexander John Bayley, born October 16, 1827, in Athens, Vermont. Bayley sailed around the Horn to California in 1849, settling in Pilot Hill, El Dorado County. He was elected to the California Assembly in 1871 and later became locally famous for his 22-room, $20,000 mansion at Pilot Hill known as "Bayley's Folly." This portly, meticulously attired, well educated and prominent California pioneer died June 8, 1896. *Historical Souvenir of El Dorado County,* Oakland, Paolo Sioli, pp. 223-224, 1883; also R. H. Watson, Clarksville, January 7, 1955, and *Georgetown Gazette,* June 9, 1896.

2. Lloyd Hawthorne, son of "One Arm" Hawthorne who left his name on the town of Hawthorne, Nevada. R. H. Watson, Tahoe City, September 2, 1955.

3. A wagon road existed between Campbell's Hot Springs and Tahoe City in the 1870's. Refer Glenbrook and Brockway chapters, 39 and 44.

4. "Big Hill," sometimes known as "Squaw Creek Hill," is located near the present "Burnham Hill" property on the Truckee River southwest of Squaw Valley's road junction with Highway 89. R. H. Watson, January 7, 1955.

5. This version of the stage accident is based upon a story told to R. H. Watson by George Lukins. See also the *Tahoe Tattler,* 2nd edition, 1931, and *Truckee Republican,* October 6, 1876.

6. Placer County Court House records, Auburn, California. Tax Rolls, Book X, 1860-61.

7. *History of Placer County, California,* Thompson and West, Oakland, 1882.

8. *Sacramento Union,* September 6, 1862.

9. *The Lake of the Sky,* George Wharton James, pp. 224-318, Boston, 1915. Actually M. L. King built and operated the first hostelry, Tahoe City Hotel, in 1864. Placer County records show it valued at $2,500 in 1865. W. Pomin(e) appears in 1869 as owner of the Tahoe Saloon between Frank Pomin(e) and Frank Trueworthy on Main (Lake) Street. W. Pomin's home (later Tahoe House) adjoined the saloon on the south side. Placer County Records, Auburn, Book X, 1864-70. E. Dyer (1865) and Samuel Bethel (1871-72) surveyed the township and Tom M. Bittencourt laid out the site of Tahoe City. Land section maps of Tahoe City under direction of L. Upson, California State Surveyor General (1865); see also Tahoe City Township map (1871-72).

10. "The first white child born on the shores of Tahoe was Harold Powers, son of P. F. Powers from Friday's Station." Grant Merrill, Woodfords, October 28, 1955. Evidence points to Tahoe Pomin being the first white girl. Refer Edgewood chapter 32.

11. The Commons, a narrow strip of shoreland confirmed as a parcel of Tahoe City in 1868 by an Act of Congress. *History of Placer County, California,* 1882.

12. Placer County Records, Book X, 1864-65.

13. Ibid.

14. Vischer was optimistic as the only private "villa" on Tahoe's shoreline in 1867 was Ben Holladay's in Emerald Bay. Sailing vessels of 2 or more tons numbered four only. Refer Early Marine History of Lake Tahoe section.

15. Colonel Alexis Waldemar Von Schmidt, born in Bauski, near Riga on the Baltic, Courland, Russia, on August 25, 1821, came to America in 1827 and later was educated in "Eastern institutions" as a civil engineer. At the age of 28 he sailed on the schooner *Pleiades* around the Horn to Mazatlan, Mexico, continuing to San Francisco on the 85-ton bark *Fanny* (greatly overloaded with 450 men, 25 head of cattle, 40 sheep, 30 hogs and 300 chickens). Von Schmidt became a United States surveyor for government lands and Spanish land grants. He was also an inventor, building the first pumping dredges on the Pacific Coast, constructing Hunter's Drydock, and blowing up "Blossom Rock" in the Golden Gate. He died on May 26, 1906, in Alameda, California. Miss Marion Mitchell, Tahoe Tavern, July 15, 1956.

16. Placer County Court House Records, Book X. Also "Colonel Von Schmidt constructed the Von Schmidt Dam at the outlet of the lake." Miss Marion Mitchell, July 15, 1956.

17. *Sierra-Nevada Lakes,* George and Bliss Hinkle, p. 308.

18. Ibid, pp. 292-93.

19. Ibid, p. 308.

20. Robert H. Watson, Lake Forest, September 2, 1955.

21. Refer Dollar Point chapter 49.

22. Lou and John A. Huntington, W. Campbell, L. Taylor, A. J. Bayley, C. Keyler, J. C. Fitger, Henry Burke. Placer County Records, Book X, 1870-73.

23. Refer Tahoe Park chapter 6.

24. *Truckee Republican,* May 10, 1869.

25. Robert Kincaid's saloon became the Grand Central Saloon in the spring of 1872. It was located on the south side of the hotel. Placer County Tax Rolls, 1871-72.

26. The gradient was actually 90 feet to the mile when track was laid in 1899.

27. *Sacramento Union,* July 28, 1870.

28. Cornelian Bay, later spelled Carnelian Bay. Refer chapter 48.

29. *San Francisco Daily Alta,* September 22, 1870, p. 2.

30. *Railroad Gazeteer,* Sacramento, 1871, pp. 122-23.

31. Ernest Henry Pomin, Tahoe Park, August 29, 1954. "Amazia Franklin Campbell, brother of J. B. Campbell, took over operation of the Custom House in 1889 after Joe Forbes sold his interest. In 1907 high water 'washed away' the old structure." R. H. Watson, October 7, 1855. Lake Tahoe crested at 6231.26 feet in 1907 and spilled over the top of Von Schmidt's dam. (Author's note.)

32. *History of Nevada County, California,* p. 77.

33. Based on a story related by Robert Montgomery Watson to his son, R. H. Watson. George Lukins claimed to be an eyewitness to the killing. Today's Stewart's "grave" is in the Tahoe City Cemetery above the golf course. Refer Sierra House and King's Beach chapters, 28 and 45, for more on Stewart.

34. *Truckee Republican,* May 22, 1877, and *Sacramento Union,* August 9, 1877.

35. Ibid.

36. R. H. Watson, Lake Forest, October 9, 1955.

37. Original issues of the *Tahoe Tattler* may be found in the Bancroft Library, University of California, Berkeley, July 9, 1881, through October, 1881. Reprints of original articles are in the Tahoe City Library in the 1936-39 issues of the new *Tahoe Tattler.*

38. Refer Early Marine History of Lake Tahoe section.

39. A post office was authorized for Tahoe City on June 21, 1871, known as "Tahoe." On October 1, 1949, it was officially changed to Tahoe City post office. "Trucky River P. O." was established on April 26, 1864, and discontinued November 1, 1864. Post Office Records, Washington, D. C. Jeanette Pomin (Mrs. Bert Watson) was postmistress for many years at the old post office.

40. "John McQueen (brother of F. W. McQueen) built the Hot Springs, Brockway's first full-fledged inn." (sic) *Sierra-Nevada Lakes,* p. 315. Refer Brockway Hot Springs chapter 44 for factual data.

41. *History of Placer County, California,* 1882, p. 147.

42. *Truckee Republican,* April 14, 1883.

43. "A. J. Bayley spent his winters at Pilot Hill, California." R. H. Watson, Lake Forest, September 12, 1955.

44. For *Pavillion,* otherwise known as the *Floating Palace* and *Burke's Barge,* refer Early Marine History of Lake Tahoe section.

45. "Worms from the trees." R. H. Watson.

46. Robert Montgomery "Bob" Watson, born in Bradford County, Pennsylvania, in 1854, staged to Tahoe in 1875. Yukon goldseeker in 1897-98, trail blazer, mountaineer, peace officer, game warden. His wife, Sarah Ann Cunningham, traveled from Maine around the Isthmus in the 1860's. Watson spoke of his five children as "3 Jacks and a pair of Queens—a full house," as he had two girls and three boys: Alice May, Edna Nevada, Herbert Sydney, Frank Gilbert and Robert Howard. The epitaph on his tombstone in Tahoe City's cemetery reads: "Trailbuilder—endeared to his friends by his gentle, kindly ways and his love of these mountains." R. M. Watson died April 6, 1932, at the age of 77 years.

47. A. M. Henry's Tahoe City Garage stands on the former site of the Grand Central Hotel. The new Tahoe Inn was built on the location of old Tahoe House and Inn. Sequence of ownership, Tahoe House; William Pomin(e)'s private home, 1865-67, leased to Captain Joe Pomin(e) in the early 1880's, bought by R. M. Watson in 1886-87, then reverted to Joe Short on a note, to A. J. Bayley

in 1896, Jerry Williams in 1897-98, Bliss Company in 1899-1901, to Sadie Wallace Gilbert, 1902-1907, Wert Tong, 1907-1919, Carl Bechdolt, Sr., Jack Mathews and Harry Cullyford in 1920, to Bechdolt, Sr., in 1929. Burned April 26, 1934, rebuilt immediately as new Tahoe Inn and now owned by William Bechdolt and Carl A. Bechdolt, Sr. R. H. Watson, Lake Forest, September 8, 1955, and Carl Bechdolt, Sr., September 21, 1955.

48. Refer Bijou and Glenbrook chapters, 30 and 39. "Engine Number One on the L. T. R. and T. Company line was the Number Two (Tahoe) on the C. and T. L. and F. Company road." *Oil Lamps and Iron Ponies,* Bay Books Inc., p. 174.

49. Placer County Tax Records, 1898-1900.

50. Jack Bell, Sparks, Nevada, September 1, 1955, and Ernest H. Pomin, Septemeber 6, 1956. "The name 'Rattler' came from the flappers installed between each window to reduce cinder and smoke barrage sifting into the car." E. H. Pomin. Ibid. "Charlie Keyser, not Frank Keyser, in cab of Number 5." E. H. Pomin.

51. Ibid. Also refer footnote 48.

52. Mrs. Donald Goodrich, Placerville, October 12, 1955.

53. Refer *Sierra-Nevada Lakes,* p. 334.

54. "A miniature sailboat placed over the entrance was the 'Toy-Yat' Club's insignia. The establishment was named for the Chinese cook that served meals to the Bliss Company employees. Originally the Bliss store (at the head of the Custom House pier) was owned by Davis and Noteware and acquired by the Blisses in 1900." R. H. Watson, September 7, 1955.

55. "Walter Scott Bickford brought suit against the L. T. R. and T. Company and Tahoe Mercantile Company to quiet community title (1919). Judgment was found for the plaintiff in 1922." *Sierra Nevada Lakes,* p. 345. Bickford and Harry Williamson built the city's first lumber yard, and connected to the main railroad line with "Bickford's Spur." In 1915 Bickford started Sierra Garage. Clarence and Katherine Atherton built Atherton's General Merchandise Store adjoining in 1917-18. This is now Kehoe's and two other grocery stores, John and A. M. "Red" Anderson's Village Store and Jack and Dinty's Market, are located in town. Tahoe Community Center, founded on December 29, 1937 as a non-profit organization for the purpose of building a structure on the Tahoe Commons (which would contain Post Office, Library and Community Hall) was made possible through the efforts of the N. R. Mayfields, George R. Bliss's, A. M. Andersons, Henry Drostes and other public spirited citizens of Tahoe. At one time it housed the Placer County Free Library Branch which is now in the present Julia J. Bechdolt Memorial Library adjoining the Post Office to the south. Mrs. A. M. Anderson, February 20, 1958.

56. R. H. Watson, October 9, 1954, and E. H. Pomin, September 4, 1956.

57. Ibid.

58. Based on an anecdote as told by R. H. Watson, September 8, 1955.

59. Refer *Oil Lamps and Iron Ponies,* Bay Books, San Francisco.

60. Walter Danforth Bliss, Glenbrook, September 4, 1954.

61. *Tahoe Tattler,* 2nd edition, 1936, Tahoe City Library.

62. Carl Andrew Bechdolt, Sr., Tahoe City, October 9, 1955. Other alleged partners in the Log Cabins —Gus Renner and Dick Joseph.

63. Ibid. Also recollections of author.

64. *Sierra Nevada Lakes,* George and Bliss Hinkle, pp. 347-48.

65. Ibid, p. 347. Water first came through to Virginia City from Hobart Creek in 1873, not Marlette. Refer Marlette Lake chapter 41.

66. Ibid. Also R. H. Watson as told by R. M. Watson.

67. Ernest H. Pomin, Tahoe City, October 2, 1954.

68. R. H. Watson, Lake Forest, August 29, 1955.

69. E. H. Pomin, Tahoe City, October 2, 1954.

70. *Sierra-Nevada Lakes,* George and Bliss Hinkle, p. 349.

Chapter 5—Tahoe Tavern

1. Mrs. Charles "Swanee" Swanson, Tahoe City, October 11, 1954.

2. Matt Green, Sacramento, October 5, 1954.

3. Ibid.

4. Robert H. Watson, January 6, 1956.

5. *"Dat-So-La-Lee," The Works of Louisa Keyser,* Nevada State Historical Society, Reno, Nevada. The name "Dat-So-La-Lee" is also interpreted in the Washoe language as meaning variously "Big hips," "Big about the sides," "Big buttress," and "Broad sides."

6. Ibid.

7. John Drum, Jr., Chinquapin Cove, Lake Tahoe, August 12, 1955.

Chapter 6—Tahoe Park

1. "Saxton, A. H., ranch house, garden, storehouse at Big Bar; horses, mules, cattle at Volcanoville." El Dorado County tax rolls, Placerville, California, 1860.

2. Based on a story related to George D. Oliver by A. H. Saxton, July 4, 1888; as retold to author September 18, 1954. Also *The Big Four,* Oscar Lewis.

3. "Ward Rush and William Ferguson settled at the outlet of the creek in the summer of 1862, having come from Volcanoville. Ward Rush gave his name to the creek." *History of Placer County, California,* p. 403. "Creek named Ward for J. Ward, resident of Tahoe City." Robert H. Watson, Tahoe City, October 15, 1955.

4. See von Leicht and J. D. Hoffmann, *Topographical Map of Lake Tahoe and Surrounding Country,* 1874.

5. Placer County Court House, Auburn, California, assessment records, Book X, July 16, 1864; July 22, 1865.

6. "Splash dams": log, rock and dirt fill obstructions in the Truckee River with gates that could be lifted when a head of water had collected. These were set about every three miles down river between Tahoe City and Truckee. Robert H. Watson, October 15, 1955. See Wheeler Survey Map of 1876-77.

7. George D. Oliver, Carson City, August 19, 1954. Statement, A. H. Saxton to G. D. Oliver.

8. *Pacific Coast Directory,* San Francisco, 1867.

9. Ruben R. Saxton: logging contractor with a "bull-moose bellow" and a reputation as a "two-fisted drinker." Ernest H. Pomin and George D. Oliver, Carson City, September, 30, 1954. "To be a great teamster you only have to know as much as the horses." Rube Saxton to William Lindsey, as told by Lindsey, Carson City, October 4, 1955.

10. Placer County Court House records, Auburn, California, Book X, 1872.

11. Ibid., 1877-1878.

12. *Health and Pleasure Resorts of the Pacific Coast,* Newton H. Chittenden, p. 148. Also *History of Placer County, California,* 1882, p. 403.

13. "The old gentleman (Saxton) had elephantiasis, and I sat up all night at his wake—a most disagreeable experience." George D. Oliver, Carson City, September 16, 1954.

14. "If my father, James Titus, could only have seen the property now and had the chance to accept the original offer." Frank Titus, Sr., Truckee, California, August 8, 1953.

15. *Sacramento Union,* December 7, 1866. Also see Chapter 48 of this work and *Sierra-Nevada Lakes,* George and Bliss Hinkle, p. 322.

16. "Sunnyside, the charming summer retreat of Mrs. Hays (sic) of San Francisco, and other wealthy California families." *Health and Pleasure Resorts of the Pacific Coast,* Newton H. Chittenden, 1881, p. 148. "Two miles north of Idlewild is Sunnyside Cottage on the lakeshore, belonging to Mrs. Hayes of Nevada State." *History of Placer County, California,* p. 403. Mr. and Mrs. Norman D. Rideout originally owned the land adjoining Hurricane Bay, southwest of Ward Creek, in conjunction with land running north to the Kent property. Their daughter, Grace Rideout, married Dr. William Ellery Briggs of Sacramento whose daughter Phebe Briggs married a McClatchy. James B. McClatchy, February 18, 1958.

17. McMurtrey, spelled McMurtley, *Tahoe Tattler,* July, 1881. "McMurtrey correct," Robert H. Watson, Lake Forest, October 25, 1955.

18. Ernest H. Pomin, Tahoe Park, September 14, 1954.

19. Robert H. Watson, Lake Forest, September 18, 1955.

20. Jack Bell, Sparks, Nevada, August 3, 1955.

21. Robert H. Watson, Lake Forest, September 18, 1955.

22. John Drum, Jr., Chinquapin Cove, Lake Tahoe, September 3, 1955.

23. Author's note.

Chapter 7—Tahoe Pines

1. *Truckee Republican,* August 12, 1883. Also David Chambers, Chambers Lodge, July 26, 1951, as told by William "Bill" Johnson, Homewood, Lake Tahoe.

2. Steamer passage to Idlewild existed from 1870 on, group parties were "dustered" over the Truckee-Tahoe-Lakeshore road by stage.

3. *Topographical Map of Lake Tahoe and Surrounding Country,* Ferdinand von Leicht and J. D. Hoffmann, 1874.

4. George D. Oliver, Carson City, October 3, 1954, as told by Augustus H. Saxton, Saxtons Mill, Lake Tahoe.

5. Hampton Craig Blackwood, North Carolina, miner, Mud Springs (El Dorado), 35 years old. *El Dorado County Great Register,* (1867), Placerville Court House, California.

6. United States Geological Survey Map, Department of Interior, Truckee Quadrangle, Edition of 1940.

7. "Thomas McConnell — 388 acres valued at $8.00 per acre." Placer County Court House, Auburn, California, Book X, 1868-73.

8. Robert H. Watson, Tahoe City, October 22, 1955.

9. Footpaths, pack trails, and wagon roads were confused on early California maps. Trappers and "mountain men" followed Indian game trails, emigrants preferred moving along stream beds to their source, mountain ridges if passable, or when necessary the shortest way up from valley to summit. See chapter 26.

10. Presumably named Idlewild by E. B. Crocker family.

11. *Truckee Republican,* July 18, 1881.

12. Eagle Cliff-Rock-Bluff: Washoe Indian legend places its naming about 1776, at the time of the Declaration of Independence, with the Washoes using the summit of the rock to spot deer, bear, and mountain lion. One early spring morning, Big Eagle, then chief of the tribe, while hunting from the vantage point of the rock, put an arrow through the heart of his child bride, Gentle Doe, believing her to be a deer. Grief-stricken when he found that his flint-headed arrow had killed her, Big Eagle prayed to the Great Spirit, pleading that she be brought back to life. His request was denied. He then asked that he be allowed to follow her. "Not yet, can you go into the land beyond the Black Mountains," ruled the Great Spirit. Instead the young chieftain would be obliged to assume the form of his namesake, and be sent to brood upon the high cliff where he had shot his loved one. For many moons thereafter his tribesmen could see a great feathered shape poised on the overhanging edge of the sheer rock —still and dark as the promontory itself. Described by "Captain Pete," last Chief of the Washoe Indian tribe, to Ethel Joslyn Vernon, Tahoe City, Lake Tahoe (edited). Eagle Rock, centered at the eastern end of Blackwood Canyon, is judged to have been carried down by glacier action during the Ice Age.

13. "Thomas McConnell, of Sacramento County, owns land. Here is also 'Wildidle' (sic) belonging to Mrs. Crocker and her daughter of Sacramento, besides others belonging to residents of Nevada who will build on lots in the summer of 1882." *History of Placer County, California,* Oakland, 1882, Thompson and West, p. 402. Also see *Health and Pleasure Resorts of the Pacific Coast,* Newton H. Chittenden, 1881, p. 148.

14. *Tahoe Tattler,* July 23, 1881, Vol. I, No. 13. Also "Cedar Grove located near the site of Fred A. Kilner's real estate office," Robert H. Watson, October 9, 1955.

15. "T. L." Sunnyside Bay, October 15, 1955.

16. Ibid. Former Edwin H. Crocker home purchased by locally famous stage driver, one Smalley, then F. W. Ackerman family. John Ernest Pomin, Idlewild, August 12, 1954. Torn down June 1, 1956.

17. Summer of 1928, recollections of author.

18. Carl Andrew Bechdolt, Sr., and Robert Scates, Tahoe City, October 25, 1955.

19. Robert H. Watson, January 7, 1956.

20. Henry J. Kaiser, industrialist, contractor, automobile manufacturer, cement, steel, aluminum.

Chapter 8—Homewood

1. Benjamin Callender, Homewood, October 17, 1954.

2. Ibid.

3. Ibid. Another version of the story: A marine shipment of canned goods sank in 25 feet of water near Homewood and Martin Lowe, knowing that he was the only diver who could retrieve the merchandise at that depth, left the cans on the bottom of the lake and dove for them whenever he was hungry. Arnold Luneman, Meeks Bay, September 14, 1955.

4. Ibid.

5. J. P. Obexer, Homewood, September 15, 1955.

6. Robert H. Watson, Tahoe City, October 24, 1955.

7. Ibid.

8. Benjamin Callender, Homewood, October 19, 1955.

9. Other early settlers who located on creeks flowing into Tahoe besides Blackwood (Tahoe Pines) and McKinney (Chambers'): Ward Rush at the influx of Ward Creek, Captain Augustus W. Pray at Glenbrook Creek, Walter Scott Hobart at Mill Creek (Incline), Griffin on "Griff" Creek (King's Beach), General William Phipps on General Creek (Sugar Pine Point), "Friday" Burke adjoining Friday's Creek (Edgewood). "A Homewood district was formed in 1889, 100-foot lots were laid out priced at $50.00 apiece (50 cents a front foot) but they did not sell. Finally they were offered free of charge to any person who would build a substantial house." George McConnell. *Tahoe Tattler* (new edition) 1936.

10. *A Century of California Post Offices,* Walter N. Frickstad, Oakland, California. A contract letter, however, from the Post Office Department, dated January 20, 1910, ordered the postmaster

at McKinney's to supply Homewood starting May 10, 1910, on an irregular schedule.

11. B. Callender and J. P. Obexer, Homewood, November 3, 1955.

12. Advertising brochure, Homewood Hotel, summer of 1922.

13. *Lake Tahoe,* Claire MacDonald, private printing, 1929.

14. Ibid.

15. Refer Tahoe Pines chapter 7.

16. J. P. Obexer, Homewood, November 3, 1955; John Drum, Jr., September 5, 1955.

17. B. Callender, Homewood, October 2, 1955.

Chapter 9—Rubicon Springs

1. Stevens-Townsend-Murphy horseback party, November, 1844. See Truckee Canyon, Chapter 2; also Sherman Day California State survey party, Spooner Station and Summit Camp chapter 40.

2. John Hunsucker, 40 years; George Hunsucker, 38 years, natives of North Carolina, miners. *Great Register of El Dorado County,* October 29, 1866, Placerville, California. Shown as stage driver and fisherman, respectively, in *El Dorado Great Register* for 1892.

3. Virginia City *Territorial Enterprise,* June 14, 1877.

4. Mrs. Mehetable Jane Phillips Sickels, Phillips Station, October 6, 1955.

5. Ibid.

6. Mrs. Alice Elaine Phillips Lyon, Phillips Station, October 6, 1955.

7. *Sacramento Daily Record Union,* September 5, 1888.

8. *Warm Springs and Health Resorts of California,* Winslow Anderson, 1890.

9. Ben Callender, Homewood, September 6, 1954.

10. George D. Oliver, Carson City, September 18, 1954.

11. Ben Callender, Homewood, September 6, 1954.

12. Rubicon post office established May 4, 1901; moved to McKinney's April 30, 1901; re-established at Rubicon March 8, 1909; to Emerald Bay September 30, 1913; Post Office Records, Washington, D. C.

13. Mrs. Mehetable Jane Phillips Sickels, Phillips Station, October 6, 1955.

14. George Chambers, Chambers Lodge, August 16, 1955.

15. Intimately associated with the Rubicon Springs country for the last half century were the Victor Wikanders. In 1922 they homesteaded on an island at Buck Island Lake, just south of Rubicon Springs, where they built a cottage. For years "Vic" Wikander was known as the "Lone Cross Country Skier," ably following the "Snow-Shoe" Thompson tradition when he made the 130-mile round trip from McKinney's to Georgetown once a week. Mrs. Ethel Joslyn Vernon, Tahoe City, August 4, 1953.

Chapter 10—Chambers' Lodge

1. *Truckee Republican,* July 7, 1887.

2. John W. McKinney: Crossed over the Central Overland Trail from Missouri in 1850, and always regretted having missed being a '49er. Settled in Georgetown, El Dorado County, California, where he constructed the El Dorado Water Ditch with partners, John Wren and John Hardin (1853-54), selling out in 1860. McKinney hunted and explored the western shores of Lake Tahoe previous to settling on Upson Bay in 1862. A barn lettered "1854" stood until the 1940's on the west side of McKinney Creek, and a log cabin was noted in the 1880's supposedly constructed in 1858 by McKinney. No documentary evidence supports these claims. "McKiney (sic), John, miner, 33 years old, from Missouri; also McKinney, John, aged 72, Missouri; occupation, 'gentleman'." *Great Register of El Dorado County,* Placerville, January 31, 1867; also *History of Placer County, California, Oakland,* 1882; *Historical Souvenir, El Dorado County,* Paolo Sioli, 1883, and *San Francisco Alta,* August 22, 1870.

3. "McKinney" Post Office established June 26, 1884, and changed to "Chamber's Lodge," November 1, 1928. United States Post Office Records, Washington, D. C.

4. Placer County Court House records, Auburn, California, Book X, 1862-65; also *Historic Spots in California,* Hoover and Rensch, Stanford Press, 1948, p. 128, p. 248.

5. "L. Upson, Surveyor General of California in 1865, gave his name to Upson Bay after 'blazing' Georgetown-Lake Bigler trail in early 1860's." Robert H. Watson, October 6, 1955.

6. Also "Hunter's Home." Ibid., footnote 4.

7. Ibid.

8. Ibid.

9. Ibid.

10. *Truckee Republican,* August 2, 1875.

11. *Carson City Appeal,* May 28, 1880.

12. *Truckee Republican,* July 27, 1880.

13. Ibid.

14. *Tourists' Guide and Directory of the Truckee Basin,* W. F. Edwards, Truckee, 1883.

15. *Tahoe Tattler,* Tahoe City, July, 1881.

16. Tallac House brochure, 1881-83.

17. *Health and Pleasure Resorts of the Pacific Coast,* Newton H. Chittenden, 1881.

18. *History of Placer County, California,* Oakland, 1882.

19. Refer Chapters 22, 23, and 27.

20. *Truckee Republican,* August 5, 1887.

21. Ernest H. Pomin, Robert H. Watson, Tahoe City, October 23, 1955.

22. McKinney's Post Office record file, Dave Chambers, July 8, 1949.

23. Murphy Brothers and Morgan, advertising brochure, 1899-1900, McKinney's; also "Iron springs owned by Dave Chambers in 1929, beyond Gardner cottage, south side of Homewood," Claire MacDonald, *Lake Tahoe,* 1929.

24. Robert H. Watson, Ernest H. Pomin, Tahoe City, October 25, 1955. "Main hotel built from rare sugar pine," Claire MacDonald, *Lake Tahoe,* 1929.

25. Chambers' Lodge brochure, 1920-21-22.

26. Recollections of author.

27. Ibid. The old Club House has been re-built several times during the last 75 years, and in 1910 the stairs ran up the northwest side of the building with quarters for the help in the attic. Present bartenders are not always early pioneer Lake Tahoe residents, but stories have been passed down to them over the decades. (Author's note.)

Chapter 11—Moana Villa

1. James Harrison Miller: Native of Tennessee, farmer, Latrobe, California, 43 years old in 1867. Gave his name in 1887 to Miller Lake and Meadow, where he drove his sheep in the summer. Miller Lake was originally Rubicon Lake. *Great Register of El Dorado County,* 1867, and El Dorado tax rolls, 1887-88.

2. See chapter 50 for further details on Homer D. Burton, who is considered to have first left his name on Burton Pass, Canyon and Creek (now McKinney). William Burton, early day surveyor from Kelsey, El Dorado County, California, is said by some authorities to have named the pass, but no evidence points to this Burton being in the specific region during the 1860's; nor is he listed in the *Great Register of El Dorado County* for 1867, 1892 or 1894.

3. Refer chapter 50 and Early Marine History of Lake Tahoe section for *Edith Batty.* For "first settlers" see *Sacramento Union,* September 6, 1862.

4. Mrs. Hattie Belle Norris Colwell Almstaden, Placerville, October 14, 1955; also *Great Register of El Dorado County,* 1867.

5. Colwell's Mill was primarily a shingle producer and considered to have been steam powered. This was one of the sawmills mentioned by Edward Vischer when he circled Tahoe in the late 1860's. See Tahoe City chapter 4. "Possibly the Colwell mill was originally water powered, as a diversion ditch from Burton's Creek could easily have supplied water for an overshot wheel," Arnold Luneman, Meeks Bay, May 18, 1955; also Mrs. Hattie Belle Norris Colwell Almstaden, Placerville, October 14, 1955.

6. Augustus Colwell to George D. Oliver, as told to writer, October 11, 1954.

7. Refer to *Topographical Map of Lake Tahoe and Surrounding Country,* Ferdinand von Leicht and J. D. Hoffmann, 1874. Ernest Henry Pomin, Tahoe Pines, September 6, 1954.

8. The Placer-El Dorado county line where it ran into Lake Tahoe was in dispute for decades. In 1874 it entered the lake at the present site of the Sydney Ehrman home on Sugar Pine Point. See von Leicht and Hoffmann's *Topographical Map of Lake Tahoe;* also *Wheeler's U.S. Geographical Survey Map,* 1876-77.

9. Benjamin F. Callender, Callender's Lodge, Homewood, October 17, 1854.

10. Carl Andrew Bechdolt, Sr., Tahoe City, September 16, 1955.

11. Ibid. Also Mr. and Mrs. A. M. Henry, Tahoe City, October 9, 1955.
12. Willie Moretz Arnhold, Kathryn Stanner, Chambers Lodge, September 6, 1955.
13. David Chambers, Chambers Lodge, July 4, 1951.

Chapter 12—Tahoma

1. *Historical Souvenir of El Dorado County* (Oakland) Paolo Sioli, 1883; also El Dorado County Court House Records, Placerville, California, 1882-83.
2. "In 1924, Mrs. Mary R. Planett and Bishop built Tahoe's first bakery facing the lakeshore road next to the only store in the settlement. Mrs. Planett did the baking, assisted by her husband, John J. Planett. Two years previously A. M. 'Joe' Henry, his wife, the former Marie Planett, and their son Al moved to Tahoma from McKinney's, where Henry operated the automobile livery and garage. The Henry family went from Tahoma to Tahoe City in 1929 and the Planett family leased Tahoe Vista in 1929, then Carnelian Bay from the Flick Brothers in 1932," Mrs. Marie Planett Henry, February 22, 1956.
3. A. M. Henry, Tahoe City, October 14, 1955.
4. Letter from H. L. Henry to Mrs. A. M. Henry, Los Angeles, December 19, 1955.
5. Ibid.
6. A. M. Henry, Tahoe City, October 14, 1955.
7. Mrs. A. M. Henry, Tahoe City, February 22, 1956.
8. *Lake Tahoe,* Claire MacDonald, W. E. Rudge, Mt. Vernon, 1929. Private printing.
9. Post office was established at Tahoma, September 1, 1946.

Chapter 13—May-Ah-Mee Lodge

1. "Grizzly bear actually existed in the Tahoe region," Robert H. Watson, October 4, 1955. "Grizzly's at Tahoe in early days," Harry Johanson, Ernest H. Pomin, August 8, 1955, Tahoe City. See *Hutchings' California Magazine,* September, 1856, Volume I, p. 107. "Negro attacked by 1100-pound grizzly at Mud Springs (El Dorado) in 1849." "Hunter attacked by grizzly in Bird Valley in 1850, badly hurt but escaped by pretending to be dead." "A large grizzly was encountered on 'Main Top' between the North and Middle Forks of the American River with six hunters tracking him down, one Wright being attacked in heavy brush with his skull torn out exposing his brain. He lived, however."
2. Lugi Barnetto, also spelled Barnette; his killing by "Old Brin" based on a report in the *Truckee Republican,* August 5, 1881, and *Carson City Appeal,* August 7, 1881.
3. Legendary "Old Brin" found in California-Nevada newspaper reports between 1868 and 1887, and said to have received his name from George "Grizzly" Davis, famous early day bear fighter with eleven heads on his fence rail as evidence of his prowess. The beast trapped by Davis in the 1860's, lost two toes on his right foot escaping.

"Old Brin" was given the name because of his peculiar brindle color and he preyed on livestock and humans for nearly two decades. Refer Edgewood chapter 32.
4. *Truckee Republican,* August 9, 1881.
5. *Lake Tahoe,* Claire MacDonald, W. E. Rudge, Mt. Vernon, 1929, private printing.
6. *Historical Souvenir of El Dorado County,* Oakland, Paolo Sioli, 1883. *History of Placer County, California,* (Oakland), 1882. Ernest H. Pomin, Tahoe City, August 24, 1954.
7. Ernest Pomin, Tahoe City, August 24, 1954. "Pomin's Lodge built in 1913, and nearly went bankrupt in 1914 due to outbreak of World War I." J. P. Obexer, Homewood, September 10, 1955.
8. Pomin's Lodge brochure, 1915-16.
9. Post Office records, M. A. Martin, post office inspector, August 13, 1914.

Chapter 14—Sugar Pine Point

1. *Carson City Appeal,* August 11, 1862 (revised).
2. Georgetown: originally Growlersburg, El Dorado County, California, in 1850. Changed to George's Town after relative of General William Phipps, then shortened to Georgetown. *Historic Spots in California,* Hoover and Rensch, Stanford University Press, 1948, p. 92; also *Great Register El Dorado County,* Placerville, California, 1871. General William Phipps: born 1813, occupation, fisherman, died at age 74 years, *Great Register of El Dorado County,* 1867, 1893.
3. El Dorado County Assessment Rolls, Placerville, 1860.
4. Ibid. 1864.
5. Refer Chapters 4, 11 and 40.
6. El Dorado County assessment rolls, 1871.
7. *Truckee Republican,* May 19, 1883.
8. "General William Phipps built two log cabins, the one now standing built in 1870 and the original cabin constructed in the early 1860's." George D. Oliver, Carson City, Otcober 11, 1954.
9. Ernest Henry Pomin, Tahoe City, September 19, 1954.
10. *Carson City Appeal,* April 21, 1888. D. Kaiser, mortgaged to W. W. Lapham in the amount of $10,000, September 26, 1887. Bellevue Hotel, $6,500; lumber, wagons, etc. "Hotel to be erected by Kaiser on 720 feet lake frontage." El Dorado tax rolls, 1887-88.
11. Post office sanctioned "Sunbeam" April 8, 1888, moved to McKinney's September 21, 1893. Post Office Records, Washington, D. C.
12. *Sacramento Daily Union,* July 8, 1889; also June 15, 1890.
13. Bellevue Hotel brochure, 1889-90.
14. Mrs. Hattie Belle Colwell Almstaden, Placerville, September 27, 1954.
15. Bellevue Hotel advertising literature, 1890-91.
16. Mrs. Hattie Belle Colwell Almstaden, Placerville, October 3, 1954.
17. Refer Chapter 23.
18. Mr. and Mrs. Sydney Ehrman, Mrs. Claude Lazard, Sugar Pine Point, August 18, 1855. Also

El Dorado County tax rolls, 1913, 1918, 1924, 1926.
19. Ibid.
20. R. Stanley Dollar landholding on Dollar Point may be considered comparable.

Chapter 15—Meeks Bay

1. "Micks Bay," McKinney's Register, 1879. "Micks Bay, Meadow and Creek," Von Leicht and Hoffmann's *Topographical Map of Lake Tahoe,* 1874. "Meegs Bay," R. J. Waters photograph, 1882. "Meigs Bay," McKinney's Register, 1881. "Buttermilk Bay," George and James Murphy's registration, McKinney's, September 14, 1879.
2. *Sacramento Union,* September 6, 1862.
3. Stephen Hall Meek, older brother of Joseph L. Meek, claimed to have trapped around Pyramid Lake and Truckee River in 1833, sending scouting parties westward looking for passes over the Sierra Nevada Mountains. The *Autobiography of a Mountain Man:* 1805-1889, Introduction and Notes, Arthur Woodward, 1948. *No Man Like Joe,* H. E. Tobie, p. 37. "Meeks Bay — for Stephen H. L. Meek, member of J. R. Walker's party in 1833—." (Sic) *The Dictionary of California Land Names,* P. T. Hanna, 1946, p. 170. *Great Register, El Dorado County* (1869), lists Bajels Meek, age 67, native of Kentucky, farmer, Placerville, but no connection with Meeks Bay.
4. "Digger Indians" indicated but they were undoubtedly Washoe's who were native to Lake Tahoe. *Placerville Herald,* July 9 and 16, 1853.
5. Ibid. Also see Cave Rock chapter 36.
6. Mrs. Harry J. Lawson, Sacramento, California, March 16, 1956.
7. Ibid.
8. Ibid.
9. Ibid.
10. Ben Callender, Callenders Lodge, Homewood, September 7, 1954.
11. Arnold Luneman, Meeks Bay, August 12, 1955.
12. Ibid. Also George Kehlet, Meeks Bay, August 4, 1954.
13. Ibid.
14. Mrs. Harry J. Lawson, Sacramento, California, March 16, 1956.
15. "Chinquapin Lodge built in summer of 1923," John Drum, Jr., Chinquapin Lodge, August 14, 1955. El Dorado tax records, however, on Drum estate, begin in 1926.
16. John Drum, Jr., August 18, 1955.
17. Ibid.
18. George Kehlet, July 21, 1955. Meeks Bay.

Chapter 16—Rubicon Park and Bay

1. *San Francisco Alta,* July 11, 1880; also "Mr. Lusk was the first to settle on what later became the Frost-Harper property," Mrs. Harry J. Lawson. Refer Meeks Bay chapter 15.
2. El Dorado County Court House, Placerville, California, Assessment Rolls, 1886-87.
3. Photographic reference, summer of 1895.

4. El Dorado County Court House, Placerville, Assessment Rolls, 1905.
5. J. P. Obexer, Homewood, May 6, 1954.
6. Ibid. Also Ernest H. Pomin, Tahoe City, August 7, 1954.
7. Ibid. Assessment Records, 1918-25.
8. El Dorado County Assessment Records, 1926-34.

Chapter 17—Rubicon Point

1. Refer Facts of Tahoe section for "bottomless depths at Rubicon Point."
2. "Called the Rubicon probably in jesting analogy to Caesar's crossing of the Rubicon River." *California Place Names,* E. G. Gudde. Also see *Topographical Map of Lake Tahoe and Surrounding Country,* 1874.
3. Grecian Bend: a wooded curve of shoreline to the south of Rubicon Point. Evidence points to it being named, in the late 1860's, after the way the American women walked, a result of the padded styling of the day. This was known as the "Grecian Bend" or, ungraciously, "colic stoop."

Chapter 18—Emerald Bay

1. Richard Barter: Native of England, seaman, naturalized in Boston, Mass., in 1832. Drowned at Rubicon Point October 18, 1873, at the age of 66 years. *Great Register of El Dorado County.* 1867, Placerville, Calif.; *Truckee Republican,* October 18, 1873; *Sacramento Union,* May 29, 1875.
2. *San Francisco Alta,* August 22, 1870.
3. Emerald Bay: originally Eagle Bay in the 1860's, being named for American eagles that were found there. Officially the name was changed to Emerald Bay on the *Topographical Map of Lake Tahoe and Surrounding Country,* Von Leicht and Hoffmann, 1874.
4. *San Francisco Alta,* August 22, 1870.
5. Ibid.
6. Ibid. Also refer Early Marine History of Lake Tahoe section.
7. Ibid.
8. Ibid.
9. Yank's Hotel, Tahoe City, Glenbrook have all been given as the departure points from which Barter sailed on his last cruise. It has been established that "Captain Dick" was on the south end of Tahoe on the night of October 18, 1873, and as Rowland's Lake House Saloon was the only bar on the water at the time, Barter unquestionably left from there. "Captain Barter was sober for once when he made his final voyage." Captain Ernest John Pomin to Miss Jessie Armstrong; to writer January 17, 1955.
10. *Truckee Republican,* October 18, 1873. "Captain Dick," an eccentric old English sailor, chose this wild mountain retreat for a home, built a cabin, chiseled out a tomb in the solid rock face on the lonely rockbound island near the entrance. Falling overboard while intoxicated, the lake became

his last resting place." *Health and Pleasure Resorts of the Pacific Coast,* 1881, Newton H. Chittenden.

11. Desolation Valley Primitive Area was originally known as Davis Valley. It contains 41,380 lake-spotted, barren, granite acres and runs from the vicinity of Rubicon Springs to Ralston Peak and Echo Lake. Eagle Falls: sometimes known as Emerald Bay Falls.

12. *Truckee Republican,* July 8, 1866; also *San Francisco Alta,* July 11, 1866. "Coquette Island, so called because of its deceptive appearance."

13. "The trapper was no relation to the William Henry Armstrong family." Miss Jessie Armstrong, Oakland, January 17, 1955. "A trail also followed around south Eagle Point to the bog at the head of the bay and then northeast along shore. Sometimes horses and pack mules swam the inlet, but there was never a bridge there." George Anderson, October 19, 1955.

14. For "trout mining at Bigler" see also the *San Francisco Alta,* January 10, 1878. Refer chapters 28 and 39 for Henry "Hank" Monk.

15. Refer *Tahoe Tattler,* July 23, 1881, for an Emerald Bay steamer excursion trip, and Early Marine History of Lake Tahoe for steamers.

16. "Kirby, Paul T. and Lucy M.: 160-120-220 acres." El Dorado County Assessment Rolls, 1884, Placerville, Calif.

17. Ibid. The Kirby-Armstrong resort cottages should not be confused with the present Emerald Bay Camp (Resort) location one mile to the northeast. Ben Holladay, Jr.'s; "The Cottage" was "robbed and burned out by tramps in 1879." Miss Jessie Armstrong, January 17, 1955. "Armstrong, Margaret J.: Hotel, Club House, 200 acres at Emerald Bay." El Dorado County Court House tax rolls, 1885.

18. *San Francisco Chronicle,* July 7, 1890.

19. Parson's Rock: also "Warden's Rock," El Dorado County assessment records, 1900. No evidence of the mineral springs exists at the bay today.

20. William Henry Armstrong, Virginia City and Gold Hill mining man, purchased the Holladay holding in 1885 and leased back to the Kirbys. It became known as Emerald Bay Resort. "The Armstrong family repossessed the property in 1900 from Mrs. Lucy Kirby Cowles, the court awarding them 6 years back rental that was due." Miss Jessie Armstrong, January 17, 1955.

21. El Dorado Assessment Rolls, 1900. See Early Marine History of Lake Tahoe section for *Lily Van.*

22. Mrs. Louis L. Cox, Carmel, May 10, 1955. Miss Jessie Armstrong, Oakland, January 17, 1955.

23. Mrs. Russell Cowles Graves, Mrs. Louis L. Cox, Carmel, May 10, 1955.

24. Miss Jessie Armstrong, Oakland, January 17, 1955. Also "Emerald Bay road, Meyers to McKinney's, was officially opened on August 13, 1913. A committee of Assemblymen and Senators made the trip in a rented Winton car." Grant Merrill, Woodfords, October 4, 1955. "I was the first to take a spring wagon and span around the

new Emerald Bay road in the summer of 1913, and I met a Stanley Steamer coming from Tahoe City." Stella Tong Watson, October 4, 1955. "Early in 1913 I drove a Pierce Arrow from Tallac to Tahoe City around Emerald Bay. It was an impossible 'trail'. We had to hire seven Washoe Indians to build crude log bridges and lay a corduroy road at Rubicon Meadows. Block and tackle had to be used to pull the car from tree to tree and the trip took two days." Lloyd Tevis, Sunnyside, August 18, 1955.

25. Emerald Bay Camp brochure, 1918; El Dorado County Court House, Assessment Records, 1918-1919. Post office officially established at Emerald Bay December 17, 1888.

26. Paul E. Gruver, Lakeview, October 19, 1955.

27. Mrs. Lora Moore Knight: Born in early 1860's in Galena, Illinois. Maiden name, Lora Small; one of two sisters who married two Moore brothers. Lora Small married James Herbert Moore of Chicago, leading financier of his day (Rock Island Railroad and National Biscuit Company). James Moore died in 1916 and Mrs. Lora Moore married Harry Knight of St. Louis, divorcing Knight in 1921 before she built *Vikingsholm.* She also had extensive estates in Santa Barbara, California, and St. Louis, Missouri.

28. Armstrong's Emerald Bay Resort brochure, *"Milflores."* Miss Jessie Armstrong.

29. Mrs. Russell Cowles Graves, Carmel, April 5, 1955.

30. "The private road into *Vikingsholm* possibly cost $30,000 to build, and in addition an electric power line, plumbing facilities and a water system had to be provided at great expense in this remote location." Matt Green, Sacramento, October 4, 1954; Lennart Palme, Tahoe Tavern, July 16, 1955. "The Armstrongs and Kirbys went in by steamer or took the trail before *Vikingsholm* was constructed." Miss Jessie Armstrong, January 17, 1955. "Mrs. Knight's bay frontage property approximated 7,000 feet." Matt Green, October 4, 1954.

31. "Local labor, not 'imported Norwegian stonecutters,' split granite for castle's foundations." Matt Green, October 4, 1954.

32. "The circular Chinese rug was not woven especially for the tower." Miss Jessie Armstrong, January 17, 1955.

33. Lennart Palme, Tahoe Tavern, July 18, 1955.

34. "The stone house on the island is built of granite boulders, not blocks." Matt Green, October 4, 1954.

35. Author's recollections, 1937.

36. Miss Jessie Armstrong, January 17, 1955.

37. Lawrence P. Holland from Sacramento, California, acquired *Vikingsholm* in 1946 for $201,000, later selling to Harvey West, a Placerville lumberman. West sold in turn to the State of California in 1953. It is now open to the public, included in the 499-acre Emerald Bay State Park, and known as the Harvey West Memorial Park. See *Sacramento Bee,* September 23, 1946, for Holland purchase.

Chapter 19—Cascade Lake

1. Dr. Charles Brooks Brigham: native of Boston, Harvard graduate; one son William Babcock Brigham and two daughters Alice Wyer and Katherine Duer Brigham. Mrs. H. R. Ebright, October 11, 1955.
2. Mrs. Harold Raymond (Katherine Brigham) Ebright, October 11, 1955.
3. Ibid.
4. Ibid.
5. Jack Bell, Sparks, Nevada, August 26, 1955.
6. Mrs. H. R. Ebright, October 11, 1955; also refer Early Marine History of Lake Tahoe section, for *Pirate.*
7. Mrs. Gladys Comstock Bennett, Brockway, August 29, 1955. Mrs. H. R. Ebright, Cascade Lake, October 11, 1955.
8. Ibid. Mrs. H. R. Ebright.
9. "My father paid twice for the property before obtaining title through a Los Angeles broker . . . something of a record." Mrs. H. R. Ebright, October 11, 1955.
10. Ibid.
11. Ibid.

Chapter 20—Fallen Leaf Lake

1. Mrs. Harriet Price Craven, Sacramento, September 4, 1954 (edited).
2. Refer to Facts of Lake Tahoe section.
3. Mrs. Harriet Price Craven, Sacramento, September 4, 1954.
4. *Sacramento Union,* June 15, 1890.
5. Refer log chute photograph, this chapter.
6. Louis Agassiz (1807-1873), professor of geology and zoology at Harvard University. Agassiz School for Boys, Auburn, California, run by W. W. Price and named for Agassiz.
7. Mrs. H. P. Craven, September 4, 1954.
8. *San Francisco Examiner,* June 29, 1913. *California—Romantic and Beautiful,* George Wharton James, p. 245.
9. Mrs. H. P. Craven, September 4, 1954.
10. Webster F. Street, Carmel, April 12, 1956.

Chapter 21—Glen Alpine Springs

1. Nathan Gilmore: emigrant from Indiana, 36 years old, resident Mud Springs, *El Dorado County Great Register,* Placerville, California, April 15, 1867. N. Gilmore: age 61, height 5 feet 5 inches, Mud Springs, farmer and stock raiser, *El Dorado County Great Register,* 1892.
2. Mud Springs: later town of El Dorado, El Dorado County, California. Placerville: originally known as "Old Dry Diggings," then Hangtown.
3. Nevett's Summit (sometimes Nevitt), Johnson Pass and cut-off is now Echo Summit. For this and Strawberry Station see The Great Bonanza Road to Washoe Chapter 51.
4. Osgood's Toll House. Refer Way Stations on the Bonanza Road section.
5. "Yank's." Refer chapter 27.

6. Glen Alpine Springs: originally Gilmore Springs. Dixwell Pierce, Sacramento, October 6, 1954, furnished reference material for early history of the Gilmore family. The Springs are 6,800 feet above sea level and the gateway to Desolation Valley primitive area. "Nowhere in the world is found a finer specimen of a glacial valley than this wild, rough, barren valley." David Starr Jordan, quoted in *California — Romantic and Beautiful,* George Wharton James, p. 246. Glen Alpine, houses, barn, 2 wagons, harness, 4 miles of wagon road, 16 horses, six colts, El Dorado County Assessment Rolls, 1895. Post office established at Glen Alpine June 23, 1904, moved to Tallac in 1918, United States Post Office records, Washington, D. C.
7. *Historical Souvenir, El Dorado County,* Oakland, Paolo Sioli, 1883.
8. Dixwell Pierce, Sacramento, October 6, 1954.
9. *Carson City Appeal,* September 28, 1880.
10. Ibid.
11. Dixwell Pierce, June 18, 1954.
12. *California, the Wonderful,* Edwin Markham, p. 300.
13. Susie Lake; also "Suzy," U. S. Department of Interior, *Geological Survey Map, Pyramid Peak Quadrangle,* 1889.
14. Dixwell Pierce, June 18, 1954.
15. Mr. and Mrs. Melvin F. Springmeyer, Bijou, October 21, 1955.

Chapter 22—Tallac

1. E. "Yank" Clement, see chapters 23 and 27. M. C. Gardner, refer chapter 24. "Yank's" Hotel located between the present George Pope (Vatican Lodge) property (former Will Tevis, earlier (1895) George P. Tallant holding) and old Tallac Point. Author's note.
2. *Carson City Appeal,* August 14, 1875.
3. *Carson City Appeal,* July 6, 1875.
4. See Early Marine History of Lake Tahoe section.
5. *Truckee Republican* and *Gold Hill News,* July 6, July 7, 1875.
6. Elias Jackson "Lucky" Baldwin: born in Hamilton, Ohio, April 3, 1828. Captained Central Overland wagon train in 1853 to California. Became horse livery operator in San Francisco and Virginia City, speculator in Comstock Lode stocks, reportedly "mining the Comstock from the other end—the stock board." Baldwin became a multi-millionaire, ranking with the barons of the Big Bonanza, and America's "original real estate trader," hotel owner (Baldwin Hotel, San Francisco; Tallac, Lake Tahoe), owner Santa Anita Rancho in Southern California, four times married, possibly five, the target of numerous breach of promise suits, seductions, accusations and sweethearts. The original basis of his fortune and nickname: he had locked stock certificates (Hale and Norcross mine) in his safe and gone big game hunting in India; on his return he sold the stock for two and one-half million dollars to Jones and Sharon. Died March 1, 1909, in San Francisco, at the age of 81 years. *Lucky Baldwin,*

C. B. Glasscock; also *An Editor on the Comstock Lode,* Wells Drury, p. 67.

7. Acreage held by Baldwin variously and erroneously given as high as 8,000 acres. "Baldwin, E. J., 1,886 acres in the year 1886, 1,800 acres in 1895, 2,647 acres in his estate in 1926." El Dorado County Assessment Rolls, Placerville, California. "Baldwin used his mill at Fallen Leaf to furnish lumber for his own construction, preserving the forest around Tallac." Ernest H. Pomin, Tahoe City, September 11, 1954.

8. Variously Captain Gorden, Gorgon. See *Health and Pleasure Resorts of the Pacific Coast,* Newton H. Chittenden, 1881, p. 153.

9. George Lord Mortimer Comstock, Sheriff of Mineral County, Nevada, in the 1860's. Managed Tallac Hotel for only six years, as died February 18, 1888. Father of Harry O. Comstock. See chapter 44. "Mrs. G. L. M. Comstock became the 'Comstock' of Comstock and Lawrence upon her husband's death. In the mid-1890's, her son, H. O. Comstock, joined with Melville Lawrence." Gladys Comstock Bennett, September 24, 1956.

10. Tallac House (Hotel) continued to be known sentimentally as "Yank's" for several years after its purchase by E. J. Baldwin. Author's note.

11. *Gold Hill News, August* 11, 1882.

12. *Tourists' Guide and Directory of the Truckee Basin,* Truckee, 1883. W. F. Edwards.

13. See chapter 19.

14. "The air up there in the clouds is very pure and fine, bracing and delicious. And why shouldn't it be—it is the same the angels breathe" is the actual quotation. *Roughing It,* Mark Twain (Samuel Clemens), Harpers, 1871.

15. See Cascade House chapter 23.

16. Tallac House brochure, 1891-92.

17. "$30,000 borrowed from John F. Elliott, New York at 9½% interest per year." El Dorado County Court House, Placerville, California, Book of Assessments, 1898, p. 134. This was to partially finance Baldwin's new hotel as he was evidently "land poor" at the time. "Baldwin had planned new hotel, and built foundations at his death in 1909. Mrs. Anita Baldwin McClaughey of Santa Anita was now to carry out the plan and make it fireproof" (sic). *California—Romantic and Beautiful,* George Wharton James.

18. Not to be confused with "Sawmill Flat" two miles from present Highway 89 on the road to Fallen Leaf Lake. (Author's note.)

19. *Sacramento Daily Union,* June 1, 1890.

20. The Tallac (House) brochure, 1900-01.

21. Ibid.

22. Ibid. Also Harry O. Comstock, Brockway, May 28, 1952.

23. George D. Oliver, Carson City, September 24, 1954.

24. Mrs. Gladys Comstock Bennett, Brockway, September 11, 1955.

25. Carl Andrew Bechdolt, Sr., Tahoe City, October 18, 1955.

26. Lloyd Tevis, Sunnyside, Lake Tahoe, September 4, 1955.

27. Carl Andrew Bechdolt, Sr., Tahoe City, October 18, 1955.

28. Maillard Bennett, Brockway, September 11, 1955.

29. Ibid. As recalled by Harry O'Callaghan.

30. "No tears shed—" *San Francisco Bulletin,* March 2, 1909. "He (Baldwin) was a great man, great pioneer and builder. I am not ashamed to say I shed tears at his death." Harry O. Comstock to C. B. Glasscock, as noted in Glasscock's book *Lucky Baldwin.*

31. Walter Danforth Bliss, Glenbrook, September 5, 1954.

32. Stella Tong Watson, September 15, 1955.

33. Tallac House, Casino, piers, and other improvements on north side of present Highway 89 gone by 1928, as $70,000 value erased from El Dorado County Assessment Rolls in that year. Baldwin house at Fallen Leaf, value $39,500, standing.

34. Ben Callender, Homewood, October 2, 1953.

Chapter 23—Cascade House

1. *Sacramento Union,* May 17, 1887.

2. El Dorado County Court House, Placerville, California, Assessment Rolls, 1885-86-87.

3. Ibid. "Yank's" "land and farm ranch," 1886; "Yank's Hotel, and Josiah H. Applegate and Mrs. McDonald" (sic), 1888; "Clements (sic), E., 47 acres plus 120 acres. Fifty foot lot deeded to J. H. Applegate; 100 foot lot to Clara Belle Gardner McDonald" (sic), 1890; "Cascade House, Clement, E. Lot One, fronting on Tahoe, 300 feet running back to Tallac Avenue, to the west, Claire McDonald (sic), lot to the east then E. J. Baldwin's property." Yank's holdings included a "hotel, barn, club house, saloon, outbuildings, and one small gas steamer." El Dorado County records, 1895.

4. Based on an eyewitness account, George D. Oliver, Carson City, Nevada, October 11, 1954.

5. *Sacramento Union,* June 15, 1890.

6. Ernest Henry Pomin, Tahoe City, September 14, 1954.

7. Mrs. Don Goodrich, Placerville, October 6, 1955. Grace Jellerson McCleary, Reno, October 9, 1955.

8. George D. Oliver, Carson City, Nevada, October 11, 1954. Revised. "Emer-villy": Emeryville, California.

9. Mrs. Katherine Brigham Ebright, Cascade Lake, October 10, 1955.

10. The Story of Tahoe, *Tahoe Tattler,* special printing, 1940, undocumented.

Chapter 24—Camp Richardson

1. Matthew (also Mathew) Culbertson Gardner: Early resident, Wooden Valley, near Suisun, California; moved to Carson Valley in 1860's; stock trader, rancher, lumberman, and recalled as "furnishing the horses for Virginia City's recruits in the Battle of Pyramid Lake where the volunteers were massacred by the Paiute Indians." Grant Merrill, Woodford's, October 29, 1955. *El Dorado County Great Register,* 1867.

2. Dr. George M. Gardner, Homewood, August 21, 1955.

3. *Truckee Republican,* June 3, 1875.

4. Dr. George M. Gardner, Homewood, August 21, 1955. Also "Mulatto in Carson Valley yoked 4 oxen to M. C. Gardner's oxen and hauled locomotive to Lake Tahoe." Grant Merrill, Woodford's, October 29, 1955.

5. Harry James, Lakeside, Lake Tahoe, August 28, 1955.

6. Grant Merrill, Woodford's, California, October 29, 1955.

7. Dr. G. M. Gardner, Homewood, August 21, 1955.

8. Ibid.

9. Ibid.

10. Mrs. Fannie Rowland Barton, Sacramento, California, May 11, 1955.

11. Dr. Gardner, Homewood, August 21, 1955.

12. Claire MacDonald, *Lake Tahoe,* private printing. 1929. Also El Dorado County Court House, Placerville, California, Douglas County Court House, Minden, Nevada, Assessment Rolls, 1881-85.

13. "My father held approximately 6,000 acres, the majority of which were timber leases and a small remainder was owned outright." Dr. M. C. Gardner, Homewood, August 21, 1955.

14. See Chapter 23. Cascade House.

15. Lloyd Tevis, Sunnyside Bay, Lake Tahoe, September 14, 1955.

16. George P. Tallant (also Talant) gave his name to Tallant Lakes, west over the ridge from Rubicon Peaks.

17. Mrs. Ray Knisley ("Sis") Richardson, Camp Richardson, September 8, 1955.

18. Ibid.

19. Copeland's Grove Brochure, 1923-24.

20. Mrs. Ray Knisley, Camp Richardson, September 8, 1955.

21. Ibid.

Chapter 25—Echo Lake

1. "A Cruise on a Mountain Sea," Henry C. Watson, in the *Sacramento Union,* January 1, 1873, concerning a Tahoe-Sierra Nevada junket made by Ramsdale Buoy and party, presumably in May, 1866. Echo Lake is actually two lakes, Lower and Upper Echo.

2. Ibid. Devil's Basin; also Davis Basin after its discoverer. Now Desolation Valley Primitive Area.

3. Refer Bijou chapter 30.

4. Nevett's Summit: See Great Bonanza Road to Washoe chapter. Osgood Lake: Named for Nemi Osgood; Osgood's Toll Station.

5. Ralph King, Berkeley, California, March 11, 1955.

6. Dr. Clark J. Burnham, Jr., Piedmont, April 26, 1956.

7. Ralph King.

8. John Kirk: Pioneer '49er El Dorado County resident, civil engineer; constructed cabin for Sherman Day survey party in the winter of 1855 at Sugar Loaf Flat below Strawberry Valley; also contracted snow hauling to Placerville in spring of 1859.

9. *Historical Souvenir, El Dorado County,* Oakland, Paolo Sioli, 1883, p. 108.

10. Echo Lake P. O. moved to Meyer's in 1910, reestablished at Echo Lake, December 11, 1926. U. S. Post Office records, Washington, D. C.

11. Hamden El Dorado Cagwin: Native of Illinois and brought to Hangtown (Placerville) in 1852 via the Isthmus of Panama. Moved successively to Markleeville, Virginia City and Carson City, where Cagwin, Sr., became a storekeeper; Hamden traveled to Oregon by wagon in 1891 and several years later he moved to Tahoe. He was given the middle name, El Dorado, as he was born during the '49 gold rush. F. L. Phelps (nephew of H. E. D. Cagwin), as told to Ralph King, Berkeley, March 11, 1955.

12. Norman and Hazel Celio, Lake Valley, October 25, 1955. Ralph King, Berkeley, California.

13. "Flood Years Were 1913-14," Norman and Hazel Celio, Lake Valley, October 25, 1955.

14. Lower Echo Lake is one and one-half miles long by one-half mile wide, and Upper Echo, three-fourths of a mile long by three-eighths of a mile wide. *U. S. Forest Service map, Lake Valley district,* 1950.

Chapter 26—Lake Valley

1. Wasson (also Wassan) Peak, now Mount Rose. Eagle Valley is the present site of Carson City, Nevada. Indian Cave is Cave Rock, and Daggett Pass the summit of the Kingsbury Grade.

2. The outlet of Lake Tahoe was discovered in November, 1844. Approximately one-third of the lake's surface is in Nevada and two-thirds in California, and the northern extremity of Tahoe was known to the emigrants. Refer Great Bonanza Road to Washoe chapter and Facts of Tahoe section, also chapter one, Squaw Valley.

3. Lake Tahoe is 21.8 miles long and 12.6 miles wide. Refer Facts of Tahoe section.

4. The type of winters, i.e., mild or heavy, determine the water level of Lake Tahoe and the height is controlled by the Truckee River dam outlet gates.

5. No law prohibited taking unlimited quantities of fish from Tahoe or its affluents in Goddard's time. The trout were evidently spawning.

6. "Johnson Hill" should not be confused with Osgood's or, later, the "Meyers Grade," which entered Lake Valley one mile to the north. For George H. Goddard's report see *Report of a Survey of a Portion of the Eastern Boundary of California and a Reconnaissance of the Old Carson-Johnson Immigrant Roads Over the Sierra Nevada* (Sacramento, 1855) in *Pamphlets on California* (Bancroft Library), Vol. XXVI, No. 28; also *Hutchings' California Magazine,* June, 1858. George H. Goddard (G.H.G.).

7. Refer Facts of Tahoe section, also chapters 15 and 20.

8. *My Overland Trip to California,* Colonel L. A. Norton, Bancroft Library, Berkeley, California. Governor John Bigler of California led rescue

party and the lake was named Bigler in his honor. See Facts of Tahoe section.

9. Martin "Mart" Smith; see chapter 27. "Smith, Martin, 320 acres, value $1,240, bounded north by Kingsbury, south by Hawley; money, stables, horses, mules." *El Dorado County Court House, Assessment Rolls,* 1860. Placerville, California. "Mr. Smith's in Lake Valley with grass and water plenty." William Bartlett's (Emigrant) Guide to California, *Placerville Herald,* August 13, 1853, p. 3, col. 1.

10. A. H. Hawley, *Lake Tahoe,* Bancroft MS, University of California.

11. Hawley, Asa Herschel: Born in Windsor County, Vermont, in 1813, and overland to Colonel Reese's Mormon Station (Genoa) in 1851, later settling in Placerville. Here he built Elkhorn Mill and then moved to Lake Valley in 1854, wintering in Coloma, California. Six Mile House (Elkhorn House) and a hotel in Latrobe, also Swift's Station on the Kings Canyon Road were operated by Hawley in the 1860's and early 1870's. "Hawley bounded north by Mac (sic), south by Lyons, wagons, horses, cattle." El Dorado County records, 1861-62. "Hawley took out a patent on his Lake Valley land on August 20, 1878, deeded to Peter Van Sickle in 1881, who sold to Nemi Osgood." Celio family Book of Deeds, Lake Valley, October 27, 1955. A. H. Hawley died in Yerington, Nevada, August 31, 1899, at the age of 86 years.

12. "The Johnson Hill grade is a 782-foot rise to summit by barometer reading." George H. Goddard, September 29, 1855, California Survey report. Gradient has been given as high as 50%.

13. Grant Merrill, Woodfords, October 19, 1955.

14. Goddard was speaking of the Stewart brothers, murdered by Mickey Free and George Wilson. See "A Cruise on a Mountain Sea," Henry C. Watson, *Sacramento Union,* January 1, 1873; also *Pioneers of El Dorado,* Placerville, 1906, p. 118.

15. The old "back road" or Placerville-Carson Valley route or "Johnson Pike" is here referred to as distinguished from the "Lakeshore Road" running to Lake House (Al Tahoe) from Yank's (Meyers) and along the shore to old Stateline.

16. The "large stream" is Trout Creek.

17. Probably Cold Creek.

18. Later Lapham's Hotel, Carney's Station, old Stateline and now Lakeside.

19. Gold Canyon: south defile of Sun Peak (Mt. Davidson) where Silver City, Gold Hill and Virginia City later mushroomed.

20. Henry James, Lakeside, October 26, 1955.

21. Dr. Charles Daggett was probably the only physician available at Genoa, although "Drs. Luce, Daggett, Chamberlain and Walters" are noted in *Hutchings' California Magazine* article, February of 1857, written by an anonymous correspondent. Other accounts give Daggett only.

22. *Overland Monthly,* Vol. VIII (2d series), October, 1866, pp. 419 through 435; also *Hutchings' California Magazine,* February, 1857.

23. *Sacramento Union,* July 14, 1857.

24. "J. M. C." (actually Jarad B. Crandall) letter to *Sacramento Union,* July 4, 1857.

25. Refer to the Great Bonanza Road to Washoe chapter 51.

26. Refer Meyers chapter 27.

27. See Way Stations on the Bonanza Road section.

28. Refer Edgewood chapter 32.

29. G. N. Douglass, partner with Martin Smith. Their land bounded south by Hawley, north by Clemente (sic), east by range of mountains, west by Kingsberrys (sic). El Dorado County Court House, Book of Deeds, April 9, 1862, p. 639. See Way Stations on the Bonanza Road section.

30. Post office moved to Tallac December 20, 1870; to Bijou November 4, 1895; to Tahoe Valley, June 12, 1940. United States Post Office Records, Washington, D. C.

31. "Stumps were located on Heavenly Valley Creek (Miller) in 1890 that broke away under the impact of an ax head and (therefore) considered to be 30 years old. Sawdust piles were also found, black with age clear to the bottom. Lake Valley residents indicated in the 1880's that this was the first mill (to be built) during the construction of the Carson-Placerville road." *Engineering Works Contributory to the Comstock,* John Debo Galloway, University of Nevada Bulletin XLI, June, 1947.

32. Refer Way Stations on the Bonanza Road section.

33. *Sacramento Union,* September 6, 1862.

34. Ephraim "Yank" Clement to George D. Oliver, July 4, 1889, as told to writer by Oliver, October 4, 1954.

35. Based on Ramsdale Buoy and party's trip in May of 1866 as described by Henry C. Watson, in "A Cruise on a Mountain Sea," *Sacramento Union,* January 1, 1873.

36. Smith's remaining land sold to Nott ran north to Osgood's Toll House, south to Hawley's, and east and west up the mountain slopes. On February 28, 1871, Nott deeded the land to Charles Warren Winstanley. Carlo Guisseppi Celio acquired the property on December 10, 1878. "Junction" was the Luther Pass-Kit Carson "Y" in Hope Valley. The station was first owned by James Green, then Alphonzo Nott (Knott spelling incorrect), then Edward M. Pickett, and called "Pickett Place." Refer *Historical Souvenir El Dorado County,* Paolo Sioli, 1883; Alpine-El Dorado counties tax rolls. Also original patents, homestead claims, bills of sale, deed records, Mrs. Frank Celio, Mrs. Hazel Celio Taylor, Norman Celio, Celio Home Ranch, October 24, 1955.

37. California State Library, Sacramento Census Records, 1870.

38. *Sacramento Union,* May 29, 1875, "Resources and Wonders of Lake Tahoe" article.

39. Mrs. Don Goodrich, Placerville, September 4, 1955.

40. Refer Hobart chapter 33.

41. *Health and Pleasure Resorts of the Pacific Coast,* N. H. Chittenden, 1881, pp. 143-144.

42. Carson and Tahoe Lumber and Fluming Company's Book of Deeds. Will M. Bliss, Piedmont, California, November 7, 1954.

43. See Meyers chapter 27.

44. Mrs. Don Goodrich, Placerville, September 4, 1955.

45. In 1927-28 the Celios built a second sawmill south of Gardner Mountain, selling to the Placerville Lumber Company in 1943. It burned in 1951 and was rebuilt by A. C. Winkleman in 1954. It was operating under the name Lake Tahoe Mill in 1957. Mrs. Hazel Celio and Norman Celio, February 1, 1956. "C. G. Celio and Sons, 2,600 acres." 1913 El Dorado County Court House records.

46. Refer footnote 6 of this chapter.

Chapter 27—Meyers

1. "Mr. Smith's station in Lake Valley," *Bartlett's Guide to California,* August 18, 1853. "Martin Smith, postmaster of Lake Valley P.O. in 1858, located one mile north of Osgood's Toll Station." Also "Smith and Douglass Ranch bounded south by Hawley, north by Clement, east by range of mountains, west by Kingsberry's" (sic). El Dorado County Court House, Book of Deeds, p. 629, April 9, 1862. "Martin Smith, age 40, Agent Wells Fargo, Strawberry." *El Dorado County Great Register,* 1867.

2. *Historical Souvenir, El Dorado County,* Oakland, Paolo Sioli, 1883.

3. *Placerville Herald,* September 24, 1853.

4. *Placerville Herald,* October 8, 1853.

5. *Historical Souvenir, El Dorado County,* Oakland, Paolo Sioli, 1883, p. 177.

6. Refer to George H. Goddard, Lake Valley chapter.

7. *Sacramento Union,* June 12, 1857.

8. Refer Meyers Station chapter 27.

9. Book of Assessments, 1862-63, El Dorado County Court House, Placerville, California. "Powers Meat Market sold to E. Clement, May 11, 1864, price $425.00." Book of Deeds, 1864, p. 639.

10. Refer Sierra House, chapter 28; Al Tahoe, chapter 29.

11. George D. Oliver, Carson City, September 5, 1954. Best known version: "I'm a Green Mountain Boy so they called me Yank."

12. *Sketches of the Washoe Mining Region,* Edward Vischer, San Francisco, 1862.

13. Based on *Reminiscences of Senator William Stewart of Nevada,* N. Y., 1908, p. 62; *Saga of the Comstock Lode,* George D. Lyman, pp. 187-189.

14. "A dinner station par excellence—from the time the stages passed Strawberry Station on their way east, or Van Sickle's going west, the meal waiting at Yank's was uppermost in the minds of the coaches' passengers." Edward Vischer, San Francisco, 1862.

15. Based on an anecdote in *Treasure Express,* Neil C. Wilson.

16. *The Big Bonanza,* Dan DeQuille (William Wright), Hartford, 1876.

17. Yank's Hotel, later Baldwin's Tallac House, see chapter 22.

18. El Dorado County Court House, Assessment Records, 1886.

19. *Great Registers of El Dorado County,* 1867-92-94.

20. Mrs. Minnie Lyons Creighton, San Mateo, January 30, 1956.

21. Ibid.

22. Judge Peter J. Shields, Sacramento, December 18, 1955.

23. Carlo (Charles) Guisseppi Celio, 33, native of Switzerland, occupation milkman 1866, Lake Valley. Station purchased from Meyers by the Celios on March 19, 1903. Sons of Carlo Celio; Frank, Armenio, Charles Guisseppi, Benjamin, Caesar, George, and daughter Henrietta Margerite. Granddaughters and grandsons: Hazel, Florence Edith, Charles Lewis, Norman, Alorna, Georgia and Arta May.—Norman Celio, Hazel Celio Taylor, Mrs. Frank Celio, Lake Valley, October 25, 1955.

24. Refer Way Stations on the Bonanza Road section.

Chapter 28—Sierra House

1. Based upon a story by Mrs. Ethel Joslyn Vernon, Tahoe City, May 27, 1954. See Lake Valley and Edgewood chapters for Henry Van Sickle.

2. For "Long Haired" Sam Brown refer *The Saga of the Comstock Lode,* George D. Lyman; also Myron Angel's *History of Nevada,* Oakland, 1881, p. 344; Sam Davis's *History of Nevada,* Vol. I, p. 249, and Eliot Lord's *Comstock Lode.*

3. Refer Tahoe City chapter 4 for details of Stewart's sudden death.

4. See Glenbrook chapter 39, also Emerald Bay chapter 18, for Hank Monk.

5. Refer Lake Valley chapter 26 and Bonanza Road to Washoe chapter. "Previous to 1890 a road led directly from Sierra House to Lake House on the Tahoe shore." Mrs. Fannie Rowland Barton, Sacramento, September 8, 1955.

6. *The History of Contra Costa County,* 1917, F. J. Hulaniski, pp. 530-531. Also "Mr. Dean preempted a tract of land—built a cabin on the road followed by the emigrants from the east. Mr. Mack appeared and claimed the land belonged to him. Finally he agreed to pay $3,500 for the improvements—and (Dean) sold out." *History of the State of California and Biographical Record of Coast Counties,* 1904, J. M. Guinn, p. 721.

7. See also *Pacific Coast Business Directory* (1867).

8. Letter from C. E. Swain to R. H. Cross, March 27, 1938, R. H. Cross Library, Berkeley, California, "Swain traded a mine he owned southeast of Hicksville (Arno) between Galt and Elk Grove with A. G. Tryon for Sierra House."

9. George Anderson, Bijou, October 21, 1955.

10. Charles Siebeck, lumberman from Diamond Valley, El Dorado County, and native of New York State, is said to have owned Sierra House in the 1870's and 1880's. Mrs. Fannie Rowland Barton, Sacramento, April 8, 1955. Possibly Siebeck took

over the way station after G. W. Chubbuck's
bankruptcy in 1886-87, although no record exists
in the El Dorado County Court House registers.

11. Mrs. W. H. (Francis Brockliss) Lampe, Gardnerville, October 26, 1955.

12. Ibid.

13. Ibid.

14. No authority for conclusion of tale.

15. Letter, Swain to Cross, March 27, 1938. Swain's
theory was that the board had "grown higher as
the tree grew" but anything driven into a tree
will remain at the same level from the ground no
matter how high the tree may grow.

Chapter 29—Al Tahoe

1. *A Peep at Washoe*, J. Ross Browne, Harpers
Magazine, December, 1860, and February, 1861.

2. Refer Sierra House chapter 28; also *History of
the State of California and Biographical Record
of Coast Counties*, J. M. Guinn, 1904, p. 721.

3. Refer Lakeside chapter 31. Van Wagener also
spelled Van Wagner.

4. Letter from Robert Garwood Dean to the *Daily
Territorial Enterprise*, Virginia City, February
3, 1870.

5. *Up and Down California*, William H. Brewer,
p. 442, 1860-64.

6. *Early Inns of California*, R. H. Cross, p. 237.

7. "A Cruise on a Mountain Sea," Henry Watson.
Refer Echo Lake and Bijou chapters, 25 and 30.

8. Thomas Benton Rowland: Native of East Corinth, Vermont, who came to California in 1862.
Mrs. Fannie Rowland Barton, September 16,
1955.

9. Mrs. Fannie Rowland Barton, Sept. 26, 1955.

10. *Carson City Appeal*, August 6, 1870; also *Truckee
Republican*, August 9, 1870.

11. Mrs. Fannie Rowland Barton, May 9, 1954.

12. Mrs. Don Goodrich, Placerville, September 4,
1955.

13. "Silver coin was found here in the water, with
the side facing down worn smooth by action of
the sand, the top side bright and shiny with its
original stamping perfect." George Anderson,
Bijou, September 24, 1955.

14. El Dorado County Assessment Rolls, 1876-77.

15. *Health and Pleasure Resorts of the Pacific Coast*,
Newton H. Chittenden, 1881, pp. 143-144.

16. George Anderson, Bijou, September 24, 1955;
also Mrs. Don Goodrich, Placerville, September
4, 1955.

17. Ibid.

18. Mrs. Fannie Rowland Barton, Sacramento, May
9, 1954.

19. George Anderson, Bijou, September 24, 1955.

20. Ibid; also Mrs. Fannie Rowland Barton.

21. Ibid; George Anderson.

22. Ibid.

23. Mr. and Mrs. Frank Globin, October 14, 1955.
El Dorado Tax Rolls show the Globins taking
over in 1927.

24. Mrs. Fannie Rowland Barton, Sacramento, May
11, 1956.

25. Mr. Grover Irey, Al Tahoe, September 12, 1955.

Chapter 30—Bijou

1. The landing was at the site of the present Bijou
pier and known variously as Taylor's Landing,
Taylor's Acres, Taylor's Ranch.

2. Based on "A Cruise on a Mountain Sea," Henry
C. Watson, *Sacramento Union*, January 1, 1873.

3. Deeds, patents, homestead claim records, Bijou,
1866-1924. Mrs. Glorene Dunlap Young, October
7, 1955.

4. More commonly Mack. El Dorado County Assessment Rolls, 1861.

5. Ibid. Assessment rolls, 1884-85.

6. Refer *United States Geographical Map*, 1889
survey, for length of line. Chubbuck's railroad
has been described as a "wooden track tramway,
log bed track faced with strap iron." El Dorado
County records show it to have been a conventional standard gauge railroad.

7. Harry James, Lakeside, Lake Tahoe, October 3,
1955.

8. *Early Engineering Works Contributory to the
Comstock*, John Debo Galloway, University of
Nevada Bulletin XLI, June, 1947. Also Mrs.
Rose Chubbuck Dodson, Carson City, October
18, 1954.

9. Ibid.

10. El Dorado County tax rolls, 1866; also George
Anderson, Bijou, October 21, 1955.

11. Ibid.

12. The post office was officially moved to Bijou
from Rowlands on September 11, 1888.

13. George Anderson, Bijou, October 21, 1955.

14. Mr. and Mrs. E. V. Fettic, Genoa, Nevada, October 24, 1955, and Harry James, Lakeside, October 3, 1955.

15. *United States Geological Survey Map* (Markleeville Sheet), 1889, shows length of pier to be
closer to 2,600 feet. During May, 1896, the pier
was extended 80 feet to accommodate the new
steamer *Tahoe* launched the following month.
See Glenbrook chapter 39, also Early Marine
History of Lake Tahoe section.

16. El Dorado tax rolls, Placerville, 1889-91.

17. Ernest Henry Pomin, Tahoe Park, September 4,
1954; also George D. Oliver, September 5, 1954.

18. George D. Oliver, Carson City, September 14,
1955.

19. George Anderson, Bijou, October 26, 1955.

20. *Great Register of El Dorado County*, 1892-94; also
George Anderson, October 26, 1955.

21. Ernest Henry Pomin, Tahoe Park, October 28,
1954; also George Anderson, Bijou, October 26,
1955.

22. Ibid.

23. "Flying-switch": The brakeman uncouples from
the still-moving cars, the switch is thrown and
the locomotive runs into a siding. The switch
is again thrown and the cars move past on the
main track. The engineer backs to the main
track, couples to the rear car and pushes the
cars to the line's terminus. Although common
practice in early day railroading at Tahoe, it was
banned after the Jim Vair killing.

24. Mrs. Frank Globin, Al Tahoe, October 24, 1955.
25. El Dorado County records, Placerville, 1889-1900.
26. Ibid.
27. El Dorado County Court House records, 1924-25.
28. Clyde Beecher, owner of Nevada Club, South Stateline. Among other casino owners at South Stateline — William Harrah, Harvey Gross, George Cannon.
29. Bijou: French name for gem or jewel was applied to the settlement during the late 1880's by (1) French-Canadian lumberjacks; (2) William S. Bliss and Cary Platt, who jointly decided the name was most suitable; (3) William S. Bliss; (4) "Bonnie" Oakley, Bijou schoolteacher. Mrs. Fannie Rowland Barton, Sacramento, August 12, 1954; Mrs. W. D. Barton, Lake Valley, September 4, 1954.

Chapter 31—Lakeside

1. William W. Lapham: Pre-empted land in Calaveras Grove in 1853, selling out to James L. Sperry in 1857. Lapham's first wife, Nancy L. Lapham, died at the age of 28, November 7, 1858, and this tragedy prompted Lapham's move to Lake Tahoe. He was the original owner (with Seneca Dean and W. Van Wagener) of Lake Bigler House (Al Tahoe) before moving to what later became Lakeside. Refer Early Marine History of Lake Tahoe section (*Governor Stanford*) and Sugar Pine Point, chapter 14.
2. Based upon an anecdote in *The Big Bonanza,* William Wright (Dan DeQuille), 1876.
3. "Frank Powers, A. M. Taylor, M. K. 'Friday' Burk(e) adjoined Lapham's holdings." Also "bound on west by stateline, north by Bigler Lake and east by Power's Ranch." El Dorado County Court House Tax Roll records, 1860-70. Douglas(s) County Tax Rolls, Minden, Nevada.
4. Boundary Bay: later Sapphire Bay (1880-1900) located between Bijou and Round Hill (Mound). Refer *Topographical Map of Lake Tahoe Region,* 1876-77; Wheeler Survey.
5. California-Nevada stateline surveys: Day-Marlette-Goddard survey, 1855; Lt. Mowry's United States War Department financed survey, 1860-61; Kidder and Ives survey, 1863; Colonel Von Schmidt's survey, 1872-74. The first state line ran through present Tahoe Meadows, 100 feet north of former Harold Leupp cottage. Kidder and Ives "corrected" this and then Lt. Mowr which they found to run 1½ miles east of their line. Von Schmidt determined that the line was 2400 feet farther east than the original survey and placed it as running through Lapham's Hotel. The present line run out in 1899 is 2000 feet farther east again. Refer *Sierra-Nevada Lakes,* George and Bliss Hinkle; *History of Nevada,* Effie Mona Mack, p. 405.
6. Refer Tahoe City chapter 4 for additional details on Colonel Von Schmidt.
7. One of the last, and best preserved, horse change stations in the Sierra. Now run by Jack Van Sickle. See Sierra House chapter 28.

8. Refer Early Marine History of Lake Tahoe section. Four major resorts then on Tahoe: Rowland's Lake House, Glenbrook, Campbell's Hot Springs and Tahoe City (Hotel). Refer Von Leicht and Hoffmann's *Topographical Map of Lake Tahoe and Surrounding Country,* 1874.
9. Letter from Mrs. Marion Hill to R. E. Cross, January 31, 1938, Cross Library, Berkeley, California.
10. John Carney: Native of Utica, New York State, born in 1828. In 1853, Carney accompanied the John Weyth emigrant train overland as outrider and settled in Placerville. Miner, wholesale butcher, hay and grain merchant, hotel keeper, Carney died in Carson City.
11. Miss Catherine Patterson, Sacramento, California, May 5, 1955.
12. Ibid.
13. Ibid.
14. Ibid.
15. George Anderson, Bijou, September 24, 1955.
16. El Dorado County Court House Assessment Rolls, 1885, page 111.
17. Mrs. Ethel Joslyn Vernon, Tahoe City, May 26, 1954; also *Truckee Republican,* July 11, 1889.
18. Ibid.
19. Letter Mrs. Hill to R. E. Cross, January 31, 1938.

Chapter 32—Edgewood

1. On April 3, 1860, the first Pony Express rider left San Francisco headed east. The route followed was Sacramento, Placerville, Johnson Pass, Lake Valley, over Luther Pass, down the West Carson Canyon past Woodford's and along the base of the east Carson Range of the Sierra Nevada to Genoa, Carson City and on to Saint Joseph, Missouri.
2. Douglas(s) County Court House, Minden, Nevada. Book of Records, 1860-64. Also, "Station called 'Friday's' because a hired hand could never remember the name of the owners." O. Dickey to G. D. Oliver, July, 1892.
3. Walton's Summit (1859-1874), now Spooner Summit at the head of Clear Creek Grade. Also known as Summit Camp (1875-1900).
4. Stations between Friday's and Van Sickle's on the Kingsbury Grade. Robb's Station, Alexander and Frank Rob(b), 160 acres (1863), later owned by John Hurley (1867-72), Peter Van Sickle's at "Peter's Flat," two log cabins on the south side of the road, one a saloon; Cary's Mill, corrals, barn, at foot of grade; Clark Station, M. N. and Rob Clark (1863-66), later W. H. Stark (1867) and then How(e) and Montrose; Stark's Ranch, and sawmill (1871). James W. Small holding to C. P. Young (1872) "Young's Station." Henry Van Sickle's Toll House north of east Kingsbury approach. Douglas(s) County Court House, Minden, Book of Deeds, 1863-67-71-72.
5. Boundary Bay lies between Round Hill and Lakeside. Burke and Company (the "Company," J. W. Small), *Sacramento Union,* September 6, 1862.

6. "Home Station," usually family owned furnishing board and lodging with horse changes often available.

7. David Wallace Park, Edgewood, September 6, 1954.

8. *The Saga of the Comstock Lode,* George D. Lyman. *Sierra-Nevada Lakes,* George and Bliss Hinkle. Also see chapter 50, Lake Forest.

9. "The fastest run of the Pony Express" will be debated for decades, and is fogged in claims and counter claims. Haslem's ride appears to have been the equal of any. (Author's note.)

10. The story is based on a personal narration of "Pony Bob" Haslem, see *The Pony Express,* William Lightfoot Vissher. Also *Via Western Express and Stagecoach,* Oscar O. Winther, p. 131.

11. *Roughing It,* Mark Twain (Samuel Clemens).

12. *Mining and Scientific Press,* San Francisco, June 22, 1861, J. Silversmith.

13. "Frank Powers transferred meat market to E. Clement, Yank's Station, May 11, 1864." Douglas(s) County Court House, Minden, Nevada, assessment records, Book H, of Deeds, 1864-65.

14. Ibid.

15. Ibid.

16. Refer to chapters 39 and 40, Glenbrook and Spooner Station.

17. Douglas(s) County Court House Records, 1870-71.

18. "Friday's Station, a relic of the palmy days of staging, established by Burke in 1859." *Crofut's New Tourist and Overland Guide,* 1880.

19. *Carson City Appeal,* August 6, 1875. Also chapter 12. "Old Wash" stems from Small's middle name, Washington; also J. W. Small, member of the Nevada Legislature.

20. *Carson City Appeal,* May 6, 1875.

21. Mrs. Fannie Rowland Barton, Sacramento, August 16, 1955. Mrs. Minnie Lyons Creighton, San Mateo, January 30, 1956. Mrs. Don Goodrich, Placerville, September 4, 1955.

22. Mrs. Fannie Rowland Barton, Sacramento, August 16, 1955. Also "Averill, John Wales, 430 acres." Douglas(s) County Land Records, 1895.

23. David Wallace Park, Edgewood, September 27, 1954. D. W. Park's father, David Brooks, born December 24, 1839; died July 16, 1906. Mottsville Cemetery, Nevada.

Chapter 33—Hobart

1. See Crystal Bay Chapter 43.

2. Walter Scott Hobart made his fortune at Virginia City. Died at age 53 in the year 1892, leaving an estate estimated at $15,000,000. See Chapter 42, also Los Angeles Times, December 13, 1955, part one, page 4.

3. Hobart's timberland holdings, southeast Tahoe: 7,845 acres in 1873; 7,962 acres in 1874-75 (value $20,000) taxes $700 per year; 8,083 acres 1882-83-84; reduced to 7,963 in 1893 (estate). Holdings (Nevada Lumber Company) acquired by C. and T. L. and F. Company, 1890-92. Douglas County

Court House, Minden, Nevada, Assessment Records, 1873-93.

4. El Dorado Wood and Flume Company, "Corporation existing by virtue of the laws of the State of Nevada." Filed December 2, 1876, in Book of Inc. folios 159-160, recorded Ormsby County Book One of Incorporation, pp. 545, 546. Filed with State of California February 26, 1930. Object, "Cutting, manufacturing, transporting and selling wood and lumber with right to buy and sell real estate, operate flumes and railroads, etc." $20,000 Cap. Stock. Trustees: H. M. Yerington (President), W. C. Ralston (Bank of California); J. W. Haynie. First timberland acquisition May 27, 1875. (Mrs. Beverly Cola, El Dorado County Court House, Placerville, January 8, 1956).

   El Dorado Wood and Flume Company; acquired J. W. Haines and partner Van Gardner's Ranch (Haines Canyon east Kingsbury Grade); Farmer's Mill, Summit Mill, wood V-flume, 3995 acres, in 1876.

   1884—5980 acres.

   1885—5990 acres, 1520 stripped; saw mill Van Sickle's Canyon.

   1893—Timber gone from 2518 acres; 3222 standing.

   1895—Timber gone from 2678 acres.

   1896—Total 5899 acres, 2678 cut. Value cut-over land, 25 cents an acre; timberland, $2.50 an acre.

   1918—Increased to nearly 8000 acres.

   Douglas County Court House Records, Minden, Nevada, Book of Assessments, pp. 92-109.

5. William Rabe, Edgewood, Nevada, August 7, 1954.

6. Ibid.

7. Mrs. Emma Frances Jewell Clifford, Reno, Nevada, October 24, 1955.

8. Ibid.

9. Abraham Day Jewell originally owned ranch north of Meyers, Lake Valley; moved to Virginia City in 1900. See Chapter 27, Meyers.

10. See Chapter 28, Sierra House.

11. Harry James, Lakeside, October 25, 1955.

12. Douglas County Court House, Minden, Nevada, page 27, assessment rolls, 1895-96.

13. Harry James, Lakeside, October 25, 1955.

14. William Rabe, Edgewood, Nevada, August 7, 1954.

15. "164 acres, less 30 acres sold to Tahoe Village and Sky Harbor." Ibid.

Chapter 34—Marla Bay

1. Marley, John, rancher, stockman, native of England; Douglas (originally spelled Douglass) County Court House, Minden, Nevada, assessment rolls, 1864, p. 30.

2. Ibid. Property valuation in 1864 was $1,000 and it dropped to $515 in 1866.

3. Pray, A. W. 150 acres (sic) value $500.00. Pray acquired Marley's holding by paying $407.10 in back taxes. Douglas County Assessment Rolls

and Delinquent Tax Book (Cave Rock Township), 1870-71.

4. Mrs. Laura McFaul Allerman, Allerman Ranch, Genoa, Nevada, August 28, 1955.

5. Ibid.

6. Ibid.

7. Assessment Rolls, Douglas County Court House, Minden, Nevada, 1890-91.

8. Martin Sorenson, Hope Valley, California, October 4, 1955.

9. McFaul, William: Born April 17, 1847, in Canada and wife Elizabeth Moore McFaul. One of 5 sons. Two brothers, George and Robert, also came to Tahoe. The children, Frederick Duke McFaul, Joseph Allen McFaul, W. A. Edward McFaul, Laura Alice McFaul and Ethel McFaul. Mrs. L. M. Allerman, Genoa, Nevada, August 28, 1955.

10. Douglas County Court House Records, Minden, Nevada, 1922-29.

11. Refer Early Marine History of Lake Tahoe section.

12. Douglas County Court House, assessment records, 1936-37.

Chapter 35—Zephyr Cove

1. The lakeshore road was variously known as the "Main Stem, the Main Drag, Lake Bigler Toll Road, Lake Tahoe Wagon Road, Butler Ives Turnpike, Johnson Pass road and cut-off." Refer Douglas(s) County Court House, Minden, Nevada, assessment rolls, also Topographical Map of Lake Tahoe, 1874.

2. Douglas(s) County Court House, Minden, assessment records, 1862-63-64.

3. Ibid.

4. Mrs. Fred Allerman, Genoa, Nevada, September 24, 1955.

5. Douglas(s) County Court House, assessment rolls and deed book, 1863-64.

6. *Sacramento Daily Union,* August 26, 1863.

7. Refer *Sierra-Nevada Lakes,* George and Bliss Hinkle; also *Sacramento Daily Union,* January 1, 1863.

8. *Carson City Appeal,* July 11, 1871.

9. Mrs. Rose Chubbuck Dodson, Carson City, May 8, 1955.

10. A. T. Wakeman: 40 acres, $300.00 personal property on Clear Creek, 1887. Douglas(s) County Register, Minden, Nevada. Also see chapter 40.

11. Mrs. Rose Chubbuck Dodson, Carson City, Nevada, May 8, 1955.

12. Refer to Way Stations on the Bonanza Road section.

13. See chapter 30.

14. The *Daily Nevada Tribune,* reporting on an article in the *Truckee Republican.*

15. Refer chapters 6 and 48 for "Subterranean fissures in Lake Tahoe connecting with the Comstock."

16. Douglas County Court House, Minden, Nevada, assessment rolls, 1938-39.

Chapter 36—Cave Rock

1. "Big Water." See Facts of Lake Tahoe section.

2. Refer Lake Valley chapter; George H. Goddard's California survey report, September 29, 1855.

3. *Placerville Herald,* July 9 and 16, 1853.

4. "No Indians will cross Tahoe as the Evil Spirit will drown them to the bottom." *Historical Souvenir, El Dorado County,* Oakland, 1883, Paolo Sioli.

5. *Placerville Herald,* July 9 and 16, 1853.

6. Ibid.

7. George D. Oliver, Carson City, August 3, 1954. Ernest H. Pomin, Tahoe City, September 26, 1954.

8. Douglas (spelled "Douglass" until circa 1870) County Court House tax roll, Minden, Nevada, 1864-65.

9. *San Francisco Daily California Alta,* July 1, 1865.

10. See *The Big Bonanza,* Dan DeQuille (William Wright), Hartford, 1876. "In the year 1879 the C. and T. L. and F. Company consolidated 2,281 acres in the vicinity of Cave Rock as timberland property," Douglas County Court House, Minden, Nevada, assessment roll, 1879-80.

Chapter 37—Logan House

1. G. E. Pierson to Robert Logan, "640 acres, more or less," signed for Logan by "Well" Stewart, July 8, 1863. Filed for reference August 28, 1863. Douglas County Court House, Minden, Nevada. Book of Deeds: Book B, p. 177.

2. Ibid.

3. "Wellington Stuart (sic) built another hotel (Logan House) one mile south of Glenbrook House," *San Francisco Alta,* September 16, 1864.

4. *Sierra-Nevada Lakes,* George and Bliss Hinkle, p. 284. Referring to article in *San Francisco Alta,* October, 1865.

5. Dan DeQuille (William Wright), *The Big Bonanza,* 1876, pp. 317-318.

6. Douglas County Court House, Minden, Nevada. Book of Mortgages and Deeds, 1864-65-66.

7. Ibid.

8. Ibid. "H. M. Yarington (sic) acquired ranch known as Logan House; 160 acres, price $500" (1870). Yerington also owner 1871-72-73-74-75. Part of C. and T. L. and F. Company land from 1876 on.

9. William Lindsey, Carson City, November 22, 1955. Ernest H. Pomin, October 6, 1954.

Chapter 38—Shakespeare Rock

1. Shakespeare Cliff, noted on the maps of 1870-80. More commonly known today as Shakespeare Rock.

2. *The Big Bonanza,* Dan DeQuille (William Wright), p. 317. Hartford, 1876.

3. *History of Nevada,* Myron Angel (Oakland, 1881), p. 380.

4. "Shakespeare Rock . . . is one thousand feet high and on its face is a well defined portrait of a man, moss formed or wind chiseled, the 'Old Bard of Stratford on Avon'." *Beyond the Sierras,* 1877. Rev. A. H. Tevis.

Chapter 39—Glenbrook

1. *Carson City Daily Appeal,* July 6, 1875.
2. Spooner Meadow, now Spooner Lake, is just north of the present junction of Highways 50 and 89 above Glenbrook. Refer Spooner Station and Summit Camp, chapter 40.
3. For further details on the opening of the Lake Tahoe Railroad refer to the *Truckee Republican, Carson City Appeal* and *Gold Hill News,* Fourth of July, 1875, accounts.
4. Captain Augustus W. Pray: Native of Vermont where Pray said "they plant schoolhouses and raise men." Pray was born September 6, 1820, and went on to become master of a vessel on the Atlantic seaboard. In 1853 he emigrated to California, where he obtained a captain's command on a vessel plying the Pacific Coast waters as far north as Puget Sound. In the late 1850's Pray moved to Lake Tahoe, where he acquired, over the next two decades, "4,000 acres (sic) of arable lands and timber tracts." Pray was a big man, a 6-footer with red hair and red, bushy whiskers, known as God-fearing, temperate in his habits, liberal with charities, countenancing no liquor or business on Sundays. He died in the early 1890's. Refer *Beyond the Sierras,* Rev. A. H. Tevis, 1877.
5. Glenbrook spelled as two words between 1861 and 1867. Glenbrook Creek also known as "Wood Creek" in 1870. Refer Douglas(s) County Court House Records, Minden, Nevada, 1860-70.
6. *Sacramento Union,* September 6, 1862; also *Alta California,* September 16, 1864.
7. *Early Engineering Works Contributory to the Comstock,* John Debo Galloway, University of Nevada Bulletin XLI, June, 1947.
8. Ibid. Also refer *Way Stations on the Bonanza Road* section. A. W. Pray: 650 acres in the Cave Rock precinct, bounded north by Ormsby County, west by Lake Bigler, south by Logan and Stewart, east by Colbath and Winter. 1 sawmill, value $8,000; 3 wagons at $50.00, 3 cows at $50.00; 7 yoke of oxen at $525; 1 horse, $200; 30,000 feet of lumber at $420.00; 20 tons of hay at $700; 8 tons of potatoes at $400; farming utensils, household furniture, $350; real estate and improvements, $6500.00. Douglas(s) County Court House Assessment Rolls, 1864.
9. Mill hands: Luke Bodie, I. Bradley, William Davis, Silas Grant, John Ditmer, Charles Monk, Knox Farrell and A. V. Grigsby among others. "Captain Augustus Pray's mill: value $10,000; capacity, 10,000 board feet per day." *Pacific Coast Directory,* 1867; also Douglas(s) County Court records, 1863-65.
10. "Orion Clemens, Mark Twain's brother—'Mr. Secretary or Poo-Bah' of Nevada Territory in Carson City." *Sierra-Nevada Lakes,* Bliss and George Hinkle, pp. 191-93. Also refer Mark Twain's *Roughing It.*
11. Ibid.
12. Douglas(s) County Court House Assessment Rolls, Minden, Nevada, 1862-63-64.
13. San Francisco *Alta California,* October, 1865, as quoted in *Sierra-Nevada Lakes,* p. 284.
14. Lake Shore House (later spelled Lakeshore House) was completed in August of 1863. Refer *Sacramento Union,* August 26, 1863. The hotel became the main stopover location at Glenbrook in the 1880's and '90's. It still stands today as the south wing of Glenbrook Inn, fronting directly on Lake Tahoe. The north wing of the Inn is old Jellerson Hotel and the center section, J. M. Short and Bliss' former over-water store.
15. Clear Creek Grade, originally Rufus Walton's Toll Road, 1860-65; also part of Eagle Valley Ranch—Johnson's cut-off emigrant road 14 years before King's Canyon turnpike became a wagon and stage road. Refer Spooner Station and Summit Camp, chapter 40.
16. "Colbath and Beaty (sic) residents of Glenbrook, liquors $500.00"; also "Colbath and Winters, 5 acres, bounded south and west by Pray. (1) barn, (1) house, known as Glen Brook House, value $10,000, furniture $5,500.00," in 1864. "Joe Winters Glen Brook House reduced in value to $9,000.00," in 1865. Delinquent Tax Rolls, Douglas(s) County Court House records, 1864-68.
17. Refer Facts of Tahoe section for depths and other dimensions of the lake.
18. *San Francisco Alta California,* October 15, 1865.
19. G. H. F. Goff had both a sawmill (Goff and Morrill) and a shingle mill (Goff and Company). "One shingle machine, one sailboat and skiff. Goff and Morrill, mill and 6 acres, Glenbrook." Douglas(s) County Court House records, 1866-70.
20. "Yarington and Co. (sic) Glen Brook House, 1869. "Glen Brook Club; a hotel known also as Glenbrook House," December 31, 1870, Douglas(s) County Assessment Rolls. William Sharon, known as the "Croesus of the Coast"; William Bonner, superintendent of the Gould and Curry mine, Virginia City; William Ralston, president of the Bank of California, San Francisco; all members of the so-called "Bank Ring."
21. Also known as the "Glenbrook Mill Company" and located one-half mile north of Pray's sawmill; value $6,000. The original "Davis Mill" was never acquired by the C. & T. L. & F. Company. Douglas(s) County Court House records, 1870-71-72.
22. Mountain howitzers were common weapons carried by early emigrant parties and the Fremont Cannon was not recorded as being fired on Fremont's trip through Carson Valley in February of 1844. This in no way detracted from the historical significance read into the discovery of the cannon ball at Glenbrook. Refer *Sierra-Nevada Lakes,* p. 318. "The saw log with the embedded shot was cut from Lake Valley." Dr. George M. Gardner, Homewood, August 21, 1955.

23. Wakeman, A. T. Refer Zephyr Cove, chapter 35. Present Highway 50 does not follow the original Clear Creek Grade from Summit to A. J. Pedroli's Meadow half-way down the grade. It was re-routed to the north. The White House, a waystation, stood where the present public campground is now located and Bath's Station was at the foot of the grade. Pedroli's was the last stop before Saint's Rest. King's Canyon Grade was used as an alternate to Clear Creek. One station only (Swift's) stood between John S. Heidenreich's ranch house and toll gate, and Spooner Station. Reference: George D. Oliver, Ernest Henry Pomin, Grant Merrill, Carson City-Woodfords, September 24, 1954.

24. Refer *Sierra-Nevada Lakes*, p. 288, for another version.

25. *Carson City Appeal*, May 7, 1872.

26. Bliss, Duane LeRoy: Born June 10, 1833, in Savoy, Mass., Bliss came to California by way of the Panama route in the spring of 1850. Moved on to the Comstock Lode in 1860, where he became a partner in the Gold Hill banking firm of Paul, Bliss and Baker that merged with the Bank of California, Virginia City branch, in 1871. Bliss was assigned the task of acquiring the right-of-way for the Virginia and Truckee Railroad, thus tying in with Henry Marvin Yerington, construction superintendent, W. Sharon and D. O. Mills. D. L. Bliss went on to become the "Grand Old Man of Tahoe," with lumbering, hotels, steamers, real estate. He died December 23, 1907. Refer Tahoe Tavern, Bijou, Spooner Station and Summit Camp chapters.

27. D. L. Bliss first acquired 160 acres of timberland near Summit (Spooner's Ranch) on August 11, 1870, where he corded wood that brought $2.25 per cord. The quarter section was purchased from John S. Richards. Bliss and Yerington formed Yerington, Bliss and Company in 1870 and acquired additional timberland in 1871-72-73 and then incorporated under the C. & T. L. & F. Company. Douglas(s) County Court House records; Book of Deeds, 1869-74.

28. Refer Spooner Station and Summit Camp chapter 40.

29. Refer Truckee River Canyon chapter 2 for log chutes.

30. Refer Early Marine History of Lake Tahoe section.

31. The Elliott Brothers, heading up the Summit Fluming Company, had 4½ acres of V-flume in Clear Creek and nearly 5 miles of V-flume running out of Marlette Lake (Meadow), by the fall of 1870. This was extended by the C. & T. L. & F. Company. Douglas(s) County Court House records, 1869-73.

32. "Lower Pray Meadow to the south, was later known as Chinese Gardens, as vegetables were raised there by Orientals. The original Chinese Gardens were in Glenbrook Meadow back of the Bliss and Pray summer homes." Ernest Henry Pomin, September 16, 1954.

33. The accepted weight of the engines has always been 23 tons. Ten tons is recorded on the Douglas(s) County Court House Assessment Rolls, 1875-79.

34. Ibid. Also George D. Oliver, Carson City, September 12, 1954.

35. Ibid. Also Ernest Henry Pomin, September 15, 1954.

36. Spur track ran out over the water for unloading wood barges in front of Mill Number One; additional track extended into the roundhouse and to the east side of each mill. Sidings were located on the west side of Upper Pray Meadow and double passing track ran above the second switchback and also served as a cordwood loading siding. Will S. Bliss, George D. Oliver, Ernest H. Pomin, September 12, 1954.

37. *History of Nevada,* Myron Angel, p. 380, Oakland, 1881.

38. Thaxter to Davis (The Glenbrook Mill), August 25, 1874. Frank Davis to George C. Thaxter, April 21, 1877; also "all chains, crowbars, boom sticks, cant hooks, office furniture. Boarding house and mill on a 2-year lease at $135.00 per month, gold coin in advance. Thaxter to have *privalege* of paying the insurance, taxes on the mill and two notes held by John King." Book A of Deeds, Douglas(s) County Court House, p. 137.

39. *Carson City Appeal,* October 28, 1880.

40. Henry J. "Hank" Monk: Born in Washington, New York, in 1829. Drove six-horse team out of Boston in his 'teens and then followed Nicaragua route to San Francisco, arriving in Sacramento in June of 1852. Hired out as a stage driver on the Auburn route until 1857, when he entered the employ of the Overland Stage Company, driving between Placerville and Genoa, Nevada. In 1859 Monk transferred to the Pioneer Stage Line following the same route, and in the 1870's and early '80's he drove the Carson City-Glenbrook run. Died in Carson City, February 28, 1883.

41. *Six Horses,* Major William Banning and George Hugh Banning, 1930.

42. William D. Keyser to his son-in-law George D. Oliver, Carson City, July 4, 1886, as related to author.

43. *Roughing It,* Mark Twain, Rinehart Editions, pp. 103-107, 1953.

44. William D. Keyser to G. D. Oliver, Carson City.

45. Ibid. Also attributed to nearly a dozen other Sierra Nevada stage drivers.

46. Ibid.

47. George D. Oliver, Carson City, September 20, 1954, as told by Walter Scott Hobart, Sr.

48. G. D. Oliver, September 22, 1954.

49. *Pony Express Courier,* Placerville, California.

50. Based on an anecdote recorded by Dan DeQuille in his *The Big Bonanza,* 1876.

51. Walter Danforth Bliss, Glenbrook, August 2, 1955.

52. The *Carson City Appeal* recorded Hank Monk's death as February 28, 1883, and his burial March

3, 1883. The inscription on his headstone is, therefore, probably incorrect as to date.

53. *Carson City Appeal,* October 29, 1880.

54. Walter Danforth Bliss, Glenbrook, August 23, 1954.

55. Ibid.

56. Davis Family Band: Mrs. Davis, C. C. Davis, George Davis, Willie L. Davis, Ivan L. Davis, Lizzie Davis and B. Fehmenam. (*McKinney's Guest Register,* 1873-95.

57. Ernest Henry Pomin, October 3, 1953; also Mrs. Jane Barnes Clark, Reno, Nevada, October 10, 1955.

58. "During the mid-1880's production of the C. and T. L. and F. Company's Number One and Two mills averaged 60,000 to 65,000 board feet of lumber per day for each mill. Four trips were made to Summit Camp each working day by the locomotives, hauling loaded cars. The average upgrade time was 45 minutes and it took only half an hour to return. Twenty-two minutes was the best time recorded on the downgrade run and this would have been improved had not a herd of cows blocked the road temporarily." George D. Oliver, Carson City, September 12, 1954.

59. *Carson City Appeal,* October 12, 1887.

60. Ibid.

61. Mrs. Grace Jellerson McCleary, Reno, Nevada, October 10, 1955.

62. Ibid.

63. Based on an anecdote of Ernest Henry Pomin's, October 6, 1955, and August 28, 1956.

64. Mrs. Jane Barnes Clark, Reno, October 10, 1955, and Ernest Henry Pomin, August 22, 1956.

65. Ibid.

66. Ibid.

67. Ibid. Also George Anderson, Bijou, October 26, 1955.

68. Douglas County Court House Assessment Rolls, pp. 14-15, 1895.

69. Refer Early Marine History of Lake Tahoe section.

70. Ibid.

71. "The annual dollar total of cordwood that went up in smoke at Virginia City amounted to $2,500,-000. 80,000,000 feet of lumber went underground; 6,000,000 alone into the Gould and Curry mine." *The Story of the Mine,* Shinn, pp. 116-118. *The Big Bonanza,* Dan DeQuille (William Wright), 1876.

Chapter 40—Spooner Station and Summit Camp

1. Based on a story in the *Carson City Appeal,* May 25, 1883.

2. "Turning north we forded a tributary of the Middle Fork of the American River (probably Rubicon River), and scaled a granite ridge which runs east and west . . . and then by a low pass entered a valley from which two small lakes (Miller and McKinney) drain into Lake Bigler." Sherman Day, Sacramento, 1855, *Report of a Survey of a Portion of the Eastern Boundary of California and of a Reconnaissance of the Old Carson-Johnson Immigrant Roads Over the Sierra Nevada.*

3. Ibid. Also refer to Chapter 26.

4. Douglas County Court House Records, Minden, Nevada, Book of Deeds, 1855-60.

5. Ibid., April 26, 1860, and July 26, 1860.

6. Ibid., Book A of Agreements and Assessments, 1863-64. The Douglas County portion of the road was assessed at $5,000. Also refer Glenbrook and Lake Valley chapters, 39 and 26.

7. Ibid. Originally spelled Carll.

8. Ibid., 1864. "Spooner's hotel and barn, $11,500, liquors, $100.00, one wagon, $100.00, two cows, $50.00, three yoke oxen, $180.00, one house, $50.00, chickens, $20.00, hogs, $75.00, furniture, $1,200, implements of husbandry, $50.00, blacksmith shop (G. W. Kenison) $50.00."

9. Douglas County Court House, Minden, Nevada, Book of Deeds, September 20, 1862.

10. Ibid. Book of Assessments, 1864-70.

11. Ibid. December 31, 1870-71.

12. *San Francisco Alta,* August 22, 1870.

13. Mr. and Mrs. E. V. Fettic, Genoa, Nevada, October 26, 1955. George D. Oliver, Carson City, August 21, 1954.

14. Refer to Glenbrook Chapter 39.

15. Mr. and Mrs. E. V. Fettic, Genoa, October 26, 1955. For liquidation of Spooner's holdings see Douglas County Court House Records, Minden, Nevada, Book of Assessments, 1884-85, p. 75; 1893, Book 2, p. 57; 1895-96-97, pp. 71, 73, 149, respectively.

16. Ibid. Tax rolls, 1896, p. 149.

Chapter 41—Marlette Lake

1. Seneca Hunt Marlette: Born New York State near Syracuse, of French parentage, fourth of seven children, on January 18, 1824. After graduating as a civil engineer, he rounded the Horn on a sailing vessel in 1849. First a railroad surveyor, then Surveyor General of California (1854-56), he moved to Washoe (Nevada) in 1860 and was elected county surveyor of Carson County, Utah Territory. Later appointed by Governor Nye as first surveyor for Storey County, Nevada. Upon retiring entered into the water and lumber business at Lake Tahoe, where he is incorrectly said to have owned approximately 85,000 acres in partnership with Walter S. Hobart. Marlette died on August 24, 1911, at the age of 87 years in Southern California. *History of California,* James Miller Quinn, p. 1214, vol. 2.

2. *Early Engineering Works Contributory to the Comstock,* University of Nevada Bulletin XLI, June, 1947, John Debo Galloway; also *The Big Bonanza,* Dan DeQuille (William Wright), 1876.

3. Ibid. Also "Pipe line has a length of seven miles and 134 feet, a diameter of 12 inches, maximum thickness of five-sixths of an inch. Delivery through the first pipe installed was 2,200,000 gallons every 24 hours, under 800 pounds pressure at Lakeview Station, 1,720 feet below Mar-

lette Lake. The inlet was 465 feet higher than the outlet at Five Mile Reservoir. Total gallonage, after three pipes were installed (1887), was 10,000,000 daily." *Picturesque California,* C. C. Goodwin, Volume 10, p. 478. "Higher gallonage than 10,000,000 every 24 hours if required." James Leonard, Virginia City, October 25, 1955. "Pipeline contracted by Dave Crosby of Carson. He used Chinese labor and burros and made a fortune." Mrs. James Leonard, Virginia City, October 25, 1955. "Five Mile Reservoir southwest of Virginia City covers a maximum of 4 acres when full, and is only 8 to 10 feet at its deepest spot." Ibid. "When they opened the pipeline's relief valves on the crests of the ridges, it made the blowing of a whale a mere whisper." *The Big Bonanza,* Dan DeQuille, p. 172.

4. Ibid. *Early Engineering Works Contributory to the Comstock,* John Debo Galloway.

5. *The Big Bonanza,* Dan DeQuille, p. 171.

6. Ibid. Contrarily, "During the celebration of the pipeline's completion at Virginia City's International House, Schussler, formerly of the Spring Valley Water Company, S. F., and designer of the watercourse, was hurriedly summoned with the cry 'the flume has broken'." Mrs. James Leonard, Virginia City, October 25, 1955.

7. Evidence points to the Elliott Brothers (Summit Fluming Company) developing Marlette Basin previous to the Bliss and Yerington combine. Refer Spooner Station Chapter 40.

8. *Early Engineering Works Contributory to the Comstock,* Galloway. See footnotes 2 and 3 of this chapter.

9. Tunnel's length given as 3,000 feet, Dan DeQuille, *The Big Bonanza,* p. 173; and other "authorities" go as high as 4,200 feet. "The tunnel was worked from both sides, blasted out with black powder. A dump car railway ran from each portal. When completed it was 7 feet high, 4½ feet wide at the top of the bore and 6½ feet at the floor level," Galloway. "The original V-flume in the center was 3 to 4 feet across the top, and the tunnel 5 feet wide in solid rock and 6 feet wide at the portals, where it was shored with timbers," James Leonard, Virginia City, October 25, 1955. "The old V-flume running through the tunnel has been supplanted with a water ditch, and daylight could be seen through the tunnel bore until some 15 years ago, when granite boulders slipped into the tunnel and the water had to be routed around them. In places the bore is polished to a jasper finish by the action of the water, tremendous two-foot-wide springs gush into the tunnel near its center (possibly fed from three small lakes above), 'set' timbers or lagging constitute half of the tunnel now (2,000 feet), and hundred foot markers are placed through its 4,000-foot length. West Tunnel House is at the west portal, 'Red House' at 'Intake' on Hobart Creek. Here, in 1910, two women were drowned when the dam broke in the middle of the night, carrying 'Red House' down canyon. 'Marlette Lake Station' lies southeast of Mar-

lette Lakes dam, where the water is just under 50 feet when maximum capacity is reached. The dam has been raised several times in the last 75 years." James Leonard, Virginia City, October 25, 1955; "Red" McGovern, Lakeview Station, October 22, 1955.

10. *Picturesque California,* C. C. Goodwin, vol. 10, p. 478; Galloway, *The Big Bonanza,* DeQuille, p. 172.

11. George D. Oliver, Carson City, October 4, 1954.

12. "After Captain Overton planted the trout they became so plentiful that suckers were planted to eat the eastern brook's spawn. Then the suckers had to be removed. The maximum size of brook trout in Marlette is 3 pounds." Mr. and Mrs. James Leonard, Virginia City, October 25, 1955.

13. Mrs. Gladys Comstock Bennett, Brockway, October 10, 1955. Mr. and Mrs. James Leonard, Virginia City, October 25, 1955.

Chapter 42—Incline

1. *Reno Evening Gazette,* October 14, 1880.

2. George D. Oliver, Carson City, September 4, 1954.

3. Little Valley, known as White Rock Valley until 1876. See Ferdinand Von Leicht and J. D. Hoffmann's *Topographical Map of Lake Tahoe and Surrounding Country,* 1874.

4. *Reno Evening Gazette,* October 14, 1880.

5. Ibid. Also see *Early Engineering Works Contributory to the Comstock,* John Debo Galloway, University of Nevada Bulletin XLI, June, 1947.

6. Mrs. James Leonard, Virginia City, November 7, 1955.

7. See Chapter 41 for additional details on tunnel and flume. The V-flume of the S. N. W. and L. Company transported lumber and cordwood to and through the water tunnel of the Virginia and Gold Hill Water Company (cut under the rim of the Carson Range above Tahoe) and followed down the eastern slope through Little Valley to the saddle at Lakeview Station between Washoe and Eagle valleys. Here flatcars on a spur track of the Virginia and Truckee Railroad transported the lumber and cordwood directly to Virginia City. Author's note.

8. Incline Mountain, known as White Cliff in 1874. Refer Von Leicht-Hoffmann, *Topographical Map of Lake Tahoe,* 1874.

9. "The present white boathouse at Sand Harbor was built in the 1880's for logging operations, and made into a clubhouse by Walter Hobart, Jr." Ernest H. Pomin, Tahoe City, August 6, 1954; Mrs. James Leonard, Virginia City, November 7, 1955.

10. Washoe County Court House, Reno, Nevada, Douglas County Court House, Minden, Nevada, tax rolls, 1880-81-82. Original locators on Hobart property: J. B. Rice, D. V. Pritchard, J. H. Maddox, S. Smith, and W. Hodges.

11. See Chapter 43 for Pacific Wood, Lumber and Fluming Company.

12. George D. Oliver, Carson City, October 3, 1954.

13. Mrs. James Leonard, Virginia City, November 7, 1955.

14. *Carson and Tahoe Lumber and Fluming Company, Land Record Register,* Will M. Bliss, San Francisco, January 6, 1953.

15. Hobart Mills, see Chapters 33 and 47. "Captain Overton decreed there would never be a church or saloon in Hobart and there never was." Mrs. James Leonard, Virginia City, November 7, 1955.

16. Pacific Wood, Lumber and Fluming Company comparison figures: 15,000,000 board feet and 75,000 cords of wood in the year 1876 alone. *Sierra-Nevada Lakes,* George and Bliss Hinkle, p. 310.

17. Based on a story told by Ernest Henry Pomin, Tahoe Pines, May 8, 1953.

18. Mrs. Jane Barnes Clark, Reno, October 25, 1955; Mr. Ellis Folsom, Carson City, November 7, 1955; Mrs. James Leonard, Virginia City, November 7, 1955.

19. John Drum, Jr., Chinquapin Cove, Lake Tahoe, August 22, 1955.

20. Ibid.

21. Ibid.

22. Ibid. See Early Marine History of Lake Tahoe section.

23. J. P. Obexer, Homewood, November 2, 1955.

24. "3,000 acres, more or less, taking in Marlette Lake's shoreline, Marlette Lake, and Hobart Creek's watershed, were retained by the Hobart estate." Mrs. James Leonard, Virginia City, November 7, 1955. "The estate (Hobart) kept 3,000 acres." George D. Oliver, Carson City, October 3, 1954.

25. Refer Early Marine History of Lake Tahoe section.

Chapter 43—Crystal Bay

1. Based on a news story by H. J. Ramsdell, *New York Tribune,* September 16, 1875.

2. General Seneca Hunt Marlette. See chapters 26 and 41. Wasson was the original name given Mount Rose in 1860's. Also spelled "Wasoo," "Wassan" and "Wasan," a corruption of Washoe.

3. Gilman Nathaniel Folsom; born in East Corinth, Maine, August 15, 1829, he married Priscilla Tibbitts in 1855 and they emigrated to California, settling at Jenny Lind, Calaveras County, in January, 1857. Here Folsom operated a lumber yard and in 1860 moved to Big Tree Ranch, Silver Valley, then Washoe Valley in 1861, where he established the Old Central Mill at Washoe City with James Norcross as partner. Later they built other mills, among them the "Little Bangor." Floods and fires wiped out his holdings, Folsom losing $150,000 alone on his Truckee Meadows operation. Finally he moved into the Tahoe basin—Crystal Bay, and then Hobart. In his lifetime Folsom was Senator from Douglas County, Nevada; a member of Constitutional Convention, County Commissioner and Justice of the Peace in Carson City. Mr. and Mrs. Ellis J. Folsom, Carson City, November 2, 1955.

4. The diary of Gilman N. Folsom. Mr. and Mrs. Ellis J. Folsom, Carson City, November 2, 1955.

5. See Incline chapter 42.

6. *Truckee Republican,* July 7, 1884.

7. "There was no road into Incline from the Hot Springs along the lake previous to the turn of the century. It was a pack trail only. Three or four emigrant wagons were discovered by Robert Montgomery Watson in the late 1880's abandoned at Crystal Bay after having been pulled over the mountain from Washoe Valley by oxen to Tahoe several decades earlier. They could go no further, and the wagons later burned in a forest fire." Robert H. Watson, October 23, 1955, Lake Forest.

8. Refer *Reno Evening Gazette,* August 21, 1887.

9. Mr. and Mrs. Ellis Folsom, Carson City, November 2, 1955.

10. Mrs. James Mather Leonard (Jessie Hobart), Virginia City, November 4, 1955. Refer Agate Bay chapter 47.

Chapter 44—Brockway Hotel and Hot Springs

1. *Up and Down California,* William H. Brewer, August 25, 1863, p. 444. Also see Squaw Valley and Tahoe Vista chapters, 1 and 46.

2. Original partnership, Lambo and Wade, with a ranch and trading post fifteen miles north of old Mormon Station (Genoa), Nevada. Douglas County Court House, tax rolls, Minden, Nevada. Also see *Historical Souvenir, El Dorado County,* Oakland, Paolo Sioli, p. 117.

3. See Tahoe Park (Saxton's Mill), chapter 6.

4. See Agate Bay chapter 47.

5. *Truckee Republican,* August 28, 1869.

6. *Truckee Republican,* August 9, 1869; also see *Sacramento Union,* May 29, 1875, C. F. McGlashan, "Resources and Wonders of Tahoe." The James Cain mentioned is not placed as a member of the famous Bodie family.

7. Placer County tax rolls, Volume X, 1868-72, Auburn, California.

8. See Tahoe City and Observatory Point chapters, 4 and 49. An early trail, later a wagon road, followed the present highway closely. Refer George M. Wheeler's *Army Engineers Topographical Map* of 1876-77, front and back inside covers, this work.

9. Contemporary handbill, lobby of Glenbrook Inn, Glenbrook, Lake Tahoe.

10. *Truckee Republican,* June 16, 1883. Official post office records give October 22, 1888, as the date "Hot Springs" post office was established.

11. Robert H. Watson, Lake Forest, October 14, 1955.

12. A granite marker was placed by the Kidder and Ives survey party in the early 1860's and showed the Hot Springs to be in Nevada. Maps from 1874 forward correctly indicate Stateline one-half mile east of Brockway, but confusion existed into the 1890's. (Author's note.)

13. "Swimming and plunge baths" but no pool until the 1920's.

14. *Lake Tahoe and Chautauqua Improvement Company Brochure,* Reno, Nevada, 1893. Bancroft Library, Berkeley, California.

15. William Lindsey, Carson City, November 2, 1955.

16. Mrs. Velma Comstock Eden, Sacramento, California, May 4, 1955.

17. *California, Romantic and Beautiful,* James, 1941, p. 245.

18. "The present building was jacked up and moved. The original hot spring bubbled up on the shoreline near the bar when the building was in its original location, making it very handy for the bartender to serve hot drinks. We handed out keys and charged 25c for the use of the mineral baths. When the pump was not running we still could bathe with buckets of hot water from the springs." Mrs. Velma Comstock Eden, Sacramento, May 4, 1955.

19. An "amusement Casino" was built straddling the California-Nevada state line above and to the east of Brockway. Named Cal-Neva because of its location in the two states, it was originally constructed to resemble Frank Bacon's cabin in the play *Lightnin'*. Immense boulders flanked a running stream with planted trout and huge fireplace. Through the dance floor ran the state boundary line. After burning to the ground several times it has been rebuilt into a nationally famous gambling and entertainment center. To the north are clustered other palatial entertainment casinos: Bal Tabarin (Cal-Vada), the massive Tahoe Biltmore Hotel, Joby's Monte Carlo, Crystal Bay Club (Ta-Neva-Ho), Sierra Lodge, and Northshore Club (Cappy Ricks).

21. Gladys Comstock and her sister, Velma, daughters of Harry O. Comstock, were raised at Tallac and Brockway Hot Springs. Velma Lakes and Gladys Lake, southwest of Lake Tahoe, named after the two girls by their father. Refer Cascade Lake chapter 19.

Chapter 45—King's Beach

1. For the killing and burial of James Stewart see Chapter 4.

2. Story based on word of mouth version; Robert Montgomery Watson to his son, Robert H. Watson, and revised by author. R. H. Watson, Lake Forest, Lake Tahoe, October 12, 1955.

3. "Griffin had a steam-powered sawmill bordering Griff Creek, and an old boiler stood on 'Boiler Point' for years," Tevis Paine, Tahoe City, March 12, 1955. "Griffin's sawmill," *History of Placer County, California,* Oakland, 1882. Thompson and West.

4. Robert H. Watson, Lake Forest, October 4, 1955.

5. Ibid.

6. Ibid.

7. Ibid.

8. Joe King, Kings Beach, October 22, 1955.

Chapter 46—Tahoe Vista

1. Cherry de St. Maurice: irresistible harlot turned madam and practically "running" Sacramento, California, at the turn of the century. Owner of the "famous little black book," murdered for her jewels and money.

2. "Trail roads" followed the northern lakeshore of Lake Tahoe starting with the '49ers. In the 1860's the Dutch Flat Wagon Road, connecting with the Central Pacific as it moved eastward, used the Martis Valley, north Tahoe, Incline Summit route for pack trains bound for Virginia City, dropping to Washoe Valley in the vicinity of Franktown, Nevada. See Chapters 1 and 42. Von Leicht and Hoffmann's *Topographical Map of Lake Tahoe and Surrounding Country,* 1874, and Wheeler's *Survey Map,* 1876-77.

3. See Squaw Valley chapter 1.

4. Wright's Pine Grove Station, not to be confused with Griffin's House and Saloon one mile east.

5. See Chapter 42.

6. Edward Paine, brother of Charles W. Paine, took over management in 1914 for three seasons. Ref. Tevis Paine, Tahoe City, March 12, 1955.

7. Ibid.

8. Ibid.

9. *San Francisco Examiner,* June 29, 1913.

10. *Lake Tahoe,* Claire MacDonald, private printing, 1929.

Chapter 47—Agate Bay

1. Washoe Indians first named the valley Tim-i-lick.

2. *Sacramento Daily Union,* August 26, 1863. Also see *Sierra-Nevada Lakes,* George and Bliss Hinkle, p. 273, and W. F. Edward's *Tourists' Guide and Directory of the Truckee Basin,* Truckee, 1883, pp. 100-102.

3. *Up and Down California,* William H. Brewer, New Haven, 1930.

4. *Sacramento Daily Union,* August 26, 1863.

5. Agate Bay quarry, still in use today.

6. Sherman Day, *"Report of a Survey of a Portion of the Eastern Boundary of California and of a Reconnaissance of the Old Carson-Johnson Immigrant Roads Over the Sierra Nevada,"* Sacramento, 1855, in Pamphlets on California, Bancroft Library, Vol. XXVI, Number 28. *Place Names of California,* Gudde, "The Whitney Survey gave the name Agate to the Bay" (sic).

7. See Early Marine History of Lake Tahoe section.

8. Mr. and Mrs. James Leonard, Virginia City, November 7, 1955. Robert H. Watson, Lake Forest, August 22, 1955.

9. Robert H. Watson, Lake Forest, August 23, 1955.

10. Ibid.

11. Newspaper clipping, George D. Oliver, Carson City, October 5, 1954.

Chapter 48—Carnelian Bay

1. *The Mystery of the Savage Sump,* Sam Davis, Bancroft Library, Berkeley, California. Also see *Sierra-Nevada Lakes,* George and Bliss Hinkle, Bobbs Merrill, 1949, for condensed version, revised here. Sam Davis' yarn is probably the most extravagant tale ever fabricated around the theory that subterranean outlets existed connecting

Lake Tahoe with the Comstock Lode. Geologists scoff at the idea. Davis, known as the "Oracle of the Sagebrush" and accepted in the 1880's as Washoe's leading pundit, undoubtedly based his fabrication on the *Sacramento Union's* news-pieces carried in the December 7, 1866, and July 31, 1883, editions.

2. *Sacramento Union,* July 31, 1883.

3. No foundation in fact has ever been established linking the waters of Lake Tahoe with the Virginia City mines. See *Carson City Appeal,* July 28, 1883, for their interpretation.

4. "Manzanita Promontory," also "Flick's Point," ref. Tevis Paine, Tahoe City, March 12, 1955. For naming the bay, see *Up and Down California* (1860-64), William W. Brewer, and *California Place Names,* Gudde, p. 57.

5. *Railroad Gazeteer,* Sacramento, 1871, pp. 122-123.

6. Dr. Bourne's original "Hygenic Establishment" on Sansome Street, San Francisco, in the 1860's, *Diary of Gilman Nathaniel Folsom,* Ellis Folsom, Carson City, Nevada, September 19, 1955.

7. *San Francisco Alta,* August 22, 1870.

8. *Truckee Republican,* August 18, 1872.

9. Ibid.

10. For Brockway "Carnelian Bay Hot Springs" see Brockway chapter. "Carnelian (cornelian) stones formed from gobs of pine pitch lying in lake over the years and swept up on the beach after southeast storms." Ben Callender, Homewood, October 21, 1954. "Smoothly worn variegated pebbles," *History of Placer County, California,* 1882, Thompson and West. "Variegated waxy quartz," *California Place Names,* E. G. Gudde, 1949.

11. Changed by public request to Cornelian Bay Hotel in summer of 1875. See *Truckee Republican,* July 8, 1875.

12. For other outsize agricultural wonders see Glenbrook and Lake Forest chapters, 39 and 50.

13. George D. Oliver, Carson City, Nevada, September 19, 1954.

14. Headstones Tahoe City Cemetery, Lake Tahoe. Harry Johanson, Tahoe City, May 6, 1954.

15. Carnelian Bay Improvement Company Brochure, 1910. Also "L. P. Delano building a high class Club House" (sic), *California, Romantic and Beautiful,* George Wharton James, 1913.

16. Refer Early Marine History of Lake Tahoe.

17. Orin Branch, Tahoe Vista, September 11, 1954.

Chapter 49—Dollar's Point

1. "Land squatter Griffin never changed his clothes and was considered 'lousy,' therefore point was named after him." Ernest Henry Pomin, Tahoe Park, May 18, 1955. Other explanations of the point's naming: "The waters off the promontory were 'lousy' with trout, hence 'Lousy Point'." Robert H. Watson, Lake Forest, September 2, 1955. "If we can just get around that lousy point," credited to Captain J. A. Todman while navigating the *Tod Goodwin* during the normally heavy afternoon chop found on the water here. George D. Oliver, September 24, 1954.

2. Chinquapin, also Chinkapin. Point so named by the Washoe tribe for the scrub trees with edible nuts they found growing there and called Chinquapin.

3. Also refer *Truckee Republican,* September 18, 1872.

4. *Register, Land and Deed Records:* C. and T. L. and F. Company, William M. Bliss, Piedmont, California, November 14, 1953. "Captain A. W. Pray, Rube Saxton and J. Lubeck also logged on Point in the 1880's." Robert H. Watson, Lake Forest, October 2, 1955.

5. *Truckee Republican,* June 28, 1887.

6. "Wychwood," also "Witchwood." Matt Green, Sacramento, November 21, 1953.

7. Refer Emerald Bay chapter 18.

8. Refer Tahoe City chapter 4.

Chapter 50—Lake Forest

1. Homer D. Burton's holding known variously as "Island Farm Ranch," "Island House," "Burton's Island Farm," and "Tahoe Island Farm." *Railroad Gazeteer,* Sacramento, 1871, pp. 122-123. Wheeler's *Topographical Map of the Lake Tahoe Region,* 1876-77.

2. Burtons Island: Actually only a small, low-lying island at high lake level.

3. Robert H. Watson, Lake Forest, September 14, 1955.

4. *Sacramento Union,* June 15, 1890.

5. See Chapters 18 and 27 for comparison stories of these men.

6. *Railroad Gazeteer,* Sacramento, 1871.

7. George D. Oliver, Carson City, October 11, 1954.

8. Ibid. (Revised.)

9. Ibid.

10. Ibid.

11. For a more factual account of the battle see *Sierra-Nevada Lakes,* George and Bliss Hinkle, pp. 163-69.

12. Robert H. Watson, Lake Forest, September 21, 1955.

13. *Sacramento Union,* June 15, 1890.

14. See "Early Marine History of Lake Tahoe" section.

15. "Homer D. Burton became known as the 'Chrize sake' man due to his habit of prefacing conversations with the expletive." Robert H. Watson, September 21, 1955.

16. Antone Russi used some of the rooms in Burton's old home for churning butter and racking his cream cans. He also had a large holding in Blackwood Creek to the south. Frank X. Walker obtained his start with Russi as a milker. In 1910, after having owned Russi's property for more than a decade, he sold a parcel which included the Burton home to Dr. George Briggs of Sacramento. Matt Green subdivided this acreage calling it Tahoe Island Park and later it was resubdivided by Henry Droste of the Tahoe Realty (who had the first real estate office on the western side of the lake) into Lake Forest. R. H. Watson, March 4, 1958.

17. A post office was not officially established under the name Lake Forest until April 16, 1947. Post Office Records, Washington, D. C.

18. Robert H. Watson, September 25, 1955.

Chapter 51—The Great Bonanza Road to Washoe

1. James E. Birch: pioneer stage line operator and first president of the California Stage Company. Refer *Express and Stagecoach Days in California,* O. O. Winther, 1936, p. 91.

2. *Mountaineering in the Sierras,* Clarence King, 1872, pp. 212-215.

3. Debate continues on the route taken by the Stevens-Townsend-Murphy horseback party over the western Sierra upon reaching Tahoe in November of 1844. George and Bliss Hinkle, in *Sierra-Nevada Lakes,* have the group "probably passing over the mountains via Squaw Valley," ignoring entirely the important fact that the well equipped young pioneers (Daniel Murphy, Mrs. Townsend, Miss Ellen Murphy, John Murphy, Oliver Magnan (Magnent) and Mrs. Townsend's servant, Francis Deland) were the first white people to set foot on the shores of Tahoe and discover the lake's outlet. George R. Stewart, in his *The Opening of the California Trail,* contends the horseback party moved over what is now McKinney Creek Pass (Burton's) to the Middle Fork of the American River by way of Rubicon River. As the group took 25 days to go from Truckee Lake Creek's junction with the Truckee River to Tahoe and over the mountains to Sutter's Fort in Sacramento Valley, it is equally plausible to believe that they continued along the lakeshore to Lake Valley and crossed over what would become the Johnson cut-off, thence down the South Fork of the American River.

4. John Calhoun Johnson: original trans-mountain mail carrier, opening and marking out what became "Johnson's cut-off" (Echo Summit). He once made the Placerville-Carson run in 26½ hours. Johnson became a Colonel in the United States Army and was killed by Apaches on September 13, 1876, in Arizona Territory. Refer *Placer Mountain Democrat,* September 23, 1876, and Paolo Sioli (*Historical Souvenir, El Dorado County,* p. 210); also *History of Nevada,* Mack, p. 123. See Cave Rock, Meeks Bay, and Lake Valley chapters for more on J. C. Johnson.

5. *History of Nevada,* Myron Angel, p. 103.

6. Luther(s) Pass: named for Ira M. Luther, who in 1854 became the first man to pass over the route with a wagon and team. Mormon Station was founded by John Reese and Stephen A. Kinsey, July 4, 1851. On September 20, 1855, the name was changed to Genoa after the birthplace of Columbus (Wren, p. 25). Also *The Overland Mail,* LeRoy R. Hafen, p. 64.

7. Daggett's Pass (Kingsbury): refer Lake Valley and Friday's Station chapters.

8. Placerville: "Old Dry Diggings" (1848-50); also "Ravine City," then "Hangtown" becoming Placerville after 1854.

9. John "Snowshoe" Thompson: born in Norway, April 30, 1827, Thompson emigrated to California during the Gold Rush. He was the first to fabricate and use Norwegian type "snowshoes" (skis) in the Far West. Eight to 10 feet long and 4 to 6 inches wide, they were described as "light, elastic wood weighing 25 pounds with a center strap for holding the boot." Thompson used a single, thick sapling instead of ski poles, balancing it in front of him, or sitting on the pole and using it as a brake when running down hill. He is credited with being the first to use "dope" (tallow) on skis. In January of 1856, he made his first mail run (Placerville to Carson City) carrying 100 pounds of mail and taking 3 days to cover the 90 miles. He never wore winter clothes and had a mountain man's true sense of direction when he could not guide himself by the stars. In storms it was his practice to dance a jig on a high rock to keep from freezing. When Thompson was 43 years old he raced 1,600 feet down Silver Mountain in 21 seconds, and one-half mile in 31 seconds (1870). He also set a jumping record of 170 feet. "Snowshoe" was never known to carry firearms on his winter mail runs and his closest brush with death came in Hope Valley when he skied slowly through a pack of timber wolves who were tearing at the carcass of a frozen deer. If he had deviated from his path they would have attacked. Thompson was never reimbursed by the Government for his mail carrying. He died on May 15, 1876, at his ranch in Diamond Valley (Woodford's). Two crossed skis mark his grave on a marble tombstone in Genoa cemetery. *The Big Bonanza,* Dan DeQuille; *Mining and Scientific Press,* October 9, 1886; *Historical Souvenir, El Dorado County,* Paolo Sioli, 1883; *History of Nevada,* Effie Mona Mack, p. 338; also refer Lake Valley chapter 26.

10. *Statutes of California,* 6th Session, 1855, pp. 180-181.

11. *Report of a Survey of a Portion of the Eastern Boundary of California and of a Reconnaissance of the Old Carson-Johnson Immigrant Roads Over the Sierra Nevada,* Sacramento, 1855; in pamphlets on California, Vol. XXVI, No. 28, pp. 81-96, Bancroft Library. Refer also to Lake Valley, Spooner Station and Summit Camp chapters 26 and 40.

12. Ibid.

13. *Sacramento Union,* April 27 and September 20, 1855; *Alta California,* November 11, 1855.

14. Actually the emigrants' Conestoga wagons and pack trains had been crossing on the Johnson cut-off since '49, so the stage coach "feat" was not incredible. Refer Lake Valley and Spooner Station chapters 26 and 40. See *Sacramento Union,* June 15, 1857, and July 8, 1857.

15. The men: J. G. McCallum, T. Foster (Foster's Halt), J. B. Crandall, C. Stump, H. Cheatum, William M. Cary (Cary's House, Placerville), and "Mr. Reporter." Eight men were actually said to have made the trip but only 7 were noted. *Sacramento Union,* June 11, 1857.

16. William Keyser: "the first stage driver to

rein a coach and four east to west over the Johnson route on a regular run." George D. Oliver, Carson City, October 22, 1954. Theo. F. Tracy (also F. F.), and his brother, E. W. Tracy, initiated "Trac(e)y's Carson Valley Express from Placerville by way of Lake Valley." *Sacramento Union,* June 17, 1857.

17. James H. Nevett (also given as Joseph H.). Present Echo Summit was first "Johnson Trail Summit or Hill" (1848-52), Mickey Free Point (1852-55), Nevett's Pass or Summit (1857-59), Hawley's Summit (1859-61), Osgood's Summit (1861-70), "Big Hill Summit" (1880's).

18. "The trip did not appear to be as happy as anticipated—got out and pushed—walked, removed obstacles—road so rough they often bumped their heads against the coach's roof." *Surmounting the Sierras,* Chester Lee White, California Historical Society Quarterly, VII (March, 1928), pp. 14-15. Also refer Lake Valley chapter 26.

19. James Green's "Junction House passed to Alphonzo Nott (incorrectly Knott), then became Pickett's, who gave his name to Pickett Peak.

20. John Cary's water-powered sawmill located near the present site of Woodford's in 1853-54.

21. *Sacramento Union,* June 15, 1857; also *Surmounting the Sierras,* C. L. White.

22. Ibid.

23. "Length of line will be 2 miles (east slope of Johnson's Summit into Lake Valley) on a grade of 5 per cent and when it is finished stages will go over at an easy trot." *Sacramento Union,* June 15 and July 8, 1857. Also "William M. Cary and A. M. Johnson were awarded the road contract to complete." *Sacramento Union,* November 30, 1858.

24. George D. Oliver, Carson City, October 5, 1954. Contrarily "Five passengers and mails ran from Carson to Placerville in 12 hours—fastest time on wheels—passengers were not obliged to get out of coach the entire trip to get along." *Sacramento Union,* July 18, 1857.

25. Silver was discovered in the summer of 1858 on the eastern slopes of Mount Davidson (Sun Mountain/Peak) and the Comstock Lode in the spring of 1859." (Paxson.) Refer also Squaw Valley chapter 1.

26. *Placerville Herald,* January 12, 1859.

27. *Up and Down California,* William H. Brewer, p. 439.

28. *History of Nevada,* E. M. Mack, pp. 354-355. Also attributed to Mark Twain.

29. Ralph H. Cross Library, Berkeley, California. Placerville-Carson Road file, August 3, 1954.

30. *My Playhouse Was a Concord Coach,* May Hélène Bacon Boggs, private printing, 1942.

31. Refer Edgewood and Lake Forest chapters 32 and 50.

32. *A Peep at Washoe,* J. Ross Browne, Harpers Magazine, December, 1860, and February, 1861.

33. *An Editor on the Comstock Lode,* Wells Drury.

34. *Sacramento Union,* April 2, 1860, via Union telegraph.

35. *History of Nevada,* E. M. Mack.

36. Ibid. Refer also *Sierra-Nevada Lakes,* Hinkle, pp. 277-78, for additional statistics.

37. Irad Fuller Berry: pre-empted land at Strawberry Valley in May of 1858; sold to Charles E. McClane (Pioneer Stage Lines) in January, 1866, who deeded to Thomas Benton Rowland in 1867. Charles Watson was landlord of Strawberry Station after Rowland. R. H. Cross Library, October 18, 1954. Refer also to Al Tahoe chapter 29.

38. *Virginia Daily Union,* March 14, 1864, and *Historic Spots in California, Valley and Sierra Counties,* Rensch and Hoover, pp. 71-72.

39. *Six Horses,* Banning and Banning (not specifically referring to Slippery Ford).

40. *Mountaineering in the Sierras,* Clarence King, 1872, pp. 212-215.

41. Ibid.

42. G. D. Oliver, Carson City, October 5, 1954.

43. *Six Horses,* Banning and Banning; also G. D. Oliver.

44. Judge Peter Shields, December 3, 1955.

45. Ibid.

46. Ibid, as related by John Woods.

47. Concord coaches were built by Abbott-Downing and Company, Concord, New Hampshire. Oval in shape, ash bodied, they were a modified enlarged form of 19th century design. Nine passengers were accommodated on the inside and 12 more on top, with "dickey seats" behind the driver. The coaches weighed 2,500 pounds light, cost $1,200 to $1,500 each. Forward and after "boots" held the mail, express and baggage. The "mud wagon" was a lower, lighter coach, generally substituted in mountain travel. Both were slung on leather supports (thoroughbraces). *Six Horses,* Banning and Banning; *Express and Stagecoach Days in California,* Winther, pp. 97-98, and *Three Years in California,* J. D. Borstwick, p. 103.

48. *Roughing It,* Mark Twain (Samuel Clemens).

49. *Reading Independent,* C. C. Bush, September 5, 1878.

50. *My Playhouse Was a Concord Coach,* Boggs, 1942.

51. Ibid.

52. *An Editor on the Comstock Lode,* Wells Drury.

53. *Pioneers of El Dorado,* Charles Elmer Upton, Placerville, 1906.

54. *A Peep at Washoe,* J. Ross Browne.

INDEX

A

Abbott, Daniel, 80, 92
Academy of Science,
    (San Francisco), 137
Adams, John, 180
Adams, Maude E., 99
Agassiz, Camp, 145
Agassiz, Louis, 145
Agate Bay, 325, 339–342
    (See also "Bay City," Lake Tahoe)
Alameda-Santa Cruz Railway, 41
Albany, New York, 204
Alexander, Douglas C., 117
Alice Lake, 141
Allen, Scotty, 53
Allison Engines, 442
Almon "Jim Poker" Taylor's
    Ranch, 215
Aloha Lake, 177
Alpine County, 19, 207
Alta California, 267
    (See also San Francisco
    Daily Alta California)
Al Tahoe; (Dean & Van Wagener's/
    Rowland's Station), 41, 186, 187,
    203–210, 243, 389, 400, 455, 459
Al Tahoe Development Company, 210
Al Tahoe Hotel (and Water
    Company), 209, 210
Al Tahoe Post Office, 210
Alverson, Frank Brockway,
    327, 333, 336
Alverson, Nellie Staples Dow
    Comstock, 327
Alverson's—, 327, 329
Alvord, William, 33
Amalfi Drive (Italy), 318
American River—North Fork, 28
    Middle Fork, 1
    South Fork, 147, 148, 176, 360,
    364, 365, 373, 461
American Tragedy, 142
Anderson, Charles, 319
Anderson, Clem, 86
Anderson, George, 209
Angel, Myron; History of Nevada; 303
Angelus Temple, 96
Angora Lakes, 150
Angora Peak, 143, 150, 466
Antone Meadow(s), 358
A Place in the Sun, 142
"Appian Way of the West," 368
Applegate, Josiah H., 167, 173
Arabian Pool, 318
Arena, Danny, 441
Arizona border, 28
Argonauts, 113, 368
Arlington Hotel, 106, 372
Arms, Ellery, 22
Armstrong—, 126
Armstrong, Jack, 287, 288
Armstrong, Miss Jessie, 131
Armstrong, Mrs. William H., 131
Armstrong's, 129, 131
Armstrong's (Glenbrook), 287
Armstrong, William Henry, family,
    129, 131
Armstrong, W. H., Jr., 131
"Army in Gray," 373
Ashe, R. Porter, 63

Aspen, Colorado, 10
Auburn, 48, 73, 175
Auburn County Hospital, 87
Audrain Reservoir, 176
    (Lake), 461
Audrain's Lodge, 378
Audrain(s) Station, 177, 189, 377, 378
Audrain, Thomas, 377, 378
"Aunt Liddy," 159, 167, 168, 169, 189,
    192, 193, 195
    (See also Mrs. Lydia Mark
    Clement)
Aurora, 112, 270
Austrian Tyrol, 10
Autan, 318
Autocar, 141
Averill, Adda, 208
Averill, John Wales, 237
Averills, 237
Avery, Captain D. W., 283, 396, 400
Azure (Gladys) Lake, 141

B

Babcock, Harry, 141, 436
"Baby Chick" Rock, 119
    (See also Hen and Chickens)
Bactrians, 223; see camels
Bailey, 283
Baker's Map of the Mining
    Regions, 462
Balancing Rock, 120
Bal Bijou, 220
    (See also Young's Bijou)
Baldwin, Anita M., 164, 165
Baldwin, Comstock and Lawrence,
    159, 161, 163
    (See also Comstock and Lawrence)
Baldwin, Elias Jackson "Lucky,"
    36, 85, 139, 145, 152, 154, 157, 159,
    164, 165, 167, 173, 180, 289, 327, 385,
    410, 418, 419, 423, 436
Baldwin Hotel (House), 445
    (See also Baldwin's Tallac House)
Baldwin Locomotive Works, 273, 403
Baldwin's Chicamauga, 415
Baldwin's sawmill, 159
Baldwin's Tallac House, (Hotel
    Tallac), 152, 156, 167, 209
Ballard, J., 445
Bancroft Publishing House, 462
Bank of California, 269, 270
"Bank Ring," 406
Banning, Major William, 275
Baranoff Island, 126
    (See also Emerald Isle)
Barbee, Stanley, 442
Bard of Avon, 262
Bardstown, 112
Barker, William Andrew, 63, 64
Barker(s) Pass, 64
Barker(s) Peak, 63, 64, 466
Barker(s) Meadow, 64
Barnes—, 287
Barnes, Gertrude, 287
Barnes, Jennie, 287
Barnetto, Lugi, 97
"Barnie"—, 61
"Barons of the Comstock,"
    141, 269, 279, 406
Barrett, Charles R., 265, 267

Barter, Captain Richard "Dick,"
    121, 122, 123, 125, 126, 135, 356,
    385, 389, 457
Bartlett, William; (Bartlett's Guide to
    California), 181, 361, 368, 461, 462
Barton, Emmy, 208
Barton, Himan (Heyman) Dana,
    195, 380
Barton, Hiram, "Hy," 195, 216, 379
Barton, Hiram; Home Ranch, 379
Barton, Mrs. Fannie Rowland, 208
Barton, Timothy Guy, 195, 379
Barton, William Delos, 105, 209, 379
Barton's—, 216
Barton's dairy, 208
"Basketry," 56
Basquette, Lina, 96
Bates, Minnie, 86, 87
"Battle of Pinnacle Mount," 233
"Battle of Pyramid Lake," 233
Battle of the Bulge, 47
"Bawker's," 63
    (See also Barker, W. A.)
Bay City (Lake Tahoe), 308, 342
    (See also Agate Bay)
Bay City (San Francisco), 63, 112, 152,
    175, 193, 225, 267, 393, 396, 407
    (See also San Francisco)
Bayley, A. A., 31, 325
Bayley, Alexander John, 23, 29, 33, 34,
    37, 39, 325, 326
Beal, Ed, 223
Bear Creek, 19, 21, 22, 28
Bear Den, 59
"Bear Slides," 309
Bear Trap, 15
Bear Valley, 20
Beatty, A. S., 267, 268
Bechdolt, Carl A., Jr., 62
Bechdolt, Carl Andrew, Sr., 45, 52,
    94, 163
Beecher, Clyde, 220
Bee, F. A., 366
"Bee's grapevine," 366
Belcher, Ernest, 96
Bell, Jack, 41, 431, 432, 433
Bell, Jack, (renegade), 197
Bellevue, 105, 106, 107
Bellevue Club House, 107
Bellevue Hotel, 107, 168, 418, 419, 436
Belmont, 113
Bemis, C. C., 395
Bence, Robert Lucius, 200, 209,
    242, 369, 384
Benham, M. T., 59
Ben Holladay's Island Cottage, 135
    (See also Holladays)
Bennett, Gladys Comstock, 329
Bennett, Maillard "Pete," 329
Benton and Phillips, 385
Benton, James "Doc," 31, 206, 207,
    269, 275, 282, 321, 326, 403, 445
Benton, Reverend J. A., 261
Benton's Stage Lines, 206, 445
Berry, Irad Fuller, 367
"Berry's" Station, 189, 365
    (See also Strawberry Station)
Bezoni, Johnny, 53
"Big Barn," 239
Big Bend, 22

"Big Blue," 193, 393, 411, 459
    (See also Lake Tahoe)
Big Bonanza (mining strike), 2
Big Bonanza Bar, 31
Big Bonanza Saloon, 38
Big Bonanza Saloon building, 38
Big Chief Camp, 14, 34
Big Chief "No Name," 14, 15, 16, 35
Big Deep of Tahoe, 460
"Big Four" (Central Pacific
    Railroad), 27, 57
"Big Four" (Comstock Lode),
    313, 316
Big Gorge, 15
    (See also Truckee Canyon)
"Big Hill" (Echo Summit), 168
Big Hill (Truckee Canyon), 23, 24, 25
Bigler, Governor "Honest John"/"Old
    John"/"Mandarin John," 205,
    461, 462, 463
Bigler, Lake, 1, 3, 5, 29, 257, 259, 268,
    293, 321, 461, 462, 463, 464
    (See also Lake Tahoe)
Bigler Lake outlet, 3
Bigler Lake Valley, 293
    (See also Lake Valley)
"Big Three," 440
Bigler Toll Road, 256
    (See also Johnson cut-off)
Big Meadow, 269
"Big Truckee Lake," 462
"Big Water," 143, 205, 251, 255,
    462, 463, 464
    (See also Lake Tahoe)
Bijou, 41, 117, 150, 168, 185, 186, 209,
    210, 211–220, 240, 289, 389,
    405, 413, 436, 438, 443, 455
Bijou House, 216
Bijou-Lake Valley railroad, 379
    (See also Lake Valley Railroad)
Bijou Pier, 215, 217, 443, 455
Bingham, Patrick, 85
Birch, Mr., 359
Birdsall, Fred K., 65
Bishop, Frederick Aubrey, 361
Bishop, Joseph, 95
Bissell(s), William, 61, 436
Black Bart, 197
Blackmore, Bill, 277
Black Rock Desert, 357
Blacks—, 73
Black, Spencer, 61
Blackwood Canyon/Creek/Gorge, 63,
    64, 65, 67, 69, 72, 91, 92, 211,
    358, 458
Blackwood, Hampton Craig, 63, 64
Blair, John, 362
Blair, Mrs. John, 371
Blair, Ned, 198, 373
Blaisdel, Honorable H. G., 389
Blanchard—, 145
Blanding, Gordon, 436
Blethen, Charlie, 308
Bliss and Yerington, 89, 92, 186, 209,
    219, 270, 273, 291, 301, 308, 417
Bliss, Charles Tobey "Bud," 42, 427
Bliss, Duane LeRoy, 51, 111, 120, 239,
    263, 270, 275, 279, 283, 288, 300, 351,
    353, 385, 393, 403, 406, 408, 411, 427,
    457
Bliss estate, 311

Bliss family, 33, 45, 51, 61, 131, 220,
    284, 289, 385, 423, 427, 431, 432, 433
Bliss, Hope, 427
Bliss interests, 159, 168, 358, 406
Bliss, Mrs. Duane LeRoy (Elizabeth
    Tobey), 120, 403, 427
Bliss railroad, 61
Bliss store (Tahoe City), 42
Bliss, Walter Danforth, 51, 107, 131
Bliss, Will M., 49, 427
Bliss, William Seth, 41, 45, 85, 215,
    407, 427, 433, 434
Bliss-Yerington-Mills combine, 171
    (See also C. & T. L. & F.
    Company)
Blue Lakes, 182
Boats (Lake Tahoe)
    Adenoid, 311
    Aileen, 436
    Alice, 437
    Amanda, 437
    Annie, 437
    Apache I, 311, 439
    Apache II, 244, 311, 439
    Arrow, 436
    Baby Skipalong, 442
    Belle Isle Bear Cats, 439, 440
    Bellevue, 386
    Bessie, 385
    Bluebird, 437
    Breathless, 442
    Brightbird, 59, 61
    Brockway, 437
    Burke's Barge, 398 (See also Pa-
        villion)
    Caroline, 386
    Catalina, 436
    Challenge, 385
    Challenger, 442
    Checog, 436, 440
    Cherokee, 439
    Chinquapin, 436
    Chipmunk, 436
    Chris Crafts, 440
    Colleen, 437
    Comanche, 439
    Comet, 439
    Consuelo, 436
    Corona, 436
    Dora, 399
    Dorothy, 437, 438
    Drinkwater, 436
    Edith Batty, 91, 211, 265, 358,
        385, 388, 389
    El Dorado, 385, 388, 389
        (See also Edith Batty)
    Ellen, 437
    Elsie, 436
    Elsie B., 439
    Emerald I, 31, 127, 151, 171, 206,
        269, 385, 391, 393, 394
    Emerald II, 289, 385, 386,
        416, 417, 429
    Eva, 39
    Firefly, 437
    Flash, 441
    Fleeter (Fleta), 36, 127, 385
    Floating Palace, 151, 319, 385, 398
        (See also Pavillion, Burke's
        Barge)
    Florence, 436

Boats—(Cont'd.)
    Florence M., 437
    Freddie, 39
    Friendship, 436
    Garizibio (Garazebio), 311, 438
    "Gar Wood," 74, 438, 440, 442
    Gazelle, 385
    Governor Blaisdel, 26, 31, 126, 171,
        206, 247, 268, 336, 385, 387
        389, 390, 391
    Governor Stanford, 28, 31, 37, 65,
        85, 95, 127, 151, 223, 225, 283,
        325, 349, 385, 386, 394, 395,
        396, 397, 398, 400
        409, 410, 413
    Greenwich Folly, 442 (See Baby
        Skipalong)
    Gypsy, 407, 437
        (See also Nomad I)
    Happy Day, 163, 436
    Hattie Belle, 94, 385, 418
    Hawaii Kai's, 442
    Hesperus, 437
    Hey-There's, 438, 440
    Hi-Yah, 385
        (See also Lady of the Lake)
    Hobo, 437, 438
    Hull Number 42, 427
    Hurricane IV, 442
    Idlewild, 67, 436
    Iron Duke, 26, 205, 265, 357, 385,
        386, 387, 400
    Jim, Jr., 440
    Kemah, 437
    Lady of the Lake, 437
    Lady of the Lake (Hi-Yah), 385, 407
    Letts-Go's, 440, 441
    Leviathan (S.S.), 311
    Lily Van, 129, 385, 410, 411, 413, 436
    Little Lucky, 441
    Lucky Strike II, 441
    Mabee Not I, 441
    Mabee Not II, 442
    Mahala, 413, 436
    Mamie, 385, 413, 414, 415, 418
    Mamie One—Twenty-Five, 415
    Marian B., 385, 433, 435
    Marin, 436
    Mary II, 437
        (See also Hesperus)
    Menina, 436
    Mercury ("Merc"), 442
    Meteor, 39, 85, 111, 127, 168, 209,
        215, 217, 247, 273, 275, 283,
        289, 349, 385, 386, 403, 404,
        405, 406, 407, 408, 409, 410, 417,
        419, 423, 427, 429, 434, 435
    Merrimac, 389
    Miduena, 436
    Minnie Moody, 385, 398, 399
    Miss Tahoe's, 440
    Mohawk, 439
    Mollie Bawn, 127, 385
    Monitor, 389
    Mount Rose, 437
    Myrno III (Reverie), 244, 437
    Nancy, 123, 125, 126, 385, 389
    Navajo, 440
    Nevada, 42, 79, 94, 115, 209, 289,
        350, 385, 418, 423, 425, 435
        (See also Tallac)

Boats—*(Cont'd.)*
  Niagara, 307, 325, 342, 385, 396, 400, 401, 403
  Nomad I, 407, 437
  Nomad II, 437
  Nyack, 437
  Osprey, 438
  Oregon, 427
  Orange Blossom, 311, 439
  Olive, 438
  Paiute, 439
  Pavillion, 39, 385, 396, 397, 398
    (See also *Floating Palace* and *Burke's Barge)*
  Pirate, 141, 436, 437
  President, 440
  Pride of the Lake, 358, 385
  Pronto I, 437
  Pronto II, 437
  Prospector, 437
  Psyche, 441
  Pueblo, 439
  Quit-Cha-Kiddin', 311, 433, 434, 437
  Ranjac's—, 440
  Red Wing, 438
  Rip Van Winkle, 437
  Rosalie, 163, 436
  Rubicon, 436
  S. A., 311
  Saxon, Jr., 442
  Sergeant, 440
  Shamrock, 437
  Sheik, 437
  Short Snorter, 442
  Sierra, 437
  Skipalong, 438
  Skipalong of California, 442
  Skylark, 437
  Solicitor, 437
  So-Long, 441
  Standard, 437
  Susie, 39
  Ta-ha-na, 436
  Tahoe, 42, 48, 69, 70, 79, 94, 107, 115, 120, 141, 246, 289, 329, 337, 348, 350, 385, 405, 410; (launching) 425, 427; (specifications) 429, 431; (sinking) 433, 434; 432, 435, 464
  Tahoe (Seattle mail boat), 435
  Tallac, 159, 289, 385, 410, 415, 418, 419, 423, 429
    (See also *Nevada)*
  Tecalote, 440
  Thelma, 437
  Thunderbird, 438
  Tod Goodwin, 81, 87, 284, 385, 408, 409, 410, 415, 423
  Tonsil, 311
  Transit, 85, 86, 385
  Truckee, 151, 171, 206, 247, 269, 321, 325, 385, 393, 394, 396, 398, 400, 418
  Uncle Sam, 442
  Viking, 437
  Viva, 437
  Walkurie, 437
  Washoe, 439
  Wasp, 438
  Water Wagon, 440
  Whoopee, 440

Boats—*(Cont'd.)*
  Wild Goose, 436
  Wildwood of Brockway, 437
  Will-Till, 437
  Wren, 436
  Ya-Ya, 311
Bodie, 270
Boiler Point, 336
Bonanza (period/days), 41, 112, 141, 168, 281, 289, 304, 308, 368
Bonanza Lines, 23, 34
"Bonanza Road to Washoe," 151, 169, 191, 201, 207, 237, 359–373
Bonanza Stage Lines, 23, 34
Bonanza turnpike, 373
Bonner, Charles, 269
Bonneville-Walker group, 17
Bonpland, Aimé Jacques Alexandre, 461
Bonpland, Lake, 360
  (See also Lake Tahoe)
Borland—, 180
Boston Creek, 347, 353
  (See also Watson Creek)
Boundary Bay, 222, 232, 395, 443
Boundary Point, 317
Bourne, Arthur K., 244, 442
Bourne, (Dr.), 347, 349, 350
Boyle, William "Bill," 43
Bradley, A. R., 67
Bradley, A. V., 326
Bradley, Charles, 131
Bradley, Katherine, 149
Branch family, 350
Branch, Mr.—, 445
Branch, Orin, 350
Brannon, William, 382
Breezes—, 74
Brewer, William H., 205, 319, 339, 341, 367, 443
Brigham, Dr. Charles Brooks, 139, 141, 142, 215, 217
Brikell and Krueger, 11, 13, 26
Brockliss—, 363
Brockliss, Annie, 240
Brockliss bridge, 379
Brockliss grade, 362
Brockway, 309, 318, 319–330, 394, 400, 425, 455, 457, 460
  (See also Brockway Hotel and Hot Springs)
Brockway Casino, 329
Brockway Hotel and Hot Springs, 319–330, 333, 345, 393, 448, 450
  (See also Campbell's Hot Springs)
Brockway golf course, 329
Brockway Hot Springs tally-ho coach, 327
Brockway-Tahoe Club, 329
Brockway Water Company, 329, 333
Brodehl, Captain Arthur Daniel, 385, 435
Brodehl, Captain Daniel Martin, 435
Brodehl, Donald, 435
Brooks, H. S., 65
Brooks, Morris, 336
Brougher, Elsie, 436, 439
Brown—, 185
Brown, Dr. Cabot, 62
Brown, Hillyer, 112
Brown, Phillip King, 436

Brown, Sam, "Long Haired/ Fighting," 197, 198
Brown, Samuel, 208
Browne, J. Ross, 203, 205, 365
Bruso, Johnny, 198
Bucke, Richard W., 1, 2
"Bucket of Blood," 67
Buck Lake, 93
Bucklands (see Fort Churchill), 233, 234
Buenaventura River, 460
Buffalo Lithia Springs, 129
Buffalo, New York, 418
Bullion Bend, 379
Buoy, Ramsdale, 175, 185, 205, 211, 389
Burke and Company, 232, 443
Burke and Small(s), 235, 236, 384, 443
Burke, Henry, 23, 24, 25, 29, 151, 319, 321, 385, 396, 397
Burk(e), Martin F. (Friday), 190, 231, 232, 235, 236, 239, 247
Burke, Mrs. M. K., 239
Burke, Widow, 239
Burke's estate, 239
Burke's land, 239
Burkhalter, Charles, 457, 460
Burlingame, 311
Burnham, James Henry, 175
Burton—, 321
Burton & Company, 91
Burton, "Captain" Homer D., 91, 102, 211, 355, 356, 357, 358, 385, 388, 389
Burton Creek, 73, 81, 83, 85, 91, 353, 357
  (See also McKinney Creek)
Burton, Mrs. Homer D., 355
Burton(s) Canyon, 80, 91, 102
Burton's Island Farm (Hotel), 26, 355, 356, 358, 388, 389
Burton(s) Pass (Road), 75, 81, 82, 91, 93, 468
Bushes—, 74
Butler, Tim, 51
"Buttermilk Bay," 109
  (See also Meeks Bay)
Buttermilk Bonanza Ranch (farm) 236
  (See also Friday's Station)
Butterworth, S. F., 33
Bryson, Mrs. Sierra Nevada "Vade" Phillips Clark, 80, 377
  (See also Clark)

C

Caesar, 119
Cagwin, Hamden El Dorado, 176, 177
Cagwin Lake, 177
Cain, James, 319
Calaveras-Mammoth Grove Hotel, 203
California and Nevada newspapers, 351
California Coast, 141
California Fish (and Game) Commission, 105, 413, 446, 448, 450
California Legislature, 362, 450, 462, 464
California-Nevada boundary (south), 223, 225

California-Nevada boundary question (north), 321, 322, 323, 324, 327
California-Nevada fishing laws, 450
California-Nevada line (north), 321, 457
California-Nevada traffic, 221
California Products of Agriculture, 186
California Senate, 361
California Stage Company, 362
California State Boundary Survey party, 179
California (State) Legislature, 10, 27, 39, 177, 207
California, State of, 79, 80, 107, 120, 147, 149, 269, 323, 351, 359, 362, 363, 364, 368; (gold fields), 379, 403, 425, 454, 458, 460, 462, 463, 464 (See also Golden and Silver States)
California State Park System, 131, 142
California Street (S.F.), 343
California the Wonderful, 19
California-Utah Territory (Nevada) boundary, 362, 460
California Wagon Road Act (1855), 3, 191, 203, 361, 362
California Wagon Road exploratory party, 291
California Wagon Road report, 181
Calistoga, 267
Callender, Ben, 70, 74, 93, 94, 112, 448
Callender Brothers, 437
Callender, Howard, 74, 112
Caldwell and Dr. Fonda, 268
Camels, Bactrian, 223
Cameron, Jack, 390, 391
Cameron, Rob, 235
Cameron, Ronald D., 235
Campbell & Forbes, 33
Campbell, Amazia Franklin (Frank), 43
Campbell, Joseph B., 31, 34, 37, 43, 237, 351, 393, 397, 399, 407
Campbell, Lulu, 33
Campbell, Mrs. Joseph B., 42
Campbell's Custom House (Bar), 33, 106, 394, 408, 415, 418
Campbell's Hot Springs, 127, 195, 206, 269, 308, 318, 319, 321, 322, 323, 325, 394, 398, 400, 410, 415, 457, 460 (See also Brockway Hotel and Hot Springs)
Campbell, William "Billy," 319, 320, 321, 325, 347, 393
Camp Bijou, 285, 416
Camp Hobart, 303, 308 (See also Incline)
Camp Richardson, 52, 171–174, 183, 195, 438, 439, 455, 458
Canada, Dominion of, 2
Canadian Hill, 3
Cannon Corner, 48
Cape Horn (Johnson Pass) 181, 231
Cape Horn (Rubicon Springs) 80, 91
Capri's Blue Grotto, 119
"Captain Billy," 225, 396, 411 (See also W. W. Lapham)
"Captain Jim" (Washoe Chief), 185, 227, 463
Captain Storey's "Virginia Rifles," 233

Cardwell, James, 23, 24, 25, 31, 34
Cardwell's Curve, 25
Cardwell's stages, 269
Carl(e)—, 293
Carl(e) & Dubois, 293
Carnegie Museum, Pittsburgh, 56
"Carnelian," (Brockway), 325
Carnelian Bay, 15, 283, 306, 325, 343–350, 351, 356, 386, 405, 415, 459 (See also Cornelian Bay)
Carnelian Bay Hotel, 349, 350
Carnelian Bay Improvement Company, 350
Carnelian Creek, 349 (See also Cornelian)
Carnelian Hot Springs (Brockway), 347
"Carnelian Hot Sulphur Springs," 325
"Carnelian Point," (Brockway), 321
Carney, Catherine, 225
Carney, Ellen, 225
Carney, John, 225
Carney, Mrs. John, 225
Carney's Stateline House (Station), 225, 384
Carson & Colorado Railroad, 41
Carson & Tahoe Lumber & Fluming Company (C. & T. L. & F. Co.), 41, 59, 91, 99, 111, 120, 171, 186, 213, 215, 216, 219, 220, 241, 247, 249, 270, 271, 273, 283, 285, 288, 289, 291, 295, 308, 353, 381, 385, 393, 405, 423
Carson Canyon, (refer West Carson Canyon)
Carson, Christopher ("Kit"), 47, 269, 460
Carson City (Eagle Valley), 31, 36, 48, 49, 54, 55, 56, 85, 86, 105, 127, 151, 154, 171, 172, 177, 186, 191, 193, 197, 199, 205, 206, 207, 223, 225, 231, 233, 234, 235, 236, 241, 242, 243, 247, 249, 255, 261, 264, 267, 269, 270, 273, 275, 277, 279, 282, 283, 284, 285, 293, 299, 300, 303, 308, 309, 321, 323, 325, 342, 353, 353, 366, 372, 389, 390, 396, 400, 403, 406, 417, 427, 429, 443, 445, 457, 463
Carson City (Daily/Morning) Appeal, 86, 87, 127, 215, 236, 245, 247, 261, 285, 341, 347, 386, 388, 394, 403, 417, 419, 446, 457, 463
Carson City-Glenbrook stage line(s), 275
Carson City State Prison, 282
Carson Immigrant Ridge Road, 361
Carson Pass (Route), 2, 17, 47, 179, 182, 236, 360, 361, 362, 365 (See also Kit Carson Pass)
Carson Pass-Hope Valley Road, 361
Carson Range (of the Sierra), 2, 48, 168, 191, 210, 231, 237, 293, 299, 301, 304, 306, 317, 353, 355, 361, 379, 460
Carson River, 17, 233
Carson Sierra-Nevada, 257, 391 (See also Carson Range)
Carson terminal yard, 283

Carson Valley, 59, 172, 176, 180, 186, 192, 200, 203, 235, 237, 240, 256, 257, 269, 279, 357, 361, 362, 365, 382, 383, 411, 454
Carson Valley Toll Road (See Rufus Walton's Toll Road)
"Carsonites," 263, 391
Cary, John, 363
Cary, William M., 236
Cary's Mill, 362 (See also Woodford's)
Cascade Canyon, 156
Cascade Falls, 139 (See also Snow/White Cloud Falls)
Cascade House, 167–169
Cascade Lake, 137–142, 156, 177, 453, 454
Casey, H. E., 342
"Casnell's Mill," 91 (See also Colwell's Mill)
Casper, Gus, 115
Caspian Sea, 457
Casta's and Kaskill's, 265
Castle in the Sky, 135
"Castle Keep," 347
Catalina Channel, 456
Cathedral Park, 145
Cave Rock, 43, 133, 231, 239, 245, 250–256, 259, 311, 456, 467
Cedar Flat, 176
Cedar Grove, 66
Cedar Heart, 15
"Celerity wagons," 372
Celestials, 217, 391
Celio, Carlo Guisseppi, 195
Celio's, 186, 195, 196, 379
Celio's Dairy House, 378
Celio's Home Ranch, 186
Celio's Incorporated Lumber Company, 196
Celio's Mill(s), 186, 196
Centerville, 205, 339
Central American Desert, 235
Central Overland Stage, 277
Central Overland Trail (Route), 147, 191, 233, 234, 235, 245, 361, 363, 372
Central Pacific Railroad, 5, 17, 23, 28, 31, 57, 58, 59, 106, 109, 195, 199, 203, 222, 236, 269, 273, 309, 319; (depot) 321, 373, 391, 396, 407
Central Sierra Nevada, 17, 181, 361, 363, 461 (See also Sierra Nevada)
Chambers, David Henry, 80, 89, 94, 329
Chambers, George C., 89
Chambers' Lodge, 81–89, 94, 386, 400 (See also McKinney's)
"Champeen Liar of the Sierry," 192
Chandler, Edward "Bud," 22
Chandler, Miss Katherine, 21, 22
Chandos portrait of Shakespeare, 261
Chaney, Lon, 96
Chanslor, Mrs. Joseph, 163
Chapel of St. Francis of the Mountains, 149, 150
"Charlies," 371
Chesroon (Chesron), James C., 26
Childers, A., 274

Child, Judge John A., 361, 363
Chimney Rock, 241
China, 217, 294
Chinese, 216, 217, 270, 273, 285, 294
"Chinese Joe," 239
Chinquapin Cove, 107
Chinquapin Lodge, 112
Chinquapin Point, 28, 319, 351, 357
  (See also Observatory/Lousy/ Dollar's Point)
Chipmunk Flat Mine, 287
Chittenden, W. A., 200
Chorpenning, Major George, 361
Chubbuck, Cora, 208
Chubbuck, George Washington, 186, 200, 212, 213, 215, 216, 247, 384
Chubbuck, Mary Lovell, 247
Chubbuck, Rose, 208
Chubbuck's dairy, 247
Chubbuck's log ramp, 215
Chuck-a-luck, 318
Church and Jones, 206
Church, Elijah "Pop," 34, 35, 354
Cincinnati Commercial, 126, 268
"City by the Golden Gate," 113
Civil War, 256, 462
Clair, Colonel, 343, 344, 345
Claraville, 7, 35
Clark and Cross, 400
Clark brothers, 235
Clark, Captain Jack, 163, 436
Clark, Eli, 378
Clark, M. B., 235
Clark, Mrs. Sierra Nevada Phillips, 75, 76, 79, 80
  (See also Bryson)
Clark, Robert, 235
Clark, Tom, 85
Clarksville, 53, 64, 191
Clear Creek (Nevada), 141, 247, 267, 279, 291, 293, 294
Clear Creek Canyon, 247, 257, 269, 270, 291, 293, 294, 300
Clear Creek Grade, 468
Clear Creek-Eagle Valley Emigrant Road, 265
Clear Creek Grade, 269, 273, 275, 279, 429, 468
Clear Creek V-flume, 270, 279, 283, 291, 294, 300
Clear Creek Station (Brockliss Grade), 362
Clear Creek Toll Road (Grade), 159, 172, 206, 267, 294, 468
Clear Lake, 436
Clear Lake (El Dorado County), 362
Cleland, James, 349, 356
Clemens, Samuel, 235, 265, 267
  (See also Mark Twain)
Clement, Ephraim ("Yank"), 86, 103, 151, 159, 167, 168, 171, 183, 189, 190, 192, 193, 195, 356
  (See also "Yank")
Clement, Lydia D. Mark, 159, 167, 168, 169, 192, 195
  (See also Percival and "Aunt Liddy")
Clement's, 169
"Cliff's Kohling Station," 67
Coachmen, 371

Coast Range, 103
  (See also Pacific Coast Range)
Coates family, 378
Cobb, W. A. B., 279
Coburn—, 17
Coburn, Guy, 163
Coburn's Station, 17, 57, 58, 339
  (See also Truckee)
Cogel family, 244
Coggins—, 6
Cohen, Abraham, 54, 56
Cohen, Philip C., 220
Cohn, "Fatty," 106
Colboth, Lou, 267
Cold Creek, 197, 198, 199, 200, 212
Cold Springs, 233, 234
Cold Stream, 27
Cole, Harvey, 172
Coleville, 47
Colfax, 317
Colfax, Schuyler, 371, 372
College of (the) Pacific, 94
Coloma, 109
Colorado, 277
Colt sixguns, 105, 167, 233
Colwell, Albert, 92
Colwell, Augustus, 91, 92, 95, 103, 208
Colwell boys, 92, 93, 94
Colwell, Elmer, 92
Colwell, George, 80, 92, 94
Colwell, Hattie Belle, 107, 418
Colwell, Ralph Lewis, 69, 80, 95, 106, 107, 385, 418
Colwells—, 80, 107
Colwell's Mill, 91
Comer's Fish Ranch, 443
Commons, 36, 48, 393
  (See also Tahoe City Commons)
Comryn, Walter "Red", 129, 413
Comryn, Mrs. Walter, 129
Comstock and Lawrence, 161, 164
  (See also Lawrence and Comstock/ Lawrence and Company)
Comstock and Sherman, 329
"Comstock Big Four," 316
  (See also "Big Four")
Comstock Club, 459
Comstock, George Lord Mortimer, 154, 165
Comstock, Gladys, 141
Comstock, Harry Oswald, 51, 141, 165, 174, 288, 289, 327, 329, 333, 423
Comstock (Lode), 1, 2, 7, 26, 76, 152, 183, 192, 194, 196, 198, 203, 211, 231, 239, 245, 247, 249, 265, 267, 270, 275, 288, 289, 299, 301, 303, 309, 316, 343, 347, 363, 364, 365, 368, 443
Comstock, Mrs. Harry O., 309
Comstock, Velma, 141
"Comstockers"—, 269
Concord coach, 159, 161, 206, 210, 367, 371, 372, 438
Conestoga wagons ("sail-tops"), 5, 181, 191, 205, 367, 368
Confederacy, 205 (See also Union)
Confederate, 256
Confederate officer, 373
Conference Point, 249
"Congress water," 149
Conkling, Roscoe, 35

Connors, George, 64
Conolley, Annie (Anna), 220
Conolley, William F., 220
Conolley's, 216, 220
Conolley's Bijou Inn, 220
Consolidated, 438
Consolidated Virginia mine, 58, 315
Coombs, Walter, 345
Copeland family, 174
Copeland, John C. "Cope," 173, 174
Copeland, Nellie, 173, 174
Copeland's Grove, 174
Copeland's Grove Hotel, 174
Copenhagen, 133
Copples Station, 360
Coquette Isle, 126, 127
  (See also Emerald Isle)
Cornelian Bay, 29
  (See also Carnelian Bay)
Cornelian Creek, 349
"Cornelian Springs Sanatoria," 347
Cornish steam pumps, 275, 309
Cortinas, Jose, 456
Cosumnes Digger Indian, 463
Cosumnes River, 217
Cothrin Cove, 64
Cothrin, William Samuel, 64
Cothrin's Store, 64
Coulten, J. H., 461
Council Grove, 360
Council Rock, 149
County Wagon Road Directors, 363
  (See also Wagon Road Directors)
"Cowboy's Inn," 215
Cowen, Joseph, 159
Cox, E. R., 259
Coy, Benjamin F., 393, 444, 445
Coyote Flat, 216
Coyot's 265
Craig, Paul, 131
Cramer, William, 261
Crandall, Colonel Jarad B., 183, 192, 362, 367
Crandall-Sunderland and Company, 362, 363
Crandall's Pioneer Stage Line, 363
Cranmer, Jack, 394, 405, 410, 416
Crater Lake, 457, 460
Craven, Frank, 171
Craven, Harriet Price, 145
Crocker, Aimeé Ashe Gillig Gouraud Miskinoff Galitzine, 66
Crocker, Charles, 33
Crocker home, 66
Crocker, Judge Edwin B., 66
Crocker, Mrs. Edwin B., 63, 65, 66
Crocker's—, 21
"Croesus of the Coast," 121
Crofut's New Overland Tourist and Pacific Coast Guide, 209
Crook, Captain, 357
"Crown chimneys," 133
Crystal Bay, 239, 306, 311, 313–318, 325, 336, 399, 410, 448
Crystal, George Iweis, 317
Crystal Mine, 225
Curry, Joe, 163
Curtis Conqueror engine, 442
Curtola, Lawrence, 52
Cushing, Alexander, 10

Custom House, 31, 36, 37, 43
  351, 399
Custom House wharf, 42, 349, 391, 396,
  403, 407, 415, 418
Cuthbert—, 129
Cuthbert's Camp, 129
Cutthroat trout, 61, 443
  (See also Lake Tahoe trout)

D

D. L. Bliss State Park, 120
Daily State Register, 463
  (See also Nevada *Daily State
  Register)*
Daggett, Dr., 183, 225
Daggett Pass (Trail), 171, 179, 183,
  193, 194, 197, 231, 233, 235,
  236, 239
Daggett(s) Ravine, 191, 192, 198, 231
  (See also Daggett Pass)
Dahl, Knute, 425
Daily California Chronicle, 385
Daily Nevada Tribune, 247
Dalles, Sir Edward, 446
Daly, Pat, 409
Damascus, 3
Dan De Quille, 363
  (See also William Wright)
Dangberg, August "Dutch Fred," 243
Dangberg, Fred, 243
Darling—, 339
Darrington, Levi, 377
Darrington, "Zack," 177, 377, 378
Dashaway Hall, 215
Dat-So-La-Lee, 54, 55, 56
  (See also Keyser, Louisa)
David—, 135
Davies, Ralph K., 117
Davis, Amaziah H., 269
Davis and Noteware (store), 33
Davis and Scott, 322
Davis Brothers, 206, 208
Davis children, 208
Davis family, 287
Davis family music, 283
Davis, Frank, 269
Davis, Fred C., 274
Davis, George W., 274
Davis Mill, 269, 271, 274
Davis, Rev. Dr. 86
Davis, S. C., 31
Davis, Sam, 261, 262, 345, 347,
  403, 405, 407
Davis, W. T. "Buck," 294, 295, 389
Day-Marlette-Goddard Survey
  (See Marlette-Day Central
  Sierra Survey), 191
Day, Sherman, 181, 191, 291, 293, 361,
  362
"Dayit's Ravine Trail," 361
  (See also Daggett Pass)
Dayton (Nevada), 213, 233
Deadman's Island, 126
  (See also Emerald Isle)
Deadman's Point (Dead Man's), 284,
  400, 408, 425, 434, 456, 458
"Deaf Bob," 326
Dean and Martin's Station, 203
Dean and Van Wagener's
  Lake Bigler House, 192

Dean and Van Wagener's
  Hotel and Fishery, 389
Dean, (Judge) Seneca, 185, 199,
  200, 203, 205, 222
Dean, Robert Garwood, 198, 200,
  203, 205
Deans—, 193, 204, 206, 211
Dean's Lake House Fisheries, 232
De Castle, William, 382
Deep Creek, Placer County, 28
  (See also Hardscramble Creek)
Deer Park Inn, 19
Deer Park Road, 21
Deer Park Springs (Lodge),
  19–22, 379
De Groot, (Dr.) Henry, 462, 463
Delano, L. P., 350
Democratic California Legislature, 462
Demon, 143
Dempsey, Jack, 342
Denny, Hiram (trading post), 378
Denver, 277
DeQuille, Dan, 208, 261, 262, 347
  (See also William Wright)
Desolation Valley (Primitive Area),
  126, 141, 150, 163, 177,
  wilderness area, 450
De Tell, Hugh, 379
Detroit, Michigan, 438, 439
DeVaux automobile, 244
DeVaux, Norman, 244, 311, 437, 439
Devil's Anvil, 35
Devil's Armchair, 35
Devil's Basin, 175
  (See also Desolation Valley)
Devil's Bluff, 35, 354
Devil's Gate, 263
Devil's Playground, 467
Devil's Post Pile, 35
Devil's Rockpile, 354
Devil's Slide, 354
De Young, M. H., 107
Diamond Springs, 379
Dibble, Honorable A. B., 445
Dick's Peak, 466
Dickey, Orsamus W., 208, 219, 413
Digger Indians, 73, 109, 227, 463
Dirego Hotel (House), 285
Dixon, Charles, 195
Dixon, Harry, 383
Dixon, Henry, 195
Dixon, James, 383
Dixon, Mr. and Mrs. Harry, 383
Dixon, "Red," 358
Dixon, Robert, 200
Dixon's House, 383
Dixon's Place, 383
Dodge, 80
Dohrmann, Bruce, 45
Dolan, Everett, 435
Dollar Hill, 358
Dollar, Robert Stanley, Sr., 353, 440
Dollar, Robert Stanley, Jr., 441, 442
Dollar's Point (Chinquapin/Old
  Lousy/Observatory), 351–354
Donner Creek, 459
Donner Lake, 17, 398
  (See also Truckee Lake)
Donner Lumber and Boom
  Company, 27, 28, 45, 289
Donner Party, 74

Donner Pass, 1, 2, 5, 17, 109, 222,
  317, 373
Donner Summit, 28, 59, 319, 339,
  353, 417
Donner Summit House (Hotel), 31
Doods—, 74
"Doolaga," 143
  (See also Fallen Leaf Lake)
Dorr, L., 185, 211
Dorsey, J. M., 362
Douglas(s) County, Nevada, 243, 259,
  297, 317, 335
Douglas(s), George N., 185, 189,
  191, 192
Downieville, 233
Downieville Buttes (California), 462
Dr. Bourne's Hygienic
  Establishment, 347
Dreiser, Theodore, 142
Dritt and Bishop, 361
Dritt, "Old Man," Jacob
  "Daddy," 361
Drum, Georgiana, 311
Drum, John, Jr., 113, 436
Drum, John, Sr., 45, 56, 112, 113, 439
"Dry Diggin's", 339 (See Placerville)
Duane L. Bliss Peak, 467
Dublin, 445
DuBois, Pierre, 316, 317
DuBois, Simon, 293, 294, 295
Ducato, Alfred, 62
Duckworth, S., 235
Duffy—, 163
Duke of Wellington, 35, 386
Dunlap baby, 42
Dunlap family, 219
Dunlap, John Eugene, 41, 209, 216,
  217, 219
Dunstall—, 129
Dutch Flat Wagon Road, 17, 339, 341
Duval, G. M., 191
Dwinell, Dr., 29

E

Eagle Bay, 121
  (See also Emerald Bay)
Eagle Creek, 131, 134
Eagle Falls, 121, 126, 127, 139
Eagle Lake, 126, 129
Eagle Point, (south/north), 111, 120,
  139, 152, 215, 389
Eagle Ranch, 293
Eagle Rock (Bluff/Cliff), 64, 65, 66
Eagle Valley, 54, 172, 175, 179, 181,
  191, 207
  (See also Carson Valley)
Eagle Valley—Lake Bigler Emigrant
  Ridge Route, 361
Eagle Valley Emigrant Ridge
  road, 231
Eagle Valley Pass, 297 (See also Sum-
  mit camp)
Eagle Valley Ranch (Carson City),
  2, 293, 361
Early Marine History of Lake
  Tahoe, 385–435
East Bay, 52, 61, 436
East Canyon flume, 294
Easton, "Big Jim," 291
Ebright, Charles, 142

Ebright, Harold, 142; Sr., 436
Ebright, Katherine Brigham, 141, 142
Echo Creek bridge, 379
Echo (Lake) Creek, 177, 378, 379
Echo Lake—Lower, 175, 176, 177
Echo Lake—Upper, 175, 177
Echo Lake(s), 150, 175–177, 186,
    377, 378
Echo Peak, 465
Echo Summit, 143, 196, 267
    (See also Johnson Pass Summit,
    Nevett's Summit, Western Summit)
Echoes, 177 (see Echo Lakes)
Eddy, W. M., 461
"Eden of Bigler," 247
Edgewood (Friday's Station),
    231–238, 243, 384
Edwards—, 59
*Edwards' Tourists' Guide &
    Directory of the Truckee
    Basin,* 445
Edwards, W. F., 445, 463
Ehmann, George "Bud," 441
Ehrman, Ester (Mrs. Claude
    Lazard), 439
Ehrman, Mr. and Mrs. Sydney,
    107, 439
"El Campo," 74
El Dorado (Gilded Man/One), 7, 95
    (See also Mud Springs)
El Dorado Campground, 456
El Dorado County, 53, 64, 75, 87,
    91, 95, 107, 112, 165, 181, 183,
    191, 195, 207, 362, 367, 381, 382
El Dorado Gravel and Deep Water
    Mining Company, 176
El Dorado-Placer County line, 81, 92
El Dorado Wood and Flume
    Company, 186, 239
Elizabethtown, 339
Elliot(t) brothers (boys), 257, 270, 293,
    294, 295
Elliot(t), Captain Frederick, 385
    398, 399
Elliott, J. F., 436
Elliot(t), John P., 270, 293, 294
Elliot(t), Thomas G., 265, 270,
    293, 294
Elliott's Mill, 270, 293
Ellis, Jack (Jock) Sargent, 185
Ellis Peak, 466
Elmore Engine, 437
Elrod, E. R., 277
Emerald Bay, 36, 111, 120, 121–135,
    139, 141, 211, 245, 283, 353, 389,
    394, 400, 405, 406, 413, 437, 438,
    453, 454, 455, 457, 458, 459, 460
Emerald Bay Camp (Resort), 127,
    129, 131, 413
Emerald Bay Gorge, 245
Emerald Isle, 126, 131, 135
    (See also Baranoff, Coquette, Dead
    Man's, Fanette, and Hermit's
    Island)
Emery, Charles, 277
Emeryville (Emer-villy), 168
Emigrant Grade (Johnson Hill), 181
Emigrant (Immigrant) Ridge Route
    road, 183, 198, 201, 241
Emigrant trail (North Tahoe), 335, 341
Engines, railroad (see locomotives)

English Channel, 464
Esberg, Milton, 45
Esmeralda, 270
Estudillo, Jesus Maria, 205
Evans, "Duke," 441
Evans, Frank, 423
Evening Bulletin, 462
Evil One (Spirit), 143
Eyre, Mary, 311

F

Facts of Lake Tahoe, 453–468
Fageol (Motors), 174
Fageol, Louis, 441
Fair, James G., 308, 313, 314, 316
Fairburn, Will, 294, 295
Fairchild, Mable French, 287
Faith and Charity Valleys, 468
Fales Hot Springs, 47
Fallen Leaf (Lake), 141, 142, 143–145,
    148, 149, 150, 152, 156, 159, 177,
    186, 196, 436, 437, 453, 454
Fallen Leaf Lodge, 145, 210
Falling Leaf (Delaware Chief), 143
Fanette Isle, 126
    (See also Emerald Isle)
Farallon Islands, 436
Fargo, J. B., 400
Farmer, Ed, 73
Farmer, Dr. Etta Smith Duffy, 72, 73
Farmers and Merchants Bank, 107
Faro, 318
"father of American mining law," 193
"Father of the Central Pacific, 367
"Father of the Ice Age Concept," 145
"Father of the Pony Express," 361
Faust—, 379
Fay, Charles, 62
Federal Revenue Agents (Prohi's)
    46, 47
Ferguson, Jack, 304
Ferguson, William Sinclair, 26,
    28, 387
Ferris, Charles, 418
Filmore, Louis, 200
Fir Crags, 467
Fish & Ferguson, 385
Fish, Ferguson, Coggins & Smith
    Company, 6, 26, 386
Fish, Al L., 386, 400
Fish, F. H., 400
"Fishery"—, 443
Fishing Facts and Fancy, 443–451
"Fish Market Landing," 443
Five Lakes, 19
Flack, Nels, 277
Flagg, A. J., 52
Flagg, John, 52
"Fleet Builder of Lake Tahoe," 59,
    386, 410
Fleishhacker, Allen, 67
Fleishhacker, Herbert, Jr., 67, 441
Fleishhacker. Herbert, Sr., 45, 67,
    436, 439, 440
Fletcher, H. F., 117
"Fleur du Lac," 67, 68
Flick brothers, 349, 350
Flick, Joseph, 349
Flick, Nicholas, 349
Flick, William, 349
Floating Island Lake, **145**

Flood, James, 308, 313, 314, 316
Flores and Salado, 31
Flugge—, 145
Flume-boat, 313, 314
"Flying Switch," 217
    (see "Hi-Daddy")
Folsom, E. B., 241
Folsom, Gilman Nathaniel, 239, 240,
    241, 247, 308, 317, 318
Folsom (Lake Tahoe settlement
    of), 247
Folsom, Priscilla, Mrs. G. N., 240
Folsom, town of, 72, 175
Folsom's Knob (Peak), 243
Folsom's land, 242
Folsom's pier, 240, 241
Folsom's shingle mill, 240
"Foot and Walker" stage line, 368
Forbes, James Olmstead, 31, 34
Forbes, Joe, 399
Ford, 145
Forest Hill, 7, 26, 27
Fork House, 2, 3, 5
Forsyth, Robert, 427
Fort Bridger, 277
Fort Churchill (Bucklands), 233, 234
Fort Tejon, 223
Foster family, 294
Foster, Freeman, 295
Foster's Halt, 362
Fountain, David Broderick, 216, 379
Fountain, Garret Washington, 379
"Fountain of Youth," 79
Fountain Place, 379
"Four Loaves of Bread," 119
Four Square Gospel, 96
Franktown, 5, 309, 317
Franktown Creek (Hobart), 299
Fred's Place, 163
Free, Mickey, 185, 191
Freel(s) Peak, 465
    (See also Mount Freel)
Freer, H. P., 425
Fremont Cannon (howitzer), 47, 48, 49
    (See also Pray Cannon)
Fremont, Captain John Charles, 17,
    47, 48, 210, 269, 360, 459, 460,
    461, 462, 463
"Fremont's Lake," 461
    (See also Lake Tahoe)
French-Canadian lumberjacks, 270,
    293, 294
"French in China," 294
French National Fair, 444
"Friday's," 171, 234, 235, 236, 240
    (See also Friday's Station, Burke
    and Small's, Small's)
Friday's Creek, 231, 236, 237
Friday's Station, 194, 231, 232, 233, 234,
    235, 236, 237, 239, 245, 256, 267,
    268, 384, 443
    (See also Edgewood)
Fries, Frank Jr., 163
Fries, Frank Sr., 163, 164
Frog Rock, 119
Frost, Amos L., 115
Frost, John "Jack," 115
Frost, Josephine "Josie," 115
"Frost's Homestead," 115
Fuller, Frank, 440
Fury—, 143

G

Gabriel, 26
Gage, Stephen T., 366
Galena, Illinois, 135
Galt, California, 382
Galliano, Joe, 287
Gamble, L. J., 62
Gaming (gambling), 318
Garcia, Mrs. Mary, 150
Gardinier (Gardner), Andrew
    Boynton, 245, 247
Gardner, Matthew Culbertson, 151,
    171, 172, 173, 186
Gardner Mountain, 171, 172, 196
    (See also Twin Peaks)
Gardner Railroad, 171, 172, 173
Gardner, Samuel W., 89
Gardner, "Uncle Jimmie" Horace, 74
Gardner's Camp, 171, 195, 209
Gardinier's Zephyr Cove House, 257
Gardnerville, Nevada, 171, 238, 242
Gay 90's, 415
Gazley, Mrs. Elizabeth, 339
"Gem of the Mountains," 9
General Creek, 105, 106, 107
    (See also Phipps Creek)
General Land Office Map of the
    Pacific States, 462
Genoa (Nevada), 171, 182, 183, 191,
    198, 203, 215, 219, 225, 233, 236, 237,
    241, 257, 291, 293, 295, 363, 366
    (See also Mormon Station)
Genoa Peak, 273, 467
George, D. S., 373
Georgetown—Burton Pass Trail, 386
Georgetown (California), 26, 75, 76,
    81, 87, 102, 105, 111, 216, 265,
    293, 378, 458
Georgetown exploration, 293
Georgetown—Lake Bigler
    Indian Trail, 75
Georgetown—Lake Bigler—Washoe
    Valley Route, 361
    (See also Placer County
    Emigrant Road)
Georgetown—Rubicon Springs—
    Tahoe pack trail, 85
Georgetown Snag, 99
Georgetown Trail, 85, 103
Georgetowners, 6
Gerhart, Curly Bob, 198
"Gertie"—, 168
Gilcrest, Samuel F., 293
Gilis, Ollie, 369
Gillard, John Montgomery, 380
Gillson and Davis, 295
Gillson, George, 294, 295, 389
Gilmore, Amanda Gray, 149, 150
Gilmore family, 150
Gilmore Lake, 150
Gilmore, Nathan, 147, 148, 150
Gilmore Point, 287
Gilmore, Susan, 149, 150
Gimp, 163
Gladiator, The, 119
Gladys Lake, 141 (see Azure Lake)
Glen Alpine Canyon, 149
Glen Alpine Springs, 21, 145,
    147–150, 156, 186
Glen Alpine tally-ho stage, 150

Glen Alpine Tonic Water, 149
Glenbrook (Glen Brook), 26, 31,
    33, 37, 39, 48, 49, 59, 72, 85, 99,
    111, 127, 151, 159, 168, 169, 171,
    172, 186, 195, 205, 206, 209, 215,
    216, 217, 219, 231, 236, 237, 239,
    243, 244, 247, 259, 261, 262, 263–
    290, 293, 295, 308, 321, 322, 325,
    351, 381, 385, 386, 389, 390, 391,
    393, 394, 396, 400, 403, 405, 406,
    407, 408, 410, 417, 425, 427, 429,
    433, 434, 435, 445, 456, 457, 458,
    459
Glenbrook Bay, 263, 264, 284, 389,
    390, 391, 393, 400
Glenbrook Creek and Canyon, 265,
    267, 273, 278, 279, 291
Glenbrook (Glen Brook) House, 26,
    29, 89, 152, 257, 262, 267, 268,
    269, 270, 273
Glenbrook Hotel Company, 269
Glenbrook Inn and Ranch, 289, 311
Glenbrook Landing, 268, 408
Glenbrook machine shops, 217
Glenbrook meadow, 257, 287
Glenbrook mills, 111, 171, 215, 270, 273,
    353, 390, 400 (See also Lake Mills)
Glenbrook's South Point, 387, 391
Glenbrookers, 270, 274, 282, 283, 287
Glide, 325
Globin, Mr. and Mrs. Frank, 210
Goddard, George H., 179, 181, 187,
    251, 341, 361, 362
Go-Devil(s), 58, 209
Goff and Morrill's *Monitor* mill,
    267, 269
Goff, G. H. F., 267
Golconda route, 372
Gold Canyon, 2, 182, 299, 363, 368
Gold Cup (races), 442
Gold Hill, 48, 85, 151, 200, 207,
    273, 303, 365
Gold Hill News, 38, 143, 323, 353, 389
"Gold Nugget Man From
    Placerville," 383
Golden Road, 259, 368
    (See also Great Bonanza Road
    to Washoe)
Golden and Silver States, 59, 373, 454
Golden West, 379
Goodman and Crowley, 345
Goodman, Joseph (Joe), 345
Goodrich, Adelman Hargrave
    ("Harry"), 207
Goodrich, Don, 41, 207
Good Spirit, 143
Goodwin, Charles, 459
Goodwin Lake, 299
    (See also Marlette Lake)
Gordinier, George F. "Little Dock," 385
Gordon—, 31
Gorilla Profile, 256
Gothic Chapel, 123
Gould and Company, 183, 191
Governor of Nevada, 389
Grand Canyon of the Colorado, 465
Grand Canyon(s), 354
Grand Central Bar, 25
Grand Central Hotel, 23, 25, 29, 31,
    33, 35, 36, 37, 38, 39, 41, 152,
    167, 282, 399, 407, 445

"Grand Highway," 368
"Grand Picnic," 326
Granite Chief, 466
Granite Lake, 126
Granite Mountain (Peak), 121, 466
Granlibaken, 42
Grant, President Ulysses S., 33,
    275, 357
Grass Lake (Desolation Valley), 143
Grass Lake (Luther Pass), 362, 455
Grass Valley, 445
Grass Valley Line, 45
Graves, Ralph, 437
Graves, Russell Cowles, 129, 131
Gray Horse Valley, 85
Gray, Joseph, 17
Great Basin, 361
Great Bonanza Road (to Washoe),
    89, 190, 191, 359–373, 382
Great Comstock, 5
    (See also Comstock Lode)
Great Deep of Tahoe, 460
Great Depression, 143
"Great Eastern," 386
Great Federal Wagon Road bill, 363
Great Highway, 365
Great Incline of the Sierra Nevada,
    306, 308, 336
    (See also Great Tramline of
    Tahoe/Sierra)
Great Lakes mackinaw, 448
    (See also Lake Tahoe trout)
Great Road, 232, 366, 368, 373
Great Sierra Mule Train, 359
Great Spirit, 15, 16
Great Sweepstakes of 1881, 445
Great Tahoe Deep, 457, 459
    (See also Great Deep of
    Tahoe/Big Deep)
Great Tramline of Tahoe, 305
    (See also Great Incline of the
    Sierra Nevada)
Great Tramline of the Sierra, 309,
    317, 342
    (See also Great Tramline of
    Tahoe)
Great Valley, 143
    (See also Sacramento Valley)
Grecian Bend, 119
Greeley, Horace, 168, 275, 277, 281
Green, Baldy, 198
"Green Bay," 145
Green, James, 459
Green, James "Jim," 362
Green, Matt, 52, 73, 112, 133, 336
"Green Mountain Boy," 167, 190
    (See also Ephraim "Yank"
    Clement)
Green, Pete, 360
Green, William Alpha, 195
Greene, Glenn, 52
Greenwood, Caleb, 360
Griffin family, 287
Griffin, John, 331, 333
Griffin, John "Johnny," 48, 284,
    287
Griffin, "Old Lousy," 351
Griffin, Oliver Franklin, 216
Griff's, 331, 333
Griff(s) Creek, 331, 333, 336
Grimshaw, Fred, 74

Grinning Negro, 119
  (See also Old Squaw/Turk in Turban)
Grizzly Bear, 379
Grizzly Bear Peak (Rabbit Rock), 466
Grosch, Ethan Allen, 1, 2
Grosch, Hosea Ballou, 1
Grouse Canyon, 59
Gruver, Robert E., 131
Gudde, *Place Names of California,* 17

H

Hacker, John, 312, 438, 439, 440
Hagen, Patrick, 379
Hagen, Rube, 331
Haines' Canyon, 236, 237
Haines, J. W., 236
Haire and Gilcrest, 293
Haire, Samuel, 293
Hale, Jack, 437
Hall, E. J., 436
Hall-Scott Motors, 174, 436, 439, 440
Halsey, S. Y., 209
Hamels—, 74
Hamilton, William, 256
Hammond—, 349
Ham, William Fenton, 407, 433, 434
Hand, William, 437
Hangtown, 109, 147, 177; (cemetery), 179, 180, 360, 461
  (See also Dry Diggin's and Placerville)
Hangtown Crossing, 384
Hanlon, William "Bill," 237
Hanscomb, John (Jack), 23, 24, 25, 31, 34
Hansen, John, 186
Happy Hunting Grounds, 15
Harbin, Matthew, 17
Hardin, Frank, 45
Hardscramble Creek (Deep Creek), 28
Harkness, Bob, 163
Harlan, Hollingsworth and Co., 403
Harmsworth Trophy, 442
Harper, Horatio T., 115, 117
Harper's—, 115, 117
Harris—, 183
Harris, Francis F., 378
Hart—, 112
Harvard University, 309
Harvey, Dr. Obed, 382
Harvey Homestead, 382
Harvey House, 382
Harvey, Charles Wesley, 382
Harvey, Miss Genevieve, 382
Haslem, Robert "Pony Bob," 231, 233, 234, 235, 237
Hatch, J. A., 26
Hatch, M. D., 269
Hawkins, Pete "Pit," 287, 423
Hawley and Company, 378
Hawley, Asa Hers(c)hel, 180, 182, 183, 191, 195, 362, 378, 459
Hawley, "Si," 277
Hawley(s) Grade Hill/Trail/Route (short-cut), 179, 180, 181, 183, 185, 372, 378, 468
Hawley's ranch, 293
Hawley's Second Elkhorn House, 180, 378

Hawthorne House, 185, 382
Hawthorne, Lloyd, 23
Hawthorne, Loyet A., 382, 396
Haydon, Thomas E., 267
Hayes, Mrs., 59
Hayes, President Rutherford B., 275, 282
Haynie, Captain John W., 186
Head, Anna, 35
Hearst, Phoebe Apperson, 112
Heather Lake, 143
Heavenly Valley Creek (Miller), 185, 199, 212, 382
Heavenly Valley Mill, 172, 185
  (See also Miller Creek mill)
Heavenly Valley Ski Lift, 187
Heller, Mrs. Claire S., 173
Hell Hole, (Lower), 6, 19, 75, 85; (Upper), 19, 80
Hellman, Florence, 107
Hellman, Isaias William, 95, 107, 436
Hellman Mansion, 107
Hellman's Paso Robles Ranch, 107
Helm, Alfred, 267
Hen and Chickens, 119
  (See also Baby Chick Rock)
Henderson—, 181
Henderson, Mrs. I. H., 112
Henley, James, 319
Henness Pass, 365
Henry, A. M. (Joe), 49
Henry, H. L., 95, 96
Hereford, J. B., 313, 314, 315
"Heritage House," 216
"Hermit of Cornelian Bay," 347
"Hermit of Emerald Bay," 121, 389, 457
"Hermit of the Lake" (Echo), 176
Hermit's Isle, 126
  (See also Emerald Isle)
Herod, Harry, 436
Herrick, Dr. L. F., 112
Hesse, Dick, 48
Hicks Engine, 436
"Hi-daddy," 217 (see Flying Switch)
Hiestand, A., 393
Higgins, Sam, 185
High Meadow, 199
High Sierra, 9, 21, 22, 29, 41, 45, 64, 107, 112, 143, 149, 161, 177, 285, 355, 368, 457
Highway 50, 196, 209, 210, 227, 237, 242, 293, 378
Highway 89, 172, 293, 353, 358, 378
Hill, Arthur, 219
Hill, Mrs. Marion, 225
Hillman and Furman, 396
Hill's, 216
Hinman—, 117
"Hippy," 331, 333
Hiram Denny's Trading Post, 378
History of Nevada, 303
Hobart (Sky Harbor), 168, 239, 240, 241, 242, 247, 318, 410
Hobart and Overton, 305
Hobart Creek, 299, 303
  (See also Franktown Creek)
Hobart Creek Dam, 301
Hobart-DeVaux race, 439
Hobart Line, 308
Hobart Mills, 308, 311, 318, 342

Hobart, Walter Scott, Jr. (Bill), 56, 74, 309, 311, 433, 437, 439
Hobart, Walter Scott, Sr., 171, 213, 239, 241, 305, 308, 309, 336
Hobart, Walter Scott, Sr. (estate), 249, 289, 342, 400
Hobarts—, 410
  (See also Hobart)
"Hobart's Ditch," 240
Hobart's Incline operation, 318
Hobart's Mill Creek sawmill, 336
Hodges, Billy, 198
Hogan, Johnny, 325
Holabird's (Holabird's Nest), 73
Holdridge, Daniel Hate, 185, 379
Holladay, Ben, 31, 121, 131, 385, 389, 391, 393, 417
Holladay, Ben, Jr., 121, 269
Holladay's, 122, 125, 127, 457
Holladay's (Cottage), 121, 125, 126, 127
Holladay's Island Cottage, 123, 135
Hollywood, 95, 142
Holt, Captain Frank, 408, 415
Holt, Captain Jack, 410
Holten, D, 26
Homewood, 64, 67, 69–74, 92, 93, 112, 435, 437, 438, 448, 459
Homewood Bay, 67
  (See also McKinney Bay)
Homewood Casino, 74
Homewood Resort, 73
  (See also Hotel Homewood)
Honey Lake, 453
"Honeymoon Cottage," 112
"Honorable Legislator," 236
  (See also Small, J. W.)
Hoover Dam, 465
Hope, Faith and Charity valleys, 468
Hope Valley (Alpine County), 19, 176, 183, 185, 191, 362, 454, 460, 468
Hopkins, Mark, 27
Horseshoe Bend (Central Pacific), 27
Hotchkiss, Captain George, 436
"Hotel de Chipmunk," 342
Hotel Homewood, 73
Hotel Tallac, 154, 156
  (See also Tallac Hotel/House)
Hotle, Robert F., 117
Hot Springs, 37, 151, 270, 321, 349, 393, 394, 396, 437
  (See also Campbell's/Brockway Hotel and Hot Springs)
Hot Springs Express (Flyer), 23, 24, 25
House of Congress, 371, 372
How(e) and Montrose sawmill, 240
Howland and Coy, 385, 393
Howland, Captain David, 385, 393
Huddleston, Mrs. Myrtle, 456
Huff, Mr. and Mrs. Donald, 73
Huffaker's, 314
Hulana, John, 191
Humboldt, Alexander Von, 461
Humbolt Sink, 360
Humbolt Sink cut-off, 63, 361
Hume, Undersheriff J. B., 379
Humiston, J., 350
Humphries, Fred, 185
Hunkin, Captain Edmund, 209, 405, 406, 423, 425, 432

Hunsucker, George, 75, 83, 85, 102
Hunsucker, John, 75, 102
Hunter's Lodge, 74
Hunter's Retreat (Home), 82, 83, 85, 91, 92
(See also McKinney's/Chambers' Lodge)
Huntington, Collis P. (Cagey Collis), 57, 58, 222, 362
Huntington, John, 24, 26, 28, 39, 103
Huntington, Lou, 26, 28, 103
Huntington, Marian, 117
Hurley, Jeremiah (Johnny), 28, 33, 42, 43
Hurricane Bay, 39, 67
Hyde, Orson, 5

I

Ichelson, Albert, 52
Ichelson, Fred, 52
Ichi-Ban, 318
I'd Do It Again, 66
Idlewild, 53, 59, 63, 65, 66, 67, 73, 406
(See also Tahoe Pines)
Illes, Francis Rawlings, 96
Illinois, 378, 380
Incline, 240, 305–312, 342, 386, 399, 400, 410, 415, 459
Incline Mountain, 306, 309, 311, 467
Incline Summit, 305
Incline Tramway, 308
(See also Great Tramline of Tahoe)
Indian Cave, 179
(See also Cave Rock)
Indian Charlie, 5
Indian legends, 221
Indian Wars, 102
Ingram, Captain Henry R., 373
Innocents Abroad, 463
Inspiration Point, 131
International Olympic Committee, 10
Interstate Commerce regulations, 431
Ireland, 379, 380
Irey, Grover, 210
Irving, Washington, 205
Irwin, George, 326
Irwin Stage Lines, 326
Island Cottage, 123
(See also Holladay's)
Ives, Butler, 223, 236, 245, 267, 460

J

"Jackass Post," 361
Jackson, Captain Thomas, 388, 389, 390
Jacks Peak, 465
Jack's Valley (cut-off), 257
Jacobs—, 183
James, George Wharton, 329
James, Harry, 241
James, "Indian Ben," 163
James, John, 182, 241
James, Will, 171
"Jehu(s) of the Sierra," 126, 277, 371
Jellerson, Amanda Jane, 285
Jellerson family, 287
Jellerson, Frank Stephens, 285
Jellerson, Grace, 287

Jellerson Hotel (House), 285
(See also Dirego Hotel)
Jewell, Emma Frances, 240
Jewell, Ruben Watson, 195
Jewell's, 216
"Jibenonasa," 458
Jim Taylor's Ranch House, 205
(See also Bijou)
Job, Moses, 465 (refer Job's Peak)
Job's Peak, 238, 457, 465
Job's Sister, 238, 457, 465
John Chinaman, 273
Johnson, Charles, 26, 444
Johnson, Charles "Chuck" Cary, 220
Johnson, Chris, Sr., 200, 220, 383
Johnson, Colonel John (Jack) Calhoun "Cockeye," 109, 143, 179, 251, 253, 360, 361, 363, 459
Johnson(s) cut-off, 180, 191, 192, 267, 293, 360, 361, 362, 363, 365, 379
(See also Johnson(s) Pass)
Johnson, Frank, 263, 264
Johnson, Fred, 216, 217
Johnson Hill (Grade), 179, 180, 181, 183
Johnson Hill Summit, 362
(See also Johnson Summit)
Johnson, Knox, 200, 201
Johnson Pass-Kingsbury Cut-off, 26, 231, 232, 389
Johnson(s) Pass Road, 2, 75, 109, 147, 159, 175, 179, 181, 185, 189, 192, 193, 203, 206, 267, 367, 371, 373, 377, 378, 379, 385, 389, 468
lakeshore turnpike, 255, stage route, 363
Johnson(s) Ranch, 444 (Lake Tahoe)
Johnson(s) Ranch, 179 (Placerville)
Johnson Route, 361, 362
Johnson, Stella Knox, 200, 383
Johnson Summit, 182, 378
Johnson Trail, 361
Johnson, Bill (El Campo), 69, 74
"Jolly Nine," 415
Jones, "Bud," 358
Jones, Dan, 241
Jones, Robert, 380
Jost, Arthur C., 73
Jost, Mrs. Arthur (Annie), 73, 74
Judah, Theodore D., 367
Judgment Day, 223
Jukes, Johnny, 217
Julesburg, 277
Junction (Hope Valley), 185
"Junction" (Johnson Pass road), 147
"Junction Station" (Hope Valley), 362
Juneau, Alaska, 219
Jurgens, Dick, 94

K

Kaiser, David, 105
Kaiser, Henry J., 67, 442
Kaiser, Mr. and Mrs. Henry J. (family), 68
Katrine Lake, 141 (see Snow Lake)
Kaufman's—, 210
Keefer, Jesse Rhodes, 378
Kehlet, Captain Fred O., 113
Kehlet family, 112
Kehlet, George, 112, 113

Kehlet, Oswald V., 112
Keiser, John, 6
Keith's Dome, 466
Kelham, George, 437
Keller, John E., 384
Kelly and Rogers, 385
Kelley, J. G., 234
Kelsey (El Dorado County), 75
Kendrick, Charles, 62, 440
Kendrick, Marron, 440
Kenison, G. W., 293
Kennedy, Mrs., 96
Kent, William, 62, 436
Kenyon houses, 337
Keyser, Charlie, 41
Keyser, Louisa, 54
(See also Dat-So-La-Lee)
Keyser, William D., 275, 326, 362, 363
Kidder-Ives Survey, 223
Kidder, John F., 223, 460
Kilner, Fred, 117
Kimball and Bartlett, 227
Kimball Manufacturing Company, 37
Kincaid, Robert, 28
King Cole, 119 (see Old King Cole)
King Emanuel of Spain, 436
King, Fred, 28
King, Joe, 45, 94, 333
King, Johnson, 7
King, M. L., 26, 28, 29
King, Mrs. E. B., 62
King, Reverend Thomas Starr, 462
Kingsbury—, 74
Kingsbury and McDonald's Daggett Pass toll road, 203, 378
Kingsbury cut-off, 236
(See also Kingsbury Grade)
Kingsbury, David Demmen, 183, 232, 378
Kingsbury Grade (Road), 159, 163, 171, 183, 186, 192, 197, 207, 231, 232, 233, 235, 236, 237, 239, 240, 245, 378, 468
Kingsbury Grade-Daggett Pass (Road), 172, 219, 237, 468
(See also Kingsbury Grade)
King's Beach, 331–333, 456
Kings Canyon Grade, 467
Kings Canyon (Lake Bigler) Toll Road, 206, 247, 267, 269, 293
King's Castle, 28, 29
"Kings of the Road," 371
Kinney, John, 265
Kiowa Indian, 278
Kirby, "Dr." and Mrs. Paul T., 36, 127, 129, 131, 413
Kirby, "Dr." Paul T., 385
Kirby, Lucy N., Mrs., 127, 129
Kirk, John, 176
Kirman, Richard, 95, 99, 242
Kit Carson Pass, 179, 461, 468
(See also Carson Pass)
Klein's—, 287
Kneass—, 438, 439, 441
Knecht, Gustave, 440
Knight, Governor Goodwin J., 10
Knight, Mrs. Lora Josephine Moore, 131, 133, 134, 135, 353, 437
"Knight of the Ribbons," 371
Knight, William Henry, 462

"Knights of the Golden Sawdust," 287, 410
"Knights of the Lash," 277, 281, 371
Knisely, Ray, 174
Knisely, "Sis" Richardson, 174, 439 (See also Richardson, "Sis")
Knox Sawmill (the "California Banks"), 271, 294
Knox, Shannon, 6, 7, 357
Knoxville, 7, 35
Knoxville's Union Clothing Store, 7
Kohl, Frederick C., 66, 67, 436
Kohl, Mrs. Frederick C., 67
Kokanee salmon, 451
Kyburz, 206
Kyburz, Samuel Elliott, 195, 209, 379

L

Lady of the Lake, 149
"Lady of the Lake," 195, 256
Lake Bigler, 1, 2, 3, 5, 179, 180, 193, 245, 293, 295, 321, 341, 388, 462, 463, 464 (See also Lake Tahoe)
Lake (Bigler) House, 185, 190, 199, 200, 203, 204, 205, 206, 208, 210, 211, 222, 443
Lake (Bigler) House Bar, 205
Lake Bigler (Tahoe) Lumber Company, 265, 267
Lake Bigler (Tahoe) Toll Road (Company), 243, 255, 257, 267, 293
Lake Bigler Valley, 361
Lake Bonpland, 461 (See also Lake Tahoe)
Lake Creek, 179, 185, 191, 208, 362, 443, 455 (See also Upper Truckee River and Lake Valley Creek)
Lake(s) Crossing (Station), 199 (See Reno)
Lake Fishery (Tahoe City), 39, 443
Lake Forest, 355–358 (See Burton's Island Farm)
Lake House Fisheries, 26, 386
Lake House (Glenbrook), 261 (See Lake Shore House)
Lake House (Idlewild), 65
Lake Mead, 465
Lake Mill (Pray's), 265, 267, 270
Lake Mill Number One, 271, 274, 283, 287
Lake Mill Number Two, 274, 283, 284, 400, 416
Lake Nyasa, 457
"Lake of the Sky," 327, 329, 429, 454 (See also Lake Tahoe)
Lake of the Woods, 177
"Laker's," 59, 87, 113, 125, 151, 185, 200, 263, 269, 319, 358, 393, 395, 427, 443, 458, 463, 464
"Lake Sanatoria," 347
Lakeshore (Lake Shore) House, 261, 267, 279, 281, 284, 287, 410, 425
Lakeshore Road, 380
"Lakeshore Turnpike," 236
Lakeside, 221–229, 241, 382, 384
Lakeside (Lapham's Hotel), 186, 389
Lakeside House (Tavern), 225, 227
Lakeside Park (Company), 227
Lake Station, 23, 273 (See also Reno)

Lake Stream, 203, 208, 361, 443 (See Lake Creek/Upper Truckee River)
Lake Street (Main), 28, 33
Lake Tahoe, atmospheric clarity at, 457; boats on (refer boats), bodies not recovered from, 456, 457; is the lake bottomless? 457; comparison statistics of, 464, 465; controversy in naming, 460, 461, 462, 463, 464; dimensions, depths and outlet of, 459, 460; feeder creeks, streams, rivers, 455; fishing facts and fancy, 443–451; facts of Lake Tahoe, 453–468; filling of, 455; formation of, 453, 454; freezing of, 455, 456; Indians at 463, 464 (refer also Paiute/Washoe Indians); lumbering, refer chapters 2, 4, 6, 7, 10, 11, 13, 14, 15, 20, 24, 26, 28, 29, 30, 33, 34, 35, 39, 40, 42, 43, 45, 49; meaning of, 463, 464; mountain passes, 465–468; mountain peaks surrounding, 465–468; natural wonders (refer Truckee Canyon, Tahoe City, Rubicon Point, Emerald Bay, Meyers, Cave Rock, Shakespeare Rock, Brockway Hotel and Hot Springs, and Dollar's Point chapters); pronunciation of, 464; railroads at, (refer Tahoe City, Camp Richardson, Bijou, Glenbrook, and Incline chapters); steam engines at (refer locomotives); swimming in, 456; trees surrounding, 457 (footnote); valleys surrounding, 468; water temperatures of, 454, 455; weather on, 458, 459
Lake Tahoe & Chautauqua Improvement Company, 327
Lake Tahoe & San Francisco Water Company, 27
Lake Tahoe Chautauqua Assembly, 327
Lake Tahoe Development Company, 52, 433, 435
Lake Tahoe Railroad (Glenbrook), 41, 48, 263, 264, 265, 273, 275, 289 (See also locomotives)
Lake Tahoe Railway and Transportation Company, 21, 41, 61, 289, 353, 358, 407, 423
Lake Tahoe Schottische, 287
Lake Tahoe Sierra Association, 51
Lake Tahoe Transportation Company, 397
Lake Tahoe, Topographical Map of (1874), 212 (See Von Leicht and Hoffmann)
Lake Tahoe trout:
cutthroat, 443, 444, 445, 446, 448, 450, 451
cross-breeds, 448, 451
Eastern brook, 450
German brown, 445, 448, 451
Mackinaw, 448, 449, 451
minnows, 450, 451
pogies, 445, 450
Rainbow, 445, 450
Royal silver, 445, 450
salmon trout, 179, 443, 445
Silver, 109, 415, 443, 444, 445, 450, 451

Lake Tahoe trout statistics, 443, 446, 448
Lake Tahoe Wagon Toll Road, 245 (See Lake Bigler Toll Road)
Lake Tahoe whitefish, 443, 445
Lake Tahoe Yacht Club Regattas, 440
Lake Tanganyika, 457
Lake Titicaca, 457
Lake Valley, 74, 105, 143, 147, 151, 167, 171, 172, 179–187, 189, 191, 192, 195, 196, 197, 198, 199, 200, 203, 215, 222, 225, 233, 235, 237, 247, 265, 293, 361, 362, 363, 368, 372, 378, 380, 382, 383, 384, 461, 463 (See also Lake Bigler Valley/Tahoe Valley, Upper and Lower Lake Valley)
Lake Valley Creek, 455 (See also Lake Creek, Upper Truckee River)
Lake Valley Diggings, 191
Lake Valley Glacier, 453
Lake Valley "Home Ranch," 379
Lake Valley Meat Market, 237
Lake Valley Post Office, 205, 382
Lake Valley Railroad, 41, 209, 215, 216, 219, 289, 379 (See also Bijou-Lake Valley Railroad)
Lake Valley ranchers, 186
Lake Valley Township, 186
Lakeview Lodge, 131
Lakeview Station, 300
Lake Wood, 17 (See Donner Lake)
Lamberts—, 62
Lambo—, 319
Lame Horse, 14, 15
"Lancers," 325
Land Office, Washington, D.C., 462
"Land Route of the Steamers," 417
Lang, Johnny, 163
Langtry, Lily, "Jersey Lily," 33
Lanigan—, 394
Lapham and Company, 385
Lapham, Captain William W. "Billy," 103, 105, 199, 203, 204, 212, 221, 222, 223, 225, 227, 283, 383, 385, 394, 395, 396, 410, 411, 436, 443
Lapham, Caroline M., Mrs., 222, 223, 395
Lapham's Fish Market and Landing, 222, 232, 389, 443
Lapham's Stateline Hotel (and Landing), 26, 105, 199, 204, 221, 223, 225, 227, 383, 384, 386, 389, 395, 396
Lapham's Station, 225
"Largo Bergler," 462 (See also Lake Tahoe)
Larson, Antonne, 186
Last Chance, 2
Latrobe, 267
Law, (Dr.) Hartland, 129, 131, 413, 437
Lawn—, 325
Lawrence and Company, 415, 418 (See also Lawrence and Comstock)
Lawrence and Comstock (Comstock and Lawrence) 129, 156, 161, 164, 174, 327, 329

Lawrence, Melville, 154, 165, 174, 327, 423
Lawrence, Mrs. Melville, 141
Lawrence, "Uncle Mel," 329
   (See Lawrence, Melville)
Lazard, Mrs. Claude, 439
   (See Ehrman, Ester)
Leamon, Charles, 215
LeConte, Joseph, 453
Lee, Dr. S. L., 54
Legendary Cave, 251 (see Cave Rock)
Leonard, Carl, 107
LeRoy, Dr., 413
Lewis, Harriet, 74
Lewright, Harley, 174
Lewright, May Copeland, 174
Liberty Engine, 439, 440, 441, 442
Lick House (Hotel), 445
Lick, James, 28, 351, 353
   (See also Lick Observatory)
Lick Observatory, 351
Lightnin', 142
Lily Lake, 91; Lily Lake (Glen Alpine), 143, 149
Lincoln, Abraham, 235, 377, 462
Lindsey, William, 431
Lindbergh, Charles, 135
Linnard Hotel interests, 45
Little Cornelian, 341
Littlefield, Big John, 198
Little, John, 185
Little King, 119
   (See also Old King Cole)
Little Round Top, 455, 461
Little Valley (White Rock Valley), 5, 299, 306, 308
"Living Waters from Lake Tahoe," 462
"L. K." Baskets, 55
Lloyd, James, 437
Lockhead, John, 393
Lockie, John, 294, 295
Lockie, Oliver and Company, 293
Locksters—, 247
Lockwood, Belva, 35
Locomotives (Lake Tahoe)
   Carson & Tahoe Lumber & Fluming Company (Lake Tahoe Railroad)
      Engine Number One (Tahoe), 274, 284, 286
      Engine Number Two (Glenbrook), 263, 264, 274, 286
      Engine Number Three, 274
      Engine Number Four, 274, 280
   Carson & Tahoe Lumber & Fluming Company (Bijou-Lake Valley Railroad)
      Engine Number One, 217
      Engine Number Three, 213, 216, 217
      Santa Cruz, 212, 213, 215, 219
   Chubbuck's Bijou-Lake Valley Railroad
      Old Morsby, 213, 216
   Gardner Railroad (Lake Valley)
      Engine Number One, 171, 172
      Engine Number Two, 171, 172
   Hobart's Incline Railroad
      Engine Number One, 308, 309, 310

Locomotives (Cont'd)
   Hobart's Incline Railroad (Cont'd)
      Engine Number Two, 308, 310
   Lake Tahoe Railway and Transportation Company (Tahoe City-Truckee)
      Engine Number One, 41, 45
      Engine Number Three, 41
      Engine Number Five, 41
      Engine Number Thirteen, 41
      Santa Cruz, 41
Logan House, 247, 257–259, 273
Logan, Robert, 257, 259
Logan Shoals, 259
Log Cabin One (Tahoe City), 45, 46, 47
Log Cabin Number One (South Tahoe), 383
Log Cabin Two (Tahoe City), 46, 47
Lonely Gulch, 33, 97, 111, 117, 405
Lone Mountain Cemetery (Carson City), 281
Lone Star State (Texas), 464
Long Meadow, 211
   (See also Siebeck's Meadow)
Long, Osgood, 369
Long Valley, 6
Long, William, 456
Loo, Fong, 400
Lookout Mountain, 467
Loomis, George, 36
Los Angeles, 95, 329
Lost Cannon Creek, 48
Lost Cannon Peak, 48
Lost Corner Mountain, 95, 109, 459, 466
Lousy Point, 351, 353, 354
   (See also Chinquapin, Dollar's, Observatory and "Old Lousy" Points)
"Love feasts," 227
Love Nest Cottage, 164
Lover's Leap, 14, 35
Lowell and Locke, 7, 20
Lowe, Martin, 69, 70, 71, 72, 73, 74, 92, 93, 94
Lower Lake Valley, 186, 235
   (See also Lake Valley)
Lower Pray Meadow, 263
"Lowery boys," 175
Lubeck family, 65
Luders—, 437
Lukens, Charles Abraham, 195
Luneman, Arnold P., 112, 113
Lusk, C. W., 109, 115
Luther(s) Pass (grade), 159, 179, 180, 181, 183, 186, 191, 207, 231, 233, 236, 293, 361, 362, 363, 378, 455, 461, 468
Lyman—, 35
Lyon, Mrs. Elaine, 377
Lyon, Robert, 259
Lyons, Charlie, 208, 237
Lyons, Lena, 208
Lyons, Mary, 195, 196
Lyons, Minnie, 208
Lyons, William Henry, 195, 196

M

MacDonald, Clara Belle Gardner, 173
MacDonald, Mrs. Alice, 167
Mackay, John W., 308, 313, 316

Mackey, Captain, 393
Mac(k), William, 198, 199, 211
Mac(k)'s Station, 192, 199
   (See also Sierra House)
Madatoll, Adeline, 287
Maes, Marcel, 95
Magee, Harry Hush, 441
Magee, William "Bill," 441
Maggie(s) Peak(s), 129, 466
Maheon Lake, 462
Maher, Frank "Waddles," 342
Maiden Rock, 129
"Mailbox," 378
Main, Fred, 442
Main Street (Tahoe City), 33, 397
   (See also Lake Street)
Main Street of the Far West, 373
Maine mill hands, 270
Maine, State of, 285, 450
Mann, Gustave, 165
Mansion House, 267
Manzanita Promontory (Flick's Point), 347
Map of California, 461
Marin County, California, 89
Marine Activity—The Gay '90's Into the Atomic 1950's, 436–442
Markham, Edwin, 19, 149
Mark Twain, 265, 327, 329, 330, 462, 463, 464
   (See also Clemens, Samuel)
Marla Bay, 240, 243, 244, 247
Marlette and Day's California Wagon Road and Boundary Survey party, 341
Marlette and Folsom, 317, 318, 325
Marlette Basin, 273, 299, 300
Marlette brook trout, 303
Marlette-Day Central Sierra Survey, 191, 362
Marlette Dam, 300, 301
Marlette Lake, 299–304
Marlette Lake flume, 304, 309
Marlette Meadow, 362
   (See also Grass Lake)
Marlette Peak, 467
Marlette, Seneca Hunt (Surveyor-General), 179, 181, 239, 269, 291, 299, 316, 317, 318, 361
Marlette tunnel, 303
Marley, John, 243
Marley, W. C., 233, 234
Marley's Ranch, 243
Marsten, Lewis A., 62
Martin, James Henry "Hank," 200, 206, 211, 213
Martin, Robert "Bob," 185
Martis Creek (Middle), 319, 341
Martis Creek Grade, 342
Martis Creek Road, 468
Martis Peak, 319, 336, 342, 467
Martis Valley (Creek) cut-off, 269, 308, 321, 323, 325, 349, 398
Martis Valley-Hot Springs road, 335
"Marty"—, 79
Mary's Lake, 460
Marysville, 366
Marysville Foundry, 403
Mathews, Jack, 48, 52
Mawdsly, George, 432
May-Ah-Mee Lodge (Pomin's), 97–99

Mayfield, Norman, 407
May, Jim, 163
Mayo and Hurley, 445
Mayo, Captain H. L., 445
Mazurka, 215
McCarty, Patrick, 264, 275
McClaskey, Eva, 240
McClaskey, Sam, 240
McClatchy, 62
McClean, James, 198, 232
McCloud, 112
McConaha, James Battson, 380
McConnell, George, 74
McConnell, J., 17
McConnell, Thomas, 64, 65, 74, 91
McConnell's, 64, 65, 396
McCormick, John, 26
McCormick, P., 185
McCumber, Charles, 383
McCumber (McComber), Freeman,
    383, 384
McCumber, George, 383
McCumbers (McCombers) Ranch,
    185, 200, 212, 247, 383, 384
McDonald, John, 211, 232, 378
McFaul children, 240
McFaul family, 243
McFaul, George, 247
McFaul, Joseph Allen, 247
McFaul Ranch, 243
McFaul, Robert, 247
McFaul, William, 243, 244, 247
McFaul's, 243, 247
McGlashan, C. F., 11, 186, 445, 446,
    457, 460
McGlaughlin, Mrs. Charles, 33
McGraw, Solly, 163
McHugh—, 295
McIntyre, George, 31, 34
McKay, Stuart, 326
McKinney Bay, 63, 64, 69, 72, 91,
    95, 117, 208
    (See also Upson Bay)
McKinney Creek, 91
McKinney, John Washington, 81,
    82, 83, 85, 86, 87, 89, 91, 92, 101,
    102, 103, 105, 385
McKinney Lake, 91
McKinney's (Resort), 37, 43, 66,
    69, 72, 73, 75, 76, 79, 81, 89, 91,
    92, 95, 99, 105, 111, 112, 127, 206
    308, 329, 396, 400, 418, 432, 436
    (See also Chambers' Lodge,
    Hunter's Retreat, Hunter's
    Home)
McKinney's (Chambers') Clubhouse,
    85, 87, 89, 94, 106
McKinney's Landing (Wharf), 76,
    321, 410
McMahon, James, 287
McMarlin, 180
McMurtrey, Thomas, 59, 61
McNutt, Jim, 19, 21
McPherson, Aimee Semple, 94, 96,
    97, 99
McQueen, F. W., 38
Meadowedge, 209
Meadow Park, 112
Medley Reservoir, 176
Meegs Bay, 109
    (See also Meeks Bay)

Meek, Joseph, 109
Meek, Stephen Hall, 17, 109
Meeker, William, 343, 344, 345
Meeks and Company, 109, 389
Meeks Bay (Meegs/Meigs/Micks),
    72, 73, 91, 97, 109–113, 117, 211,
    251, 386, 389, 405, 448, 456, 459
Meeks Bay Camp, 437
Meeks Canyon, 109, 111, 123
Meeks Creek, 109, 448
Meigs Bay, 109
    (See also Meeks Bay)
Mein, William Wallace, 61, 62, 437, 440
Merrill, Bruce, 437
Merrill, Charles, 437
Merrill, John L., 42
Messenger, "Pall," 308
Metcalf family, 440
Metcalf, Mrs. John B., 117
Methodist Campgrounds, 358
Mexican miners, 2
Meyers, 189–196, 215, 216, 329, 378,
    379, 382
    (See also Smith's/Yank's
    Station/Celio's)
Meyers family, 196
Meyers, George Henry Dudley, 186,
    195, 196
Meyers Grade, 177
    (See also Osgood's Grade)
Meyers Hotel, 196
    (See also Yank's Station)
Meyers Station, 196
    (See also Meyers Hotel)
Michel(e) Spooner and Company, 293
    (See also Spooner, Michel(e))
Michigan Bluff, 27
Michigan Yacht and Power
    Boat Company, 436
Micks Bay, 91, 109
    (See also Meeks Bay)
Middlemas and Bool, 395
"Mike"—, 80
Milflores, 131
Mill Creek (sawmill), 306, 308, 309,
    317, 342
Miller, Albert K., 62
Miller Creek (mill), 172, 199, 212, 382
    (See also Heavenly Valley)
Miller Engine, 441
Miller House, 382, 383
Miller, John G., 382, 383
Miller Lake, 91
Miller Meadow(s), 91, 383
Miller Range, 383
Miller, Sam, 400
Miller's barn, 383
Milleson's Map of the Southern
    and Middle Mines, 462
Milliser, Samuel, 380
Mills, Darius Ogden, 33, 270
Mills, Everts, 67
Milton, Maxwell, 438
Minden, 238, 243
Miner's Union, 287
Mink Harbor, 322
Miguels, Henry R., 458
Miskinoff, Mrs., 66
"Miss Amanda," 285
Miss Banning's School (Carson
    City), 225

Missouri, 360
Missouri "sail tops," 368
Moana Villa, 69, 79, 80, 91–94, 95, 418
Modiosho, 339
Modjeska Falls, 149
Modjeska, Madame Helena, 149
Moffitt, James F., 61
Moffitt, Jim, 437
Mogenburg, Mrs., 268
Mogul Locomotives, 273
Monitor mill, 267, 269
Monk, Henry James "Hank," 126,
    127, 149, 168, 197, 198, 275, 277,
    278, 279, 281, 282, 403, 405
Mono region, 453
Monte Carlo Canyon, 339
Monterey Bay, 141
Monument Peak, 465
Moody, John F., 37, 385, 397, 407
Moody, Mrs. John F., 398
Morgan and Pomin, 446
Morgan, Luke Daniel, 87, 89, 111,
    112, 418
Morgan, William (Billy), 31, 34,
    39, 54
Mormon (settlers), 5, 277, 279, 363
Mormon Station, 180, 182, 191, 291,
    361, 362 (see Genoa)
"Mormon wives," 279
Morrill, George H., 267
Morten, S., 185
Mother Lode, 6
Mott, "Old Lady," 295
Mottsville, Nevada, 237
Mountain Lake(s), 360, 459, 461, 462
    (See also Bonpland/Tahoe)
Mount Davidson, 353
    (See also Sun Mountain,
    Sun Peak)
Mount Ellis, 94, 95
Mount Freel, 210, 238, 384, 458, 465
    (See also Freel(s) Peak)
Mount Hamilton, 353
Mount Pluto, 15, 319, 354, 453,
    457, 467
Mount Richardson, 150
Mount Rose, 307, 453, 467
    (See also Wasson/Wasan/Peak
    and Rose Mountain)
Mount Rose Pass, 468
Mount Shasta, 448
Mount Tallac, 150, 157, 201, 450, 465
Mount Watson, 15, 41, 457, 467
Mowry, Lt. Sam, 223, 460
"Mr. Red Crown," 74
"Mr. Tahoe," 329
    (See also Comstock, Harry O.)
Muchie—, 53
Mud Lake, 91
Mud Springs, 1, 64, 91, 147
    (See also El Dorado)
"Mud Wagon," 159, 206, 210, 282, 372
Mueller, Adolph, 73, 437
Muir and Smith, 192
    (See also Smith and Muir)
Muir, James, 189, 192
Muir, John, 82, 107, 141
Mullen, George, 396
Murdock, George S., 361
Murdock, N. E., 265, 267
Murphy, Daniel, 459

Murphy, Frances (Morgan), 111
Murphy, George Thomas, 43, 69, 72, 87, 109, 111, 113, 115
Murphy, James Andrew, 87, 89, 109, 111, 113, 115, 418
Murphy, J. Phillip, 62, 442
Murphys, 89, 112, 113
Murray, Pembroke, 397
"Mysterious Petrified Squaw of Cascade Lake," 137
"Mystery of the Savage Sump," 343–345

N

Napoleon, 386
"Napoleon of the Plains," 121
Navonne, Louis, 52
Needle Peak, 467
Neff, Sam, 431, 433
Neptune City, 339, 341
Nevada, State of, 28, 75, 78, 79, 82, 99, 105, 133, 141; (governor of), 149, 182, 203, 247; (newspapers) 274, 313, 323, 353, 357, 359, 362, 363, 403, 419, 425, 427, 453, 454, 457, 458, 459, 460, 461, 463, 464, (See also "Sagebrush State"/ "Silver State")
Nevada-California boundary, 28, 231, 267
    (See also California-Nevada boundary)
Nevada City, 459
Nevada Journal, 385
Nevada Lumber Company, 171, 213, 241, 308
Nevada National Bank, 107, 345
Nevada State Historical Society Museum, 55
Nevada State Museum, 49, 56
Nevada State Register, 321, 395
Nevada Territory, 245, 365, 367, 462
Nevada Washoe Times, 462
Nevett (Nevitt), James H., 362, 363
Nevett's Summit, 147, 175, 231, 267, 362, 363
    (See also Echo/Johnson/Western Sierra summits)
New Chambers Lodge, 89
    (See also Chambers' Lodge)
Newhall, Carrie, 311
Newhall estate, 117
Newhall, George, 117, 311, 436, 439
New Hampshire, 378
"Newport," 325
New York (State), 91, 277, 379, 380, 464
New York Tribune, 313
Nichols, Al, 37, 326
"Nick of the Woods," 195
Nielson, Chris, 61, 163, 437
Nielson, Hulda, 61
Nixon, Senator George, 437
North American House, 377, 378
North American Indian, 54
North Canyon, 273
North Canyon flumes, 294
North Fork of the American River, 28, 459
    (See also American River)
North Meadow, 317

Northshore Club, 47
North Stateline, 47, 329
North Wood Camp, 289
Norton, Colonel L. A., 361
Norton, F. O., 350
Norway, 134
Noteware, W. C., 31
Noteware's, 287
Nott, Samuel Alphonzo, 185
Nott's Station, 185
Nunes—, 441
Nutting family, 176
Nye, Governor James, 367
Nye, Thomas, 265

O

Oakland, 27, 417
Oakland Estuary, 436
Oakland Mole, 79
Obexer, J. P. (Jake), 72, 74, 437, 438, 440
O'Brien, William S., 308, 313, 316
Observatory Point, 48, 319, 347, 353, 393, 456, 457
    (See also Dollar's/Chinquapin/ Old Lousy Points)
O'Callaghan, Harry, 164, 329
Ogden and Moody, 385
Ogden, R. L., 407
"Ogilby's Grade," 183
    (See also Meyers grade)
O'Grundy, Eustace, 229
Ohio, 378
"Old Betsy," 284
"Old Bill," 99
"Old Brin," 97, 236
"Old Dry Diggin's," 339
    (See also Hangtown/Placerville)
"Old Friday('s) Ranch" (Station), 236, 239
Old Gabriel (Gabe), 121, 126, 283, 291
"Old Gabriel's Voice," 123
Old Griff, 351
Old King Cole, 119
    (See also King Cole)
(Old) Lousy Point, 351, 353
    (See also Chinquapin/Observatory and Dollar's Points)
Old Man, 35
Old Monogram, 79, 408
Old Morsby, 213, 216
Old Ridge Route, 3
Old Road Station, 42
Old Squaw, 119
    (See also Grinning Negro/Turk in Turban)
"Old Tom" (Rowland), 207
"Old Wash," 236
    (See also Small, J. W.)
Old Woman, 35
Oliver, "Bud," 441
Oliver, Edwin Letts, 438, 440
Oliver, Frank S., 431
Oliver, George D., 400, 416
Oliver, Thomas, 279
Oliver, William, 441
Olson, Neal, 220
Olympic Club, 72
Olympic Hill, 53
"One-Eyed Dick," 207
"One-Eyed John," 101, 195

"One Hundred Drinks Legislature," 462
"Oracle of Washoe," 403
    (See also Davis, Sam)
Oregon line, 28, 322
Ormsby County Poorhouse, 297
Ormsby House (Carson City), 105 154, 207
Ormsby, Major William, 233, 357
Ortman family, 437
Osborne, "Billy," 413
Osborne's—, 74
Osgood, Neamiah ("Nemi"), 183, 378
Osgood's Creek, 183 (Echo)
Osgood's Grade, 177, 181, 378
    (See also Meyers Grade/Osgood's cut-off)
Osgood's Lake, 175 (see Echo Lake(s))
Osgood's Toll House (Station), 147, 177, 183, 186, 192, 196, 378, 379
Osgood's Trail Cut-off, 177, 183, 378
    (See also Meyers' Grade/Ogilby's)
Oslo Viking ship, 134
Outlet Point, 53
Overland, 45; (train), 79; (sleeper), 180; (trail), 369
Overlook Point, 237
Overton, Captain John Bear, 303, 305, 306, 308, 318, 342, 399

P

Pacific Coast, 35, 103, 107, 149, 154, 159, 267, 283, 330, 335, 361, 364, 377, 403, 419
Pacific Coast Magazine, 450
Pacific Confederacy, 462
Pacific House, 371
Pacific Improvement Company, 289
Pacific Railroad, 17
Pacific Range, 353
Pacific Tourist Guide, 172, 209
Pacific Wood, Lumber and Fluming Company, 308, 313, 315
Packard, 141
Packard "Four," 335
Page family, 53
Page, John, 53
Page, Lou, 53
Page Meadows, 53
Page, Sam, 53
Pah-Utah's, 137
    (See also Pai-Utes/Paiutes)
Paine, Charles W., 336
"Painted Hills," 238
Paiute (Indians), 5, 17, 101, 172, 221, 227, 233, 234, 251, 326, 335, 357, 365, 460, 463
    (See also Pi-utes/Pa-Utah(s)
Palace Hotel, 159, 400, 445
Palmer House (Chicago), 445
Panama Canal, 464
Park, David Brooks, 237
Park, David Wallace, 237
Park, Maggie, 240
Parkell, H. H., 225
Parisienne Quadrille, 325
Parmeter, Joseph, 173
Parmeter's—, 174
Parrish, Charles Halsey, 206, 213, 215, 216, 219
Parrish, Elizabeth, 213

Parrishes—, 219
Parson's Rock, 129
Paso Robles, 107
Patton—, 295
Paula Loves Pearls, 66
Pauson, Fred, 397
Peavine Hill, 362
Pedrol(l)i, Anson J. (Ranch), 269
Pedrol(l)i's Meadow, 269, 283
Pennoyer, Paul G., 117
Pennsylvania, 382
Percival—, 168, 169
Percival, Mrs. Lydia Clement, 169
     (See also "Aunt Liddy"/
     Clement, Mrs.)
Perry—, 437
Persing, O. A., 172
Peter—, 121
Peter's Flat, 235, 237
     (See also Van Sickle, Peter)
"Phantom of the Desert," 233
Phillips, Dan, 177
Phillips, Joseph Wells Davis, 75, 377
Phipps Creek, 105
     (See also General Creek)
Phipps, General William, 101, 102,
     103, 105, 389
Phipps Lake, 105
Phipps Peak, 466
Pickle Meadows, 48
Pictorial Views of California, 26
Pierce-Arrow, 80, 174
Pierce, Dixwell, 149
Pierce, George, 361
Pierce, George W., 149
Pierce, President Franklin, 363
Pierce, Susan, 149
Pierson, George E., 257
Pike (region), 279; driver, 359, 360
Pillsbury, Arthur, 437
Pilot Hill, 29
Pine Grove House/Station (Lake
     Valley), 185, 380, 382
Pine Grove Station (Tahoe Vista),
     103, 335, 336
Pine Nut Mountains, 238
Pioneer (Lines) Coach, 363, 367, 372
Pioneer Sierra Nevada Stage
     Company, 192
Pioneer Stage Line(s) (Company),
     183, 198, 232, 237, 267, 293, 372
Piper's Opera House, 149
"Pisicultural Establishment of
     Morgan, Pringle and Early," 39
"Pitching Betsies," 193, 368
Pi-utes, 463
     (See also Paiute Indian(s))
Pizini, Frank, 61
Placer County, 2, 3, 5, 7, 26, 58,
     321, 460
Placer County and Washoe
     Turnpike Company, 5
Placer County Directory, 126
Placer County Emigrant Road
     (Route), 2, 19, 361, 468
Placerville, 109, 147, 163, 175, 176,
     182, 191, 192, 193, 195, 201, 207,
     208, 209, 225, 232, 235, 255, 267,
     277, 360, 361, 362, 363, 365, 366,
     367, 371, 373, 379, 383, 461
     (Also Dry Diggin's/Hangtown)

Placerville-Carson-Johnson Pass
     back road, 185, 199, 222, 382
Placerville-Carson Valley Route, 360,
     372, 382, 383
Placerville Herald, 109, 191, 251,
     253, 367, 459
Placerville Mountain Democrat, 463
Placerville Recorder, 458
Placerville road, 163
Placerville-Sacramento stage line, 362
Placerville-Tallac stage line, 174
Plains Indians, 101
Planett family, 95
Planett, Mr. and Mrs. John J., 95
Pleasant Valley, 313
Poett, Harry, 437
Pomin and Morgan's, 31, 349, 445
Pomin(e), Captain Ernest John, 141,
     217, 405, 416, 431, 432
Pomin(e), Captain Joseph H., 31,
     39, 163, 396, 400, 408, 409, 413,
     415, 418, 423, 436
Pomin, Ernest Henry, 48, 49, 287, 431
Pomin family, 287
Pomin(e), Frank, 41, 94, 99, 117, 287
Pomin, Fred, 418
Pomin, Ida, 287
Pomin, Jeanette, 287
Pomin, John Ernest, 163, 413, 415, 436
Pomin, Maggie, 287
Pomin, Robert, 437
Pomin, Tahoe, 26
Pomin(e), William, 26, 28, 29, 39,
     41, 385, 415, 445
Pomin's Lodge, 94, 95, 99, 117
     (See also May-Ah-Mee Lodge)
Pomin's Tahoe House, 37, 396
     (See also Tahoe House)
Pomin's Tahoe House Bar, 28
Pony Express, 196, 231, 232, 233,
     234, 235, 237, 377, 379
Pope family, 173
Pope, George, 173, 437
Pope, Kenneth, 442
Port Chicago, 113
Potter, Clark (Springs), 75
Potter School Camp for Boys
     (San Francisco's), 131
Powell, Captain James, 399
Powell, Elija, 378
Powers, Frank, 235, 239, 383
Powers, P. F. "Cy," 192, 235, 239,
     240, 383
Powers Ranch, 240
Pray, Captain Augustus W., 48, 243,
     247, 257, 263, 265, 267, 268, 270,
     274, 381, 385, 389, 390
Pray, Chester, 287
Pray family, 287
Pray, Mrs. Augustus W., 48
Pray(s) Cannon, 48, 284, 429
     (See also Fremont/Sheldon
     Cannon)
Pray's Cove, 416
Pray's Mill (Lake Mill), 265, 270,
     390, 391
Pray's Social Hall, 283, 288
Prentiss family, 73
Prescott and Barth, 403
Prescott Brothers, 7
Preuss, Charles, 360, 461, 462

Price, Mrs. William Whitman, 145
Price, William Whitman, 145, 210
"Prince Fortunas," 309
     (See also Hobart, Walter
     Scott, Jr.)
"Prince of the Ribbons," 371
Pringle and Hurley, 39, 443
Pringle, Prentiss, 28
"Prison of the Genii," 253
Putman, Jacob "Big Jake," 198
Pyramid Lake, 172, 233; battle of,
     357, 365
Pyramid Peak, 465

Q

Quadrille Band, 31
Quail Lake, 85, 87
Queen, Captain W. C., 394, 407
"Queen of the Lake," 289, 385, 410,
     427, 433
Quill, Jack, 48
Quills—, 287

R

Rabe, Chris (family), 242
Rabe, Elizabeth, 242
Rabe, William, 242
Ragtown, 180
Ralston, William Chapman, 33,
     113, 269
Ralston's—, 173
Ralston(s) Peak, 466
Ramsdell, H. J., 313
Ramsey, Anthony Wayne, 208,
     215, 220
Ramsey, Arthur, 240
Ramsey, Charles, 177, 240
Ramsey, Elliott, 240
Ramsey, Mrs. Anthony Wayne, 215
Ramsey, Mrs. Charles, 288
Raney, C., 373
Raney, R. P., 383
Rantz, William D., 195, 212
"Rattler," 41
Rayburn, John W., 46
Raymond family, 436
Ray, W. S., 438
Rea, H. F., 267
Red Lake Peak, 465
Red, White and Blue Mining
     District, 205, 319, 339, 341
Reed's Station, 233
Reiselt, Freddie, 46
Remington rifles, 167
Reno, 23, 41, 45, 48, 56, 59, 207, 215,
     269, 309, 327, 333, 349, 350, 427,
     437, 445
     (See also Lake(s) Crossing/
     Station)
Reno Evening Gazette, 11, 14, 317,
     399, 463
Reno Opera House Troupe, 207, 208
"Resources and Wonders of
     Tahoe," 186
Reusenberg, Ed, 45
Rhodes, "Dusty," 369
Rice, Captain William, 390, 391
Rice, Carrie, 261
Richardson, Alonzo (Al) DeRoy
     "Rich," 52, 174, 439

Richardson, "Bud," 174
Richardson, C. A., 321
Richardson, I. B. "Bart," 150, 177
Richardson, Johnson, 233
Richardson, "Sis" (Knisley), 174
Richardson's Camp, 407, 433
    (See also Camp Richardson)
Richer, G. T., 26
Richmond, Virginia, 171
Rickard, "Tex," 163
Ricker, Reverend R. A., 322, 323
Riddle, William, 319
Rideout, N. D., 65
Ridge Route (west), 5; (east), 181
Ridinger, John, 245
Rigby, James A. (H.), 270, 274,
    294, 393
Rim of the Lake Highway, 94, 129
Rim of the Lake-Mount Rose
    Highway, 306
Ripley's *Believe It or Not,* 349
Risdon Iron Works, 300
Ritz Carlton Hotel, 66
River House, 382
Robbers Roost, 35
Roberts, Oliver, 106
Robinson, L. L., 33
Robinson's Flat, 3
Rocky Point, 256, 259
Rocky Point House, 195, 256
Rogers, Fred, 456
Rogers, Will, 51, 142
Rome, 278
Rondo, 318
Rooney, Dr. Robert F., 175
Roop, Alexander Wilkshire, 208
Roos, Leon, 440
Rose, Captain Henry, 432
Rose Cottage, 164
Rose Knob, 467
Rose Marie, 131, 142
Roosevelt, Theodore, 342
Rother, Gus, 48
Rouge-Et-Noir, 318
"Roughing It," 265, 277, 329
Round Hill (Mountain/Mound), 236,
    243, 244, 245, 442, 443, 467
    (See also Folsom's Knob/Peak)
Round Hill Resort, 244
Round Lake, 455
Rounsevel, Walter, 52
Rowland, Fannie, 208, 237
Rowland, Flora, 208, 219
Rowland, Mrs. Sophronia Dow, 209,
    210, 219
Rowland properties, 210, 212
Rowland, Thomas Benton, 200, 203,
    206, 207, 209, 219, 413
Rowland's Custom House Saloon,
    208, 210
    (See also Rowland's Station
    Custom House)
Rowland's Great Ball, 206, 207
Rowland's Lake House and Station
    (Hotel), 37, 200, 203, 207, 208,
    209, 210, 212, 215, 393, 396, 400,
    444, 457
    (See also Al Tahoe)
Rowland's Landing, 410
"Rowland's sawmills," 209
Rowland's Station Custom House, 379

Rubicon Bay, 33, 109, 111, 115,
    117, 436
"Rubicon Flyer," 79, 80, 94
Rubicon (Mineral) Springs Hotel,
    21, 85, 418
Rubicon Park, 109
Rubicon Park and Bay, 115–117
Rubicon Park Lodge, 115, 117
Rubicon Park Tract, 115
Rubicon Peak(s), 105, 109, 111,
    245, 453, 466
Rubicon Point, 53, 97, 117, 118, 119, 120
    125, 126, 406, 415, 425, 433, 457
Rubicon River, 6, 75, 79, 85, 91
Rubicon (River) Gorge, 75, 79, 85, 91
    109, 251, 459
Rubicon (Mineral) Springs, 75–80, 83,
    85, 91, 92, 94
    (See also Rubicon Mineral
    Springs Hotel)
Rubicon Springs Hotel, 76, 78, 79, 80,
    418 (See also Rubicon Mineral
    Springs Hotel)
Rubicon Springs mineral water, 75,
    78, 79
Rubicon wilderness country, 19
Rubicon's "Fountain of Youth," 80
Ruckstell—, 145
Rufus Walton's Toll Road, 269
    (See also Clear Creek Grade)
"Ruler of the Lake's Navee," 396
    (See also Avery, Captain)
Rush, Ward, 26
Russ House (Hotel), 445
Russi, Antone, 358

S

Sacramento (City), 29, 31, 52, 64,
    65, 74, 87, 115, 126, 133, 176,
    183, 191, 193, 194, 198, 206, 225,
    304, 335, 337, 341, 347, 357, 358,
    362, 364, 368, 385, 393, 427, 455
Sacramento County, 19, 115, 362
Sacramento (Daily Record) Union,
    86, 115, 119, 192, 199, 339,
    459, 462, 463
Sacramento Placer Times, 361
Sacramento Valley, 20, 27, 64, 78,
    361
    (See also Valley of the
    Sacramento)
Saddle, Charles "Coon Hollow," 198
Sagebrush State, 78, 85
"Sailor Jack," 129
St. Louis, 47, 135, 353
St. Louis Arsenal
    (See United States Armory)
St. Maurice, Miss Cherry de, 335, 337
Saint's Rest, 247, 269, 291, 295
Salmon trout *(salmo clarkii),* 17,
    443, 451
    (See also Lake Tahoe trout)
Salmon Trout River, 17, 360, 459, 461
    (See also Truckee River)
Salt Lake City, 180, 235, 277, 361
Salter, Nelson L., 131, 437
Sanderson, Sybil, 141
Sand Harbor, 306, 307, 308, 309,
    342
Sand Springs, 233, 234

San Francisco (Bay City), 21, 22,
    26, 27, 28, 33, 35, 45, 61, 63, 65,
    66, 79, 80, 89, 95, 107, 112, 113,
    117, 121, 129, 137, 139, 152, 154,
    159, 165, 173, 175, 185, 193, 194,
    211, 213, 217, 219, 223, 265, 283,
    300, 311, 322, 337, 343, 345, 347,
    351, 353, 364, 389, 391, 393, 400,
    403, 407, 413, 415, 417, 418, 419,
    427, 429, 436, 462, 464
San Francisco Bank Ring, 269
San Francisco Bay, 436, 464
San Francisco Board of Trade, 22
San Francisco Bulletin, 351, 457
San Francisco Call, 413
*San Francisco Daily Alta
    California,* 29, 154, 245, 267, 393
San Francisco Herald, 385
San Francisco Marina, 441
San Francisco-Stockton run, 441
San Jose, 267, 322
San Leandro, 205
San Quentin, 379
Santa Barbara, 135
Santa Clara Valley, 353
Santa Cruz, 267
Sapphire Bay, 241
    (See also Boundary Bay)
"Saratoga Anecdote," 281
"Saratoga, of Nevada," 268
"Saratoga of the Pacific," 161, 268
Saratoga trunk(s), 36, 156, 281, 337
Saroni, Alfred B., 62
Sartor, Mr. and Mrs. S. D., 96
Saunders, "Peg-Leg," 73
Savage, Joe, 107
Sawmill Flat, 342
Savage Mine, 343, 345
Saxon, Lloyd, 433, 434
Saxton, Augustus H., 26, 34, 57, 58,
    59, 62, 269, 270
Saxton, Ruben R. (Rube), 58, 59,
    95, 168, 172, 415
Saxton's Mill, 57, 58, 59, 172, 270
Saxton's wharf, 59, 61, 62
Scha(e)ffer, George (sawmill),
    294, 319
Schilling, Else, 117
Schmidel—, 436
Schottische Glide, 215
Schumacher—, 67
Schumachers (Tahoma), 95
Schussler, H., 299
Scoffield, Charles, 191
Scoffield family, 287
Scoffield, Norman, 287
Scott—, 41
Scott, Alice Riggins, 19
Scott, Bert Carlisle, 62, 439
Scott, Captain Fred, 393
Scott, Ed, 20, 21
Scott family, 22
Scott, Fred A., 33
Scott, Herbert, 20
Scott, John Brown, 19, 20, 21
Scott, J. Chester, 20, 379
Scott, John P., 19, 20
Scott, John T., 425
Scott, Leland Stanford, 438, 442
Scott, Mrs. John P., 20, 21
Scott, Sir Walter, 149

Scott, William "Bill," 215
"Scotts Route," 2
Scripps, 440
Sears, Ralph, 62
Second Elkhorn House, 180
    (See also Hawley's Second
    Elkhorn House)
Secret Harbor, 311, 406
"Secretary's Secretary," 265
Secret Springs House, 3
Seller's—, 26
Selma, 133
Shakespeare Rock (Cliff/Bluff), 195,
    260, 261, 262, 467
Shakespeare, William, 261, 262
Sharon, William, 269, 279, 463
Sharp Brothers, 154
Sharp's rifles, 357
Sheehy, John, 216
Sheldon—, 48
Sheldon Cannon, 48
    (See also Fremont/Pray cannon)
Sheridan, General Philip H., 33
Sherman, General William
    Tecumseh, 275
Sherman, Robert P., 329, 333
Shivel(e)y, A. R., 31, 396
Shock, Casper, 9, 20
Short, Eva, 287
Short, Evelyn, 287
Short, Frank, 287, 288
Short, Joseph M., 99, 243, 274, 283,
    326, 396, 408
Short's—, 287
"Shorty"—, 185
Sickle, John, 277
Sickels, Mrs. Mehetable Jane, 377
Siebeck, Charles, 186, 212, 213, 216,
    219, 225; (logging camp) 383
Siebeck holdings, 220
Siebeck's Meadow, 211
Sieger, A. B., 200
Sierra Battalion, 233
Sierra House (Station), 186, 197–201,
    207, 212, 215, 247, 382, 383, 384
Sierra Lake, 462
Sierra-Lake Valley crossing, 205
Sierran barrier, 190, 372
Sierra-Nevada (Range), 1, 2, 3, 5,
    11, 19, 36, 39, 46, 47, 48, 51, 71, 76,
    79, 80, 82, 85, 91, 94, 107, 109,
    119, 129, 143, 147, 152, 165, 168,
    175, 176, 179, 180, 182, 183, 191,
    192, 193, 194, 197, 198, 203, 206,
    207, 225, 231, 233, 234, 235, 236,
    237, 238, 256, 265, 275, 291, 299,
    301, 304, 313, 329, 331, 339, 359,
    360, 361, 362, 363, 365, 366, 373,
    378, 379, 383, 385, 397, 413, 450,
    453, 454, 458, 459, 460
Sierra Nevada Tourist, 349
Sierra Nevada "whips," 326
Sierra Nevada Wood and Lumber
    Company, 305, 306, 308, 316,
    318, 325, 342, 399
Sierra Power Company, 80
Sierra Rocks, 256, 259
Sigouney, Mrs., 464
Silver City, Nevada, 151, 365
Silver Creek Station, 362, 363

Silver Lake, 139
    (See also Cascade Lake)
Silver Mountain, 453
Silver Road, 369
    (See also Bonanza Road to
    Washoe)
Silver Springs, 363
Silver State (Nevada), 28, 59, 229,
    265, 303, 321, 323, 353, 373, 454
Silver trout, 443
    (See also Lake Tahoe trout)
Silvey, Martin, 152
Simplex, 163
Sinclair, Walton, 379
Singer Sewing Machine Company, 244
"Sinkhole of Mormon Deseret," 235
Sink of the Carson, 233, 234, 235
Sioli, Paolo, 95
Sioux scrip, 267
Sisson—, 349
Sisson Hatchery, 448
Sisson, James, 182, 183
Sisson, Wallace and Company, 326
Six Horses, 275
Six Mile Canyon, 2, 233, 299, 363, 368
Six Mile House, 182, 195
"Sixty Mile Bend," 378
Sixty Mile House, 378
Skinner, Carol, 74, 437, 440
Sky Harbor Airport, 242, 410
Slade, Bill, 279, 281
"Slapdash Sage of Sand Harbor,"
    309, 438
Slaughterhouse Canyon, 264
Sleeping Lady, 119
Slide Mountain, 307, 453, 467
Slippery Ford (Grade/Hill), 147,
    180, 182, 206, 231, 362, 363, 364,
    367, 368, 372
"Sluice Box," 91
Small, Della, 208
Small, J. G. "Doc," 236, 237
Small, James Washington
    ("Big Jim"), 231, 232, 236
Small, Josie, 208, 237
Small, Mary, 208
Small's, 236, 237, 239
    (See also Friday's Station)
Small's Buttermilk Farm, 236
Small's Buttermilk Bonanza
    Ranch, 236
Smart and Son, 186
Smith and Douglas(s), 192, 379
Smith and Muir(s), 183, 192, 379
Smith, Charlie, 14
Smiths, C. J., 22
Smith, E. B. "Starvation," 225, 227, 241
Smith, "Gassy," 369
Smith, Guy C., 227
Smith-Hill holdings, 227
Smith, Martin "Mart," 180, 183,
    185, 189, 191, 192, 362, 363
Smith, Mrs. E. B., 227
Smith, Sue, 113
Smith's Creek, 233, 234
Smith's land, 180
Smiths, Ray, 200
Smith's Station, 181, 191, 362,
    363, 379
Smithsonian Institute, 145
Smith Valley, 173

Smith, W. "Coffee," 371
Smith, W. H., 362
Smith, Winnie, 67, 342
Snow Ball Specials, 45
Snow Falls, 138
    (See also White Cloud Falls)
Snow Lake, 17
    (See also Donner Lake)
Snow Lake (Katrine Lake), 141
Snowslide House, 377
Snow Valley Peak, 467
Snowy Range (Great), 147; mountains,
    361, 460
Soda Springs, 28
Somerset House, 373
Sonora Pass, 48
Sourdough Hill, 83
South Camp Peak, 467
South Eagle Point, 415
    (See also Eagle Point)
Southern, Captain Gordon, 154
Southern Pacific Railroad (Company),
    45, 107, 159, 429
    (See also Central Pacific)
South Point (Glenbrook), 287, 387,
    391, 416
    (See also Gilmore's)
South San Francisco, 456
South Wood Camp, 289
Southworth, Dr. S. S., 115
Spanish explorers, 463
Spencer, Absalom, 308
Spencer, "Newt," 198
Spencer rifle, 233
"Spirit of St. Louis," 135
"Spirit's Cave," 251
"Splash dams," 35, 58
Spooner and Dubois, 293, 294
Spooner and Lockie, 294, 295
Spooner, Camille, 287, 288
Spooner Junction, 304
    (See also Spooner Station)
Spooner Lake, 297
    (See also Spooner Meadow)
Spooner, Louis, 294
Spooner Meadow, 264, 283, 293
Spooner, Michel(e) E., 95, 103, 257,
    293, 294, 295, 297
Spooner, Michel(e), Lower mill, 270
Spooner, Michel(e)'s New Mill, 271
Spooner(s), Michel(e) Station, 103
    240, 241, 247, 256, 264, 269, 271,
    291–297, 300
Spooner, Olivene, 287
Spooner Ranch, 293, 297
Spooner's Saloon, 295
Spooner Station and Summit Camp,
    291–297
Spooner Summit, 265, 297, 389
Sportsman's Hall, 362, 371
Sprague, "Al," 209
Spriggs, Fred, 163
Springmeyer, Marjorie Johnson, 150
"Square sets," 275
Squaw Creek, 6, 7, 28
Squaw Peak, 3, 466
Squaw Valley, 1–10, 19, 20, 21, 26,
    42, 63, 357, 386
Squaw Valley Charlie, 6
Squaw Valley Development
    Company, 9

Squaw Valley Pass, 15
Squaw Valley Ranch, 6, 7
Squaw Valley road, 5
Squaw Valley "Silver Rush," 81
Squaw Valley Trail, 7
Squirrel Inn, 94
Stack, James, 440
Stack, Robert, 440
Standard Oil Company, 74, 115
"Stan-ford," 145
Stanford Camp (Hill), 145
Stanford, Leland, 27
Stanford Rock, 67, 466
Stanford University, 142, 145
Stanley Steamer, 145
Staples, Big Mose, 31
Staples, Deputy Sheriff Joseph, 373
Star engine conversion, 441
Star Lake, 210
Stateline Beach, 456
Stateline Hotel, 384
Stateline Monument (south), 219
Stateline, north, 317, 318, 457, 467
    (See also Boundary Point)
Stateline Point, 467
Stateline, south, 105, 176, 187, 237,
    379, 381, 382, 385, 395
Station Five, 275
Stead, William, 442
Steamboat Valley, 313
Steam engines
    (See also locomotives)
"Steamer for Bigler," 389
Stebbens, Miss Carrie, 445
Steinbeck, John, 142
Stein, Isaac, 319
Stein, Nat, 39, 48, 95, 103, 403
Stephens Bros., 437, 439, 440
Stephens, Roy, 440
Stetson and Dean, 445
Stevenson, Miss Carrie, 59
Stevens Peak, 465
"Stevens" River, 17
    (See also Truckee River)
Stevens-Townsend-Murphy Party, 17,
    360, 459
Stewart brothers, 185, 191
Stewart, Charles, 149
Stewart, James (Silent Terror), 33,
    34, 198, 331, 333
Stewart, Wellington, 257, 259
Stewart, William Morris, 193, 459
Stockton, 113, 337, 437, 439
Stone Seal, 119
Stone, Thomas G., 89
Stony Ridge Lake, 448
Stratford on Avon, 261
Strawberry (House) Station, 147,
    193, 206, 366, 367
Strawberry Valley, 177, 361, 362,
    367, 368
Street, Frances Park, 145
Sugar Pine Peak, 466
Sugar Pine Point, 53, 63, 81, 91,
    101–107, 109, 111, 122, 168, 389,
    390, 400, 405, 410, 418, 419, 425,
    436, 437
Summit (Johnson's/Echo), 378
Summit (Walton's/Clear Creek), 267,
    269, 294, 295, 309

Summit Camp, 241, 263, 264, 273, 284,
    291–297, 300
Summit Fluming Company, 270,
    293, 294, 295
Summit Lake (Spooner Lake),
    294, 297
Summit Mill (Elliott Bros.), 270,
    274, 293
Sumpter, Andrew Jackson, 406
"Sunbeam," 105
"Sunken Cliffs," 354
Sun Mountain, 1, 2, 229, 363, 365
    (See also Mt. Davidson)
Sunnyside, 59, 61, 65, 436
Sunnyside Bay, 59, 61, 62, 437
Sunnyside Cottage, 59
Sunnyside Lodge, 61, 62
Sun Peak, 299
    See also Sun Mountain/Mt.
    Davidson)
Sun Valley, Idaho, 10
Susie Lake, 150
Sutro, Adolph, 235
Sutro Tunnel Company, 213
Sutters Fort, 47, 360
Sutton, Tom, 46
Swain, Charles Stevens, 200
Swain family, 200
Swain, Haskin Calvin, 199, 200
Swan, George W., 367
Swan's (Slippery Ford) Toll
    House, 189, 235
Swan's Upper Toll House, 367, 377
Sweeney, John J., 377, 378
Sweetzer, Captain "Jack Tar," 126,
    127, 129
Swifts Station, 269
Swind, Frank, 95
Swisler, Charles Albert, 145, 176
Switzerland, 148, 327

T

Tagg, Michel, 191
Taggerts, 210
Tahoe (see Lake Tahoe)
Tahoe Boat Company, 49
Tahoe Cedars Tract, 95
Tahoe City, 7, 14, 21, 23–49, 51, 57,
    61, 63, 65, 66, 67, 73, 85, 87, 96,
    99, 103, 105, 106, 112, 115, 121,
    127, 151, 152, 156, 167, 168, 205,
    206, 207, 211, 219, 225, 247, 269,
    270, 282, 283, 285, 289, 308, 309,
    319, 325, 333, 335, 336, 342, 343,
    349, 350, 351, 353, 358, 386, 388,
    389, 391, 393, 395, 396, 397, 398,
    399, 400, 403, 406, 407, 408, 410,
    415, 417, 419, 423, 425, 433, 434,
    435, 437, 443, 445, 446, 450, 455,
    457, 458, 459, 460
Tahoe City Commons, 23, 26, 31,
    34, 42, 47, 48, 49, 87, 398, 407,
    418, 419
Tahoe City Custom House, 394
    (See also Campbell's Custom
    House)
Tahoe City Fish Hatchery, 358
Tahoe City golf course, 42, 49
Tahoe City Hotel (Lake Hotel or
    House), 28

Tahoe City Mercantile "Merc," 42, 437
Tahoe City "Y," 42
Tahoe cutthroat, 207
    (See also cutthroat/Lake
    Tahoe trout)
Tahoe Development Company,
    336, 337
Tahoe Fish Ranch and Toll House,
    34, 39
Tahoe House Bar, 28
Tahoe House (Inn), 26, 29, 37, 39,
    41, 42, 43, 45, 47, 49, 52, 163,
    396, 445
Tahoe Mountain, 465
Tahoe Park (Saxton's Mill/
    Sunnyside), 57–62
Tahoe Pines (Idlewild), 63–68, 456
Tahoe Ranch, 26, 28
Tahoe range, 319
Tahoe Royal Silver trout, 347
    (See also Lake Tahoe trout)
Tahoe-Sierra Explorations, 143
Tahoe silversides, 207
    (See also Lake Tahoe trout)
Tahoe Tattler, 35, 36, 38, 39, 59,
    65, 75, 156, 282, 325, 349, 445,
    460, 464
Tahoe Tavern, 42, 48, 51–56, 61,
    73, 79, 94, 107, 289, 431, 436,
    446
Tahoe Tavern Annex, 51
Tahoe Tavern Casino, 42, 51
Tahoe Tavern Pier(s), 42, 51, 52, 53,
    354, 456
Tahoe Tavern Properties, 45
Tahoe trout (refer Lake Tahoe trout)
Tahoe-Truckee High School, 17
Tahoe-Truckee-Martis Valley
    road, 331
Tahoe-Truckee Railroad, 41, 42, 45
Tahoe-Truckee Stage Lines, 31, 34,
    35, 37, 407
Tahoe-Truckee (Turnpike) Toll Road,
    26, 28, 39
"Tahoe Typhoon," 39
Tahoe Valley "Y," 187, 209, 379
Tahoe Village, 242
Tahoe Vista, 335–337, 386, 437
Tahoe Vista Hotel, 335, 336, 337
Tahoe Vista Inn, 337
Tahoe's Marine Activity—The Gay
    90's Into the Atomic 1950's,
    436–442
Tahoma (Resort), 95, 96, 99
"Taho" P. O., 185
Tait, John, 165
Tait, "Pop," 172
Tallac, 36, 37, 61, 85, 115, 129, 141,
    145, 149, 151–165, 168, 174, 209,
    237, 327, 329, 400, 410, 415, 423,
    436, 450
    (See also Yank's Hotel)
Tallac Casino, 161
Tallac Glee Club, 37, 157
Tallac Hatchery, 450
Tallac Hotel (House), 51, 85, 107,
    137, 139, 143, 145, 149, 156, 159,
    165, 167, 174, 308, 410, 413, 415,
    418, 419; (brochure), 423, 432,
    436
    (See also Hotel Tallac/The Tallac)

Tallac Meadows, 139, 142
Tallac, Mount, 143, 149, 150, 450
Tallac Point, 156
Tallac(s) range, 139
Tallac wharf (pier), 415, 419
Tallant, George P., 173
Tallant Lakes, 109, 448
Tallant Lakes Basin, 119
Tallant, Melita J., 173
Tallants—, 21
Tally-ho-coach, 327
Talmud, 278
Tamarack Lake, 177
Tapem, Dan, 209
Tay-Ho Canyon (Truckee
    River), 211
Tay-ho-Sierry Country, 97, 190
Taylor, Almon M. "Poker Jim," 175,
    185, 186, 211, 212, 213, 215,
    220, 223
Taylor, C. M. "Fiddler," 215
Taylor Creek, 137, 145, 151, 156,
    157, 159, 413, 450
Taylor, Elizabeth Mott, 211
Taylor homestead, 212, 213
Taylor, Mr., 363
Taylor's Ranch and Landing, 175, 206
    209, 211, 212, 215, 389
Tell's Peak, 465
"Tennessee," 385
Territorial Enterprise, 261, 268
    (See also Virginia City Territorial
    Enterprise)
Tevis family, 173, 436
Tevis, Lloyd, 436
Tevis, William Saunders, Sr., 173
    219, 413, 436
Texas Railroad, 41
Thaxter, George C., 269, 274
"The Bank Land," 209
The Big Bonanza, 208
The Cottage, 121
The Great Bonanza Road to
    Washoe, 359–373
"The Grove" (Camp Richardson),
    173, 174
The Grove (Phillips Station), 377
"The House of Holladay," 129
The Hut, 74
"The Lovers," 126
    (See also Eagle Falls)
Thieriot, Charles, 62
The Six Companies, 68
"The Tallac," 159, 161, 165
"The Whipped Murderess of
    Hangtown," 201
Thomas—, 436
Thompson, John A. "Snowshoe," 177,
    182, 183, 361, 363, 459
Thunder Cliff, 467
Thunderbird Castle, 438
    (See also Whittell's Castle)
Tillman, Mr. and Mrs. M. J., 141
Tim-i-lick Valley, 339, 341
    (See also Martis Valley)
Tinker(s) Knob, 65, 467
"Tip-Over," 172
Titus, Frank, 41
Titus, James C., 59
Tobey, Ada, 427
Tobey, Walter D., 427

Tobriner family, 287
Todman, Captain Joseph A., 48,
    59, 223, 283, 284, 385, 386, 387,
    394, 395, 400, 408, 409, 410, 411,
Todmans, 287
Tom Rowland's Custom House, 125
    (See also Rowland's Custom
    House Saloon)
Tom Rowland's Station, 127, 237
    (See also Rowland's Station)
Tonopah Line, 41
Topographical Map of Lake Tahoe
    and Surrounding Country, 64,
    212, 460
Towne, 62
Town and Country Lodge, 67
Townsend, Charles, 440
Townsend, Dr. John, 17
Toy-Yat Club, 42
Tracey, James, 7, 26, 28
Trac(e)y, Theo. F., 362
"Trail Junction," 231
Treat, Archibald, 450
Tro-ko-nene River, 253
"Trolling with Rod in Shallow Water
    on Lake Tahoe," 450
Trough, Bill, 163
Trout (Tahoe), 443–451
    (See also Lake Tahoe trout)
Trout Creek, 185, 199, 212, 379,
    381, 382
"Trout Mining at Lake Bigler," 127
Truckee (French Canadian), 17
Truckee (Indian), 17
Truckee (town of), 14, 21, 23, 25,
    26, 27, 28, 29, 31, 34, 35, 37, 41,
    43, 45, 58, 61, 67, 74, 79, 86, 105,
    106, 151, 159, 247, 269, 270, 319,
    323, 325, 327, 333, 336, 342, 349,
    353, 357, 391, 395, 397, 398, 399,
    407, 415, 418, 445, 446, 457, 463
Truckee Basin, 331
Truckee Canyon (Gorge), 11–17, 59,
    289, 386, 410, 415, 418, 453, 454
Truckee Canyon Road, 468
Truckee Hotel, 31, 37, 398, 399
Truckee (Truckey) Lake, 1, 17, 360,
    (Tahoe), 361, 461
    (See also Donner Lake)
Truckee Meadows, 101, 313
Truckee Pass, 179
    (See also Donner Pass)
Truckee Republican, 11, 14, 25, 31,
    33, 39, 65, 125, 137, 156, 215,
    303, 321, 347, 355, 394, 395, 398,
    399, 403, 407, 413, 463, 464
Truckee River, 3, 5, 6, 11, 13, 15, 17,
    19, 22, 26, 27, 28, 42, 43, 46, 49,
    54, 58, 341, 360, 399, 445, 446,
    459, 460, 461
Truckee River bridge, 6
Truckee River and Tahoe Lake
    Turnpike Company, 28
Truckee River Canyon (Gorge),
    11–17, 28, 41, 109, 159, 342,
    354, 453
    (See also Truckee Canyon
    (Gorge)
Truckee River Lumber Company,
    13, 14, 26, 225

Truckee River outlet, 321, 397, 398, 465
    (See also Truckee River)
Truckee's Brass Band, 398
Truckee Station, 34
Truckee-Tahoe arterial, 319
Truckee-Tahoe-Hot Springs
    Circle route, 269, 394
Truckey, Trucky, Truckey's Lake, 17
    (See also Truckee Lake)
Trueworthy, Frank, 26
Tryon, A. G., 199
"Tuck Holdridge's Range," 379
Tula Tulia, 462
    (See also Lake Tahoe)
Tulare, California, 350
"Turk in Turban," 119
    (See also Grinning Negro/Old
    Squaw)
Turner, W. H., 396
Turpin, Dick, 281
Turrill, Charles B., 347
Twain, Mark, 141, 156, 277, 278, 371
    (See also Samuel Clemens)
Twigg and Son, 436
Twin Crags, 467
Twin Lakes, 461
Twin Peaks (Blackwood Creek
    watershed), 59, 466
Twin Peaks (Gardner Mountain), 465

U

Uncle Sam, 326
Union, 205, 232, 256; (causes), 339,
    373; (forces), 389
Union Clothing Store, 7
Union Gas Engine Company, 436
Union Hotel, 7
Union Iron Works, 417, 419, 427
Union Pacific, 58, 273
United States Armory (St. Louis), 47
United States Coast and Geodetic
    Survey, 457
United States Department of the
    Interior, 462
United States Exploring Map of Upper
    California, 461
United States Geological Service, 48
United States Land Office, 317
United States Observatory, 457
United States Topographical
    Engineers, 460
University of California, 448
Up and Down California, 443
Upper Glenbrook Meadow, 247
Upper Lake Valley, 177, 180, 181, 186,
    191, 362, 378
Upper Pray Meadow, 263, 273
Upper Truckee River, 179, 180,
    181, 183, 186, 209, 321, 361, 378,
    379, 382, 393, 443
    (See also Lake Creek/Lake
    Bigler Creek)
Upson—, 231
Upson Bay, 64, 81, 91, 102, 265
    (See also McKinney's)
Utah Territory-California
    boundary, 267, 293
Utah Territory (Nevada), 179, 233,
    362, 363

V

"Vade"—, 75, 76, 377
Vair, Bessie, 240
Vair, James R., 216, 217, 240
Valley of Grass, 15
    (See Sacramento Valley)
Valley of (Lake) Bigler, 179, 192
    (See Lake Valley)
Valley of the Carson, 368
Valley of the Sacramento, 2, 47, 460
    (See also Sacramento Valley)
Van Blerk Engine, 439
Van Nuys, California, 456
Van Sickle, Henry, 198
Van Sickle, Lily, 411
Van Sickle, Peter, 237
Van Sickle's (Station), 171, 232, 233
Van Wag(e)ner, William, 204, 206,
    211, 222
Van Wagener's Hotel, 203
    (See also Lake (Bigler) House)
Varney, Professor James W., 325, 400
Vatican Lodge, 173
V-booms, 171, 215, 247, 273, 307,
    342, 416
Veazie, Colonel and Mrs. Horace M.,
    269, 273
Veazie, Ed, 263
Veazie House, 281
    (See also Lakeshore House)
Velma Lakes, 141
Venetian Water Carnival, 52
Vermont, 450
V-flume, 269, 270, 273, 279, 283,
    291, 294, 300, 305, 306, 307, 308,
    313, 315, 316
Viking's Castle, 133, 353
    (See also Vikingsholm)
Vikingsholm, 131, 133, 135; great hall,
    133; north room, 133; south tower,
    133; north tower ("Tower Room"),
    134
Viljoen, W. E., 407
Vineland, New Jersey, 247
Virden, Mrs. W. H., 323
Virginia, 380
Virginia and Gold Hill Water
    Company, 299, 301, 305, 306
Virginia and Truckee railroad, 171,
    269, 273, 309, 429
Virginia City, 1, 26, 31, 33, 48, 57,
    58, 63, 76, 85, 129, 141, 149, 151,
    169, 190, 194, 199, 207, 212, 233,
    245, 247, 263, 267, 269, 270, 273,
    275, 289, 299, 300, 301, 303, 309,
    321, 322, 325, 343, 345, 353, 357,
    363, 365, 366, 368, 371, 385, 391,
    427, 443
Virginia City Chronicle, 353
Virginia City *Evening News,* 443
Virginia City *Territorial Enterprise,*
    75, 183, 347
    (See also *Territorial Enterprise*)
Virginia Range, 313
Virginia Reel, 215
Vischer, Edward, 26, 193, 462
Visel, Morlan, 441, 442
Volcanoville, 57
Von Leicht, Ferdinand and
    Hoffmann, J. D., 64, 460

Von Schmidt, Colonel Alexis
    Waldemar, 27, 28, 223, 225,
    322, 454
Von Schmidt dam, 45, 445
Von Stroheim, Eric, 163
Voorhees, Senator, 73
Vosburgh—, 363
Vulcan Iron Works, 213

W

Wade, W. B., 183
Wadsworth, 445
Wagon Road Directors, 362, 363
Wakeman, Albert Town, 247, 269, 295
Wakeman, Nellie, 247, 269, 295
Wakenreuder, V., 462
Waldorf Astoria, 163
Walker, Brooks, 437, 440, 441
Walker, Clinton, 437
Walker, Frank, 358
Walker, Jimmie, 139
Walker, Randolph, Sr., 440
Walker River, 47, 48
Walker, Tom, 67
Walker's bar, 67
Wallace, William, 26
Wallace, William and Lambo
    Company, 319
Wallace, W. J., 210
Wallenrodt, George, 378
Walton, Izaak, 43
Walton, Rufus, 265, 267, 293, 385
Walton's Landing, 231, 265, 386, 389
Walton's Mills, 265
Walton's Summit, 231, 293
    (See also Spooner)
Walton's Toll Road (Summit), 293
Waltz Quadrille, 325
Ward Creek, 39, 42, 57, 59, 61,
    358, 455
Ward Creek Canyon, 57, 59, 61, 62
Ward Peak, 59, 466
Warner, Frank, 406
Warren and M. Upton Company, 211
Warren, G. W., 265, 267
Washington, George, 277, 462
Washoe, 1, 5, 6, 38, 86, 147, 183,
    185, 189, 192, 194, 197, 203, 231,
    232, 233, 243, 245, 257, 261, 267,
    293, 295, 299, 308, 317, 339, 345,
    353, 364, 365, 367, 372, 382, 445
Washoe City, 265, 317
Washoe County Road, 327
Washoe dialect, 463
Washoe-Eagle Valley saddle, 300
Washoe freighters, 368
Washoe Indian(s), 5, 6, 54, 64, 95,
    109, 111, 112, 113, 137, 142, 156,
    163, 175, 179, 180, 185, 186, 195,
    200, 205, 207, 221, 227, 240, 251,
    253, 255, 262, 326, 335, 351, 385,
    436, 443, 457, 462, 463, 464
Washoe Indian Legends, 14, 143,
    251, 253, 255
"Washoeites," 463
Washoe Lake, 299
Washoe mines, 379, 386
    (See also Washoe)
Washoe nabob(s), 59, 141, 193, 368
Washoe Sink, 5, 299

Washoe Valley, 306, 357, 454
Washoe wagons ("sail-tops"), 193,
    206, 233, 365, 382, 389
    (See also Washoe freighters)
Washoe Zephyr, 459
"Wash-oos"
    (See also Washoe Indians)
Wasson Peak, 179, 316, 317
    (See also Mount Rose/Rose
    Mountain)
Waterloo, 386
"Waterniche," 115
Waters, Gerald Dee, 22
Waters, R. J., 410
Watkins family, 287
Watkins, Jetora, 287
Watkins, Richard, 48
Watkins, Wilbur, 287
Watson, Bert, 431
Watson, Bill, 216
Watson, Charlie, 198, 373
Watson, Johnny, 287
Watson, Joseph Wheeler, 131
Watson Lake, 41
Watson, Robert H., 42, 48, 61, 333
Watson, Robert Montgomery, 21,
    41, 42, 333
Way Stations (Placerville-Carson
    Valley), 365
Way Stations on the Bonanza Road
    to Washoe (Phillips Station/
    Friday's Station), 377–384
Weatherwax, Cliff, 66
Weatherwax, J. M. B., 362
Weaverville, 3
Weeks, Anson, 94
Wehrman, Captain Henry, 425
Wellington, Duke of, 35
Wells Fargo Express (Company),
    34, 106, 159, 194, 197, 232, 237,
    239, 294, 297, 367, 373, 397, 423
Wentworth Springs, 75
West Carson Canyon (route), 181,
    183, 293, 361, 362, 363, 365, 372
Western Company, 115
Western Sierra, 2
    (See also Sierra Nevada)
Western Union, 294
Western Utah Camps, 1
    (See also Virginia City)
Westhoff family, 89, 111, 329
Westhoff, Louise, 87
Westhoff, William, 87, 89
Weyant, S. D., 186, 200, 213
Weyant, F. D., 216
Wheeler Survey Map, 17
Wheeler's U. S. Geographical Map
    (1876-77), 64
Wherner, Captain Pete, 410
Whippoorwill Farm, 28
whips, 371
whipsters, 371
White Cloud Falls, 139, 156
    (See also Cascade Falls/Snow
    Falls)
White, George, 156
Whitehall, boats, 31, 102, 121, 167,
    368, 446
"White House," 269
White Oaks township, 64
Whitney Brothers, 80

Whitney Survey party, 205, 319, 339, 347, 367
Whitney, Vincent, 22
Whittell, "Captain" George, 249, 311, 438
"Whittell's Castle," 312, 438
Whitten, J. S., 48
Wichart, W. R., 403
Wieland, Charles, 436
Wieslander, Leslie R., 117
Wiggins, George Washington, 103, 186, 331
Wiggins Station, 331
Wilbur, Brayton, 113
Wilcut(t), George B., 21
William Pomin's Tahoe House Saloon, 121
(See also Pomin(e), William)
Williams—, 21
Williams and Company, 180
Williams family, 117
Williams, John, 234
Williams Station, 233
Williamson, "Doc," 349
Williamson, Harry S., 437
Wilmington, Delaware, 403
"Willow Walk," 121
Wilson, George, 185, 191
Wilton, Thomas G., 26, 31
Winnemucca, Chief, 17
Winstanley, Charles Warren, 177, 195
Winter Olympic Games, 10, 52
Winters, Joseph D., 265, 267
Winters and Colbath, 267
Wolf "Wolfy," 201
Woodburn, Robert, 172, 185, 265, 380, 381, 382
Woodburn's—, 216, 380, 381, 382

Woodburn's (sawmill), 172, 185, 192, 201, 233, 265, 380, 381, 382
Woodford, Daniel, 183, 362
Woodford, Mrs. Daniel, 362
Woodfords, 361, 362
(See also Cary's Mill)
Wood, Robert E., 35, 36, 38, 39, 65, 75, 282, 283, 397, 460, 464
Woods, John, 163
Woodland, 73
Woodward, Absalom, 361
Woodward Gardens, 113
Wood Wharf, 358
World War I, 145, 173
World War II, 45, 47
Wren, John, 81
Wright, D. H., 335, 336
Wright, William, 289
(See also Dan De Quille)
"Wuthering Heights," 312
Wyatt, Homer, 217
"Wychwood," 131, 353
"Wyntoon Castle," 112

Y

Yankee Jim's, 6, 27
"Yank," 151, 152, 167, 168, 190, 191
(See also Clement, E.)
"Yank's" (Tallac), 151, 152, 154, 400
"Yank's" Cascade House, 86, 107, 167–169
Yank's Hotel, 151, 152, 167, 398
"Yank's Landing" (Cascade House), 168
Yank's Saloon, 193

Yank's (Station), 148, 151, 167, 183, 185, 189, 192, 193, 194, 195, 196, 231, 235, 293, 378, 379, 380, 381, 382, 383
(See also Smith and Muir's/ Celio's/Meyers)
"Ye Old Mustang Oil," 283
Yerington and Bliss, 89
(See also Bliss and Yerington)
Yerington, Henry Marvin, 65, 186, 259, 270, 294, 300, 308, 351
Yolo County, 362
Yosemite's Half Dome, 119
Yosemite Valley, 131, 306
Young, Brigham, 5, 279
Young brothers, 117, 220
Young, Charles P. (Ranch), 207, 219, 236
Young, Charles Rowland, 219
Young, Dr. Malon W., 219
Young, Homer, 349
Young, Thomas A., 3, 5, 460
Young, Wilton Richard, 219
Young's Bijou (Bal Bijou), 220, 225

Z

Zaletto, Alonzo, 137
Zephyr Cove, 212, 243, 245–249, 251, 311, 384, 459
Zephyr Cove House (Hotel), 245, 247, 257
Zephyr Cove Point, 249
(Conference Point)
Zephyr Meadow, 245
Ziegler—, 174
"Ziegler's Grove," 174
Ziese (propeller), 405

TYPOGRAPHY *by The Filmer Brothers Press*

TEXT: *10 Point Century Schoolbook leaded 4 points*

TITLES: *24 Point Perpetua Titling*

DESIGN: *Reinhard Steinley, Harry Moore*